D1267390

Measurement
of Risks

ENVIRONMENTAL SCIENCE RESEARCH

Editorial Board

Recent Volumes in this Series

Continuation Order Plan is available for this series. A continuation order will bring
delivery of each new volume immediately upon publication. Volumes are billed only upon
actual shipment. For further information please contact the publisher.

Measurement of Risks

Edited by

George G. Berg and **H. David Maillie**

The University of Rochester School of Medicine and Dentistry
Rochester, New York

PLENUM PRESS • NEW YORK AND LONDON

Library of Congress Cataloging in Publication Data

Rochester International Conference on Environmental Toxicity (13th : 1980 :
    University of Rochester) Measurement of risks.

    (Environmental science research ; v. 21)
    Proceedings of the Thirteenth Rochester International Conference on En-
vironmental Toxicity held June 2-4, 1980, at the University of Rochester,
Rochester, N.Y.
    Includes bibliographical references and index.
    1. Environmental health—Evaluation—Congresses. 2. Environmental
health—Statistical methods—Congresses. 3. Environmentally induced diseases—Congresses.
I. Berg, George G., 1919-   . II. Maillie, H. David. III. Title. IV. Series.
[DNLM: I. Probability—Congresses. 2. Environmental exposure—Congresses. 3. Environmental pollutants—Toxicity—Congresses. W L EN986F
v. 21 / WA 671 I59 1980m]
RA565.A2R6 1980   616.9'8   81-13969
ISBN 0-306-40818-X   AACR2

Proceedings of the Thirteenth Rochester International Conference on
Environmental Toxicity, entitled Measurement of Risks, held June 2 – 4, 1980,
at the University of Rochester, Rochester, New York. This was conference
number CONF-800601.

© 1981 Plenum Press, New York
A Division of Plenum Publishing Corporation
233 Spring Street, New York, N.Y. 10013

Printed in the United States of America

ACKNOWLEDGEMENT

We gratefully acknowledge the support provided for this conference by the U.S. Department of Energy, Environmental Protection Agency, Nuclear Regulatory Commission, and Department of Health, Education and Welfare (including the National Institute of Occupational Safety and Health, the National Institute of Environmental Health Sciences, the F.D.A. Bureau of Drugs and the N.I.H. Fogarty International Center), and by the University of Rochester.

We are especially indebted to Dorris Nash for efficient administrative and secretarial service in preparation for and support of the conference, to Florence Marsden for assistance during the conference, and to Rose Gering for her high-quality typing of the discussion sections.

The Conference Committee

George G. Berg, Co-Chairman
H. David Maillie, Co-Chairman
George W. Casarett
James R. Coleman
Solomon M. Michaelson
Morton W. Miller
Paul E. Morrow
Gunter Oberdorster

CONTENTS

INTRODUCTION

*In chapters with multiple authors, the participant in the
  Conference is identified with an asterisk.

**Two papers in this section present expanded versions of parts
  of Conference reports and are consequently not followed by
  discussion.

INTRODUCTION

THE RISKS OF MEASURING RISK

George G. Berg

Department of Radiation Biology and Biophysics
University of Rochester
School of Medicine and Dentistry
Rochester, NY, 14642

The Thirteenth Rochester International Conference on Environmental Toxicity examined both the logical soundness of the inference of risk and the validity of the experimental evidence of damage. Examples were drawn from current research by the participants on environmental hazards of toxic chemicals and ionizing radiation. Contributions by twenty-two researchers were grouped under six headings:

- Statistical Inference of Risks
- Risks of Prenatal Exposures
- Risks of Contaminated Air and Drinking Water
- Comparative Risks of Energy Sources
- Genetic and Cancer Hazards
- Extrapolation to Low Doses

Environmental toxicologists measure and evaluate a growing number of risks. Of necessity, standardized and simplified procedures are being chosen. In each of the four examples that follow, the current trend in risk assessment is shown first, and an alternate choice second.

(1) Single factor models: exposure-response relationships, in preference to models of competing risks.

(2) Population responses: "body counts" or increases in incidence, in preference to population effects (e.g. life shortening or duration of hospital stay).

(3) Conservative inferences: based on worst-case statistics, in preference to objective best fit values for dose-effect relationships.

3

(4) Linear extrapolation: to <u>zero risk only at zero exposure</u>,
    in preference to a "<u>de minimis</u>" acceptance of a threshold
    to damage.

Are the currently accepted shortcuts sound enough to yield reliable approximations of true risks? Can we progress to more
precise measurements and more accurate models? Or have we tak-
en logically flawed shortcuts that mislead us into counting
imaginary victims and overlooking real casualties? Such questions were posed by Conference organizers.

The Conference was opened by Dr. Kates with a reminder that
in measuring risk in terms of the number of people damaged we
may be counting three quite different kinds of victims. Are
they the projected victims who might exist only on paper, or
people actually damaged by the exposure in question, or victims
of the situation related to the exposure? The latter include
the victims of the risk estimate, that is people who became
sickened or impoverished by a mistaken belief that they have
been hurt by the exposure. There has always been that kind of
health risk in prophesying risks, just as there was a health
benefit in promising healing. Psychopharmacology is a tool for
a physician: have toxicologists fallen into the practice of
psychotoxicology? Variants of this question came up repeatedly
in Conference discussions, with studies at Love Canal as a case
in point.

Statistical inference is an essential, but not necessarily
understood tool for scientists in the epidemiological and experimental areas of risk measurement. Two philosophers spe-
cializing in the logic of inference challenged the scientists
with examples of routine misuses of this tool. The termination
problem was an example: when do we stop testing and choose a
course of action based on test results? Dr. Seidenfeld showed
that the best decision was reached by estimating correctly the
number of people who stood to benefit from the correct action
(or suffer from the wrong choice of action). An overestimate
can stall useful action indefinitely, on the incentive of gath-
ering better information before taking the plunge. Policies
based on such overestimates of the population at risk are currently mistaken for scientific conservatism by lawmakers and
regulators, as witnessed by the handling of radioactive
wastes. An underestimate, on the other hand, can trigger action prematurely, so that the chance of finding the right thing
to do is minimized. An extreme underestimate would be for a
physician choosing a treatment to treat each appearance of an
ailment as a case of one, instead of testing alternate treatments in suitably balanced groups; yet human experimentation is
discouraged in the name of humanitarianism.

The second example dealt with the possibility of misinter-
preting significance tests. When the damages we are scoring
occur rarely, a high level of significance is entirely compatible with a high error rate. A 99% confidence level in the diagnostic test need not keep us from making a false positive
diagnosis most of the time. Dr. Spielman showed how to derive
reliable decisions from tests by including additional appraisals. We need to estimate the incidence of the response that we
have set out to measure: just how rare is it, as compared to an
identical (and improbable) outcome of a control test? This, in
turn, depends on how small an effect we chose to score as damage. Consequently, decisions aimed at unobservably small consequences are likely to be wrong. Here statistical decision
theory supports the legal principle that "de minimis non curat
lex". It also removes logical foundations from various official attempts to prevent an undetectable event, such as the one
extra case of cancer in a population of one million. By the
same token, however, the theory confirms the key importance of
detecting very low levels of damage with very little error.
This, of course, is just where the best experimentalists and
epidemiologists have been concentrating their efforts: much of
the elegant work reported in this volume was devoted to improving the sensitivity and accuracy of dose-effect measurements.

Effects far below the level of damage were scored precisely
and reproducibly in mice and humans. This realm of subcritical
effects was covered for prenatal exposures by Drs. Liane Russell, Broman and Stein, and for adults by Drs. Bender, Ferris
and Hackney. Readings of cytological, anatomical, physiological and chemical changes are being calibrated into exquisitely
sensitive biological dosimeters. Here are future tools for
assaying exposures that would be out of reach of direct measurements of doses. For example, respiratory function tests
will measure the extent of exposure to air pollutants in a Canadian tourist in Los Angeles, or in a child whose mother has a
roast cooking in a gas oven. Here also is an opening for
abuse, by the simple-minded device of confusing signs of exposure with signs of damage. Sources and consequences of such
confusion were examined by Drs. Sagan and Cohen.

What are the standards for accepting or rejecting the evidence of damage? The philosophers advised us, on theoretical
grounds, that the decision depended in large part on the investigator's assessment of the situation under test. Dr. Utidjian, speaking from experience, set forth professional criteria
for coming up with a reliable assessment. When judged by his
standards, some of the currently permissible occupational
exposures to heavy metals come entirely too close to the danger
line.

Real and tragic incidents of illness and premature death provided data bases for reports by Drs. Land, Clarkson, Broman, Stein and Forbes. The last three dealt with common, everyday exposures. If science could ever be said to justify an activist, rally-rousing political movement, then these reports would make a brief for a revival of temperance societies. Cigarettes and liquor were the main malefactors. Even the environmentally ubiquitous lead was found at raised levels in smokers, yielding an interesting clue to a mechanism of heart trouble. Drinking and smoking by pregnant mothers stood out among the hazards to prenatally exposed babies. Urinogenital infections and low socioeconomic status of mothers ranked next. Here is a place where social anthropology may make a major contribution to future studies of environmental toxicity, just as experimental psychology contributed to the studies in this volume.

Historically, atomic energy furnished the training ground for the development of modern methods and concepts of environmental risk management. Risks of other energy systems have been subjected to comparable measurements only in the last few years, with results presented by Drs. Cohen, Pott and Inhaber. Dr. Inhaber's objective and well-documented analysis went beyond establishing coal at the bottom, and atomic fuel near the top of the safety ratings: it posed the general problem of optimizing a mix of energy sources. These range from fully decentralized installations, such as wood stoves or solar homes, to highly centralized ones, epitomized by a nuclear power station that can feed an electric power grid for six months from a single, sealed-in load of fuel. At issue was not just a summation of current risks, but also a comparison of each system's potential for correcting mistakes. Such a comparison is at hand in the contrast in historical accident patterns between travel by private car and travel by commercial airline. Whatever the merits of decentralization of power sources, they do not promise to include a saving of lives.

Where do the mutagenic and carcinogenic effects of ionizing radiation fit into the pattern of environmental risks? Dr. Stein's study of chromosomes in human reproduction and Dr. Liane Russell's data on oocytes in mice documented the ability of genetic systems to filter out deleterious mutations. Epidemiological studies of Dr. Land, occupational exposure data of Dr. Cohen, animal experiments of Drs. Abrahamson and William and Liane Russell all converged to show that doses of ionizing radiation would have to be raised many fold above background levels before causing detectable increases in reproductive wastage, genetic errors or cancer. This stood in sharp contrast to the evidence that many chemicals caused measurable

increases in cancer and reproductive defects at levels currently encountered by the general population or by workers.
The hazards inherent in the sheer diversity of pathways to
chemical damage were illustrated by Dr. William Russell's
discovery that male mouse gametes were exquisitely susceptible to mutation by an otherwise unremarkable alkylating compound.

Measurements of risk in terms of population genetics were
presented by Dr. Crow, who showed that selection may have been
more of a factor than mutation. Our high technology civilization has shielded enough generations from environmental hard-
ships to enrich the gene pool in technology-dependent traits.
The imminent societal risk is not one of mutations by waste
products of energy systems. On the contrary, it is the risk of
a technological failure of supply which would trigger a die-off
among those who depend on technology for survival, whether for
genetic or environmental reasons or both. In terms of survival
of the next few generations, we are boxed into a situation
where the need to make energy available is critical, while the
risk of mutation pressure is relatively minor.

What are the appropriate terms for measuring and evaluating
risk? Exposure-response models such as the two-term linear-
quadratic model were featured in reports on ionizing radiation,
but a comparable dosimetry for chemicals was still missing.
Evidence for the existence of a non-linear threshold to the
onset of dose-dependent damage was brought out in an epidemiological study of brain damage in people (by Dr. Clarkson) and
in an experiment on carcinogenesis in mice (by Dr. Cranmer). A
more fundamental question, however, concerned the choice of
units for measuring damage. Conventionally, this is done by
counting the incidence of a specified response, such as individual tumors (which could then exceed 100% in control mice),
or deaths classified by cause (often on the strength of a death
certificate). Yet no statistic is more open to abuse. The
simple arithmetic device of converting a projected incidence
into a body count lets an undetectable (and possibly imaginary)
increase in cancer mortality be inflated into thousands of
corpses. More realistic and more informative measures were
called for by Dr. Weinberg, reviewed by Dr. Cranmer and developed further by Dr. Thompson. The key is to evaluate cancer as
one of many competing causes of death, in order to measure
toxic damage in terms of life shortening. Dr. Crow pointed out
that even the prolongation of life may be a misleading measure
without a correction for the ensuing quality of life. By including the potential both for the degradation and for the
shortening of life in our measurements of risk we may help to

safeguard the most happy sum of lifespans for the living and for the generations to come.

In the light of the Conference, established approaches to risk measurement have not withstood the test of experience and logic, in spite of initial popularity and official acceptance. By attempting to be conservative in reporting numbers and impartial in interpreting statistics, the professionals in risk measurement managed to reap the worst of both policies: they encouraged simple-minded interpretations of biased measurements. This contributed to the neglect of well known hazards, and to an overkill of others that caught the scientists' interest and the body politic's fancy. Alternate approaches were clearly called for. Whether investigating ionizing radiation or polluted air, brain damage or cancer, the participants preferred the scientifically soundest estimate of risk to the worst case estimate, and then evaluated it by asking "compared to what?"

The alternate approach to risk measurement then, is to be objective in reporting and realistic in interpreting; to provide decision-makers and the public with scientifically most accurate estimates tempered by situation-relevant statistics.

More than a review of advances in measurement of risks to health by leading specialists, this volume may have a lasting value as a landmark of a change in scientific opinion.

_____

This paper is based in part on work performed under Contract No. DE-ACO2-76EVO3490 with the U.S. Department of Energy at the University of Rochester Department of Radiation Biology and Biophysics and has been assigned Report No. UR-3490-1986.

SESSION I

STATISTICAL INFERENCE OF RISKS

CHAIRMAN:

ROBERT W. KATES

INTRODUCTION TO SESSION I

Robert W. Kates

Graduate School of Geography
Clark University
Worcester, MA 01610

Statistical inference is essentially a measure of ignorance and helplessness. This is often forgotten. If this were a meeting on automobile safety, we would never have had the session. People understand the difference between a car crashing at 2 miles per hour and a car crashing at 60 miles per hour, that such crashes obey well-known laws of physics and that causal mechanisms allow a great deal to be said about hazards.

Nonetheless, statistics are the most common language of science. More people have a smattering of statistical knowledge than of mathematical knowledge - especially as you go across the spectrum of sciences, including the biological, social and behavioral sciences.

Statistics serve as our defense against hubris. Statistical inference is our defense against fooling ourselves. Yet it is surprising, for something that is a measure of ignorance and helplessness, how ignorance becomes knowledge and conventional assumptions become facts. We raise eyebrows at 5%, we agree at 1% and we think we know at 0.01%.

We talk about the power of a test, not the weakness of the idea that is tested. Language gets inverted in that peculiar way. Statistical significance somehow becomes common sense significance and people seem to interpret statistical significance as having some real world meaning other than a sign of our ignorance. We have debates where a change in a statistical test is seriously mistaken for a change in reality. My current favorite in this regard deals with interpreting whether cancers are caused by occupational exposures in lead smelter and lead battery workers, depending upon whether a one-tailed or two-tailed test is used.

    If scientific understanding hinges on one- or two-tailed tests,
or the like, a simple prescription is to do more studies, make more
observations. Sometimes this is not possible. To use Al Weinberg's
expression, it may be a trans-scientific problem. Either we know how
to do it but we can't do it, or we are just not smart enough to think
of an experiment, or we cannot think of an ethical experiment. But
these limitations do not apply to most cases. Rather, we just can't
wait for more findings, we must act on whatever we know. Therein
lies the rub and this is what we will be discussing for the next
couple of days.

    This is the dilemma. As scientists, we should delay until we
know much more. As responsible citizens, we appreciate the need to
act, whether we advise industry, government, or public interest
groups.

    In risk assessment, the distinction has been made between known
victims and statistical victims. Especially in the past year, that
distinction has broken down considerably. You can see what has happened in the poignant faces of the people of Love Canal, in the vet-
erans exposed both to Agent Orange in Viet Nam and to fallout of
atomic weapons in the U.S., in the people of Middletown affected by
Three Mile Island, in the women in Oregon who suspect they have
been affected by aerial sprays. All of a sudden, the unknown victims become known, at least to themselves.

    We are working under a new pressure. We are under a time limit
not only for the decision makers we advise and report to, but also
for the people who feel they are victims - albeit, in many cases,
mistakenly. I am not sure how we can cope with that. In the coming
days we must sharpen our science and our consciences as well.

THE PROPER INTERPRETATION OF SIGNIFICANCE TESTS IN RISK

ASSESSMENT

Stephen Spielman

Department of Philosophy
Lehman College and the Graduate Center of the City
University of New York
Bronx, New York 10468

In experimental and epidemiological assessments of potential carcinogens, two complementary techniques of data analysis are commonly employed. Data are cranked through an appropriate test of significance to determine whether or not the substance or factor is risk increasing. If the data are statistically significant, the magnitude of the risk to humans is estimated. Such estimates are highly controversial if the study involves extrapolation from data of a large dose animal study. In those cases where the substance tested is a food additive, the main burden falls on the first pattern of analysis under the so-called Delaney clause of the Food, Drug and Cosmetic Act. This is especially true when the substance is weakly, if at all, carcinogenic. In such cases, no clear dose response curve is exhibited by the data, and significance tests play a crucial role.

Four general rules are usually employed in the interpretation of tests of significance in the area of risk assessment. Some definitions are required before they can be described. Let E be an experiment or epidemiological survey designed to test the hypothesis H_R of a positive correlation between exposure and response rate against the null hypothesis H_N of no correlation. E involves a comparison of a test group against a control. Let D be the set of all possible data points for the outcome of E and X a suitable test statistic. X is usually either the familiar chi-square statistic or the z-statistic which is a measure of rate differences between test and control samples. If d* is the actual data point obtained, $P_N(X \geq X(d*))$ is the probability that X would take on a value equal to or greater than the actually observed X-value if H_N is true. This probability may be called the "observed significance probability" or simply, the P-value for the test. Since H_R is an hypothesis of increased

13

risk or positive correlation, the test is one-tailed.

Rule 1. (a) If the P-value for E is "statistically significant" (usually ≤ 0.05), the data point d* so strongly disconfirms
the null hypothesis H_N that it may be rejected. In other words, d*
provides very strong evidence against the hypothesis that the observed differences between test and control groups are due to chance.
(b) Moreover, the lower P is, the stronger is this evidence.

The next rule is thought to be a corrollary of Rule 1.

Rule 2. (a) If the P-value for E is statistically significant,
the hypothesis of increased risk is strongly confirmed by the data
d*. (b) The lower the P-value the stronger the confirmation.

The next two rules govern "negative" results.

Rule 3. (a) If the P-value exceeds the set level of significance, d* provides some weak evidence for the view that the null
hypothesis is close to the truth. The larger the sample size, the
stronger is this degree of confirmation. Very large sample sizes
are required for "negative" data to have the evidential weight that
"positive", ie. significant, data have. (b) Moreover, the larger
P is, the stronger the evidence in favor of H_N is.

Rule 4. (a) If the P-value is not significant, the data weakly
disconfirm H_R, the degree of disconfirmation increasing with sample
size and (b) increasing with the size of P.

The concept of evidence is central to these rules. As a result,
modern theory does not support them. The authors of the currently
received theory of statistical testing, Jerzy Neyman and E. S.
Pearson, explicitly rejected use of the concept of evidence. In an
important early paper[1] they remark:

> We are inclined to think that as far as a particular
> hypothesis is concerned no test based upon the theory of
> probability can by itself provide any valuable evidence
> of the truth or falsehood of that hypothesis...Without
> hoping to know whether each separate hypothesis is true
> or false we may search for rules to govern our behavior
> with regard to them, in following which we will insure
> that, in the long run of experience we shall not be too
> often wrong.

As Neyman elaborates this idea in subsequent works[2], significance tests are to be viewed as a branch of decision theory, of the
art of gambling with truth, and not as a branch of the art of
weighing evidence. We gamble with truth by making decisions in

accordance with a predesignated rule (test) to either declare H_N false or to declare H_N true on the basis of E's outcome. A good test-experiment pair is an instance of a type of "similar" pairs which will only rarely lead to erroneous decisions in the long run when the background assumptions are true. Tests with the same error probabilities, but with different subject matter, are "similar" in the relevant sense. Similarity of subject matter and experimental procedures, plus similarity of error probabilities involves a more relevant criterion of similarity, but presumably, as long as error probabilities are the same, tests with true background assumptions will yield the same error rates.

Diagnostic screening tests are simple paradigms for this conceptual framework which embody the narrower criterion of similarity. In his only textbook[3], Neyman presents a fictitious example which describes a mass screening procedure in which patients who show no signs of clinically advanced cases of tuberculosis are given five X-rays. Let X be the number of "positive" X-rays, H_N the hypothesis of no disease and H_T the hypothesis that the individual in question has tuberculosis. Under H_T the test statistic X has a binomial distribution with parameter 0.6 and under the H_N the parameter is 0.01. The relevant table of probabilities is presented in Table 1. If we set 0.05 as our level of significance, do not consider randomized tests* and treat H_N as the hypothesis tested, H_N will be rejected if $X \geqslant 1$. When employed over a large range of cases, this procedure will issue false positives only 4.9% of the time and false negatives only 1% of the time. The error rate for such a class of diagnoses would be between 1% and 4.9%, depending on the incidence of tuberculosis in the class of patients tested. So it is a good bet before an individual is examined that the diagnosis issued will be accurate.

Table 1. Frequency Distribution for Number of Positive X-rays.

X =	0	1	2	3	4	5
H_N true	0.951	0.048	0.001	10^{-5}	4.95×10^{-8}	10^{-10}
H_T true	0.01	0.077	0.234	0.346	0.259	0.078

---

*For example, to achieve an exact 5% level of significance, pure NP theorists would introduce a game of chance G with a chance event B whose probability is 0.001/0.951. Then H_N is rejected iff $X \geq 1$ or X = 0 and B occurs on a trial of G.

The main differences between such simple tests and gambling with
truth in risk assessment is that while the chance of a false
positive (erroneously rejecting H_N) is controlled, the chance of a
false negative (misleading non-significant outcome) is not measure-
able by a single number. However, the chance of a false negative at
specified levels of increased risk can be determined. Hence, an
upper limit of this chance for all levels of risk above a certain
practically important level can be ascertained. This security level
increases with sample size for a fixed level of significance. Large
samples are required for a high security level at a 0.05 level of
significance. For example, in a one dose animal study, sample sizes
of 223 for both test and control groups are required to achieve even
a 50% security level for detecting an increase of 5 percentage points
or more over a 5% background risk for the control population[4]. For
a 90% security level of detecting such a difference, sample sizes of
551 would be required. National Cancer Institute guidelines recommend sizes of 100 (50 of each sex).

The gambling with truth versions of Rules 1 - 4 are not very
different from the originals. The difference between them may appear
to be of only theoretical interest. Of course they exclude the (b)
part of each rule and talk about evidence. Moreover, the magnitude
of P is irrelevant; the only relevant question is whether or not it
is greater than the chosen level of significance. Rule I corresponds
to both Rules 1 and 2.

Rule I. If a significant value of X is observed, it is a good
bet to take those actions appropriate if H_R is true, e.g., publish
a report of an important finding of increased risk. It is a good
bet because only a small proportion of decisions of this sort will
be wrong in the long run, unless the experiment is so huge that
trivial departures from H_N will be reliably detected.

Rule II. If a non-significant outcome is observed, declare the
study to be negative, i.e., declare that either H_R is false or the
level of increased risk is not high enough to be reliably detected
by a study of this size. However, if the experiment is large enough
to reliably result in significant outcomes if H_R is substantively
true, declare that H_R is not substantively true. Such judgments will
be wrong in only a small proportion of cases and represent good bets.

The fact that the theory of testing which dominates recent statistics textbooks is antithetical to the evidential pattern of interpretation expressed in Rules 1 - 4, does not prove that the rules are
incorrect. These rules are handed down from a biometric tradition
whose leading representative was the great statistician R. A. Fisher.
In Fisher's view, the P-value of an experiment is a direct measure
of the objective credibility of the null hypothesis in relation to
test data, a measure of the weight of evidence which is more prim-

itive than--and does not justify any statement about--the probability
of the null hypothesis[5]. The lower P, the less credible the null
hypothesis in light of the data. So far, so good, since the lower
P, the higher the value of the test statistic X--which is an ordinal
measure of the intuitive discrepancy between what we would expect if
H_N is true and what we observed. The crucial step involves trans-
forming P from a purely ordinal measure whose numerical values merely
serve to rank data with respect to disconfirmation, to a scale with
some of the properties of absolute scales. This is accomplished by
treating low values of P (≤ 0.05) as such a high level of disconfirmation as to warrant provisional rejection of H_N on the grounds that
the data strongly disconfirm it.

It is not crystal clear to all competent statisticians that the
level of significance has this special measurement property. For
example, the well known biostatician Joseph Berkson confessed that
his experience as a consulting statistician exposed him to situations
where

(1) it was patent to all competent people who viewed the data,
that the null hypothesis, on the evidence, was not true, but
a small P did not result, (2) a small P did result, but it
was obvious to all who examined the data, that the null hypothesis was substantially true....[6]

After years of accepting Rules 1 and 2, Berkson came to the view
that a low P-value provides evidence against a null hypothesis if and
only if such low P's would occur frequently were the alternative
hypothesis true, that no conclusions can be drawn from a low P alone.

Neyman also had serious doubts about the logical cogency of the
Fisherian mode of interpretation and put forward very strong formal
criticisms of the Fisherian approach[7].

In response to such mounting criticism, Fisher undertook to lay
the opposition to rest by the following argument. Suppose that the
observed P-value is low. Then it follows that either we have observed a rare experimental outcome or the null hypothesis is false[5].
The second (unspoken) premise is that it is reasonable to suppose
that if the observed outcome were rare, it would not have occurred
in just one trial of E. It follows from the fact that it did occur,
that it is reasonable to judge that it is not a rare outcome and
hence that the null hypothesis is false. The lower the P-value, the
more reasonable the judgment that it is not rare, hence the lower P
is, the greater our warrant for rejecting the null hypothesis.

This Fisherian rationale for Rules 1 and 2 is seductive, but
a little reflection shows that if the second premise were sound in
all applications to chance phenomena, it would lead to the conclu-

sion that we would never be justified in regarding any wheel of
fortune or any roulette wheel as being fair, since under the fair-
ness hypothesis all specific outcomes are rare. Clearly if this
premise has merit, it is only in connection with the classification
of experimental outcomes in terms of P values. But even for this
case it is dubious. Consider the following example. At a recent
meeting of the American Heart Association, a researcher presented a
paper which claimed that there is clear statistical evidence that
pet ownership increases the chance of survival among patients recovering from a heart attack. Of 39 patients who did not own pets, 11
died within the first year of the study and only 3 of 53 pet owners
died during this period. The P-value for this data is 0.007. Let
us apply Fisher's premise to this case. Is it reasonable to suppose
that if observing this great difference between pet owners and non-
owners were as rare as the P-value indicates, such a difference would
not have been observed? Hardly! Rare statistical quirks occur all
the time. If enough people go on enough fishing expeditions in the
murky waters of statistical data, plenty of rare experimental outcomes will be encountered. I am inclined to judge this study outcome as being one of them, because it is initially implausible to me
that there exists a large enough difference in survival rates between
pet owners and non-owners to frequently produce such low P-values in
studies of this type. In other words, it is implausible that significant outcomes are not rare in such studies. Of course there may
exist such a difference, but unless it is initially plausible that
significant differences are regularly replicable if the null hypothesis is false, no conclusion can be drawn from this study.

    It is worth noting that Fisher, in another context, explicitly
endorsed this view.

    ...no isolated experiment, however significant in itself,
    can suffice for the experimental demonstration of any nat-
    ural phenomenon;.... In relation to the test of signifi-
    cance, we may say that a phenomenon is experimentally
    demonstrable when we know how to do an experiment which
    will rarely fail to give us a statistically significant
    result[8].

Fisher's second premise is applicable only when (a) it is reasonable
to suppose that significant outcomes would not be rare if the alternative hypothesis is true; (b) this alternative is initially plausible. The correctness of (a) cannot be guaranteed by good experimental design, although the larger the sample size the more reasonable it is to endorse (a). Conditions (a) and (b) represent scientific judgments which may be fairly subjective in particular cases.

    The point I have been driving at is that when the conditions
required for Fisher's rationale to be cogent are unpacked, it is

clear that the rationale undermines Rules 1 and 2; no conclusions can be drawn from a low P-value alone. A conclusion may be reasonably drawn only from a low P-value in conjunction with judgments of types (a) and (b). Such judgments are justified in particular cases on the basis óf an extensive record of experiments similar to the one in question. I know of no plausible argument for Rules 1 - 4 as they stand. In fact, it is clear that unless we are prepared to open the Pandora's box of subjective judgments of plausibility, the gambling with truth approach is more attractive.

Unfortunately, its rules for significance tests are logically untenable, in spite of their apparent obviousness. The reasons why may be seen through a reconsideration of the example used to illustrate the conceptual foundations of the approach. It was shown above that in the long run only 4.9% of patients will receive false positive diagnoses, and only 1% false negatives. But as any person trained in public health is aware, it does not follow that only a small proportion of positives will be incorrect, and that only a small proportion of negatives will be incorrect. Let Z be the incidence of cases of tuberculosis per hundred examinees. The average frequency of diagnoses per hundred examinations is given in Table 2. Among those positively diagnosed, the proportion of those incorrectly diagnosed is $.049(100 - z)$ divided by the total number of positives. If z is realistically small, say, .5, this proportion is .908. In other words, only 9.2% of positives are correct! Even if z is as high as 10, 31% of positives are incorrect. Similarly, the proportion of negatives which are incorrect may be very low or very high, depending on z.

The situation is even worse than the table shows. The above formulas represent averages over the different kinds of diagnostic cases $(X = 0, 1, ...5)$. The error rates for each of these cases are substantially different. For example, among those diagnosed positive by virtue of having an X-value of one, the proportion of persons receiving erroneous diagnoses is $.048(100 - z) \div (.077z + .048(100 - z))$. If z = 10, this proportion is .848, which is 275% greater than the overall error rate for positives.

Table 2. Frequency of Diagnoses

Diagnosis	Positive	Negative	Total
Has TB	.99z	.01z	z
No disease	.049(100 - z)	.951(100 - z)	100 - z
Total	.99z + .049(100 - z)	.01z + .951(100 - z)	100

    The only thing that the low error probabilities of .049 and .01
guarantee is an overall error rate of between 1 and 4.9%. But this
is compatible with a high rate of error for diagnoses that do not
occur frequently, or for cases that do not occur frequently. This
holds true in general, hence our simple arithmetic calculations show
that the gambling with truth rules for significance tests are falla-
cious. For, contrary to Rule I, there is no guarantee that significant experimental outcomes are only rarely misleading, i.e., that
decisions to declare the null hypothesis false are only rarely incorrect. Moreover, even if a test is so designed that non-significant
outcomes are rare when the null hypothesis is substantively false,
the proportion of negatives which are correct may be quite low. As
the example shows, the relative frequency of true null hypotheses
among the class of null hypotheses tested is a controlling variable.

    The simplicity of the tuberculosis example is no objection to
our critique. If the gambling-with-truth approach does not work for
its paradigms, it does not work for those cases in which our insight
is clouded by mathematical complexity. In fact, it works less well
with general problems of testing because in these cases the frequency
of false negatives is as unknown as the frequency of true null hypotheses. It is quite clear that Fisher's complaint that the approach
is applicable only to industrial quality control has much force. On
the other hand, it fares no worse than the Fisherian theory. Our
analysis shows that on either approach two sorts of judgments must
be combined with the level of significance in order for intelligent
decisions and/or data analyses to be made. The frequency of significant outcomes when the null hypothesis is false must be "guess-estim-
ated". The plausibility (Fisher) or the truth frequency of null
hypotheses must be evaluated, and these two appraisals combined,
somehow, with the level of significance to arrive at a judgment about
the import of the experimental data. This process is not program-
mable into the statistical packages found at your computer center.
One could, of course, decide to stick with the old rules on the
ground that there is nothing better around. But having tasted the
subjective worms which inhabit the core of the P-value, we may decide
to throw away the fruit.

    There is no way of avoiding the need for subjective judgment in
the analysis of data. What is wrong with the use of the P-value is
that there is no straightforward way of combining it with the requi-
site judgments to achieve an intelligent overall judgment. Subjective Bayesians have a sophisticated model for combining objective
probabilities with subjective judgment, but it is mathematically complicated. A useful substitute for the P-value in risk assessment
would be an easily computable objective measure of the import of data
which can be combined with subjective judgment in a direct, easily
comprehended manner.

I now propose a measure which has these properties. The conceptual scheme which underlies it is that of the gambling-with-truth
approach, but it is given a new direction. The tuberculosis example
provides a clear illustration of it. Suppose that you were to issue
diagnoses without taking X-rays by flipping a coin, or using a pair
of dice. Your ratio of correct to incorrect positive diagnoses would
be $z/(100 - z)$. Compare this ratio with the ratio of correct to incorrect positives when X positive X-ray pictures are observed. The second ratio equals the first times the chance of X given tuberculosis
divided by the chance of X given no disease. Thus the ratio of these
two chances equals the improvement of the success:failure ratio of
positive diagnoses issued on the basis of X over the success:failure
ratio for positives made on a gambling device. Let us call this
the relative success:failure ratio for positives based on X. The
inverse of this ratio is the relative success:failure ratio for negatives based on X. For example, the relative success:failure ratio
for negatives based on X = 0 is 95.1, a substantial improvement over
chance. If X = 1 the ratio for positives is only 1.6. In this case we
are not much better off than guessing by chance. On the other hand,
when X is greater than 2, the ratio for positives is so high that
virtual certainty in the correctness of the diagnosis is guaranteed.

Our proposed substitute for the P-value is based on the relative
success:failure concept. An application of it to one dose animal
studies of potential chemical carcinogens is sketched below. It can
be applied more generally, but space does not permit a general account.
Since animal studies have a practical objective, we must identify it
carefully if intelligent analysis is to be achieved. Suppose that we
are concerned with the association of the substance tested with a particular type or site of malignancy.We begin by setting a minimum
level for a practically important increase in rates between the unexposed target human population and the same population at a probable
average level of exposure to the substance. Instead of using a virtually safe dose concept, I propose what I call a detectability criterion. A practically important increase is one which is detectable
through standard epidemiological methods based on a year's complete
data for the population in question.(There are obvious complications
if the population already has some exposure, but these cases can be
handled with a little cleverness.) If the incidence is 100,000 cases
annually for a population of 200 million, a minimum detectable increase is .5%, or 500 additional cases. On the other hand, if the population is 100,000 and the baseline incidence is 100 cases a year,
a 16.4% increase would be the minimum detectable level under present
criteria. The criteria could be made less stringent, to let's say
one standard deviation from normal, but even still you are talking
about a 10% increase. The practically important increase appropriate
for the problem at hand is translated into an equivalent increase in
rate for the animal population at the experimental dose. This translation depends on the assumed shape of the dose-response curve and

the method of translating animal doses to equivalent human doses. Such assumptions are likely to command only limited agreement, since the proliferation of ideas on these matters is not going to be reduced by empirical means in the near future. However, such controversies are unavoidable in the end; it makes sense to bring them in right at the beginning so that we are really clear about the import of data with respect to the questions they are supposed to answer.

Let k be the minimum practically important level of increase for the animal population. Suppose that x_1 of n_1 controls develop the disease in question and x_2 of n_2 test animals do. We estimate the exact chance of observing what we observed under the null hypothesis by pooling the data to obtain an estimate of the hypothetical binomial parameter. The pooled estimate $p = (x_1 + x_2)/(n_1 + n_2)$. The estimated probability under the null hypothesis is

$$C(n_1, x_1) p^{x_1} (1-p)^{n_1 - x_1} \ C(n_2, x_2) p^{x_2} (1-p)^{n_2 - x_2} \ .$$

The second estimate is of the probability of getting what we observed under the assumption that the rate for the test population is k times greater than that for the control population. The rate for the control population is estimated by the value of q which satisfies the formula $n_1 q + n_2(1+k)q = x_1 + x_2$. Let $r = q(1+k)$. The estimated probability is thus

$$C(n_1, x_1) q^{x_1} (1-q)^{n_1 - x_1} \ C(n_2, x_2) r^{x_2} (1-r)^{n_2 - x_2} \ .$$

Suppose that we were to bet on the truth of the hypothesis that the response rate is increased by a factor of k or more (H_k) in a gamble in which we lose if H_N is true, but neither win nor lose if the truth is "in between" H_N and H_k . The relative success:failure ratio for such bets is the relative frequency with which our data will occur among the class of all tests for which H_k is true divided by the relative frequency with which our data will occur among those cases for which the null hypothesis is true. Of course, we don't know these relative frequencies (unlike the situation for the tuberculosis example). However, since they are defined over a class of experiment-hypothesis pairs which is similar to ours in terms of structure and subject matter, we can use our data to estimate these relative frequencies. We already have an estimate of the denominator of the success:failure ratio in the first estimated probability given above. I propose that a reasonable estimate of the numerator is the second estimated probability. A thorough defense of this proposal would be too tedious to present here. However, it should be noted that it is conservative in that when x_2/n_2 is greater than x_1/n_1 by much more than k, the second probability is lower than that calculated by setting k higher, except for unrealistically high values of k.

An illustration of the above ideas is provided by the 1977 Canadian two generation saccharin study which prompted the Canadian government to issue a ban on diet soft drinks containing saccharin.[9]

Let us assume an average population exposure equivalent to one can of diet soda per person per day for life. The minimum detectable proportional increase in rates for the U.S. population is set at .325%. Assuming a linear dose-response curve (which results in a high k), the animal dose of 5% of food weight translate on a mg/kg basis to a k of 2.6 . The number of bladder tumors observed in the second generation group of control males was 0/42 and the number observed in the test group was 12/45 (P = .0029). Plugging these data into the above formulas yields an estimated relative success:failure ratio of 346. This is the estimated improvement of wins to losses over betting on H_k if a coin(fair or otherwise) falls heads up, for all the experiments in the relevant similarity class. Does this high ratio justify betting on H_k for the experiment at hand? It does if there is no reason to think that H_k's are only rarely true. Another requirement, of course, is that no real loss is experienced if neither H_N nor H_k is true. Our selection of k guarantees that this is so for this study.

A major advantage of this approach over use of the P-value as a decision criterion is that it does not embody a decision criterion at all. What one does with an estimated success:failure ratio depends upon what judgments about the ratio of the proportion of true H_k's to the proportion of true H_N's one is willing to make. For, the product of this ratio and the success:failure ratio for the data is the absolute ratio of wins to losses for cases with similar data. If one judges this ratio to be low, i.e., that one would lose frequently betting on H_k by chance, a high relative success:failure ratio is required to offset it. On the other hand, if one judges the ratio to be moderately high, a moderately high estimated relative success: failure ratio may justify the declaration of a "positive" result. Since such judgments are subjective, even though based on extensive research experience, a reasonable policy is to declare a positive result only when a high estimated relative success:failure ratio is obtained. Irresolvable controversy is thereby.avoided.

Another advantage of not incorporating an arbitrary decision criterion is that there is no sharp dichotomy, as there shouldn't be, between data which are just barely significant and those which just barely aren't. For example, among first generation male rats in the Canadian study, 1/36 of the controls and 7/38of the test group had tumors. The published P-value was .075, although the more proper one tailed value is slightly less than .05. As a result, it was claimed that the study shows no carcingenicity among first generation male rats of the type studied. The estimated relative success:failure ratio is 11.4, a moderate level of support for H_k . Our analysis also resolves confusion about results in which there is no apparent sample difference between test and control groups. For example, the second generation females in the Canadian study showed ratios of 0/49 for the control group and 2/49 for the test group. It would not be correct to say that these data support H_N. Rather, they fail to favor H_k over H_N by much. This is reflected in the success:failure ratio of 2.5 .

Relative success:failure ratios are multiplicative over similar studies of a substance for different strains and/or species if the hypotheses involved are formulated with proper generality. Thus two or three studies which yield moderate ratios in favor of the general version of H_k can result in a strong case.

It may be felt that a serious defect of the gambling-with-truth approach outlined above is that different researchers or institutions will arrive at different estimated relative success:failure ratios if they use different methods of translating animal doses into equivalent human doses,even when the detectability criterion is agreed upon. The k value for a surface area mode of translation will be about five times greater than that arrived at by a straight dose/weight projection, if rats are the test species and a linear dose-response curve is assumed. It will be still larger if the projection is based on mg/kg/lifetime. Another major source of disagreement is different assumptions about the shape of the dose-response curve used in the projection from minimum practically important human increases at probable average human doses to corresponding animal increases at the chosen experimental doses. At present there are few empirical grounds for choosing between linearity for low doses, which is compatible with a "one hit" model, a "two hit" quadratic curve, probit-log dose models and others. [10] The National Academy of Sciences and several biometricians recommend use of the "one hit" model on the ground that it is the most "conservative" of the alternatives, and fits observed dose-response patterns reasonably well.[10] The question people in the chemical industry will be quick to ask is "Conservative with respect to whose interests?" What is "conservative" from the perspective of a guardian of the public health, may be flagrantly biased from a farmers or manufacturer's point of view. Appeals to conservativism represent concealed value judgments and do little to clear the air. The only hope for resolving these issues in the short term is for guardians of the public health and the producing sectors of our society to agree on standards that each can live with. In other words, the issues should be taken out of a narrow regulatory arena and set in a political one. This appears to be the only way in which all the interests of society can be protected at the present time.

REFERENCES

1. Neyman, J. and Pearson, E.S.: On the problem of most efficient
    tests of statistical hypotheses. Philosophical Transactions of
    the Royal Society A, CCXXXI: 289-337(1933)

2. Neyman, J: "Inductive behavior" as a basic concept of philoso-
    phy of science. Ruvue. Inst. Int. de Stat. 25: 7-22 (1957)

3. Neyman, J.: First Course in Probability and Statistics. Holt,
    Rinehart and Winston, Inc., New York (1950)

4. Fleiss, J.L.: Statistical Methods for Rates and Proportions.
    John Wiley and Sons, New York, Chapt. (1973)

5. Fisher, R.A.: Statistical Methods and Scientific Inference,
    2nd Edition. Oliver and Boyd, Edinburgh, p. 43(1959)

6. Berkson, J.: Experience with tests of significance: a reply
    to Professor R.A. Fisher. J. Amer. Stat. Assn. 38: 242-246
    (1943)

7. Neyman, J.: Lectures and Conferences on Mathematical Statistics
    and Probability. U.S. Dept. of Agriculture, Washington (1952)

8. Fisher, R.A.: Design of Experiments, 8th Edition. Hafner,
    New York, p. 14 (1966)

9. Cancer Testing Technology and Saccharin, OTA, Congress of the
    United States (1977)

10. Hoel, D.: Low dose and species-to-species extrapolation for
    chemically induced carcinogenesis. In Banbury Report 1, Ed.
    by V. McElheny and S. Abrahamson. Cold Spring Harbor
    Laboratory (1979)

DISCUSSION

WEINBERG: In the last paragraph of your abstract you talk about levels below which you can not see anything. Do you want to elaborate on that paragraph?

SPIELMAN: You have to make certain assumptions. The first would be a practically significant increase in risk for the human population. Then you have to translate that into an equivalent increase for animal testing, and specifically, into an equivalent increase in the group of animals chosen for your test. This is the problem of estimating comparative dose response curves. To predict responses at low doses for the human population, you have to scale down from higher doses used in animal tests. The likelihood ratio that you would compute depends on the scale of projected animal studies and on the formula for translating results from animal studies to human studies. This is a controversial area and there are different models for doing this.

The last remark in my abstract related to this question of whether or not you should follow so-called conservative procedures, such as assuming a linear dose response curve at low doses. I don't want to rely on that type of argument because when you start saying "let's use this dose-response curve and the linear extrapolation because it is conservative", it is going to be an overestimate relative to alternate models. I think the question that people in the chemical industry are likely to ask is, conservative with respect to whose interests? What is conservative from the perspective of the guardian of public health may be flagrantly biased from, say, a farmer's point of view or a manufacturer's point of view. And appeals to conservatism really represent concealed value judgments. I want to suggest that the way you can resolve the basic issues in estimation, at least in the short term, is for the guardian of the public health and the producing sectors of our society to agree on standards that each could live with.

CROW: There's a genetical problem that is analogous to the one you're talking about. If one is asking about detecting linkage between two loci, the null hypothesis is 50% recombination, which means independent genes. You state how large a linkage value you're interested in detecting, say 2%. For a known pedigree, you can then write the likelihood of the probability of this pedigree under the 2% assumption and under the null assumption. That, I think, is quite equivalent to what you are doing.

Now, here's my question. It is often possible in this field to assign a prior distribution to the probabilities of the various recombination values. Then you have a prior odds ratio and a likelihood ratio from which one can get a posterior odds ratio. Is there any systematic way of doing this in the real world where the prior odds are imperfectly known?

SPIELMAN: My own feeling is that a thorough-going Bayesian approach is logically the soundest, because the weighing of evidence is subjective and you might as well acknowledge it and introduce your subjective bias right away. However, there's an extreme resistance to operate with prior distribution among scientists because it smacks of subjectivism. And if you were going to introduce prior probabilities to calculate posterior probability (or prior odds to calculate posterior odds), then you might as well go whole hog and give full-blown Bayesian analysis. But that becomes too complicated, with double integrals to evaluate, and it is beyond the scope of the average experimentalist. So he needs something that he could just plug formulas into, simply, which is close enough to a fairly realistic Bayesian approach, and still gives the kinds of answers you want. This is what I offered - a substitute which does the job reasonably well.

LAND: I think your example was a little bit deceptive because the reason for testing a hypothesis is not to be right more often than wrong. I don't see that it is so terribly disturbing that, depending on the distribution of tuberculosis in the population, your probability of false positives might be small. One kind of error is more important than the other kind of error.

     The preferred way to treat this kind of thing may be in a decision-theoretic framework where you differentially weight the various kinds of error.

SPIELMAN: Yes, this is the standard game of Neyman-Pearson. First, what you have to do is decide which type of error is most serious, and then you want to control that type of error. That's the approach. Neyman used an example in which the most serious type of error is to let a case of tuberculosis go undetected. And so he concluded that what we want to do is to control that. But what is it that we control? It's type 1 error, the probability of issuing a false negative. That approach is inverted from the way I did it.

     The probability of a false negative can appear very low, .01, and that looks like it's a great test, one might think "only 1% of my negatives are likely to be erroneous". Actually, it just doesn't work out that way: the likelihood was 10%.

     So I think even on a Neyman-Pearson approach in any kind of decision theoretical framework you must be concerned with your error rates. Then you can bring in, if you want, the seriousness of the error, and combine those from a decision theoretic point of view. We have to clarify first what error rates we should use in a decision

theoretic approach.   That is my objection to the orthodox Neyman-
Pearson approach.

STEIN: In the public health area today, it seems to me that what
you discussed has practical implications for prenatal screening,
which is done in two steps.   First, screening serum for the level of
alpha-fetoprotein.   Then, at whatever level you decide to score as a
positive response, there is a problem of false positives and false
negatives, because a decision has to be made to do to the second
level of screening, amniocentesis, which introduces a hazard to the
patient.   The risk-benefit ratio will be different where there is a
difference in analytical methods - a highly sensitive method of
analysis will yield more false positives, a highly selective method
may reject some true positives.   Even with a highly sensitive and
highly specific test on accepted criteria, there will be important
differences in the risk-benefit ratio between applying the same two-
step procedure in the U.S. and applying it in Britain.   The decision
to do or not to do amniocentesis does come out of the numerical value
chosen as a positive response in the first test, but you should not
use the same value under different conditions.

KATES: The TB example is fascinating in a broader perspective.
What turned out to be important was not the likelihood of type 1 or
type 2 error, but the risk of the procedure.   We were probably increasing the incidence of cancer by exposing people to routine
screening from chest X-rays.   Only a persistent bias on the part of
the doctors, i.e., the assumption that people are ill rather than
healthy, can account for the prolongation of screening long after
any good decision analysis would call for abandoning the procedure.

There was also a second adverse effect, the Three Mile Island
phenomenon, which is the anxiety created in people who get those
little cards, as I used to get, saying "please come in for a second
test, you probably have TB."   We have only very poor measures of worry
and anxiety, but I think increasingly we will be factoring them in.

WEINBERG: There is an unstated assumption in your assertion that
people are getting cancer because of diagnostic X-rays.   The point
that Dr. Spielman made is that this depends upon what extrapolation
to low dose we use.   And on certain extrapolations to low dose, that
assertion is not correct.   Let's remember that.

REMARKS ON SEQUENTIAL DESIGNS IN RISK ASSESSMENT

Teddy Seidenfeld

University of Pittsburgh
Department of Philosophy
Pittsburgh, PA 15260

Part 0 - Preliminaries

My primary aim in this talk is to review some of what I consider to be the special merits of sequential designs in light of
particular challenges that attend risk assessment for human populations. In advance of a discussion of sequential experimentation,
let me remind you of a distinction that I think is especially
important given the title of this morning's session "Statistical
Inference of Risks." There are two kinds of "inference" that are
commonly called "statistical inference," and we must take care to
distinguish them if we are to avoid unnecessary confusion about
the relevance of values (as opposed to facts) in statistical inference of risks. First, we may understand a statistical inference to be an argument whose conclusion is a statement of, what
philosophers tend to call, "a rational degree of belief," i.e. a
statement of evidential support. For example, we can think of
statistical conclusions, inference, of the form: on the basis of
data E, the probability of H: that $quantity_1 \geq quantity_2$, is
roughly .9; that is, $p(H;E) \approx .9$. Here the quantities may be
place holders for risk levels (or risk indicators), e.g. a quantity
may be the chance of premature death (to agents of a given type)
due to increased exposure to chemical X. In Bayesian terms, the
"inference," then is to a statement of posterior probability for
H, given E; where H may, itself, refer to chances (objective probability). Those who try to follow "orthodox" statistics, yet who
wish to retain this sense of "inference" (contra Neyman's own
warnings) attempt to cite the size and power (or confidence level)
in lieu of a posterior probability. However, this attempt is
known to suffer from "after-trial" deficiencies. That is, the
Neyman-Pearson standards (of low size and high power, say) do not

apply after-trial, once the data are fixed.

I shall not be involved, here, with this sense of "statistical inference," as the problem of design I hope to address does not fall under this sense of "inference." We will, however, become involved (in Part 2) with the clash between Neyman-Pearson and Bayesian programs of sequential design--so we will not avoid the foundational disputes altogether.

A second sense of "inference," the sense I shall use, treats a statistical inference as a <u>decision</u>. In the orthodox statistical parlance (of Neyman-Pearson theory), the inference is whether to <u>accept</u> or to <u>reject</u> the hypothesis H (or, as we shall include, whether to postpone that decision in order to experiment first). Here too we must be cautious and distinguish a pair of senses for "acceptance." The "orthodox" sense, paradigmatically given in problems of quality control, sees the statistical acceptance (or rejection) of an hypothesis as shorthand standing for selection of a limited course of action, e.g. send the items on for sale or send them back for recyling. That is, the options (accept/reject) are non-cognitive acts: the investigator chooses between two courses of action, neither of which involves coming to believe a hypothesis is true or false (let alone coming to believe to some degree that it is true). In Neyman's terminology, the investigator faces a problem of <u>inductive behavior</u> (what to do), not <u>inductive inference</u> (what to believe). The decision is with respect to practical consequences (payoffs), e.g. sending out a defective batch of goods, and the concern with $type_1$ and $type_2$ errors is the "orthodox" way of expressing the concern with carrying out the inappropriate act (inappropriate given the agent's practical goals and preferences). We shall (part 2) examine the propriety of using the probabilities of $type_1$ and $type_2$ errors to express such preferences in sequential designs. In short, this first sense of "acceptance" is one in which a statistical inference is a decision taken with respect to practical goals.

As an alternative, some philosophers (notably Levi [9] and Hempel [7]) have suggested theories of cognitive acceptance: <u>deciding</u> what to believe, decisions taken with purely cognitive goals as payoffs, e.g. Levi trades off truth of hypotheses against their cognitive content (including informativeness, simplicity, etc.). These philosophers adopt a Bayesian form of decision making. (We shall review Bayesian decision theory in the next section.) But, as I will suggest, I do not think that the problem of experimental design can be dealt with decision theoretically if only cognitive goals are recognized. (Basically, I can make no sense of "cost" with respect to cognitive goals that would

justify terminating inquiry in order to decide what to believe.
Note: I do not dispute the possibility of identifying cognitive
goals that would serve to rank alternative experiments according
to respectable cognitive standards. Only I do not see how to
identify a cognitive "cost" that would justify ceasing further inquiry prior to deciding what to believe. This concern addresses
Levi's program as developed in [9].)

In outline, then, my talk contains three parts. First, I
want to rehearse with you the decision theoretic grounds for choosing a sequential design (where possible) over a fixed sample size
design. I shall begin with a Bayesian decision theory for this
purpose. Throughout, I shall treat statistical inference as decision theoretic with at least some non-cognitive costs associated
with the decision. Second, I want to review a comparison of
Bayesian and orthodox N-P sequential designs--the application is
to sequential medical trials (and the comparison is taken from the
recommended plans of P. Armitage [orthodox] and F. Anscombe
[bayesian]). I hope to shake your confidence in the N-P recommended
tests (if you retain conviction in orthodox statistics) by remind-
ing you that the before-trial/after-trial problem, which plagues
orthodox statistical inference when inference is understood in the
first (of the two) sense(s), i.e. as evidential, also surfaces
when N-P theory is interpreted in the recommended fashion, i.e.
when inductive behavior is at stake.

Third, and last, I want to sound a warning about a danger
which arises in the general case of sequential decision theory,
and to speculate that this danger sets up a dilemma for the philosophical debate between utilitarians and non-utilitarians, as these
two parties might approach the sequential medical trials problem,
discussed in part 2.

Part 1- The value of sequential designs.

A canonical decision presents a choice among a (finite) list
of (terminal) options $A_1,...,A_m$. There is uncertainty about which
relevant state of nature $S_1,...,S_n$ obtains. The agent represents
this uncertainty by a subjective probability $p(S_i)$. (I assume,
for simplicity, that the states are probabilistically independent
of the acts, i.e. $p(S_j;A_i) = p(S_j)$, all i,j.) Outcomes of each
act, A_i for a given state of nature, S_j, are known: o_{ij}. Moreover, it is assumed that there is a well defined (von Neuman-
Morgenstern) utility $U(o_{ij})$, defined over the outcomes, $U(o_{ij}) =
u_{ij}$. This information is conveniently summarized in the standard
decision matrix:

Table I Decision Matrix

$$p(S_1) \qquad p(S_2)\ldots. \; p(S_j)\ldots. \; p(S_n)$$

	u_{11}	u_{12}		u_{1n}
A_1	u_{11}	u_{12}		u_{1n}
A_2	u_{21}	u_{22}		u_{2n}
A_i			u_{ij}	
A_m	u_{m1}	u_{m2}		u_{mn}

The expected utility of option A_i is just the sum: $\sum_j u_{ij} \cdot p(S_j)$,
and (Bayes') policy of maximizing expected utility is to declare
as admissible any option A* whose expected utility is maximum
(among the declared options).

Suppose that, in addition to the m terminal options (above),
there is the option to perform a cost-free experiment E, with
outcome in the sample space $\Omega = \{e_1,\ldots,e_k\}$, and then choose from
among the terminal options after observing the experimental outcome. Let us assume, for simplicity, that the unknown states S_j
each provide a simple statistical model for the experiment, i.e.
$p(e_i;S_j)$ is well defined. Also, let us suppose that the experiment E is not trivially irrelevant to the uncertainty about the
unknown states, i.e. for at least one possible outcome e*,
$p(e^*;S_j)$ is, as a function of j, not a constant. (That is, the
likelihood is not unity for at least one possible experimental
outcome.). This insures that $p(S_j;e_i) \neq p(S_j)$ for some experimental outcome and some unknown states. After the experiment is
run Bayes' rule advises choosing an option $A_{\bar{e}}^*$ that maximizes
expected utility against the posterior probability $p(S_j;e_i)$, where
e_i is the experimental outcome observed. The value of $A_{\bar{e}}^*$ will
depend (usually) upon which outcome is observed. For some outcomes it will be above the value of A* (the best option available
without experimenting first), for other possible experimental
outcomes it may be below the value of A*. However, if we calculate
the expected value of the new option to postpone decision until
after performing the experiment by averaging the value of $A_{\bar{e}_i}^*$
against the probability of the outcome e_i, so that the expected
value of waiting to see the outcome and then choosing the best
(Bayes') terminal option is:

value of waiting: $\sum_i u(A_{\bar{e}_i}^*) \cdot p(e_i) = u(A_{\bar{E}}^*)$,

A_E^* is strictly preferred to A^* (see Good [5]). That is, it is an interesting mathematical fact that decision theoretically, it always pays to postpone a decision in order to acquire cost-free information. (Here, I assume that there is no cost in "processing" the data as well.)

The point is clear. If we are to take advantage of decision theory in deciding when to "stop looking" and decide the question, there must be some cost to looking--otherwise the advice is to procrastinate. In the next section I want to take advantage of this forced concern over costs in inquiry by letting "cost for looking" include typically eithical costs when "looking" involves experimenting with human subjects. But first, let me rehearse (with the aid of a simple example) the argument in favor of sequential design over fixed sample design (see deGroot [6]).

Suppose we are faced with a decision between two options, with only two relevant states of uncertainty, and payoffs as follows:

$$p(S_1) = \pi \qquad\qquad p(S_2) = 1-\pi$$

	$p(S_1) = \pi$	$p(S_2) = 1-\pi$	
A_1	0	-b	
A_2	-b	0	$(b > 0)$

The expected gain from A_1 is $-(1-\pi)b$ and from A_2 is $-\pi b$, which are equal iff $\pi=1/2$. Otherwise, choose A_1 iff $\pi > 1/2$ and choose A_2 iff $\pi < 1/2$.

Next, consider the opportunity to perform an experiment with one of three possible outcomes: e_1, e_2 and e_3. If e_1 occurs we know for certain that S_1 obtains, i.e. $p(S_1;e_1) =1$. Similarly, if e_2 occurs we learn that S_2 obtains, i.e. $p(S_2;e_2) = 1$. Finally, let e_3 be irrelevant to S_1, S_2, i.e. $p(e_3;S_1) = p(e_3;S_2) = \alpha$. Let the cost per trial of this experiment be constant, c, and we have the opportunity to repeat (independent) trials, subject to the constant cost per trial, stop when we want, and then choose one of the two terminal options A_1, A_2, (There are no added costs for delaying the decision, by assumption.)

Examine the alternative designs that involve running the experiment n times and then deciding between A_1 and A_2. That is, consider the choice of a fixed sample size experiment. After n trials either an "e_1" or "e_2" will have resulted (but not both), or else all n trials will have outcomes e_3. In the former, we will have learned which of S_1, S_2 obtains and we will lose nothing from the choice between A_1 and A_2, though we will have paid out c.n units in experimental fees. If all outcomes are "e_3" our posterior probability, $p(S_j;e_3^n)$, equals our prior probability,

$p(S_j;e_3^n)$, equals our prior probability, $p(S_j)$ and the best decision after-trial is just the same as our best decision before-trial, with the same expected return less the c·n units for experimental fees. For simplicity assume that $\pi \leq 1/2$ so that A_2 is then "best" with expected value $-\pi b$. As before, the value (pre-trial) of this experiment is obtained by weighting the values after-trial by the probability of the appropriate experimental outcome. There are only two "kinds" of outcomes to consider. With probability $(\alpha)^n$ all outcomes will be "e_3". In which case the pre-trial value of the experiment with constant result e_3 is:

$$-(\alpha)^n[\pi b + cn].\qquad\qquad(1)$$

If at least one outcome is other than an "e_3", which has probability $1 - (\alpha)^n$, the loss is just the fee. Thus, the pre-trial value of the experiment with a decisive result is:

$$-[1- (\alpha)^n](cn).\qquad\qquad(2)$$

Summing these two values, the total pre-trial value of the design with fixed sample size $\underline{n}$ is:

$$-(\pi b\alpha^n + cn).\qquad\qquad(3)$$

We can solve for the best fixed sample design by minimizing (3) over choices of $\underline{n}$. Let us assume that b, c, and π are such that it is better to take at least one observation instead of deciding without any experimentation. Then the n* that minimizes (3) is such that the expected value of the design with n* observations prior to deciding between A_1 and A_2 equals

$$-([c/\log(1/\alpha)] + cn*) = -(\pi b\alpha^{n*} + cn*)\qquad\qquad(4)$$

where $n* = [\log(\pi b\log[1/\alpha]/c)]/\log(1/\alpha)$ (5).

Suppose, next, that the investigator has the opportunity to perform an instance of the experiment, observe the result, and then decide whether or not to continue experimenting in advance of a terminal decision between A_1 and A_2, with n* an upper bound on the total number of trials affordable. Clearly, once an experiment leads to a decisive result; i.e. if any trial has "e_1" or "e_2" as its outcome, it is a waste of resources to continue experimenting. In a sequential design of this sort the expected value is strictly greater than the value of the best fixed sample design, as can be seen from the following considerations.

Because of the symmetry in the statistical models, i.e. in $p(e_i/S_j)$, the probability of stopping the experiment on the $\underline{m}$-th trial $(m \leq n^*)$ is independent of the true unknown state, S_j. The pre-trial value of the sequential design is merely the sum of the expected cost for looking, i.e. $c \cdot E(N)$ where $N \leq n^*$, plus the added risk of performing the maximum n^* trials where all n^* results are "e_3", i.e. $\pi b \alpha^{n^*}$. Thus, the total value of this sequential design is:

$$-[\pi b \alpha^{n^*} + cE(n)]. \tag{6}$$

But since $E(N) < n^*$ (in fact, $E(N) = (1-\alpha^{n^*})/(1-\alpha)$), (6) is more (a smaller negative number) than (4) and the sequential design with bound at n^* is preferred to the best fixed sample size design, if at least one observation is worth taking. The general result is easily stated: fixed sample size designs do not offer advantages over sequential designs and typically the sequential designs are strictly preferred (if available).

Before I turn to a comparison of sequential designs using Neyman-Pearson considerations (type$_1$ and type$_2$ errors) against the Bayesian styled sequential designs (as illustrated above), let me point out that the sequential design described above (with value given by (6)) is not optimal amongst sequential designs. For the problem just examined, (6) represents an improvement over the optimal fixed sample design, but (6) is a bounded design: a maximum of n^* observations was permitted. If we drop the constraint that there is an upper bound to the total purchasable observations and require merely that observations have a constant cost of c units each, there is an optimal design: experiment until a decisive result $(e_1$ or $e_2)$ obtains, stop experimenting and choose between A_1, A_2--which choice carries no risk since we then know which state S_j is real. The cost for this design is solely the fee for "looking" and, since with probability 1 "looking" terminates, the pre-trial value is $cE(N)$ (where N is the number of observations taken):

$$-c \cdot E(N) = -c(1/[1-\alpha]) \tag{7}$$

Note, however, that this optimal design can, with bad luck, lead the investigator into "ruin," for there is no upper bound on the number of observations that may be taken! At each stage the investigator queries, "Is it better to decide now or to try another instance of the experiment first?" Until a decisive result is seen (and assuming that even the first trial was worth making), the answer is always, "Try again." Of course, in this case, the probability of ruin is decreasing fast enough to make the open-ended strategy best among all designs. In the final section of this talk I shall return to this matter and point out a danger lurking in open-ended designs.

Part 2: Neyman-Pearson vs. Bayesian sequential designs.

In section 1 we examined an artifical statistical decision
(inference) in order to highlight the advantages of sequential
designs over fixed sample designs. However, with reckless abandon
I introduced the full Bayesian machinery, "prior probabilities"
π in particular, so that Bayes' theorem was available to fix posterior probabilities, after-trial, and to permit post-trial evaluations of expected gains with these posterior probabilities. I
am certain that you are familiar with the "orthodox" objections
to this Bayesian approach; specifically, the charge that Bayesians
introduce "prior" probabilities over statistical hypotheses (i) at
the expense of a conceptual error--all probabilities must have
objective bases and there just is no chance process underlying the
determination of which state S_j obtains-- or (ii) the "prior" is
ad hoc -- merely a subjective preference expressed by the investigator which has no place in scientific inference.

The program of statistical inference tracing back to the work
of Neyman-Pearson attempts to avoid this "mistake" by relying on
"objective" probabilities of type$_1$ and type$_2$ errors to gauge the
merits of statistical tests. That is, for a test of a given size
(probability of type$_1$ error--rejecting the null hypothesis when
true) one attempts to maximize the power (1 - probability of type$_2$
error -- accepting the null hypothesis when false).

Let us review the application of size and power considerations to sequential tests. The following example is borrowed from
P. Armitage's Sequential Medical Trials [2]. Imagine an investigation into the relative merits of two treatments, T_1 and T_2. The
treatments may stand for most any contrast where, as usual, it is
assumed that presence of a treatment is causally relevant to the
observed quantity measured by the test. For simplicity, assume
also that there is a linear model connecting treatments with
"effects," so that in "like" individuals difference in observed
effects is a sum of two components: treatment difference --
which is constant across individuals, plus "random" effects (un-
correlated with treatment effects) -- which, for simplicity, is
of known constant variance σ^2 = 1. Armitage adopts a Normal statistical model for paired differences. That is, each trial consists of a pair of readings (x_i,y_i)--x getting T_1 and y getting
T_2-- and $z_i = (x_i - y_i)$ is Normally distributed with mean μ (treatment difference) and known variance σ^2. [Depending upon the correlation due to matching factors, precision will improve with
positive correlation.]

Armitage considers a context in which the investigator has
three terminal options: declare (">" for "is preferable to")
$T_1 > T_2$, $T_2 > T_1$, or decline the judgment of preference, i.e.

suspend judgment regarding preference. He takes the "null hypothesis" to be the state where $\mu = 0$, under which it would be "wrong" to express a preference between the treatments. In order to fix concern with the <u>power</u> of a test, Armitage requires the investigator identify a minimal critical difference (expressed in units of $\delta_1 = \mu/\sigma$) that is worth identifying. Once the <u>size</u> of a test is fixed (he uses .05--see Table II) the challenge is to find the best sequential plan whose power is at least .95 if a critical difference exists. (Note: power here measures the chance of a correct preference.) For example, if $\delta_1 = .4$ (row three of Table II) then a bounded (closed) design with a maximum of 111 trials is available--whose graph has the shape of the region in figure 1.

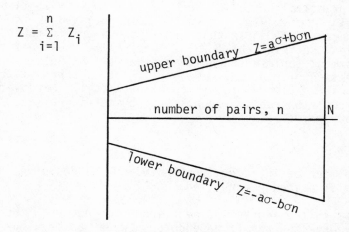

$$Z = \sum_{i=1}^{n} Z_i$$

Fig. 1 Schematic representation of restricted design, with "continuation region" and "termination boundaries".

Table II

Critical value of μ/σ δ_1	Coefficients in upper and lower boundaries a	b	Maximum number of pairs allowed N
0.2	18.19	0.10	445
0.3	12.13	0.15	198
0.4	9.09	0.20	111
0.5	7.28	0.25	71
0.6	6.06	0.30	49
0.7	5.20	0.35	36

What is the underlying motive for considering sequential designs? As we noted before, unless there is some "cost" associated with making an observation, there is no decision theoretic ground for stopping experimentation prior to making a terminal choice. In medical trials there are two kinds of "costs" that spring to mind: a practical cost associated with running and processing the trials, but second (in the case of human subjects and where the terminal decision involves a recommended course of action for treating people) there is an "ethical" cost to be identified with using human subjects as a source of information.

Let us follow Neyman's advice and understand the terminal decision, whether or not to declare T_1 preferable to T_2, as a shorthand for adopting a practical course of action, say, deciding to administer (adopt) T_1 over T_2. Moreover, let us suppress (as negligible) the practical costs and focus attention on what might count as "ethical" costs. With regard to those involved in the study, i.e. with regard to those observed in the n trials taken prior to a terminal decision, half (n of them) will have received an inferior treatment (unless the null hypothesis is true). Adopting a suggestion of F.J. Anscombe's [1], let us approximate this "ethical" cost by a moral regret function $n \cdot |\delta_1|$. Moreover, if our terminal decision really amounts to recommending a treatment, then let our payoff (loss) be

$$-k \cdot \max (0, -\delta_1 \cdot \text{sgn } \bar{z}),$$

where $\underline{k}$ is the number of individuals affected by the decision, and $\bar{z}$ is the average of paired observations.

At any stage in the sequential decision we do not know the value δ_1, so our expected payoff depends upon what has been observed. That is, at any stage in the sequential design, using these payoffs we find that our expected gain from stopping the inquiry and deciding is

$$-(n \cdot E(|\delta_1|) + k \cdot E(\max[0, -\delta_1 \cdot \text{sgn } \bar{z}]). \qquad (3)$$

(3) depends, in addition to what has been observed ($\bar{z}$), on $\underline{k}$ and the prior $\pi(\delta_1)$ through the expectations taken over the posterior probability for δ_1. Since my purpose here is to compare the sequential design when Neyman-Pearson standards are used in place of Bayesian considerations, the most charitable approach is to use a prior that duplicates standard N-P inference in this example. That prior is a familiar "ignorance" prior--which is relatively flat, i.e. the "uniform" prior. Finally, in accord with Armitage's closed plans, let us consider closed (bounded) designs where at most $N = n + k/2$ pairs can be sampled. Thus, $\underline{k}$, those affected by the decision decrease (by 2) each time a new pair is sampled.

Given all these assumptions, one can fix an optimal Bayesian sequential decision as a function of N. (The solution is obtained by a "backwards induction" argument--which is analytically quite intractable.) Anscombe provides a respectable guess at the shape (and size) of the stopping boundary: see Figure 2.

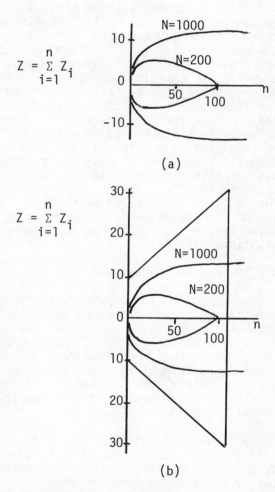

(a)

(b)

Fig. 2 Stopping boundaries for the comparison of two treatments. The abscissa is n, the number of pairs of patients. The ordinate is Z. (a) Two optimal stopping boundaries. (b) Armitage's stopping boundaries, from line 3 Table II, superimposed on (a).

How does Armitage's "orthodox" plan compare with the Bayesian solution from Anscombe's analysis? I have superimposed Anscombe's diagrams to show the great disparity of the two methods. To paraphrase Anscombe's interpretation: Armitage's boundary for a restricted sample (of at most 111 pairs) increases as though tens of thousands of individuals might be involved in the decision, but then terminates abruptly as though at most a few hundred might be involved.

If we assume a "payoff" function and "cost" function at all similar to Anscombe's "ethical" judgments, then it is quite evident that the Neyman-Pearson styled sequential tests of Armitage do not maximize expected "utility" under the standard "ignorance" prior. (Armitage's plan may be reasonable if the null hypothesis: $\delta_1 = 0$, has a high prior probability.) With these two sequential plans we confront the well known conflict between the "before-trial" concerns of Neyman-Pearson and the "after-trial" concerns of Bayesian expected utility. Prior to experimentation, Armitage's plan has the advertized low size and high power. But after experimentation, the investigator is not entitled to retain confidence in the pre-trial benefits of the plan. This is just the point of difference with the Bayesian sequential plans. True, with poor luck the optimal sequential plan may terminate well beyond the expected (pre-trial) stopping point. However, under the Bayesian plan, whenever one finally stops inquiry and makes a terminal decision it is in light of all the evidence acquired up to that point. One stops looking because, given the data actually acquired, it no longer pays to continue looking.

Part 3: Two warnings with sequential designs.

I would like to close my collection of remarks with related warnings (alerts) about the use of sequential designs. The first danger is more a mathematical point, namely, that optimal designs do not always exist and if, ignoring this fact, one proceeds with what otherwise would be a good strategy certain ruin may await. The second warning is more a philosophical point on the controversial status of the ethical theory that stands behind the kind of argument offered in the preceding section of this paper, e.g. Anscombe's "ethical" payoff functions.

(a) On dangers with unbounded designs. If the design problem has constraints that fix the options so that there is an upper bound on the number of observations that may be taken prior to a terminal decision, e.g. if the funding runs dry after n-trials, or if there is a time constraint preventing postponement beyond a given deadline, the existence of an optimal design is assured. (Solving for it, however, may be a formidable task.) Nevertheless, as we noted in part 1, the optimal design may lie outside the

class of bounded plans. In the example discussed earlier, the
assumption of a constant cost per observation led to the optimal
open-ended design: sample until an "e_1" or "e_2" results. Do such
optimal solutions always exist? No! And the following example
(due to Chow, Robbins and Siegmund [4]) reflects the seriousness
of the problem.

Suppose, for simplicity, at stage $\underline{n}$ of the decision problem
one has a choice between stopping at $\underline{n}$ and receiving the reward
x_n, or continuing on with another trial, where the expected reward
of stopping after $\underline{n}+1$ (one more) trial is $E_n(x_{n+1})$. Define the
set A_n as follows: $A_n = \{E_n(x_{n+1}) \leq x_n\}$ (1)
That is A_n is the set of n-fold sequences for which it does not
pay to take another trial before deciding. In a choice between
deciding now (at stage $\underline{n}$) and deciding at $\underline{n}+1$, it is not better to
delay. Define the monotone case as one where

$$A_1 \subset A_2 \subset \ldots \tag{2}$$

That is, in the monotone case once one proceeds beyond the point
where it pays to stop, one continues to face ever non-increasing
expectations for terminating after another trial. A most natural
candidate for an optimal stopping plan in the monotone case (one
that works in bounded monotone cases) is the rule, stop at the
first $\underline{n}$ such that the sequence enters A_n.

Consider, however, the following stopping problem. We are to
flip a fair coin until we decide to stop, at which point we receive one of two rewards: at stage $\underline{n}$ receive $2^n(2n/n+1)$ if all
n-flips have landed "heads," and receive nothing otherwise. (This
problem is something like "double-or-nothing" with incentive for
continuing.) At any stage $\underline{n}$, the expectation of playing one more
flip before collecting the reward is:

$$2^{n+1}(n+1)/(n+2) > x_n, \text{ if } x_n > 0 \tag{3}$$
and $\qquad\qquad\qquad 0 \;\; = x_n, \text{ if } x_n = 0.$

Thus, we have the monotone case since it no longer pays to play
once more before stopping only when we have already "lost." But
the natural candidate (identified above) for the monotone case
leads us to certain ruin, as we are directed to play until a "tail"
shows, i.e. until we lose! [That there is no optimal strategy here
is evident as the pre-trial value of the strategy: play $\underline{n}$ times
and stop is just

$$2n/(n+1), \tag{4}$$

which is increasing (in $\underline{n}$) with limit value 2--but the limiting
strategy (letting $\underline{n} \to \infty$) is identical in value to what the natural
candidate for the monotone case led to.]

What is the point in raising this riddle-example for your
consideration? Simply this: if one approaches sequential decision
problems with myopic vision; "Shall I stop here or continue on for
one more trial?" the upshot of a sequence of reasonable choices
may be unreasonable. That is, it is not enough to be aware of the
sequential nature of experimental design problems. One must also
face the difficult question of fixing the horizon of choices that
exists-or else risk the unpleasant consequences that attend the
strategy of looking only one step ahead.

(b) On sequential decision theory as a tool for the moral
philosopher (moral investigator): Welfarism is hardly the accepted
ethical banner of contemporary moral philosophy. The strategy of
resolving ethical decisions involving groups of persons which we
find in, say, Anscombe's sequential design is not merely welfarish
but straightforwardly utilitarian. His idea is to take account of
the "ethical" rewards (or, more accurately, the expected "ethical"
rewards) each member of the group receives and to attempt to maximize the $\underline{sum}$ of these expectations by a clever choice of stopping
rule for the experiment. However, whether or not the $\underline{n}$-th person
is exposed to what, at stage $\underline{n}$, is thought to be the less desirable
treatment depends crucially on $\underline{k}$, the estimated patient horizon
(that number waiting to be treated or to be affected by the choice
of treatments). Where $\underline{k}$ is large (yet), the subject next in line
has two roles to play. He represents one of the $\underline{N}$ subjects in the
total population; hence, he contributes his fair share to the total
"ethical" reward. However, he also represents a potential source
of information about the treatment difference--which is of upmost
importance for correctly treating the $\underline{k}$ agents waiting in the wings.
Those fortunate ones who stand at the back of the line (of $\underline{N}$), do
not represent as important a source of information since, by the
time they are observed it will be too late to alter the treatments
of those who have preceded. Thus, though all $\underline{N}$ individuals are
seen as "ends," each contributes an equal amount to the total
"ethical" reward, those coming first are also seen as a "means" of
acquiring data valuable to securing the desired "ends" for those
remaining, i.e. the $\underline{k}$ next in line.

A simple answer to the question of how to temper this ethical
utilitarianism is to shrink $\underline{k}$, to make the estimate of the patient
horizon modestly small. The extreme case is to abandon all utilitarian standards, to recommend what is best for that agent, as if
k=0 and to take due note of what has been learned to that point.
But now you see the dilemma that strikes me (at least) as unavoidable. The simple solution to excessive utilitarianism amounts to
adopting the myopic stand and that risks falling into the worst
strategy over the long run. The ethical dilemma arising from the
choice of sequential decision procedures is the conflict between
utilitarian and non-utilitarian standards translated into the conflict between strategic and myopic strategies. It would appear,

then, that the very machinery of sequential decision theory pre-
supposes a commitment to utilitarianism. I will not venture here
to offer a verdict on the plausibility of sequential decision
theory as a neutral tool for the moral investigator. Instead I
will rest content with having alerted you to the dilemma and then
stop!

References

1. Anscombe, F.J., "Sequential Medical Trials," J.A.S.A., 58
    (1963), 365-383.
2. Armitage, P., Sequential Medical Trials, Charles C. Thomas:
    [Springfield, IL., 1960].
3. _____,Statistical Methods in Medical Research,
    Blackwell Scientific Publications: Oxford, 1974.
4. Chow, Y.S., Robbins, H., & Siegmund, D., Great Expectations:
    The Theory of Optimal Stopping, Houghton Mifflin Co.:
    Boston, 1971.
5. Good, I.J., "On the Principle of Total Evidence," B.J.P.S.,
    17, #4 (1966), 319-321.
6. DeGroot, M., Optimal Statistical Decisions, McGraw-Hill Book
    Co.: New York, 1970.
7. Hempel, C.G., "Deductive-Nomological vs. Statistical Explana-
    tion," Minn. Studies in the Phil. of Sci., 3 (1962), 98-169.
8. Hoel, D.G., Sobel, M., & Weiss, G.H., "A Survey of Adaptive
    Sampling for Clinical Trials," in Perspectives in Biometrics,
    Vol. 1, R.M. Elashoff, ed., Academic Press: New York, 1975.
9. Levi, I., Gambling With Truth, A. Knopf: New York, 1967.

DISCUSSION

CROW: Where does the concern for the population at large come in this procedure?

SEIDENFELD: In which procedure? The Neyman-Pearson version used by Armitage, or the Bayesian style? The Bayesian style comes in after you agreed what the size of capital N is. If you look at the table - little n is the sample size, capital N is the size of the population of people who will be affected as a result of your inquiry and action. What you're doing then is subtracting to get K as the number of those not involved in your sample. The sampling, of course, may be passive, merely deciding to let the situation go on. You may be looking at two medical centers, and you are just going to decide to let the centers continue their different practices and not recom, end which is the better practice until you have seen enough data. Then N would be the estimate of how many people in total are going to be treated by these two centers.

KATES: There is a direct parallel between the Love Canal situation and the kind of situation in which the total population is to some extent unknown. In fact, that seems to be the issue. How do you react to the notion that the 36 blood samples were sufficient? The current situation, I gather, is that some of the people are going to prohibit any further testing on themselves until they get some guarantee of a pay-off, namely government-financed relocation. How do you react to this situation within the framework of choices you discussed?

SEIDENFELD: I think it is a bad mistake to think you can enter these problems, try and identify something like an ethical cost for letting a person continue in the study and not face the very difficult problem of what does this capital N look like. How many people are involved as a result of your decision? I don't think at this point it is proper to retreat to a cognitive decision and say, after all, all I'm trying to decide is which is the right theory or which is the more risky situation. If you do that, I think you're going to start to use Neyman-Pearson type considerations and get designs like the Armitage one, in which the capital N term will be overinflated for that case. It will be as if you thought your investigation is so important that tens of thousands of people's lives are in the balance. The result of not trying to be honest about this capital N is, in fact, to overestimate K, which means to devalue the life of those people actually at risk in the study.

BERG: I don't know how familiar the group here is with Love Canal, but I think the example is apt because an arbitrary decision has to be made. It is clear that many people in Love Canal, as in Utah downwind from Frenchman's Flats, are victims of a placebo-effect

disease. That is, they are genuinely sick for imaginary reasons,
a well-known phenomenon. If you accept that notion, then indeed the
number of people so affected across the United States, where timidity
is currently fashionable, is going to be very, very large. And that
number of psychotoxically afflicted and consequently sick people can
be incremented by one chemical or radiological scare after another.
Then the whole population of the United States would benefit, in
your terms, if we reduced the scare: the small group at Love Canal
would be milked for information to estimate the ratio of chemically-
afflicted people to placebo-afflicted people, with the understanding
that the investigation will not help the subjects.

The alternative view is that we are concerned with a small number
of afflicted people within the probable range of a chemical spill and
that we are trying to make a true distinction between the medically-
deserving and the economically-deserving individuals. In that case,
I don't see where the distinction helps them, because members of
both groups will need reimbursement for medical expenses and for
real estate losses. As I look at the compromise testing programs
now being reached by Federal and State authorities, I don't see where
they make any sense.

KATES: I asked Dr. Crow last night about chromosome breaks and the
issue is whether the situation is exactly as you stated. Is it only
an economic one? Does anyone here feel that the information that
someone had chromosome breaks (let's assume that we can accept the
measurements) is of any value to an individual to know?

BERG: Forgive me, I merely said that with chromosome damage not
being repairable by any treatment, you will not do any good to that
person by identifying him, while the damage of loss of valuation on
one's house is repairable and indeed, you can help that person. Now,
someone can claim remuneration for having his probability of coming
down with cancer increased in one part in a hundred thousand, but I
don't see where paying him will change his probability of getting
cancer.

KATES: You're coming close to all the issues of genetic screening,
and I'm sure there must be some dissent in the room on that.

UPTON: Since reference has been made to chromosome damage, I think
it is important to understand whether in fact the test data that have
been reported in the press can be interpreted to indicate chromosome
damage related to exposure to chemicals in the Love Canal dump. It
is my understanding that it was not a statistically-designed study
and, in fact, that the information that has been derived is, to all
intents and purposes, uninterpretable. So, until we have reason to
suppose that there is a relationship between damage to chromosomes
and exposure to chemicals, we may prejudge the outcome by assuming
a linkage.

SEIDENFELD: But wouldn't this be an opportunity for introducing the machinery which was just very hastily sketched here, because if there is no causal relation, then whatever recommendation is made in terms of health effects will be irrelevant. You won't be altering people's health by telling the occupants either to leave or to stay there. There may be economic differences, but the ethical ones will at least be minimal. In some sense the ethical regret would be measured by how much damage had been created by the wrong recommendation. You can decide, if you get some sense about this sample size, and how much damage goes with the difference between staying and leaving. Then you can decide how ethical loss grows with change in damage, and how many people can be allowed to stay and be used as subjects. Assuming, of course, that those who stay are willing to stay.

UPTON: I think it would be useful to determine whether there was in fact evidence of toxicity to lymphocyte chromosomes associated with residence in the Love Canal area. Whatever that toxicity would mean in terms of a long-run health impact is a second question.

SEIDENFELD: I'm trying to suggest that the way to ask the question should not be the cognitive way - just does it affect them or doesn't it? Rather, try to think about the number of people who are involved by the decision whether or not they're affected. The statistics are used here for a recommendation on how to act, not a recommendation on what to believe.

BERG: Just for clarification, I think there are two problems related to the Love Canal experience. One is the significance of cytogenetic change, should there be any, and the other is the design of the investigation itself. I think everybody agrees, with respect to the second problem, that it was irresponsible to carry it out without controls, though the investigator may not be the one to blame. But with respect to the first question, should the study have been done at all, competent or not, I think I would disagree with Dr. Upton, because I don't believe that we know what the health significance is of an increased frequency of cytogenetic change, either to the people involved or their offspring. Now, the geneticists in the room might disagree with me on that.

SEIDENFELD: I hope an answer will be given from the other side of the table, that this information would help in assessing some sort of loss of function.

SAGAN: I would like to expand on Dr. Berg's last point regarding the unknown significance to health of cytogenetic changes in circulating lymphocytes. It is clear that many deviations from normality are reflections of a physiological response to a new environment. For example, if any of us takes a ride on a roller coaster, changes will occur in pulse rate and hormone levels. As our knowledge increases and our ability to measure physiological parameters improves, we

increasingly encounter phenomena such as cytogenetic changes where
we cannot with certainty discriminate between physiological adaptation and pathological reaction. The point of this is that members
of the press or of the public are not likely to understand this distinction and are likely to consider any effect to be adverse under
these circumstances, there is a responsibility to be very much aware
of possible misinterpretation before embarking on health surveys such
as those around Love Canal.

UPTON: I just wanted to clarify what I intended to say. That is,
that having seen a suggestion of chromosome damage, I think it would
be useful scientifically to pursue the finding and determine whether
that suggestion can be corroborated with a carefully designed study.
But as to whether one should have done the study to begin with, that
question involves considerations which I'm not prepared to evaluate
now since I don't know enough about the situation.

        I would agree with the caveat you have expressed.

ABRAHAMSON: The field of environmental mutagenesis has been directing
itself, at least for the last 10 years, to trying to get a somatic
risk estimate from the somatic cell and translate that ultimately
into a germinal risk estimate, so that we may project genetic effects
in subsequent generations. Are you saying you don't want to provide
us with the bridge because you are afraid the public is going to be
upset by that bridge?

SAGAN: I didn't say that. I say, don't do it in such a politically
charged and sensitive situation as one has at Love Canal. No, please
go ahead and collect useful information wherever available. We need
that information, preferably from exposures where there is a way to
get a reliable estimate of dose, something not available at Love
Canal. But don't do it in a place or in a manner likely to be mis-
interpreted, to have economic and psychic costs not only to people
involved, but to the nation as a whole and provide no useful scientific information to boot.

KATES: I suggest that three points of view have been raised in this
last interchange that are worth remembering. The speakers, especially
our philosophers, have been trying to get us to focus on the difference between knowing something (or learning something) and observing something. They have been asking us to distinguish between knowing enough to decide which seems most correct (or whether something
is true or false) and knowing enough to decide what to do. I suggest
that there is a third factor that I have not heard and, in fact, we
seem to shy away from. That is the question of what would anyone's
doctor, for any one of the people in the Love Canal area, prescribe
as a reasonable battery of tests for that particular person. This
just shows what I naively expect from people who are MD's instead of
PhD's. It seems to me that we PhD's tend to turn people into numbers.

EPIDEMIOLOGIC STUDIES OF TOXIC RESPONSE -

SIGNIFICANCE REQUIREMENTS

H. Michael D. Utidjian, M.D.

Associate Corporate Medical Director
Union Carbide Corporation
270 Park Avenue, New York, N.Y. 10017

INTRODUCTION

The epidemiologic approach to the study of human
toxic response is attractive, at first glance, for two
main reasons. Firstly it circumvents the considerable
ethical problems of deliberate experimental exposures of
human subjects to toxic agents. It is opportunistic and
seeks to utilize for study exposures and responses which
are already active in a population, inadvertently as far
as the investigator is concerned. Secondly, by its very
essence, epidemiology studies statistically the response
to exposure of relatively large numbers of individuals
who, in many community-based studies, may represent a
very broad cross-section of the human population with
respect to age, sex, health and socio-economic status,
and even, in some cosmopolitan communities, to race.
Thus such studies should fundamentally accommodate one
of the biggest sources of variation in quantitative toxic
and therefore of individual risk, individual biological
variability. As is generally well known the animal toxicologist handles this factor by exposing a substantial
number of animals at each dose level and, in the case of
lethality studies, generates the familiar LD50 or LC50
and employs logit and probit statistics. It is perhaps
not so generally appreciated how much the effective lethal
dose for certain substances may vary in human subjects

however. To take a tragically commonplace example, ethylene glycol, the main constituent of most commercial anti-
freeze formulations for automobile cooling systems, seems
to exhibit a wide range of lethal dose by ingestion, even
in small children of similar body-weight. Fatalities have
been reported following the ingestion of as little as one
teaspoonful and yet, exceptionally, estimated doses as
large as a pint have been survived.

A community-based epidemiologic study of toxic response therefore has claims to "representativeness", as
being valid in a "real life" situation. However, the
foregoing advantages are more theoretical than real, that
is to say they fully apply in only an unattainably ideal
situation. Epidemiology may paint its picture on a very
large, even at times grandiose, canvas, but it uses a very
coarse brush indeed. The brush-work is crude both with respect to estimated exposures, be they via community air or
water pollution or occupational exposures, and to the
detection of effects. There is, in addition, the enormous
problem of concomitant and potentially confounding variables. Although ingenuity in the selection of appropriate
control groups may be hoped to solve the problem of the
confounding variables, the extent to which it can really
do so is limited by the "state of the art" awareness of
all the potentially significant confounding variables
which the investigator ought to be taking into account.
It is primarily because of this overwhelming problem that
the "significance requirements" for epidemiologic studies
of toxic responses in risk assessment cannot be formulated
with mathematical precision.

Epidemiologic studies of human toxic response have
been concerned with effects ranging from trivial morbidity such as subjective eye irritation or headaches associated with photochemical oxidant air pollution, to excess
or accelerated mortality from all causes, again associated
with air pollution, or mortality from ischemic heart disea
associated with characteristics of the municipal drinking-
water supply of certain cities. Studies have been conducte
for the most part, of the strictly speaking prospective
type in the sense of looking forward from a perceived toxi
exposure to an outcome or effect, the toxic response,
Often, for expediency, these studies have been conducted
in an historic mode, that is from records of events which
have already taken place, rather than in the temporally
prospective sense. Strictly retrospective studies in

which the study population has been defined by manifestation of a particular disease or other effect, and has
then been investigated for differential exposure to a
suspect toxic agent or agents in comparison with a control
group without the disease, have also been undertaken.
These are often referred to as "case-control" studies.

OCCUPATIONAL MORTALITY STUDIES

        Occupational mortality studies, that is the study of
overall and cause-specific mortality rates in certain specified occupational groups, with or without job-specific
chemical exposures, have become increasingly popular in
recent years. In the United Kingdom it has been the practice for many years to publish decennially (1) Standardized Mortality Ratios (SMR's) for many officially categ-
orized occupational groups, based upon underlying causes
of death and customary occupation of the deceased, as
stated on the death certificate. The denominator populations at risk in each occupational group are derived from
a different source, the decennial census. This expedient
of combining occupational data from two possibly dispar-
ate sources has been criticized. It has been suggested,
with some cogency, that "usual occupation" as declared by
the surviving relatives of the deceased on the death certificate is likely to "flatter" the deceased, while more
confidence is placed on the occupation claimed by the
living worker in the census. The Standardized Mortality
Ratio is here defined as the ratio between the observed
deaths in each occupation divided by the number of deaths
that would have occurred in the same population, had suitably adjusted national rates applied, multiplied by 100.
(In Britain the industrial age-range is taken as 16 to 65
years and for the industrial occupations studied the population has traditionally been overwhelmingly male.)
Thus an SMR of 100 would denote "national average" mortality experience, whereas an SMR above 100 would indicate
and increased, below 100 a decreased "relative risk" of
mortality in the occupational group under study, compared
with the general population.

        In this country the investigation of mortality by
occupation on a large scale has been pioneered by Dr.
Samuel first in Washington State from 1959 to 1971 (2) and
later, in collaboration with Dr.Gerald R. Petersen in the
State of California for the years 1959 to 1961 (3). In
these two studies the Proportional Mortality Ratio (PMR)

rather than the SMR was calculated. This is because in the
first (Washington State) study the denominator population
at risk was not known with precision. The same index was
used in the second (California) study in the interest of
comparability. In general the Proportional Mortality Ratio,
an estimate of the proportion of a given number of deaths
from a specific cause compared with the corresponding proportion for some standard population, is considered to be
a very inferior statistic, compared to the Standardized
Mortality Ratio because only the latter can be used as an
estimate of risk. By definition all PMR's must sum to 100
so that an abnormally high or low frequency of any particular cause of death must produce a balancing deficit or
excess of all other causes in the set, regardless of their
actual risk. PMR's, being much easier to perform, are
commonly calculated for occupational groups purely as a
preliminary "screening" type of study, to be followed by
the more definitive SMR study. In the case of Milham and
Petersen's two studies however (2) and (3), these are
based on such large state-wide populations, that considerably more confidence may be invested in their findings.
The findings of these two studies on Washington State and
California populations are quite thought-provoking, especially for those commoner occupations for which there are
upwards of 1,000 deaths available for analysis. In many
instances the results are quite similar not only between
these two American populations but also in comparison
with British and New Zealand data. Of course, studies on
whole industrial and occupational groups of this kind
relate only indirectly to specific toxic agents, but in
some cases a salient toxic exposure would appear to be
the most likely explanation of a consistently observed
increased proportion of mortality from a particular cause.

Occupational mortality studies have particularly lent
themselves to the search for or quantification of the
risk/potency of occupational chemical (and a few physical)
carcinogens. This is for several reasons. Firstly, most
occupational cancers, except for those of the skin, have
a high case fatality rate and therefore the mortality
rate tends to closely follow incidence. It is, after all,
the abnormal incidence of a disease in which we are mainly
interested in evaluating toxic response. Secondly, the
long and variable latency periods seen in most occupational
cancers, which are likely to obscure causal relationships
in purely anecdotal and clinical observations, do not so
readily escape epidemiologic scrutiny, providing cohorts
with sufficiently long duration of exposure and time lapse
between onset of exposure and point of death, are studied.

The successes of occupational mortality studies in
identifying or confirming occupational carcinogens include
those on workers exposed to asbestos, arsenic, beta-naph-
thylamine and benzidine, bischloromethyl ether (BCME),
certain chromates, certain nickel compounds, radon-daughters
(uranium miners and hematite miners), ionizing radiation
from radiological equipment. I have not included vinyl
chloride workers on this list quite deliberately. I happened to be involved, while working with doctors Tabershaw,
Cooper and Gaffey in Berkeley in 1973-74, in the largest-
to-date, industry-wide mortality study on vinyl chloride
manufacturers and polymerizers in this country, sponsored
by the Chemical Manufacturers' Asspciation. When we were
at least six months into the study, the clinical observation, initially of only three cases of hemangiosarcoma
of the liver at a single plant was made by Drs. Creech
and Johnson at the Louisville plant of B.F.Goodrich (4)
among vinyl chloride polymerization workers (i.e. manufacturers of polyvinyl chloride). This anecdotal finding
was corroborated by animal studies in Bologna, Italy by
Professor Cesare Maltoni (5). However, as you will see
by observing the key SMR table from the Equitable Environmental Health/CMA study (by Gaffey,Tabershaw and Cooper),
which I reproduce here on the following page as the Final
Report has still not been published in the open literature,
hemangiosarcoma of the liver, of which five cases were
identified, did not even obtrude. They are included and
as it were "buried" in the category "Malignant Neoplasms,
Digestive Organs and Peritoneum (150-159)", which otherwise had a deficit so that the final SMR for the rubrick
was only 75. This is because hemangiosarcoma of the liver
is so exceedingly rare that at that time the mortality
rates for this specific tumor were not available from the
National Center for Health Statistics. It has since been
estimated by Dr. William Lloyd then of NIOSH, now at OSHA
that during the relevant decades the annual mortality from
hemangiosarcoma of the liver for the entire U.S. population
was approximately 25 per year (6). This points up an interesting feature of epidemiologic studies, employing published
statistics for comparison purposes, that is for generating
expected rates - if the condition is of excessive rarity
it may be missed. At the same time it was the great rarity
of the tumor which drew the attention of Drs. Creech and
Johnson to the fact that with three cases occurring at one
plant over a few years (it later turned out that there
were three or four more cases buried in different types of
record at that plant) they almost certainly had a "cluster",
that is a greatly excessive number of cases over what they
should have expected, on their hands.

Table 1.   Observed/Expected Deaths and Standardized
           Mortality Ratios for Selected Causes of Death
           in 9,677 Vinyl Chloride Workers.

Cause of Death with ICD No. (a)	Obs./Exp.	SMR (b
All causes	707/795.0	89**
All malignancies (140-205)	139/141.4	104
Malignant neoplasms, buccal and pharynx (140-148)	5 / 5.2	102
Malignant neoplasms, digestive organs and peritoneum (150-159)	29 /40.8	75
Malignant neoplasms, respiratory system (160-164)	45 /44.3	107
Malignant neoplasms, genital organs (170-179)	4 / 7.2	59
Malignant neoplasms, urinary organs (180-181)	8 / 6.9	123
Malignant neoplasms, other and unspecified sites (190-199)	28 /20.2	147
Malignant neoplasms, brain & other parts of nervous system (193)	12 / 5.9	215*
Leukemia and aleukemia (204)	9 / 6.7	143
Lymphomas (200-203, 205)	11 /10.4	112
Major cardiovascular and renal diseases (330-334,400-468,592-594)	347/385.2	95
Cirrhosis of liver (581)	14/ 26.5	56**
All other certified causes	169/241.9	74**
Number of workers at risk	9,677	
Number of person-years	120,203	

(a) Cause-specific numbers indicate categories in the 1955
    (7th) revision of the International Classification of
    Diseases.
(b) SMR's (other than for All Causes) adjusted for 38
    deaths with no death certificates by factor of +5.68%
*   Significant at the 0.05 level
** Significant at the 0.01 level

(Table taken from "Epidemiological Study of Vinyl Chloride
Workers-Final Report" prepared for the Chemical Manufacturers' Assoc., 1825 Connecticut Ave. NW, Washington,D.C.
20009, by Equitable Enviromental Health, Inc.,6000 Executive Blvd., Suite 400, Rockville,Md. 20852,submitted Jan.
1978.)

There are two other points of interest on this table I
I should like to briefly discuss. The first is the overall
SMR for deaths from all causes of 89, significantly below
100 or expectation at the 0.01 probability level. This is
a manifestation of the so called "Healthy Worker Effect"
which is almost invariably seen in occupational mortality
studies (7). It is not so much, alas, an indication of the
unusual salubriousness of working conditions in the industry
as a reflection of the fact that any employed population,
by definition, has to be fit enough to be working and will
not include certain elements of the general population,
including very small children, the aged and the permanent-
ly infirm who have an inherently higher-than-average mortality rate and contribute negatively to the mortality experience of the general population. It has even been suggested further that, at least in western industrial society,
a state of chronic unemployment among the physically fit,
may also be associated with a higher mortality experience.
The second point of interest is the finding of the only
significantly raised SMR, that of 215 for malignant tumors
of the brain and other parts of the nervous system, based
on 12 cases. This observation is of particular concern to
my corporation, Union Carbide, at this time because we are
currently aware of an apparently excessive frequency of
primary brain tumor deaths, mainly from glioblastoma multiforme, at one of our largest general chemical plants. I
say "apparently" because, as of this time we have only a
raised PMR to go on. A comprehensive historical prospective (cohort) mortality study of the plant population since
its inception in 1942, is currently being undertaken joint-
ly by NIOSH and OSHA with the full cooperation of the corporation. To date some 17 confirmed cases of primary brain
tumor have been identified, of which two had extremely
short durations of employment at this plant (29 and 38
days respectively). Be that as it may, whether the appropriate number is 15 or 17,there would appear to be an excess
of the order of four-fold over expectancy. Now the curious
thing is that, although this plant has both manufactured
and polymerized vinyl chloride at this plant, not a single
case of primary brain tumor has so far appeared among the
cohort of some 400 "vinyl chloride exposed workers" identified at this plant for the purposes of the Equitable Environmental Health/CMA Study. In fact only one of the cases
has any suggestion of occupational exposure to vinyl chloride during part of his work history at our plant. Of the
original 12 primary brain tumors identified in the earlier
study two were contributed by Union Carbide, but they were
both from our South Charleston, West Virginia plant, which
is more than 10 years older than the plant now under invest-

igation. Waxweiler et al in 1976 (8) collected some 19
primary brain tumors from the vinyl chloride industry,
including the 12 already described, found that all but one
were classifiable as glioblastoma multiforme, and opined
that vinyl chloride must be the causal agent. Maltoni, in
his continuing large scale rat-exposure studies, has found
primary brain tumors in some of the animals, among a great
variety of other tumors (9).

Making the problem even more complicated however is
the presence of "clusters" of primary brain tumors, in
almost certainly excessive numbers in at least two other
plants in the same part of Texas. One of these plants has
employed vinyl chloride, the other not vinyl chloride but
acrylonitrile, which has been shown to produce brain tumor
in animals experimentally. In April, 1979 Terry Thomas
from the NCI presented a paper at the AOMA Annual Meeting
of a proportional mortality study performed on death certificates made available by the Oil, Chemical and Atomic
Workers' Union from their membership in the petroleum and
petrochemical industries, which showed more than a two-
fold excess of primary brain tumors. In the meantime Dr.
Patricia Buffler, now of the School of Public Health of
the University of Texas Health Center, Houston, is perform
ing a mortality study in the Texas, Gulf-Coast counties
in which all the plants mentioned lie, and is so far under
the impression that the incidence of primary brain tumors
appears to be above the national level, although that for
Texas as a whole is not.

Before leaving the subject of occupational mortality
studies, I should like to point out that not all have been
positive for cancer, although "negative" studies do not
seem to enjoy the esteem of the "positive", however well
the former are conducted, particularly in government circ-
les. A series of three studies conducted by NIOSH and its
predecessor bureau of occupational health on the small but
specialized beryllium industry, were in fact negative,
although certain witnesses at the Public Hearings held by
OSHA in the summer of 1977, went to extreme lengths of
casuistry to claim that beryllium had in fact been shown
to be a "weak" pulmonary carcinogen, (10,11,12). Many other
studies have been performed, looking for confirmation of
a suspected occupational excess of one type of cancer or
another, with "negative so far" results. I personally
categorically reject the governmental assertion that negative epidemiologic studies of carcinogenesis are, by definition, invalid.

Finally, it should not be assumed that occupational mortality studies are exclusive to cancer in their utility. Cardiovascular disease mortality is also of great interest in certain occupational groups, notably carbon disulfide workers in the viscose-rayon industry. This story came about in a rather unusual way. Back in 1967 in Great Britain, Dr. Richard Schilling and his colleagues from the London School of Hygiene were investigating the allegation that occupational exposure to carbon disulfide, a particularly pernicious toxic solvent with a very broad spectrum of toxicity, might be associated with hypertension. They were engaged on a blood-pressure survey in a viscose-rayon plant when one of the plant staff commented on the seemingly high rate of coronary "heart attacks" in the work force. On performing a mortality study, the investigators in fact confirmed an excess risk of death from "coronary heart disease" (13). This initial study, published in 1968, has triggered a whole series of similar studies, particularly in Scandinavia (14,15,16,17) all of which have tended to confirm the hypothesis that carbon disulfide exposure, at levels somewhere in excess of 20 ppm and possibly lower, is indeed associated with an increased risk of coronary heart disease or ischemic heart disease mortality. Recently however, one study has been reported from the Netherlands by Vertin (18) which purports to be negative and strongly challenges all the foregoing studies. It is to be hoped that the four-plant U.S. study currently being undertaken by Professor Brian Mac-Mahon of Harvard, may resolve this controversy, at least for the United States' rayon industry.

There is no reason why other non-malignant diseases should not be investigated by the occupational mortality study approach, such as chronic obstructive pulmonary disease, severe renal disease, etc., providing that the disease of interest carries a significant mortality, and furthermore that that disease is likely to be credited as the underlying cause of death on the death certificate. These two prerequisites of course considerably restrict the number of disease states which lend themselves to study by this method, but I am convinced that there is more scope in this field.

OCCUPATIONAL MORBIDITY STUDIES

Studies of the differential incidence of disease, that is morbidity rates in particular occupational groups appear, at first glance, to offer much more scope in terms of the range of diseases, or toxic responses, which

could be studied in a living work force. However, this
area of research has been much less exploited than the
occupational mortality study, to date. One of the reasons is the extreme difficulty of performing morbidity
studies on an historical prospective basis, with the
great economies in real time of that mode, because records
of morbidity are never as well defined, let alone certified, as the mandatorily recorded and certified fact of
death. Many segments of industry, especially in the chemical and oil industries, are currently engaged in extensive
R & D work in the development of Occupational Health Surveillance Systems, to use but one of the formulae which
are in vogue. The common idea of all such systems is to
somehow standardize and computerize medical and biological
data, derived from periodic medical examination programs,
clinic visits, hospitalization records etc. and any biological monitoring data which may be collected with respect
to certain recognized exposures (e.g. urine and blood analyses for toxicants or their metabolites or enzymatic or
other changes they may produce) and enter into the same
computerized data storage system industrial hygiene data
reflecting specific environmental exposures from the workplace, and somehow make the system self-instructing in ter
of automatically and on an ongoing basis detecting any
meaningful relationships between (toxic) exposures and
morbid responses. The ideal is, of course, for industry
to equip itself with a fail-safe early warning system to
prevent any further unpleasant, even tragic surprises, as
the vinyl chloride denouement. Even as I write this however, many will recognize that this ideal is never likely
to be achieved, when there is such an infinity of parameters to examine.

Be all that as it may, there have been some important
applications of the morbidity study in the past, one of
which, more than 40 years ago, served to establish an
approximate threshold for the toxicity of a potentially
extremely dangerous industrial metal, mercury. In the
1930's P.A.Neal and his associates of the Public Health
Service performed surveys of the workers in the felt-hat
industry in New York and Connecticut (19). They found sign
of chronic mercurialism (mostly manifestations of neurotox
icity) in workers in environments with mercury in air leve
down to 0.1 mg Hg per cubic meter of air. This level then
was taken as the Threshold Limit Value and remained such
for more than 30 years (20). It is only unfortunate that,
in the politico-social climate of the thirties, it was not
deemed necessary to implement any safety margin between
what a toxicologist would call the minimum effect level

and a permissible occupational exposure level. The NIOSH
Criteria Document, published in 1973, calls for only a
modest reduction of the 8-hour time-weighted-average exposure standard to 0.05 mg mercury per cubic meter of air
(20) a figure which is also endorsed by the current list-
ing of Threshold Limit Values by the American Conference
of Governmental Industrial Hygienists (ACGIH). This remains
the occupational exposure standard for which the epidemiological basis is the most solid.

COMMUNITY-BASED EPIDEMIOLOGICAL STUDIES

Epidemiologic studies of community or regional as
opposed to occupational populations, with respect to the
effects of potentially toxic exposures in the environment,
be it from air or water pollution or dietary sources,
would appear to offer much broader scope. Such studies
have the initial attraction of being of a more broadly
representative population than a specific occupational
group. However, as must be immediately apparent it is
much more difficult to characterize exposures, either
qualitatively or quantitatively, for individuals in a
"free-living" community environment. Even with widely
dispersed ambient air contaminants such as sulfur or
nitrogen oxides or various types of particulates, for
example, considerable differences for all these classes
have been demonstrated as between indoor and outdoor environments. Furthermore air monitoring stations must be
limited in number and especially where industrial stationary
sources of air pollution are local to a metropolitan
area, considerable variations in the concentrations of
air pollutants occur in different localities, influenced
by location relative to the pollution source, prevailing
winds, other meteorological conditions etc.

The Air Quality Act of 1967, requiring as it did the
declaration of certain pollutants as "Criteria Pollutants"
mandating in turn the setting of ambient air quality standards, provided a great stimulus to the epidemiological
appraisal of the effects of air pollution, attributed to
each of the "criteria pollutants" in turn, upon health.
Each of the Air Quality Criteria Documents (for Sulfur
Oxides and Particulates originally published in 1969; for
Photochemical Oxidants 1970; Nitrogen Oxides in 1971)
devotes a major and important chapter to "epidemiological
appraisal". Both mortality and morbidity data were reviewed
for each of these major pollutants in turn, both in relation to acute episodes of severe air pollution, usually
associated with thermal inversions and air stagnation

phenomena, and temporal or geographic comparisons between
differing general pollutionlevels. One problem which was
immediately recognized was the virtual impossibility of
separating or differentiating health effects from exposure
to one pollutant, from effects attributable to the others,
for at ambient air concentrations the effects of each of
the criteria pollutants are to all intents and purposes
indistinguishable, and moreover none of these pollutants
ever occurs in isolation. With a candor which is as comm-
endable as it is unusual in a governmental research publication this fact is acknowledged in the Air Quality Criteria
for Sulfur Oxides document (21):

> "Because sulfur oxides tend to occur in the same
> kinds of polluted atmospheres as particulate
> matter, few epidemiologic studies have been able
> adequately to differentiate the effects of the
> two pollutants. It follows, therefore, that the
> studies presented in this chapter are frequently
> identical with those described in the companion
> document, Air Quality Criteria for Particulate
> Matter."

So much for the relationship between sulfur oxides and
particulates (in the case of sulfate aerosols, the two
overlap in any case), but virtually the same could be
said of nitrogen oxides and photochemical oxidants. The
fact that individual studies tend only to report on the
concentration of those particular pollutants to which they
are directed does not mean that other pollutants were not
concomitantly present and acting.

Because the epidemiologic studies available in the
literature for review in the first round of Air Quality
Criteria documents suffered severe limitations from not
having been expressly designed for the purpose of elucid-
ating hypothetical thresholds for adverse health effects,
and most were seriously lacking in objective environmental data, the newly founded Environmental Protection Agency
through its National Environmental Research Center, attempted to carry out studies expressly designed to remedy these
limitations. Known as the CHESS (Community Health and Environmental Surveillance System) studies, these were laudably ambitious and innovative. However, only the series
addressing sulfur oxides was ever formally reported on,
and these only by an interim report: "Health Consequences
of Sulfur Oxides: A Report from CHESS, 1970-1971" (22)
The analyses of the studies seemed to be flawed by a desire
on the part of the analysts to draw conclusions consonant
with already established agency policy. In late 1974
(the above CHESS report having been released in May of

that year) a consulting firm with whom I was then associated received a contract from the Federal Energy Administration, to perform a critical analysis, officially of
the aforementioned "...Report from CHESS"(22) but unoffic-
ially and more urgently, of a draft paper which was entitled "Health Effects of Increasing Sulfur Oxides Emissions".
This position paper, though never officially published, had
been widely circulated within E.P.A. , other governmental
agencies and the academic community during 1974, and seemed
to represent E.P.A.'s "position" on atmospheric sulfur oxides, and especially "acid sulfate aerosols". It went considerably further than the published "...Report from CHESS"
(22) and presented an apocalyptic vision of what would be-
fall the public health if sulfur oxides emissions of all
kinds, but especially those from "stationary fossil fuel
combustion sources" (i.e. the electric power utilities),
were not drastically curbed. We had less than two months to
perform our task and were not in a position to challenge
the data, whether health or environmental parameters, of
CHESS, but only to critique the methodology employed and
in that light to comment upon E.P.A.'s conclusions. We realized at the outset that we were not likely to win any popularity contests either with E.P.A. or with the adherents
of the environmental movement.

Our report was submitted to the F.E.A. in February 1975
(23) and led to, among other things, a summons to testify
before Senator Muskie's subcommittee on the Clean Air Act
and its implementation, in April of that year. Basically
we found that the data, as presented, did not support E.P.A.'s
more extreme positions, that there was conflicting evidence on sulfur oxides, particulates and health effects both
from mortality studies in New York City (24,25) and clinical
morbidity studies in London (26) that militated strongly
against the prominent attribution of adverse health effects
to sulfur oxides. We also found that the attempts to establish thresholds for sulfur oxides-mediated health effects
by "hockey-stick functions" were statistically flawed. It
was also commented that much of the morbidity data, especially that based on self-administered questionnaires, diaries,
parents' reporting on their asthmatic children, were inherently weak, highly subjective, prone to bias, and that certain
well established validation techniques (such as the inclusion
of "hooker questions") had been avoided. Predictably this
criticism was not well received and it was suggested that
we also had been biased in our criticism in order to accommodate our client agency, the Federal Energy Administration,
whose mission could be seen to be in conflict with that of
E.P.A. over a large area. However, our report was more than

vindicated when on Labor Day of the same year there was
published a lengthy investigative report of a special congressional committee set up to study in depth the conduct
of the CHESS studies. (This investigation had, in part,
been instigated by an attack earlier that year, in the Los
Angeles Times, on one of the principal CHESS investigators,
suggesting scientific improprieties, which in turn triggere
congressional hearings.) The investigative report went much
further than ours, not only confirming all our criticisms
but, having access to the raw data and more than five montl
of working time, exposed much of that too as being quite
spurious. The lesson to be learned from this rather sad
history is that when epidemiology is made subservient to
political expediency, or forced to support previously adopt
policies and positions, it can be perverted as readily as
any other science of probabilistic estimation.

What the CHESS studies had laudably set out to do was
to determine thresholds for the toxic response to communit
air pollution by epidemiologic means, to provide a rationa
basis for Federal Ambient Air Quality Standards. However,
further level of sophistication is necessary in considerin
the threshold concept in the context of air pollutants and
their evaluation by epidemiological - as opposed to toxicological means. Basically the threshold so determined is f
the smallest detectable increase in incidence, above basel
of a particular health effect (whether mortality or one of
a range of respiratory or cardiopulmonary symptoms), as
registered by individuals of a particular community, as
detected by a particular survey method. Seen in this light
it becomes apparent that the "threshold" will be as much
a function of general pathological, psychological and sociological variables as of the fundamental toxicity of the
air pollutant in question.

SIGNIFICANCE REQUIREMENTS

Significance requirements for epidemiological studies
of toxic response are the obligatory second part of the
title of this presentation, and I am a little concerned
that some of the audience might have been led by such a
title to expect a magic number, or range of numbers, or
rubric, which can be applied universally to determine
whether an epidemiologically (that is to say statistically
demonstrated association between exposure, at a particular level to a toxicant and a particular level of respons
is significant in the sense of biologically meaningful.
However, the statistical association as a mathematical
attribute is only one of several criteria which should

be satisfied in an epidemiological study in order to support the proposition that a demonstrated association is causal, rather than secondary or entirely spurious. These criteria include:

        (i) a correct temporal relationship (i.e. putative cause must be shown to precede observed effect)

        (ii) there must be a graded response (or dose-response relationship, which usually will be positive)

        (iii) there should be consistency of results between different studies of the same association in different populations, and preferably by different methods.

        (iv) it should be "biologically plausible" that the association is causal, in other words, it should be possible to postulate a mechanism in the light of current biological knowledge and theory

        (v) the statistical association should be "strong"

        (vi) intervention to change the level or intensity of the suspect causal factor (independent variable) should be followed by some diminution in the incidence or severity of the effect (the dependent variable).

By strength of statistical association one tends to imply "significance" of a Chi^2 or other appropriate test at conventionally the 0.05 probability level or higher. Some authors like to present not only Chi^2 values, and or probability numbers but also confidence limits and standard errors, to give a feeling of the robustness of the differential data. In the case of the Relative Risk estimate such as a Standardized Mortality Ratio, in addition to a conventional index of "significance" most investigators feel that a Relative Risk of less than two-fold is unlikely to be biologically, as opposed to purely statistically significant, because of the relative insensitivity of the mortality study. However, it must be borne in mind that a very highly significant statistical association alone is just as likely to occur with a secondary or non-causal, as with a causal association. On the other hand, a series of consistent small deviations, individually lacking statistical significance, may well indicate a weak, or diluted causal association.

REFERENCES

1. OPCS - Office of Population Censuses and Surveys, 1971.
   The Registrar General's Decennial Supplement, England
   and Wales, 1961, Occupational Mortality Tables. London:
   Her Majesty's Stationery Office.
2. Milham,S. Jr., 1976. Occupational mortality in Washingto
   State 1959-1971, H.E.W. Publication No.(NIOSH) 76-175-C.
   NIOSH Research Report, 3 volumes.
3. Petersen,G.R. and Milham,S.Jr.1980. Occupational mortality in the State of California 1959-1961 H.E.W. Public
   ation No. (NIOSH) 80-104. NIOSH Research Report.
4. Creech,J.L. and Johnson,M.N., 1974: Angiosarcoma of
   liver in the manufacture of polyvinyl chloride.
   J occup Med, 16:150-151, 1974.
5. Tabershaw I.R. Editor's note, J occup Med, 16:150-151,
   1974.
6. Lloyd,J.W.1974: Personal communication.
7. McMichael,A.J. 1976: Standardized Mortality Ratios and
   the "Healthy worker effect": Scratching beneath the
   surface. J occup Med 18(3):165-168
8. Waxweiler,R.J.;Stringer,W.;Wagoner,J.K. and Jones,J.
   1976: Neoplastic risk among workers exposed to vinyl
   chloride. Ann N Y Acad Sci 271:40-48
9. Maltoni,C.: Personal communication to American Society
   of Toxicology, Washington D.C., April, 1980.
10. Bayliss,D.L.;Lainhart,W.S.;Cralley,L.J.,Ligo,R.;Ayer,H.
    and Hunter,F.: 1972: Mortality patterns in a group of
    former beryllium workers. NIOSH Unpublished research
    report.
11. Bayliss,D.L. and Lainhart,W.L.:Undated. Mortality
    patterns in beryllium production workers. NIOSH
    Unpublished research report.
12. Bayliss,D.L. and Wagoner,J.K. 1977: Bronchogenic cancer
    and cardio-respiratory disease mortality among beryl-
    lium production workers. NIOSH Unpublished research rep
    report.
13. Tiller,J.R.;Schilling,R.S.F. and Morris,J.N.:1968:
    Occupational toxic factor in mortality from coronary
    heart disease. Brit med J 4:407-11
14. Hernberg,S.; Nurminen,M. and Tolonen,M.:1973:Excess
    mortality from coronary heart disease in viscose ray-
    on workers exposed to carbon disulfide. Work environ
    Health 10:93-99
15. Tolonen,M.;Hernberg,S.;Nurminen,M. and Tiitola,K. 1975:
    A follow-up study of coronary heart disease in viscose
    rayon workers exposed to carbon disulphide. Brit J
    indust Med 32:1-10

16. Hernberg,S.;Tolonen,M.and Nurminen,M.1976: Eight-year follow-up of viscose rayon workers exposed to carbon disulfide. Work environ Health 2:27-30.

17. Nurminen,M.1976: Survival experience of a cohort of carbon disulphide exposed workers from an eight-year prospective follow-up period. Int J Epidemiol 5:179-85

18. Vertin,P.G..1978:Incidence of cardiovascular diseases in the Dutch viscose rayon industry. J occup Med 20: 346-350.

19. Neal,P.A.;Jones,R.R.;Bloomfield,J.J.;Dallavalle,J.M. and Edwards,T.I.1937:Study of chronic mercurialism in the hatters' fur-cutting industry. Public Health Bulletin 234. Federal Security Agency, U.S.Public Health Service.

20. NIOSH. 1973: Criteria for a recommended standard... Occupational exposure to inorganic mercury. DHEW. (NIOSH) HSM 73-11024 p.72.

21. U.S. Dept. of H.E.W.,Public Health Service,Environmental Health Service, National Air Pollution Control Administration 1969: Air Quality Criteria for Sulfur Oxides. Publication AP-50, p.117

22. U.S. Environmental Protection Agency, O.R.D., N.E.R.C., Health Consequences of Sulfur Oxides: A Report from CHESS, 1970-1971. EPA-650/1-74-004, May 1974

23. Tabershaw-Cooper Associates: A critical evaluation of current research regarding health criteria for sulfur oxides. A Technical Report prepared for the Federal Energy Administration, February 1975.

24. Schimmel,H. and Greenberg,L. 1972: A study of the relation of pollution to mortality, New York City, 1963-1968. J Air Pollut Control Assoc 22: 607-616

25. Schimmel,H.;Murawski,T.J. and Gutfeld,N.1974: Relation of pollution to mortality,New York City, 1963-1972. Presented at the Air Pollution Control Association meeting in Denver,Colorado, summer 1974.

26. Emerson,P.A. 1973: Air pollution, atmospheric conditions and chronic airways obstruction. J occup Med. 15(8):635-638

DISCUSSION

SEIDENFELD: The calculation of the levels of significance in the
group listed under "all malignancies" may provide further support
for the caveat listed at the end. In particular (I'm guessing now),
these levels of significance were obtained by just considering that
entry against all the others combined as opposed to doing a simultaneous analysis. It's as if you were testing side 1 on a 9-sided
die against all the other 8 sides as opposed to asking simultaneously if all sides were showing in a way that would correspond to
a fair die. With such a die, you could reject up to a third of the
sides individually as being unfair, and yet if you did a simultaneous test the die would be listed as fair. So, if you just listed
the ones that showed significant derivations against the combined
rest, of course there will be the one that is most abnormally high
and the one most abnormally low. What you must do instead, of
course, is to look at the simultaneous distribution since the die
can only land on one side or a person only die of one malignancy,
according to this table.

UTIDJIAN: There is also the inherent limitation that you can die of
only one malignancy in a legal sense (or National Center for Health
Statistics sense). Attempts have been made to introduce a classification with multiple causes of death, and there have been some pilot
studies. It becomes extraordinarily complex and with all our computerized records, I can't visualize this coming about before the
millennium. This is a serious problem. When you're on the path of
cancer and you come across the death certificate and the individual
died with the cancer of interest, but in fact was done in by a bus
accident or a gunshot wound, by convention the death has to be classified under the traumatic cause. You can't enter the cancer into
your analysis if you are using the National Center for Health
Statistics rates for comparison purposes.

The only hope of getting around that is by doing cooperative
studies between industries on such a large scale that they can generate their own expected rates from their own selected controls and
not rely on national statistics. And then you can set up your own
criteria to interpret all death certificates yourself.

UPTON: I think you have illustrated very nicely how one can miss a
major carcinogenic effect if the type of tumor in question is a rare
tumor. In the past we have naively tended to lump cancers in large
classes and expect too often that a carcinogen would increase the incidence of all leukemias, or all gastrointestinal tumors. It is really important to break down the different kinds of tumors and look
at each tumor type, perhaps even within a given organ. How do you
see that need being met? Is that something that you think is feasible if anyone plans to have a small number of cases to begin with?

UTIDJIAN: If you have a strong index of suspicion and you know what you are looking for, I think you have a better chance. I guess that now it would be possible to generate expected rates for angiosarcoma of the liver because we know about it. The problem is that you are usually on a fishing expedition, where rarity is a two-edged sword. By virtue of its rarity, the appearance of angiosarcoma hit a physician in the eye at Louisville, Ky. It did not take a statistician to tell this physician that even three cases were, in a sense, an epidemic.

Sometimes people ask why do we go on studying asbestos. It has been known for a number of years that asbestos is a potent carcinogen, but there is the unresolved issue of induction of pleuromesothelioma. The type of asbestos is in question: whether it is primarily a chrysotile or whether is can be amosite, and whether it is specific to fiber dimensions or to a physicochemical property of the fiber. So these in-depth studies are justified as the only way in which we will identify the specific carcinogenic factors.

Again, there is a political pressure here. There are people who want to incriminate vinyl chloride for causing as many types of cancer as possible. I was privileged to hear Maltoni talk just a few weeks ago down in Bethesda about his 10,000 rat studies. And in a sense he was telling us that it is only a matter of time until he will be able to produce any tumor you name in some rats, at least at some level of exposure. I think it is important to investigate the possibility that vinyl chloride is also a brain carcinogen on the basis of that study, and Waxweiler at NIOSH is investigating on a sort of case control basis the possibility that it's a pulmonary carcinogen. We are in an epidemiological sense fortunate -- where a disease is rare, as in the case of hemangiosarcoma of the liver, which is almost but not quite unique to vinyl chloride exposures. We know it is also associated with thorotrast and certain arsenical compounds. Such patterns help our attempts to define the whole spectrum of risks for one kind of exposure.

To respond to your question, I think it is a matter of first doing serial studies as hypothesis-generating fishing expeditions, and then focusing on the suspected effects and continuing the study to test each hypothesis critically. Eventually we may say we are getting no new information, this kind of asbestos is a carcinogen, we need not investigate asbestos any more.

POCHIN: I'm sure it is important to look at the individual types of cancer, provided one doesn't suffer too much from the two penalties: firstly, as you go to the smaller groups you are paying a bigger and bigger price from the smaller absolute numbers and the expanding confidence limits of your statistical distributions, and secondly, that the more individual cancers you study, the greater

the likelhood that one will reach a certain level of apparent significance by chance and you may suffer as much by going to individual cases as you gain.

BERG: I just would like to follow this with a suggestion that even
in dealing with people of good will and some technical competence,
there is a serious hazard of their mistaking an explanation that was
made up to fit the data for a theory that was tested by a prospective study. With some skill in subdividing cancers, it is possible
to select a cluster of cases and correlate some peculiar and unique
circumstances with their particular cancers, and then, of course,
predict an enormous increase in incidence of those particular cancers under circumstances that you happened to find. This is what
Dr. Spielman called "fishing in murky waters."

     Now, if people understood that this can only lead to a hypothe-
sis which has yet to be investigated by looking forward and seeing
if the correlation is real, we could speculate freely. But this
hasn't been made clear in the literature, has it?

UPTON: Not often enough. I think the problems that you and Sir
Edward have pointed out are very real problems. In this era one is
all too prone to seize on what appears to be a meaningful cluster
without remembering all of the necessary caveats that have been
brought up this morning.

SAGAN: There is another kind of interpretive error that I should
like to comment upon, and that is the tendency to seize upon only
the positive associations as meaningful and to ignore the negative
associations as meaningless. We are not psychologically prepared
to consider negative effects. For example, in the case of vinyl
chloride we have focused on the three excess cancers and neglected
the fact that there is a significant deficit of cirrhosis. This, I
think, reflects the fact that we live in a society which is intensely
cancerophobic, where we seem to prefer to avoid cancer rather than
to extend life or reduce overall mortality.

     A real possibility exists that exposure to chemical agents may
alter the spectrum of disease without altering the overall risk of
disease or of mortality. For example, in the case of vinyl chloride,
it is just possible that what the vinyl chloride has done is to induce liver cancer at the expense of other liver disease so that
some prospective cases of cirrhosis of the liver end up as a malignancy. Under such a scenario, the overall frequency of liver disease
would not be affected, survival would not be affected, but only the
cause of death. I believe that this information is consistent with
the data which we have just seen, but is an interpretation which is
rarely considered either because of our preoccupation with cancer,
or because it does not fit with our models of disease or both.

UTIDJIAN: I would like to correct the impression that this is a
study of vinyl chloride workers as a whole. At our particular plant,
the current brain tumor problem, which remains a completely baffling
enigma as far as I'm concerned, is not apparently a vinyl chloride
problem. The work force includes a small subcohort of vinyl chloride
workers. If you pull together Terry Thomas' OCAW/PMR study and the
plant clusters that we are aware of in Texas in our own corporation,
the salient common exposure factor in all the cases is ethylene gas.
Applying Criterion #4 on my list, biological probability seems to
be rather low, but not out of the question. At CIIT they have been
doing some work on biotransformation of ethylene. They have found
evidence of activity by very sensitive radioisotope techniques, but
they think that less than 1/10th of 1% of ethylene is metabolized by
rodents to some unidentified transient and ephemeral epoxy form,
possibly ethylene oxide or something closely related. This aroused
great interest, because switching from epidemiology to toxicology we
are confronted with the high probability that ethylene oxide itself
will prove to be a human carcinogen. We have animal studies which
strongly suggest it, and we've known for some years that it is a
mutagen.

BIOLOGICAL MODELS IN EPIDEMIOLOGY:

RADIATION CARCINOGENESIS

Charles E. Land

Environmental Epidemiology Branch
National Cancer Institute
Bethesda, Maryland, USA 20205

INTRODUCTION

There is general agreement that ionizing radiation is
the best understood of the common environmental causes of
cancer. Although the mechanisms by which radiation damage
to tissue leads to cancer are not known precisely, a considerable body of radiobiological theory has evolved,
providing valuable guidelines for the analysis of observa-
tional data. The existence in man of a cancer risk from
ionizing radiation is well established. It appears to
affect all or nearly all tissues in which cancer commonly
occurs. It is the nature of this risk that now excites
our interest, including 1) the relative sensitivities of
various tissues to the carcinogenic effects of ionizing
radiation, 2) the influence of sex, age at exposure, hormonal status and other host factors at the time of exposure, and the influence of cancer risk factors other
than radiation, on the carcinogenic response to radiation,
3) the distribution over time following exposure of the
excess cancer risk from radiation, and 4) the influence of
various dimensions of exposure, including dose, radiation
quality (linear energy transfer, or LET), and fractionation and protraction of dose. These factors are not unrelated, particularly the dimensions of exposure, but it is
the cancer risk from low-dose, low-LET radiation that is
of most concern for public policy, and about which there
is the most controversy.

Although the literature of theoretical and experimental radiobiology is vast, statistically reliable estimates
of risk based on human experience, if they can be ob-

tained, are preferable to those based on animal data. The
epidemiology of radiation carcinogenesis rests primarily
on studies of patient populations exposed to therapeutic
or substantial diagnostic x ray, or who were injected with
radioactive materials, workers who ingested or inhaled
radioactive materials in their occupational environments,
and the survivors of the atomic bombs dropped on Hiroshima
and Nagasaki, Japan.

    By far the most informative human data on radiation-
induced cancer pertain to high-dose exposures. The
reasons for this are statistical: as dose decreases, so
also does the excess risk due to exposure, and the amount
of data needed to obtain a usefully precise estimate of
the excess risk increases as its inverse square. That is,
if excess risk is proportional to dose, and if an exposed
population of 1,000 is necessary to estimate the excess
risk from a 100-rad exposure, then about 100,000 will be
necessary to estimate that from a 10-rad exposure, and 10
million for a 1-rad exposure. For example, the risk of
breast cancer is estimated to be about 6 excess cases per
million women per year, after a minimal latent period of
about 10 years, for a single x-ray exposure of 1 rad to
breast tissue.[1] Assuming an idealized study in which half
of a large group of women, all 35 years old, were given a
single mammographic examination delivering 1 rad to both
breasts, and the other half were not exposed, about 100
million women would require to be studied in order to have
a reasonable chance of obtaining an estimate close to the
(assumed) true value.[2] A case-control study would require
many times the number of breast cancer cases expected
annually in the United States among women in the age range
45-54, in order to produce an estimate of comparable
precision. A "small" study, involving a cohort of around
1 million women, could be expected to yield either a negative risk estimate, a positive but statistically non-
significant estimate, or one significantly greater than
zero but greatly exaggerated (in this example, at least
660% too high).[2] In other words, except in situations
where the cancer risk from low-dose radiation is high
relative to the underlying normal risk in the absence of
added radiation (and prenatal exposures from x-ray pel-
vimetry may be such an exception), studies of populations
exposed to low-dose radiation are likely to be unhelpful
or even misleading, even if quite large.

    The above discussion ignores another consideration,
that may be even more important than the requirement for
enormous sample sizes. If the effect to be measured is
small relative to normal risk, subtle biases in the ascer-

tainment of morbidity or exposure are far more important
than if the effect is large relative to normal risk.
Controlling for such biases calls for exceptional attention to detail at the same time that considerations of
statistical power require that this attention be extended
to unmanageably large numbers of subjects. Thus the
demands on scientific and economic resources are multiplied, further detracting from the feasibility of
epidemiological studies of populations exposed to low
doses of radiation.

     Since it is so difficult to answer questions about
low-dose risk directly, it is necessary to proceed indirectly, to rely on the considerable body of theoretical
and experimental radiobiology to provide a theoretical
framework of what makes sense and what doesn't, so that
the range of possible relations is limited to a manageable
few. Also, it is necessary to rely on the basic scientific principle of consistency of results among different
populations, differently exposed, to determine the
validity of objections to the use of any one of them.

SOME RADIOBIOLOGICAL THEORY

     The presumed mechanism by which ionizing radiation
affects cancer risk is the breaking or weakening, by
ionization, of chemical bonds in the genetic material of
somatic cells.[3],[4] Radiobiological models relating the
probability of cell damage to the frequency of ionizing
events in cell nuclei, their spatial and temporal disper-
sion, and the ability of DNA to repair damage caused by
ionization, form the basis for theoretical dose-response
models for radiation carcinogenesis. Radiation dose,
expressed in rads or Grays (1 Gray = 100 rads) gives the
amount of energy released in tissue by ionizing radiation,
and therefore the relative probability that an ionizing
event will occur at a given locus. Radiation quality or,
more precisely, ionization density or linear energy transfer (LET), expresses the tendency of ionizing events
caused by a particular kind of radiation to be dispersed
evenly or in clumps along radiation tracks. Low-LET
radiations, like gamma rays or high-energy x rays, produce
ionizations sparsely along radiation tracks, except at the
ends of the tracks, which are somewhat densely ionizing.[5]
Thus along most of a gamma-ray radiation track two
closely-spaced ionizing events are unlikely except where
the track is intersected by another. In the high-LET
tail, however, closely-spaced ionizing events are the
rule. Here, if an ionizing event occurs at a given locus,
the chances are very high that at least one more occurs

close by. For neutrons or alpha particles, whose radiation tracks are densely ionizing, the probability that two or more ionizing events occur within the volume occupied by a single molecule, for example, is proportional to dose. For the low-LET portion of tracks from gamma rays or high-energy x rays, this probability is proportional to the square of dose while for the high-LET tails it is proportional to dose.

It is believed that the damage caused by a single, isolated ionizing event is easier to repair than that from two closely spaced events.[6] Assuming further that unrepaired, or erroneously repaired, damage to a single cell can cause cancer, the probability of radiation-induced cancer should be proportional to dose for high-LET radiation, but for low-LET radiation this probability should be proportional to a weighted linear sum of dose and the square of dose, the sum of the probability of cancer from a single ionizing event plus the probability of cancer from two closely-spaced ionizing events.

Cell killing or cell sterilization is a competing effect of ionizing radiation that reduces the number of cells available for the induction of cancer. A cell that cannot divide cannot become cancerous. The functional form for a dose-response model for cell killing should be similar to that for the induction of cellular changes that may result in carcinogenesis, although the the coefficients may of course be different. The usual way of combining the concepts of cellular changes leading to carcinogenesis and cell killing as a competing effect is to express the risk of cancer due to radiation exposure as a quadratic function of dose, times the negative exponential of another quadratic function of dose, this one representing the reduced population of cells with the ability to divide further.

The form below gives cancer risk as a function of dose (D) from low-LET radiation:

(1) $Risk = (a_0 + a_1 D + a_2 D^2) \exp(-A_1 D - A_2 D^2)$.

An example of such a curve is shown in Figure 1. The structure imposed by the model is greater than that of a fourth degree polynomial approximation, because all the parameters in the model are non-negative, and all have radiobiological meaning. The intercept is the normal risk of cancer, in the absence of the extraneous radiation represented by dose D. The linear coefficient of dose is the additional risk of cancer per unit dose at very low

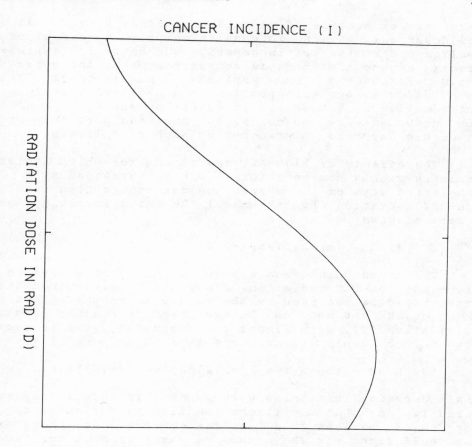

Fig. 1.   General dose-response model for radiation car-
          cinogenesis, including adjustment for the compet-
          ing effect of cell killing.

doses of radiation. It represents the sum of the effects
of isolated ionizing events from the main parts of radiation tracks and the closely-spaced events occuring in the
high-LET tails. The coefficient of dose-squared in the
quadratic form expresses the effect of closely-spaced
ionizing events produced by the interaction of two radiation tracks. The coefficients in the exponential expression are similarly defined, except that they correspond to
a biological effect qualitatively different from the initiation of a cancer. Cell killing is important here only
insofar as it affects cells that might develop into can-

cers, either because of radiation or other causes. At
low doses cell killing is considered to be an effect of
smaller order than carcinogenesis, and hence its expression in exponential form is acceptable under the approximate relationship, $1-x = \exp(-x)$, when x is small. This
formulation allows both positive and negative curvature,
but positive curvature, if it occurs at any dose level,
must occur at very low doses, and negative curvature, if
it occurs anywhere, must occur at high dose levels.

The effects of high-LET radiation, for which isolated
ionizing events can be ignored, can be expressed as a
simplified form of the expression for cancer risk from
low-LET radiation, by taking out the terms involving the
square of dose:

(2) Risk = $(a_0+b_1D)\exp(-B_1D)$.

The cancer risk from exposures involving a mixture of
high- and low-LET radiation, e.g., the mixed neutron and
gamma-ray dose received by the survivors of the Hiroshima
and Nagasaki A-bombs, can be expressed as a generalization
of equation (1), with linear and quadratic terms in gamma
dose (γ), but only linear terms in neutron dose (ξ):

(3) Risk = $(a_0+a_1\gamma+a_2\gamma^2+b_1\xi)\exp(-A_1\gamma-A_2\gamma^2-B_1\xi)$.

The theoretical reasoning upon which this formulation is
based implies that the linear coefficient for gamma ray
dose should be less than that for neutron dose, whenever
the coefficient for the square of gamma dose is positive.
That is, if two closely spaced ionizing events have a
biological effect greater than that of two isolated ionizing events, the effect of a given dose of neutron radiation should be greater than that of the same dose of gamma
radiation, especially at low doses where interactions
between low-LET radiation tracks are unlikely and where
the competing effect of cell killing is slight for both
types of radiation. Conversely, if the dose-response
curves for gamma radiation and neutron radiation are the
same, they should be linear.

According to the crude theory outlined above it does
not necessarily follow that if the dose-response curves
for gamma and neutron radiation are different there is
marked curvature in the gamma-ray curve over the dose
range observed, because the above theory does not specify
the relative magnitudes of the coefficients a_1 and a_2.
The highly sophisticated Theory of Dual Radiation Action
developed by Rossi and Kellerer[7] specifies a functional

relationship between the size of the biological target and the a_1/a_2 ratio of the dose-response curve for purely low-LET radiation, but the adequacy of the theory has been challenged by Goodhead,[8] who found that results obtained from in vitro studies of mutagenesis and inactivation using radiations of similar LET but different track length were inconsistent with the predictions of the model. The characterization of the dose-response relationship as a quadratic function of dose with positive coefficients for dose and dose-squared was not challenged, however. Brown[5] has estimated the ratio a_1/a_2 for different biological systems, obtaining typical values of about 130 for chromosome aberrations and much larger values for cell killing from in-vitro studies. In-vivo carcinogenesis obviously is a more complex phenomenon than mutagenesis, the induction of chromosome aberrations, or cell killing. Nonetheless, the models outlined in equations (1)-(3) are general enough to encompass most variations that have widespread support among radiobiologists.

STUDIES OF THE JAPANESE A-BOMB SURVIVORS

The role of studies of the Hiroshima and Nagasaki A-bomb survivors is crucial to the estimation of dose-response functions for radiation carcinogenesis and to compare the relative effects of neutron and gamma-ray radiation. The Life-Span Study (LSS) sample,[9] defined from a list of persons identified as A-bomb survivors from the 1950 Japanese national census and who were living in Hiroshima or Nagasaki in 1950, is large (82,000 exposed plus 26,000 non-exposed controls) and, unlike medically exposed populations, was not selected for exposure because of disease. Its age distribution represents that of the population of the bombed cities in 1945, and therefore offers a fairly complete picture with respect to age at exposure and its relationship to dose response for radiation-induced cancer. An additional sample includes persons exposed in utero and controls. The Japanese family registry system enables virtually complete mortality followup at the level of death certificate diagnosis. Until recently there was an active autopsy program, and at the level of incidence the research program benefits from a clinical program and local tissue, tumor, and leukemia registries.

Of primary importance is an elaborate dosimetry program based on location and shielding at the time of the bombings, which has yielded individual dose estimates for about 97% of the exposed members of the LSS sample.[10] The dose distribution is such that there are enough high-dose

survivors for useful risk estimates to be obtained for
many cancers. Most of the survivors were exposed to low
doses, however, which allows theoretical models of dose
response to be tested against the data to an extent not
possible with other exposed populations. Thus the LSS
sample data have the potential to define estimates of risk
at low dose levels with minimal arbitrary assumptions
about the shape of the dose response curve, and to estimate models to be applied to other data. The LSS sample
data have indeed played that role, to the extent possible,
in recent authoritative reviews of data on radiation induced cancer in man.[11],[12] Recently, the capacity for
analyzing dose response for specific cancer sites has been
greatly improved by the development of algorithms for
converting estimates of kerma ("kinetic energy released in
matter," a whole-body measure of exposure) to organ-
specific dose estimates.[13]

        The applicability of the LSS sample data to the es-
timation of low-dose risk for low-LET radiation like x ray
is limited to some extent because the larger part of the
data, that pertaining to the Hiroshima survivors, corresponds to individual doses having a substantial neutron
component. For Nagasaki survivors the neutron component
of dose is very small, but for Hiroshima survivors this
component is about 30% of the total at all dose levels.
Because of this, inferences about the shape of the dose
response for low-LET radiation from curve fitting alone
are effectively limited to what can be obtained from the
Nagasaki data.

Example: Leukemia incidence, Nagasaki A-bomb survivors

        The most extensive existing information on dose-
response relationships for leukemia induced by sparsely
ionizing radiation are the 1950-1971 incidence data from
the LSS sample of survivors of the Nagasaki A-bomb.[14]
Table 1 gives average bone marrow dose in rads, person-
years at risk (PY), and leukemia rates by kerma interval.
Rates are adjusted to the age distribution of the entire
LSS sample, including both cities. In this example the
neutron component of bone-marrow dose, because it is
small, has not been distinguished from the gamma-ray component. The age-adjusted rates have been assumed to have
the covariance structure of rates based on independent,
Poisson-distributed random variates. Curve fitting has
been by an iterative weighted least-squares algorithm
described elsewhere.[15] The data have been fitted to a
quadratic function of dose D, here denoted linear-
quadratic (LQ) to emphasize its dependence on both dose

Table 1. Leukemia incidence among members of the LSS
         sample, Nagasaki 1950-1971, by kerma interval.

Kerma int.	Av. dose	PY at risk	Rate per 10^4
0	0	90,944	2.44
1-9	2.1	128,288	4.77
10-49	11.8	71,676	4.41
50-99	38.9	25,643	0
100-199	79.0	27,355	18.6
200-299	132.	14,714	57.4
300-399	186.	5,415	35.1
400+	286.	6,981	93.7

and dose-squared,

(4) $LQ(D) = a_0 + a_1D + a_2D^2$,

and to a pure linear (L) model,

(5) $L(D) = a_0 + a_1D$,

and a pure quadratic (Q) model,

(6) $Q(D) = a_0 + a_2D^2$.

Since the coefficients a_0, a_1, and a_2 are all assumed to
be non-negative, models L and Q are the extreme forms of

Table 2. Summary of curve-fitting analyses of
         Nagasaki leukemia data.

Model[b]	Estimates±sd[a] a_1	a_2	Goodness of Fit chi-sq.	df	p
LQ(D) (4)	1.0±1.2	.010±.008	6.3	5	.28
L(D) (5)	2.5±0.6	---	6.9	6	.33
Q(D) (6)	---	.016±.004	7.7	6	.26

[a]Parameter estimates and standard deviations (sd)
[b]scaled by 10^6.
  See numbered equations in text.

the more general model LQ giving, respectively, the
highest and lowest low-dose risk estimates consistent with
the general model. For simplicity, the possible influence
of cell killing has been ignored.

        The results of these analyses are given in Table 2.
As seen from the chi-square values for lack of fit, and
from the curves drawn in Figure 2, the fitted curves do
not differ markedly in their closeness of fit to the data.
The models give similar risk estimates at around 150 rads.
Estimates of risk at low doses, on the other hand, differ

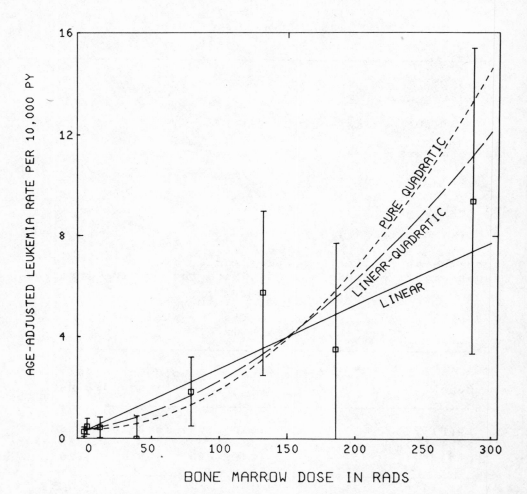

Fig. 2.   Age-adjusted leukemia incidence, LSS sample,
           Nagasaki 1950-1971, and fitted dose-response
           curves.

greatly among the different models. At 1 rad, for example, the estimated excess incidence per million PY
varies from .016 (±.004) for the Q model, to 1.0 (±1.2)
for the LQ model, to 2.5 (±0.6) for the L model.

Our inability to distinguish statistically, in terms
of goodness of fit, among models giving such diverse low-
dose risk estimates is a consequence of small sample size.
Suppose the LQ model estimate were correct, i.e., that at
dose D the expected risk per million PY were given by

(7) Risk per million PY = $33 + D + .01 D^2$,

and that the standard deviation of the risk were equal to
the expected risk divided by the number of PY of observation for risk. Then the least-squares estimate of the
linear coefficient a_1, using the LQ model, would have
expected value 1.0 per million and standard deviation 1.1
per million. Using the usual normal theory approximation,
this gives approximate power .24 for a_1 at level .05, that
is, for testing the hypothesis $a_1 = 0$ against the alternative $a_1 > 0$. In other words, power would be low for testing the LQ model against the Q model. Similarly, the
least-squares estimate of the dose-squared coefficient a_2
would have mean 0.01 per million and standard deviation
0.007 per million, corresponding to power .43. Thus power
also would be low for testing the LQ model against the L
model, although slightly higher than for the LQ vs. Q
comparison. If the numbers of PY at risk were increased
10-fold at all dose levels, the standard deviations of the
parameter estimates would be decreased by a factor of
3.16, giving power values of .906 for a_1 and .998 for a_2.
If, on the other hand, the numbers of PY were decreased by
a factor of 10, power would be only .09 for a_1 and .12 for
a_2. A 10-fold increase in only the PY corresponding to
under 100 rad kerma, where the linear term dominates under
the assumed model, would increase power to .65 for a_1 and
.64 for a_2. A 10-fold increase in only the PY for over
100 rad kerma, where the dose-squared term dominates,
would increase power somewhat more, to .71 for a_1 and .99
for a_2.

In general, if the L model is used to estimate risk
when the true dose-response relationship is that given in
(7), the quantity corresponding to the linear coefficient
is not a_1, the excess risk per rad at very low doses, but
a_1', the average excess risk per rad over the entire dose
range represented by the data. In the example, according
to (7), this value is 2.34 per million PY. Its estimate
has standard deviation 0.61 per million, giving statisti-

cal power of about .987 for a_1'. Similarly, if the Q
model is fitted to the data, the quantity estimated by the
coefficient for dose-squared is not a_2 but a_2', the
average excess incidence per unit of dose-squared, which
has value .0175 per million PY in the present example.
The estimate of this quantity has standard deviation .0038
per million, corresponding to approximate power .999 for
a_2'. The assumed true dose-response model is shown in
Figure 3, with 95% prediction intervals at the average

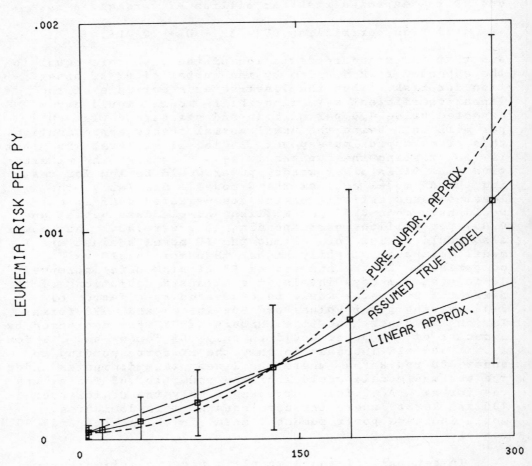

Fig. 3.   Expected values and 95% prediction intervals for
          leukemia incidence, assuming the LQ model es-
          timate and the sample size and dose distribution
          of the LSS sample, Nagasaki 1950-1971. Approx-
          imate curves correspond to the L and Q models.

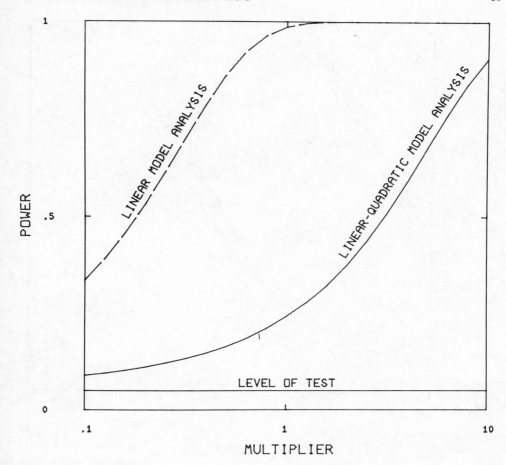

Fig. 4.   Power of the LQ and L model tests for a_1 at level
.05 as functions of sample size, assuming the LQ
model estimate and the dose distribution of the
LSS sample, Nagasaki 1950-1971.   Multiple = 1
corresponds to the LSS sample size.

dose values given in Table 1, and with the closest approximations to the true dose response according to models
L and Q, respectively.   Figure 4 compares power for a_1
using the LQ model with power for a_1' using the L model,
as functions of sample size.   Figure 5 similarly compares
the LQ and Q model analyses for a_2 and a_2', respectively.

    The message of Figures 4 and 5 is that if the true
dose response were given by equation (7), simple analyses

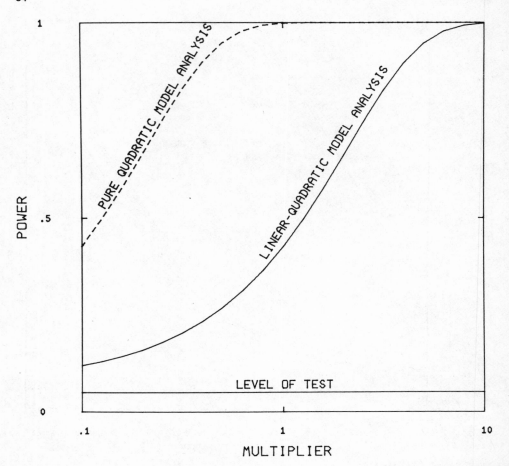

Fig. 5. Power of the LQ and Q model tests for a_2 at level
         .05 as functions of sample size, assuming the LQ
         model estimate and the dose distribution of the
         LSS sample, Nagasaki 1950-1971. Multiple = 1
         corresponds to the LSS sample size.

assuming a response proportional either to dose or to
dose-squared would have high power for showing the existence of a dose response, given the sample size and dose
distribution of the LSS sample data for leukemia incidence
among the survivors of the Nagasaki A-bomb, or even somewhat smaller sample sizes. An analysis incorporating
linear dependence on both dose and dose-squared, without
specifying the relative values of the coefficients, would
have poor power for showing the need for such a complex

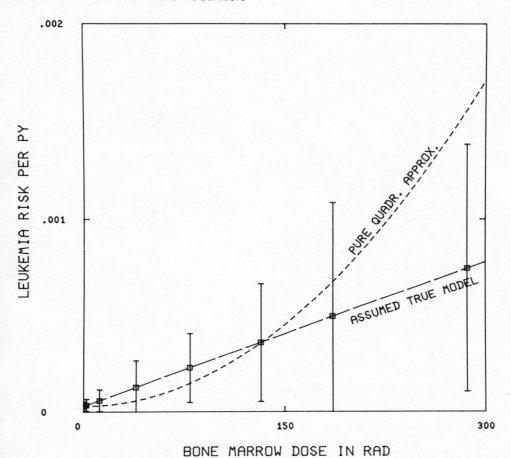

Fig. 6. Expected values and 95% prediction intervals for
leukemia incidence, assuming the L model estimate
and the sample size and dose distribution of the
LSS sample, Nagasaki 1950-1971. Approximate
curve corresponds to the Q model.

model unless the sample size were drastically increased.

If the true dose response relation were a simple
linear or a pure quadratic function of dose, would the
analysis be able to show this? Figure 6 shows expected
values and 95% prediction intervals assuming the L model
estimates in Table 2, and the closest Q-model approximation to this dose-response function. Figure 7 shows power
for a_1 as a function of sample size using the LQ and L

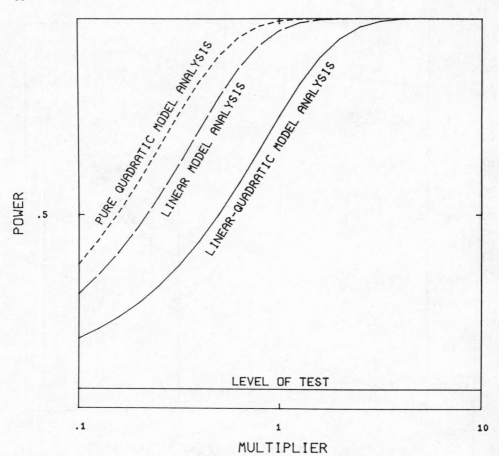

Fig. 7.   Power of the LQ and L model tests for a_1, and of
           the Q model test for a_2', at level .05 as func-
           tions of sample size, assuming the L model es-
           timate and the dose distribution of the LSS
           sample, Nagasaki 1950-1971. Multiple = 1 cor-
           responds to the LSS sample size.

model analyses, and for a_2' (= .0187 per million PY per
increment in dose-squared) using the Q model analysis.
Both the L and Q model analyses have high power for detection of a dose effect, even for sample sizes substantially
less than those given in Table 1. The Q model has more
power, presumably reflecting the relative strength of the
data above 100 rads. Although not as high, the LQ model
has acceptable power (.71) for a_1, much higher than in

Figure 4. Thus if the L model curve in Figure 6 were a
true representation of the dose response relationship, it
is likely that estimates obtained using the LQ model would
fit the data significantly better (at level .05) than
estimates obtained using the Q model, i.e., that the
analysis would discriminate between the L and LQ models on
the one hand and the Q model on the other. Under the
assumption $a_2 = 0$ the LQ analysis has power .05 for a_2,
regardless of sample size. Thus there is a 5% chance that

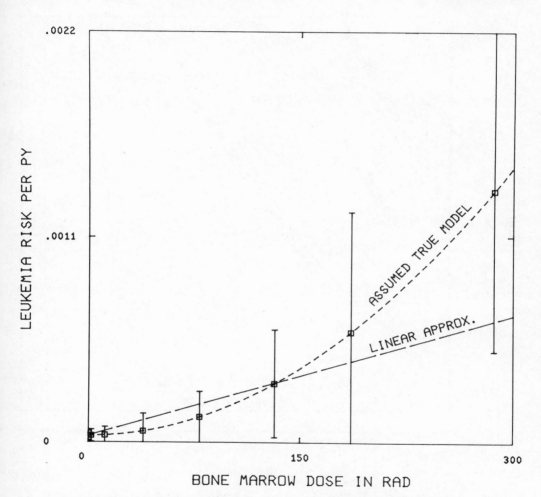

Fig. 8.   Expected values and 95% prediction intervals for
          leukemia incidence, assuming the Q model estimate
          and the sample size and dose distribution of the
          LSS sample, Nagasaki 1950-1971. Approximate
          curve corresponds to the L model.

the LQ model analysis would falsely discriminate between
the L and LQ models.

Figure 8 shows the true dose response and the L model
approximation assuming the Q model estimate in Table 2.
Figure 9 shows power for a_2 corresponding to Q and LQ
model analyses, and power for a_1' (= 2.14 per million PY
per rad) corresponding to an analysis using the L model.

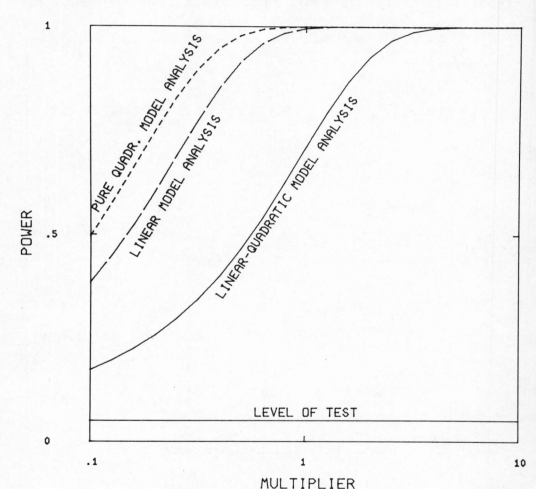

Fig. 9.   Power of the LQ and Q model tests for a_2, and of
           the L model test for a_1', at level .05 as func-
           tions of sample size, assuming the L model es-
           timate and the dose distribution of the LSS
           sample, Nagasaki 1950-1971. Multiple = 1 cor-
           responds to the LSS sample size.

The message of Figure 9 is analogous to that of Figure 7: assuming the dose response of Figure 8 and the sample size and dose distribution of Table 1, both simple dose-response analyses would have high power for detecting the existence of a dose response, and the LQ model analysis would be likely (power = .75) to discriminate between the LQ and Q models on the one hand and the L model on the other.

Considering for the moment only those power values in Figures 4, 5, 7, and 9 corresponding to the actual sample size, the results summarized in Table 2 suggest that neither of the two simple dose-response models is correct, and that the greater complexity of the LQ model is needed. This inference is a weak one, based on the observation that if either the L or Q model were correct the LQ model analysis would be more likely than not to yield statistically significant estimates of a_1 or a_2, respectively. A stronger inference, based on statistically significant values for both a_1 and a_2, would be likely only if the sample size were increased by a factor of 3 or more.

Example: Breast cancer incidence, Nagasaki

Tokunaga et al. have reported breast cancer incidence among female survivors of the Hiroshima and Nagasaki A-bombs and non-exposed controls for the period

Table 3. Breast cancer incidence among female members of the LSS sample, Nagasaki 1950-1974, by breast tissue dose interval in rads.

Dose interval	Av. dose	PY at risk	Rate per 10^4
0 [a]	0	149,365	1.70
1-3	1.9	40,933	1.87
4-9	5.6	38,769	1.75
10-19	13.0	26,568	1.65
20-49	33.6	18,288	3.10
50-99	70.8	15,962	2.09
100-199	143.0	17,883	5.43
200-299	240.5	5,844	10.68
300-399	343.7	2,456	4.53
400+	585.6	2,394	11.13

[a]Includes non-exposed controls.

1950-1974.[16] This study, and other studies of breast
cancer incidence among patients given x-ray therapy for
benign breast disease[17-19] or who were given high cumulative doses of diagnostic x ray,[20,21] establish the female
breast as perhaps the human tissue most sensitive to the
carcinogenic effects of ionizing radiation.[22] Average
dose levels, PY at observation for risk, and age-adjusted
incidence rates are given by breast tissue dose interval
for the Nagasaki portion of the LSS sample, in Table 3.
The rates are adjusted to the age distribution of the
female portion of the entire LSS sample, including both
cities. Curve-fitting analyses with respect to models LQ,
L, and Q, similar to those given in Table 2, are summarized in Table 4. The analyses of the breast cancer data
differed from those of the leukemia data in that the LQ
model analysis yielded a negative estimate of the coefficient a_2, but a statistically significant estimate of a_1.
Under the constraint that all coefficients be non-negative
the fitted curves under the LQ and L models are identical,
and since the LQ model fits the data significantly better
than the Q model, there is strong statistical evidence for
the existence of a linear component of dose in the breast
cancer response to radiation. The dose-response data fit
the L model somewhat better than might be expected assuming it to be true (chi-square = 3.3 with 7 degrees of
freedom). Thus the (least-squares) estimated standard
deviations of a_1 under both the L and LQ models are less
than those expected assuming the L model to be true. This
is a reason for caution in interpreting the statistically
significant estimate of a_1 according to model LQ. Assuming the estimated L model curve to be the true dose-
response function, power for a_1 under the LQ analysis

Table 4. Summary of curve-fitting analyses of
         Nagasaki breast cancer data.

Model[b]	Estimates±sd[a]		Goodness of Fit		
	a_1	a_2	chi-sq.	df	p
LQ(D) (4)	2.7±0.8	−.0018±.0021	2.9	7	.89
L(D) (5)	2.2±0.4	---	3.3	8	.91
Q(D) (6)	---	.0062±.0024	9.4	8	.31

[a]Parameter estimates and standard deviations (sd)
  scaled by 10^6.
[b]See numbered equations in text.

should be only .27. The weighted least squares algorithm
used to obtain the fitted curves summarized in Table 4
does not take non-linear constraints, such as the requirement that all coefficients be positive, into account when
computing estimates of standard deviations,[15] but the
fitted curve using the LQ model without these constraints
yields a lower level .95 confidence limit of 2700 for
a_1/a_2. Thus the breast cancer incidence data suggest a
dose-response curve that is more nearly linear than that
suggested by the leukemia data.

Example: Leukemia incidence, Hiroshima and Nagasaki

        As we have seen, the Nagasaki LSS sample data are not
sufficient to determine the functional form of the dose
response for radiation-induced leukemia, even when the
family of possible curves is limited to those described by
the LQ, L, and Q models. Most of the LSS sample pertains
to the Hiroshima survivors, but analyses of the entire

Table 5. Leukemia incidence and average gamma and neutron
         bone marrow dose, LSS sample, Hiroshima and
         Nagasaki 1950-1971, by kerma interval and city.

Kerma Interval	Av. Dose Gamma	Neutron	PY at Risk	Rate per 10^4
		Hiroshima		
0	0	0	569,266	3.68
1-9	1.7	0.2	262,511	2.57
10-49	10.0	1.1	204,738	8.79
50-99	32.2	3.5	51,456	13.3
100-199	61.9	7.9	32,384	40.6
200-299	106.4	14.8	12,632	45.4
300-399	146.3	23.9	7,048	135.
400+	219.4	37.5	9,535	151.
		Nagasaki		
0	0	0	90,944	2.44
1-9	2.1	0	128,288	4.77
10-49	11.8	0	71,676	4.41
50-99	38.8	0.1	25,643	0
100-199	78.7	0.3	27,355	18.6
200-299	131.1	0.9	14,714	57.4
300-399	184.	1.4	5,415	35.1
400+	283.7	2.7	6,981	93.7

sample must take into account the substantial neutron
component of dose for the Hiroshima survivors. If we
continue to ignore the possible competing effect of cell
killing, equation (3) reduces to a model quadratic
(linear-quadratic) in gamma dose γ and linear in neutron
dose ξ, which we denote LQ-L for short:

$$(8) \quad LQ-L(\gamma,\xi) = a_0 + a_1\gamma + a_2\gamma^2 + b_1\xi.$$

Just as we defined models L and Q as the extreme forms of
model LQ for analyses with respect to gamma dose alone, we
define a model linear in both γ and ξ, denoted L-L,

$$(9) \quad L-L(\gamma,\xi) = a_0 + a_1\gamma + b_1\xi,$$

and a model pure quadratic in γ and linear in ξ, denoted
Q-L,

$$(10) \quad Q-L(\gamma,\xi) = a_0 + a_2\gamma^2 + b_1\xi.$$

Table 5 gives numbers of PY, age-adjusted leukemia
rates, and average values of gamma and neutron dose to
bone marrow by city and kerma interval, for the period
1950-1971.[14] Table 6 summarizes the results of curve-
fitting analyses of these data with respect to models
LQ-L, L-L, and Q-L. In the analyses the intercept a_0 was
allowed to depend on city. The analyses of data from the
two cities show hardly any change from the analyses of the
Nagasaki data alone with respect to the coefficients for
gamma dose and its square. The lack of change reflects
the strong linear dependence of ξ on γ within each city, a

Table 6. Summary of curve-fitting analyses of LSS sample
          leukemia data, Hiroshima and Nagasaki 1950-1971,
          by gamma and neutron dose.

Model[b]	Estimates±sd[a]			Goodness of Fit		
	a_1	a_2	b_1	chi-sq.	df	p
LQ-L (8)	.99±.93	.0085±.0056	28.±7.5	10.4	11	.49
L-L (9)	2.2±0.6	---	25.±7.5	11.5	12	.42
Q-L (10	---	.014±.004	31.±6.9	12.3	12	.49

[a] Parameter estimates and standard deviations (sd) scaled
by 10^6.
[b] See numbered equations in text.

dependence that causes the estimates of a_1 and a_2 to
depend almost entirely on the Nagasaki data, and the estimates of b_1 to depend on the contrast between the two
cities.

In the narrow sense of inferences based on the estimates of coefficients a_1 and a_2, and on chi-square
values for lack of fit, the additional data corresponding
to the Hiroshima survivors are uninformative about the
dose-response relationship for leukemia induction from
low-LET radiation. The relative values of the coefficients for gamma and neutron radiation are informative,

Table 7. Breast cancer incidence and average gamma and
         neutron dose to breast tissue, LSS sample, Hiro-
         shima and Nagasaki 1950-1974, by dose interval
         and city.

Kerma Interval	Av. Dose Gamma	Neutron	PY at Risk	Rate per 10^4
a		Hiroshima		
0	0	0	680,372	24.2
1-3	1.5	0.2	82,913	27.2
4-9	5.4	0.8	63,099	25.2
10-19	11.1	1.7	75,610	22.5
20-49	27.3	4.3	55,856	35.3
50-99	59.3	9.9	30,240	37.7
100-199	118.5	21.5	17,057	79.9
200-299	202.9	41.6	6,913	34.9
300-399	277.9	63.2	3,212	74.3
400+	450.5	128.2	2,690	203.8
		Nagasaki		
0	0	0	149,365	17.0
1-3	1.9	0	40,933	18.7
4-9	5.6	0	38,769	17.5
10-19	13.0	0	26,578	16.5
20-49	33.5	0.1	18,288	31.0
50-99	70.6	0.2	15,962	20.9
100-199	142.1	0.9	17,883	54.3
200-299	238.2	2.3	5,844	106.8
300-399	339.7	4.0	2,456	45.3
400+	578.4	7.2	2,394	111.3

a
Includes non-exposed controls.

however, in view of the theoretical relationship between
the shape of the dose response for low-LET radiation and
the relative biological effect (RBE) of high-LET radiation. The RBE of neutrons relative to gamma radiation is
constant under the L-L model. It is interesting that
under this model, the estimated RBE is 11.3±5.7, i.e., the
estimate is significantly greater than 1. This suggests
that neutrons are more leukemogenic than gamma rays, and
that therefore the true dose-response curve for the
leukemia risk from gamma radiation is curvilinear. Unfortunately, this information does not specify the dose level
beyond which the dose-squared term dominates. The region
where interactions between tracks are important could well
be outside the range of doses represented in the data.
The LQ-L model analysis results correspond to a lower 95%
confidence limit of 33 rads for a_1/a_2, but an infinite
upper limit.·

Example: Breast cancer incidence, Hiroshima and Nagasaki

Table 7 gives age-adjusted rates, PY at risk, and
average gamma and neutron breast tissue doses by city and
interval of total breast tissue dose, for female A-bomb
survivors and controls.[16,23] Analyses using the LQ-L,
L-L, and Q-L models are summarized in Table 8. The
analyses gave virtually the same coefficients for a_1 and
a_2, and the same evidence favoring linearity and rejecting
a pure quadratic dose response in γ, as the analyses summarized in Table 4. The importance of the Hiroshima data
is that the estimated coefficient for ξ, b_1, is not significantly different from the estimate of a_1. On the

Table 8. Summary of curve-fitting analyses of LSS sample
         breast cancer incidence data, Hiroshima and
         Nagasaki 1950-1974, by gamma and neutron dose.

Model[b]	Estimates±sd[a]			Goodness of Fit		
	a_1	a_2	b_1	chi-sq.	df	p
LQ-L (8)	2.5±0.8	-.0012±.0021	3.2±3.6	8.2	15	.92
L-L (9)	2.2±0.5	---	3.1±3.6	8.4	16	.94
Q-L (10)	---	.052±.021	8.5±4.6	17.0	16	.39

[a]Parameter estimates and standard deviations (sd) scaled
 by 10^6.
[b]See numbered equations in text.

other hand, the L-L model estimate of the ratio b_1/a_1 is
1.4±1.9, with one-sided upper 95% confidence limit 4.5.
Thus, unlike the analyses of the leukemia data in Table 6,
the breast cancer data do not rule out linearity in γ
according to the RBE criterion, and the data strongly
suggest that the RBE for neutrons is less than 5. Thus
little bias should be introduced by treating gamma and
neutron dose alike, or by pooling of Hiroshima and
Nagasaki breast cancer data after adjustment for age differences.   The unconstrained LQ-L model analysis yields a
lower 95% confidence limit of 1350 for the ratio a_1/a_2, a
number suggestive of at most slight curvature.

The consequences of ignoring cell killing

     The possibility of a competing effect from cell kill-
ing has been ignored in the examples given above, mainly
because the additional complication of extra parameters to
allow for cell killing would reduce power for the
parameters of greatest interest, a_1 and a_2, to such an
extent that only inconclusive results could be expected.
The effect of even so basic a complication as going from
the L or Q model to the LQ model is amply demonstrated in
Figures 3 and 4. In the case of the A-bomb survivor data,
however, there is little evidence that suggests the need
for terms allowing for cell killing. Cell killing is
primarily a high-dose effect, and the whole-body exposures
from the A-bombs precluded survival following exposures
much above 500 to 600 rads kerma. The data themselves do
not suggest an appreciable cell-killing effect. Any such
effect, if present, should be stronger among the Hiroshima
survivors than among the Nagasaki survivors, because of
the presumably greater lethality of neutrons. Neither the
breast cancer data nor the leukemia data, however, show
evidence of a high-dose turnover for the Hiroshima dose
response, either graphically or in curve-fitting analyses.
Allowance for possible cell killing does appear to be
indicated, however, in analyses of data from medically
irradiated populations receiving high-dose, partial-body
exposures, e.g., for treatment of mastitis.[18,23]

Example: Effect of fractionation of exposure

     Parallel analyses have been performed of breast can-
cer data from different doses by breast tissue dose interval and age at first exposure for Hiroshima and Nagasaki
A-bomb survivors and former patients at two Massachusetts
tuberculosis sanitoria who received multiple chest
fluoroscopies during the course of pneumothorax therapy.[21]
We consider women in the ranges 10-19, 20-29, and 30-39

years of age at exposure, with assumed minimal latent
periods of 20 years for those less than 15 years old at
first exposure, 15 years for those between 15 and 19, and
10 years for those over 20. These minimal latent periods
are based on the observation that radiation-induced breast
cancer tends not to occur before ages of significant
breast cancer risk in non-irradiated populations.[23,24]
The ages represented are those present in sufficient numbers in both populations to allow comparisons of age-
specific risk estimates.

       The two populations are interesting bases for com-
parison because breast cancer rates are very different in
the United States and Japan, the circumstances of exposure
were very different but were not related to the presence
of breast disease in either population, and the A-bomb
exposure affected the entire body while the fluoroscopy
exposures were only to the upper torso. The most interesting difference, however, is that the A-bomb exposure
was delivered in a very short time, while the total
cumulative doses from fluoroscopy were delivered over
periods of about 2 years on the average in bi-weekly examinations delivering about 1.5 rad to breast tissue per
examination.[21] The radiation was sparsely ionizing in the
spatial sense because it was in the form of x rays, and
also sparsely ionizing in the temporal sense. The relative lack of opportunity for different radiation tracks to
interact except over periods of weeks to years is consistent with a linear dose response with respect to cumulative dose at the end of the treatment series, regardless
of the shape of the curve for unfractionated exposures.[5]
Substantial curvilinearity of the dose response for unfractionated exposures, that is, a strongly positive value
for a_2, would be expected to result in a much lower
average excess risk per rad from highly fractionated
exposures, like those received by the pneumothorax
patients, than from unfractionated exposures, like those
received by the A-bomb survivors.

       The given dose values for the A-bomb survivors assume
equivalence of neutrons and gamma rays. Any true difference consistent with an effect of LET (i.e., with a
strong positive curvature in the dose response) should
bias the results in favor of higher age-specific risks for
the A-bomb survivors as compared to the fluoroscopy
patients, that is, in the direction consistent with a
fractionation effect.

       Table 9 compares age-specific estimates of excess
risk per rad, computed according to the L model, between

Table 9. Age-specific linear estimates of breast cancer risk, from two irradiated populations.[23]

Series	Age at first exposure	Estimated absolute risk per 10^6 PY-rad: estimate±sd
Massachusetts tuberculosis patients[21]	10-19	8.9±3.1
	20-29	3.8±2.1
	30-39	6.9±4.8
Japanese A-bomb survivors[16]	10-19	8.9±2.1
	20-29	2.9±0.8
	30-39	4.7±2.5

the two populations. Sample sizes are low because of the subdivision of the sample by age at exposure, with consequent instability of the estimates, but the pattern is clear. The age-specific risk estimates are closely comparable. The results in Table 9 suggest that for breast cancer induction, fractionation of dose is of relatively little importance. Therefore, especially in view of the apparently small effect of LET and the apparently linear observed dose response for the Nagasaki survivors, the results strongly suggest linearity for breast cancer induced by low-LET radiation. One possible criticism of the above inference, that a fractionation effect in the fluoroscopy patients was counterbalanced by a greater sensitivity of American women to radiation-induced breast cancer as compared to Japanese women, is answered by observing that data from a third exposed population, of American women treated by (relatively unfractionated) x-ray therapy for acute postpartum mastitis, and analyzed in exactly the same way, gave similar age-specific risk estimates.[23]

DISCUSSION

In the field of radiation carcinogenesis, the application of biological models to epidemiological data is successful to the extent that such models suggest simple hypotheses that are testable using the data available. The advanced development of radiobiological theory suggests multiple ways by which one important question, the level of risk from low-dose, low-LET radiation, can be attacked. This is possible because three questions, the

shape of the dose response curve for unfractionated low-
LET radiation, the effect of LET, and the effect of fractionation of dose, are interrelated in specific ways. In
the case of radiation-induced breast cancer in women, the
results of various comparisons point to a boundary-value
solution, that of linearity of the dose response and independence between risk and changes in LET and fractionation
of dose. This result implies that the risk of breast
cancer from a one-rad mammography examination, for example, can be estimated by proportional scaling of an
appropriate estimate of risk from a high-dose exposure.

Similar analyses with respect to leukemia risk, but
not including the effects of fractionation of dose, lead
not to a boundary-value solution but to the conclusion
that there is some curvature in the dose response to low-
LET radiation, and that at low doses high-LET radiation is
more leukemogenic than low-LET radiation. The data suggest that the dose-response relationship has non-
negligible linear and quadratic components, but the relative values of these components are not estimated with any
precision. It appears, however, that usable upper limits
of risk at low doses can be defined under the assumption
of linearity, an assumption that should lead to conservative estimates and that, because of its simplicity, is
well suited to the analysis of sparse data.

Although epidemiological data cannot be created to
fit the requirements of a specific question in the way
that experimental data often can, their use avoids certain
problems of extrapolation from inbred animal strains to
human experience that are unavoidable when reliance is
placed on experimental studies. Also, it would be extremely difficult to duplicate in an experimental setting
the numbers of subjects represented by the A-bomb survivors or many medically exposed populations.

In the study of radiation carcinogenesis the dependence of radiobiological theory on epidemiological observations is not trivial. We have seen how in the case of
radiation-induced breast cancer the influence of changes
in LET and fractionation of dose appears to be minimal, a
finding that contradicts a substantial body of experimental data involving carcinogenesis, mutagenesis, and the
induction of chromosomal aberrations. It is interesting
that the epidemiological results are consistent with experimental observations of radiation-induced mammary
adenocarcinoma in rats.[25] While the the experimental
finding might easily have been ignored or ascribed to
special experimental conditions, it is difficult to ignore

the epidemiological evidence that different tissues may
have very different carcinogenic responses to ionizing
radiation. Thus it would seem futile, for example, to
search for a common ratio of the LQ model coefficients a_1
and a_2 to be applied generally to radiation carcinogenesis. Rather, an experimental search for mechanistic
explanations of the apparent difference in dose response
between radiation-induced leukemia and breast cancer could
conceivably lead to a more comprehensive theory of radiation carcinogenesis, and eventually to refined estimates
of risk when new models are applied to epidemiological
data.

REFERENCES

1. National Academy of Sciences Advisory Committee on
    the Biological Effects of Ionizing Radiation: The
    Effects on Populations of Exposure to Low Levels of
    Ionizing Radiation. National Academy of Sciences-
    National Research Council, Washington, D. C. (1972)
2. Land, C. E.: Cancer risks from low doses of ionizing
    radiation. Science 209:1197 (1980)
3. Casarett, A. P.: Radiation Biology. Prentice-Hall,
    Englewood Cliffs, New Jersey (1968)
4. Upton, A. C.: Physical carcinogenesis: radiation--
    history and sources. In Cancer, a Comprehensive
    Treatise, Vol 1, Ed. by F. F. Becker. Plenum Press,
    New York, p. 387 (1975)
5. Brown, J. M.: The shape of the dose-response curve for
    radiation carcinogenesis: extrapolation to low
    doses. Radiat. Res. 71:34 (1977)
6. Elkind, M. M. and Han, A.: Neoplastic transformation
    and dose fractionation: does repair of damage play a
    role? Radiat. Res. 79:233 (1979)
7. Kellerer, A. M. and Rossi, H. H.: The theory of dual
    radiation action. Curr. Top. Radiat. Res. Q. 8:85
    (1972)
8. Goodhead, D. T.: Inactivation and mutation of cultured
    mammalian cells by aluminum characteristic ultrasoft
    x-rays. III. Implications for theory of dual radia-
    tion action. Int. J. Radiat. Biol. 32:43 (1977)
9. Beebe G. W. and Usagawa, M.: The Major ABCC Samples.
    Atomic Bomb Casualty Commission TR 12-68, Hiroshima,
    Japan (1968)
10. Jablon, S.: Atomic Bomb Radiation Dose Estimation at
    ABCC. Atomic Bomb Casualty Commission TR 23-71,
    Hiroshima, Japan (1971)
11. United Nations Scientific Committee on the Effects of
    Atomic Radiation: Sources and Effects of Ionizing
    Radiation, Report to the General Assembly. Publ.

E77IX1, United Nations, New York (1977)

12. National Academy of Sciences Advisory Committee on
    the Biological Effects of Ionizing Radiation: <u>The
    Effects on Populations of Exposure to Low Levels of
    Ionizing Radiation, III</u>. National Academy Press,
    Washington, D. C. (1980)

13. Kerr, G. D.: Organ dose estimates for the Japanese
    atomic bomb survivors. Health Phys. 37:487 (1979)

14. Ichimaru, M., Ishimaru, T. and Belsky, J. L.: In-
    cidence of leukemia in atomic bomb survivors belong-
    ing to a fixed cohort in Hiroshima and Nagasaki,
    1950-71. Radiation dose, years after exposure, age
    at exposure, and type of leukemia. Jpn. Radiat.
    Res. 19:262 (1978)

15. Knott, G. D.: MLAB--A mathematical modelling tool.
    Computer Programs in Biomedicine 10:271 (1979)

16. Tokunaga, M., Norman., J. E., Jr., Asano, M.,
    Tokuoka, S., Ezaki, H., Nishimori, I. and Tsuji, Y.:
    Malignant breast tumors among atomic bomb survivors,
    Hiroshima and Nagasaki, 1950-1974. J. Natl. Cancer
    Inst. 62:1347 (1979)

17. Mettler, F. A., Jr., Hempelmann, L. H., Dutton, A.
    M., Pifer, J. W., Toyooka, E. T. and Ames, W. R.:
    Breast neoplasms in women treated with x rays for
    acute postpartum mastitis. A pilot study. J. Natl.
    Cancer Inst. 43:803 (1969)

18. Shore, R. E., Hempelmann, L. H., Kowaluk, E., Mansur,
    P. S., Pasternack, B. S., Albert, R. E. and Haughie,
    G. E.: Breast neoplasms in women treated with x-rays
    for acute postpartum mastitis. J. Natl. Cancer Inst.
    59:813 (1977)

19. Baral, E., Larsson L. and Mattsson, B.: Breast can-
    cer following irradiation of the breast. Cancer
    40:2905 (1977)

20. MacKenzie I: Breast cancer following multiple
    fluoroscopies. Br. J. Cancer 19:1 (1965)

21. Boice, J. D., Jr., Monson R. R.: Breast cancer in
    women after repeated fluoroscopic examinations of the
    chest. J. Natl. Cancer Inst. 59:823 (1977)

22. Mole, R. H.: The sensitivity of the human breast to
    cancer induction by ionizing radiation. Br. J.
    Radiol. 51:401 (1978)

23. Land, C. E., Boice, J. D., Jr., Shore, R. E., Norman,
    J. E., Jr., and Tokunaga, M.: Breast risk from low-
    dose exposures to ionizing radiation: Results of an
    analysis in parallel of data from three different
    exposed populations. J. Natl. Cancer Inst. 65:353
    (1980)

24. Land, C. E. and Norman, J. E., Jr.: Latent periods
    of radiogenic cancers occurring among Japanese a-bomb

survivors. In <u>Late Biological Effects of Ionizing
Radiation</u>, Vol I. (Proc. IAEA Symp. on Late Biol.
Effects of Ionizing Radiat., March 1978, Vienna)
International Atomic Energy Agency, Vienna, p. 29
(1978)

25. Shellabarger, C. J.: Effect of short-term dose frac-
tionation on mammary neoplasia incidence in the rat.
In <u>Radiation Research</u>, Ed. by S. Okada, M. Imamura,
T. Terashima and H. Yamaguchi. (Proc. IV Intern.
Congr. Radiat. Res., May 1979, Tokyo) Toppan Print-
ing Co., Tokyo, p. 199 (1979)

26. Shellabarger, C. J.: Modifying factors in rat mammary gland carcinogenesis. In <u>Biology of Radiation
Carcinogenesis</u>. Ed. by J. M. Yuhas, R. W. Tennant,
and J. D. Regan. Raven Press, New York, p. 31 (1976)

DISCUSSION

W. RUSSELL: Charles, I understand you are taking these three models to bring out your statistical points, but I think the possibility should be introduced that none of these models represents the true response. For example, if you introduced the possibility of repair and dose dependence of repair, then you would have a much more complicated model than any of these.

LAND: The linear-quadratic model is very simple, and the linear and pure quadratic models are even simpler, representing the two extremes of the linear-quadratic. The models, which have some radiobiological respectability, were used to illustrate the problems of making even such crude discriminations as those between the implications of the two extremes. Sometimes, however, looking at the data in a totally different way can be informative about more subtle questions. For example, if there really were dose dependence of repair in the case of breast cancer induction, there would have been dose-related differences in the temporal distributions of the malignancies following exposure, and there wasn't any evidence of this.

W. RUSSELL: Yes, you might exclude that particular case. I don't think it should be generalized that one of these three models fits all cancers.

LAND: I agree, but much of the time we are asking only limited questions, such as which of a limited selection of models is best for risk prediction. It is of course important to approximate reality with radiobiologically plausible models, and I will use more plausible models when they are developed, provided only that they are simple enough to work within applications like the ones I have described.

FORBES: Two questions, one on the data and one on the model. In your data, at the high dose rates, had you thought of adjusting for competing risks? For somebody who gets a high dose rate, there is the risk of more than one cancer. I take it the distribution did not show any outliers and the residuals were well behaved.

LAND: I did not treat it here, but I don't see any evidence in the A-bomb survivors that there really is a competing effect. But that is a very complicated model, and if you compare two complicated models, you're apt not to find any difference.

FORBES: Have you looked at multi-stage models to see which stage might be affected by ionizing radiation?

LAND: No, I think that is a more complicated question and we're just trying to answer simple questions here. However, the models we tested are not linear approximations. These models are from radiobiology. Each of these coefficients has a meaning. That's a little bit different than just trying to see, well, if you added a cubic term and a quartic term, what would happen. There would be no radiobiological reason to do the latter kind of manipulation.

FORBES: Unless you want to model a particular disease and that gives you hard information to build your model.

LAND: I think that the staging hypotheses are better handled by looking at the temporal distribution of the occurrence of radiation-induced cancer rather than by looking at the dose response. Because you see, in this case everybody got their dose at the same time, even the fluoroscopy patients who got their doses over a period of two years. You can follow the temporal distribution of the occurrence of excess breast cancer following that exposure and you can learn a lot about the problem.

ABRAHAMSON: There's an inherent assumption in the breast cancer data, and you have said that you are dealing with an induction phenomenon by radiation. Is it not possible, on the evidence that there was no RBE effect, that there was also no dose-rate effect? Then you might not be dealing with an induction phenomenon with respect to radiation, but with a promotion or secondary phenomenon. In that case your model of induction would not be the correct model to apply to data for breast cancer. The data do not seem to conform to any of the radiobiological phenomena that we look at with chromosome aberrations, with the induction of other cancers, or with gene mutation. And maybe it just isn't induction.

LAND: If it were a promotion effect, would you expect to see more of a risk in women who were exposed at earlier ages than women who were exposed at later ages? This is what you do find. Wouldn't promotion be stronger if it had more time to work?

ABRAHAMSON: It depends on what you mean by later ages. Isn't there a point where hormonal differences might affect your results?

LAND: Let's just take the age range 10 to 40 of the women who are exposed, in all these studies. Women between the ages of 10 and 20 had much more excess breast cancer on an absolute basis than women who were exposed between 20 and 30 and between 30 and 40. Yet the older women have had more chance of exposure to the other initiators which you postulated.

BERG: If it were a promotion effect, then you would expect to have a pool, let's say, of leukemia-induced subjects, and the exposure to radiation would shorten the latent period before the appearance of leukemia. Then, as time went on, the pool in that population would be drained prematurely, and leukemia rates would be expected

to drop, before the control rates drop some 30 years after exposure.
Now, my understanding is that this may be appearing now in the
Japanese A-bomb populations. I don't know if this is true and I
invite comments.

UPTON: I think in that connection it would be instructive to compare
each distribution of leukemias as a function of dose and the age at
irradiation; similarly, to analyze the age-distribution of breast
cancer, lung cancer, and cancers of other sites. It is my understanding that with respect to breast cancer, there was no observable
excess among women who were irradiated before puberty until they
reached 30 or 40 years of age. The latency was a long latency in
that case. Acceleration, if you will, did not occur to the degree
that allowed the tumors to manifest themselves within a 10- or 15-
year latent period when irradiation was received before puberty.

      Conversely, among women who received their atomic-bomb radiation
at age 45 or beyond, the latency was shorter. There is some evidence
that it was less than 10 years, for breast cancer.

LAND: Let us look at women of similar ages in 1945 and at the curve
of cumulative incidence of breast cancer versus time for those who
were not exposed to radiation. Women who received over 100 rads
have 3 times as much breast cancer, so it is reasonable to assume
that 2/3 of these cancers are radiation induced. The shape of the
cumulative curve was the same in the two groups. If you follow the
same procedure for lung cancer, you get the same result.

      If you do the same thing for leukemia, you get something which
indicates there was a wave of excess incidence. You can see the
wave only indirectly, but the technique is sensitive to the kind of
thing you see in leukemia.

BERG: Biologically, promotion would be expected to be a multi-hit
phenomenon because it would involve disabling redundant repair
mechanisms. Induction, which is stochastic, would give a one-hit
probability distribution. Do you think this is at least consistent
with the kind of data you presented? You see, a promoter would have
to score more than one hit to really promote because there is more
than one repair mechanism sitting in that cell.

LAND: In terms of radiobiology, if LET makes a difference then
don't initiators have to do the same thing?

BERG: No, they may only have to do it to escape from repair.

LAND: Do you know of any case where repair isn't involved in carcinogenesis?

TOTTER: Many of these questions were based on what Dr. Berg expressed a moment ago as a target theory. And a target theory is based on the fact that cumulative cancer incidence goes up with about 4th or 5th power of age. If one looks at vital statistics, that gives a better fit than say the Gompertz curve, but it is possible to find a still better fit to vital statistics which have nothing to do with hit phenomena. With this expression, if you had to answer questions about the kind of mathematical relationships found in vital statistics, all the questions as well as the answers would be different.

SESSION II

RISKS OF PRENATAL EXPOSURES

CHAIRMAN:

ARTHUR C. UPTON

INTRODUCTION TO SESSION II

Arthur C. Upton

Department of Environmental Medicine
New York University Medical Center
New York, NY 10016

This afternoon we are going to deal with problems relating to
susceptible subpopulations. Susceptibility is generally taken to
mean the relative sensitivity of an indivudal or a population when
exposed to a given risk factor, rather than merely the likelihood of
being exposed, although one does occasionally see susceptible subpopulations so designated because of their likelihood to be exposed.
Sensitivity can be increased qualitatively as well as quantitatively
when one is dealing with malformations in the developing embryo, as
Dr. Russell will bring out. There are critical periods or critical
gestational ages when exposure finds the organism at a particularly
high risk. And if exposure is deferred until substantially later in
development, the qualitative difference may be enormous, may be
virtually absolute.

By the same token, when one is concerned with heritable abnormalities or genetic risks, one refers to the genetically significant
dose for the population for whom reproduction remains likely or
feasible, and women exposed during post-menopausal age are no longer
sensitive in the same sense at all.

Quantitative increases are still not well understood, but are
very important. The commonest form of cancer arises on the skin and
it is well known that fair-skinned individuals are more sensitive to
sunlight than dark-skinned individuals. The problem is presumably
largely one of dosimetry, because skin pigmentation effectively pro-
tects the germinal cells in the basal layer which would otherwise
suffer damage to their DNA. We now know that the exquisite photo-
sensitivity and extremely high susceptibility of individuals with
xeroderma pigmentosum, an autosomal recessive, is not a problem of
dosimetry as such. It's that the X-P individuals are incapable of
repairing damage to their DNA with the same efficiency as normal individuals. Here we have a simple genetic trait controlling sensi-

109

tivity, and more and more is known now about how genetic differences influence not just the repair capability but the whole process of activation of carginogen precursors, detoxification, and so on.

We've mentioned age in reference to sensitivity of the fetus and sensitivity to genetic effects, we've referred to inherited differences. Sex is certainly an influence on susceptibility to many kinds of toxicity, and so is exposure to other environmental factors which may condition the susceptibility of an exposed individual. The factors can be additive with the particular risk factor in question. They can be multiplicative as in the case of asbestos and tobacco smoke. Or they can be inhibitory. The startling diminution in the incidence of stomach cancer in recent decades argues, in the eyes of many observers, to the protective effects of fresh dietary factors such as fresh fruits, vegetables and milk.

To make any assessment of risks, one must take into account the distribution of risks in a population. This involves taking into account the special susceptibilities of subpopulations. To do this adequately, one will ultimately need to know much more about mechanisms. This is true in the case of cancer whether one is dealing primarily with the so-called initiators or with late stage risk factors, including promoting agents. Here, epidemiologic studies and laboratory studies should go hand in hand and be mutually complementary.

DOSE-RESPONSE RELATIONSHIPS FOR ADULT AND PRENATAL EXPOSURES TO METHYLMERCURY

Thomas W. Clarkson   Division of Toxicology
                          Department of Radiation Biology
                             and Biophysics

Christopher Cox   Division of Biostatistics

David O. Marsh   Department of Neurology

                          University of Rochester School
                             of Medicine and Dentistry
                          Rochester, New York 14642

Gary J. Myers   Center for Developmental and
                             Learning Disabilities
                          The University of Alabama in
                             Birmingham
                          Birmingham, Alabama 35294

Sadoun K. Al-Tikriti   Medical College, Baghdad
                             University,
                          Baghdad, Iraq

Laman Amin-Zaki   Medical College, Baghdad
                             University,
                          Baghdad, Iraq

Abdul Ruzak Dabbagh   Republican Hospital
                          Erbil, Iraq

INTRODUCTION

Public concern over the health hazards of methylmercury was aroused by the two outbreaks of poisoning in Japan: in Minamata in the 1950s and in Niigata Prefecture in the 1960s (for details,

see reference 26). The cause of the mass poisoning was the consumption of fish that had been contaminated by industrial discharge of
methylmercury compounds.

A more widespread threat from methylmercury became apparent
when Swedish investigators discovered that methylmercury was synthesized from inorganic mercury by micro-organisms living in fresh
water aquatic sediments (for review, see reference 28). Woods's
work[29] in the United States had indicated that methanogenic bacteria
could produce dimethylmercury from inorganic mercury. The dimethylmercury compounds could break down to monomethylmercury depending
upon water pH and other conditions, and lead to uptake of methylmercury by fish (for review see reference 22). Methylation probably
occurs also in the oceans since the mercury in muscle tissue in most
oceanic fish is almost entirely in the form of methylmercury

Several countries proposed standards for maximum safe levels
of methylmercury in edible tissues of fish and shellfish, and the
World Health Organization advised a tolerable weekly intake of
methylmercury.[27,28] These standards were based on the best available evidence at the time but there remained an important need for
quantitative data on dose-response and dose-effect relationships in
man, and for identification of the stage of the human life cycle
most sensitive to methylmercury. This need is now all the more
urgent in the light of current evidence that acid rain, resulting
from consumption of fossil fuels, is leading to further elevation
of methylmercury levels in affected bodies of fresh water (for
discussion, see references 6 and 16).

An opportunity to obtain quantitative data was provided by the
large outbreak of methylmercury poisoning that took place in rural
Iraq in the winter of 1971-72.[5] Farmers and their families consumed homemade bread prepared from wheat treated with a methylmercury fungicide. Consumption of the contaminated bread was restricted to a few months (three in most cases). Over 6000 cases
were admitted to hospital and about 450 deaths in hospital were
attributed to methylmercury poisoning. A great many more must have
been affected but not recorded as hospital admissions. All ages and
both sexes were victims of the poisoning. The outbreak itself and
its immediate sequalae have been reported.[5,8,9,17,24,28] The results of follow-up studies of prenatally exposed children and their
mothers are now becoming available.[4,18,19,20] This report is a new
dose-response analysis of previously reported data on both non-
pregnant adults and on prenatally exposed children.

DOSE-EFFECT, DOSE-RESPONSE IN ADULTS

Methylmercury compounds belong to a class of short-chain alkyl-

mercurials whose toxic effects in man have been known since members
of this class were first synthesized in 1865(for review, see reference 13). An outbreak of poisoning due to occupational exposure to
methylmercury compounds was the occasion for the now classic description of signs and symptoms of poisoning.[14,15]   Methylmercury
damages, primarily, the sensory and coordination functions of the
central nervous system, resulting in limb and perioral sensory
symptoms and signs, concentric constriction of visual fields, ataxia,
dysarthria and, in more severe cases, mental changes, involuntary
movements and sometimes death.

The data in figure 1 are derived from a group of people admitted to hospital in Baghdad, Iraq for intensive study, and a group
from nearby villages. Details on the estimation of the amount of
methylmercury ingested have been described elsewhere.[8,5]   The
frequencies of a number of signs and symptoms, together with fitted
lines, are plotted against the maximum estimated body burden for
cohorts of people of approximately equal size (about 20 people per
cohort). Each graph in figure 1A has a characteristic shape. At
lower body burdens the lines are horizontal, indicating no relationship of occurrence of signs and symptoms with the dose of methylmercury. At a certain level of body burden, a sharp change in the
slope of the line is evident, indicating linearly increasing frequency of signs and symptoms with increasing body burden. The point
of intersection of the two straight lines can be interpreted as a
"practical threshold" body burden at which signs and symptoms due
to methylmercury become detectable above the background frequency.

This type of data analysis, first reported by Bakir et al.[5]
has been proposed[12] and used[30] by others and is commonly referred
to as the "Hockey Stick" Regression Method. Parameters of the
Hockey Stick model are estimated by the method of maximum likelihood.
The method does not require the assumption of an absolute threshold
for the general population. It does, however, recognize the existence of a background frequency for all signs and symptoms, the
magnitude of which will depend upon a number of factors such as the
"specificity" of the sign or symptom and the degree of severity of
the effect. In the case of methylmercury, severity ranges from mild
symptoms of paresthesia to incapacitation and death.

In the example given in figure 1A the background frequency was
estimated to be 8.6% for paresthesia and 2.5% for ataxia. The EC50
(the 50% frequency over and above the background frequency) was calculated to be 2.1 (standard error 0.43) mg Hg/kg for paresthesia
and 2.7 (standard error 0.18) mg Hg/kg for ataxia (Table I). The
standard errors reflect both the true variances of thresholds for
paresthesia and ataxia in the population as well as errors in measurement of body burden and frequency of signs and symptoms.

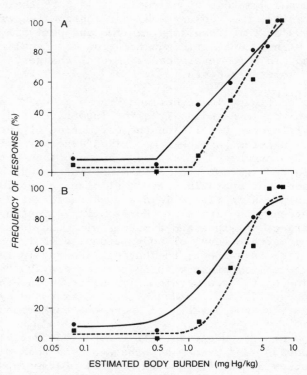

Fig. 1. The frequency of signs and symptoms of methylmercury poison-
        ing versus the maximum estimated body burden of methylmercury
        in adults. In fig. 1A the data are plotted according to the
        Hockey Stick method and in fig. 1B according to logit anal-
        ysis. The data are taken from Bakir et al.[5] The values
        for the body burden correspond to the lower values estimated
        by Bakir et al.[5] and are divided by the body weights to
        yield units of mg Hg/kg. Bakir et al.[5] also estimated body
        burden by a second method that yielded values about 50%
        higher than the ones quoted in this figure.

        ●————————— paresthesia

        ■--------- ataxia

The same data are presented in Fig. 1B, together with response frequencies estimated by logit analysis, modified to include a background frequency.[1] The model does not provide a threshold value for this population, rather the frequency of response is a smoothly increasing function of (log) dose. As in the case of the "Hockey Stick" model, parameters are estimated by the method of maximum likelihood.[1] The EC50s, 2.1 and 3.0 for paresthesia and ataxia respectively, were similar to those calculated by Hockey Stick analysis (Table I). The background frequencies, 6.8% for paresthesia and 2.8% for ataxia, were also similar to the values obtained by Hockey Stick analysis.

Despite the fact that the Hockey Stick differs from the logit model, the former representing frequencies of signs and symptoms as having a discontinuous rate of increase at the threshold dose and the latter using a continuously increasing function of dose, the two models yielded an equally good fit to the data and gave essentially similar quantitative estimates for such parameters as background frequency, EC50 values, and the standard errors.

Table I.   Comparison of the EC50s[a] for adult (non-pregnant) and prenatal exposures to methylmercury compounds.

ADULT EXPOSURES			PRENATAL EXPOSURES		
Signs and Symptoms	EC50 ± SEM mgHg/kg[a]		Signs and Symptoms	EC50 ± SEM mgHg/kg[b]	
	Hockey Stick	Logit		Hockey Stick	Logit
Paresthesia	2.1±0.43	2.1±0.41	Motor Retardation	0.52±0.11	0.56±0.19
Ataxia	2.7±0.18	3.0±0.33	CNS signs	1.23±0.82	1.01±0.44

[a]The average concentration of methylmercury in the body expressed as mgHg/kg body weight associated with a 50% frequency of signs and symptoms corrected for background frequency. The EC50s are calculated from the data in Fig. 1.

[b]The average peak concentration of methylmercury in mothers during pregnancy associated with a 50% frequency of signs and symptoms in their children corrected for background frequency. The EC50s are calculated from the data in Fig. 5. The average concentration of methylmercury in the body was calculated by dividing the hair concentration by 175 as explained in the text.

It was therefore of interest to see if the models would be successful in describing dose-response relationships for prenatal exposure
to methylmercury.

DOSE-EFFECT, DOSE-RESPONSE IN PRENATAL EXPOSURE

A number of prenatally exposed infants had been admitted to
hospital during the outbreak in Iraq.[5] Clinical observations at
that time[2] and follow-up studies after the infants had returned
home [3,4] established the main clinical features of severe prenatal
poisoning. The manifestations were essentially similar to the
22 cases of cerebral palsy reported in the Minamata outbreak.[11]
Both the Iraqi and Japanese cases exhibited severe psychomotor retardation, but cases of blindness were reported in Iraq whereas
none were reported in Japan. Autopsy examinations of two cases in
Japan[25] and two cases in Iraq[2] indicated disturbed development of
brain tissue.

The Minamata cases suggested that the prenatal stage might be
more sensitive to methylmercury than the adult stage of life inso-
much that the mothers had mild transient symptoms as contrasted to
the severe effects in their children. Amin-Zaki et al.[2] reported
six mothers and six infants who had signs of intoxication but in
only one infant-mother pair was the infant clinically affected and
the mother asymptomatic. Thus the early observations in Iraq
tended to conflict with the data from Japan and a major question
was raised as to the sensitivity of the fetus versus that of the
adult.

In order to answer this question, a much larger number of
infant-mother pairs had to be identified, covering a wide range of
exposures to methylmercury. Furthermore, it was necessary to
develop a means to recapitulate exposure of the mother during pregnancy if dose-response and dose-effect relationships were to be
established quantitatively.

A means was discovered in the longitudinal analysis of samples
of head hair (for detailed discussion see reference 10). In the
example given in Figure 2, a sample of hair consisting of about
100 strands, was collected from a mother in February 1973, cut as
close to the scalp as possible. The sample was cut and analyzed
for mercury in one centimeter segments measured from the scalp.
Each centimeter represented approximately one month's growth of
hair and is represented as such on the abscissa of this graph. An
allowance is made of 1 month for the time taken for freshly formed
hair to emerge above the scalp to occupy the first 1 centimeter of
the sample. Blood samples had been collected on certain dates and
mercury concentrations are plotted according to the date of collection. Clearly, the concentration of mercury in hair, at the time

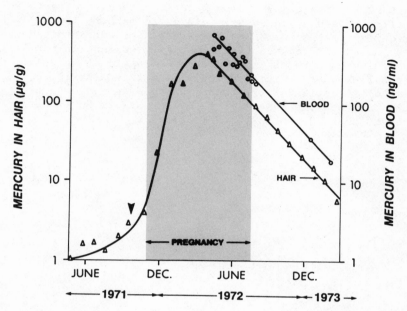

Fig. 2.   An example of the longitudinal analysis of a sample of head
hair, measured centimeter by centimeter from the scalp,
and the comparison of these results with mercury concentrations in samples of blood collected at the estimated time
of formation of the 1 cm hair segments. Distance in centi-
meters from the scalp were converted into date (month) of
formation of the segment assuming the hair grows at about
1 cm per month. For further details, see text. This
figure was adapted from Fig. 6 in Amin-Zaki et al.[3]

of its formation, is directly proportional to the simultaneous concentration in blood. When concentration is expressed in the same
units, the concentration of total mercury in hair is about two hundred and fifty times the concentration in blood in people exposed
to methylmercury compounds. Individual variation in the value of
the ratio has been described elsewhere.[23]

Longitudinal analysis of hair samples thus provided a means of
recapitulating blood concentrations. In the example in Fig. 2, it

was possible to go back as early as June 1971 - almost two years
prior to the date of collection of the hair sample. Of special importance, maternal blood concentration may be reconstructed throughout the entire period of pregnancy. We decided to test the possibility that the frequency and/or severity of toxic effects in the
prenatally exposed children are related to mercury levels in the
mother during gestation. Many rural villages were visited and hair
samples collected from nearly all mothers resident in the villages
who had children born at times corresponding to the possible period
of prenatal exposure. This period, illustrated in Fig. 3, includes
the time of ingestion of the contaminated bread (about one to three
months), and the time taken for methylmercury to be excreted from
the mother (about 9 months to one year).

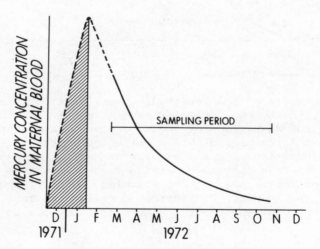

Fig. 3. A diagrammatic representation of the mercury concentrations
        in mothers' blood during (shaded area) and after (open area)
        the consumption of contaminated bread. Infants that were
        conceived during this time period would have received pre-
        natal exposure to methylmercury. Adapted from Fig. 1 of
        Amin-Zaki et al.[2]

A standard form was completed for each family with sufficient detail to allow subsequent identification by a clinical follow-up. A polaroid picture was taken of each infant-mother pair and attached to the sampling form. A 35mm color picture was also taken and, after development, matched against the polaroid picture to provide a permanent photographic identification.

An important item in this study was determining the date of birth of the child. Unfortunately, exact birth records are not available in rural areas and the birth dates have to be determined by interview of the mother and other members of the rural "extended" families. It turned out that their recollection of the date of the mercury outbreak was the most reliable reference point.

The clinical investigators were provided with names that included controls and infant-mother pairs who had been exposed to methylmercury. They had no knowledge of the results of the hair analyses. Standardized forms were used to record the histories and results of physical examinations. The mothers were questioned about pregnancy, labor and delivery, about early milestones of development, their opinion about the child's mental and physical progress with reference to their siblings, any manifestations of seizures and other medical history. The neurological examinations were performed in the home, outdoors or in the village dispensary. It began with a period of observation, followed by a standardized neurological examination. The following criteria for abnormalities were adopted: motor retardation if the child was not walking at 18 months, speech retardation if not talking by 24 months, mental retardation or seizures (or convulsive-like attacks) according to the history provided by the mother and neurological signs according to two independent examiners. No standards are available for head circumference or height for Iraqi children so these observations were evaluated in terms of standard deviations below the mean for the group.

Findings on 29 infant-mother pairs are depicted in Fig. 4. The pairs were divided into three cohorts of approximately equal size according to the maximum maternal mercury levels (2 to 11, 12 to 85, and 99 to 384 ppm). Visual signs and symptoms appear to be more frequent in the group with the highest maternal hair levels. Statistical tests reveal that the highest group differs significantly ($P<0.05$) from the lower group for motor and speech retardation and seizures. Maternal paresthesias, not reported in Fig. 2, also occurred with a significantly higher frequency in the high exposure group.

This study is limited by the small number of infant-mother pairs. Nevertheless, it suggests that, in terms of frequency of response, the mother does not differ from her prenatally exposed infant. However, mother and infant do differ markedly in the severity and permanence of damage. Transient paresthesias were the most

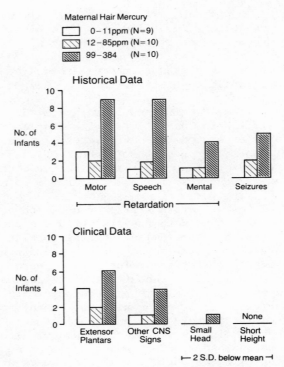

Fig. 4.   Infants' symptoms and signs related to maternal hair
          mercury concentration. Adapted from the figure in
          Marsh et al.[19]

common manifestation in the mothers as compared to psychomotor retardation which was severe in some infants in the high exposure
group. For example, the four mothers with the highest peak hair
concentrations (384, 209, 204 and 165 ppm) were either asymptomatic
or had transient mild symptoms during pregnancy whereas all the infants had neurological abnormalities on examination, retarded speech
and mental development.

     Similar findings were made in a more extensive study of
82 infant-mother pairs which included the original 29 pairs discussed above.[20] Data from this study are plotted in Fig. 5 using
76 of the 82 pairs reported by Marsh et al.[20] In Fig. 5A the frequencies of motor retardation and of CNS signs were estimated by
the Hockey Stick method. The logit analysis of the same data is

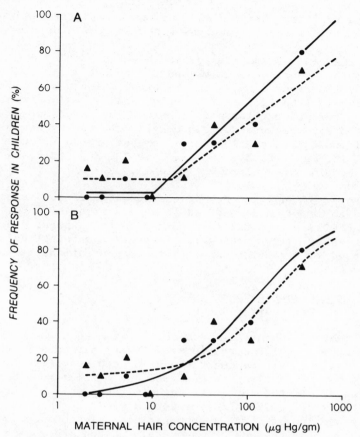

Fig. 5. The frequency of abnormalities in prenatally exposed
children versus the estimated maximum body burden in the
mother during pregnancy. In Fig. 5A, the estimated frequencies were obtained by the Hockey Stick method and in
Fig. 5B by logit analysis. The data are taken from Marsh
et al.[20]

● —————————— Motor retardation is defined as failure to
walk by the age of 18 months

▲ - - - - - - - - CNS signs, moderate to severe central nervous system (CNS) signs were defined accord-
ing to a scoring system ranging from mild
(unity) to most severe (ten). Children with
a score greater than three were defined as
having CNS signs. The scoring was based on
the results of examination by two independent neurologists.

presented in Fig. 5B. Grouped data points are plotted in Fig. 5 although the fits were obtained using the ungrouped data.

As in the case of adult exposures both the Hockey Stick and the logit method gave an equally good fit to the data. This is evident from the figures and from the usual Chi-square goodness-of-fit statistics. A background frequency of 3.3% was estimated by Hockey Stick for motor retardation whereas the three parameter logit fit indicated zero background frequency. Both Hockey Stick and logit model indicate a similar value for background frequency for CNS signs - 10.8% and 10.2% respectively. The EC50 values estimated by the two models agree closely (Table I).

Both types of analyses may be used to compare the relative sensitivity to methylmercury of adult versus prenatal life. In Table I, the EC50 values for adult and prenatal exposures are compared in the same units (mgHg/kg). To convert maternal hair concentrations (used in Fig. 5) to whole body concentrations, a value for the ratio r where

$$r = \frac{\text{Hair concentration}}{\text{Whole body concentration}}$$

must be estimated. Shahristani et al.[24] obtained a value for r of 137 based on empirical observations on thirty patients in the Iraq outbreak. Maximum hair concentrations in each centimeter were determined by neutron activation analyses and maximum body burdens were estimated from the intake of methylmercury in the contaminated bread using a whole body half-time determined for each patient from the rate of decline of mercury concentrations in consecutive segments of hair after the end of exposure. On the other hand, a value of 175 may be obtained if we assume a hair to blood ratio of 250, and that 5% of the body burden is contained in the blood compartment as indicated by radioactive tracer data in adult volunteers.[21]

The adult whole body concentrations reported in Fig.1 and Table I (EC50 values) were calculated in part from concentration of mercury in whole blood. Bakir et al.[5] used two methods of estimation with the high estimate being about 50% higher than the lower estimates. In Table I the EC50 values are based on the lower estimate for adults and the lower estimate for prenatal exposure - in this case using a value of r of 175.

The EC50s calculated in this way indicate that prenatal life is more sensitive to methylmercury than adult (non-pregnant) life. This conclusion would not be substantially changed had we used the higher estimate of body burden for adults according to Bakir et al.[5] and for prenatal exposure using a value of r of 137. Comparison of the EC50 values in Table I suggests there is roughly a factor

of three to four in relative sensitivity. However, the dose-response
curves for adult versus prenatal exposure are not parallel so that
different values of relative sensitivity will be obtained if comparisons are based on body concentrations at other frequencies such
as EC84 and EC16 and in terms of practical threshold concentrations.

A number of cautionary statements must be made. The effects in
adult are not the same as those in the infant except that both are
due to damage to the central nervous system. The body burdens in
the mother were estimated from hair concentrations. Artifacts due
to misalignment of the hair strands during collection and to differences in growth rate of individual strands may reduce the observed maximum hair value below the true values (for discussion,
see reference 10). Shahristani et al.[24] claimed that these artifacts were insignificant in their study but they cannot be dis-
counted in our studies at this time. Further work is in progress
in our laboratories to check the analytical data in hair analysis
and the contribution of methodological artifacts to the results of
this report.

Having presented the logit and Hockey Stick models, we conclude by discussing the two approaches more fully. The traditional
justification for either probit or logit analysis in quantal-response
bioassay has been the concept of the tolerance distribution for a
population of subjects at risk. Both approaches provide a probability model for this distribution, in terms of the population
frequency of response as a (smoothly) increasing function of stimulus intensity. It may be debated, however, whether the concept of
a tolerance distribution has much biological reality in a particular situation. In any case, the mathematical model does provide a
useful description of quantal, dose-effect data and it can be used
as such. The same considerations apply to the Hockey Stick approach.
The method was originally used[5] to simply summarize two striking
properties of the data. The first is the presence of a clear background or spontaneous frequency of response, as indicated at the
lowest doses by small proportions which do not increase with dose.
In contrast, the second striking feature is a clear, approximately
linear (in the logarithm of the dose) increase in the response proportions at higher doses. This linearity is consistent with the
fact that both the probit and logit models are nearly linear in
the range of doses around the EC50 (see Fig. 1B).

No assumption of a biological (population) threshold is required to use the Hockey Stick model. (In reality, the assumption
of a discontinuous rate of increase in the frequency of response
for an entire population, as opposed to any individual subject, is
probably somewhat unrealistic.) However, the method does provide
a practical threshold which can, for example, help set limits for
acceptable dosages.

REFERENCES

1. W. D. Ashton,"The Logit Transformation with Special Reference
    to Its Use in Bioassay", Hafner Publishing Company, New York,
    (1972).
2. L. Amin-Zaki, S. B. Elhassani, M. A. Majeed, T. W. Clarkson,
    R. A. Doherty, and M. R. Greenwood, Intrauterine methyl-
    mercury poisoning in Iraq, Pediatrics, 54:587 (1974)
3. L. Amin-Zaki, S. B. Elhassani, M. A. Majeed, T. W. Clarkson,
    M. R. Greenwood, and R. A. Doherty, Perinatal methylmercury
    poisoning in Iraq, Am. J. Dis. Child. 130:1070 (1976).
4. L. Amin-Zaki, M. A. Majeed, S. B. Elhassani, T. W. Clarkson,
    M. R. Greenwood, and R. A. Doherty, Prenatal methylmercury
    poisoning, clinical observations over five years, Am. J.
    Dis. Child. 133:172 (1979).
5. F. Bakir, S. Damluji, L. Amin-Zaki, M. Murtadha, A. Khalidi,
    N. Y. Al-Rawi, S. Tikriti, H. I. Dhahir, T. W. Clarkson,
    J. C. Smith, and R. A. Doherty, Methylmercury poisoning in
    Iraq, Science 181:230 (1973).
6. J. A. Bloomfield, S. O. Quinn, R. J. Scrudato, D. Long, A.
    Richards, and F. Ryan, Atmospheric and watershed inputs of
    mercury to Cranberrry Lake, St. Lawrence County, New York,
    in: "Polluted Rain", T. Toribara, M. W. Miller, and P. E.
    Morrow, eds., Plenum Press, New York (1980).
7. B. H. Choi, L. W. Lapham, L. Amin-Zaki, and T. Saleen, Abnormal
    neuronal migration, deranged cerebral cortical organization
    and diffuse white matter astrocytosis of human fetal brain.
    A major effect of methylmercury poisoning in utero, J.
    Neuropath. Exp. Neurol. 37:719 (1978).
8. T. W. Clarkson, and D. O. Marsh, The toxicity of methylmercury
    in man: dose-response relationships in adult populations,
    in: "Effects and dose-response relationships of toxic metals",
    G. F. Nordberg, ed., Elsevier, Amsterdam (1976).
9. T. W. Clarkson, J. C. Smith, D. O. Marsh, and M. D. Turner,
    A review of dose-response relationships resulting from human
    exposure to methylmercury compounds, in: "Progress in Water
    Technology" vol 7., P. Krenkel, ed., Pergamon Press, Oxford,
    1975.
10. T. Giovanoli-Jakubczak, and G. Berg,Measurements of mercury in
    human hair, Arch. Environ. Health, 28:139 (1974).
11. Y. Harada, Study group on Minamata Disease, in"Minamata Disease"
    M. Katsuma, ed., Kumamoto University, Kumamoto, Japan (1966).
12. V. Hasselbad, Regression using "hockey stick" functions. Paper
    presented at the Statistical Section 101st Meeting, American
    Public Health Association, San Francisco, Nov. 8
13. D. Hunter, Diseases of Occupations, Little Brown & Co.,
    London (1969).
14. D. Hunter, R. R. Bamford, and D. S. Russell, Poisoning by methyl-
    mercury compounds, Quart. J. Med., 33:193 (1940).

15. D. Hunter, and D. S. Russell, Focal cerebral and cerebellar atrophy in a human subject due to organic mercury compounds, J. Neurol. Neurosurg. Psychiatr., 17:235 (1954).

16. A. Jernelov, The effects of acidity on the uptake of mercury by fish, in: "Polluted Rain", T. Toribara, M. W. Miller, and P. E. Morrow., eds., Plenum Press, New York (1980).

17. G. Kazantzis, A. Al-Mufti, A. Al-Jawad, Y. Al-Shahwani, M. A. Majid, R. M. Mahmoud, M. Soufi, K. Tawfig, M. A. Ibrahim, and H. Dabagh, Epidemiology of organomercury poisoning in Iraq, Bull. WHO, vol 53 suppl., pp 37-38 (1976).

18. D. O. Marsh, G. J. Myers, T. W. Clarkson, L. Amin-Zaki, and S. Tikriti, Fetal methylmercury poisoning: New data on clinical and toxicological aspects, Trans. Amer. Neurol. Assoc., 102:1 (1977).

19. D. O. Marsh, G. J. Myers, T. W. Clarkson, L. Amin-Zaki, S. Tikriti, M. A. Majeed, Fetal methylmercury poisoning: Clinical and toxicological data on 29 cases, Ann. Neurol., 7:348 (1980).

20. D. O. Marsh, G. J. Myers, T. W. Clarkson, L. Amin-Zaki, S. Tikriti, M. A. Majeed, A. R. Dabbagh, Dose-response relationship for human fetal exposures to methylmercury. Presented at the International Congress of Neurtoxicology, Varese, Italy, Sept. 24-30 (1979).

21. J. K. Miettinen, Absorption and elimination of dietary mercury (Hg^{2+}) and methylmercury in man, in: "Mercury, Mercurials and Mercaptans," M. W. Miller and T. W. Clarkson, eds., Charles C. Thomas, Springfield, ILL. (1973).

22. National Academy of Sciences, An assessment of mercury in the environment, National Academy of Sciences, Washington, D.C. (1978).

23. R. W. Phelps, T. W. Clarkson, T. C. Kershaw, and B. Wheatley, Interrelationships of blood and hair mercury concentrations in a North American population exposed to methylmercury, Arch. Environ. Health 35:161 (1980).

24. H. Shahristani, K. Shihab, and I. K. Haddad, Mercury in hair as an indicator of total body burden, Bull. WHO, vol 53 suppl., pp 105-112 (1976).

25. T. Takeuchi, Pathology of Minamata Disease, in:"Minamata Disease," M. Kustuna, ed., Kumamoto University, Kumamoto, Japan (1968).

26. T. Tsubuki, and K. Irukayama, Minamata Disease. Methylmercury poisoning in Minamata and Niigata, Japan, Elsevier, Amsterdam (1977).

27. WHO, Evaluation of mercury, lead, cadmium and food additives amaranth, diethylpyrocarbonate and octyl gallate, Food Additive Series No. 4, WHO, Geneva (1972).

28. WHO, Environmental Health Criteria 1. Mercury, WHO, Geneva (1976).

29. J. M. Wood, F. S. Kennedy, and C. G. Rosen, Synthesis of methyl-
    mercury compounds by extracts of methanogenic bacterium,
    Nature, 220:173 (1968).
30. T. Yanagimeto, and E. Yanamoto, Estimation of safe doses:
    Critical review of the Hockey Stick Regression Method
    Environ. Health Perspectives, 32:193 (1979).

─────────────

This paper is based in part on work performed under a Center grant
#ES 01247 and a Program Project grant #ES 01248 from NIEHS and
in part on work performed under Contract No. DE-AC02-76EV03490 with
the U.S. Department of Energy at the University of Rochester Department of Radiation Biology and Biophysics and has been assigned
Report No. UR-3490-1988.

DISCUSSION

ABRAHAMSON: You mentioned earlier that methylmercury might have a genetic effect. Ramel and Magnusson, in Sweden, reported increased non-disjunction in Drosophila scored in the offspring of female parents that were fed methylmercury either as larvae or adults. This was increased non-disjunction but not chromosome loss. I think they also extended that work to plant root tips. So it did at least induce non-disjunctional events in some systems.

CLARKSON: That is correct. I don't know of any other test where it was shown to be a mutagen. I think the standard microbial tests haven't worked out.

ABRAHAMSON: Nor have they for any metallic ion as far as I know. That's not surprising.

CLARKSON: We have discussed this aspect with Dr. Doherty and his opinion is, as far as Iraq is concerned, that the size of the exposed population just wouldn't be big enough to test for genetic effects.

ABRAHAMSON: Are you looking for increased incidences of, for example, Down's syndrome in the children of mothers who have higher doses?

CLARKSON: Dr. March and Dr. Meyers have, so far, examined 83 children. These are the ones in which we have precise information about exposure levels during pregnancy. We'd have to have a very high frequency of Down's syndrome to pick it up.

BERG: You are speaking of two different populations. Chromosomal aberrations leading to Down's syndrome could be expected only in children of women who became pregnant after exposure or in grandchildren of mothers exposed during pregnancy.

CLARKSON: Yes, I see your point. Still, the number of mothers whose exposure level we know precisely is limited. It is certainly measured only in the hundreds. Again, you'd have to have a very high frequency of an abnormality before it could be detected.

FORBES: I think your second slide shows the relation between brain and blood concentrations, and you get a surprisingly linear relation in animals. Would you not expect that the body burden from an exposure would follow a different course than the level measured in the blood? I wonder if you have any information on that. Also, you mentioned you have ten cases per plotted point. Do you have any evidence for outliers? What was the distribution of those 10 points?

CLARKSON: The first point is well taken. There have been a number of tracer studies on humans carried out in Finland and in Sweden in

which a radioactive and non-radioactive dose of methylmercury has
been ingested by a number of volunteers. About 20 have been studied
this way. The amount going to the brain seems to be a constant frac-
ton of the body burden, about 10%. And the half-time in the brain
as determined by regional whole-body counting is about the same as
the half time for the whole body. It's about 70 days. These are
only tracer studies, of course. There is certainly evidence, though,
that methylmercury is highly mobile in the body. It is not like
other forms of mercury. It readily crosses the placenta and it
readily crosses the blood/brain barrier. So that, in general, it
is not being accumulated like lead in bone or something like that.

    The statistics, with regard to your second question, have not
really been finished on the data. Certainly this hockey stick plot
for instance, is somethin that we're interested in.

STEIN: Two points: one, hospital admissions were given for March,
1972. I don't know when the actual exposure occurred, whether exposures were in December or January or whether the victims went
straight to the hospital. In either case, you must have a distribution over time of when the mothers whose infants you examined were
exposed and at which stage of gestation. Even if the numbers are
small, you must have a feeling for that.

    The second point arises from Dr. Abrahamson's remark. If you
think that non-disjunction occurred, it could have occurred in the
prospective father or the mother to appear subsequently, who knows
when, in reproduction. It probably would manifest itself as spontaneous abortion, since 99% of trisomic conceptions abort before the
mother comes to term. So you might, if it's worthwhile, have a
chance to check that, whereas I agree that you wouldn't find an increased Down's syndrome.

CLARKSON: The question of stage of gestation is something that
Dr. Marsh, Dr. Cox and I are looking into. There have been previous
papers from Iraq which certainly indicate that the third trimester is
important; that is, infants had severe brain damage if the mother
ingested the contaminated bread only in the third trimester.

STEIN: It would be puzzling if there were not as many women who
were exposed in midtrimester or early trimester.

CLARKSON: Oh yes, there are. But we do know that exposure in the
last trimester will produce damage. We can't exclude the others as
yet. We're trying to look into it, but there is some difficulty in
precisely determining the birthdate in Iraq, which limits how finely
we can do that.

W. RUSSELL: Could you summarize very briefly the parts of your paper
that you said were most interesting, but which you didn't get to in

your talk?

CLARKSON: One other thing I would have liked to say was that besides the dose-effect relationship, there are some interesting kinetic differences in the behavior of methylmercury in people. Methylmercury is an example of a poison for which we know the range of biological half times in man, at least we have a distribution for it. In future estimates of risk, we would like to take into account not only the distribution of estimated doses but also the distribution of biological half times into the calculations that may indicate a threshold. For example, when you are relating long-term daily intake to risk, then of course you go first through the blood level calculation and then to the risk of an adverse effect. There is evidence in Iraq that there is a bimodal distribution of elimination half times. A statistical analysis is being made in which both these distributions have been taken into account and it yields a rather broad range of risks from the same level of exposure.

UPTON: You looked at a pulse exposure, for the most part, and have shown us hockey stick-shaped dose-response curves. Do you have any reason to suppose that the same blood level or tissue concentration sustained over a long interval in prenatal development would increase or decrease the toxicity?

CLARKSON: Quite frankly, we don't know the answer to that. In adults, Dr. Marsh and Dr. Turner and others have examined a population in Peru where people were exposed to a more or less steady state level all their lives. The levels really didn't get into the toxic range seen in Iraq, but if there were substantial effects of duration of exposure we would have expected some severe cases in Peru, which we did not see. But time differences between weeks and months are probably important and we have not really tackled that.

SAGAN: I'd like to ask about a possible mechanism. The early slide suggests to me that it's the amount of mercury in brain tissue that is toxic. The hockey stick plot suggests that there is a threshold. Those two observations suggest in turn that the threshold may be at the blood-brain barrier, and the differences in the blood-brain barrier among species and perhaps among individual humans may account for differences in responses. That, I should think, would be fairly easy to test in animal models.

CLARKSON: Yes, it would. There is a change in kinetics and a change in distribution, slightly, just before a toxic outcome in the animals. So there may be some change in the properties of the blood-brain barrier. Certainly, methylmercury does cross the blood-brain barrier readily in all species. Tracer data are quite conclusive on that point.

SAGAN: But tracer data won't tell you whether the material is intra-cellular or extracellular.

CLARKSON: No, they will tell you whether the material is in the brain as a whole.

SAGAN: It could be in the vascular compartment, for example.

CLARKSON: Well, there is more evidence than that. We do have auto-radiographs.

BERG: There is a technical point. The blood-brain barrier concept is probably not applicable to methylmercury, which does not exist as a compound in solution anywhere in the body. It exists only in bound form, and piggy-backs or exchanges between alternate ligands. It also dissolves in lipids and moves readily across cell mem-branes. So what you rather have is a biochemical distribution be-tween alternate binding sites and the molecular target site, what-ever that may be. We have published some of the relevant kinetics which look different than blood-brain barrier kinetics, but do not exclude the concept of threshold.

POCHIN: Just a small point. A logarithmic horizontal scale is an awfully good way of making a relationship look as though it had a threshold. It still looks like a threshold on a linear plot, though, doesn't it?

CLARKSON: Not quite as well.

BERG: Dr. Pochin cautioned us against a fallacy of similar plots which simulate an inflection by extending the abscissa down toward the log of zero, at minus infinity. In the case we are discussing, however, the lower end of the horizontal scale is anchored to a sizeable background concentration of methylmercury. This would tend to validate the plot.

RISK FACTORS FOR DEFICITS IN

EARLY COGNITIVE DEVELOPMENT

Sarah H. Broman

National Institute of Neurological and
Communicative Disorders and Stroke
Bethesda, Md. 20205

The current emphasis on risk assessment, a methodology introduced in the early fifties (1), has been attributed to a decreased public tolerance for exposure to potentially harmful
events, particularly if the exposure is perceived as involuntary
and widespread (2). Efforts to identify risk factors are certainly
not new, nor have they been unproductive. What has become increasingly urgent is the need to carry out the complex tasks involved in quantifying risks so that their relative importance can
be evaluated. It is well-recognized that all segments of the population are not at equal risk following similar exposure to an
injurious event. Examples of susceptible subpopulations are pregnant women, infants, and young children. In this paper, methods
of identifying and evaluating risk factors for cognitive deficits
in infancy and early childhood are illustrated by findings from
a large-scale longitudinal study of the developmental consequences
of complications in pregnancy and the perinatal period. Between
1959 and 1974, the offspring from 53,043 pregnancies were followed
from gestation through eight years of age in the Collaborative
Perinatal Project of the National Institute of Neurological and
Communicative Disorders and Stroke. Women in the study were selected by site of prenatal care. Abnormal outcomes of particular
interest were cerebral palsy, mental retardation, congenital malformations, and learning disorders. Causes of perinatal death and
prematurity were also investigated, as were factors related to
physical and cognitive growth. The goals of the Perinatal Project
were heavily influenced by the work of Lilienfeld, and Knobloch
and Pasamanick and colleagues who carried out a series of retrospective studies to investigate the concept of a continuum of
reproductive casualty, an hypothesis that complications in pregnancy and the perinatal period can produce a spectrum of abnor-

malities ranging from fetal or neonatal death through severe to mild
neurological deficit (3,4).

From a series of five studies of psychomotor and cognitive
development, factors found to be independently related to delays or
deficits ranged from cultural and social characteristics of the
family to physiological status and drug exposure of the neonate.
These studies demonstrate the value of a multivariate approach not
only for controlling potentially confounding variables, but also
for yielding estimates of the relative importance of a given risk
factor. In the first three studies, the sequalae of low birthweight, perinatal anoxia, and exposure to medication during labor
and delivery were investigated using multiple regression analyses.
In the last two studies, predictors of severe mental retardation
and of unexpected school failure were identified in discriminant
function analyses.

Low birthweight, a sign of immaturity, has long been considered
a potent risk factor related to survival and to mental and motor
development (5). The control of birthweight and of preterm delivery is seen as central to improving fetal and perinatal health,
a top priority of pediatric research (6). Unexpected findings
emerged from an early study in the Perinatal Project of the relationship of birthweight to psychomotor development in infancy and
to later IQ scores in the preschool period (7). Although mean
scores at eight months of age on the Bayley Mental and Motor Scales
increased linearly with birthweight as predicted, with the lightest
group ($\leq$ 2000g) scoring about two standard deviations below the
heaviest group ($\geq$ 3501g), birthweight explained only 5% to 6% of
the variance in test scores in this population of 31,000 infants.
Other variables included in the multiple regression analyses were
gestational age and sex of child, and ethnicity and education of the
mother. Together, these variables explained only an additional
2% to 3% of the variance in Bayley mental and motor scores. These
results show that while low birthweight is a risk factor for delayed psychomotor development, the effect of birthweight on outcome
is small. Most of the variance in infant test scores was unexplained
in these analyses.

The relationship between birthweight and Stanford-Binet IQ
scores at age four was examined within demographic subgroups of the
population because ethnicity and educational level of the mother
had moderately high correlations with four-year IQ (r = .41 and .33,
respectively). Mean IQs increased with birthweight but differences
were smaller than at eight months of age. Among white children
in each of two maternal education groups, and among black children
whose mothers' had more than a high school education, the lightest
birthweight group scored about one-third of a standard deviation
below the heaviest group (5 to 6 points). The largest difference
was found among black children whose mothers had not completed

high school. In that group, children with birthweights of 2000g
or less scored about two-thirds of a standard deviation, or 9 IQ
points, below those with birthweights over 3500g. In a regression
analysis that included six covariates, birthweight explained less
than 1% of the variance in IQ scores at age four. Ethnicity and
maternal education were the best predictors, accounting for 16%
and 6% of the variance, respectively. Bayley Mental Scale scores
at eight months accounted for more of the variance in IQ (3%) than
did Bayley Motor Scale scores, or gestational age, or sex of child
(< 1%). These results show that birthweight has less of an effect
on measures of cognitive development at age four, when verbal skills
are assessed, than at age eight months. The most important predictors of preschool IQ were cultural and social characteristics
of the family. While this study did not focus on the development
of the most immature neonates, the findings indicate that low
birthweight is not a major risk factor for cognitive deficit.

Perinatal anoxia has been recognized as a possible cause of
mental and physical handicaps in childhood for over a century (8).
Recent studies of the association between perinatal anoxia — defined as reduction in oxygen level below the physiological requirements of the organism during labor and delivery — and intellectual functioning have been reviewed by Gottfried (9). It
was noted that inconsistencies in findings were related to important
variations in research design. Studies in this area differ in
definition of the independent variable, introduction of control
variables, and use of retrospective or prospective methods of data
collection. Some of these methodological issues were addressed in
an investigation of ten clinical signs of perinatal anoxia as risk
factors for cognitive deficit among children in the Collaborative
Perinatal Project (10). Bayley Mental Scale scores at eight
months were consistently lower within demographic subgroups for
infants with a clinical judgement of respiratory difficulty in the
newborn nursery, and for those who had suffered mutiple apneic
episodes. In multiple regression analyses, the ten signs of perinatal anoxia together explained only 2% to 3% of the variance in
Bayley Scale scores in the white and black samples. A more in-
clusive set of perinatal and demographic predictors accounted for
9% to 15% of the variance in eight-month scores with the best predictors being birthweight and gestational age.

At age seven, IQ scores on the Weschler Intelligence Scale for
Children (WISC) were lower among children with respiratory difficulty as newborns and among those with low Apgar scores of three
or less at one minute after birth. However, differences between
these children and the unaffected controls were not consistently
significant (p < .01) within the demographic subgroups based on
ethnicity, social class, and sex. The ten clinical signs of perinatal anoxia explained less than 1% of the variance in seven-year
IQ scores in the white and black samples. The larger set of

perinatal and demographic predictors accounted for 25% of the
variance in scores among whites and 13% among blacks. The best
predictors were a composite index of socioeconomic status of the
family, educational level and non-verbal IQ score of the mother,
head circumference at birth, and among whites, a clinical diagnosis
of brain abnormality in the newborn nursery. In summary, prediction
of cognitive outcome from signs of perinatal anoxia alone or with
other predictors resulted in an estimate of the magnitude of the
relationship which was very small in infancy and even smaller in
childhood. Results obtained from other methods of analysing these
data, including lower mean scores for anoxic groups and a higher
frequency of clinical signs among the retarded, indicate that anoxia
accounts for so little of the variance in cognitive scores not
because it is unrelated to outcome, but because relatively few
newborns are affected.

The effects of drugs given during labor and delivery on the
fetus and newborn are a matter of concern to pediatricians and
obstetricians (11). In a third prospectively designed study currently in preparation, relationships between obstetric medication
and physical and cognitive development through age seven were investigated in a sample of children followed longitudinally (12).
The cohort was drawn from white registrants at two of the hospitals
participating in the Collaborative Perinatal Project. Subjects were
1944 full term infants with birthweights over 2500g who were born
to mothers with uncomplicated pregnancies and vaginal vertex de- ·
liveries. Pharmacological agents evaluated were inhalation anesthetics and six other drugs administered during labor and delivery.
Outcomes in the first year of life included items from pediatric
examinations at birth and at four months, a psychomotor assessment
at eight months, and a pediatric neurological examination at one
year. Later outcomes were scores from psychometric examinations
at age four and at age seven, and items from a pediatric neurological examination at age seven. Univariate associations between
outcomes and drugs were identified with hospital of birth controlled. The significant relationships were examined in multiple
logistic regression analyses with other relevant risk factors
included. A standardized relative risk was then computed for each
outcome - drug relationship.

The results suggest that inhalants are associated with deficits
in psychomotor and neuromotor functioning in the first year, and
that oxytocin is also associated with psychomotor deficit. Scopolamine and secobarbital are related to respiratory difficulties in
the newborn, and inhalants, scopolamine, and secobarbital are
associated with palpable liver at 4 months. At older ages, scopolamine is associated with slightly lower scores on some cognitive
tasks, and oxytocin is associated with lower achievement test
scores. These findings suggest hypotheses that require independent
confirmation. With the large number of covariates included in each

analysis, overcontrolling rather than confounding may well be the major analytic problem. However, some of the significant associations found could be due to chance. Drug-free groups of sufficient size were not available for comparative study in this sample of normal pregnancies from the Perinatal Project. Further research on risks associated with drugs given in labor and delivery is needed within the context of current obstetric practice.

A major goal of the Collaborative Perinatal Project was to investigate prenatal and perinatal causes of mental retardation. In a retrospectively designed study, maternal urinary tract infection during pregnancy was identified as a risk factor for severe mental retardation in children without motor deficit or other major CNS abnormality (13). In a univariate screen for perinatal antecedents of severe mental retardation at age seven, it was found that mothers of children with IQs under 50 but without major neurological signs had a significantly higher frequency of urinary tract infection during pregnancy (40%), than mothers of the severely retarded children with neurological abnormalities (5%) or those of children with IQs in the borderline, average, or superior ranges, where the frequency decreased linearly from 21% to 9% of women affected. A discriminant function model was used to investigate the independent contribution of maternal urinary tract infection to cognitive deficit. Of the 92 children with IQs under 50 at age 7 in the white population of the Perinatal Project (N = 17432), 26 were free of major neurological abnormality. The prospectively ascertained pre- and perinatal characteristics of this group were compared with those of the neurologically abnormal severely retarded children, and with those of a large group of normals with seven-year WISC IQs in the average range of 90 to 119 (N = 12667). Maternal urinary tract infection during pregnancy was a significant independent discriminator in both comparisons. The only other significant pre- and perinatal discriminator between the two groups of severely retarded children was a clinical diagnosis of brain abnormality in the newborn nursery. Other significant discriminators in the comparison with the average IQ group were maternal seizures, weight gain, and anemia during pregnancy, breech delivery, fetal heart rate, apneic episode, non-CNS malformations, sex ratio, housing density, and maternal intelligence test score.

Mothers with urinary tract infections may also have endotoxemia, which, in turn, can cause fetal damage (14). Within the Perinatal Project population, this pregnancy complication has been related to excess perinatal deaths (15) and to fetal leukoencephalopathy in infants who died in the first month of life (16). The present findings are based on a small sample, but they suggest that maternal urinary tract infection is a significant risk factor for severe cognitive deficit in children.

In a study of a less handicapping condition, risk factors related to unexpected school failure at age seven were investigated in a retrospective design using discriminant function analyses (17). The target group of low achievers was defined as children with normal IQ scores and below average achievement test scores. Subjects were the 430 white children and 564 black children in the Perinatal Project seven-year sample of 35,000 who had IQs of 90 or above on the WISC and reading or spelling scores on the Wide Range Achievement Test that were more than one year below grade placement. Low Achievers were compared with IQ-matched academically successful controls of the same ethnic group on prospectively ascertained medical, psychological and environmental characteristics beginning in the prenatal period. Subgroups of low achievers including those rated as hyperactive at age seven were also studied. Approximately three percent of children in both ethnic groups were low achievers, a proportion in agreement with the lower limit of most prevalence estimates of learning disabilities (18). These children who were required by study criteria to have seven-year WISC IQ scores of at least 90, had mean scores of less than 100 (98 $\pm$ 7 among whites and 96 $\pm$ 5 among blacks). Results from discriminant function analyses comparing low achievers and controls showed that even when IQ scores are held constant and are fixed at or above a normal level, poor academic performance of young school children is related primarily to the sociocultural factors of large family size and low socioeconomic status, and to the biocultural factor of sex of child with males most frequently affected. Some adverse or potentially adverse perinatal events were more frequent among low achievers than controls, but only longer first stage of labor in the black sample was a relatively powerful discriminator. Speech and language problems at three years of age were more frequent among low achievers than controls, but were weaker discriminators than a lower four-year IQ score, a more comprehensive index of lag in cognitive development.

Unexpectedly, a set of seven-year psychological, neurological, and demographic characteristics had only a slightly higher relationship to low achievement than did the early characteristics from the prenatal period through age four. Sex of child and family size remained among the most important discriminators. Signs of deviant behavior and non-verbal as well as verbal cognitive deficits were more frequent among low achievers. Several neurological signs at age seven were significant discriminators but not among the most efficient ones. Only a few of the low achievers had definite neurological or sensory abnormalities. Neurological "soft" signs including right-left confusion and impaired position sense were more common, and pointed to problems with spatial orientation among low achievers. A subgroup rated as hyperactive at age seven differed from nonhyperactive low achievers primarily on other behavioral characteristics, but they also had a higher frequency of obstetric complications and neuro-

logical soft signs. For low achievers as a whole, these findings
suggest that although they differed in several developmental areas
from their academically successful controls, the largest and most
consistent differences of etiological significance were in aspects
of family environment closely associated with opportunities for
verbal-conceptual stimulation.

REFERENCES

1. Lilienfeld, A.M.: Advances in quantitative methods in epide-
    miology. Public Health Rep., 95:462 (1980)

2. The risks of assessing risks. Br. Med. J., 281:1374 (1980)

3. Lilienfeld, A.M. and Pasamanick, B.: The association of
    maternal and fetal factors with the development of cerebral
    palsy and epilepsy. Am. J. Obstet. Gynecol., 70:93 (1955)

4. Nelson, K.B: The 'continuum of reproductive casualty.' In
    Clinics in Developmental Medicine No. 27, Studies in Infancy,
    Ed. by R. MacKeith and M. Bax. Spastics International Medical
    Publications, London, p. 100 (1968)

5. Caputo, D.V. and Mandell, W.: Consequences of low birthweight.
    Dev. Psychol., 3:363 (1970)

6. Court, S.D.M.: Context and priorities for paediatric research
    in the eighties. Pediatr. Res., 14:1290 (1980)

7. Broman, S.H.: Birthweight, infant development and preschool
    IQ. Unpublished manuscript (1973)

8. Little, W.J.: On the influence of abnormal parturition,
    difficult labor, premature birth, and asphyxia neonatorum on
    the mental and physical condition of the child, especially in
    relation to deformities. Trans. Obstet. Soc. London, 3:293
    (1862)

9. Gottfried, A.W.: Intellectual consequences of perinatal
    anoxia. Psychol. Bull., 80:231 (1973)

10. Broman, S.H.: Perinatal anoxia and cognitive development in
    early childhood. Chapt. 3 in Infants Born at Risk, Ed. by
    T. Field. Spectrum Publications, Jamaica, New York, p. 29
    (1979)

11. American Academy of Pediatrics, Committee on Drugs. Effect
    of medication during labor and delivery on infant outcome.
    Pediatrics, 62:402 (1978)

12. Broman, S.H. and Brackbill, Y.: Obstetric medication and early development. In T. Sedick (Chair), The international year of the child: A retrospective consideration of perinatal factors influencing pregnancy outcome and development. Symposium presented at the annual meeting of the American Association For the Advancement of Science, San Francisco (1980)

13. Broman, S.H.: Perinatal antecedents of severe mental retardation in school-age children. Paper presented at the 86th annual convention of the American Psychological Association, Toronto (1978)

14. Leviton, A. and Gilles, F.: Maternal urinary-tract infections and fetal leukoencephalopathy. N. Engl. J. Med., 301:661 (1979)

15. Naeye, R.L.: Causes of the exesssive rates of perinatal mortality and prematurity in pregnancies complicated by maternal urinary-tract infections. N. Engl. J. Med., 300:819 (1979)

16. Leviton, A., Gilles, F.H., and Dooling E.: Epidemiology of the perinatal telencephalic leukoencephalopathy characterized by hypertrophic astrocytes and amphophilic globules. Neurology (Minneap.), 29:571 (1979)

17. Broman, S.H.: Early development and family characteristics of low achievers: A multivariate analysis. Paper presented at the Scientific Research Workshop on Neurological Aspects of Learning and Behavior Disorders, 15th International Conference of the Association for Children with Learning Disabilities, Kansas City, Mo. (1978)

18. Minskoff, J.G.: Differential approaches to prevalence estimates of learning disabilities. Ann. N.Y. Acad. Sci., 205:139 (1973)

DISCUSSION

FORBES: Would you like to comment briefly on the methods used for checking your models? Also, were there any results which were particularly surprising or unexpected on the basis of past information, or were they consistent with anecdotal evidence?

BROMAN: There were several surprises. The relationship between birth weight and cognitive performance is still considered by many people to be substantial, and when one reports that it isn't, that is surprising. This results from the kinds of statistical methods people ordinarily use. They usually use t tests, and don't talk about the amount of variance explained. These two methods give somewhat different answers from the same set of data.

Examining a subgroup of extremely low birth weight babies gave a somewhat different picture from examining a group where the whole range of weights is represented. Findings from the latter approach were unexpected in terms of the state of the art.

I mentioned the unexpected finding about academic difficulties being associated with parental social class, even when I.Q. of the child is controlled.

We were encouraged to find that maternal urinary tract infection in pregnancy is related to mental retardation because this provides a lead that something can be done about. This finding agrees with some animal data and with some autopsy data.

With regard to checking models, I can't think of any variables with distributions that were particularly disturbing, either to me or to the consulting statistician. There was a great deal of checking of the data before we got to the analytic stage, and both continuous and dichotomous variables were used.

STEIN: Did it make a difference if the mothers were treated or untreated for urinary infections? And secondly, did I understand you to say that no effect of nitrous oxide inhalant remained after the child was one year old?

BROMAN: There were a few findings for inhalation anesthetics after the first year, but they were scattered, and they had to do with behavior. The exposed children were more often rated as dependent and nonassertive. The major findings for inhalants were deficits in motor development in the first year.

UPTON: How about the treatment of urinary tract infections?

BROMAN: Unfortunately, the data on treatment in the Collaborative

Study are not always complete. Most of the women were treated with sulpha drugs, according to their medical records.

SAGAN: How did you identify the urinary tract infections? Were they looked for in a standardized fashion?

BROMAN: Yes, there were a series of prenatal interviews with the women by the attending obstetricians.

SAGAN: So the infections were diagnosed only by symptoms?

BROMAN: If the women were symptomatic, laboratory tests were done.

SPIELMAN: I am surprised not to see cigarette smoking among the prenatal influences. Is that because at the time you did the study people weren't alert to that relationship?

BROMAN: I think they were alert to the relationship between cigarette smoking and birth weight. I have reported elsewhere that there is a correlation between the number of cigarettes smoked during pregnancy and birth weight of about -.20.

SPIELMAN: Oh, I was asking not only about birth weight but about childhood development.

BROMAN: There are some data from the Collaborative Study that shows an association between maternal cigarette smoking and hyperactivity.

SAGAN: What about the use of other drugs throughout the pregnancy? You have only talked about drugs at the time of delivery.

BROMAN: I am looking at those in the context of the study of drugs during labor and delivery. They will be entered as covariates in the analysis.

SPIELMAN: I did not see alcohol intake mentioned. Did that get factored out or was it not taken into account in this study?

BROMAN: The interest in that came much later in the Collaborative Study. Detailed data on maternal alcohol intake were not collected. However, data from the Collaborative Study have been pooled with data collected in Seattle in a study of the fetal alcohol syndrome.

BOURDEAU: It seems that one of the main factors associated with deficits in cognitive development was the head circumference. This was a positive relationship?

BROMAN: Yes.

BOURDEAU: The smaller the head, the bigger the deficit?

BROMAN: Yes.   Head circumference was consistently, at every age, the best of three physical measurements in predicting cognitive development.   Height and weight were also positively associated with scores on cognitive tests.

CROW: Is this big head adjusted for body size or not?

BROMAN: No.   Although Dr. Stanley Garn did look at the three measurements together in analyses of growth data from this study.   The results are not much different.

CROW: You said that you were surprised to find an influence of socioeconomic status of the parents on the development of the child when parental I.Q. was held constant.   I don't find it surprising and maybe we're thinking differently about it.   I should think that parents had many influences on children other than through their I.Q.

BROMAN: Yes, of course.   We controlled on I.Q. of the child which is highly related to his or her achievement test scores.   And then we know that social class of the family is highly related to I.Q. of the child.

CROW: Well, I guess we differ in our surprise level.   I realize all of these are correlated.

UPTON: There has been concern about undernutrition causing physical and mental underdevelopment.   Do your data argue against this?

BROMAN: We don't have any direct information on nutrition; all we have are maternal height and weight and we have weight gain during pregnancy, birth weight, placental weight and the measurements that I named on the child.   We find small but positive correlations of all those variables with cognitive development.   It is a very indirect approach.

POCHIN: Was it possible to look at whether the correlation with oxytocin could be separated from any correlation with the factors for which oxytocin was given?

BROMAN: We attempted to do that in two ways: by restricting the cohort to so-called normals -- that is, vaginal vertex deliveries without complications, and by statistical controls, or the covariates entered into the logistic regression analyses.   I think this pretty effectively gets rid of confounding factors.   Also, oxytocin was not given for induction of labor.   Induced women were excluded from the sample.   It was given for augmentation.   The reasons given in the charts for augmentation did not indicate that specific problems were present.

SAGAN: You did not report on this but I find myself very interested with the effects of what the pediatricians call bonding. There's probably no standard measure of bonding, but breast feeding might be an indicator. Children who are breast fed in hospital, who have early, close association with mothers, could be considered to be better bonded than bottle fed children. Did you examine the variable?

BROMAN: No, but Dr. Stein has done some analysis of the Collaborative Study data.

STEIN: It is extremely hard to isolate that factor from social class. Especially in 1959-62, the better-off mothers were less likely to breast feed. Breast feeding was not fashionable then.

CROW: I should think that the fact that habits have changed so widely would make it easier to study, by comparing the two groups, where the habit of nursing changed for people of the same economic status.

BROMAN: From the point of view of a psychologist, one of the gaps in the Collaborative Study is the lack of behavioral data. I would not have thought of looking at breast feeding because I don't think we have an appropriate behavioral outcome to relate it to.

KATES: There's an immunological outcome as well.

UTILIZATION OF CRITICAL PERIODS DURING DEVELOPMENT TO STUDY

THE EFFECTS OF LOW LEVELS OF ENVIRONMENTAL AGENTS

Liane B. Russell

Biology Division
Oak Ridge National Laboratory
Oak Ridge, TN 37830

I. INTRODUCTION

The identification of susceptible subpopulations serves basic
as well as applied purposes. The biological properties by which a
subpopulation differs from less susceptible individuals furnish
important clues about the basic mechanisms by which an environmental agent impinges on biological material of *all* organisms
(e.g., repair deficiencies shed light on repair in general); they
also provide information on the pathways between the original
interaction and the finally expressed endpoint. From a more
applied point of view, the existence of susceptible subpopulations
may lead to limitations in permissible doses of an environmental
agent. Where a subpopulation cannot be physically separated from
the main population, such limitations must be to the overall
population. Alternatively, the susceptible subpopulation may
have to be restricted from certain environments, e.g., the
workplace -- a procedure that can have social and legal implications.

The developing embryo and fetus have long been known to be
particularly vulnerable to ionizing radiation. In part, this
excessive vulnerability is the result of the fact that a developing
organism is capable of endpoints which no longer exist in an adult.
For example, one would not expect a fully formed structure (a hand,

*Research sponsored by the Office of Health and Environmental
 Research, U.S. Department of Energy under contract W-7405-eng-26
 with the Union Carbide Corporation.

or an eye) to become drastically malformed by irradiation, whereas
such an effect is quite logical when the formative stages of a
structure are exposed. But even where endpoints are more directly
comparable (e.g., death of the whole organism), the intrauterine
mammal responds at lower doses than does the adult.

To consider the embryo as a whole as a single subpopulation
is, however, a simplification that can lead to great loss in
sensitivity in the detection and measurement of risk, i.e. to an
underestimation of risk. Conversely, it may lead to overestimation
of risk in the process of extrapolating from single to protracted
exposures. The embryo is, of course, a dynamic system with rapidly
changing patterns of sensitivity. As we showed 30 years ago (9,
10, 17), a given effect can be induced readily by exposure at a
well-defined developmental stage, but not at all induced by the
same exposure at other stages -- even those occurring only a day
before or after the sensitive one. This pattern, which we worked
out for certain endpoints in the mouse, was named the pattern of
critical periods.

The critical periods define subpopulations of a subpopulation
whose special properties of sensitivity should be exploitable in
studying risk at low levels of exposure to environmental agents,
and for the development of methods for extrapolation. Only a
limited amount of such exploitation has occurred to date. This
paper will describe three systems that may be well suited for more
extensive future work in this area.

II.   SYSTEMS THAT UTILIZE CRITICAL PERIODS TO STUDY LOW-LEVEL EFFECTS

A.   Cell Kinetics as an indicator of nervous-system maldevelopment

In man, nervous-system formation occupies a relatively much
greater proportion of the period of intrauterine development than
in experimental mammals, and abnormalities involving the nervous
system (e.g. microcephaly, mental retardation) are thus, under-
standably, among the most frequently reported human teratogenic
effects (16). The developing nervous system of experimental
mammals has long been known to be highly sensitive (4). In spite
of this, most observations have been of a qualitative nature, and
little effort was made until recently to develop sensitive quantitative indicators of developmental damage.

The device of working at the stage of maximum sensitivity has
led to an experimental system whose endpoints permit extrapolation
to low levels. Using at first moderate to high doses of X-rays,
Kameyama, Hoshine, and Hayashi (5) investigated the undifferentiated
matrix cells in the ventricle walls of the developing telencephalon

during embryonic stages spanning a major part of cerebral-cortex
formation in the mouse. They found day-13 postconception to be
most vulnerable with respect to a number of parameters: (a) cell-
cycle changes in the first postirradiation cell division, (b)
incidence of pyknotic cells 4-5 h postirradiation; and (c) reduction
in cortical cells 7 weeks later.

Having discovered the stage of maximum sensitivity, they
extended their investigations to lower doses, down to 10 R. They
found that the prolongations of the (G_2 to 1/2 M) phase of the cell
cycle were a linear function of the logarithm of the dose. The
line did not extrapolate to zero dose, but to a point between 5 and
10 R, indicating a probable threshold below 10 R.

Although the fate of the matrix cells exhibiting an alteration
of their cell-cycle times has not been directly determined, there
is enough indirect evidence available to link this endpoint with
damage to the cerebral cortex. Inasmuch as the finally perceived
damages (e.g., cortical cell reduction in the adult, behavioral
changes) are probably not as easily amenable to quantitative
studies in the low dose range, the cell-cycle changes in the
telencephalon, induced *at the stage of maximum sensitivity*, may be
regarded as useful sensitive indicators of teratogenic activity.

B.   Oocyte depletion

The second example, like the first, deals with an effect
measured at the cellular level. It illustrates, in addition, that,
in order to estimate risk for the intrauterine period of man's
life, it may occasionally be necessary to investigate postnatal
stages in those experimental mammals that are born at a considerably
less mature stage of development than is the human infant.

Our fertility studies with female mice of various ages showed
that newborns did not become sterilized by doses of X rays that,
in young adults, caused permanent sterility after only one or two
litters; but that, at early postnatal ages, the ovary appeared to
be exquisitely sensitive (18). The pattern is similar when the
end point is oocyte count, rather than fertility. Peters (8) found
heavy destruction of mouse oocytes after only 20 R given at 7, 14,
or 21 d postnatally. By administering single doses of 18 rad γ
irradiation at various ages between birth and 47 d, Dobson et al.
(3) later found a distinct, and very low, minimum in oocyte
survival following exposure in the second or third postnatal weeks.

Once investigators had identified the sensitive period, they
were able to demonstrate effects of very low doses. In pioneering
work, Oakberg (7) showed that a single dose of 3 rads γ on day-10
postnatally significantly reduced oocyte numbers. Dose-response

curves give no evidence for a threshold (2). Throughout the sensitive period, LD$_{50}$'s for oocyte killing are considerably lower than
any known LD$_{50}$'s for other types of cell death. Reported values
include 8.4 rads (2.9 rad/min γ irradiation) for stage-1 oocytes at
10 days (7), 7 rads (1 rad/min γ) at 18 days (2), and 4.5 rads
(tritium in body water) administered through the drinking water
during the entire period (2).

It should be noted that the mechanism by which oocytes are
depleted is unknown. Since the cells are nondividing, depletion
is not through aneuploidy death. Most oocytes of late fetal and
newborn mice are in meiotic prophase (pachytene or diplotene).
Shortly after birth, the cells enter the arrested, dictyate, stage,
and it is this newly attained dictyate that appears to be particularly sensitive. Working at the height of the sensitive period,
days 10-12, Oakberg (7) found a lower oocyte survival when irradiation was administered at 2.9 r/min than when it was given at
0.01 r/min. This indicated the existence of repair processes in
the newly attained dictyate oocyte. Subsequent investigations (2)
clearly confirmed the dose-rate effect during the second and third
prenatal weeks, but also showed that the oocyte's ability to
recover was limited. The age pattern in sensitivity that has been
demonstrated with radiation, appears to be closely paralleled when
newborn, juvenile, or young adult mice are treated with 3-
methylcholanthrene (3) and appears thus to be the result of
intrinsic features of the early dictyate oocyte.

While early dictyate oocytes are present during juvenile
stages of the mouse, they are found during fetal stages in primates,
including man (Oakberg, private communication). Oocytes of women
and adult monkeys, in contrast to those of rodents, have been
notoriously radioresistant; however, there is increasing evidence
(summarized in ref. 3) for elevated radiosensitivity during the
last trimester of primate development. Using the spider monkey,
Dobson et al. (3) found an LD$_{50}$ of, at most, 5.6 rads from tritiated
drinking water (less, should only a portion of the last trimester
be sensitive). It appears, therefore, that the sensitive test
system developed for the juvenile mouse may be directly applicable
to human risks.

The susceptible stages of the ovary obviously provide good
experimental material for measuring risk in a subpopulation. Not
only is the endpoint of clear practical importance (in that it
concerns human fertility), but it is not far down the chain of
events between initial lesion and scorable effect and lends itself
readily to quantitative analysis. The time span during which
oocyte killing can be profitably used to investigate low-level
effects is a fairly long one -- perhaps 2 weeks in the mouse. This
makes the end point amenable to studies involving dose fractionation
or protraction. It also theoretically provides a good chance for

detecting effects in epidemiological studies. From a practical
standpoint, however, such detection is unlikely, since oocyte
counting is ordinarily not feasible, and fertility impacts would
probably not occur until near the end of the normal reproductive
period, when few women conceive in any case.

C.   Homeotic shifts in the skeleton

Morphological aberrations ("birth defects") are, for obvious
reasons, perceived by man as major risks from prenatal exposure to
harmful agents. Because of this, it seems advisable to design one
or more test systems around morphological endpoints. In doing so,
one must bear in mind the possible complexity of the pathways
between the initial lesion and the observed effect (Fig. 7 in
ref. 17). Because of the likelihood, moreover, that several targets must be hit before a malformation pathway is even initiated
(e.g., death of a single cell presumably does not produce polydactyly), simple dose-effect relations are not to be expected.

The early work on critical periods already showed that certain malformations had high thresholds, i.e., they were readily
induced by 300 R, but not induced at all by 200 R (9, 10). It also
demonstrated the complexity of interpreting quantitative relations
when both incidence and degree of an abnormality could vary with
dose (9).

We have endeavoured to find morphological endpoints that are
serviceable in a low dose range in order to make use of a sensitive subpopulation for the detection of teratogenic potential of
environmental agents. One prerequisite is that such endpoints
should be suitable for quantitative analysis, with incidence and
degree being part of the same scale.

Certain problems with, as well as opportunities for, quantitative analysis of morphological effects are illustrated in Fig. 1.
It may be assumed that the genotype fixes the position of the mean
value on a scale of developmental potencies. Variability about
this mean is caused by a multiplicity of normally occurring small
environmental variables in development. Body weight is a readily
comprehended example of such a situation, in which the finally
observed character -- *as well as* the underlying developmental
potencies -- are capable of continuous variation. Where, however,
the final character must vary by discreet steps, rather than
continuously, as is the case for many quantitative morphological
features (e.g., 13 vs. 14 ribs, 7 vs. 8 teeth), canalization
occurs through the superimposition of thresholds, and the areas
under the curve on each side of the threshold can be translated
into histograms. This type of analysis is based on Sewall Wright's

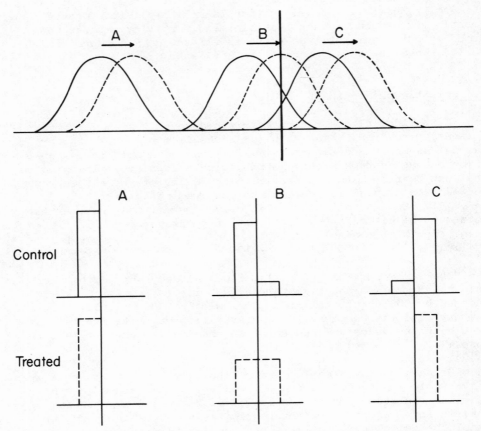

Fig.1. Hypothetical distributions relating to a specific character in
three strains of mice, A, B, and C. -- The top portion of the
figure illustrates continuous variability about a mean, fixed
by the genotype, on a scale of developmental potencies. Solid
lines represent normal position, broken lines new position
following an environmental interference in development; in
this example, all three strains are shifted to the same
degree. -- The bottom portion of the figure illustrates distribution of a discontinuously varying character, derived from
the continuous distributions shown in the top portion when
presence of a threshold causes canalization. The histograms
are derived from the areas under the curve on each side of the
threshold. Solid and broken lines, as well as strain designa-
tions, correspond to top portion of the figure. -- Although
the treatment in this hypothetical case has shifted all
strains equally, strain B is the most useful of the three for
quantitative studies of small effects (see text).

classical study of toe development in different inbred strains of guinea pigs (19, 20).

One may note, by looking at distributions A, B, and C, that shifts of the same magnitude can have very different probabilities of being detectable and/or measurable. In the case of A, the shift would not be detectable at all, because neither the old nor the new distribution crosses the threshold; in the case of B, the shift would be both detectable and measurable; while, in the case of C, the shift would be detectable but not measurable, since the new distribution no longer crosses the threshold, and the position of the mean can thus not be fixed. The ideal situation to aim for is thus B; that means finding an *inbred* strain that possesses a great deal of normal variability with regard to the character being studied.

During our early exploration of critical periods, we found that the development of the last rib (thoraco-lumbar border) could be affected in different ways by irradiation administered at different stages. Thus, exposure on day $8\frac{1}{2}$ postconception (p.c.) shifted the border posteriorly, while exposure on day $11\frac{1}{2}$ p.c. shifted it anteriorly (10, 17). These and similar numerical effects have been referred to as homeotic shifts (12). The strain of mice used in the early investigations (actually, an F_1 between two inbred strains) was, in the absence of radiation, quite *invariable* with regard to this feature and to other quantitative characteristics of the axial skeleton. The constancy indicated that this genotype probably did not provide the most favorable material for working with the desired end points (cf. strain A in Fig. 1). A subsequent exploration of other strains led us to select the BALB/c.

The question of stage sensitivity for the homeotic shifts in the axial skeleton was reinvestigated using the BALB/c, since different genotypes may have slightly different developmental time-tables. As had been the case for the (C57BL x NB)F_1 in our earlier work (10, 17), the BALB/c was quite sensitive on day $8\frac{1}{2}$ to the induction of posterior shifts. Clearcut effects had been found with 25 R (11), the lowest dose then tested. The stage of maximum sensitivity, however, has recently been established to be 18 hours later, on day $9\frac{1}{4}$ (12). This was true of 4 different characters: position of the thoraco-lumbar border, position of the lumbo-sacral border, number of sternebrae, and number of costo-sternal junctions (Fig. 2). (The first of these characters showed an *anterior* shift when treatment was three days later, day $12\frac{1}{4}$.)

The BALB/c strain on day $9\frac{1}{4}$ p.c. thus provides a potentially sensitive system for the detection of environmental insults to the embryo. We have concentrated on day $9\frac{1}{4}$ and are in process of determining the lowest dose of X-rays that can be readily detected. For two of the four characters, clearcut shifts are apparent after

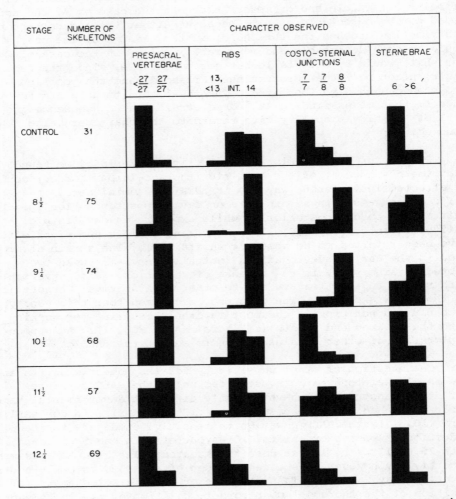

Fig.2. Frequencies of various quantitative skeletal characters in newborn BALB/c mice following 100 R irradiation at different stages in embryonic development. (Reproduced from ref. 12 by permission of the Wistar Press).

12.5 R.   Experiments with 5 R are in progress, and it appears that effects will be detectable by one of the characters, namely expression of the fourteenth rib.

III.   APPLICATION OF THE SENSITIVE SYSTEMS TO THE TESTING OF CHEMICALS

Since the homeotic shifts by themselves are presumably not damaging to the organism, the endpoints are used as sensitive indicators that an agent is capable of affecting developmental processes.   The quantitative relation between given degrees of shift and selected anomalies for which day-9¼ p.c. is also the critical stage has been worked out at higher doses of X rays.   Is this particular quantitative relationship peculiar to the teratogen (in this case, X rays), or is it a function of the existing developmental conditions?   If the latter is the case, then the system can be used not merely as a sensitive detector of agents capable of causing developmental interference but as a predictor of actual levels of teratogenicity.   Doses of chemical agents teratogenically equivalent to certain doses of X rays can then be determined readily.

We have approached this question with one chemical, benzo(a)-pyrene, BaP (Ref. 15, and Russell, unpublished).   With regard to homeotic shifts (Fig. 3), an exposure to 100 mg/kg was found to be somewhat less potent than irradiation with 100 R X rays administered at an effectively equivalent stage.   (Note that the BaP was injected into the pregnant female 18 hours prior to the maximum sensitive stage, day 9¼, in order to allow time for formation and transport of active metabolites.)   Subsequent experiments have indicated that, with respect to homeotic shifts, 100 mg/kg BaP is indeed equivalent to an X-ray dose somewhere between 50 and 100 R; and 50 mg/kg BaP is equivalent to an X-ray dose between 25 and 50 R.   Significantly, this equivalence extends also to an array of axial skeleton defects induced at the corresponding stage (13), i.e., there is no clearcut qualitative difference between the actions of these two teratogens. Thus, for at least one chemical, it appears that the conditions for extrapolating from homeotic shifts to abnormalities may hold.

Both of the other low-dose systems that have been discussed, oocyte depletion and cell-cycle alteration in the telencephalon, use endpoints that in themselves are damaging to the organism.   It is, therefore, perhaps not as important as in the case of the homeotic shifts to build bridges to other effects.

Some of the guidelines currently governing teratogenicity testing require preconception, postconception, and postnatal administration of the test substance; and some protocols even specify a three-generation test.   Quite apart from the fact that these

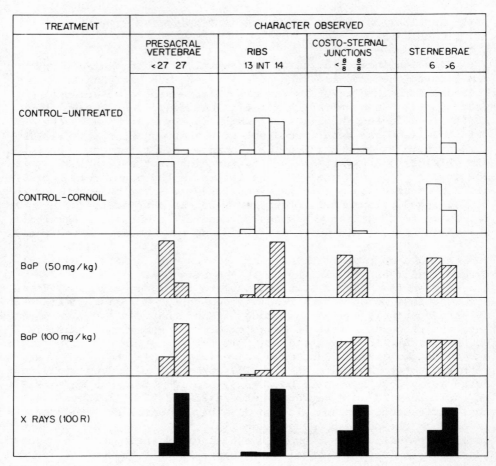

Fig.3. Homeotic shifts in four features of the axial skeleton in the
BALB/c strain of mice treated on day-9¼ postconception with
X-rays, or at a developmentally equivalent stage (see text)
with Benzo(a)pyrene dissolved in cornoil. Note that all dis-
tributions are shifted to the right by the treatments, with
100 mg/kg BaP being somewhat less effective than 100 R X rays.
Cornoil alone has no effect. (Figure based on data by
Russell and McKinley 1978.)

procedures confuse genetic and teratogenic effects, they also dilute the probability for discovering specific developmental damages, because only small fractions of the total dose will be received during specific critical periods. It may be suggested that tests such as the three discussed in this paper, which have been developed with strict attention to specific critical periods, can provide rapid and sensitive means for revealing whether an agent is capable of causing developmental interference. More extensive teratological investigations could then follow, if necessary. Because of metabolic differences between species (and even strains) of experimental mammals, and because of the possible tissue specificity of some chemical agents, it might be well to develop a *battery* of indicator tests. A possible battery that would include different species, target tissues, and developmental stages, might consist of the homeotic-shift test in the mouse, oocyte killing in another species, and telencephalon changes in yet another.

IV. THE ROLE OF SENSITIVE STAGES IN ESTIMATING RISK

    Embryonic, fetal, and even early postnatal periods each consist of as a succession of stages that are sensitive to the induction of different arrays of effects. In experimental animals, the pattern has been determined for certain classes of endpoints but is unknown for the vast majority of possible effects. What may be surmised for man comes mainly from extrapolation to developmentally equivalent stages of the data from experimental animals.

    When investigating effects of short-term exposures to environ-mental agents, epidemiological studies should pay strict attention to stage of exposure -- if possible, by week postconception. If this is not done, it is easy for a real effect to become so diluted as to be imperceptible. A specific effect inducible during only one of 38 weeks of pregnancy, for example, would virtually disappear if the sample included equal numbers derived from exposures during any one of the 38.

    This may be illustrated by actual data for an endpoint that is apparently sensitive during several successive weeks, and therefore not quite as dilutable as if the critical period were more strictly limited. Fig. 4 depicts the microcephaly data for Hiroshima (6, 1): the plot for exposures during weeks 6-11 of pregnancy shows a steep dose-response curve (albeit with wide error bars due to the small-ness of the samples), while the plot for the entire period of pregnancy (with different mixes of stages at each dose point) indi-cates a much shallower curve of different shape at the lower end. Extrapolation to low doses could presumably be different from the two tabulations. This epidemiological study was a very large one, and the sample size and dose range are not likely to be duplicated for other agents. It is thus improbable that one will be able to

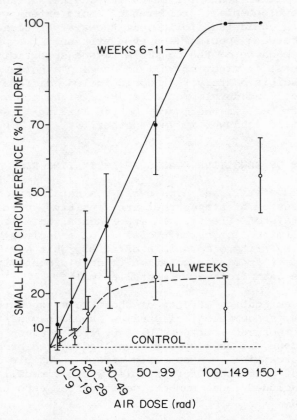

Fig.4. Incidence of microcephaly in children who had been exposed to
       the atomic bomb in Hiroshima while in utero. Solid line
       derived from children exposed weeks 6-11 postconception,
       broken line from all children. Error bars are standard
       errors of the proportions. (Figure based on data by Miller
       and Mulvihill 1976; control incidence from Blot 1975.)

deduce, from human data alone, critical periods for other endpoints. If one can*not* do so -- and therefore has to work with a smear of stages -- the low-dose extrapolation will always be an underestimate as far as the real sensitive subpopulation is concerned.

On the other hand, the circumstances that most critical periods for specific damages are probably short, may lead one to overestimate the risk from that particular damage if one assumes that protraction or fractionation of a given dose will not (or will only slightly) reduce the response. Such a spreading out of the exposure is likely to result in only a very small portion of the dose being received during the short period that is sensitive to the induction of the specified effect. For example, a single dose of 200 R administered at one of various times during the first two weeks postconception produced a number of very severe damages; but spreading out the same dose over the entire two weeks eliminated virtually every effect (14).

V. SUMMARY

Careful definition of critical periods in the development of selected characters can result in experimental systems that may be highly useful in studying risk at low levels of exposure. Three examples are presented. Epidemiological investigations can lose much of their value unless critical periods are known for the endpoints being studied.

REFERENCES

1. Blot, W. J.: Growth and development following prenatal and
    childhood exposure to atomic radiation. J. Radiat. Res.
    Suppl., 82-88 (1975)

2. Dobson, R. L. and Kwan, T. C.: The tritium RBE at low-level
    exposure -- variation with dose, dose rate, and exposure
    duration. Current Topics in Radiation Research Quarterly
    12:44-62 (1977)

3. Dobson, R. L., Koehler, C. G., Felton, J. S., Kwan, T. C.,
    Wuebbles, B. J., and Jones, C. L.: Vulnerability of female
    germ cells in developing mice and monkeys to tritium, gamma
    rays, and polycyclic aromatic hydrocarbons. In Developmental
    Toxicology of Energy-Related Pollutants, Ed. by D. D. Mahlum
    et al. Techn. Info. Center, U.S. Dept. of Energy, CONF-771017
    pp. 1-14 (1978)

4. Hicks, S. P. and D'Amato, C. J.: Low dose radiation of the
    developing brain. Science 141:903-905 (1963)

5. Kameyama, Y., Hoshine, K. and Hayashi, Y.: Effects of low-
    dose X-radiation on the matrix cells in the telencephalon
    of mouse embryos. In Developmental Toxicology of Energy-
    Related Pollutants, Ed. by D. D. Mahlum et al. Techn. Info.
    Center, U.S. Dept. of Energy, CONF-771017, pp. 228-236
    (1978)

6. Miller, R. W. and Mulvihill, J. J.: Small head size after atomic
    irradiation. Teratology 14:355-358 (1976)

7. Oakberg, E. F.: Gamma-ray sensitivity of oocytes of immature
    mice. Proc. Soc. Exptl. Biol. Med. 109:763-767 (1962)

8. Peters, H.: Radiation sensitivity of oocytes at different
    stages of development in the immature mouse. Radiat. Res.
    15:582-593 (1961)

9. Russell, L. B.: X-ray induced developmental abnormalities in
    the mouse and their use in the analysis of embryological
    patterns. I. External and gross visceral changes. J.
    Exptl. Zool., 114:545-602 (1950).

10. Russell, L. B.: X-ray induced developmental abnormalities in
    the mouse and their use in the analysis of embryological
    patterns. II. Abnormalities of the vertebral column and
    thorax. J. Exptl. Zool., 131:329-395 (1956)

11. Russell, L. B.: Effects of low doses of X-rays on embryonic development in the mouse. Proc. Soc. Exp. Biol. Med. 95: 174-178 (1957)

12. Russell, L. B.: Sensitivity patterns for the induction of homeotic shifts in a favorable strain of mice. Teratology 20:115-125 (1979)

13. Russell, L. B.: Sensitivity of the homeotic-shift prescreen for environmental teratogens. Teratology 19:45A (1979)

14. Russell, L. B., Badgett, S. K., and Saylors, C. L.: Comparison of the effects of acute, continuous, and fractionated irradiation during embryonic development. Internat. J. Radiation Biol., Suppl.:343-359 (1960)

15. Russell, L. B. and McKinley, Jr., T. W.: Application of a sensitive in vivo teratological system to the testing of Benzo(a)pyrene. In Developmental Toxicology of Energy-Related Pollutants, Ed. by D. D. Mahlum et al. Techn. Info. Center, U.S. Dept. of Energy CONF-771017, pp. 175-187 (1978)

16. Russell, L. B. and Russell, W. L.: Radiation hazards to the embryo and fetus. Radiology 58:369-376 (1952)

17. Russell, L. B. and Russell, W. L.: An analysis of the changing radiation response of the developing mouse embryo. J. Cellular Comp., Physiol., 43, Suppl. 1:103-149 (1954)

18. Russell, W. L., Russell, L. B., Steele, M. H., and Phipps, E. L. Extreme sensitivity of an immature stage of the mouse ovary to sterilization by irradiation. Science 129: 1288 (1959)

19. Wright, S.: An analysis of variability in number of digits in an inbred strain of guinea pigs. Genetics 19:506-536 (1934)

20. Wright, S.: The results of crosses between inbred strains of guinea pigs, differing in number of digits. Genetics 19: 537-551 (1934)

DISCUSSION

STEIN: In the experiments of Dobson and Oakberg, did the oocytes disappear or was it possible to score for chromosomal abnormalities?

L. RUSSELL: They disappear. The score is actually a count of surviving oocytes. Dobson counted three days, and Oakberg two days after treatment. Non-surviving oocytes disappear almost immediately. It is a very rapid death, apparently followed by dissolution, because investigators report finding empty follicles very soon after treatment.

BOURDEAU: I'm sorry that you didn't have time to talk about your experience with testing chemicals. You described three very sensitive test systems and you know that it is very important at this time everywhere in the world to design screening systems for chemicals. Do you see any chance of having one of your procedures developed to the point where it can be made into a sophisticated test to predict possible hazards from chemicals?

L. RUSSELL: I think all of them have that potential. As far as I know, the mitotic delay in the telencephalon has not been used in chemical studies. Oocyte killing has been employed fairly extensively in studies with chemicals and has been found quite useful. The homeotic shift system has so far been used only with benzo(a)-pyrene. With benzo(a)pyrene, the correspondence between given levels of homeotic shifts and certain frequencies of malformations was similar to that found in X-ray experiments over a fairly wide range of effects. So we are trying to develop rad equivalent doses.

BOURDEAU: You believe in a rad-equivalent system?

L. RUSSELL: Not for everything, but I think in this particular case we can validate it. I'd like to see whether a dose of chemical that has a certain rad-equivalence with respect to percentage of homeotic shifts will also have the same rad equivalence with respect to percentage of malformations in the axial skeleton.

ABRAHAMSON: Didn't Dobson test about 50 chemicals on the oocytes? All those that were known carcinogens were very effective in the oocyte test, as I recall.

WEINBERG: I'd like to ask an unfair question. If you had been advising Governor Thornburgh at Three Mile Island, would you have recommended that the pregnant women be evacuated?

L. RUSSELL: I'm so glad I was out of the country, in Argentina, I think. What dose levels was he concerned with?

WEINBERG: About 100 MR per person.

L. RUSSELL: No, I wouldn't.

UPTON: As I recall, the concern there was not how it would come out at that time, but the instability of the reactor. The public was made aware of some problem on Wednesday or Thursday, and then there seemed to be a continuing problem. I understood it was the concern about what might transpire that caused the evacuation.

WEINBERG: I think the underlying point was the belief that the fetus is very much more sensitive than the adult, but I guess my impression was that that belief was based on the Stewart-Kneale/Oxford study rather than on the findings you're reporting here.

L. RUSSELL: I don't want to comment on the transplacental carcinogenesis because I'm really not an expert on that. If you think that the decision was made in relation to possible effects later in life on offspring exposed in utero, then it might have been rational to evacuate pregnant women. But on the basis of congenital malformations from a dose of 0.1 R to pregnant women I would not have recommended that.

WEINBERG: Your figures are still inconsistent with the alleged sensitivity that the Oxford study claimed. The Oxford study claimed that you double the carinogenic effect at about 2 R, I think that was the figure. John Totter claims to have disproved that point in a recent paper.

TOTTER: It is highly unlikely that there is any such sensitivity for carcinogenesis.

L. RUSSELL: Oocyte studies reveal very clear effects of low doses of radiation. As I mentioned, Oakberg found a statistically significant reduction in oocyte numbers at 3 R, and the LD50 has been shown to be only 5 R. Dobson's work indicates that there is no threshold. I think that in exposing human female fetuses, you might have to worry about cutting down oocyte numbers.

BERG: Would the speaker reconsider her choice of words? How many oocytes do you expect the exposed female offspring to use for the production of children, and what is the surplus in there?

L. RUSSELL: I discuss this in one part of the paper I had to cut out of the oral presentation. It would probably be impossible to demonstrate any such damages, because women run out of oocytes near the end of their reproductive life span, when they are usually not procreating in any case.

BERG: I am moved to consider the slaughter among epidermal cells of my palms when I chop wood, since at that site the ax handle is a great deal more harmful than 5 R. Could we differentiate between effects which are merely evidence that a dose has been administered, and those effects that in the parlance of toxicologists are called critical because they lead to some permanent damage? Are you drawing that line?

L. RUSSELL: I don't want to make any value judgments as to what is going to be harmful and what is not. I look upon the systems that I have described as indicators that something is happening. They're not designed to measure actual damage (and damage is presumably occurring elsewhere in the developing body). I think they are indicators to help us explore dose-effect relations.

BERG: Biological dosimeters of great sensitivity?

L. RUSSELL: They are dosimeters, yes. It is for that reason that I really want to be able to build some of the bridges between these "indicator" effects and effects that are generally recognized as harmful, e.g., malformations. This will be hard to do at low doses, but I think we can calibrate several of them at higher doses. Not all, because some of the malformations will have high thresholds.

CROW: What is known about the repair systems in these early egg stages that you're talking about, i.e., highly sensitive egg stage?

W. RUSSELL: Were there dose-rate effects in experiments on oocyte killing?

L. RUSSELL: There must be some repair system in oocytes but I am not aware of any studies.

CROW: I am reminded of effects on reproduction in fruit flies following urethane treatment, where following it with caffeine enhances the death rate by cutting back on the repair system, but it lowers the mutation rate because the repair system that's being cut out is an error-prone repair system. Possibly oocyte killing also has the effect of lowering the frequency of later abnormalities.

COHEN: You mentioned a treatment where 200 R did not produce a response. As a non-biologist I am surprised that there was not more variation in susceptibility among individuals.

L. RUSSELL: The endpoint was a very gross morphological effect - in that particular case a skull defect. We are dealing with an inbred strain of mice, i.e., animals are totally uniform genetically. So, any variability would be environmental rather than genetic.

SAGAN: Mutagenesis, carcinogenesis, teratogenesis -- there are a number of agents that produce all three effects. Is it a reasonable hypothesis that all three effects operate through the same mechanism?

L. RUSSELL: Carcinogenesis very probably has a somatic mutation component, but I am inclined to think that somatic gene mutation is not a major mechanism in teratogenesis. The evidence for this comes from the clear pattern of critical periods for specific types of malformations. If malformations were due to mutations, one would expect a random pattern of altered differentiations. But the pattern is strictly or very closely determined by the stage of development. I have been vividly reminded of this in the course of some recent mutagenesis experiments involving the somatic mutation test, popularly called the "mouse spot test." Animals are treated at a specific stage in development, namely day 10-1/4, and we subsequently look for somatic mutations at specific coat-color loci. This test provides, as a byproduct, some teratological information because, as we look at the animals for pigment spots, we also score malformations of features that can be seen externally -- feet, hands, tail, ears. It turns out that, with every chemical we have tried, the only externally detectable teratogenic effect is polydactyly of the hind feet. It is always of exactly the same type -- it always affects the first toe primarily on one side, I think the right side. It is remarkable how constant this end result is, and how dependent it is on stage of exposure, rather than on the chemical or agent that has been used. The pattern of teratogenic response changes with stage, and within a few hours one can produce a totally different effect by the same treatment. I think this indicates a mechanism of action through cell killing, or division delays, at sites that have a transitory high susceptibility to such disturbance.

UPTON: If you define teratogenic effect as an effect that occurs after fertilization and interferes with normal growth and development of the zygote, then would the X/O offspring represent a teratogenic effect or a genetic effect?

L. RUSSELL: The slide that I showed referred to the pronuclear stage, which I really consider an extension of the germ-cell stages. Prior to the first cleavage, the male and female pronuclei exist separately in the zygote; they have not fused. I consider sex-chromosome loss induced in pronuclei to be a genetic effect.

UPTON: You really have two haploid nuclei in the same cell.

L. RUSSELL: Of course, you can probably induce X/O's in later cleavage stages too, we just haven't looked for them. A problem in the mouse, and in all mammals, is that the embryo is formed from only a small percentage of cleavage cells. The inner-cell-mass (ICM) of the blastocyst, which actually forms the embryo, is made

up of only a few of the cells that have gone through cleavage.
Therefore, if treatment during cleavage stages were to induce an X/O
condition in one cell line, this event need not always result in a
mosaic individual. The X/O line could end up constituting the entire
ICM (resulting in a whole-body X/O), or be totally excluded from it
(resulting in a whole-body X/X). Because of that circumstance, one
always underestimates the incidence of mosaics.

UPTON: It has been reported by a number of observers that killing
of cells is linear with dose in the low dose range. At higher doses
there is a shoulder where the slope becomes steeper. Theoretically,
even with the smallest dose, one would occasionally kill some cells.
But you're arguing that in the developing embryo there's enough redundancy, if you will -- or reserve -- so that the loss of an occasional cell wouldn't itself lead to malformation.

L. RUSSELL: That's right. I would guess that even for the differentiating primordia of organs it would take more than one killed cell
to produce a morphological change. In the case of oocytes, on the
other hand, one killed cell would be detected because you are counting them. You can pick that up directly.

EPIDEMIOLOGIC STUDIES OF ENVIROMENTAL EXPOSURES

IN HUMAN REPRODUCTION

Zena Stein, Jennie Kline, Bruce Levin, Mervyn Susser
and Dorothy Warburton
New York State Psychiatric Institute and
Gertrude H. Sergievsky Center
Columbia University
630 West 168th Street
New York, New York 10032

Human offspring, although in general well protected between conception and birth, are by no means invulnerable to the external environment. In this and a companion paper (14) based on the same data set from a case-control study of spontaneous abortions, we illustrate this vulnerability by setting out the quantitative relations between two maternal behaviors - cigarette smoking and alcohol drinking - and two effects on the fetus - spontaneous abortion and reduced birthweight. We interpret the observed associations of these maternal behaviors and fetal effects as causal. The evidence indicates that the effects relate to post-conceptional exposures, and that their origin is <u>not</u> pre-conceptionally determined pathology in the fetus. These interpretations rest on clinical history, cytogenetic analysis, statistical control, and biological coherence.

<u>Biological considerations</u>: <u>The pre-conception period</u>.

We begin with some guiding concepts and speculations. The immediate opportunity afforded by our case-control study is to distinguish, among the triad involved in the reproductive process, which individual was exposed to a given hazard and what the timing of the exposure was likely to be. Some of the possibilities are explored here by way of an introduction. These possibilities will make the reader aware that the new data to be shown below are but one facet of a varied set of findings.

Parental influences on the offspring fall into three classes:

(a) maternal and paternal genetic transmission in a strict
    sense, that is, alterations in the chromosome number or
    structure of the germ cell, or inherited defects;
(b) non-genetic maternal transmission, through the agency of
    oocyte cytoplasm, uterus, or breast milk;
(c) non-genetic paternal transmission, through the agency of
    the sperm cytoplasm and the seminal fluid.

The transmission of hereditary material by either parent is
determined at the time of meiosis of the germ cells. The unique
chromosomal composition of each oocyte and sperm arises at the
first meiotic division (when haploid cells develop from the diploid cells of the primordial germ plate in the female or the primary spermatocyte in the male) During meiosis I, the twenty-three
chromosomal pairs of a diploid cell line up together and bridg-
ing strands ("chiasmata") are seen to connect them, enabling
exchange of chromosomal material ("crossing over") to take place.
Next, one member of each of the chromosome pairs in the diploid
cell (which originated in turn from the germ cell layer) is
selected at random to pass into a single germ cell, which then
contains a set of 23 chromosomes, each of which is unpaired, or
haploid. The second meiotic division in the haploid cell is a
process analogous to mitosis in the diploid cells: two identical
copies of the parent haploid cell are produced, of which only one
is retained as a germ cell.

In the human female, the first meiotic division begins while
the infant girl is still in utero, but the process is not finally
completed for a given germ cell until the time of ovulation. At
each ovulation, that is, roughly every 28 days from menarche until
menopause excepting for the interruptions of pregnancy,
lactation or oral contraception, one or more oocytes ripen,
meiosis I is completed, and ova are released from the ovary into
the fallopian tubes and pass to the uterine cavity. The second
meiotic division of the oocyte is not completed unless and until
fertilization takes place. In the human oocyte there is therefore
a long resting phase - lasting from before birth until puberty at
a minimum, and up to the menopause at a maximum - during which
meiosis I is suspended and homologous chromosomes lie paired in
readiness for separation.

It has been suggested that the long resting phase of the
oocyte in the female affects the probability that the genetic
material will be altered. There are at least three ways in which
this might come about. First, the vulnerability of the genetic
material to both extrinsic and intrinsic factors could increase
with the age of the oocyte. Second, factors which are intrinsic

to the aging process may influence the genetic material. Third, the possibility of exposure to extrinsic factors and any risks associated with such factors must increase simply by virtue of the greater duration of potential exposure (25).

How then should one interpret the over-representation of trisomic abortuses and of Down's syndrome infants occurring among births older women? Recent experiments in mice (19) are compatible with epidemiological inferences that the main source of the excess of trisomy in pregnancies of older women is maternal and not paternal. Such experiments, carried out in controlled environments, may seem on the face of it to point to influences which are intrinsic to the aging process. Yet, in humans, the rate of aging and maturation is not impervious to environmental influences; both the age of menarche and of menopause vary with environment. For example, malnutrition is associated with later age at menarche (2) and cigarette smoking appears to accelerate the menopause (11). Even so, only one specific factor, namely   X-irradiation, has so far been suspected of affecting oocytes in the resting phase of meiosis I. Some far from conclusive evidence, fully reviewed elsewhere (3,5), suggests that diagnostic irradiation in women can produce at conception, one or two decades later, a slight increase in the risk of triploidy and possibly trisomy (1).

The time taken to conceive increases with maternal age (14). This relative infecundity could arise because the ovulatory cycle becomes irregular or because the frequency of sexual intercourse decreases with age. It could also arise because in older women the oocyte has been impaired and impairment need not be confined to errors in meiosis, which lead in turn to the conception of a chromosomally abnormal zygote. Thus we have found that the risk of spontaneously aborting a chromosomally normal conceptus increases with maternal age no less strongly than does the increase of trisomy with age. Impairment of the oocyte cannot be excluded as contributing to this association of maternal age with eukaryotic abortions, although hormonal and systemic factors which change with age must also be considered.

Overall, however, abortion studies are compatible with the view that the genetic material is relatively well-protected during the long resting phase of meiosis I. Among offspring at term the sole adverse effect of maternal age about which one can   be sure so far is the excess of trisomic errors (trisomy 13,18,21). Other disorders among the offspring whether transmitted in the mendelian, polygenic or sporadic mode do not relate consistently to maternal age. Nor is there evidence of more subtle impairments. In fact quite the contrary, for indeed the offspring of older mothers have a slight but consistent benefit in terms of

measured intelligence and general health (32).*   In sum, any
disadvantage of prolonged meiosis of the oocyte appears to be
limited to the special circumstances of trisomy. With trisomy,
the major influence may well be the intrinsic aging process.
Although extrinsic factors are not excluded, the invariable
relation of maternal age with trisomy in diverse geographic areas
suggests that their influence is less important.

The chronology of the developmental cycle of the male gamete
(the sperm) differs markedly from that of the oocyte, and leads
to different predictions and hypotheses about both intrinsic and
extrinsic factors. In the male, meiosis I does not begin until
puberty. Only then do the diploid primary spermatocytes appear and
begin to be transformed into haploid spermatocytes, spermatids
and spermatozoa.   Spermatozoa are produced in batches and
at most survive two or three months. In animal experiments, it
has been shown that depending on species, dose, and substance,
some environmental exposures may affect the spermatogonia, others
the spermatocytes, while some distort or destroy the spermatozoa
themselves (4,18,31).

Experimentally, damage to the genetic material of spermatogonia
in the permanent cell layer may occur in some not very obvious
forms such as point mutations, and this effect could be life-long
and transmissible to all subsequent generations. (Perhaps this
is the mechanism for one human finding involving increasing paternal
age which is that it is associated with an unusual risk of a rare
dominant mutation, achondroplasia)(26). Damage to spermatocytes leading to chromosome rearrangements, which can effect the offspring and
their germ cells, have been induced experimentally (20); the
effects may be lasting in the progeny, but shortlived in the
sire, since newly generated spermatocytes will not show the
changes. Damage to the genetic material of the spermatozoa may
be marked, but this will be shortlived as are the spermatozoa
themselves.   There are proven human examples of changes in the sperm
related to paternal exposures as with lead (15) and DBCP (29,30).
Exposure to DBCP (29) has been associated with infertility but
not with the birth of an infant with defects.   The parental origin
of trisomic conceptions has been traced to the father several
times (perhaps in one-fifth of cases successfully assigned to
either parent).   In addition, about two-thirds of triploid conceptions result from fertilization by two sperm (10) but maternal
influence cannot be ruled out here: there is possibly a failure
of the egg to recognize the fertilization by the first sperm, or
a failure of the first sperm to "communicate" its entrance.

---

*This statement may not hold for births over 4 5 years (6).

In one study (16), paternal exposure to irradiation was associated with chromosomal anomaly in the aborted conceptus. There have, to our knowledge, been no systematic attempts to relate paternal exposures to trisomic conceptions where the origin of the genetic error is paternal, nor to triploid conceptions which are owed to dispermy. The considerable geographic variation in the frequency of triploidy, as well as the variation in the proportion of cases which are due to dispermy suggests that enviromental factors may relate to the genesis of triploidy (27). Paternal exposure to vinyl chloride monomer and anaesthetics have been reported to relate both to spontaneous abortion and malformation, but the work at this time is no more than suggestive and awaits confirmation (19, 21, 8, 23).

We have suggested that chronological age is a measure of duration of exposure to the environment. Excepting trisomies, the fact that age seems not be impair the genetic material in any obvious way either in the female during the prolonged first stage of meiosis of the oocytes nor in the male during the equally long pre-meiosis stage of the spermatogonia suggests that in these developmental stages, at least, the genetic material is well protected from the environment.

The same may not be true for the period immediately preceding conception. It seems possible that the ovum ripening in the ovarian follicle, the circulating spermatocytes and spermatozoa, and the newly formed zygote may be vulnerable to environmental factors. Four observations support this view:

First, the susceptibility of the spermatozoa to several factors (irradiation, DBCP and cottonseed) is well established. Second, in a study of induced abortions, maternal drug taking around the time of conception was associated with an increase in the frequency of all chromosomal anomalies (28). Third, among conceptions that take place while women are taking oral contraceptives it has been suggested that births with trisomy 21 are more frequent (7). Fourth, we have shown that spermicides may disturb the first cleavage division of the zygote leading to conceptions with a rare chromosomal anomaly (24). These four observations perhaps allow us to entertain the notion of a critical period for oocyte, sperm, and zygote around the time of conception.

The post-conception period

We turn now from effects of maternal or paternal exposure before conception and around conception to consider effects after conception. The particular effects we shall discuss are those of maternal smoking and alcohol drinking on spontaneous abortions

and birthweight. In order to properly assess these post-conceptional effects, they must be isolated from pre-conceptional effects
owed to the same exposure. With regard to spontaneous abortion,
the most salient descriptive criterion at hand to effect this
isolation is the karyotype of the abortus. We can be reasonably
sure that chromosome anomalies (excepting for a few very rare
anomalies) do not arise after conception. When an aborted
conceptus is karyotypically normal, the possibility that the
abortion relates to an exposure which occurred after conception
may be entertained. About one-half to two-thirds of spontaneously
aborted conceptions are chromosomally normal and for this majority,
causes acting after conception may pre-dominate. Specification
of the karyotype therefore sharpens the hypotheses regarding the
likely timing of exposure and greatly increases the statistical
power to detect effects (12). When we began our studies in 1973,
we found that this differentiation of karyotypes had nowhere been
made in a systematic way in the research literature (22). Figure
I sets out a model which helped us to develop the differentiation
between the rate of abortion and timing of insult for conceptuses
with different chromosomal and morphologic features.

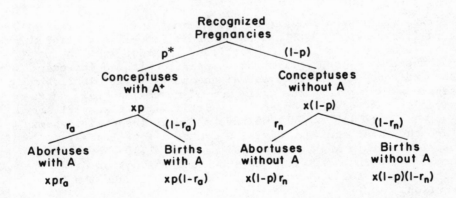

*p could be taken as a function of gestational time
+ for the moment only one "A" per fetus is assumed

Fig. 1. Diagram showing relationships between incidence of anomalies,
         fetal loss and birth defects among recognized pregnancies.
         (Stein et al. Spontaneous abortion as a screening device
         American Journal of Epidemiology, 1975, 102(4) 275-290)

With regard to the time of exposure to the hypothesized causal factors, we rely on the history given by the mother to characterize her exposure. We shall discuss ways of controlling potential bias below. For a reason unrelated to reporting bias, the factors we have chosen pose a special problem in the separation of pre- and post-conceptional exposure. Smoking and drinking are habitual behaviors, and a woman who smokes or drinks during pregnancy seldom starts that activity anew at the time of conception. If she continues at the same level during pregnancy as before, then her case is uninformative in separating pre- and post-conceptional effects. Fortunately, changes in habit with pregnancy are common. We find that a substantial number of women reduce their frequency of alcohol drinking as well as altering their diets. This reduction in alcohol consumption with pregnancy permits us to attempt to separate the effects of postconception alcohol drinking from those of preconception drinking. For smoking, the presence of both ex-smokers and smokers in our sample permits us to examine the relation of both preconception (often long in the past) and post-conception exposure to spontaneous abortion.

Methods

The data to be presented draw on an ongoing epidemiologic study which is being carried out in three New York City hospitals. Over the past six years, we have identified all women admitted with spontaneous abortion to either the private or public facilities of the hospitals (cases). Over this period, 2802 women have been interviewed and in about 30% of these cases we have completed a cytogenetic examination of the aborted conceptus.* A comparison group, matched for maternal age and payment status (private or public patient), has also been selected and interviewed. This group is comprised of women who sought prenatal care at the same three facilities and whose pregnancies continued longer than 28 weeks gestation (controls). We have included 1343 interviewed controls in the comparisons with women experiencing spontaneous abortion; data on 972 singleton livebirths to those women have been processed so far and are available for the birthweight analyses. In some of the analyses to be presented here we include a subset of the data: 657 interviewed cases using the public facilities of the hospitals are compared with their matched control, who was also treated in the public facilities of the hospitals. The study design and the sample are described fully elsewhere (13,14).

---

*We enumerate here women aged 15-40 years at their last menstrual period since only these women are included in the analysis presented here.

Three different comparisons are made:

(1) First we compare the frequency of exposure in women with spontaneous abortions(cases), and in women who carry their pregnancies 28 weeks or more (controls). The interview where the history of smoking and drinking is taken is carried out after the abortion for cases,and during the first two trimesters of pregnancy for nearly all controls. Since the responses of a woman who suspected that smoking or drinking could have caused her miscarriage might be colored by her experience (perhaps she would report more, perhaps less, than her actual consumption), this case-control comparison may be affected by reporting bias.

(2) In our second comparison, we contrast the frequency of exposure in cases of eukaryotic spontaneous abortions with that in controls, destined to have longer gestations and (with rare exceptions) eukaryotic offspring. This is, for many purposes, the most cogent comparison in the case of miscarriage, because neither the interviewer nor the patient knows at the time of interview, whether the abortus will prove to be chromosomally normal or abnormal. Thus the association of an exposure with chromosomally normal abortions but not with chromosomally abnormal abortions provides compelling evidence that an association observed in the case-control comparisons is not a reflection of reporting bias.

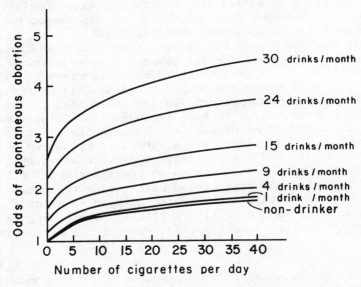

Fig. 2.   Increases in the odds of spontaneous abortion with increases in the number of cigarettes smoked each day for women defined in seven alcohol consumption categories.

(3) In our third comparison we examine the relation of exposures to birthweight, among the liveborn singleton infants of controls. The findings come from histories taken prospectively, and are therefore in the genre of cohort studies. In these data we need have no worry that the outcome has colored the history.

At this point, it may be useful to comment on the chromosomal anomalies grouped as 'other aneuploid' in the tables to follow. Anomalies may be split or grouped and what is distinctive about each subgroup may be as important in determining specific causes as what all have in common. Still, at the present preliminary stage of knowledge some tentative lumping must be imposed for analytic purposes, and we have put together all autosomal trisomic forms, as if they formed a single entity. This grouping of trisomies is not without some support since there are two observations which suggest that autosomal trisomies may relate to the same causes. First, all trisomies tend to be associated with raised maternal age, although not all to the same degree. Second, if a woman has two spontaneous abortions and the first is trisomic, there is a raised probability that the second will also be trisomic and this second trisomy is not usually of the same chromosome. Likewise, the risk of bearing a child with Down's syndrome (trisomy 21) is raised in a woman who previously or subsequently had an abortus with trisomy of some other chromosome.

On the other hand, there is reason to group trisomy/normal mosaic forms among trisomies rather than among 'other aneuploid' as we have done here. Both the frequency of the trisomic component and the raised maternal age in such cases suggest that the zygote was initially trisomic and became mosaic in the post-conception period. For this and other reasons, the group that is designated other aneuploid' and that comprises all anomalies other than trisomy, is a grouping that should not be taken to imply homogeneity within the group. Thus bigger numbers and more homogeneous groupings may be required to examine the relation of exposure to each of the chromosomally abnormal conceptions included here.

RESULTS

Comparisons of the first kind-cases vs. controls:

Figure 2 shows the estimated dose-response curve relating the odds of spontaneous abortion to the number of cigarettes smoked per day. The odds of an abortion increase with each additional cigarette smoked for women who did not drink (the lower curve), for women who drink daily (the uppermost curve) and for women drinking at intermediate frequencies. The odds of spontaneous abortion increased by 46% for the first ten cigarettes smoked and

Table 1.   Percent distribution of non smokers, exsmokers
           and current smokers among women experiencing
           spontaneous abortions (cases) and women
           experiencing deliveries at 28 weeks gestation
           or later (controls).

	% Cases	% Controls
Never smoked	50.0	51.4
Current smoker	32.2	24.9
Exsmokers		
Stopped smoking 1-7 months prior to interview.	6.9	11.9
Stopped smoking 8-24 months prior to interview.	3.1	3.8
Stopped smoking more than two years before interview.	7.8	8.1
Total Number	2748	1340

Table 2.   Frequency of drinking twice a week or more during
           pregnancy among women experiencing spontaneous
           abortion (cases) and controls for the categories
           of drinking prior to pregnancy.*

Frequency of drinking prior to pregnancy	Percent drinking twice a week or more during pregnancy (number)	
	Cases	Controls
Never	1.7(121)	0.7(149)
Less than once a month	3.1(259)	1.8(273)
Less than twice a week	9.3(118)	4.5(111)
Two to six times a week	55.4(112)	34.4(96)
Daily	80.0(40)	41.2(17)
Total	17.7(650)	7.9(646)

*Table includes public patients, aged 15-40.

Taken from: Kline et al. Drinking during pregnancy and spontaneous
           abortion, 1980, in press.

by 61% for the first twenty cigarettes smoked.* The level of
drinking in no way alters the relationship of smoking to spontaneous abortion.

Figure 3 shows the estimated dose-response curves relating
the frequency of drinking alcohol to spontaneous abortion for
three levels of cigarette smoking. Maternal age and education
were again controlled. The best-fitting curve is linear. The
odds of spontaneous abortion increases 3% with each additional
day on which alcohol was consumed. The odds of spontaneous abortion for a non-smoker who drinks daily are 2.53 times that of a
non-drinker. The odds of abortion for a woman who smokes one
pack of cigarettes each day and who drinks daily are 4.08 times
over those of a non-smoking abstinent woman.

We examined whether the associations of both smoking and
alcohol drinking were likely to be owed primarily to exposure
during pregnancy only, or to pre-conception exposures as well.
In Table 1 we contrast the proportion of women who never smoked,
who smoked during pregnancy, and who have stopped smoking.
Among cases and controls there is a slight, but statistically
significant, excess in the proportion of controls who stopped
smoking either immediately prior to pregnancy or during the
first few months of pregnancy (stopped smoking 1-7 months prior
to interview) compared to cases. The data provide strong support
for the hypothesis that it is smoking during pregnancy, not prior
to conception, which is associated with spontaneous abortion.

Similarly, in Table 2 we contrast the frequency of drinking
twice a week or more for women experiencing spontaneous abortion
and controls for five categories of frequency of drinking prior
to conception. The association of drinking during pregnancy
with spontaneous abortion is similar for all categories of preconception drinking. There is, however, a marked overlap in the
women who drink frequently both prior to pregnancy and during
pregnancy. Thus although the data suggest that the association
with abortion is primarily owed to drinking during pregnancy, the
possibility that frequent consumption prior to conception is a
necessary antecedent can not be ruled out.

Comparisons of the second kind-karyotyped cases and controls:

The second strategy takes account of the karyotype of the
aborted conceptus. Our anticipation was, in terms of the model

---

*These curves were fitted using maximum likelihood logistic
regression, with maternal age and education controlled. The
shape of the best fitting curve is a linear function of the
logarithm of one plus the number of cigarettes smoked each day.

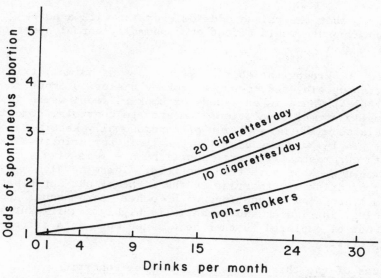

Fig. 3. The odds of spontaneous abortion with increases in the number of days each month on which alcohol was consumed for women defined in three smoking categories.

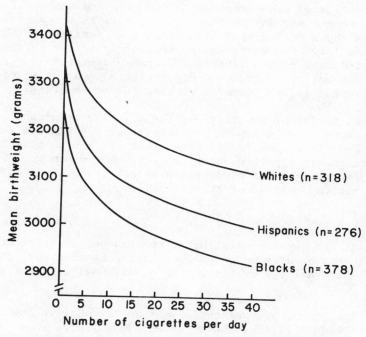

Fig. 4. Decrease in the predicted mean birthweights of 972 singleton liveborns with increases in the number of cigarettes smoked each day: Whites, Hispanics and Blacks.

shown above, that the raised odds of abortion with a postconception exposure would affect chromosomally normal abortions
entirely.

Table 3 groups the abortus karyotypes as normal, trisomic,
and other aneuploid, and compares smoking histories among these cases
with controls. There is an excess of smokers among women aborting
chromosomally normal conceptions compared to controls. Smoking is
not associated with the abortion of chromosomally abnormal conceptions. Table 4 shows a similar analysis for drinking. Again,
women with chromosomally normal abortions are more likely to
drink twice a week or more than controls. There is also a raised
frequency of drinking, aberrant in the light of our anticipations,
among women aborting conceptions with "other" chromosomal anomalies.
This finding, intriguing and potentially highly significant as it
is, will not be explored further here since more data are needed
to interpret it.

Comparisons of the third kind – the control cohort:

Using exactly the same independent variables as in the first
and second comparison we next examined mean birthweight in the
offspring of control women. Figure 4 is based on 972 infants of
women whose pregnancies went longer than 28 weeks gestation. It
shows the estimated dose-response curves relating number of
cigarettes smoked per day to mean birthweight. The dose-response
curves* are shown for each of the three races separately (White,
Black, Hispanic). For women who smoke ten cigarettes each day,
the predicted mean birthweight is 205 grams lower than for non-
smokers. For women who smoke 20 cigarettes each day predicted
mean birthweight is 260 grams lower than for non-smokers.

In this series of maternities, the drinking of alcohol, in
contrast, shows no relation to prematurity or low birthweight.
The published literature is not consistent at this point. If the
effects previously reported occur chiefly among women who drink
every day, they might not be detected in our study since daily
drinkers comprise only 2% of the cohort.

Discussion

None of the results relating to spontaneous abortion nor to
birthweight can be attributed to confounding by such obvious
factors as maternal age or race. Our questionnaire is extremely

---

*Maternal age, race, prepregnant weight and alcohol intake
were controlled in fitting these curves. This curve is a
logarithmic function of one plus the number of cigarettes
smoked each day

Table 3. Frequency (%) of smoking among women with euploid
          abortions, trisomic abortions, and other aneuploid
          abortions compared to controls.*

Number of Cigarettes Per Day	Percent Distribution Karyotyped Abortions			
	Euploid	Trisomic	Other	Controls
None	61.3	75.0	67.2	69.8
1-13	22.6	13.3	15.5	20.0
14-80	16.1*	11.7	17.2	10.2
Total	261	60	58	645

*The adjusted odds ratio for smoking 14-80 cigarettes per day
compared to non-smokers for euploids versus controls is 1.63; 95%
confidence interval = 1.06-2.52.

*Table includes public patients, aged 15-40.

Taken from Kline et al.   Enviromental influences in early
                          reproductive loss in a current New York City
                          Study, 1980, in press.

Table 4.   Frequency (%) of alcohol consumption during pregnancy
           among women with euploid abortions, trisomic abortions
           and other aneuploid abortions compared to controls.

Frequency of alcohol consumption	Percent Distribution Karyotyped Abortions			
	Euploid	Trisomic	Other	Controls
Never	40.2	48.3	36.2	43.7
Twice a month and less	30.7	33.3	36.2	38.0
Less than twice a week	11.5	11.7	12.1	10.4
Two to six days a week	11.9*	5.0	10.3	6.5
Daily	5.7*	1.7	5.2	1.4
Total number	261	60	58	645

     *Adjusted odds ratios were calculated controlling for an
association between maternal age (15-19, 20-29, and 30-40 years)
and karyotype, and for an association between smoking (non-smoker
versus smoker) and karyotype.

     For euploid abortions versus controls:

          Odds ratio for drinking daily versus never = 4.11
          95% confidence interval = 1.73 - 9.75
          Odds ratio for drinking two to six times a week versus
             never = 1.86.
          95% confidence interval = 1.11 - 3.14.

     Taken from Kline et al. Environmental influences in early
                            reproductive loss in a current
                            New York City Study, 1980, in press.

detailed on these and other points, many of which we have controlled
in the analysis. Maternal education, however, is one variable that
cannot be entirely set aside as an influence on fetal survival.
Thus the odds of abortion with smoking is greater among better-
educated than among poorly educated women. The converse is true
for drinking, and the odds are lower among better educated women (14).
Neither of these relationships is statistically significant, but
they leave open the possibility that in a bigger series, or in an
independent study, they may become more convincingly manifest.
Maternal education may be associated with differences in smoking and
drinking behaviors which have not been investigated here. For
example, the type of cigarette smoked (low or high tar and nicotine),
the amount smoked (to the butt or not), the type of beverage drunk,
whether drinking is accompanied by eating, and the frequency of
binge drinking are all aspects of these habits which may vary with
maternal education and may effect the association with spontaneous
abortion. In our own data there is additional evidence to suggest
differences between better educated and less-educated women;
chromosomally normal fetuses comprise a larger proportion of miscarriages among public (primarily less-educated) than among private
patients.

It is possible that a fetal influence or feto-maternal interaction in itself induces changes in habit with pregnancy, for
instance, a reduction in alcohol intake or smoking, and that the
capacity to induce change portends a healthy outcome. Women might
change their behavior because they have a healthy pregnancy, rather
than the reverse. For example, nausea and vomiting, which tend to
be associated with pregnancies with healthy outcome, may well bring
about such behavior change. Analyses controlled for nausea and
vomiting, and for the stage of gestation at which the history was
taken, however, do not alter the results reported here. It is our
best judgement that the effects we show are indeed causal. However,
epidemiological studies must always lack the precision afforded
laboratory experiments, and sceptics (ourselves included) await
replication and confirmation by other approaches.

With regard to risks associated with smoking, it is reasonable
to see a common thread in the outcomes in which the odds are high,
namely, miscarriage of normal fetuses, and low birth weight (intrauterine growth retardation). The shape of the curves for each outcome are not dissimilar, they are not moderated by ethnicity, by
alcohol intake, by pre-pregnant weight, or by maternal age. There
is also no evidence of malformations among the eukaryotic aborted
fetuses of women who smoke (Byrne, 1980). One might see the spontaneous abortion and intrauterine growth retardation as competing
fates for essentially normal conceptuses exposed to smoking.
Among pathogenetic theories advanced to explain reduced birthweight with smoking are decreased oxygen supply, nicotine toxicity,

and under-nutrition. Anoxia or toxicity seem the more likely to cause spontaneous abortion; infants who survive this insult may then proceed to encounter the process which leads to low birth-weight.

With regard to drinking, we have shown a marked association between moderate maternal drinking and the odds of spontaneous abortion: at this level of intake there is, on the other hand, no effect on birthweight, although at least part of the excess of abortion was contributed by eukaryotic abortuses.

In general, there must be some factors that specifically influence the abortion of a eukaryotic fetus but that do not affect intrauterine growth in survivors; other factors may have both effects.

In conclusion, our data show that the post-conceptional period is one in which everyday exposures, exemplified by maternal cigarette smoking and alcohol drinking, can be hazardous to the survival of a fetus presumably normal at conception. Environmental effects on the fetus can be studied in quantitative terms, just as can be done for cancer, and in addition, hazards can be compared according to their effects on different reproductive outcomes. With the adoption of a combined cytogenetic and epidemiologic approach, we can begin to study the physical and social environment, using human experience in reproduction as the ultimate criterion.

REFERENCES

1. Alberman, E., Polani, P.E., Fraser Roberts, J.A., Spicer, C.C., Elliott, M. and Armstrong, E. Parental exposure to X-irradiation and Down's syndrome. Ann Hum Genet 36: 195-207, 1972.

2. Bongaarts, John. Does Malnutrition Affect Fecundity? A Summary of Evidence. Science, Vol.208,9:564-569, 1980.

3. Brent, R.L. Effects of ionizing radiation in growth and development. In M.A. Klingberg and J.A.C. Weatherall, Eds., Epidemiologic Methods for Detection of Teratogens, Vol. I, Contributions to Epidemiology and Biostatistics, pp. 147-183, S. Karger, Basel, 1979.

4. Chandley, A.C. and Speed, R.M. Testing for nondisjunction in the mouse. Environmental Health Perspectives 31:123-129, 1979.

5. Cohen, B.H., Lilienfeld, A.M., Kramer, S. and Hyman, L.C. Parental factors in Down's syndrome -- results of the second Baltimore case-control study. In E.B. Hook and I.H. Porter, Eds., Population Cytogenetics: Studies in Humans, Academic Press, New York, 1977.

6. Goldberg, M.F., Edmonds, L.D. and Oakley, G.P. Reducing birth
    defect risk in advanced maternal age. JAMA 242:2292-
    2294, 1979.
7. Harlap, S., Shiono, P., Pellegrin, F., Golbus, M., Bachman, R.,
    Mann, J., Schmidt, L. and Lewis, J.P. Chromosome
    abnormalities in oral contraceptive breakthrough
    pregnancies (letter). Lancet 1:1342, 1979.
8. Hatch, M., Kline, J. and Stein, Z. Power considerations in
    studies of reproductive effects associated with vinyl
    chloride and some structural analogues. Presented at
    Conference to Reevaluate the Toxicity of Vinyl Chloride,
    Polyvinyl Chloride and Structural Analogues, March 1980.
    Environmental Health Perspectives, in press.
9. Infante, P.F., Wagoner, J.K., McMichael, A.J., Waxweiler, R.J.
    and Falk, H. Genetic risks of vinyl chloride. Lancet i:
    734-735, 1976.
10. Jacobs, P.A., Angell, R.R., Buchanan, I.M., Hassold, T.J.,
    Matsuyama, A.M. and Manuel, B. The origin of human
    triploids. Ann Hum Genet Lond 42:49-57, 1978.
11. Jick, H., Porter, J. and Morrison, A. Smoking and menopause.
    Lancet ii:459, 1977.
12. Kline, J., Stein, Z., Strobino, B., Susser, M. and Warburton, D.
    Surveillance of spontaneous abortions: power in
    environmental monitoring. Am J Epidemiol 106:345-350,
    1977.

13. Kline, J., Shrout, P., Stein, Z., Susser, M. and Weiss, M.
    II. An epidemiological study of the role of gravidity
    in spontaneous abortion. Early Human Development 1:
    345-356, 1978.
14. Kline, J., Levin, B., Stein, Z., Susser, M. and Warburton, D.
    Epidemiologic detection of low dose effects on the
    developing fetus. Presented at First Annual Symposium
    on Environmental Epidemiology, Pittsburgh, April, 1980.
15. Lancranjan, I., Popescu, H.I., Gavanescu, O., Klepsch, J. and
    Serbanescu, Maria. Reproductive Ability of Workmen
    Occupationally Exposed to Lead. Arch Environ Health
    Vol. 30: 396-401, 1975.
16. Lazar, P., Gueguen, S., Boue, J. et al. Epidemiologie des
    avortments spontanes precoces: a propos de 1469 avort-
    ments caryotypes. In Les Accidents Chromosomiques de la
    Reproduction. Edited by A. Boue, C. Thibault, Paris,
    Institut National de la Sante et de la Recherche Medicale,
    317-331, 1973.
17. Leridon, Henri. Human Fertility: The Basic Components.
    University of Chicago Press, Chicago and London, 1977.
18. Manson, J.M. and Simons, R. Influence of Environmental Agents on
    Male Reproductive Failure. In: Work and the Health of Women,
    Ed. Vilma R. Hunt. CRC Press, Florida, 1980.

19. Maudlin, I. and Fraser, L.R.   Maternal age and the incidence of aneuploidy in first-cleavage mouse embryos. J Reprod Fert 54:423-426, 1978.

20. Russell, W.L.   Studies in mammalian radiation genetics. Nucleonics 23:53-4, 62, 1965.

21. Spence, A.A., Cohen, E.N., Brown, B.W., Knill-Jones, R.P. and Himmelberger, D.U.   Occupational hazards for operating room-based physicians: analysis of data from the United States and the United Kingdom.   JAMA 238:955-959, 1977.

22. Stein, Z., Susser, M., Warburton, D., Wittes, J. and Kline, J. Spontaneous abortion as a screening device: the effect of fetal survival on the incidence of birth defects. Am J Epidemiol 102:275-290, 1975.

23. Strobino, B.R., Kline, J. and Stein, Z.   Chemical and physical exposures of parents: effects on human reproduction and offspring.   Early Human Development 1:371-399, 1978. Reprinted in Birth Defects Reprint Series, National Foundation - March of Dimes, 1979.

24. Strobino, B., Kline, J., Stein, Z., Susser, M. and Warburton, D. Exposure to contraceptive creams, jellies and foams and their effect on the zygote.   To be presented at the Society for Epidemiologic Research, Minneapolis, June, 1980.

25. Susser, M.   Environment and the biological characteristics of aging.   Presented to NIA/NAS Committee on Aging Workshop on the Biology and Behavior of the Elderly, Woods Hole, June, 1980.   In press.

26. Vogel, F.   Mutation in man.   In S.J. Geerts, Ed., Genetics Today, Vol. 3, Proceedings of the 11th International Congress of Genetics, Pergamon Press, New York, 1963.

27. Warburton, D., Stein, Z., Kline, J. and Susser, M.   Chromosome abnormalities in spontaneous abortion: data from the New York City study.   Presented at New York State Symposium on Birth Defects, October, 1979.   In press.

28. Watanabe, G.   Environmental determinants of birth defects prevalence.   In M.A. Klingberg and J.A.C. Weatherall, op. cit., pp. 91-100.

29. Whorton, D., Krauss, R.M., Marshall, S. and Milby, T.H. Infertility in male pesticide workers.   Lancet ii: 1259-1261, 1977.

30. Whorton, D., Milby, T.H., Krauss, R.M. and Stubbs, H.A. Testicular function in DBCP exposed pesticide workers. Journal of Occupational Medicine 21:161-166, 1979.

31. Wyrobek, A.J. and Bruce, W.R. The Induction of sperm shape abnormalities in mice and humans. In A. Hollaender and J.F. Serres, Eds., Chemical Mutagens: Principles and Methods for their Detection, Vol. 5:257-285, Plenum Press, New York, 1978.

32. Zybert, P., Stein, Z. and Belmont, L. Maternal age and children's ability. Perceptual and Motor Skills 47: 815-818, 1978.

Acknowledgements

We are indebted to Mr. Robert Cautin, A. Mark and Ms. S. Zayac for programming and data processing, to Mss. Callery, Downey, Jozak, Kornhauser, Silverstein and Wilson, who carried out the fieldwork, to Mss. Chih-Yu and Peters who carried out the laboratory work, and to Professor R. Vande Wiele, Dr. R. Neuwirth, Dr. T.F. Dillon and Dr. A. Risk and their colleagues for facilitating our work on their services.

This research was supported by grants from the New York State Department of Mental Hygiene and by grants (5R01-HD-08838, 5T32-HD-07040, 5R01-HD-12207, and 1R01-DA-02090) from the National Institute of Health.

DISCUSSION

CROW: First, what are those other abnormalities and second, did you measure head circumference in view of Dr. Wellman's results?

STEIN: We have measured head circumference but we haven't analyzed it yet in the newborn. The other abnormalities were aggregated because we are only beginning to understand them. One of them, for instance, is mosaic trisomy. We would now put mosaic trisomy with trisomy because we've got quite a big series of mosaic trisomy and their distribution is like the overall trisomies. Then we've got monosomy X of which we now have a big enough number to study separately. And the third group is triploidy and tetraploidy. We feel that triploidy is the most sensitive to the environment. We have 47 triploidies now and it's just coming to the stage where we may be able to study them separately.

ABRAHAMSON: Concerning the abortuses that are not associated with a gross chromosome abnormality, it seems to me it would be useful to put them in a deep freeze so we can study the cells at some subsequent time when techniques are available for doing more precise cytogenetics or even enzyme biology on them.

STEIN: I have been urging this on my colleagues. It is what epidemiologists do, they store things, whereas geneticists look them over and turn away. We are now going to store cells. The chromosomally normal abortus should also be put in frozen storage in case biochemical analysis could later become feasible.

ABRAHAMSON: White blood cells from the fetus may be moving into the maternal circulation as well as the reverse. With very precise cell sorting techniques, one could pull out fetal blood cells from a mother and then grow those without the need for amniocentesis. In the next 5 or 6 years, I would think that it could become one way of being able to detect cytogenetic defects rapidly without amniocentesis.

STEIN: Would you think that if a woman aborted, the fetal blood cells would still be in her circulation? She's the one who's most likely to have a karyotypic anomaly in fetal cells.

ABRAHAMSON: It is possible. If the first is true (and people are working on the first statement - finding if they can pick up fetal cells) these cells could be circulating in the mother for quite a while. But I cannot answer that now.

FORBES: It is known that cigarette consumption or alcohol consumption can be underestimated by a large margin, between 30% to 70%. Comparing the controls to the cases of abortion, could not the trauma of abortion affect the degree of underestimation? Have you thought of checking this on a subsample, by comparing the reported amount of smoking with a measurement of carboxyhemoglogin?

STEIN: We have thought of it but we have not done it. I didn't mention that the birth weights of offspring of the control women who reported drinking alcoholic bevarages were no different from the birth weights of offspring of the control women who did not drink. So they're probably not underestimating their drinking. This also seems to be the case with cigarettes.

FORBES: For the women in your study who gave up smoking, have you thought of interpreting this as a generally more health-conscious attitude?

STEIN: We considered that, but a more serious question is why do so many women give up smoking and drinking during pregnancy? We did test and control for nausea and vomiting. It may not be generally known that women who abort have less nausea and vomiting than women who go to term. It is really quite a big difference in our study. I don't know yet whether the improvement is in the chromosomally normal or chromosomally abnormal, or at what time of abortion, or whether it is associated with any morphological difference.

I have worried as to why they give up smoking and drinking. They change their diet in many ways, they give up coffee, they give up all sorts of things. We've watched this carefully, but we controlled just for the answer to the question "have you had nausea and vomiting?". We have not controlled for more subtle changes.

FORBES: With regard to your graph of the birth weights of children of women who smoke, just a word of warning. If you want to use this in public education programs to discourage women from smoking, there was an example in Britain where this was evaluated, and the reverse effect was observed. Many women felt that smaller birth weight made for easier pregnancies and they therefore tended to smoke.

ABRAHAMSON: Carr, in his first work on abortuses, also published the observation that triploidy was increased in women who used contraceptive agents. Now, subsequent to that, I thought there was a larger scale study that did not indicate that was true. What is the status of that now?

STEIN: The pill itself has changed a lot since the first study and that may have to do with the inconsistency. But Eva Alberman in London, and ourselves too (although we have not published it) suspect that taking the pill for a year before you become pregnant may slightly decrease the chromosomally normal abortions. There is a suggestion of that. And that's the only effect of the pill found so far that holds up. Not the triploids.

Talking about critical periods, it looks as if the perifertil-
ization period may be one on which we should spend a lot more effort.
Dr. Russell's review of 1965 on mice showed that the oocyte seemed
susceptible for a couple of months and resistant afterwards. I
thought maybe the point was that during the development of the first
polar body, perhaps a couple of weeks before fertilization might be
a vulnerable period for the egg. Whereas the long latency periods
we've always looked at may be less important. There is a suggestion
by Watanabe who studied systematically induced abortions that more
of all kinds of chromosome anomalies were found in women who have
taken drugs about a month before fertilization. We need to look at
that period.

WEINBERG: As I understand it, the methodology you use is called the
case control method, which is a retrospective study. I've been told
by people who know more about this than I, that there are methodological questions with retrospective studies. Assume that abortions
are of two classes: those caused by drinking and the idiopathic abortions. The problem in a retrospective study is to correct for the
abortions that would happen anyhow. One of the conditions required
to make the case control method work is that at least it must be
plausible that idiopathic abortions must have the same prior history
as the controls that carried to term.

I have two questions. First, have you examined your two populations to see whether this seems plausible? And second, in view of
the enormous public interest, do you have any plans to make a prospective study of this whole question?

STEIN: We had a lot of information in the case histories and information that seemed in any way relevant to having a spontaneous abortion has been controlled in what I've shown you. That is, the
mother's age, whether she has had a previous spontaneous abortion,
ethnic factors. We also had information about smoking, that 50% of
them have not smoked. Now that's rather close, that suggests that
they were well matched for a lot of factors, including smoking.
They use the same services, live in the same area. We have controlled the things we can think of.

But I think the argument that smoking causes spontaneous abortion rests most strongly on data on incidence of karyotypically
normal abortuses. I think that is really the key, because why would
a chromosomally normal fetus abort? Case control studies don't
usually have that sort of hidden relevance.

WEINBERG: So you don't think a prospective study is indicated?

STEIN: I didn't say I wouldn't like to do it.

WEINBERG: What would it take to do a prospective study to get 3,000 aborted specimens?

STEIN: I would say to the women "you may smoke or not as you like, but choose before you start because you are going to have to sign an informed consent." If I were doing such a prospective study, I would have to share with them what I think about smoking during pregnancy. That may make it difficult to find volunteers for the smoking cohort.

UPTON: What fraction of conceptions do abort?

STEIN: Of recongnized conceptions in a population, it is probably somewhere between 12% and 16%. You can say to women who aborted "don't worry, it is a common experience -- next time the odds will be in your favor." And a great majority of women who abort will go on to have successful pregnancies. Only a very small fraction of women have recurrent spontaneous abortions which is a health problem in its own right.

On the other hand, if a spontaneous abortion has a trisomy, that raises the mother's risk of having a trisomy. In other words, there is an indication of susceptibility. Therefore, if we did find some factor that caused the incidence of trisomy to change, the same factor could be related to Down's syndrome at birth.

UPTON: I was struck by the marked difference in birth weight between whites, hispanics, and blacks. Is that related to socioeconomic factors or age at delivery?

STEIN: These factors were held constant -- maternal age and economic class. But there is an interesting thing in a slide I did not show, which compares 15 years ago with the present at the same hospital. You will see that the differences between white, hispanics and blacks were bigger 15 years ago than they are now. For blacks, in particular, babies are getting heavier. There are class differences in birth weight among blacks, as among whites and hispanics, but they never explain totally the birth weight differences.

CLARKSON: With regard to drinking, the people who drink today, I presume, drink a lot more at one session than they used to some years ago.

STEIN: They do drink more. We have several measures of drinking, such as what you drink, how much you drink, binge drinking -- we have examined drinking exhaustively. And the frequency of drinking, oddly enough, is the best predictor. That is why I have been showing it here. The amount of alcohol consumed can be estimated, too, and gives much the same picture, but actually just the frequency of drinking covers alcohol-related problems.

It is not so surprising. If you look at an ultrasound picture
of the fetus in a woman who has a glass of alcohol you notice a
change of fetal movement. They have been noticing the same thing
with smoking cigarettes. I think we were defining teratology and
teratogenesis earlier and we are not saying that this effect is
necessarily teratogenic. Alcohol may be an abortifacient or a fetal
toxin which does not produce morphological anomalies, and may be
relevant to reproductive outcome in these ways.

SAGAN: What is known, if anything, about effects on the fetus of the
smoking of marijuana by the pregnant woman?

STEIN: Marijuana smoking has perhaps less of an effect than cigarette smoking but we have not yet completed the analysis of data on
marijuana. Heavier effects are with heroin, and methadone gives the
heaviest effect of all. There are some things we are very good at
testing in New York City, and that is one of the areas where we have
a lot of data.

MAILLIE: Have you done any studies in areas other than New York
City?

STEIN: We have collected data in New York City. In Hawaii there is
a group that we have pooled data with. One of the earliest studies
was done in Paris. There is a group in London, a group in Arhous in
Denmark and one in Japan. These are all the world's studies. I
think we have the only epidemiological plus cytogenetic study, but
the other groups have cytogenetic data which fit very well with ours.

SESSION III

RISKS OF CONTAMINATED AIR AND DRINKING WATER

CHAIRMAN:

PAUL E. MORROW

INTRODUCTION TO SESSION III

Paul E. Morrow

Department of Radiation Biology and Biophysics
University of Rochester School of Medicine
Rochester, NY 14642

This morning we will be dealing with the risk of inhaled contaminants and contaminated drinking water. Probably the session should be renamed somewhat to reflect the emphasis on air pollution. Problems of environmental pollution, particularly air pollution, represent a major challenge to risk assessment. Many of us, after studying air pollution over the years, feel uncertain about the risks to the public health that it represents. What are the important pollutants? What is the evidence? What do we know about causality? How effective have our efforts been to measure and control? What are we doing to assess the risks associated with air pollutants or environmental pollutants in general?

We can accept the fact that there is a problem, but I think most of us feel that we don't understand its dimensions nor its importance. Human studies, both epidemiologic and experimental, have clearly revealed features that will be paramount in risk assessment. We are dealing with effects of low doses. Despite the fact that acute air pollution episodes brought the hazard to our attention, the real problem must be regarded as one of large numbers of people continuously exposed at low levels. We are also dealing with the thorny issue of the synergism of mixtures. Finally, we are dealing with policies which have a serious impact on every level of society. The costs of doing something about air pollution are convincingly large and impressive. They tax our ingenuity to make as few mistakes as possible.

Out distinguished speakers this morning are here to tell us what is being done and how it's being done, and some of its limitations and successes.

HEALTH RISKS OF LEAD AS JUDGED FROM AUTOPSY MATERIAL

M.D. Krailo, K.S. Brown, W.H. Cherry and W.F. Forbes

Department of Statistics
University of Waterloo
Waterloo, Ontario, Canada N2L 3G1

INTRODUCTION

Clinical poisoning by lead has long been recognized[1] and may result from a single "high" dose (acute poisoning) or from the accumulation of "low" doses (chronic poisoning). More recently, metabolic poisoning by lead[2] has been identified -- for example, the inhibition of ALAD activity[3]. Between these extremes, it is possible that the long-term exposure of large populations to general environmental levels of lead is a cause of chronic human health effects due to sub-clinical poisoning. For example, there is some evidence[2] of a role for lead in the pathogenesis of one or more of the major fatal degenerative disease processes, such as cardio-vascular disease and cancer; also, behavioural dysfunction in children has been related to lead at levels below those which usually produce clinical symptoms of lead poisoning[4]. However, the problems associated with collecting and analyzing data to elucidate these matters have led to considerable dispute about the validity of the various claims; the resolution of these disputes is an important area of work in environmental health.

It is generally not practicable to estimate directly an individual's exposure to the trace-element(s) of interest from sources such as food and beverages, air and tobacco smoke. An alternative is to determine elemental levels in samples of one or more tissues from appropriate donors, and to assume that these levels provide an estimate of exposure; however, metabolic differences among donors and the chemical form(s) of the element(s) to which they are exposed may also be reflected by tissue levels. The next step is to search for differences in elemental levels (or burdens) between the "experimental" and "control" groups of donors; this is often hindered by the presence of other factors which may influence both the magnitude and the variability of these levels, and which may also, in some instances, affect the donor "response". For example, cigarette smoking is (causally?) related to elevated lead levels in bone[5 6 7 8] and to an increased incidence of cardiovascular diseases[9].

    In carrying out studies investigating possible health effects of low-level exposure, the question arises as to which tissue samples will best reflect the total, long-term exposure. A large amount of data has been obtained on lead levels in blood and urine, which are poor indicators of long-term exposure. If, on the other hand, tissues such as bone, which have relatively low turnover rates, are selected, a number of difficulties arise with respect to sample collection, sample preparation, contamination control, sample storage and the appropriate anatomical sampling site. Base-line values for lead in all important human tissues are not known reliably. Another difficulty is that, if autopsy samples are used, it is frequently difficult to obtain satisfactory data on variables of interest, such as occupational history and smoking status, which are important for the appropriate statistical analyses. Consequent-ly, although it is known that food, air, cigarette smoking and drinking water affect total body burdens of lead, the relevant associations between these types of exposure and lead levels in many tissues are difficult to quantify.

    The approach in the present study was to obtain autopsy sam-ples, to determine lead concentrations in bone, and to obtain retospectively information on the relevant independent variables, such as occupational exposure and smoking status, in order to investigate the appropriate associations. The data were also analysed to estimate the relevant health risks from lead with respect to cardiovascular disease mortality. No information is available on this point at present, although Crawford[10], on the basis of unadjusted data, suggested that an association may exist between elevated lead levels in bone and cardiovascular disease (CVD) mortality. This hypothesis has also been investigated in a preliminary manner on a subset of the present data set, at a time when only a smaller number of samples were available[8]. In another report[11], the base-line values obtained for the present data set (see Table I), and also the factors associated with lead concentra-tions in rib, have been investigated (see Table II). The results show that the variable pack-years smoked and evidence of occupa-tional lead exposure are associated with lead concentrations in rib (see Table II). Perhaps not surprisingly, age itself does not appear to be very significant in predicting lead concentrations in rib; in fact, age may be even less important, if other environ-mental factors could be delineated more precisely. The results of multiple regression analyses suggest that in future studies of lead levels in human tissue, donor smoking histories, occupational

TABLE I   LEAD CONCENTRATIONS IN RIB BY SEX, SMOKING HISTORY
AND AGE

	AGE GROUP	n	SAMPLE MEAN	SEM	RANGE		AGE GROUP	n	SAMPLE MEAN	SEM	RANGE
	MALES						**FEMALES**				
NON-SMOKERS	0-34	5	5.35	0.76	2.37- 6.58	NON-SMOKERS	0-34	2	3.85	3.81	2.62- 5.07
	35-44	2	34.38	4.03	30.34- 38.41		35-44	3	12.82	1.95	9.19- 15.87
	45-54	9	21.82	3.06	12.76- 43.36		45-55	8	20.29	4.38	8.14- 45.35
	55-64	10	21.46	3.28	10.72- 42.37		55-64	19	22.40	1.95	12.84- 46.89
	65-74	6	28.43	3.29	18.42- 39.98		65-74	16	21.74	2.24	10.06- 38.08
	75+	5	35.94	12.66	20.62- 86.39		75+	7	26.80	5.56	15.60- 57.42
	OVERALL	37	23.15	2.46	2.37- 86.39		OVERALL	55	21.27	1.42	2.62- 57.42
SMOKERS	0-34	11	19.98	2.50	9.71- 32.61	SMOKERS	0-34	3	13.92	3.05	9.49- 19.76
	35-44	10	23.44	1.97	15.40- 33.70		35-44	10	17.90	2.38	9.75- 33.68
	45-54	43	32.91	2.45	15.05- 88.02		45-54	10	23.06	2.76	10.87- 37.60
	55-64	34	36.69	3.65	15.90-104.59		55-64	15	33.10	3.50	15.71- 68.82
	65-74	23	29.19	2.59	8.59- 62.00		65-74	10	29.91	4.15	15.00- 63.26
	75+	8	35.90	3.74	26.96- 57.00		75+	0	--	--	--
	OVERALL	129	31.59	1.44	8.59-104.59		OVERALL	48	25.98	1.82	9.49- 68.82
EX-SMOKERS	0-34	3	14.86	2.82	9.42- 18.92	EX-SMOKERS	0-34	0	--	--	--
	35-44	3	22.94	1.91	19.30- 25.75		35-44	1	11.79	-	11.79- 11.79
	45-54	6	26.05	3.33	16.41- 34.72		45-54	3	23.36	3.50	17.04- 29.13
	55-64	15	35.28	3.56	17.69- 62.41		55-64	3	26.61	3.11	21.03- 31.79
	65-74	10	34.68	7.71	13.77-100.39		65-74	2	42.77	18.12	24.64- 60.89
	75+	5	25.44	5.73	9.87- 42.35		75+	0	--	--	--
	OVERALL	42	30.31	2.50	9.42-100.39		OVERALL	9	27.47	4.65	11.79- 60.89
UNKNOWN SMOKING HABIT	0-34	9	9.04	1.64	2.69- 17.76	UNKNOWN SMOKING HABIT	0-34	1	16.11	-	16.11- 16.11
	35-44	5	16.48	2.10	8.39- 20.65		35-44	5	20.24	6.95	6.71- 46.11
	45-54	0	--	--	--		45-54	0	--	--	--
	55-64	1	8.63	--	8.63- 8.63		55-64	0	--	--	--
	65-74	0	--	--	--		65-74	0	--	--	--
	75+	8	34.05	5.13	12.44- 56.08		75+	19	23.73	4.04	7.78- 74.13
	OVERALL	23	19.34	3.01	2.69- 56.08		OVERALL	25	22.73	3.33	6.71- 74.13

NOTES: 1. The rib samples were 3 cm sections ("Section B") of rib shaft,
taken immediately adjacent to the costochondral junction

2. The notation used in this and subsequent tables is:

n = number of tissue donors
SEM = standard error of the sample mean

TABLE II   SUMMARY OF REGRESSION MODELS FOR VARIOUS SUBPOPULATIONS

	CONSTANT	YEARS SMOKED	PACK-YEARS (PACKS/DAY × YEARS SMOKED)	FREQUENCY SMOKED (PACKS/DAY)	OCCUPATIONAL EXPOSURE TO LEAD †	AGE (YEARS)	AGE^2 (YEARS^2)	AGE$^{1/2}$ (YEARS$^{1/2}$)	BIRTH YEAR POST 1920 †	YEARS SINCE RETIREMENT	ASH WEIGHT SECTION B RIB	DEATH DUE TO CANCER †	DEATH DUE TO CARDIOVASCULAR DISEASE †	PRESENCE OF NEPHROSCLEROSIS †	ASH AS A FRACTION OF WET WEIGHT
MALE SMOKERS — Coefficient (Standard Error)	53.30 (10.65)		.51 (.13)	-13.18 (5.08)	13.72 (4.05)		-.0050 (.002)		-6.27 (4.05)			28.83 (6.93)			-56.73 (23.91)
Accumulated R^2 (Order of Entry)			.21 (1)	.39 (4)	.28 (2)		.44 (6)		.46 (7)			.35 (3)			.42 (5)
MALE EX-SMOKERS — Coefficient (Standard Error)	19.76 (6.42)		.20 (.068)	*	10.75 (3.37)		.0033 (.0012)				13.00 (5.61)	*	*	-7.24 (3.23)	-80.51 (22.24)
Accumulated R^2 (Order of Entry)			.28 (1)		.50 (2)		.70 (5)				.65 (4)			.77 (6)	.60 (3)
MALE NON-SMOKERS — Coefficient (Standard Error)	140.5 (75.2)	*	*	*	42.04 (6.90)	9.46 (4.4)	-.04 (.02)	-72.58 (36.40)			11.95 (8.7)	*			
Accumulated R^2 (Order of Entry)					.40 (1)	.62 (4)	.67 (5)	.61 (2)			.62 (3)				
FEMALE SMOKERS — Coefficient (Standard Error)	221.51 (106.43)	-.48 (.15)	.10 (.06)	*	*	13.23 (5.79)	-.064 (.023)	-95.4 (47.7)	-23.4 (3.6)	*		*	4.91 (2.43)		
Accumulated R^2 (Order of Entry)		.81 (4)	.83 (5)			.77 (3)	.71 (2)	.87 (7)	.70 (1)				.84 (6)		
FEMALE NON-SMOKERS — Coefficient (Standard Error)	2.38 (13.09)							2.48 (1.34)		1.60 (.45)	15.41 (7.92)		5.81 (2.87)		-61.40 (24.03)
Accumulated R^2 (Order of Entry)								.24 (1)		.33 (2)	.44 (5)		.36 (3)		.40 (4)

* Variable was not relevant for this subpopulation

† Entered as an indicator variable (0 if trait is absent, 1 if trait is present)

histories and indicators of environmental exposure must be considered and should be obtained in as comprehensive a form as
possible in order that the variability in concentrations may be
investigated more fully.

Using the same set of data, a search was also made for associations between the observed lead levels and the hardness of water
for the area in which the individual donor resides, but no significant associations could be observed. However, additional data
may well reveal some association. The main question to be addressed
by this paper is whether the observed trace metal levels are associated with a higher incidence of cardiovascular disease mortality.

METHODS

In principle, it would be desirable to use a technique such as
multiple logistic regression. With this method, the response
variable "CVD death" (1=yes, 0=no) could be investigated for its
relation to the joint action of several concomitant variables such
as age, smoking status, sex of donors, and lead concentrations.
However, this was not possible since many donors came from a centre
of cardiology, and hence this sample contained a disproportionate
number of young CVD deaths. Consequently, a matched pairs analysis
was employed in which individuals who died of causes other than CVD
were considered as "controls" and were matched with individuals
from a pool of "cases" which was comprised of individuals who died
of CVD (ICD codes, 8th Revision, 400-429; 444-448). In this way
the relationship of variables such as age to CVD would not be masked
by an overabundance of young donors dying of CVD in centres of cardiology. This may lead to the difficulty that most of the "cases"
come from one source and most of the "controls" from another source.
However, this is not a problem in the present study as it has been
established that source of sample is not associated with rib lead
concentrations on the basis of a regression analysis[11]. In order
to determine variables which were to be matched between cases and
controls, a non-parametric analysis was carried out to identify
factors associated with lead levels in bone. The relationship
between lead concentration in rib and age at death and pack-years
smoked was examined using Kendall's τ; a non-parametric measure
of correlation[12]. A regression analysis (see [11]) was performed to
estimate the effects of the factors associated with variations in
lead concentrations. The results of this and the non-parametric
analysis indicated that matching should be performed on the basis
of the following criteria:

  (1) age at death (within 2 years)
  (2) sex of donor
  (3) smoking status (smoker or ex-smoker versus non-smoker)
  (4) occupational exposure (exposed versus non-exposed).

Variables such as "ash as a fraction of wet weight of bone",
"frequency smoked (pack/day)" and "years smoked" were matched as
closely as possible within pairs. Fifty-eight pairs matched in
this way were available for analysis.

The differences in bone lead levels between controls and cases,
d_i, were calculated for the 58 pairs. Under the hypothesis that
mean lead levels are the same for the non-CVD and CVD groups, there
should be approximately the same number of positive and negative
differences, and the average of these differences should be approximately 0. On the other hand, a significantly greater number of
negative values would imply that those who died of CVD, that is the
cases, have higher lead concentrations in bone, and consequently
there is a positive association between CVD death and lead levels
in rib. A test of the hypothesis of no difference in lead levels
between controls and cases was carried out by a paired t-test[13],
assuming that the differences are distributed normally ($N[\mu, \sigma^2]$),
and by the Wilcoxon signed rank test[12], which makes no assumption
about the distribution of the d_i's, except that it is continuous
and symmetric. The former method tests the hypothesis:

$$H : \mu_D = 0 \ldots (i)$$

and the latter method:

H : median of the underlying distribution of the d_i's is zero;
i.e. med(D) = 0, ... (ii),

where D is the random variable associated with d_i .

The conditions of symmetry of distribution and zero median are met
if the distribution of lead in cases and controls is identical. The
significance levels for hypothesis (ii) were obtained from
McCormack[14]. The Wilcoxon test was performed if there was evidence
contradicting the assumption of normality of the d_i's, an assumption which was checked using Quantile (Q-Q) plots[13].

RESULTS

Non-Parametric Analyses

Sample statistics for lead levels in rib for various age, sex
and smoking status subpopulations were calculated and are summarised
in Table I. The results indicate lead levels differ between strata
used. Specifically, it appears that age, sex and smoking status
are related to lead levels. To examine the statistical significance
of these trends, the population was divided into the following
sub-populations:

(1) Male Smokers   (2) Male Non-Smokers
(3) Male Ex-Smokers   (4) Male, Unknown Smoking Habit
(5) Female Smokers   (6) Female Non-Smokers
(7) Female Ex-Smokers   (8) Females, Unknown Smoking Habit.

The following definitions were employed:

(1) X_{ij} is the lead concentration in section B rib of the jth individual in the ith subpopulation, $i=1,2,\ldots,8$;

(2) Y_{ij} is the age at death of the jth individual in the ith subpopulation, $i=1,2,\ldots,8$;

(3) Z_{ij} is the number of pack-years smoked for the jth individual in the ith subpopulation; $i=1,3,5,7$;

(4) n_i is the number of individuals in the ith subpopulation; $i=1,2,\ldots,8$.

$\tau(X_i,Y_i)$ was calculated for each subpopulation (see Table III). The results indicate significant positive association between lead levels and age in the Male Smokers and Non-Smokers, Female Smoker and Non-Smokers, and Males of Unknown Smoking Habit. The absence of trends in the Male and Female Ex-Smokers may be due to diverse smoking histories within these groups, especially with regard to years since cessation of smoking (see Table IV). Previous analyses of this data set indicated that pack years smoked may be related to lead concentration in rib. To investigate this finding $\tau(Z_i,Y_i)$ and $\tau(Z_i,X_i)$ were calculated for $i=1,3,5,7$, that is, for Male Smokers, Male Ex-Smokers, Female Smokers and Female Ex-Smokers (see Table V). This table shows that, in Male Smokers and Ex-Smokers, there is a significant positive association between lead concentration and pack-years smoked, but there is also a positive association between pack-years smoked and age at death. Thus, with this technique, it is not possible to separate the effects of age and pack-years smoked.

There does not seem to be a positive association between pack-years smoked and lead concentration in the Female Smokers, although there is a positive association between pack-years smoked and age. This suggests that there may be another variable influencing bone lead levels in Female Smokers, or that smoking histories obtained were less accurate than those obtained for Male Smokers (see also below).

It is also interesting to note the average amount smoked (in pack-years) for each of the subpopulations (see Table VI). The average amount smoked and variance in amount smoked may be ranked:

TABLE III   NON-PARAMETRIC CORRELATION COEFFICIENTS (KENDALL'S τ)
            BETWEEN AGE AT DEATH AND LEAD CONCENTRATION IN RIB
                       FOR VARIOUS SUBPOPULATIONS

	MALES				FEMALES			
	SMOKERS	NON-SMOKERS	EX-SMOKERS	UNKNOWN	SMOKERS	NON-SMOKERS	EX-SMOKERS	UNKNOWN
n	129	37	42	23	48	55	9	25
τ	0.16	0.32	0.16	0.64	0.33	0.25	0.44	0.07
S.L.*	0.008	0.005	0.132	0.001	0.001	0.008	0.095	0.639

* S.L. is the approximate level of significance, i.e., the
approximate probability of a value as large or larger than $|\tau|$,
if the traits are independent.

TABLE IV   YEARS SINCE CESSATION OF SMOKING
            FOR MALE AND FEMALE EX-SMOKERS

SUB-POPULATION	n	SAMPLE MEAN	SEM	MEDIAN	RANGE
MALES	42	6.4	.91	5	.2-23
FEMALES	8	4.6	1.65	4	1-15

TABLE V   NON–PARAMETRIC CORRELATION COEFFICIENTS (KENDALL'S τ)
           BETWEEN PACK–YEARS SMOKED AND (i) LEAD CONCENTRATION
           IN RIB AND (ii) AGE, FOR VARIOUS SUBPOPULATIONS

	MALES				FEMALES			
	SMOKERS		EX–SMOKERS		SMOKERS		EX–SMOKERS	
	PACK–YEARS AND LEAD	PACK–YEARS AND AGE	PACK–YEARS AND LEAD	PACK–YEARS AND AGE	PACK–YEARS AND LEAD	PACK–YEARS AND AGE	PACK–YEARS AND LEAD	PACK–YEARS AND AGE
n	87	87	27	27	30	30	7	7
τ	0.24	0.30	0.42	0.44	0.18	0.36	0.14	−0.05
S.L.*	0.001	0.001	0.002	0.001	0.153	0.005	0.652	0.881

* S.L. is the approximate level of significance, i.e., the
approximate probability of a value as large or larger than
τ if the traits are independent.

TABLE VI   REPORTED NUMBER OF PACK–YEARS FOR SELECTED
                         SUBPOPULATIONS

	SUB-POPULATION	n	SAMPLE MEAN	SEM (SAMPLE VARIANCE)	MEDIAN	RANGE
MALES	SMOKERS	87	51.2	3.3 (953.18)	45.0	1.5–147.0
MALES	EX–SMOKERS	27	42.6	4.7 (605.83)	45.0	1.5– 90.0
FEMALES	SMOKERS	30	34.5	4.1 (510.79)	31.6	0.9– 93.0
FEMALES	EX–SMOKERS	7	19.5	3.3 (76.63)	24.0	5.0– 28.0

        Male Smokers > Male Ex-Smokers > Female Smokers >
        Female Ex-Smokers.

This ordering is similar to that of the strength of the relationships between pack-years smoked and lead concentration in rib (see
Table II). This suggests that there may be a threshold of smoking,
below which there is little connection between smoking and lead
concentration, but that above this threshold level (for example,
in the Male Smokers and Ex-Smokers) there is such a relationship.
Alternatively, the absence of a strong relationship for female
smokers may also be ascribed to the small variation in the amount
smoked by this group (see Table VI).

        In summary, it appears from this analysis that sex, age,
smoking status and pack-years smoked (within smoking subpopulations)
are associated with lead levels in rib, suggesting that these variables should be matched between case-control pairs.

Matched Pair Analyses

        The results for all 58 pairs are shown in Table VIIa, which
shows that the hypothesis of equality of mean level concentration
between cases and controls is not rejected on the basis of the
paired t-test [hypothesis (i)], but that there is some evidence
against the hypothesis (ii) from the Wilcoxon signed rank test. A
possible reason for these contradictory results emerges from
inspection of Table II, which indicates that CVD death represents
a significant predictor of lead concentration in the female subpopulations and in the male non-smokers subpopulation, when juvenile
deaths are excluded[II]. This suggests that there may be differences
in bone lead levels depending on whether an individual died of CVD
or not, but only in certain subpopulations. Consequently, cases
and controls were separated into four groups, namely, (1) male
smokers and ex-smokers, (2) male non-smokers, (3) female smokers
and ex-smokers, and (4) female non-smokers, and the same two tests
were performed for each subpopulation (see Table VIIb).

        The results showed that there is no evidence of a difference
in lead levels between CVD deaths and non-CVD deaths in group (1)
(male smokers), but that there is evidence in groups (2) and (3)
for a positive association between CVD death and lead concentrations; for these two groups, the significance levels for the test
of hypothesis (i) in each case were less than .1 . The results
for group (4) (female non-smokers) appear to be contradictory. The
test of hypothesis (i) had a significance level of .58, but the
test of hypothesis (ii) had a significance level between .10 and
.20. However, examination of the normal Q-Q plot indicated two
outliers, and these two points were therefore omitted in a subsequent analysis; the Q-Q plot then appeared linear, as incidentally did the Q-Q plots for all the other groups. The analysis with

TABLE VIIa   MATCHED PAIRS ANALYSIS FOR FULL DATA SET

n	TEST	VALUE OF TEST STATISTIC[2]	S.L.[3]
58	PAIRED t	−1.06	.29
	WILCOXON	614 (855.5)	.05−.10

TABLE VIIb   MATCHED PAIRS ANALYSES FOR VARIOUS SUBPOPULATIONS

	SUB-POPULATION	n	TEST	VALUE OF TEST STATISTIC[2]	S.L.[3]
MALES	SMOKERS AND EX-SMOKERS	30	PAIRED t	.31	.76
			WILCOXON	236 (232.5)	>.90
	NON-SMOKERS	4	PAIRED t	−2.5	.09
			WILCOXON	0 (5)	.125
FEMALES	SMOKERS AND EX-SMOKERS	13	PAIRED t	−1.92	.08
			WILCOXON	21 (45.5)	.05−.10
	NON-SMOKERS	11	PAIRED t	−.56	.58
			WILCOXON	12 (33)	.10−.20
	NON-SMOKERS[4]	9	PAIRED t	4.80	<.001
			WILCOXON	1 (22.5)	<.01

[1]
The paired t test tests hypothesis (i), i.e. $\mu_D = 0$.
The Wilcoxon test tests hypothesis (ii), i.e.
med(D)=0.

[2]
The value of the test statistic for the Wilcoxon
test is the sum of the positive ranks. The expected
value of this sum under the hypothesis med(D)=0 is
given in brackets (see reference 12, page 165).

[3]
Significance levels for two-tailed tests.

[4]
Female non-smokers after removing two outlying
observations.

the two outliers removed (see Table VIIb) now showed a positive
relationship between lead levels and CVD death.

Hence there appears to be a positive association between lead
levels and CVD death in three of the four groups (groups 2,3 and
4) but no such relationship in group 1 (male smokers). Moreover,
this latter finding could not be explained by discordance of place
of residence (urban or rural) within pairs, although it should be
noted that this information was sometimes incomplete. Incidentally,
for the females, groups 3 and 4, the weakest (least significant)
evidence was noted in group 3 (female smokers and ex-smokers),
suggesting that the variables "years-smoked" and "frequency smoked"
may affect the results in the smoking groups, particularly since
these variables could often not be matched exactly. Also, it seems
certain that reporting errors occur in the smoking histories and
hence the pairs may in fact not be closely matched with respect to
smoking habit. Incidentally, differences in occupational exposure
delineated by the crude "0-1" classification may also confound the
results for males.

Comparing the strengths of the significant relationships between lead concentration and CVD death, it may be noted that the
evidence for such a relationship is weakest in group 2 (male non-
smokers), but this is presumably mainly because of the small sample
size. The evidence for the relationship is strongest in group 4
(female non-smokers), and it is in this group that the matching is
likely to be closest, as there are fewer confounding variables such
as smoking history or occupational exposure, as there were no
females with occupational exposure to lead in the present study.

It should be noted that the results obtained may not reflect
a cause and effect relationship, since sampling fluctuations or a
third variable, associated with both lead concentrations in bone
and CVD death, may account for the observed associations. For
example, lead and calcium are antagonistic with respect to their
absorption in the body, and a higher lead uptake may lead to a
lower absorption of calcium, and calcium may exert a protective
effect with respect to CVD[15].

It should also be emphasized that since this study is retrospective, the effect of lead on CVD incidence cannot be assessed.
That is, lead levels in bone may discriminate with respect to the
cause of death, but this assumes that an individual has died, and
therefore gives no direct information on the effect of lead on CVD
incidence. Nor do the data provide evidence of relative CVD mortality rates in populations which have relatively high or low bone
lead levels (see Fig. 1).

However, the results indicate a relationship between lead
levels and CVD death. Additional matched pair analyses,

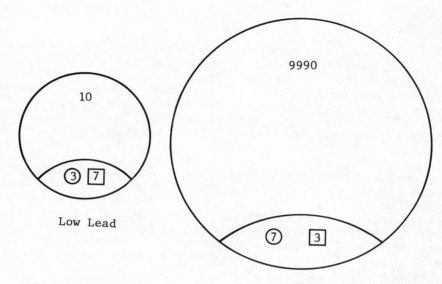

Low Lead

High Lead

Figure 1.   Schematic representation of two hypothetical populations containing relatively high and low lead levels. The circled figures represent the number of CVD deaths, the figures within squares represent the number of non-CVD deaths, and the remaining numbers represent the number of survivors; that is, these latter individuals are not members of the study group since they have not died. In this example, lead discriminates among the type of death, that is, given that a person has died, they are more likely to have died of CVD death if they are from the "high lead" population. P(CVD death|death and low lead) = 3/10; P(CVD death|death and high lead)=7/10. However, the CVD mortality rate is higher in the low lead group 3/20 than in the high lead group (7/10,000).

particularly for male non-smokers, may assist in strengthening the association, and also more accurate information regarding smoking history and occupational exposure would improve the matching and may well help to clarify the apparent anomaly for the male smoker sub-group.

Concluding Remarks

This paper investigates the relationship between CVD and lead levels under normal conditions prevailing at this time. The word "normal" is intended to describe the levels of lead which occur, on average, in a general population. The data set comprised a number of documented autopsy samples, and estimates of lead in a specified section of rib. This represents one approach, although it should be borne in mind that it is possible that trace metals such as lead have an effect on a variety of diseases and in this way increase mortality for most diseases, and that consequently an analysis of the type undertaken may not indicate associations between trace metal concentrations and higher mortality from specific diseases. Also, the method searches for an association between lead concentrations and mortality and the results do not therefore necessarily apply to morbidity. Also other variables, for example, those related to diet or income, may account for the observed association. With these qualifications, the results indicate that CVD appears to be related to lead levels in bone.

It should be noted that the absence of any association does not preclude adverse health effects of lead. This follows since it is possible that the data set was not representative of the general population at this time, or because the method employed was not sufficiently sensitive to detect an association, or because lead increases the possibility of dying from a number of different diseases in a similar way, which would preclude the identification of a relatively higher mortality from a specific disease. With respect to the last point it should be noted that, in fact, many environmental hazards, for example, cigarette smoking, have initially been identified because of their association with specific diseases (lung cancer) and, in that particular instance, associations with other diseases were identified subsequently. In the case of lead therefore, this paper presents what is believed to be the first report of an association between lead concentration in rib and CVD, after allowing for factors which influence lead concentrations in rib. Establishing a definite link between lead and CVD nevertheless remains a formidable task, because of the possible presence of a large number of complex and interrelated factors, such as socio-economic class and diet, which could not be estimated in the present study. However, more rigorous case-control and prospective studies may provide better evidence for the association suggested by the present analyses.

REFERENCES

1. P. Grandjean, Lead in Danes. Historical and Toxological Studies, in: "Lead", T.B. Griffin and J.H. Knelson, eds., Geo. Thieme and Academic Press, Stuttgart and N.Y. (1975).
2. H.A. Waldron and D. Stöfen, "Sub-Clinical Lead Poisoning", Academic Press, London (1974).
3. "Environmental Health Criteria 3. Lead", World Health Organization (1977).
4. H.L. Needleman, G. Chari, A. Leviton, R. Reed, H. Peresie, C. Maker, and P. Barrett, Deficits in Psychologic and Classroom Performance of Children with Elevated Dentine Lead Levels, N. Eng. J. of Med. 300:689 (1979).
5. R.E. Nusbaum, E.M. Butt, T.C. Gilmour, and S.L. DiDio, Relation of Air Pollutants to Trace Metals in Bor _, Arch. of Env. Health 10:227 (1965).
6. R.B. Holtzman and F.H. Ilcewicz, Lead 210 and Polonium 210 in Tissues of Cigarette Smokers, Science 153:1259 (1966).
7. R.B. Holtzman, H.F. Lucas and F.H. Ilcewicz, The Concentration of Lead in Human Bone, in: Argonne National Laboratory, Radiation Physics Division Annual Report, July 1968 through June 1979 (1979).
8. S.R. Esterby, "Lead Levels in Human Rib, Vertebra and Lung-Within Tissue and Between Individual Comparisons", Doctoral Thesis, University of Waterloo, Waterloo (1976).
9. "Smoking and Health. A Report of the Surgeon General," U.S. Dept. of Health, Education and Welfare, Wash., D.C. (1979). D.C. (1979).
10. M.D. Crawford and D.G. Clayton, Lead in Bones and Drinking Water in Towns with Hard and Soft Water, Brit. Med. J. 2:21 (1973).
11. M.D. Krailo, K.S. Brown, W.H. Cherry, and W.F. Forbes, Factors Associated with Lead Concentrations in Rib. For presentation to the 14th Annual Conference on Trace Substances in Environmental Health, University of Missouri, Columbia (1980).
12. J.D. Gibbons, "Non-parametric Statistical Inference", McGraw Hill Book Company, New York (1971).
13. J.G. Kalbfleisch, "Probability and Statistical Inference", Springer-Verlag, New York (1979).
14. R.L. McCornack, Extended Tables of the Wilcoxon Matched Pairs Signed Rank Statistics, J. Amer. Stat. Assn 60:864 (1965).
15. "Geochemistry of Water in Relation to Cardiovascular Disease", National Academy of Sciences, Washington, D.C. (1979).

ACKNOWLEDGMENT

The authors are indebted to Dr. Arthur Finch for many helpful discussions. Financial support has been provided by the Ontario Ministry of the Environment.

DISCUSSION

CROW: I didn't see any numbers about amount of lead in the two groups.

FORBES: That was a test slide, just the scatter diagram. You are going up about a factor of 5. I can give you the actual figures. Lead in autopsy material goes up, reaches a maximum, and then for those levels often goes down. Now, the age measurements were squared. This might mean that people who lived earlier got less exposure when they were young. Maybe early life exposure is important.

CROW: I was just interested in the numerical values.

FORBES: I haven't given you the raw data. I've given you the means. The two groups differed roughly by a factor of five.

BOURDEAU: What units were used to express lead concentrations?

FORBES: Micrograms per gram of ash. Now, that makes a difference too because it's one of the chemical difficulties. Some people use lead per wet weight, or ash -- they all have problems. The proper way to do it I think is to give all data. Wet weight gives problems if the tissue has been standing about for a long time. Ash weight has the problem that ash tends to be hygroscopic.

WEINBERG: Did you examine the presence of other heavy elements at the time you looked at lead? There is an old belief that cadmium may be involved in cardiovascular disease.

FORBES: Yes, we did. We did lead, cadmium and zinc. You're quite right. Basically, the long-term aim is to see if the trace metals are important. There is anecdotal evidence of some trace metal interaction, no question. There are experimental difficulties. It is a question of which instrumentation you use. For lead, cadmium and zinc, we believe that atomic absorption is the best method.

We have not yet processed the data for cadmium and cardiovascular disease although there are some WHO data available. Unfortunately, the WHO data do not always include smoking status and smoking affects cadmium to a large extent.

WEINBERG: Is there a high correlation between the level of lead and the level of cadmium?

FORBES: There is some correlation, but that is not unexpected since, for example, both lead and cadmium are associated with cigarette smoking and occupational exposure.

WEINBERG: You are aware of studies that were done 25 years ago on this correlation between cadmium and cardiovascular disease?

FORBES: Yes, but confounding variables can confuse the issue. That is, you want to make sure that smoking, education, income, or something else you haven't adjusted for, did not account for the observed association.

BOURDEAU: What was the difference in age at death between the cardiovascular deaths and the others in the group that gave you the highly significant relationship?

FORBES: Matching was done by age, within two years.

BOURDEAU: So those were people who died from cardiovascular disease at a given age and who died from other causes who have the same age, plus or minus one.

FORBES: Yes. One of the problems is how lead causes disease. If it contributes to a number of diseases, conceivably by poisoning several enzyme systems, it could be that following lead exposure, the diseases will occur more frequently. In that case, one could not pick up a particular disease. In practice, one usually starts with a particular disease, looking for a cause. In the case of cigarette smoking, the correlation with lung cancer was observed first, and then other health consequences were found.

BOURDEAU: In the literature data seem to show that lead accumulates in bone. Concentration increases over the years but does not decrease, whereas it seems here you found a decrease above a certain age.

FORBES: That is correct. What have you found?

BOURDEAU: A continuous increase but with a plateau maybe, but no decrease.

FORBES: There is a flattening at the higher ages and some of our cohorts show decreases. It could be that bone structure alters significantly with age, and the observed changes may then depend on whether you report results on the basis of ash weight, dry weight or wet weight.

STEIN: Did I read correctly that you didn't get a lead effect?

FORBES: We did not get an effect for male smokers, but there was an effect in the other groups. One interpretation is that there is too much noise in the data for the male smokers. We rely on postmortem records. Somebody goes through the records and gets as much information as possible. On admission, a patient is asked about his smoking status, and there is a good chance that his or her smoking habit is not reported accurately.

However, there were four groups. The effect showed up in two, it did not show up in one, and in one it became apparent after removal of outliers.

BERG: I have a comment and a question. The comment is on lead in bone. I take it that you had one special bone picked out, which was a good way to get reproducible data. In such material there could be a loss of lead at an older age because there is resorption of calcified material, and the collagen matrix becomes a significant part of dry weight. So that a local loss of lead would not be unexpected, even if the whole skeleton continued to accumulate lead in the long bones.

The question concerns a recent paper by Dr. Taves indicating a negative correlation between fluoride in diet and cardiovascular deaths. Now, if lead in cardiac muscle is a contributor to cardiovascular deaths, then Taves' correlation could be explained by a mechanism of sequestering lead, particularly in mitochondrial deposits, if this was accomplished more effectively with an increase in fluoride. A little more lead would be sequestered out of harm's way.

Wouldn't it be reasonable to include, in your multifactorial analysis, the fluoride level in the community's drinking water?

FORBES: Your first point is relevant and correct. It represents one of the possibilities to explain the data.

With respect to your second point, we looked at the water hardness but have no data on fluoride content. It is a good suggestion. Thank you.

USE OF TESTS OF PULMONARY FUNCTION TO MEASURE EFFECTS OF

AIR POLLUTANTS

B. G. Ferris, Jr., F. E. Speizer and J. H. Ware

Harvard School of Public Health and The Channing
Laboratory, Department of Medicine, Harvard Medical
School, and Peter Bent Brigham Hospital
Boston, MA 02115

This conference is concerned with the measurement of risks.
I would like to restrict my comments to the use of tests of pulmonary
function to assess the risks associated with air pollutants.

Pulmonary function testing as an objective measure of morbidity
in health effects of air pollution research has been used since the
early 1950's. Generally, simple maneuvers which give reliable and
reproducible measures of some component of lung function have been
used in a standardized manner in population groups. These have been
used along with more sophisticated techniques in the clinical
assessment of volunteer subjects undergoing controlled exposure
studies. In each situation exposed versus unexposed conditions are
compared. Generally, in population studies the vast majority of
pulmonary function measured is in the "normal range," and what is
compared is the relative degree of normality in the exposed and
unexposed groups. In the clinical studies deviations from the pre-
exposed state is monitored, with usually some information on how
long it takes for the subject's function to return to normal. Thus,
the effect of exposure can be determined. However, before we can
measure such effects we need to define what constitutes an adverse
or unacceptable effect. Adverse risk implies an effect on health
such as death, life shortening or some permanent change or decrement
in functional capacity. The fact that one can measure a temporary
functional or physiologic change does not necessarily indicate that
this is an adverse effect. With carbon monoxide exposure, for
example, we are willing to accept an increase in carboxyhemoglobin
up to 2-2.5 per cent as a measurable effect but as an acceptable
risk, even in patients with angina (2). Slightly higher levels
would be acceptable in normal healthy persons and not pose an
unacceptable risk. Thus, these are measurable effects that can be

statistically significant but are not considered to be medically important. This can also occur if one studies very large population groups where very small changes can be statistically significant but have little or no medical significance. In another instance the change may not be in the direction suggested by the expected response. For example, there may be an improvement in pulmonary function during a period when concentrations of air pollutants are elevated or such an increase might occur over time when a decrease would be expected. This has been observed in younger working populations (4), which implies that no effect has occurred, but merely normal random variation. Another example is the observation of Van der Lende et al. (15) of a temporary decrease in pulmonary function in an urban population associated with an increase in air pollution. This was a retrospective observation in which an improvement in pulmonary function was observed during a follow-up study. A reappraisal of the conditions at the time of the earlier study indicated increased levels of air pollution. A careful search was conducted for possible other explanations for the reduced lung function levels. None was found. The authors concluded that the temporary decrease in pulmonary function was related to the elevation of air pollution. Later studies (10) have shown the usual decrement expected with aging. It would thus seem that there was a temporary decrease in pulmonary function. From these observations it is not possible to infer whether repeated episodes of this sort would carry an increased risk of permanent impairment and eventually indicate an adverse risk.

A partial answer to the effect of repeated insults of this sort may be obtained from our unpublished observations in Steubenville, Ohio, where we have been taking advantage of the days with high pollution when an "alert" has been called. Our procedure is to measure baseline pulmonary function in the fall in about 200 children at school. When an air pollution "alert" is called, the children's pulmonary functions (forced vital capacity (FVC), and forced expiratory volume (FEV) in 0.75 and 1.0 second) are measured at the time of the alert and at weekly intervals for three weeks thereafter. Figure 1 represents an example of our data from 1978 on the forced vital capacity. Note that with the increase in concentration of the pollutants during the alert there was a decrease in pulmonary function. This decrease persisted for the three weeks of post-alert observation, although air pollution abated. The other measurements of pulmonary function showed essentially the same pattern. We repeated this alert study in 1979. An actual alert was slow in appearing, so we called a sham alert to see whether our observations were related to our study protocol. The results on the sham-alert day were essentially unchanged from baseline data. An actual "alert" was called a couple of days later. Again, a similar pattern to that seen in 1978 emerged even though the mix of pollutants was slightly different. In 1978 the alert was largely due to particulate pollution. In 1979 SO_2 was more elevated. Also,

in 1979 the pollution levels were elevated on the follow-up days
when pulmonary function was measured. Initially one might conclude
that this was an adverse reaction. When we compare, however, our
results of pulmonary function in Steubenville children with results
from the other cities in our study we note that the pulmonary
function in Steubenville is second best for FVC and $FEV_{1.0}$ for both
boys and girls. Best is Portage, Wisconsin, a clean community.
These results are presented in Table I where the residuals in lung
function from a prediction equation are listed for white children.
Even correcting for cooking fuel in the home, presence of air
conditioning, parental educational level and parental smoking does
not significantly alter this observation (Tables II, III). This
suggests that persistent effects of such episodes in Steubenville
must be small relative to other sources of variation between
communities, if such effects exist at all.

We have done some preliminary analyses in a prospective manner
to see whether the children's lungs in the different communities are
growing in a comparable fashion. As far as can be determined to
date there do not seem to be discrepancies. This is an area where
further analyses are indicated in order to give adequate assurance
to our present conclusions or to require that the conclusions be
modified.

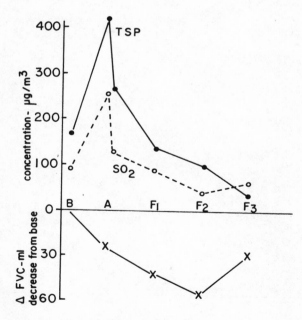

Fig. 1. Change in forced vital capacity in children associated
         with an air pollution "alert".

TABLE I

Children's Lung Function Residual Means
Standardized to Population Totals by Age
(Intake: White children ages 6-8 whose height for age
is 0.5-99.5% of NCHS standards)

	FVC (ml)		$FEV_{1.0}$ (ml)	
	Mean	S.E.	Mean	S.E.
M A L E S				
Portage	60.4	8.4	50.7	8.0
Topeka	-28.0	7.4	-9.6	7.0
Watertown	-17.4	8.1	14.4	7.4
Kingston-Harriman	18.5	7.9	6.5	7.1
St. Louis	5.5	6.9	13.4	5.9
Steubenville	25.1	7.4	24.7	6.7
F E M A L E S				
Portage	26.8	8.4	18.0	7.8
Topeka	-34.7	7.0	-32.0	6.1
Watertown	-17.3	7.9	-14.5	7.2
Kingston-Harriman	16.6	7.8	-3.3	6.9
St. Louis	-3.7	6.2	-8.5	5.6
Steubenville	12.0	6.3	13.3	5.6

TABLE II

Children's Lung Function Residual Means Standardized to Population Totals
By Age and Home Variables

(Intake: White children ages 6-8 whose height for age is 0.5-99.5% of NCHS standards)

MALES	(ml)	Cooking Fuel		Air Conditioning		Parental Educational Level		Parental Smoking	
		Mean	S.E.	Mean	S.E.	Mean	S.E.	Mean	S.E.
Portage	FVC	59.0	8.6	59.0	9.0	57.7	11.9	61.3	9.0
	$FEV_{1.0}$	50.1	8.0	50.1	8.9	52.8	11.9	50.7	8.5
Topeka	FVC	-26.7	8.6	-38.1	9.5	-27.1	8.7	-28.1	7.6
	$FEV_{1.0}$	-7.7	8.0	-14.4	9.1	-7.6	8.2	-9.2	7.2
Watertown	FVC	-0.5	28.7	-20.8	15.8	-16.2	8.1	-17.4	9.1
	$FEV_{1.0}$	26.2	21.2	13.2	12.6	14.0	8.5	12.4	8.6
Kingston-Harriman	FVC	9.8	34.4	13.1	9.0	16.8	9.2	16.9	8.7
	$FEV_{1.0}$	24.6	27.6	-0.4	7.9	6.3	8.5	4.6	7.9
St. Louis	FVC	5.9	10.5	3.3	7.3	-1.8	10.3	6.6	7.1
	$FEV_{1.0}$	7.2	8.8	13.1	6.2	8.7	8.1	13.3	6.1
Steubenville	FVC	25.3	7.8	27.3	7.6	15.1	7.9	21.0	7.5
	$FEV_{1.0}$	24.0	7.1	26.1	6.8	20.1	7.1	21.4	6.8

TABLE III

Children's Lung Function Residual Means (Cont'd)

(ml)	Cooking Fuel		Air Conditioning		Parental Educational Level		Parental Smoking	
	Mean	S.E.	Mean	S.E.	Mean	S.E.	Mean	S.E.
F E M A L E S								
Portage								
FVC	29.4	8.6	23.7	9.4	27.8	10.2	24.2	9.2
$FEV_{1.0}$	20.0	8.1	14.1	8.2	17.1	11.0	13.0	8.2
Topeka								
FVC	-33.1	7.6	-28.3	8.6	-37.4	9.1	-34.9	7.4
$FEV_{1.0}$	-31.0	6.4	-28.0	7.2	-33.3	7.7	-32.2	6.5
Watertown								
FVC	-23.2	17.9	-7.8	13.0	-13.8	9.0	-18.9	9.1
$FEV_{1.0}$	-31.7	17.8	-18.2	9.9	-10.1	7.9	11.1	8.6
Kingston-Harriman								
FVC	14.9	20.4	16.3	8.2	19.8	8.8	16.8	8.6
$FEV_{1.0}$	-14.8	18.7	-3.2	7.2	-0.8	7.8	-5.7	7.8
St. Louis								
FVC	-6.5	9.7	-0.9	6.3	-1.9	7.0	-4.1	6.4
$FEV_{1.0}$	-6.4	9.1	-6.7	5.7	-4.5	6.4	-8.2	5.7
Steubenville								
FVC	11.7	6.5	14.2	6.6	17.3	6.8	13.3	6.7
$FEV_{1.0}$	12.6	5.9	15.2	5.8	20.7	5.8	14.6	5.8

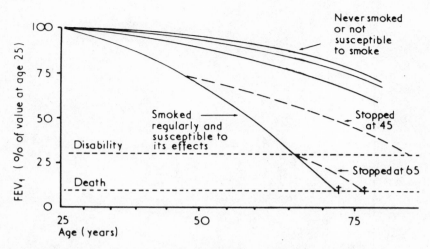

Fig. 2.   Idealized curves representing changes in $FEV_{1.0}$ with age
under different smoking habits. Change is related to per
cent change from value at 25 years of age.

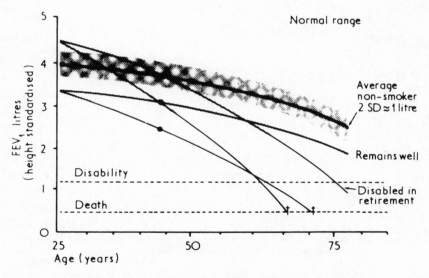

Fig. 3.   Idealized curves representing changes with age in $FEV_{1.0}$
in absolute values.

Figures 2 and 3 reprinted by permission of the British Medical
Journal as published in Brit. Med. J., 1: 1645 (1977).   (see ref. 7)

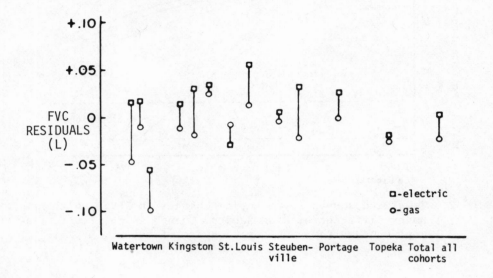

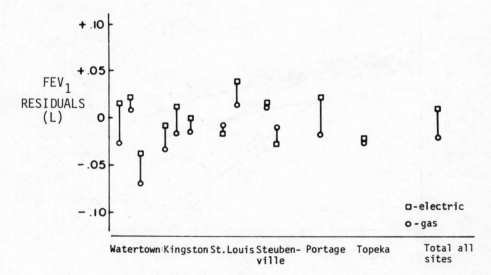

Fig. 4.   Residuals of pulmonary function values for children in
          homes where gas is used for cooking vs. electricity.
          (Figure reprinted by permission of the American Lung
          Association as published in Am. Rev. Resp. Disease,
          121: 3 (1980). (See ref. 13.))

Another example of the use of tests of pulmonary function is shown in Figures 2 and 3. These are idealized curves from data from a prospective study in Great Britain (7). Figure 2 represents the change in $FEV_{1.0}$ as a per cent of the value at age 25. For non-smokers and those not susceptible to cigarette smoke $FEV_{1.0}$ declines with age at a rate which increases slightly in older age groups. This decline does not cause the $FEV_{1.0}$ to reach a level where disability could occur. For all cigarette smokers there would be a range of curves representing varying degrees of susceptibility. The important points here are: 1) that susceptible cigarette smokers tend to lose $FEV_{1.0}$ more rapidly than non-smokers or non-susceptible smokers and thus can reach a level of $FEV_{1.0}$ that can cause disability or result in death; 2) if the susceptible smoker stops at a relatively early age, e.g. 45 years, then the rate of decline parallels that of the non-smoker but is set lower due to irreversible changes that have occurred - the decline is slowed and may not reach a level that would cause disability; 3) if the smoker stops at age 65 or as he or she approaches the level of disability, then the rate of decline will be slowed but, because there is so little leeway, death can still result due to low $FEV_{1.0}$, albeit postponed to some extent.

Figure 3 shows another aspect of this same phenomena. Here the $FEV_{1.0}$ is in absolute numbers rather than per cent. The lines represent the decline in $FEV_{1.0}$ over time and the shaded area represents 2 standard deviations around the line for the average non-smoker. A person may have a low $FEV_{1.0}$ but be within the "normal" range and remain so throughout life. His $FEV_{1.0}$ at 45 years of age is represented by the dark circle in the shaded area. Another person with a comparable $FEV_{1.0}$ at age 45 may have reached that level even though at an earlier age he had a high "normal" value. These two can be distinguished if earlier results of pulmonary function testing are available or by following them prospectively. Thus persons who fall in the low "normal" range, and for whom early results are not available, should be followed prospectively. If they are cigarette smokers, they should be strongly encouraged not to smoke. The other solid circle represents a person who has already fallen below the "normal: range. He, too, if a smoker, should be encouraged to stop smoking. Thus, the $FEV_{1.0}$ can be used to identify those smokers more susceptible to the effects of cigarette smoking and, therefore, at greater risk.

We have also used simple tests of pulmonary function to assess the possible effects of NO_2, produced by gas cooking stoves, on children (Fig. 4). Here the residuals as calculated from a prediction equation generated from our data are plotted for the various cohorts in each of our six cities. For the $FEV_{1.0}$ the values for children living in homes where gas is used as cooking fuel are lower in all but two instances and for FVC in all but one cohort. There is quite a range of differences between cities and even between cohorts within cities which are likely to represent real differences between the cohorts.

In another study (5) the results of pulmonary function testing proved to be more discriminatory than the responses to a standard questionnaire. This occurred in the comparison of Berlin, New Hampshire, and Chilliwack, British Columbia. No differences were noted between the two communities with respect to percent positive responses to questions concerning respiratory symptoms using a standard questionnaire. This occurred despite a considerable difference in the levels of air pollution - Berlin being more polluted. The tests of pulmonary function, adjusted for sex, age, height and smoking habits, however, did show better function in Chilliwack; the same spirometer was used and the observers were the same, so that these sources of bias were minimized.

Bouhuys and Zuskin (3) have used tests of pulmonary function to show that men exposed to hemp dust have a greater decline in $FEV_{1.0}$ than their controls. This was particularly evident in the 20- to 40-year-old group that were non-smokers.

McKerrow et al. (12) have monitored the $FEV_{0.75}$ during the day and during the week in cotton workers and have shown that they can separate out various degrees of response (i.e. decrease in $FEV_{0.75}$) and the persistence of the response and thus classify varying severity of disease. In addition, those men who show the more pronounced acute response had more persistent response and appeared to be at greater risk of developing permanent disability than those who had a less pronounced acute response. This observation identified a susceptible group that either must be removed from the work place or for whom better engineering controls must be installed to reduce their exposure.

These various examples have demonstrated the usefulness of the simple tests of pulmonary function as measured by spirometry in assessing the possible effects of air pollutants even at rather low levels of exposure. In general, these simple tests have proven to be most applicable, serviceable and reproducible whether used in the field or in chamber studies.

A number of other measurements can be taken from the spirogram or obtained by other techniques. These are the mid-maximal expiratory flow (MMEF) and flow at various lung volumes usually expressed as flow at a certain per cent of vital capacity.

Some observers (9,14) have found the MMEF to be as good as or better than the $FEV_{1.0}$ or $FEV_{0.75}$. The results of these tests are all very highly correlated and since it is not too difficult to obtain all measurements from a tracing, especially when the data

can be interfaced with a computer or digitizer, all three
measurements should be obtained.

Flow-volume data can be taken from the spirogram or measured
directly. It is generally believed that the values obtained at less
than one-half the vital capacity are more indicative of lower (small)
airways disease (11). There is, however, considerable intersubject
variation (up to 30-35%) even when done under well-controlled
laboratory conditions (11,8).

In instances where interstitial disease is expected - as with
asbestos exposure - diffusing capacity as well as simple spirometry
is recommended (6), as it can detect early changes consistent with
an increased risk of developing severe asbestosis.

There are a number of other more complicated tests that can
be used in selected studies. Most of these may be time consuming,
demand too much of the subject - such as obtaining a blood sample,
or have considerable variation. Some of these are discussed in a
standardization project report prepared for the Division of Lung
Diseases by an American Thoracic Society Committee (6).

In summary, much can be learned from the simple tests as shown
above. They fit the fundamental requirements of being reasonably
sensitive although often not very specific. They are not invasive
and take relatively little time. They do require some cooperation
from the subject, but most everyone can learn how to perform with
a rather brief training time. A most important factor is to be
sure that the instrument used meets certain standards and that the
tests are done in a standard manner (6,1). Under such conditions
small changes can be detected and are useful in estimating possible
risks of exposure to air pollutants, or to identify susceptible
population groups.

ACKNOWLEDGEMENT

Supported in part by grants from the National Institute of
Environmental Health Sciences (ES0002, ES01108), Electric Power
Research Institute Contract No. RP1001 and EPA Contract No. 68-02-
3201.

REFERENCES

1. American Thoracic Society: ATS statement. Snowbird Workshop on standardization of spirometry. Am. Rev. Resp. Dis., 119: 831(1979)

2. Aranow, W. S. and Isbell, M. W.: Carbon monoxide effect on exercise-induced angina pectoris. Ann. Int. Med., 79:392 (1973)

3. Bouhuys, A. and Zuskin, E.: Chronic respiratory disease in hemp workers: A follow-up study, 1967–1974. Ann. Int. Med., 84:398(1976)

4. Ferris, B. G., Jr., Puleo, S. and Chen, H. Y.: Mortality and morbidity in a pulp and a paper mill in the United States; a ten-year follow-up. Brit. J. Indust. Med., 36:127(1979)

5. Ferris, B. G., Jr. and Anderson, D. O.: Epidemiological studies related to air pollution: A comparison of Berlin, New Hampshire and Chilliwack, British Columbia. Proc. Roy. Soc. Med., 57(part 2):979(1964)

6. Ferris, B. G., Jr.: Epidemiology standardization project. Am. Rev. Resp. Dis., 118(part 2):1(1978)

7. Fletcher, G. and Peto, R. The natural history of chronic airflow obstruction. Brit. Med. J., 1:1645(1977)

8. Green, M., Mead, J. and Turner, J. M.: Variability of maximum expiratory flow-volume curves. J. Appl. Physiol., 37:67(1974)

9. Higgins, M. W. and Keller, J. B.: Seven measures of ventilatory lung function. Am. Rev. Resp. Dis. 108:258(1973)

10. Holland, W. W., Bennett, A. E., Cameron, I. R., Florey, C. duV. Leeder, S. R., Schilling, R. S. F., Swan, A. V. and Waller, R. E.: Health effects of particulate pollution: Reappraising the evidence. 4. Exposure to particulates: morbidity in adults. Am. J. Epidemiol., 110:580(1979)

11. Knudson, R. J., Slatin, R. C., Lebowitz, M. D. and Burrows, B.: The maximal expiratory flow-volume curve: Normal standards, variability and effects of age. Am. Rev. Resp. Dis. 113:587 (1976)

12. McKerrow, C. B., McDermott, M., Gilson, J. C. and Schilling, R. S. F.: Respiratory function during the day in cotton workers: A study in byssinosis. Brit. J. Ind. Med. 15:75 (1958)

13. Speizer, F. E., Ferris, B., Jr., Bishop, Y. M. M. and
    Spengler, J.: Respiratory disease rates and pulmonary function
    in children associated with NO_2 exposure. Am. Rev. Resp. Dis.
    121:3(1980)

14. Tager, I. B., Weiss, S. T., Rosner, B. and Speizer, F. E.:
    Effect of parental cigarette smoking on the pulmonary function
    of children. Am. J. Epidemiol., 110:15 (1979)

15. Van der Lende, R., Huggen, G., Jansen-Koster, E. J.,
    Knijpstra, S., Peset, R., Visser, B. F., Wolfs, E. H. E. and
    Orie, N. G. M.: A temporary decrease in ventilatory function
    of an urban population during an acute increase in air
    pollution. Bull. Physiopathol. Resp., 11:31(1975)

DISCUSSION

SAGAN: You spoke about lung function with respect to indoor air
pollution. I'd like to ask two questions related to energy conser-
vation measures and possible effects on indoor pollution and lung
function. With increased insulation and reduced air flow in homes,
what changes would you expect in indoor concentrations of pollutants?
Secondly, what specific changes in pollutants would you anticipate
from the increased use of firewood as an energy source?

FERRIS: From our information on the types of homes we knew whether
they use gas for cooking. We also asked whether they had vents over
the stoves and whether they vented into the room or outside. We
didn't even bother asking them whether they turned the fan on or not.
The homes that had outside venting showed levels of oxide of nitrogen
indoors more similar to those of electric homes. They weren't quite
as low but were very close to it. So that venting is enough to do
a very adequate job whether you turn it on or not, provided it goes
to the outside.

To answer your question the other way, with tightened up homes
and these sources in the homes, we shall probably find higher concentrations of pollutants. To say whether this is going to be bad
for health is more difficult. We need to collect data over a longer
time period rather than just use these initial observations. I know
that in Great Britain and in Scandinavian countries they have tightened the houses so much that they also accumulate other products of
combustion, such as water vapor. In the damp climates of England
and Scandinavia, this moisture in their homes causes other problems.
Now they leave a window open much of the time to get rid of the water
vapor. I think we're just going to have to have a certain amount of
ventilation whether we like it or not.

With respect to wood, we're just beginning to see more wood
being used. A lot will depend upon the type of burner that it's in.
If it is in an open fireplace, we can detect the smoke out in the
room by an increase in the amount of sodium in the air. If they have
a good, tight stove, they should have less contamination but they
have to open the stove to charge it. I know of no detailed studies
of wood burning and its effects on health.

A piece of anecdotal information is that in Vail, Colorado, they
found this a very serious problem, and now they have a regulation
that you are allowed to burn wood in your fireplace in Vail only one
day out of six or something like that. This is because they're getting excessive air pollution from wood smoke because of inversion
effects in the enclosed valley.

POCHIN: I think we open the windows to get rid of radon, too.

FERRIS: To us, that's secondary. We are not looking at that.

ABRAHAMSON: What's the physiological mechanism that reduces the lung capacity so rapidly in those school children right after the alert? How does it operate?

FERRIS: I don't think we know. Presumably it may have something to do with a bronchospasm. We have analyzed the responses in all the children that we saw five times. We don't always see all the same children each time. In this case, we looked at only the ones we saw each time. If you separate out those children who have a history of having had lung problems, they're the ones that are producing most of the fall, whereas the children who have no history of lung problems do have a little fall but it's not statistically different from the baseline data. So this is all being driven by the children who have a history of respiratory disease.

FORBES: Was there any information on smokers of different types of cigarettes, or on pipe smokers?

FERRIS: Yes, we do have that. The pipe or cigar smoker is nowhere as badly off as the cigarette smoker. He is like a very light cigarette smoker or often just like an ex-smoker. The variables that we're looking at do not respond to the modifications in the cigarette as do the carcinogenic effects, where they are looking at changes in tar content. I think the major component that we see here is probably oxides of nitrogen and other gaseous components rather than particulates of the smoke, which might be filtered out by filter tips.

BOURDEAU: On the point you just raised, we started some time ago a study on the relationship between air pollution and respiratory symptoms in school children in various countries in Europe. We found that the most significant factor related to respiratory symptoms was not air pollution outdoors but smoking by the parents. The exception was France, where the quality of the tobacco is markedly different from what is smoked elsewhere. I don't know if there is an indication there.

And incidentally, the function tests that we carried out did not give good results at all, whereas the questionnaire worked out fine. But we used a peak flow rate meter and maybe this is the reason. Would you have anything to say about that versus the spirometer?

FERRIS: It's an attractive instrument because it doesn't depend on electricity and you can just read it. But you have to be sure they are all carefully calibrated and checked regularly and they just give one point per test. They do not give a lot of other information. And you can't go back and check the data, you don't have any records.

Whether parental smoking has an effect on health is still up for grabs. We are not able to demonstrate it in our data, either from a questionnaire or from lung function tests. Some people find it and some don't.

CROW: What's the state of the art in regard to portable detecting instruments that a person could carry and not be too badly encumbered thereby? Also, would you are to comment on Lester Lave's studies?

FERRIS: I think Lester has the same problem as most of the economists. That is, that they'll take any sort of data and crank it through to get an answer. And believe it! I think the big problem is that he does not have a lot of physiological and medical advice to inform him what is making medical sense. Furthermore, in his methodology, the model is highly sensitive to the assumptions he puts into it. And he does not take into account all the confounding variables.

Similar sorts of studies have been made by a number of other economists. You might call them statistical manipulators. And the more confounding factors they put into their model, and depending upon their assumptions, they can make all the effects of air pollution disappear. And with the Lester Lave model, he picked out minimum sulphate levels as the driving force. Why did he pick out minimum sulphate? Well, it just happened to fit better. But it doesn't make sense. It ought to be the maximum sulphate rather than the minimum. And there are a lot of other things in there that he did not take into account. I would not believe it.

To answer the question about personal monitors. They are commercially available, although we think we've built a better one because it has to be more rugged than the commercial ones. We have been using this portable device to sample mass respirable particulates on a 24-hour basis. This meant that we had to improve our analytical techniques to measure down to a microgram of sulphate. These samples work quite successfully, but you have to be sure the flow rates are maintained. The units do offer a bit of encumberance to the individual walking around. We haven't been able to put them on day laborers because you can not swing a pick and have this thing hang around you. You can not get them into certain businesses because the manager will not allow them in the factory. But we do have people who have worn them and carried them around.

For the oxides of nitrogen - these take 24-hour samples, so you miss a peak during the daytime. You get the rise for that day but not an hourly value. Ed Palms, at New York University, has developed a NO_2 monitor, that you hook on your pocket. It is probably not as big as a piece of chalk. It is a passive diffusing device which works quite well, but you have to expose it for five days or seven

days to get a big enough sample of oxide of nitrogen to measure. It
misses all of the peaks for that period of time and just gives an
average value. We have been using it and it gives us some information. But, it makes me nervous to try to plot such data against
effects. Effects are probably more related to the peaks which are
not measured by these integrating monitors.

KATES: You were very careful to circumscribe what you said about
the health effects of pulmonary impairment. Could you just reverse
that? Tell us what, in a positive sense, do you think, is the relationship between evidence of early childhood pulmonary impairment
and later health?

FERRIS: I didn't say anything about that because first of all, we
do not have any data and we do need to have the results from the
prospective studies. There are reports in the literature, both from
England and from this country, in which they have seen people in
older age who have a lot of pulmonary problems and then they find
that they have a history of chilhood disease. They have concluded
that this is an early incidence of childhood disease that now begets
the elderly pulmonary cripple. But that study is subject to a lot
of bias because what you really need to do is to set it up prospectively. A person who is now sick as an older person may say, oh yes,
I remember my mother said I had a lot of pneumonia as a kid. Whereas a guy who is healthy says, oh, I was never sick at all. But he
had a serious bout back at the age of 3 but it never stuck so he
never remembered it. And you need to follow this in a prospective
way to be able to give good credence to that observation. So I do
not believe I can answer that.

KATES: Are any longitudinal studies of that sort under way?

FERRIS: They might be able to get some of these data out of the
studies in Tecumseh, Michigan, although they have not been doing as
much pulmonary function testing. It might be available in some of
the Framingham data, but they generally pick up the people as adults
and they have not followed them from childhood. Whether this study
will be done depends on whether somebody has the determination to
stick with it for another 40 years. I do not think I can.

KATES: Cogeneration plants are about to become major air polluters.
Were you seriously planning to monitor the pulmonary function of the
people in the neighborhood?

FERRIS: I do not know whether I would bother with pulmonary function
measurements. I think they ought to measure what the concentrations
are. And I have strongly urged that they do this, but I do not think
they are.

L. RUSSELL: Of the five locations you used, I am familiar with
one, the one at Kingston/Harriman, which is fairly close to us at
Oak Ridge. Was that study made before or after the tall stacks for
a coal fired steam plant?

FERRIS: The reason we picked the place was that the tall stacks
were up and they had not started to be used. So our observations
were first with the small stacks and then with the high stacks. The
tall stacks modified the levels of pollution in Kingston quite considerably. There are no longer any of the smoke pollution incidents
or fumigations that used to take place regularly. They now disperse
pollution over the hill into Harriman, and they probably dump it
farther up the valley near Oak Ridge.

     I do not think we have an answer to pollution control by the
use of tall stacks. Certainly they make airborne waste products
go farther downwind, and if your solution to pollution is dilution,
that is one way to do it. But if you are concerned about the long-
range transport of SO_2 and acid rain, this is not a good thing, unless the scrubbers are placed on stacks to remove a large amount of
SO_2. I do not think we have the answers on the amount of waste removal needed.

COHEN: What about the Brookhaven studies on SO_2?

FERRIS: They suffer from the same problems as Lave and Seskin's
studies, by and large. They take Lave and Seskin's data -- or the
same sources, do similar analyses and say "See, we get the same answers, they must be right." We have disagreed with this regularly.

MORROW: You mentioned the fact that some effects such as those observed in school children are reversible. Therefore, there might be
some question as to whether or not these exposures increase risks.
Can there be much doubt about this in the case of the children who
might have respiratory disease or perhaps in the older age segment?
Should we conclude that there is no appreciable risk in this type of
physiological adjustment or temporary dysfunction?

FERRIS: I would like to follow them for a longer period of time to
be sure that I can substantiate my information. I think a lot of
the studies, in fact practically all of them, have been just cross-
sectional. Very few have been longitudinal. Looking at the people
in Time A we can not make a prediction whether the effects that
happened back here are having influence at Time B. Until we do
more longitudinal studies, I do not think we can really answer that
question.

MORROW: But these are the kinds of effects that were probably important in episodic pollution, nonetheless.

FERRIS: In Steubenville we have been trying to get alert data there for three years and we got it for 2 out of 3. These children are 8, 9, 10 years of age and have been exposed at alert levels a number of times. And yet we see very little residual, at least so far.

BOURDEAU: You get continual information then.

FERRIS: Yes, because we see the children every year. The "alert" study is a special study done in the fall whereas the annual survey occurs in the spring.

WEINBERG: You were showing pulmonary function with the parents smoking and without the parents smoking. There seemed to be a very large variation, at least in the numbers on your slides, between what presumably were the normal levels of function from one place to another. You had a number like 59 for Watertown, something like 6 for Kingston. Did I misunderstand what that slide was saying?

FERRIS: Those were developed by having a regression equation, based upon all the children and putting their data together. Then for each child, we predicted what this value would be. We then subtracted his observed from his predicted. That was a residual. If it was positive, it was bigger than expected. If it was negative, it was smaller. There was a considerable range. Portage had the best data and they were around 60.

WEINBERG: Was this a measure of the variation in the population or a measure of the actual level of function?

FERRIS: Well, it should be a measure of the difference between the populations. We're trying to standardize and measure them against some sort of standard. There are also standard errors given around those numbers, and those are also fairly big because we have a fairly large, heterogeneous population.

WEINBERG: Is there really a large normal variation in the FVC or FEV-1 that you speak of?

FERRIS: Yes, and because of that almost any prediction formula that you use is terrible. They all have standard errors of the order of half a liter. So that in essence they are all the same. It is one of the difficulties of using a cross-sectional observation and then using a prediction equation. That was what I was trying to point out with the British data, namely that a person could fall in a number of different categories. You do not know how he got into that category, unless you have earlier data. A super normal person who comes in complaining of symptoms may have a normal pulmonary function in terms of standard values, even though he is ill with depressed function. You will miss it. So it is much better to follow them

prospectively, using each individual as his own control, which is
what we propose to do. That was the situation we used in the
Steubenville alert. We have boys and girls together and we have a
few blacks. Each one is used as his own control. In absolute numbers, the whites would be higher and the blacks lower on the scale,
but the differences from control readings are roughly the same across
the groups.

HACKNEY: I noticed on your Steubenville "alert" slide that apparently the FEV didn't come back to normal for the duration of observation, which was about three weeks. Was there any association with
clinical indications of respiratory infection, for example: How did
you deal with the possibility of a confounding effect of just inci-
dental respiratory infection in looking at these data?

FERRIS: We generally record whether they currently have respiratory
symptoms or whether they have had them in the past week. I don't
know why FEV took so long to come back to normal, unless just a few
of the children in the group are taking much longer to recover than
the others. We need to check this.

EXPERIMENTAL EVALUATION OF AIR POLLUTANTS IN HUMANS

AS A BASIS FOR ESTIMATING RISK

Jack D. Hackney and William S. Linn

Rancho Los Amigos Hospital Campus, University of
Southern California School of Medicine
Downey, California 90242

INTRODUCTION

The purpose of this paper is to provide a brief "guided tour"
of human experimental studies of air pollution exposure. This field
of investigation is rather new and small compared to the related
fields of animal toxicology and epidemiology, which are discussed in
some of the accompanying papers. In human studies--sometimes called
"human toxicology" or "clinical toxicology" or "clinical environmental stress testing"--the investigator creates or finds a polluted
air environment of interest, recruits volunteer subjects, exposes
them to the pollution under well-controlled conditions, and looks
for responses which could in any sense be considered adverse effects
on health. Controlled human exposure studies play an important part
in environmental risk assessment as it relates to air pollution,
because they can often provide firm, credible scientific information not available otherwise. Needless to say, human experimentation has strict ethical and practical limitations. Nevertheless,
a broad range of environmental problems can be investigated, given
proper concern for the health and welfare of the subjects. Investigation of any real risks--those to which the subject is, or could
reasonably be, exposed in the course of his normal activities--
presents few ethical problems. Investigation of potential risks--
those which the subject has not previously experienced, but could
reasonably encounter in the future--likewise can be justified. Such
activities provide benefits to the individual subjects, since they
obtain potentially valuable information on their responses to certain
environmental stressors.

We present here a highly selective review of the historical
development of human exposure studies as they apply to risk

231

assessment. This is intended to illustrate some of the problems
faced in the design and conduct of these studies, and some of the
resulting uncertainties in applying the scientific results to air
quality policy decisions. Finally, some suggestions will be made
concerning possible future improvements in planning of research and
its application to public policy. This discussion will be limited
to respiratory irritant pollutants; inhalable systemic poisons
present equally important but different problems. In exploring these
issues, it will be useful to refer to what we consider the basic
needs in research applied to risk assessment. These can be expressed
as the "three R's"--rigor, relevance, and redundancy.

Rigor, of course, means the scientific reliability of an
experiment--the conditions necessary to minimize the chance that we
will mistakenly associate an environmental cause with a health
effect, or fail to recognize a real association between environment
and health. Animal toxicology is usually the most rigorous scientific tool for risk assessment, in that the ability to control all
the important variables is maximal. But to be useful in policy
decisions, research must be equally concerned with the second "R"--
relevance to human health concerns. The relevance of laboratory
animal data to humans is always more or less controversial. On the
other hand, in epidemiology relevance is seldom in question but rigor
is always a problem. The diversity and unpredictability of human
behavior and of the air environment make it nearly impossible to
control the many potential interfering variables. For the same
reasons, epidemiology has problems with the third "R"--redundancy.
The uncontrollable conditions vary with time and location, making it
impossible to verify a past epidemiologic study by replicating its
conditions and its results. But when studying humans in the laboratory, we have the chance to reduce interfering variables to a minimum,
and to document the conditions and results of the exposure to the
extent that the experiment can be repeated independently. Ideally,
then, we can achieve high degrees of rigor, relevance, and redundancy all at once in human exposure studies. Of course, reality
often falls short of ideals, as will be discussed in reviewing the
past and present development of the field.

WHERE WE HAVE BEEN--SOME HISTORICAL DEVELOPMENTS

While most important developments in human exposure studies
occurred in the 1970's, scientific literature on the subject goes
back more than 100 years. In 1876 a British physician, Benjamin
Ward Richardson, published a monograph including a discussion of
the health effects of ozone (1). Richardson and his associates
performed inhalation experiments on themselves and documented the
respiratory irritant effects of ozone. They also did animal toxicology, using more extreme exposures to demonstrate lung injury
unequivocally. Their human and animal experiments were an attempt
to confirm their previous epidemiologic observation that the

presence of ozone in ambient air was associated with increased incidence of febrile illnesses. Richardson clearly was aware of issues recognized by modern air pollution epidemiologists, although he was not concerned with a man-made pollution problem. He noted that pollutant variables are strongly correlated with meteorological variables, that concentrations vary substantially over short distances, that technological resources are often inadequate to monitor ambient pollution with the needed accuracy and detail, and that it may be difficult to identify a few people severely affected by exposure among many who are less susceptible or less exposed. His experimental observations were of course crude and sometimes inaccurate by modern reckoning, yet Richardson was remarkably insightful in recognizing the need and the possibility to investigate air quality problems by combining epidemiologic, animal toxicologic, and human laboratory investigations.

Earlier in this century, there were only a few human exposure studies, generally rather crude and concerned with subjective responses to pollutants of occupational concern. Interest in scientific studies of community air pollution grew in the 1950's and '60's. Studies published during that period were reviewed in some detail in the 1969-70 Air Quality Criteria documents (2,3). In North America, western Europe, and Japan, respiratory function measurement was (and still is) chosen as the predominant investigative tool, since the respiratory tract is the first target of inhaled irritants. In the Soviet Union, attention was focused on subtle neurological responses, which were commonly observed at exposure concentrations much lower than required to produce a demonstrable pulmonary response. The Soviet reports have not received much serious attention in the West, perhaps because they seldom include detailed documentation of experimental methods.

The investigations by Mary O. Amdur, Robert Frank, and coworkers at Harvard University provide noteworthy examples of respiratory-effect studies from the 1950's and '60's (4-7). The important methodological issues which had to be addressed by these and other investigators included choice of adequately sensitive and objective physiological measures of response, verification of the reproducibility of these measures, choice of experimental atmospheres to simulate "real-world" pollution realistically, and development of a satisfactory means of exposing the volunteers to the experimental atmospheres. Practical limitations in each of these areas were severe initially, and are still important despite technological advances. Sulfuric acid aerosol, sulfur dioxide, and sulfur dioxide mixed with sodium chloride aerosol were studied in brief exposures (15-30 min). Significant effects were found at concentrations realistic for occupational exposures, though higher than expected in ambient air. In the earliest of the studies cited, sulfuric acid aerosol was administered via a face mask and response was measured in terms of changed respiratory flow rates and tidal volumes. Later, sulfur dioxide effects were studied by measuring resistance of the subject's airways in a whole-body plethysmograph or "body box" which also served as the exposure chamber. Other measures of respiratory response were made, but resistance seemed most sensitive. However, baseline resistance measurements and responses to exposure varied considerably from day to day in any given subject, limiting the ability to detect real but small exposure effects.

Overall, these studies at high concentrations did not provide firm information concerning health effects of ambient exposure, but they did provide a valuable foundation of experience to be drawn upon in later investigations. Constriction of airways in response to sulfur dioxide was shown to develop within a very few minutes after exposure began, and to reverse quickly after it ended. However, if a second exposure took place on the same day, the response was substantially less than in the first exposure. Coexisting sodium chloride aerosol did not significantly increase the response to sulfur dioxide in these studies, but sodium chloride did appear to have some potentiating effect in similar studies by others. Gas-aerosol mixtures were (and still are) important to study because aerosols, which nearly always coexist with gases in ambient pollution, can adsorb soluble gases such as sulfur dioxide and deliver them to the deep lung when inhaled. In the absence of aerosol, the gas would be largely scrubbed out in the nasopharyngeal area and thus might be less hazardous.

A major advance in human exposure studies came about through the work of David V. Bates and associates at McGill University in Montreal in the early 1970's. These investigators directly addressed the problem of establishing exposure conditions which would realistically simulate real-world experiences (8). To eliminate the need for unnatural breathing through a tube or confinement in a body box, they designed an exposure chamber large enough to allow some freedom of movement for the subject inside. A stationary bicycle allowed the subject to exercise intermittently during exposure, increasing his ventilation and thus his pollutant dose as would occur during typical outdoor activity. Ozone and sulfur dioxide were the pollutants of interest in these studies. A two-hour exposure period was adopted since high ambient levels of ozone commonly persist for about that length of time. Although a variety of sophisticated pulmonary physiological measurements were used to assess response, attention was eventually focused on the relatively simple measurements of a maximal forced expiration--the forced vital capacity (maximum expirable volume) and maximum expiratory flow rates. These indices are much more stable under control conditions than airway resistance or most other respiratory measurements, thus even small exposure-related changes can be detected as statistically significant. Bates and coworkers found clinical and physiological effects of ozone at concentrations experienced regularly in ambient Los Angeles air, and occasionally elsewhere (9,10). Their experimental approach has been adopted in many more recent human studies, and their findings on ozone have been confirmed repeatedly. Ozone's salient effect is irritation of the lower respiratory tract, producing cough, chest pain, and reduced forced expiratory performance. The effect develops more slowly and reverses more slowly than the effects of sulfur dioxide. With ozone and sulfur dioxide present together, an apparent marked enhancement of the irritant effect was observed (11), although the sulfur dioxide was at a concentration too low to produce any effect by itself.

The experimental approach of Bates presents a problem in that large quantities of pollutants and background air are needed to supply the relatively large exposure chamber. Controlling the atmospheric conditions may be more difficult on this scale than when mouthpiece or mask exposures are used. Bates's group did not purify their chamber air supply, they simply made use of air-conditioned laboratory air. This was reasonable since resources were limited (interest and funding for environmental studies were still not great), the area was not heavily polluted, some filtration was provided by the building air conditioning, and the levels of the test pollutants were shown to be negligible in the supply air. However, one could not be sure that the exposure atmosphere was free of other pollutants, since there was no means of monitoring them. An extraneous pollutant in the background air might affect the accuracy of the instruments monitoring the test pollutant, interact with the test pollutant and modify the subject's biological response, or react chemically with the test pollutant to form an undetected third species with undetermined biological effects. Obviously, any of these occurrences might invalidate the experiment. This probably did not happen in the ozone studies of Bates et al., but may have happened in the ozone-plus-sulfur-dioxide study, as will be mentioned later. It must be emphasized that these problems relate to limitations of technology and material resources, not to inadequate experimental design or investigators' lack of ingenuity. They are present to a greater or lesser extent in every controlled-exposure study. Careful purification and monitoring of exposure air can reduce but cannot eliminate the likelihood of interferences, since no purification or monitoring system is perfect.

A further advance in human studies came about with the use of large-scale exposure chambers provided with air purification systems and high-capacity air conditioners allowing simulation of a range of weather conditions. The authors' laboratory at Rancho Los Amigos Hospital near Los Angeles provides an example. Its exposure chamber (12) is sheathed with stainless steel and other chemically unreactive materials to minimize reactions between atmospheric substances and surfaces. It is large enough to accommodate several subjects at a time. The supply air is purified by passage through a high-temperature metal oxide (hopcalite) catalyst, a regeneratable sorption bed also containing hopcalite, chemical filters containing

activated carbon and permanganate-impregnated alumina, and high-
efficiency particulate filters. Gases and particulates commonly
monitored in ambient air are reduced to negligible levels inside the
chamber. Very few facilities with this degree of environmental
control have been built: they are costly in terms of capital investment, construction time, technical personnel requirements, and
maintenance. The majority of exposure laboratories currently in
operation use only chemical and particulate filters, which provide
air purification adequate for many experimental purposes.

Initial studies in our exposure chamber, conducted during the
mid-1970's, dealt with ozone and other pollutants found in Los
Angeles smog (12-14). The exposure protocol was similar to that of
Bates et al. Their findings concerning ozone were confirmed qualitatively, but the quantitative dose-response curves were different,
our Los Angeles subjects being generally less reactive than the
Montreal residents studied by Bates's group. The discrepancy might
have been an effect of interfering factors in one or both studies.
This possibility was examined in a collaborative study (15) in which
both Montreal and Los Angeles subjects were exposed to ozone, and
measurement techniques were compared. No interfering factors or
methodological differences adequate to explain the different results
were found. The results of the previous separate studies were
generally confirmed: some Canadians were considerably more reactive
than any of the Los Angeles subjects in terms of symptomatology and
lung function test results. Thus, although other possibilities
could not be ruled out, it appeared that Los Angeles residents
somehow developed an adaptation to ozone as a result of frequent
ambient exposures. This hypothesis was supported in another experiment comparing long-term residents and new arrivals in a student
population (16). Since then, adaptation has been demonstrated
directly in several laboratories by exposing volunteers to ozone
repeatedly (17-19). The clinical and physiological responses dimin-
ish markedly after two or three exposures. Whether these findings
relate directly to the apparent reduced reactivity in Los Angeles
residents is not clear, since the laboratory-induced adaptation
appears to require exposures more severe than those typically experienced in Los Angeles ambient air. The underlying biological mechanism of the adaptive response is not understood, nor is it known
whether any long-term benefit or harm results.

When volunteers in our laboratory were exposed to mixed ozone
and sulfur dioxide, little enhancement of response was observed
relative to ozone alone, in contrast to the results of Hazucha and
Bates (11). A second collaborative study was undertaken to investigate this discrepancy (20). Marked reactivity to the mixed gases was
confirmed in some Montreal subjects; but we were not able to compare
their responses to ozone alone, and thus could not directly test for
ozone-sulfur dioxide synergism. However, an important observation
was made in the atmospheric monitoring: large numbers of very small

particles formed in the exposure chamber when the mixed gases were present. These appeared to be sulfuric acid, formed by a reaction between ozone and sulfur dioxide catalyzed by trace hydrocarbon contaminants. The total mass of particulate formed in the Rancho Los Amigos chamber was small, but a much larger amount appeared to form in the Montreal chamber when it was examined retrospectively. Thus it appeared that sulfuric acid (or some other particulate substance) might have contributed to the effects observed in the Montreal study of ozone and sulfur dioxide. This issue is still not completely resolved. A more recent similar study by Bedi et al. (21), in which relatively little aerosol should have been present, showed no substantially enhanced effect of the mixed gases compared to ozone alone. Thus overall it seems unlikely that ozone and sulfur dioxide per se act synergistically in producing respiratory effects. Still of public-health concern is the possibility that they interact with particulates, since in ambient exposures particulates are virtually always present along with gases.

Deliberate (as opposed to inadvertent) investigation of particulate pollutants has not been carried out on a substantial scale until recently, since generation and monitoring are much more difficult with particulates than with gases. Particles in ambient air are difficult to analyze reliably, thus there is usually some uncertainty as to how the ambient material should be simulated in the laboratory. The size distribution (critically dependent on relative humidity) as well as the mass concentration of the laboratory aerosol must be given careful attention. Possible reactions with trace exposure-chamber contaminants must be investigated since they may change the character of the exposure atmosphere substantially. For example, an acidic aerosol may be neutralized by traces of ammonia exuded by the subjects. In our laboratory, an apparatus to generate water-soluble aerosols over a wide range of concentrations and size distributions has been developed, and volunteers have been exposed to sulfuric acid and its ammonia neutralization products (22) and to ammonium nitrate (23). Little or no effect of these substances on respiratory function has been detected in two-hour exposures to concentrations potentially attainable in severely polluted ambient air. Other recent studies of sulfate and nitrate salts (24,25) have employed shorter exposure times and substantially higher concentrations; again, little or no effect has been found.

Rather than create synthetic (and invariably somewhat unrealistic) pollutant exposure atmospheres, one may study real ambient pollution by setting up an exposure experiment at an appropriate location. This requires a means of exposing volunteers under blind conditions to purified air as well as to unaltered ambient air. Some rigor is lost in this approach: the ambient exposure conditions will vary unpredictably, and it will not often be possible to identify a specified pollutant as the cause of an observed effect. On the other hand, the relevance of the findings to real-world exposure problems is considerably more clear than in conventional laboratory studies. We conducted a field study in an oxidant-polluted area near Los Angeles, employing a mobile laboratory designed to duplicate the capabilities of a fixed human exposure laboratory on a smaller scale (26). When subjects breathed ambient air during peak oxidant hours, slight but statistically significant respiratory physiological and clinical decrements were found, relative to control studies in which the exposure air was passed through chemical and high-efficiency particulate filters (27).

The series of developments just discussed related primarily to improvements in experimental exposure capability. Another area in which improvements are continually sought is the sensitivity of biological measures of response. As suggested earlier, physiological indices considered highly sensitive to exposure effects are likely to be highly variable under control conditions, so there may be difficulty in distinguishing between "signal" and "noise" in the data obtained.

One potentially very sensitive response test involves quantitating the reactivity of the airways to irritant stimuli by challenging the subject with increasing doses of a bronchoconstricting drug (histamine or an acetylcholine analog). If exposure to a pollutant subtly damages the respiratory tract, there may be no overt symptoms or changes in function tests used in previously-mentioned studies. However, the effect might still be detected by an increased response to a given dose of bronchoconstrictor administered during the pollutant exposure. (Bronchoconstrictor response is measured as increased airway resistance or reduced forced expiratory performance.) This approach was employed by Jean Orehek and coworkers of Marseilles, France in a study of asthmatic volunteers' responses to nitrogen dioxide (28). The subjects were exposed for one hour to 0.1 or 0.2 ppm of the gas, thus receiving a dose easily attained in ambient exposures and considerably lower than required to produce significant effects directly (judging from other studies). Many, though not all, of the subjects appeared to be more responsive to the bronchoconstrictor during the pollutant exposure than under control conditions. This would suggest that, if natural airborne allergens or other irritants acted similarly to the bronchoconstricting drug, nitrogen dioxide pollution might potentiate their tendency to cause asthmatic attacks. Although these results were published several years ago and have provoked some controversy, there have been no serious efforts to confirm them until very recently.

Another possibly very sensitive response index which has been investigated by another European group is arterial blood oxygen tension. This might be disturbed, even in the absence of overt respiratory changes, if a pollutant exerted most of its effect on small peripheral airways or on the alveolar-capillary interface.

Ozone is one pollutant which acts in just such a fashion, at least in animal toxicologic studies. G. von Nieding and associates of Moers, Germany (29) investigated arterial oxygenation in healthy volunteers exposed two hours to 0.1 ppm ozone--again, a dose well within the ambient range and much lower than those found to produce respiratory function changes in other studies. Ear lobe capillary blood was sampled after "arterialization" by application of heat and a vasodilator--a procedure less difficult and uncomfortable than direct arterial sampling, but potentially more subject to inaccuracies. A modest but statistically significant decrease in blood oxygen tension was reported to occur with ozone exposure. A similar study in our laboratory employed both ear lobe blood sampling and direct arterial sampling in volunteers exposed to 0.2 ppm ozone (30). No major differences between ear lobe and arterial measurements were found, and changes in oxygen tension attributable to ozone were not significant. The reasons for the discrepancy between ours and the German findings are not clear, although adaptation to ambient ozone in Los Angeles area residents might be suggested as a contributing factor.

Blood biochemistry is still another area of concern in the search for sensitive response indices. Blood is the only internal tissue which can be sampled readily in human subjects, and the first target of inhaled pollutants which pass beyond the respiratory tract. Oxidation of red-cell enzymes by ozone and stimulation of anti-oxidant defenses during ozone exposure have attracted considerable interest. Initial studies of these phenomena in our laboratory showed significant and apparently dose-related effects occurring in conjunction with respiratory changes (14,31). In one study of asthmatics, small significant biochemical changes were found in the absence of any meaningful physiological or clinical effects (32). However, it has become apparent that these biochemical responses are not specific to pollutant exposure, but also occur with other stresses such as heat and exercise, even in clean air (33). At present, it is not clear whether they are of any significance in relation to adverse health effects of pollutant exposure.

The foregoing review has obviously left out much of scientific and public-health importance. It is limited to experimental studies which, besides being familiar to the present authors, serve to illustrate important problems and means of addressing them. Hopefully, it has adequately illustrated that there are many worthwhile avenues of investigation which can be most productively followed through human exposure studies, but that all such studies are beset with complex scientific and practical problems which dictate a continuous search for better solutions. The usefulness of human-study results in risk assessment of course depends on careful design and execution of the experiments. Even with optimum design, the degree to which inherent problems can be overcome is limited by available resources and the current technological state of the art. (The same could of

course be said of other fields of investigation.) As with any other
application of scientific data in the evaluation of public-health
risks, the inherent limitations of the particular experimental
approach should be taken into account carefully when translating the
results into public policy.

WHERE WE ARE NOW--CURRENT KNOWLEDGE OF AIR POLLUTION HEALTH RISKS
FROM HUMAN STUDIES AND OTHER FIELDS

Comprehensive reviews of the effects of various pollutants have
been published recently by the National Academy of Sciences and the
World Health Organization, as well as by the Environmental Protection
Agency in the form of Air Quality Criteria documents. The following
very brief survey attempts to define the current state of the information base applicable to risk assessment, in terms of firm knowledge, controversial or unconfirmed findings, and identifiable gaps
in knowledge which should be the focus of additional research
efforts.

Ozone is the respiratory irritant pollutant most thoroughly
investigated by human studies, and the only one which has consistently shown adverse exposure effects at doses attainable in ambient
exposures. Firm dose-response relationships have been determined for
the effects on forced expiratory performance, and data from different
laboratories are in reasonably good quantitative agreement (34).
Lung function decrement and symptom responses have been well documented at concentrations of 0.3 ppm and above. Slight responses have
been suggested but not confirmed at 0.25 ppm with light intermittent
exercise, and at 0.15 ppm with heavy continuous exercise. As mentioned previously, disturbance of blood oxygenation has been reported
in one study at 0.1 ppm, but not in another at 0.2 ppm. These findings relate to exposure times of 2 hr or less. The few epidemiologic
studies of short-term clinical effects generally are in agreement
with the controlled-exposure studies, in that they have found significantly increased incidence of respiratory complaints at times of
high ambient ozone levels. Ozone effects have not been investigated
to any meaningful extent, by controlled studies or by epidemiology,
in certain population groups likely to be at increased risk from
ambient exposure. These include children, the elderly, and people
with chronic respiratory diseases. People with mild to moderate
asthma have been studied fairly extensively; they have sometimes
appeared more reactive than healthy people, but the evidence for
this is not conclusive. In animal toxicologic studies, distinct
pulmonary pathological lesions have been shown to occur in exposures
only slightly beyond the ambient range, in terms of concentration
and exposure time.

Nitrogen dioxide is an oxidizing pollutant like ozone, but
appears substantially less toxic in animal studies. Respiratory

function and symptoms have been studied in asthmatics and mild
chronic bronchitics as well as in healthy people exposed to nitrogen
dioxide. At concentrations representative of severe ambient exposures (0.5 to 1 ppm, exposure times of one or more hours), little or
no effect has been found. As previously discussed, one group of
asthmatics exposed to 0.1 ppm appeared to have increased bronchial
reactivity. Further studies of this phenomenon are needed, and
several are now in progress. Epidemiologic investigation of nitrogen
dioxide has been difficult, and its results inconclusive, since other
potential respiratory irritants are nearly always present with it in
ambient exposures.

Relatively few human studies of sulfur dioxide have been
published, and those which dealt with concentrations relevant to
ambient exposures (below 1 ppm) generally have shown little effect.
Animal studies likewise generally have not shown obvious harm at
these low concentrations. However, elevated ambient sulfur dioxide
levels have been associated with excess respiratory morbidity and
mortality in a considerable number of epidemiologic studies, including some conducted fairly recently (when exposure levels were much
lower than in earlier studies, thanks to pollution control improvements in the interim). Explaining the discrepancy between laboratory
and epidemiologic findings on sulfur-containing pollutants is one of
the more important current problems in risk assessment. It has been
suggested that particulate sulfate compounds rather than sulfur dioxide are responsible for the epidemiologically-observed effects.
However, no sulfate or other particulate substance has shown substantial toxic effects in human studies at ambient concentrations.
Synergistic interaction between sulfur dioxide and other gases or
particulates remains a plausible explanation for increased morbidity
during sulfur pollution episodes, although laboratory evidence for
synergism is not convincing overall. One must also consider the
possibility that either the epidemiologic or the laboratory results
are invalid. Undetected and uncontrolled interferences could well
produce spurious positive epidemiologic findings. Negative laboratory findings could be misleading if insufficiently sensitive test
populations or response measurements were used, or if exposure
conditions did not adequately represent ambient exposure stresses.
Exposure times are one area in which typical human studies may not
be fully adequate to simulate ambient exposures to sulfur compounds.
Practical concerns usually limit laboratory studies to a few hours,
whereas ambient episodes may last for several days. This currently
unresolvable controversy over the health consequences of sulfur
pollution exposure illustrates the need to exercise caution in interpreting the results from any one field of investigation: even if
they are highly consistent within themselves, they may be called
into question by information from a different but related field.

WHERE WE SHOULD BE GOING--SOME SUGGESTIONS CONCERNING FUTURE
RISK-ASSESSMENT STUDIES OF AIR POLLUTION

Having discussed some of the accomplishments and problems of
air pollution health research, we conclude with some comments on
appropriate courses of action to provide improved risk-assessment
information in the foreseeable future. Specific investigative goals,
more general policies for research planning, and means of applying
results to public policy will be mentioned.

Hopefully, the preceding sections have illustrated the continuing need to extend controlled human studies to more sensitive measures of response, more sensitive populations, and more realistic
exposure conditions. The most immediate need in the area of response
indices is to confirm the validity of techniques such as bronchial
reactivity measurement in detecting responses to low pollutant
concentrations. If this is done, it will then be necessary to
address the question whether these subtle physiological changes truly
represent adverse health effects (or increased risk thereof), or
merely reflect normal homeostasis. The possibly excessively sensitive population groups which need to be studied have been mentioned
previously. Ethical issues arise, of course, when "high-risk" people
are deliberately subjected to an environmental stress. Such actions
are readily justifiable if it can be demonstrated that the stress
bears a clear relationship to the subject's normal environment and
that adequate precautions have been taken, i.e. that the exposure
and the subject's condition are carefully monitored and that predictable emergency situations can be dealt with. On the issue of
more realistic exposure conditions, the need to study more lengthy
exposures and more complex pollutant mixtures has been mentioned.
To insure reasonable choices of conditions, extensive ambient air
monitoring data must be collected and evaluated.

Increased interaction and coordination of effort can and should
be achieved among investigators, funding agencies, and policymakers
with interests in applied risk-assessment research on air pollution.
(More basic research, e.g. that intended to elucidate mechanisms of
physiological response to toxicants, also contributes importantly to
risk assessment, but in a less predictable manner.) The potential
health risks are already reasonably well identified, and the scientific means of evaluating them are reasonably well established. The
problem is to apply the science in the manner which produces information most needed for public-health protection with the least
possible delay, then to apply that information quickly and correctly
to air quality policy decisions. The present framework for policy
decisions is the existing set of EPA Air Quality Criteria documents
and the schedule for revising them at regular intervals. Reference
to this can facilitate scheduling of research projects to obtain
results at opportune times.

Having in mind some fairly clear scientific goals and target dates for achieving them, one then needs to choose an effective investigative strategy. Again, rigor, relevance, and redundancy should be the overall criteria for judgment. Similar but independent studies should be conducted within a given field of investigation. If their results are similar, they will inspire a high degree of confidence; whereas if results are conflicting, the reason for this may be identified and used to design further experiments to resolve the issue. Coordination among different but complementary fields of investigation is also essential to an effective overall strategy. For example, acute, readily reversible exposure effects can be assessed most reliably in human exposure studies. The critically important question whether acute effects eventually lead to chronic irreversible effects cannot be addressed directly in human studies, but can be in animal toxicology. If links could be established between acute and chronic effects observable in animals, and also between acute animal effects and acute human effects, one could then rationally predict what chronic effects were likely in humans receiving long-term ambient exposures. An experimental hypothesis could be developed out of that prediction and tested epidemiologically in appropriate populations. To be sure, coordination of effort among different investigative groups is difficult, since it requires that those involved sacrifice some of their freedom of scientific inquiry. Overly strict and badly planned coordination must be avoided, since it might well result in a multiplication of errors rather than a multiplication of knowledge. Nevertheless, coordination should be encouraged to the extent that it has a reasonable chance to expand the public-policy data base and improve its reliability. Air pollution research consumes large amounts of public funds, and its results can have tremendous impact on public economic health as well as physical health. Those involved should therefore have a special commitment to high productivity and responsiveness to public needs, as well as to traditional scientific values.

The translation of scientific evidence into environmental standards and control regulations is an inherently political process--it involves choices among competing alternative sets of costs and benefits not amenable to objective analysis. Health scientists have no unique competence to make decisions in this process, but they do have a unique responsibility to insure proper use of their findings. Since the regulatory process is generally concerned with recent findings (older, well-established information having been taken into account in previous regulatory decisions), gaps and apparent inconsistencies are usually present in the data base being considered. Thus each competing interest group may be tempted to interpret the data selectively for its own benefit, subverting the scientific evaluation process. This tendency should be vigorously opposed, as it may lead non-scientists to the conclusion that there can be no objective assessment of environmental

health risks, and that researchers deliberately bias their results
to please those who pay for them. The self-interests of all factions
in a regulatory debate require that objective scientific evaluation
of pollutant effects be carried as far as possible before subjective
political debate takes over. Scientists must make and report their
observations without regard to their employers' apparent short-term
self-interests, must insist that their colleagues with competing
self-interests do likewise, and must take pains to demonstrate their
objectivity to other participants in the regulatory process.

We have argued elsewhere (35) that traditional scientific criteria for relating diseases to specific causal factors can be applied
to environmental risk assessment studies, and that these criteria
should be met before experimental findings are accepted as a basis
for public policy decisions. (Exceptions might be made when the exposures in question are easily prevented or the suspected health effects
are catastrophic.) This approach encourages a priori agreement by all
factions on rules for evaluating scientific evidence. The ensuing
scientific debate can then be largely separated from the ultimate political debate, and can provide the latter with the best possible fac-
tual basis. In addition, this process focuses attention on inconsistencies among different studies, encouraging efforts to identify and
overcome methodological deficiencies and to design and perform new
experiments to further advance our understanding of environmental
risks.

ACKNOWLEDGMENTS

The more recent work in our laboratory discussed here has been
supported by the Electric Power Research Institute, the Coordinating
Research Council, and Southern California Edison Company. Among the
many people who have contributed to our field over a number of years,
one to whom we are especially indebted is Dr. David Bates, who has
provided us with invaluable scientific and historical insights.

REFERENCES

1. Richardson, B. W.: Diseases of Modern Life. Macmillan and Co.,
      London, pp. 61-66 (1876)

2. Air Quality Criteria for Sulfur Oxides, Publication No. AP-50,
      National Air Pollution Control Administration, Washington,
      D. C., pp. 91-112 (1969)

3. Air Quality Criteria for Photochemical Oxidants, Publication
      No. AP-63, National Air Pollution Control Administration,
      Washington, D.C., Chapt. 8 (1970)

4. Amdur, M.O., Silverman, L., and Drinker, P.: Inhalation of
   sulfuric acid mist by human subjects. Arch. Indust. Hyg.
   Occup. Med., 6: 303 (1952)

5. Frank, N.R., Amdur, M.O., Worcester, J., and Whittenberger, J.L.:
   Effects of acute controlled exposure to SO_2 on respiratory
   mechanics in healthy male adults. J. Appl. Physiol. 17: 252
   (1962)

6. Frank, N.R., Amdur, M.O., and Whittenberger, J.L.: A comparison
   of the acute effects of SO_2 administered alone or in combination
   with NaCl particles on the respiratory mechanics of healthy
   adults. Int. J. Air Water Pollution, 8: 125 (1964)

7. Speizer, F.E., and Frank, N.R.: A comparison of changes in
   pulmonary flow resistance in healthy volunteers acutely exposed
   to SO_2 by mouth and by nose. Brit. J. Indust. Med., 23: 75
   (1966)

8. Bates, D.V., Bell, G., Burnham, C., Hazucha, M., Mantha, J.,
   Pengelly, L.D., and Silverman, F.: Problems in studies of human
   exposure to air pollutants. Can. Med. Assoc. J., 103: 833
   (1970)

9. Bates, D. V., Bell, G.M., Burnham, C.D., Hazucha, M., Mantha, J.,
   Pengelly, L.D., and Silverman, F.: Short-term effects of ozone
   on the lung. J. Appl. Physiol., 32: 176 (1972)

10. Hazucha, M., Silverman, F., Parent, C., Field, S., and Bates, D.
    V.: Pulmonary function in man after short-term exposure to
    ozone. Arch. Environ. Health, 27: 183 (1973)

11. Hazucha, M., and Bates, D.V.: Combined effect of ozone and sulfur
    dioxide on human pulmonary function. Nature, 257: 50 (1975)

12. Hackney, J.D., Linn, W.S., Buckley, R.D., Pedersen, E.E., Karuza,
    S.K., Law, D.C., and Fischer, D.A.: Experimental studies on
    human health effects of air pollutants. I. Design consider-
    ations. Arch. Environ. Health, 30: 373 (1975)

13. Hackney, J.D., Linn, W.S., Mohler, J.G., Pedersen, E.E.,
    Breisacher, P., and Russo, A.: Experimental studies on human
    health effects of air pollutants. II. Four-hour exposure to
    ozone alone and in combination with other pollutant gases.
    Arch. Environ. Health, 30: 379 (1975)

14. Hackney, J.D., Linn, W.S., Law, D.C., Karuza, S.K., Greenberg, H.,
    Buckley, R.D., and Pedersen, E.E.: Experimental studies on
    human health effects of air pollutants. III. Two-hour exposure

to ozone alone and in combination with other pollutant gases.
Arch. Environ. Health, 30: 385 (1975)

15. Hackney, J.D., Linn, W.S., Karuza, S.K., Buckley, R.D., Law, D.C.,
    Bates, D.V., Hazucha, M., Pengelly, L.D., and Silverman, F.:
    Effects of ozone exposure in Canadians and Southern Californians:
    evidence for adaptation? Arch. Environ. Health, 32: 110 (1977)

16. Hackney, J.D., Linn, W.S., Buckley, R.D., and Hislop, H.J.:
    Studies in adaptation to ambient oxidant air pollution: Effects
    of ozone exposure in Los Angeles residents vs. new arrivals.
    Environ. Health Perspectives, 18: 141 (1976)

17. Hackney, J.D., Linn, W.S., Mohler, J.G., and Collier, C.R.:
    Adaptation to short-term respiratory effects of ozone in men
    exposed repeatedly. J. Appl. Physiol., 43: 82 (1977)

18. Farrell, B.P., Kerr, H.D., Kulle, T.J., Sauder, L.R., and Young,
    J.L.: Adaptation in human subjects to the effects of inhaled
    ozone after repeated exposure. Am. Rev. Respir. Disease,
    119: 725 (1979)

19. Folinsbee, L.J., Bedi, J.F., and Horvath, S.M.: Respiratory
    responses in humans repeatedly exposed to low concentrations
    of ozone. Am. Rev. Respir. Disease, 121: 431 (1980)

20. Bell, K.A., Linn, W.S., Hazucha, M., Hackney, J.D., and Bates,
    D.V.: Respiratory effects of exposure to ozone plus sulfur
    dioxide in Southern Californians and Eastern Canadians.
    Am. Ind. Hyg. Assoc. J., 38: 696 (1977)

21. Bedi, J.F., Folinsbee, L.J., Horvath, S.M., and Ebenstein, R.S.:
    Human exposure to sulfur dioxide and ozone: Absence of a
    synergistic effect. Arch. Environ. Health, 34: 233 (1979)

22. Avol, E.L., Jones, M.P., Bailey, R.M., Chang, N.N., Kleinman,
    M.T., Linn, W.S., Bell, K.A. and Hackney, J.D.: Controlled
    exposures of human volunteers to sulfate aerosols: Health
    effects and aerosol characterization. Am. Rev. Respir. Disease,
    120: 319 (1979)

23. Kleinman, M.T., Linn, W.S., Bailey, R.M., Jones, M.P., and
    Hackney, J.D.: Effect of ammonium nitrate aerosol on human
    respiratory function and symptoms. Environ. Res., in press

24. Sackner, M.A., Ford, D., Fernandez, R., Cipley, J., Perez, D.,
    Kwoka, M., Reinhart, R., Michaelson, E.D., Schreck, R., and
    Wanner, A.: Effects of sulfuric acid aerosol on cardiopulmonary
    function of dogs, sheep, and humans. Am. Rev. Respir. Disease,
    118: 497 (1978)

25. Utell, M.J., Swinburne, A.J., Hyde, R.W., Speers, D.M., Gibb, F.R., and Morrow, P.E.: Airway reactivity to nitrates in normal and mild asthmatic subjects. J. Appl. Physiol., 46: 189 (1979)

26. Avol, E.L., Wightman, L.H., Linn, W.S., and Hackney, J.D.: A movable laboratory for controlled clinical studies of air pollution exposure. Air Pollut. Control Assoc. J., 29: 743 (1979)

27. Linn, W.S., Jones, M.P., Bachmayer, E.A., Spier, C.E., Mazur, S.F., Avol, E.L., and Hackney, J.D.: Short-term respiratory effects of polluted ambient air: A laboratory study of volunteers in a high-oxidant community. Am. Rev. Respir. Disease, 121: 243 (1980)

28. Orehek, J., Massari, J.P., Gayrard, P., Grimaud, C., and Charpin, J.: Effect of short-term, low-level nitrogen dioxide exposure on bronchial sensitivity of asthmatic patients. J. Clin. Invest., 57: 301 (1976)

29. von Nieding, G., Wagner, M., Lollgen, H., and Krekeler, H.: Acute effects of ozone on the pulmonary function of man. VDI-Berichte, 270: 173 (1977)

30. Linn, W.S., Jones, M.P., Bachmayer, E.A., Clark, K. W., Karuza, S.K., and Hackney, J.D.: Effect of low-level exposure to ozone on arterial oxygenation in humans. Am. Rev. Respir. Disease, 119: 731 (1979)

31. Buckley, R.D., Hackney, J.D., Clark, K., and Posin, C.: Ozone and human blood. Arch. Environ. Health, 30: 40 (1975)

32. Linn, W.S., Buckley, R.D., Spier, C.E., Blessey, R.L., Jones, M.P., Fischer, D.A., and Hackney, J.D.: Health effects of ozone exposure in asthmatics. Am. Rev. Respir. Disease, 117: 835 (1978)

33. Hackney, J.D., Linn, W.S., Buckley, R.D., Collier, C.R., and Mohler, J.G.: Respiratory and biochemical adaptations in men repeatedly exposed to ozone. In Environmental Stress: Individual Human Adaptations, Ed. by L.J. Folinsbee et al. Academic Press, New York, pp. 111-124 (1978)

34. Folinsbee, L.J., Drinkwater, B.L., Bedi, J.F., and Horvath, S.M.: Influence of exercise on the pulmonary function changes due to exposure to low concentrations of ozone. In Environmental Stress: Individual Human Adaptations, Ed. by L. J. Folinsbee et al. Academic Press, New York, pp. 125-145 (1978)

35. Hackney, J.D., and Linn, W.S.: Koch's postulates updated: A
    potentially useful application to laboratory research and
    policy analysis in environmental toxicology. Am Rev. Respir.
    Disease, 119: 849 (1979)

DISCUSSION

ABRAHAMSON: Would this study represent a realistic laboratory exposure?

HACKNEY: For humans "realistic laboratory exposures" are determined
by ambient exposure levels that have been documented or are predicted
for the near future. If ethically permissible, we typically use
worst-case conditions and look for effects in healthy subjects. If
effects are found, then we look for dose-response relationships at
lower concentrations. If no effects are found, and the ethics of it
can be dealt with, we recruit sensitive subjects for testing. Or,
perhaps, go higher in concentrations to relate to other areas such
as occupational environments. This, again, must be justified ethically.

BERG: You spoke of two goals. One was to improve the reliability
and sensitivity of the tests, and the other to identify the high
risk subpopulation. I would like to suggest that this is ethically
mandated by what two philosophers told us in the first session.
Because by extending the dose-effect functions, we do what Dr.
Spielman suggested and reduce the frequency of erroneous decisions
based on the test. And in identifying the high risk population we
do what Dr. Seidenfeld suggested and reduce the lower case k, which
is the number of people for whom we should really try to provide
protection. And so we hasten some workable decision to protect them.

BOURDEAU: On the basis of your experiment, would you be able to
recommend primary standards for ozone?

HACKNEY: I think standard setting is a process which involves both
the data base, hopefully a verifiable data base, and the judgments
of acceptability of risk. I think that this kind of experimental
information is a good starting point for the verifiable data base,
and will be helpful to the decision makers who have to consider other
issues as well. I think that investigators ought to stay out of that
area (judging acceptability of risk). I certainly want to stay out
of it because I don't have any expertise in it.

BOURDEAU: Have you had a chance to look at the effects of PAN?

HACKNEY: Others have looked at PAN (peroxyacetyl nitrate) in similar
kinds of studies, and have not found irritant effects on the respiratory system. Eye irritation has been reported; I don't remember

what the concentrations of PAN were, but respiratory tract irritation was not shown at realistic concentrations.

MORROW: Dr. Hackney, since there are thousands of materials involved in air pollution, the use of something like your field test is obviously very attractive because you have a complex mixture involved in the exposure. Do you find this to represent a particular advantage for human studies, or do you think there are disadvantages that offset this in relation to you laboratory studies?

HACKNEY: Well, you lose some control of exposure variables and the hassle for the investigators is worse. But I think that in general it isn't any more expensive to do it this way, and it makes a lot of sense to try it where possible. The situation I showed is a good one for field tests. It's the first one we've tried. Fortunately, the environment turned out to be very cooperative the summer we were in the San Gabriel Valley. It was so predictable that only a very few days didn't have concentrations that were of some interest; on one or two days it rained. It was almost like going to the laboratory and turning on the switch. You didn't know quite what concentration you were going to get each day, but it was something of interest.

A disadvantage of this kind of work is that you have to try and keep the subjects guessing as to which is the control day and which is the exposure day.

MORROW: These are all single blind experiments, in that case?

HACKNEY: In some of our laboratory work we're able to make it quasi-double blind except for the safety officer, but in this situation it would be very difficult to fool the staff. We're going to repeat the San Gabriel Valley study this summer at a much higher exercise level than we used in the study I talked about. And we think we know enough about it now, based on our experience, to randomize the exposure. Before, we had to do all of the exposures first and then match them three weeks or so later. That is, match the temperature and the humidity and clean up the air for the appropriate control. And although we didn't tell the subjects about that, they may or may not have known it. We plan to randomize clean air and ambient exposures in the next San Gabriel Valley study. In our field laboratory studies, we lose rigor with the single blind design, but gain relevancy by using ambient pollution.

MORROW: Did you undertake many more analyses than you would ordinarily, say for hydrocarbons?

HACKNEY: In the first studies in the San Gabriel Valley and the ones in the Hawthorne area, we measured the criteria gases as well as the particulates, by a variety of methods. We sampled inside and outside the chamber for total suspended particulates; we looked at various size fractions. We determined sulphates, nitrates, the metals, and we'll be doing even more extensive analyses this coming summer.

ALBERT: Did you say that Bates got a bigger response with the combination of ozone and SO_2 than you did because there was more sulphuric acid in his chamber?

HACKNEY: That seems the most likely explanation, based on our experimental results.

HACKNEY: First, the Montreal chamber was really the earliest one; this kind of work, as I mentioned, started early in the seventies. It's a plexiglas chamber and they used building air as the source. There was no absolute filtering, no HEPA filtering, and no gas scrubbing. In retrospective studies background pollutants were found to be high.

Second, the gases were introduced in such a way that they impinged on each other at fairly high concentrations and were then swept into the chamber. That's another potentially good way of producing sulphuric aerosols, if you have some other contaminants present.

And finally, in retrospective sampling significant amounts of particulates were formed under operating conditions that supposedly were the same as in the previous study.

TOTTER: Is there no need to postulate some adaptation to these exposures? Or do you still think it's possible for people to adapt to them?

HACKNEY: There are several pieces of experimental evidence suggesting that at least some Los Angeles residents adapt after repeated oxidant exposures. There is direct evidence in the laboratory showing that symptoms and respiratory function changes go away with repeated exposures to ozone. One remaining difficulty is that the studies in the laboratory have been at slightly higher concentrations than are typical for Los Angeles, although they're reached in Los Angeles occasionally. So, laboratory studies have not been extended to really low concentrations; adaptation may be more difficult to demonstrate directly if they are extended. Still, experimental studies suggest that this phenomena (called adaptation) does occur and is occurring in Los Angeles.

SAGAN: I'd like to ask about that interaction between ozone and sulphuric acid. As I understand it, there was a strong interaction, a synergistic effect beyond an additive effect. Is that correct?

HACKNEY: The Montreal studies showed what would reasonably be interpreted as a more than additive effect. But this doesn't rule out alternate explanations, such as some combination of ozone plus particulates plus SO_2.

Other possible explanations are that other pollutants could have interfered with the measurements, or that with relatively few subjects results may have been spurious; such methodologic issues must be faced. The study has not been replicated and the results have not been confirmed.

SAGAN: The Clean Air Act requires that standards be established for the primary gases. Now, if there are strong interactions and if mixtures of gases produce effects that can't be predicted on the basis of knowledge of individual gases, how do you reconcile those laws, or do those observations make nonsense of such a legal requirement?

That's part one of the question. Part two of the question I'd like to direct to Dr. Pochin. I believe that in England you have no air pollution regulations. Does that mean that you agree that regulating individual gases is not a reasonable way to control health effects of air pollution?

HACKNEY: As far as I know there are no convincing replicated studies showing that synergism is a problem in the sense that you're asking about.

POCHIN: I think I haven't an answer there because we've taken pretty strong and clearly effective action against the release of particulates within towns in which there were previously fogs, and liability to fogs in certain inversion weather conditions. But I don't think we have regulations against gas concentrations. It is regulation at the source rather than in the medium.

PROBLEMS AND POSSIBILITIES OF DETERMINING THE CARCINOGENIC POTENCY

OF INHALABLE FIBROUS DUSTS AND POLYCYCLIC AROMATIC HYDROCARBONS

Friedrich Pott, René Tomingas, and Johann Koenig

Medical Institute for Environmental Hygiene at the
University, Duesseldorf, and Fraunhofer-Institute for
Toxicology and Aerosol Research, Muenster, FRG.

ABSTRACT

The mechanism of tumor induction by asbestos fibers seems to
depend on the elongated shape of the particles (fibers, needles).
Thus even non-asbestos fibers may be carcinogenic under certain
conditions. A hypothesis is presented describing the gradual transition between the maximal and the minimal carcinogenic potency of
fibers in relation to their lengths and diameters. At workplaces
there are normally considerable differences between asbestos and
vitreous mineral fibers concerning the effective dose, i.e., the
carcinogenic potency of a defined concentration of dust. Therefore the substitution of asbestos by man-made mineral fibers is
justified from the view of the preventive medicine. However, when
using extremely thin glass fibers precaution is necessary.

An essential contribution of the PAH content in the atmosphere
to the incidence of lung cancer has not been proven, but this cannot be excluded, particularly in Europe, because of the relatively
high PAH concentrations. In the atmosphere much more than 100 PAH
are found; however, measuring a few PAH seems to be sufficient for
assessing the carcinogenic potency of the PAH content in the atmosphere. An index has been elaborated to characterize the PAH level;
the PAH units are based on the concentrations of 5 PAH in the air
and on 5 evaluation factors.

The cancer risk for the common people due to inhalation of
fibers or PAH cannot be determined scientifically. Consequently
there is no possibility of establishing air quality standards. In
Germany, however, the establishment of preventive guides for car-

cinogenic substances has been considered in order to restrict the risk of cancer.

INTRODUCTION

Inhalable fibrous dusts and polycyclic aromatic hydrocarbons (PAH) are physically and chemically two completely different groups of substances. However, with regard to their occurrence as air pollutants they have one dangerous fact in common: both consist of a mixture of carcinogenic, non-carcinogenic and weakly carcinogenic components, although the mechanisms causing carcinogenic effects are not similar for fibers and PAH.

The presence of an airborne group of related substances which differ significantly with respect to their individual carcinogenic potency leads to the following questions:
- Is it possible to determine the total carcinogenic potency of such a mixture of substances by way of a measuring technique providing a set of data for a specific evaluation model?
- Or, are evaluation systems not sufficiently reliable so that it would be better to limit the analysis to a single well-known carcinogenic component and to neglect the others because of lack of sufficient knowledge of their actual influence?

For the purist, only models based upon precise knowledge are scientifically acceptable. However, from the view point of preventive medicine, it is better for the prevention of cancer to have pragmatic assessments of the carcinogenic potency of pollutants than waiting for the exact scientific results in the distant future.

Moreover, whether it would be reasonable to set exposure limits for carcinogens, although dose-response relationships are unknown, must be considered.

Part I: FIBROUS DUSTS

Why does asbestos induce tumors? What is the carcinogenic agent? In recent years, animal experiments have established strong evidence for the old hypothesis that the elongated shape of an asbestos particle represents a carcinogenic agent: very thin glass fibers as well as other non-asbestos fibers induce tumors in rats after intrapleural or intraperitoneal administration [1,2,3]. In contrast, granular dusts which, by chemical composition are similar to asbestos, induce no or only a few tumors. These results were confirmed repeatedly. They suggest a mechanism of tumor induction not yet described as a characteristic of any other carcinogen: the fibrous shape must be regarded as being physically carcinogenic.

On the basis of these facts and in view of the increasing number of asbestos-induced tumors in man, it seems to become more

and more mandatory to establish a correct definition of a carcinogenic fiber.

The significance of length and diameter of a fiber with regard to its carcinogenic potency

A suitable yardstick or index for measuring the dose of a
chemical carcinogen is the total mass of the agent incorporated.
In the situation that the particle shape respresents the carcinogenic agent, the mass is not a suitable criterion of the effective
dose, but rather the number of particles possessing a specified
shape.

Then, the question arises as to what is the characteristic
shape of a carcinogenic fiber: Figures 1a - 1f show a variety of
fibers. Obviously, there are extensive variations of the shape,
e.g., length, diameter, length/diameter or aspect ratio, and other
characteristics. If the incomplete incorporation of a fiber in a
cell proves to be the first important step for tumor induction [4],
then it appears reasonable to assume that a fiber could be too short
to induce a carcinogenic effect, because its dimension is less likely
to irritate a single cell. Besides, the aspect ratio may make it
almost a granular particle. Furthermore, it may also be assumed
that a fiber might be too thick to irritate single cells and consequently to be carcinogenic.

Anyway, it was a step into the right direction, when the fiber
number instead of the fiber mass was evaluated in workplace atmospheres. However, at that time there were indications, with regard
to fibrosis, that longer fibers show more activity than shorter
ones, and it was further clear, that fibers with diameters above
3 µm do not reach the alveolar space. Therefore, to be pragmatic,
it was decided that fibers should only be counted if they were
longer than 5 µm, thinner than 3 µm, had a length/diameter ratio
above 3 [5,6].

Today, asbestos fibers in workplaces are counted according to
this definition and the threshold limit value of 2 fibers/ml of air
refers to it, also. However, this threshold value was only established in order to prevent the development of asbestosis. It must
be pointed out here that asbestosis does not appear to be a pre-
condition for the development of asbestos-induced mesothelioma.
In numerous cases, after exposure to asbestos, mesothelioma were
found without asbestosis [7,8,9,10]. Either "carcinogenic fiber
sizes" and "fibrogenic fiber sizes" are not identical, or fewer
numbers of fibers may be sufficient for tumor induction than for
fibrosis.

Certainly, the present definition of fibers is a pragmatic
convention and justified as such. However, it should be kept in

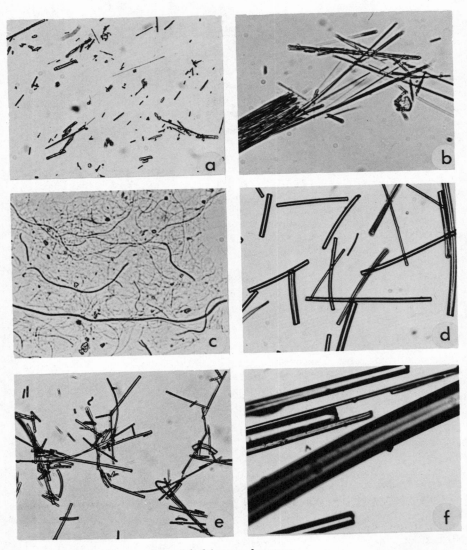

Fig. 1   a   Crocidolite asbestos
         b   Crocidolite (split bundle of fibers)
         c   Chrysotile asbestos
         d   Glass fibers (Safil)
         e   Glass fibers (JM 100)
         f   Rockwool fibers

mind that it has no sound scientific basis. General evidence exists
that a long thin fiber possesses a high carcinogenic potency, therefore, if the carcinogenicity decreases with the decreasing length
of a fiber or with the increasing diameter, we may conclude that a
continuous transition must exist between the fiber dimensions of
maximum carcinogenic potency and those that are not carcinogenic.
It would be illogical to assume that there could be a huge step
function for the carcinogenicity or fibrogenicity of a fiber of
4.9 μm length compared to another one 5.1 μm long. At present however, such a relationship is an implicit consequence of the fiber
definition for the Threshold Limit Value [TLV] of the U.S.A. or the
Technical Guiding Concentration [TGC] of West Germany.

    Figure 2 [11] illustrates the working hypothesis regarding the
carcinogenic potency of a fiber as a function of its dimensions.
Each size category requires two of three related parameters: length,
diameter and length/diameter ratio. The curves rising from the left
to the right describe, in principle, the increase of the carcinogenic potency of fibers with increasing length. The vertical coordinate of a point on the curves is supposed to indicate a carcinogenicity factor of the fiber size characterized by the coordinate

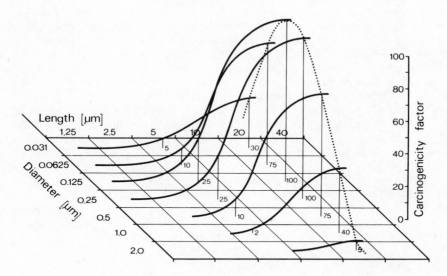

Fig. 2   Hypothesis on the carcinogenic potency of a fiber as a
          function of its size with some data on "carcinogenicity
          factors" [11]. This three-dimensional model requires the
          fiber sizes of a sample to be divided into numerous cate-
          gories. The size categories include three parameters:
          length, diameter and the length/diameter ratio.

location in the length vs. diameter plane. The highest degree of
the carcinogenicity factors is defined as 100. The carcinogenicity
factor decreases not only when the fiber becomes shorter, but also
when it becomes thicker or extremely thin. The curve in the fore-
ground and the background of the three-dimensional graph do not
rise to the level of the curves in between. This suggests that
extremely thin fibers will probably be less carcinogenic than fibers
that are slightly thicker.

The hypothesis outlined above is a general qualitative approach.
It is supported by experimental results [3,12,13], the most extensive
of which were carried out by Stanton [13]. However, at present it
is impossible to give quantitative data for this relationship. For
example: it does not strain the imagination that a large number of
fibers of 2 μm length may possess the same carcinogenic potency as
one 20 μm long fiber. But there is no proof; possibly the true
curves may run along a different slope and/or may be shifted to the
right or left.

The greatest problem for the detection of the carcinogenic
potency of specific fiber sizes in animal experiments is due to the
lack of suitable fiber samples. In order to determine the carcinogenicity factors for the supposedly most important size categories
shown in Figure 2, it would be necessary to have 10 - 20 samples
with fibers of specific and identical length and diameter in each
sample. The more the size intervals of different fiber samples
overlap, the more samples needed to ascertain the carcinogenicity
factor for specific size categories. The problem of developing a
scale or index to determine the carcinogenic potency of fibers in
relation to their dimensions would be merely academic if the fiber
size distribution of different real dust samples were all similar.
For a specific dust, the measurement of a definite, representative,
and easily detectable group of fibers would be sufficient. In
reality, however, the fiber size distributions at workplaces as well
as in the atmosphere show large differences [14,15,16,17].

The present method of evaluation of the carcinogenic potency
of a dust sample containing fibers is very unreliable. Today, however, we cannot yet offer a significantly better dosimetry model
which would appropriately take care of different fiber dimensions
and other relevant factors that are mentioned below.

Further determinants for the carcinogenic potency of a fiber

The hypothetical carcinogenicity factors assigned in Figure 2
are based on the assumption that all fibers are of cylindrical shape
and identical stability and, on inhalation, have the same probability
of being deposited in the lung and reaching the pleura or the
peritoneum. However, for a complete dosimetric assessment of the
carcinogenic potency of a fiber sample, there are actually some

further parameters influencing the effective dose [18]. Following, they are listed without discussion:

- deposition probability (aerodynamic diameter)
- ability to migrate from the airways to the serosa
- change of the number of fibers in the tissue:
    number increase by split up of fibers
    number increase by fracture of long fibers
    number decrease by fracture into non-fibrous pieces
    number decrease by dissolution of fibers
- deviation from cylindrical shape
- elasticity

Some of these parameters, especially the migratory ability of particles to move from the airways into the body and to the serosa, are important only for the induction of a mesothelioma, but others might be essential for the induction of bronchial carcinoma as well.

Man-made mineral fibers - a recommendable substitution for asbestos

From experimental results, the following conclusions appear to be justified: for man, there is a definite probability of a carcinogenic potency of man-made mineral (vitreous) fibers in the same range as asbestos fibers under certain conditions:

- the number of fibers inhaled at work in the glass fiber industry is the same as in the asbestos industry,
- the sizes of the inhaled vitreous and asbestos fibers are the same,
- the durability of vitreous and asbestos fibers in the body is the same.

However, it has to be emphasized that the stated conditions are certainly not fulfilled with regard to the fiber numbers and the fiber sizes in workplaces. The bulk of man-made mineral fibers is greater than 1 μm diameter. Glass fibers cannot split up like the bundles of asbestos fibers which produce many thin fibrils usually with a higher carcinogenic potency (compare figure 1b with figure 1f). Moreover, the workplace concentrations of glass fibers in relation to those of asbestos fibers are mostly much lower [19]. Nevertheless, during the last 20 years, glass fibers with diameters less than 1 μm have been produced in increasing quantities. In view of this increase, the present lack of evidence of mesothelioma in glass fiber workers may pertain to the latent period: this is, for asbestos dust, of the order of 15 to 50 years between the first inhalation and the occurrence of mesothelioma.

Another point of potential difference is the durability of asbestos and vitreous fibers in the tissue. There seem to be significant differences between crocidolite and chrysotile asbestos

as well as between the different kinds of vitreous fibers. There
is a potentially favorable aspect in that it may be possible to
produce very thin vitreous fibers which dissolve in the body after
a relatively short period of time and, thus, lose their carcinogenic
activity.

From the view point of preventive medicine, the substantial
differences between asbestos fibers and vitreous fibers justify the
request to substitute asbestos fibers with vitreous fibers or rock
wools wherever it is technically feasible. However, protective
measures are necessary when the diameters of the vitreous fibers
are less than about 1 μm. For these fibers, a Threshold Limit Value
should be adopted. The recommendation for establishing a size limit
discriminating carcinogenic and non-carcinogenic diameters for
vitreous fibers in the range of 1 μm is problematic and may be
justified only from the pragmatic point of view.

Part II: POLYCYCLIC AROMATIC HYDROCARBONS

For ages, polycyclic aromatic hydrocarbons (PAH) - formed by
combustion of organic material - have been emitted into the environment together with soot. More than 200 years ago, skin cancer was
observed in chimney-sweeps and later on in workers of tar factories:
findings were correlated to the intensive contact with soot and tar.
Since about 50 years, the carcinogenic potency of these materials is
explained by their content of certain PAH, which proved to be carcinogenic in animal experiments. Benzo(a)pyrene (BaP) turned out
to be the best-known compound of this kind.

Today the risk of occupational skin cancer caused by contact
with products containing PAH has been widely reduced due to protective regulations in workplaces and factories. Instead, the question
has arisen as to what extent the relatively low PAH content of the
atmosphere may be responsible for the incidence of bronchial car-
cinomas in workers in specific plants and workplaces as well as in
the common population. There is a large discrepancy between the
enormous efforts in fundamental research made with regard to the
effects and the biochemistry of carcinogenic PAH in comparison with
the limited attention given to PAH as air pollutants potentially
capable of inducing lung cancer.

In Germany, tumors of the respiratory tract of workers in tar
and coke plants are not yet specifically registered as occupational
diseases. During the period between 1963 and 1977, only five cases
with tumors of the respiratory tract were acknowledged to be trace-
able to the effects of tar fumes, tar dust and smoke-box exhaust
and were compensated under a general workmen compensation act [20].

This low number of incidences may give the impression that the
inhalation of PAH, even at high concentrations as found in some

workplaces, seems to be almost without effect. However, any law
suit to get acknowledgement of lung cancer as an occupational disease
will fail when the victim was a smoker - most workers do smoke. To
some extent epidemiological studies in the U.S.A. and in Great
Britain revealed a considerable increase in lung cancer incidence
in workers exposed to polluted air with high PAH concentrations [21,
22,23]. About 20 out of more than 100 PAH detected in the atmosphere were found to be carcinogenic in animal experiments. Inhalation experiments are sill rather rare. However, in one recent study
benzo(a)pyrene did induce numerous tumors in Syrian golden hamsters
after inhalation [24]. Whether or to what extent the incidence of
lung cancer in the common population is due to air pollution, is
controversial. Some authors who investigated this particular
question take the position that air pollution is a relatively insignificant factor [25,26,27]. In this context, an annual mortality
rate of 5 to 10 per 10,000 inhabitants is quoted, a figure
that in no way can simply be neglected. Besides PAH, the polluted
atmosphere includes numerous other substances known to be carcinogenic in men and/or animals [28]. However, many of the carcinogenic
non-PAH compounds appear only in certain locations; elsewhere, their
concentrations are rather low and the influence on lung cancer
incidence may be assumed negligible compared to that of PAH. Next to
smoking, the content of carcinogenic PAH in the atmosphere will
give us in Germany the most reasonable and obvious explanation for
the increase of lung cancer incidence during this century. This is
because the benzo(a)pyrene concentrations in several German cities
were very high; some examples are given in Figure 3. However, in
the last years the concentrations decreased significantly [41].

    In the Federal Republic of Germany, there are about 25,000
victims of lung cancer per year. In Northrhine-Westfalia (this is
that state in West Germany, which has the highest population and
the highest industrialization) the mortality rates of respiratory
tract cancer in males increased from 36 per 100,000 in 1952 to 82
per 100,000 in 1977 [45]. No data are available as to how many
cases may be caused by smoking or by common air pollution and which
fraction of the latter is related to PAH. The present situation
of epidemiological research in this field, the insufficient knowledge
about potential synergistic effects among the various carcinogens
and the presently scarce analytical measurements of the constituents
of general air pollution leave little hope that this question can be
answered within the next 20 years. However, even without detailed
knowledge of the dose-response relationship between PAH concentrations
in the air and lung cancer incidence, the existence of such a
relationship can be anticipated.

    As a consequence, ideas should be promoted with respect to the
scale, or index, by which the carcinogenic potency of the mixture of
carcinogenic, weakly carcinogenic and non-carcinogenic PAH in the
atmosphere could be assessed. For the sake of simplicity, the

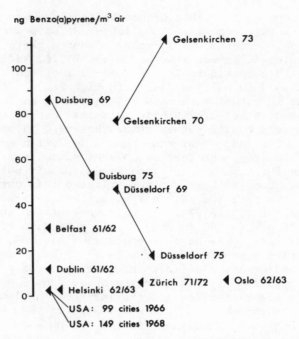

Fig. 3   Benzo(a)pyrene concentrations in the atmosphere (average
         over one year): U.S.A. [29, 30]; Belfast, Dublin, Helsinki,
         Oslo [31]; Zeurich [32]; Duesseldorf [33]; Gelsenkirchen
         [34].

potential influence of all other air pollutants on the carcinogenicity of the PAH will not be taken into account (see Fig. 4).
Otherwise, the problem would have no approximate solution.

Relative proportions (or profiles) of PAH in emissions and in
airborne particulates

     There are several possibilities to establish such an index.
Hitherto, the prevailing idea was to assess the carcinogenicity of
a PAH mixture in relation to the content of a single carcinogenic
component, namely benzo(a)pyrene. In contrast, the analysis of
benzo(a)pyrene is frequently considered as insufficient for serving
as a single indicator for the total group of PAH and its carcinogenic potency because of the relatively unstable structure of
benzo(a)pyrene. To overcome such objections, the analytical techniques of today enable analysts to quantify more than 100 PAH in
the atmosphere [35,36,37]. But what is the use of such numerous
data for a scientist who wants to find a dose-response relationship?

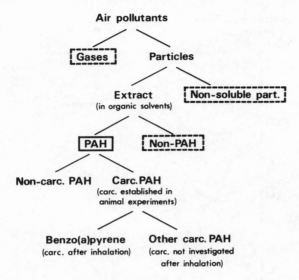

Fig. 4 Separation scheme of air pollutants for isolating PAH.
(In addition to PAH also gases, nonsoluble particulates
and non-PAH generally might contain substances which possess a carcinogenic potency for men, or substances which
can interact chemically or biologically with carcinogens.)

An important objective of research is then to find out as to
whether and to what extent the various PAH may occur in the atmosphere in constant relative proportions. The relations between PAH
found in source emissions do not support an indicator system based
on the concentrations of a few PAH. The analysis of a number of
PAH in effluents from different sources revealed some large differences in relative occurence of different PAH [38,39]. Figure
5 shows the PAH profiles of the emissions from burning different
species of coal, from an oil stove and from an automobile engine.
In view of these large variations it does not seem to be a good basis
for an assessment of the ambient concentrations of the remainder of
the PAH, when only one or a few PAH are analyzed. However, if each
type of emission or ambient pollution has its specific and basically
constant PAH profile, the following measures required for a subsequent assessment of the carcinogenic potency would be:

1.   Separation of the PAH fraction from every source emission
      of importance and from typical residential areas; analysing
      of the PAH profile.

2.   Investigation of each of these PAH fractions in order to

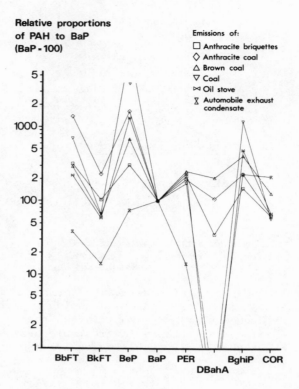

Relative proportions of PAH to BaP (BaP - 100)

Emissions of:
☐ Anthracite briquettes
◇ Anthracite coal
△ Brown coal
▽ Coal
⋈ Oil stove
Ⴟ Automobile exhaust condensate

Fig. 5   PAH profiles in exhaust of several coal species, oil stove
         [38], and automobiles [39]. The values are expressed as a
         ratio to BaP (BaP = 100). Abbreviations: BbFT = benzo(b)
         fluoranthene, BkFT = benzo(k)fluoranthene, BeP = benzo(e)
         pyrene, BaP = benzo(a)pyrene, PER = perylene, DBahA =
         dibenz(a,h)anthracene, BghiP = benzo(ghi)perylene, COR =
         coronene.

         evaluate its carcinogenicity in several tests (determin-
         ation of the dose-response relationship).

3.   Comparison of the results and derivation of specific
         parameters or evaluation factors, which may characterize
         the carcinogenicity of each PAH fraction in relation to
         the others.

4.   Setting up an index for the assessment of the carcino-
         genicity for PAH profiles with large deviations. This
         index must include data of several PAH concentrations
         and the evaluation factors.

   The strict execution of this program would be expensive and
time consuming. This is indicated by the pace of some existing
research projects following this aim for the last 10 years. In view
of this difficulty, it is mandatory to take advantage of the fact
that the profiles obtained for PAH extracted from particulate air
pollutions - as quoted below - are highly uniform.

   Since 1974, atmospheric particulate matter has been collected
on glass fiber filters at several sampling sites in the western part
of Germany and 8 PAH were determined by means of thin layer chromatography and direct fluorimetric measurement: benzo(b)fluoranthene,
benzo(k)fluoranthene, benzo(e)pyrene, benzo(a)pyrene, perylene,
dibenzo(a,h)anthracene, benzo(ghi)perylene, and coronene [40,41].
The sampling sites cannot be considered as representative for all
types of residential areas, but they were located in areas with
different emission sources: industrial complexes, urban residential
districts adjacent to major traffic arteries and rural districts.
A total of 54 PAH profiles were measured, 32 of which were determined
after a sampling period of 24 hours while 22 profiles were obtained
after a sampling period of more than 2 months. The deviations among
all of these profiles are relatively small. Figure 6 shows the
relative amount of each of the 8 PAH based on the total amount of
all of them. The small standard deviation of the average values
indicates a close similarity of the PAH profiles.

   Apparently, the different PAH profiles as obtained from various
emission sources have been mixed during their period of residence
in the atmosphere to a rather persistent PAH profile. The standard
deviation of some PAH reveal that, occasionally, larger deviations
from the "normal" profile may occur. This may be characteristic for
a distinct atmospheric situation, or it may be a chemically induced
change of PAH on the filter, brought about by particular air pollutants like SO_3 or NO_2. Finally, it may be due to errors of the
analytical method applied.

   The thin layer chromatography method permits a simultaneous
quantitative PAH determination only for a small number of PAH. To
obtain more information, the PAH content of 5 samples of particulate
matter were analyzed by means of the gas chromatography combined
with the mass spectrometric techniques [37]. These samples were
collected in 5 cities (Bremen, Duisburg, Frankfurt, Karlsuhe,
Muenchen) during the winter of 1978/79. The PAH totaled 135 in
number, and were compared quantitatively. In Figure 7 the amounts
related to chrysene are shown. This form of presentation illustrates the similarity of the PAH profiles in the 5 samples examined.

Animal experiments with PAH fractions from airborne particulates

   PAH fractions with corresponding PAH profiles consequently must
yield similar tumor rates in animal experiments. After subcutaneous

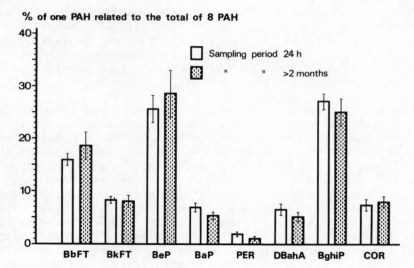

Fig. 6   Percentage of one PAH related to the total of 8 PAH;
          average of 32 sampling periods of 24 hours and 22 of 2 to
          4 months. For the meaning of the abbreviations see Fig. 5.
          (The average values characterize the "standard profile".)

injection of 4 PAH fractions from samples collected in 3 cities and
1 rural district, the results confirm the expectations (Figure 8).
Prior to the animal tests, each of the 4 total extracts as well as
the PAH fractions obtained from the extracts were concentrated in
such a way, that all fractions contained the same benzo(a)pyrene
level. They were then subcutaneously injected into mice using 4
doses in 0.5 ml tricapryline as vehicle. Since the extracts were
standardized for a distinct benzo(a)pyrene dose, the differences in
BaP concentrations in the atmosphere of the different sampling sites
are no longer accounted for.

      Another aspect of the results is of special importance: the
total extracts from samples of urban atmosphere produced more tumors
than the PAH fractions separated from each of these total extracts.
This indicates that besides the PAH, there are other extractable
substances in the suspended matter which are also carcinogenic.

      The results of the carcinogenicity tests are few compared to
the abundance of analytical data. Furthermore, due to the relative
small number of animals, only large differences in the dose-response
relationship are statistically reliable.

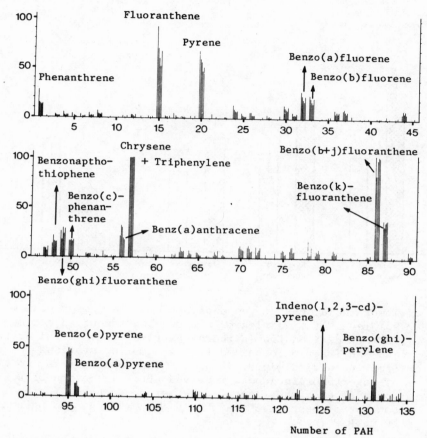

Fig. 7 Relative proportions of 135 PAH (chrysene = 100) isolated
from suspended particulate matter collected in 5 cities of
the Federal Republic of Germany (the 5 peaks in each group
count in the sequence of Bremen, Duisburg, Frankfurt,
Karlsruhe, Muenchen [37].

An index for the carcinogenic potency of airborne PAH

The two following hypotheses are mainly based on the results
of the PAH analysis:

1. The PAH profiles in the atmosphere of residential areas with a
    distinct economic and civic structure are, at least on an
    average over months, basically the same.

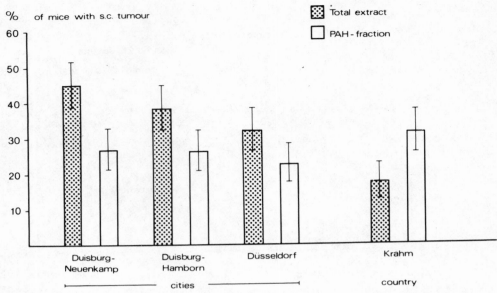

Fig. 8   Tumor incidences at the application site in per cent with
         95% level of significance after subcutaneous injection of
         extract derived from airborne particulates.   Total extract
         and PAH fraction obtained from 4 sampling stations.
         Sampling period winter 1975/76.   The columns refer to the
         average tumor incidence received after injection of 4
         doses of each substance.   Dose per mouse based on the
         content of benzo(a)pyrene: 0.16 µg, 0.63 µg, 2.5 µg and
         10 µg BaP [42].

2.   The analysis of a small number of PAH extracted from collected
      airborne particles is sufficient for establishing a scale rep-
      resentative of the carcinogenicity of the total PAH fraction.

      Certainly, both hypotheses suffer from a simplification of the
actual conditions and do not represent an exact scientific statement.   However, from the view point of preventive medicine, it is
advisable to evaluate the airborne carcinogenic PAH burden of the
population by means of a simple routine analysis.   Then, it seems
to be justified to take both hypotheses as a basis for a pragmatic
approach.   (The error possibly encountered here may be of far
smaller proportion than in the case of an indiscriminate evaluation
of all sizes of asbestos fibers above 5 µm in length and below 3 µm
in diameter [see part I]).

      With the above assumptions, an index based on several PAH can be established according to the average PAH values shown in Figure 6 which base of the analytical results of several years. The determination of 5 PAH will probably suffice to average the analytical errors of the individual PAH measurements or the deviations in the PAH profiles. We selected the four PAH with the highest concentration of the 8 PAH and the traditional benzo(a)pyrene. The average relative proportions of these 5 PAH calculated from the analytical results constitute the standard profile. Since each PAH in this standard profile is in a fixed relation to the other 4 PAH, each PAH is of the same significance with respect to the evaluation. By the same token, the individual carcinogenic potency of one of these PAH is immaterial, because the concentration of a non-carcinogenic PAH indicates the concentration of the others, and thus, that of a carcinogenic PAH too. To establish the same statistical weight for each of the different concentrations in the profile, special evaluation factors must be defined. They make sure that the high concentrations of benzo(e)pyrene will have the same weight in the evaluation as the relatively low concentration of benzo(a)pyrene. The values of the 5 evaluation factors are derived from the per cent amount of the 5 PAH in the standard profiles (see Table 1). The factors are defined in such a way that each of the 5 selected PAH in a standard profile contributes 20% to the PAH index.

As Figure 6 and Table 1 show, the different periods of sampling have little influence on the profile. A distinct difference is seen in the case of benzo(a)pyrene due to its well-known instability. However, even this deficiency is averaging out in the evaluation, when other PAH are included.

Table 1. Definition of evaluation factors providing equal weight of five selected PAH in the standard profiles. The "standard profile 24 h" is derived from 32 determinations of PAH profiles after a sampling period of 24 hours, – the "standard profile > 2 m" from 22 determinations after a sampling period longer than 2 months (compare with Fig. 6; abbreviations see Fig. 5).

	Percentage in "standard profile 24 h"	Evaluation factor	Percentage in "standard profile > 2 m"	Evaluation factor
BbFT	19.0	1.1	21.7	0.92
BkFT	9.9	2.0	9.5	2.1
BeP	30.5	0.66	33.5	0.6
BaP	8.3	2.4	6.3	3.2
BghiP	32.5	0.62	29.0	0.69
	100.0		100.0	

Based on the measured concentrations of the 5 PAH in a dust
sample collected from the air, PAH units can be calculated by means
of the evaluation factors. See Table 2. The total of the PAH units
indicates the PAH level in the atmosphere; simultaneously the PAH
units are the index for the carcinogenic potency of the airborne
PAH. In particular, the selection of the 5 PAH mentioned above is
presented as a practical example and may serve only as a basis for
discussion. In principle, the selection of PAH will depend on the
analytical procedure applied. Furthermore, it must be kept in mind
that PAH with a relatively high vapor pressure are incompletely
deposited in filters and further losses occur after extended sampling periods [43,44]. In case data obtained by gas chromatography
as given in Figure 7, the selection of PAH would be a different
one. Even the evaluation factors would change. But the principle
of establishing an index for the PAH level and the carcinogenic
potency of PAH by averaging numerous similar PAH profiles may still
be retained.

Part III: "PREVENTIVE GUIDES" FOR CARCINOGENS INSTEAD OF AIR
            QUALITY STANDARDS

The problems and possibilities of developing scales or indices
for measuring the carcinogenic potency of airborne fibrous dusts
and PAH mixtures have been discussed. A summarizing evaluation is
contained in Table 3. However, the indices are at best suitable for
comparing the burden or exposure at a given period of time and/or at
a given location. It is impossible to assess the carcinogenic risk
to the general population exposed to fibrous dusts and PAH, because
the dose-response relationships are unknown. If the hypothesis is
accepted, that the presently measured concentrations of fibrous dusts

Table 2.   Illustration for the calculation of PAH units from the
           concentrations of five PAH in the atmosphere after a
           sampling period of 24 hours and that of the evaluation
           factors according to "standard profile 24 h" (see Table 1).

	[ng/m3]	Evaluation factor	PAH units
BbFT	9.74	0.92	9.0
BkFT	4.6	2.1	9.7
BeP	30.99	0.6	18.6
BaP	6.49	3.2	20.8
BghiP	14.83	0.69	10.2
			68.3

Table 3. Evaluation of established and potential indices of the
          carcinogenic potency of airborne fibrous dusts and PAH.

Index for carcinogenic potency concerning...	Fibrous dusts	PAH
	established	not establ.
Workplace	(very imprecise)	(would be imprecise)
Ambient air	not establ. (would be very imprecise)	not establ. (would be relatively precise)

and PAH in the atmosphere are at a significant response level in
many locations, then there is reason for the demand that these substances should be reduced as much as possible.

Such a requirement is supported by the meaning and the letter
of the Air Quality Guidelines. Therefore, a "preventive guide"
(Vorsorgewert) for benzo(a)pyrene of 10 ng/m^3 in the atmosphere was
proposed [45]; it could be modified and improved by using PAH units
as explained in part II. This value was proposed in order to promote
the fundamental discussion as to whether or not preventive guides
should be established for carcinogens instead of waiting for scientifically backed-up air quality standards which shall avoid health
effects but are very often hard to achieve. A value of 10 ng BaP/m^3
in ambient air is a high level in the U.S.A.; in Germany, however,
it would require some effort to stay within this limit in all
industrial and urban areas.

In the end, the decision on an acceptable risk is a socio-
political problem of great significance. In Germany, the discussion
of this subject is still at the beginning. Up to now, politicians
and industrial managers have, in general, two prevailing views:

1. As long as an increase of tumor incidence caused by air pol-
    lutants has not been proven, the carcinogenic effects of
    present air pollution levels cannot be significant.

2. Air quality standards for carcinogens will be established as
    soon as scientific data warrant them.

Comment to the first statement: A quantitative definition of
the term "significant" is always avoided. Politicians would never
accept an annual cancer death rate of 5 - 10 cases per 100,000

inhabitants caused by air pollutants. This level was called "relatively low" by Althouse [27] from the International Agency of
Cancer Research in Lyon. However, it accumulates to 11,000 to
22,000 cases in the U.S.A., or 3,000 to 6,000 deaths per year in
West Germany.

Comment to the second statement: Everybody who is dealing with
these problems scientifically will acknowledge that, for lack of
facilities and money, the required sufficient scientific data will
not be collected within the next twenty or more years; thus, a decision on standards for carcinogens in the air and preventive actions
would have to be postponed into the next century. Meanwhile, the
carcinogens, because of the long induction time for the malignant
tumors, might work as a "time bomb".

Up to now there has been an inconsistency in the German method
of providing legal regulations for environmental protection. On
the one hand, restrictive actions against new chemicals are presently
planned relating to "positive" results in a few tests. On the other
hand, a strong hesitation can be observed regarding the planning of
suitable actions to limit relatively well-investigated carcinogens.
In this situation, a resolution of the 11 German Federal State
Ministers for environmental protection could bring about the turning
point. They recommended to the Federal Government the adoption of
preventive guides for carcinogenic substances in the atmosphere in
order to limit the risk of cancer [46]. So far, however, no decision has yet been taken.

There is no doubt that also the scientists have to think more
about the relationship between socio-economical realities and the
level of public health. We need an answer to the question: What
is a reasonable balance between these two interests which can be
accepted by human society?

ACKNOWLEDGEMENTS

The authors wish to thank Prof. Dr. W. Stoeber for his help
with the translation and critical review of the manuscript. Moreover, they express their thanks to Mrs. U. Ziem-Hanck, Dipl. Biol.,
and Mrs. C. Baumert for their accurate assistance.

REFERENCES

1. Stanton, M.F. and Wrench, C.: Mechanisms of mesothelioma in-
      duction with asbestos and fibrous glass. J. Nat. Cancer
      Inst., 48:797 (1972)
2. Pott, F. and Friedrichs, K.H.: Tumoren der Ratte nach i.p.
      Injektion faserformiger Staeube. Naturwissenschaften,
      59:318 (1972)

3. Wagner, J.C., Berry, G., and Timbrell, V.: Mesotheliomata in rats after inoculation with asbestos and other materials. Brit. J. Cancer, 28:175 (1973)

4. Beck, E.G.: Biologische Wirkung von faserfoermigen Staeuben. Arbeitsmed. Sozialmed. Praeventivmed., 10:178 (1975)

5. Asbestos Standard: Revised Recommended. U.S. Dept. of Health, Education and Welfare. Publ. Health Service Center for Disease Control, Nat. Inst. for Occupat., Safety and Health, Washington, D.C. (1976)

6. Deutsche Forschungsgemeinschaft: Maximum Concentrations at the Workplace 1979. Harald Boldt Verlag, Boppard (1979)

7. Ashcroft, T.: Epidemiological and quantitative relationships between mesothelioma and asbestos on Tyneside. J. Clin. Path., 26:832 (1973)

8. Whitwell, F., Scott, J. and Grimshaw, M.: Relationship between occupations and asbestos-fibre content of the lungs in patients with pleural mesothelioma, lung cancer, and other diseases. Thorax, 32:377 (1977)

9. Vianna, N.J. and Polan, A.K.: Non-occupational exposures to asbestos and malignant mesothelioma in females. Lancet, II:1061 (1978)

10. Otto, H.: Versicherungsmedizinische Probleme bei der Beurteilung berufsbedingter Krebskrankeiten am Beispiel des Mesothelioms. In Krebsgefaehrdung am Arbeitsplatz. Arbeitsmedizinisches Kolloqium, Hrsg. von K. Norpoth. Gentner Verlag, Stuttgart, p. 87 (1979)

11. Pott, F.: Some aspects on the dosimetry of the carcinogenic potency of asbestos and other fibrous dusts. Staub-Reinhalt. Luft, 38:486 (1978)

12. Pott, F., Huth, F. and Friedrichs, K.H.: Tumoren der Ratte nach i.p. Injektion von gemahlenem Chrysotil und Benzo(a)-pyren. Zbl. Bakt. Hyg. I. Abt. Orig. B, 155:463 (1972)

13. Stanton, M.F. and Layard, M.: The carcinogenicity of fibrous minerals. In Proceedings of a Workshop on Asbestos: Definition and Measurement Methods, 18 to 20 July, Gaithersburg, MD. Ed. by C.C. Gravatt, P.D. LaFleur, and K.F.J. Heinrich. National Bureau of Standards, Washington, p. 143 (1978)

14. Nicholson, W.J.: Recent approaches to the control of carcinogenic exposures. Case study 1: Asbestos - the TLV approach. In Occupational Carcinogenesis. Ed. by U. Saffiotti and J.K. Wagoner. The New York Academy of Sciences, New York, p. 152 (1976)

15. Friedrichs, K.H., Hoehr, D. and Grover, Y.P.: Messung des Fasergehaltes im Gewebe und in der Aussenluft. In Luft-hygiene und Silikoseforschung, Jahresbericht 1978, Hrsg. von der Gesellschaft zur Foerderung der Lufthygiene und Silikoseforschung e.V., Dusseldorf. Verlag W. Girardet, Essen, p. 28 (1979)

16. Gibbs, G.W. and Hwang, C.Y.: Dimensions of airborne asbestos
    fibres. Paper of the Symposium on Biological Effects of
    Mineral Fibres, September 1979, Lyon. International
    Agency for Research on Cancer, Lyon (in press)

17. Rendall, R.E.G. and Skikne, M.I.: Submicroscopic fibres in
    industrial atmospheres. Paper of the Symposium on Biolog-
    ical Effects of Mineral Fibres, September 1979, Lyon.
    International Agency for Research on Cancer, Lyon (in press)

18. Pott, F., Friedrichs, K.H. and Huth, F.: Ergebnisse aus
    Tierversuchen zur kancerogenen Wirkung faserfoermiger
    Staeube und ihre Deutung im Hinblick auf die Tumorentstehung
    beim Menschen. Zbl. Bakt. Hyg. I. Abt. Orig. B, 162:467
    (1976)

19. Riediger, G.: Kuenstliche Mineralfasern in der Atemluft -
    Eine Pilotstudie fuer den Arbeitsplatz. Staub - Reinhalt.
    Luft, 37:147 (1977)

20. Wendland, M.E. and Wolff, H.F.: Die Berufskrankheiten-
    verordnung (BeKV), 2. Lfg. VIII. Erich Schmidt Verlag,
    Berlin (1978)

21. Doll, R., Vessey, M.P., Beasly, R.W.R., Buckley, A.R., Faer,
    E.C., Fisher, R.E.W., Gammon, E.J., Gunn, W., Hughes, G.O.,
    Lee, K. and Norman-Smith, B.: Mortality of gasworkers -
    Final report of a prospective study. Brit. J. Ind. Med.,
    29:394 (1972)

22. Redmond, C.K., Ciocco, A., Lloyd, J.W. and Rush, H.W.: Long-
    term mortality study of steel workers. VI. Mortality from
    malignant neoplasms among coke oven workers. J. Occup.
    Med., 14:621 (1972)

23. Hammond, E.C., Selikoff, I.J., Lawther, P.L. and Seidman, H.:
    Inhalation of benzpyrene and cancer in man. Ann. N.Y.
    Acad. Sci., 271:116 (1976)

24. Thyssen, J., Althoff, J., Kimmerle, G. and Mohr, U.: In-
    halation studies with benzo(a)pyrene. In Luftverunreinigung
    durch polycyclische aromatische Kohlenwasserstoffe -
    Erfassung und Bewertung. VDI-Verlag, Duesseldorf, p. 329
    (1980)

25. Lawther, P.J. and Waller, R.E.: Coal fires, industrial emis-
    sion and motor vehicles as sources of envrionmental carcin-
    ogens. In Environmental Pollution and Carcinogenic Risks.
    International Agency for Research on Cancer, Lyon, p. 27
    (1976)

26. Higgins, I.T.T.: Epidemiological evidence on the carcinogenic
    risk of air pollution. In Environmental Pollution and
    Carcinogenic Risks. International Agency for Research on
    Cancer, Lyon, p. 41 (1976)

27. Althouse, R.: Pollution and lung cancer in humans. In Luft-
    verunreinigung durch polycyclische aromatische Kohlwasser-
    stoffe - Erfassung und Bewertung. VDI-Verlag, Duesseldorf,
    p. 189 (1980)

28. Sawicki, E.: Analysis of atmospheric pollutants of possible
     importance in human carcinogenesis. In Environmental
     Pollutants: Detection and Measurement. Ed. by T.Y.
     Toribara, J.R. Coleman, B.E. Dahneke, and I. Feldman.
     Plenum Press, New York, London, p. 69 (1978)
29. Air Quality Data for 1968 from the National Air Surveillance
     Networks and Contributing State and Local Networks,
     Division of Atmospheric Surveillance. Environmental
     Protection Agency, Research Triangle Park, N.C. (1972)
30. Olsen, D.A. and Haynes, J.L.: Air Pollution Aspects of
     Organic Carcinogens. Litton Industries, Inc., Bethesda,
     Maryland (1969)
31. Waller, R.E. and Commins, B.T.: Studies of smoke and poly-
     cyclic aromatic hydrocarbon content of the air in large
     urban areas. Environm. Res., 1:295 (1967)
32. Waibel, M. and Wanner, H.U.: Schwebestaubmessungen und
     Bestimmungen des 3,4-Benzpyrengehaltes in Zuerich. Zbl.
     Bakt. Hyg. I. Abt. Orig. B, 159:169 (1974)
33. Brockhaus, A., Weisz, H., Friedrichs, K.H. and Kraemer, U.:
     Das Vorkommen von Benzo(a)pyren und partikulaerem Blei bei
     unterschiedlichen Immissionssituationen. In Immissions-
     situationen durch den Kraftverkehr in der Bundesrepublik
     Deutschland. Gustav Fischer Verlag, Stuttgart, p. 183
     (1974)
34. Brockhaus, A., Roenicke, G. and Weisz, H.: Benzpyren-Pegel
     des Luftstaubs in der Bundesrepublik Deutschland.
     Deutsche Forschungsgemeinschaft, Bonn (1975)
35. Lao, R., Thomas, R.S., Oja, H. and Dubois, J.: Application
     of a gas chromatography – mass spectrometer – data
     processor combination to the analysis of the polycyclic
     aromatic hydrocarbon content of airborne pollutants. Anal.
     Chem., 45:908 (1973)
36. Lee, M.L., Novotny, M. and Bartle, K.D.: Gas chromatography/
     mass spectrometric and nuclear magnetic resonance deter-
     mination of polynuclear aromatic hydrocarbons in airborne
     particulates. Anal. Chem., 48:1566 (1976)
37. Koenig, J., Funcke, W., Balfanz, E., Grosch, B., Romanowski,
     T. and Pott, F.: Vergleichende Untersuchung von atmon-
     phaerischen Schwebstoffproben aus 5 Staedten der Bundes-
     republik Deutschland auf ihren Gehalt an 135 polyzyklischen
     aromatischen Kohlenwasserstoffen. Staub-Reinhalt. Luft,
     (1981, in press)
38. Brockhaus, A. and Tomingas, R.: Emission polyzyklischer
     Kohelwasserstoffe bei Verbrennungsprozessen in kleinen
     Heizungsanlagen und ihre Konzentration in der Atmosphaere.
     Staub-Reinhalt. Luft, 36:96 (1976)
39. Grimmer, G., Boehnke, H. and Glaser, A.: Investigation on
     the carcinogenic burden by air pollution in man. XV. PAH
     in automobile exhaust gas – an inventory. Zbl. Bakt. Hyg.
     I. Abt. Orig. B, 164:218 (1977)

40. Tomingas, R., Pott, F. and Voltmer, G.: Profile von poly-
    zyklischen aromatischen Kohlenwasserstoffen in Immissionen
    verschiedener Schwebstoffsammelstationen in der westlichen
    Bundesrepublik Deutschland. Zbl. Bakt. Hyg. I. Abt. Orig.
    B, 166:322 (1978)

41. Tomingas, R.: Untersuchung der PAH-Belastung in Ruhrgebiet -
    Vergleich mit einer Reinluftstation. In Luftverunreinigung
    durch polyzyklische aromatische Kohlenwasserstoffe -
    Erfassung und Bewertung. VDI-Verlag, Duesseldorf, p. 147
    (1980)

42. Pott, F., Tomingas, R., Brockhaus, A. and Huth, F.: Unter-
    suchungen zur tumorerzeugenden Wirkung von Extrakten
    und Extrackfraktionen aus atmosphaerischen Schwebstoffen im
    Subkutantest bei der Maus. Zbl. Bakt. Hyg. I. Abt. Orig.
    B, 170:17 (1980)

43. Tomingas, R.: Remarks on the sampling procedures for poly-
    cyclic aromatic hydrocarbons from the atmosphere.
    Fresenius Z. Anal. Chem., 297:97 (1979)

44. Koenig, J., Funcke, W., Balfanz, E., Grosch, B. and Pott, F.:
    Testing a high volume air sampler for quantitative col-
    lection of polycyclic aromatic hydrocarbons. Atm. Environm.,
    14:609 (1980)

45. Pott, F. and Dolger, R.: Problems involved in finding an
    exposure limit for polycyclic aromatic hydrocarbons. In
    Luftverunreinigung durch polyzykische aromatische Kohlen-
    wasserstoffe - Erfassung und Bewertung. VDI-Verlag,
    Duesseldorf, p. 375 (1980)

46. Beschluss der 14. Umweltbundesministerkonferenz vom 10./11.
    Februar 1980 in Duesseldorf

DISCUSSION

FORBES: If one is interested in lung cancer, the most important factor is cigarette smoking. In Germany, the lung cancer mortalities have continued to increase and in Britain they have leveled off and gone down. I believe there are also large variations in the lung cancer mortality data for different parts of Germany. Are you suggesting that benzo(a)pyrene in the air and other pollutants account for these differences?

Also, could it be that under-estimation of smoking habits, and/ or under-diagnosis of lung cancer is different in Germany than in the United States and Britain?

POTT: Yes, I suggest -- but it is impossible to furnish proof -- that the relatively high lung cancer rates in Great Britain and in Northrhine-Westfalia are partly caused by high concentrations of some PAHs and other pollutants in the air. These high concentrations were almost entirely the result of coal burning and might have decreased earlier in Great Britain after the Clean Air Act of 1956 than in the urban and industrial areas of Northrhine-Westfalia.

To your second question: I don't believe that the differences in lung cancer incidences of the United States, Great Britain and West Germany can be explained by differences of the quality of diagnosis. I think it is impossible that the strong increase of lung cancer incidence in men in West Germany is caused by better diagnosis in the last 30 years, because we have no real increase of lung cancer incidence in women up to now. From 1965 to 1977, we could not establish an increase in Northrhine-Westphalia in females. There is a weak increase from 1952 to 1965 from about 8 to 11 per 100,000; this weak increase could be caused by better diagnosis.

CRANMER: On your slide showing the information on mice, was I correct in inferring that the same amount of air was sampled?

POTT: It is not the same amount of air, it is the same amount of benzo(a)pyrene; in the rural area much more air must be filtered than in urban districts for obtaining the same amount of benzo(a)- pyrene.

CRANMER: In looking at your cigarette smokers in those areas with the higher ambient benzo(a)pyrene etc. levels, did you find an augmentation of the lung cancer rates in the smokers as opposed to the non-smokers?

POTT: It is a pity that we have no epidemiologic data about lung cancer of smokers in West Germany. So it is not possible to calculate the effect of air pollution and of cigaratte smoking. I'm interested to know why lung cancer incidence in females didn't

increase considerably in Germany in the last 20 years. Sometimes I
wonder whether it may be a genetic difference between men and women
as it is known between male and female golden hamsters after intra-
tracheal instillations of benzo(a)pyrene. Have you any other idea?

CRANMER: Wasn't there a greater lag period between the times that
women began smoking heavily in Germany than there was in the other
countries that you are trying to compare to? And you would expect a
displacement of the increase?

POTT: I remember that in the Second World War men and women got
smoking ration cards and they could both buy cigarettes but I don't
know how many cigarettes the women gave to their husbands.

ALBERT: You showed a slide relating the length and diameter of asbestos to a carcinogenic potency. You had a maximum for diameter of
about 0.125 microns. You also showed a drop-off in the carcinogenicity at thinner fibers, that is smaller diameters. Do you have any
experimental or theoretical basis for that?

POTT: No experimental but only theoretical. The metabolism of a
cell is changed after incomplete incorporation of a long fiber. We
think that a fiber makes a lesion in the cell wall and it could be
that a thinner fiber makes a smaller lesion.

ALBERT: The slide that showed subcutaneous tumors of mice had a difference between whole extract and something called PAH. Now, before
you said that you could characterize the PAH profile of spectrum in
the air by 5 of the PAHs. Are you talking about relating tumors to
these 5 PAHs or were you talking about the total PAH content of the
air?

POTT: We are talking about the total PAH fraction and these are more
than 100 PAHs. About 20 of them are proved to be carcinogenic in
animals.

ALBERT: But when you said that you could characterize PAHs on the
basis of 5 of them, you have tested this out experimentally? Because
after all, the characterization of PAHs has got to have some practical use, namely the prediction of carcinogenic effect. Have you
checked the carcinogenic potency of, for example, these 5 PAHs
against the total PAH?

POTT: We have checked the carcinogenic potency of several PAHs but
this is not the reason for the selection of these 5 PAHs. They
were chosen since when you have the in-air PAH profile and if all
profiles are exactly the same, then it would be necessary to analyze
only one PAH for calculating the levels of all the other PAHs as
well as the relative carcinogenic potency of the total PAH group.

But there can occur errors in the analysis of the chosen PAHs. Therefore, we think it would be better to analyze not only one PAH but five.

The following slide (Fig. 7) which was omitted in the oral presentation shows the PAH profiles of five cities in West Germany: each group of lines approximately has the same level. This underlines that it is not necessary to analyze a lot of PAHs for obtaining a correct PAH profile of the atmosphere and justifies the selection of some PAHs.

ALBERT: The Environmental Protection Agency in this country is considering characterizing atmospheres from a carcinogenic standpoint in terms of benzo(a)pyrene. I wonder whether or not you really know if the characterization of the atmosphere in terms of the 5 polycyclic aromatic hydrocarbons gives you a better measure of the carcinogenic potency of that mixture than if you were to take benzo(a)-pyrene by itself.

POTT: As to benzo(a)pyrene, it's durability on the filter is not so good. If there are pollutants in the air like NO_2 or SO_3, benzo(a)-pyrene can be oxidized on the filter; therefore it is not the best leading PAH for evaluating the carcinogenic potency of the total group.

SESSION IV

COMPARATIVE RISKS OF ENERGY SOURCES

CHAIRMAN:

PHILIPPE F. BOURDEAU

INTRODUCTION TO SESSION IV

Philippe F. Bourdeau

Directorate General for Research, Science
   and Education
Commission of the European Communities
1049 Brussels, Belgium

Up to now we have been concerned with the measurements of estimation of risks from specific pollutants. We heard about statistical
inference problems, about the interest in and importance of susceptible subpopulations, and about some aspects, at least, of the measurement of risk from specific pollutants such as lead and mercury,
or classes of pollutants such as PAH fibers. Now we are moving to
the estimation of risk from technologies, in this case energy generation, and looking at the whole cycle from the extraction of the raw
material to final disposal. This implies another type of problem.
It implies the aggregation of many different types of risk of varying
duration. It implies also not only direct risks to human health, but
also risks to targets other than human beings. Another facet of the
overall problem of risk is not only the scientifically objective estimation of what the probability of damage is, but also the response
of the public. This risk perception is an attitude made up of the
reaction to many factors, the least of which is often the scientific
evidence. Of course, this has tremendous political consequences and
nowhere is this more topical and more important for the moment than
in the field of energy generation.

283

SOME PROBABILISTIC ASPECTS OF SAFETY ASSESSMENT

W. A. Thompson, Jr.

University of Missouri-Columbia

Statistics Department
University of Missouri
Columbia, Missouri 65211

"But in this world nothing can be said to be certain, except death and taxes" - Benjamin Franklin

INTRODUCTION

Recent events at Three Mile Island have focused national attention on the task of assessing the safety of complex industrial facilities, see Lewis (1980). Prior to Three Mile Island a Reactor Safety Study (1975) was prepared. The purpose of the report is indicated by its subtitle "An Assessment of Accident Risks in U. S. Commercial Nuclear Power Plants." This Reactor Safety Study (R.S.S.) is the state of the art of safety assessment, at least for energy related problems. Evaluating the risk of a technological innovation such as a nuclear power plant is a difficult interdisciplinary problem. A new discipline, risk analysis, is being developed to treat such questions. Risk analysis has significant probabilistic and statistical components but as yet there has been little input from professional statisticians, see Easterling (1980). In the case of the R.S.S., presumably this is because the problem was perceived as being in the domain of the nuclear engineer.

This paper introduces several probabilistic considerations which go beyond the R.S.S. methodology. The common characteristic of these considerations is that they recognize explicitly that accident analysis is time dependent whereas the R.S.S. purports to take a "per demand failure rate" approach obscuring important time dependencies.

285

2.   DETERMINATION OF PROBABILITIES

    Actually, the architects of the R.S.S. are aware that safety
analysis is time dependent and to allow for this they don't really
take a per demand failure rate approach as they claim. They are
capable scientists working with a time constraint partly outside
their field; they do not use the best tools. Thus, for example, on
page 167 of the R.S.S. we find that P_{IE}, which is the probability of
an initiating event is ten transients per reactor year. There is a
huge literature of probability extending back for several hundred
years, all of it requiring that probabilities be dimensionless quantities between zero and one. Thus a probability is not per anything
and it cannot be ten. Part of this literature is the multiplication
rule: $P(A \text{ and } B) = P(A) \cdot P(B \text{ given } A)$.

    Let's simplify the R.S.S. problem to the following: Suppose
that transients occur at random in operating time at the rate of ten
per reactor year and that when a transient occurs the conditional
probability that the safety system does not function and an accident
results is $10^{-10} (= q = 1 - p)$. The methodology of the R.S.S. would
then yield that the probability of an accident is $10 \cdot 10^{-10} = 10^{-9}$ per
reactor year. The rationale given is the multiplication rule, which
is valid for dimensionless probabilities which do not exceed one.
Hence this rationale does not justify the above multiplication.
Nevertheless, the answer here is correct under one set of assumptions.

    The proper probabilistic tool for handling time dependencies is
the stochastic process. That transients occur at random at the
expected rate (not probability) of ten per reactor year is the assumption of a homogeneous Poisson process. This entails stationarity, no
simultaneous failures and that events defined on non-overlapping
intervals are probabilistically independent. Stationarity implies
that safety equipment does not wear out, that operators become
neither more skillful with experience nor more prone to error due to
boredom, and that all reactors are equally prone to accident. The
assumption of no simultaneous failures rules out so called common
mode failures where the reactor fails in several ways at once due to
a common environmental condition. Independence of events on adjacent
intervals precludes the possibility that operators under stress may
be more prone to error.

    If we wish to ignore all of these considerations, assuming a ho-
mogeneous Poisson process, then the probability of one or more tran-
sients in a <u>short</u> interval of length Δ is $10 \cdot \Delta$. The probability of one
or more transients in (not per) a reactor year is then

$$\sum_{i=1}^{\infty} (1 - p^i) \, 10^i \, \exp(-10)/i! = 1 - \exp(-10q)$$

$$\simeq 10 \cdot q = 10^{-9},$$

the answer given by the R.S.S. methodology but by quite a different route.

In some instances the time sequencing of events may be the heart of the matter. Consider the following safety system effectiveness problem.

The rate of reaction in an atomic power plant is controlled at a safe level by the insertion of control rods. The times at which control is needed (called transients) are assumed to be a Poisson process with rate μ per year. Failure of the safety control system is assumed to go undetected until inspection and repair occurs at the fixed time t_0. Control system failure time is assumed to have the exponential density $\theta \exp(-\theta t)$, $t > 0$. Transients and control system failures are assumed independent.

Within time t_0, no transient will occur when the safety system is inoperable if, first, the safety system operates for time t_0, or second, the safety system fails at time t but no transient occurs before the end of the interval. Hence the probability of this event is:

$$P(t_0) = \exp(-\theta t_0) + \int_0^{t_0} \theta \exp(-\theta t) \cdot \exp[-\mu(t_0 - t)]dt$$

$$= [\mu \exp(-\theta t_0) - \theta \exp(-\mu t_0)]/(\mu - \theta), \quad \mu \neq \theta .$$

Next assume that inspection occurs at N regularly scheduled times per year. The probability that within a year a transient will occur at a time when the safety system is inoperable, is $1 - [P(N^{-1})]^N$. Thus we have a second entirely different basis for computing the annual probability of an accident.

3. COMPARISON OF RISKS

Assessing the safety of a complex industrial activity, such as a nuclear power plant, potentially involves several kinds of negative consequences to society. Some of these negative consequences will be measured in terms of monetary loss, compromised quality of living, and premature death. The mortality of mankind imposes a constraint on any realistic safety analysis. Here we see that the quotation from Franklin is precisely to the point. The question is not whether to gamble, it is how to gamble. There is no zero risk and all risks are only relative. Perhaps it is the unpleasantness of the human condition which causes this obvious fact to be omitted from many safety analyses. The statistical discipline of competing risks is a proper framework within which to analyse this set of problems.

The R.S.S. presents nuclear risk in comparison with the risk of other types of accidents. For example, the individual chances of fatality per year are given as one in four thousand for motor vehicle accident and one in five billion for nuclear reactor accident (one hundred plants). While it is clear that the latter risk is much preferable to the former, still the average person has difficulty relating to such a comparison of very small numbers.

Our presentation is in the spirit of the R.S.S. but it goes one step further. Using competing risk theory the effect on probability of death and life expectancy of adding an additional risk, such as nuclear, and eliminating an old risk, such as motor vehicle, is calculated.

Competing risk theory hypothesizes a number of risks (diseases, accidents, etc.) which compete for the lives of individuals. For each individual, one of these risks will "win," and the individual will die from that risk. The theory then attempts to predict the consequence of removing or adding a risk. For example, what would be the effect on life expectancy if a cure for smallpox were found? Similarly, we might ask: What would be the effect on life expectancy if 100 nuclear power plants were added to the community?

Let Y, the random life of an individual from the community, have distribution $G(y)$ and density $g(y)$. The overall force of mortality is defined by

$$r(y) = \lim_{\Delta \to \infty} P(y \le Y < y + \Delta \mid Y \ge y)/\Delta.$$

Writing $\overline{G}(y) = 1 - G(y)$ then $r(y) = g(y)/\overline{G}(y)$, and

$$\overline{G}(y) = \exp[- \int_0^y r(t)\,dt]. \qquad (1)$$

The overall force of mortality has the interpretation that if an individual reaches age y then the probability that he will survive for an additional short time Δ is approximately $r(y) \cdot \Delta$. If there are k distinct risks and J denotes the random cause of death then cause specific forces of mortality are defined by

$$r_j(y) = \lim_{\Delta \to 0} P(y \le Y < y + \Delta, \, J = j \mid Y \ge y)/\Delta.$$

We have that

$$r(y) = \sum_1^k r_j(y),\tag{2}$$

the probability that the jth risk causes death is

$$P(J = j) = \int_0^\infty r_j(y)\overline{G}(y)\,dy,\tag{3}$$

and expected length of life is

$$\mu = \int_0^\infty \overline{G}(y)\,dy.\tag{4}$$

The formulae (1)-(4) allow us to examine the consequences of deleting or adding risks. For example, accepting the controversial R.S.S. figure of $2 \cdot 10^{-10}$ fatalities per year as the nuclear accident cause specific force of mortality due to adding one hundred nuclear power plants, in Thompson (1979) it is calculated that elimination of motor vehicle accidents would increase life expectancy from 72.8 years to 73.6 but addition of the nuclear risk would reduce life expectancy by only 18 seconds. These are numbers which most people can appreciate.

The above calculation assumes that the new risk is added to all of the old ones. Another interesting problem would be to calculate the change in life expectancy if the new risk is substituted for one or more of the old ones. Thus, for example, we may be considering replacing a fossil fuel plant by a nuclear plant. This could conceivably result in an increase of life expectancy (a reduction of total risk). Application of formulae (1)-(4) to this new problem would be straightforward except that a R.S.S. type study of fossil fuel plants would be required to determine their cause specific force of mortality. Perhaps the most practical problem would be to consider that new power generation capacity is needed and that this need is to be met by adding either a nuclear or a fossil fuel plant. The equations (1)-(4) can then be used to weigh the alternative risks.

4.   DELAYED FATALITIES

Fatalities due to accident may be classified as immediate or delayed. As Lewis (1980) points out, it is the delayed fatalities which are of primary interest for nuclear reactors. Competing risk analysis applies equally well to delayed as to immediate fatalities but the cause specific forces of mortality will be radically different.

For the moment consider that the new risk is the only risk and that life length is the sum of age at exposure and a delay before the exposure takes effect: $Y = A + D$. These quantities will in general be subject to chance. Suppose that the density functions of Y, A, and D are $h(t)$, $\lambda \exp(-\lambda t)$, and $f(t)$ respectively. The cause specific force of mortality of the new risk will be

$$r_{new}(y) = h(y) / \int_{y}^{\infty} h(t) d(t)$$

where

$$h(y) = \int_{0}^{y} \lambda \exp[-\lambda(y - t)] f(t) dt.$$

We may calculate that $r_{new}(y) = \lambda F(y) + 0(\lambda)$; $0(\lambda)$ is a quantity which if divided by λ goes to zero.

In particular, if the effect of a new constant risk of exposure is delayed for exactly time d then $F(y)$ will be zero or one according as y is less than or greater than d. For small

$$r_{new}(y) = \begin{cases} 0, & y \le d \\ \lambda, & y > d. \end{cases}$$

The probability that the new risk is the eventual cause of death is, from (3),

$$P_d = \int_{d}^{\infty} \lambda \exp(-\lambda y) \overline{G}(y) dy$$

$$= \lambda \int_{d}^{\infty} \overline{G}(y) dy + 0(\lambda).$$

Expected life length with the new risk postponed is, from (4),

$$
\mu_d = \int_0^d \overline{G}(y)\,dy + \int_d^\infty \exp(-\lambda y)\overline{G}(y)\,dy
$$

$$
= \mu - \int_d^\infty [1 - \exp(-\lambda y)]\overline{G}(y)\,dy
$$

$$
= \mu - \lambda \int_d^\infty y\overline{G}(y)\,dy + O(\lambda).
$$

Table 1 is a short tabulation of the integrals needed to calculate P_d and μ_d. Thus, if $\lambda = 10^{-6}$ then $P_{20} = 5 \times 10^{-5}$ and $\mu_{20} = 72.8 - 2.6 \times 10^{-3}$ while $P_0 = 7 \times 10^{-5}$ and $\mu_0 = 72.8 - 2.8 \times 10^{-3}$. Thus we see that delay of the effect of exposure for exactly twenty years changes the risk but little from the immediate fatality situation.

Table 1. Probability that the new risk is the eventual cause
of death and life expectancy as a function of delay*

d(yrs.)	P_d/λ	$(\mu_d - 72.8)/\lambda$
0	72.8	2813
1	71.8	2812
5	67.9	2800
10	63.0	2764
20	53.2	2617
30	43.5	2375
40	34.0	2041
50	24.7	1624
60	16.0	1146
70	8.5	662
80	3.2	263

*Based on average lifetime in the
United States, 1976, as given in
the Statistical Abstract of the
United States (1978).

REFERENCES

Easterling, Robert G., 1980, Reactor safety study, Amer. Statisti-
     cian, 34:61.
Lewis, Harold W., 1980, The safety of fission reactors, Sci. Amer.,
     242:53-65.
Nuclear Regulatory Commission, Reactor Safety Study, 1975, NRC Report
     WASH-1400 (NUREG-75/014), NTIS.
Statistical Abstract of the United States, 1978 ed., U. S. Department
     of Commerce, Bureau of the Census, GPO.
Thompson, W. A., Jr., 1979, Competing risk presentation of reactor
     safety studies, Nuclear Safety, 4:414-417.

DISCUSSION

WEINBERG: You have done a very interesting thing, Dr. Thompson;
very relevant to the broader questions of the measurement of risk.
What you have shown is that on an actuarial basis, even the worst
reactor accident really doesn't make that much difference. This,
somehow, misses the point in that, as far as the public's perception
of the danger from reactors is concerned, the first moment of the
probability distribution of consequences -- that means the number of
people killed per incident weighted with the probability of the occurrence of the incident -- is not what worries people. What worries
people are the higher moments: that there is a non-zero probability
that an accident could be a major catastrophe. The perceived rise
is not determined by the mean number of casualties; it is determined
as much by the maximum estimated casualties, regardless of how small
the probability.

     Having said that, I would like to put before this conference
the fundamental question which was raised. In talking about any of
these environmental insults that result in fairly large numbers of
casualties distributed over a long period of time, is it correct to
report the risk as simply the total number of casualties without comparing this to the number of natural deaths that would occur in the
absence of the insult? Should we start talking not of the increment
in total number of casualties integrated over all time, but rather
of the difference in the force of mortality, which you called the
difference in the expected lifetime with and without the insult?
That is a very fundamental question.

THOMPSON: Our third speaker is going to discuss issues like that.

FORBES: Among your first models, it seemed to me there was not that
much difference between the two and three parameter models; hence
your beta isn't terribly important. Is that right?

THOMPSON: You are asking is there a threshold or not? You are saying it looked like there wasn't, and you're right. In all 8 of these
sets of data I found one threshold which was statistically significant, but it was so close to zero it wasn't practically significant.
So there was no threshold.

FORBES: Your last slide says that if we're concerned about human
life, we should be concerned about motor vehicle accidents and not
about nuclear energy. I have two comments. First, even if all cancers were removed, we would add only about another two years to the
life span, because people would still be dying from other diseases.
On the other hand, if no one were to smoke in the United states, you
would gain about 3 years in life span and smoking should therefore
perhaps be included in discussions on relative risks. Secondly,
would you comment on the problem of waste disposal as a possible
long-term hazard?

COHEN: I am pretty sure that the reactor safety study for 100 reactors reduces life expectancy by about 7 minutes rather than 18
seconds, if it makes any difference. If you use the Union of Concerned Scientists number, this turns out to be 12 hours. The waste
disposal problem, if you use my evaluation (of course it's not in
WASH 1400) reduces life expectancy by about 9 seconds.

UPTON: Is your conclusion to stop driving or to move next to a nuclear power plant, in your personal computation? I am serious, because this has been done often, it is a common method in risk assessment literature. Almost every suggestion for displaying mortality
figures was used and manipulated for various purposes. Schwing, for
example, has several good papers on using the time of life saved. I
am curious, therefore, what your conclusion is.

THOMPSON: My personal conclusion is that our time and money would be
better expended by trying to make the highways more safe and perhaps
not quite as much effort trying to get the last gnat's eyebrow of
safety from the nuclear power industry.

STEIN: What is the substantive basis for the numbers used in the
calculation? Maybe it's coming up later, but otherwise one does not
know what to make of them. What do we use as the basis of the risk?

THOMPSON: Actuarial tables for the year 1976 in conjunction with the
controversial Rasmussen Safety Study figure of $2 \cdot 10^{-10}$ fatalities per
year as the nuclear accident cause specific force of mortality due
to adding 100 nuclear power plants...

ABRAHAMSON: ...as compared to the total number of deaths that are
being produced by that specific set of accidents, predicted deaths,
including the deaths that would accrue after the 20-year latency
period.

<u>LAND</u>: I would object to presenting risk in this form. The risk
that seems to me most relevant is the risk to the people who are
around and who are vulnerable. You could say that the risk from
coal mining is maybe a few seconds a day, on the average, to the
whole population, but is makes more of a difference to the coal
miner who is the one most likely to suffer.

<u>WEINBERG</u>: The risk is pretty well distributed over the entire pop-
ulation, so there's not much of an error involved in that.

WHAT IS THE TOTAL RISK OF ENERGY SYSTEMS?

Herbert Inhaber

Atomic Energy Control Board
Ottawa, Canada K1P 5S9

Although the toxicity of substances plays a large part in determining their effect on human health, much of the damage to health from producing energy comes from sources other than toxicity. Both toxic and non- toxic effects should be considered in calculating this damage. This paper will (a) discuss occupational disease in generating energy, (b) outline briefly the major sources of risk (defined as loss of health or death) in its production, and (c) review some of the calculations and rankings which either appear in or are deducible from the literature.

I can state without hesitation that with the exception of radioactivity, my knowledge of environmental toxicity is limited. As a result, this paper will discuss broad questions of risk, rather than specific questions of toxicity.

OCCUPATIONAL DISEASE IN ENERGY SYSTEMS

We may divide the overall risk of an energy system into two parts: occupational and public. These two aspects are sometimes called voluntary and involuntary, respectively, although there is some doubt as to exactly what the latter two terms imply.

In calculating the overall risk attributable to an energy system, many analysts count not only the activities exclusively related to a particular system (e.g., uranium mining or roof repair to a solar collector), but activities such as transportation, construction, etc., which are more general. Of course, one has the option of considering only these "exclusive" activities in evaluating energy risk (see, for example, Schurr et al[1]). However, this is done only rarely.

What are the relative proportions of disease and accident risk
in producing energy? Generally speaking, in the United States the
number of non-fatal man-days lost due to illness - which can generally be taken as related to the toxicity of substances produced at
work - is much lower than that from accidents[2]. The ratio of the
first quantity to the second varies from industry to industry, but
is generally of the order of a few percent. To take a few examples,
the man-days lost due to accidents in metal mining (per 100 man-
years) is 112; that due to illness is 2.0[2]. Corresponding values
for the steel industry are 80 and 2.0. In Britain, the ratio of
working days lost to occupational diseases to that of accidents is
about 0.035[3]. The International Commission on Radiological Protection[4] gives a somewhat higher ratio of 0.05, but it is still quite
small.

Quite frankly, when I first considered occupational health
statistics in evaluating over-all risk, I was somewhat surprised
at these ratios. One hears through the media of industrial diseases
like those caused by vinyl chloride production and of asbestosis.
The layman might anticipate epidemics of occupational illness. If
they are occurring, they do not seem to be reflected in the official
statistics.

According to Pochin and others who have studied this question,
most incidents which are classified as industrial illness are short-
term, i.e., lasting only a few days at most. However, those who
are concerned with toxicity of substances found in the workplace
generally deal with long-term effects. How these two viewpoints
can be reconciled is not clear.

One area where the above statements do not always hold is coal
mining. U.S. statistics list 200 man-days lost per 100 man-years
for non-fatal accidents in hard coal mines, and 5.2 man-days lost
for illness, for a ratio of 0.026[2], similar to those discussed
above. However, other values are not in accordance with this. The
largest divergence seems to be in Britain, where in 1974 of a total
death rate of 0.26 per 100 man-years, 0.02 was attributed to accidents and 0.24 to disease, primarily pneumoconiosis[5]. This is almost a complete reversal of the ratios mentioned previously. Of
course, one has here a typical problem of incorporating long-term
effects in one-year statistics, since it is evident that many of
those dying in 1974 of coal industrial diseases became ill some
years before.

As a perhaps less dramatic example, one can use the U.S. data
of Comar and Sagan[6] and Morris et al[7] to deduce that the ratio of
disease-related to non-disease related deaths in U.S. coal mining
is about 0.15-0.3. This ratio is less than that of Britain, but
still considerably above the ratios for non-fatal diseases and
accidents in coal mining.

In summary, the effect of toxic substances in the workplace, whether radioactive or not, is a matter of concern. Up to the present, however, their effect does not seem to be reflected in official statistics, except in the case of coal mining deaths. This situation will tend to produce underestimates of total energy risk.

TOTAL RISK OF ENERGY PRODUCTION

In determining the risk to society of various energy alternatives, a variety of risk sources can be considered. These are indicated in Figure 1. Not included here are aspects which may have an indirect effect on health, such as resource depletion, weapons proliferation, climate change, etc. While important, they deserve fuller discussion elsewhere.

Some of the risk components noted in Figure 1 pertain solely to particular energy systems, and others are more general. For example, since uranium has only slight civilian use outside of nuclear reactors, mining of this substance is an "exclusive" activity. On the other hand, steel is used in most energy systems. The total risk of an energy system is made up of both exclusive and non-exclusive activities.

As mentioned above, a minority of risk analysts consider only the "exclusive" activities in risk computation: uranium mining, repairing solar collectors, etc. However, this neglects substantial portions of risk from other sources which are necessary to produce energy from a given system. The analogy of producing automobiles might be drawn here. Some aspects of their production, like assembly lines, are exclusive to this industry. Others, such as making chrome, copper, aluminum and so on are not. If we want to determine the economic cost of a car, we have to consider both the exclusive and non-exclusive activities.

Figure 1 is a simple diagram. But how does one actually calculate each of the components? As might be expected, computation is more difficult than conceptualization. Before discussing the details, some explanatory notes and caveats must be given. Some of these have been given elsewhere[8,9]:

(a) Risk cannot be considered in isolation, since the size of systems varies considerably. The risk of a massive coal-fired plant should not be compared to that of a small solar panel. Most analysts have calculated risk per unit energy output. This is usually taken as one megawatt-year or the annual output of a large coal or nuclear plant (around 700 megawatt-years). The unit used is not of great consequence as long as consistency is maintained.

It is also possible to calculate risk per unit power capacity (rate of energy production) or use other units. Since society is

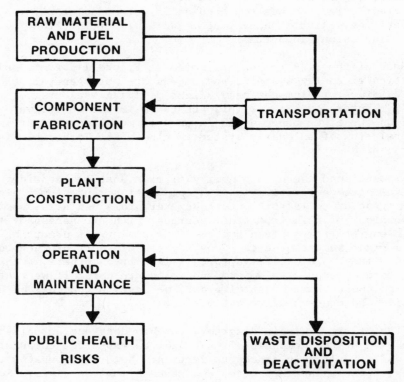

Fig. 1.   Sources of risk in energy production. The relative impor-
          tance of the components depends on the energy system. For
          some systems, energy back-up and storage may be required
          to increase reliability. Transportation is shown as inter-
          acting with a number of components.

generally more interested in the quantity of energy produced than
in the ability to produce it, the more conventional unit (the megawatt-year) is used here.

(b) Component lifetime plays an important part in risk calculations. Some risk may be produced in capital construction (building a reactor or wind turbine) and some may be incurred as a running
cost (operation and maintenance, or mining coal and uranium). To
take account of both aspects, the total risk is divided by the total
energy produced over the lifetime of the system.

The lifetimes of many systems are not accurately known. Often
replacement is made, not because parts have worn out, but because
of economic obsolescence. A lifetime of 30 years has been assumed
for most of the systems discussed here. The major exceptions are
solar space heating and windpower, with estimated lifetimes of 20
years, and hydroelectricity, at 50 years.

(c) Risk data is often given as so many deaths, accidents and
diseases per unit energy. A natural question then arises: Can
these be combined into an overall index of risk?

Physically, they cannot, but mathematically, they can. For
example, the American National Standards Institute and occupational
health bodies often use the value of 6000 man-days lost per death.
Obviously, the value in particular cases will vary strongly, ranging
from the premature death by a week of a 90-year old due to air pollution to the accidental death of a 20-year old in a coal mine.
Nonetheless, this approximation can be a useful one. One document[9]
shows both deaths and total man-days lost separately. The risk
rankings of the eleven systems considered there are similar for
both approaches.

(d) Some solar or wind systems may require energy storage
capabilities. When the sun doesn't shine or the wind doesn't blow,
the consumer still needs energy. Storage can take many forms -
rocks, liquids, batteries, pumped air or other systems. In the
present work, a rock-and-oil system was assumed. This probably
constitutes a lower limit to risk; risk attributable to manufac-
turing batteries is likely higher.

If the reliability aimed for in "baseload" electrical distribution (usually one hour of power loss in a year) is taken as a
guide, the storage required to meet this guideline could be huge.
To avoid these storage problems, a back-up, of ordinary electrical
energy, must be available. This back-up can come from one particular source, such as coal-fired or nuclear plants, or from a
"mix", based on the national proportions of electrical supply. The
latter assumption is used here.

(e) The risk of transmitting energy, as well as producing it, could be considered. This can be accomplished by evaluating the risk of building and operating transmission lines or pipelines. In the case of both, the risk attributable to transmitting energy forms only a small fraction of the total risk of the system[10,11]. As a result, this aspect of risk can be disregarded as a first approximation.

(f) Present-day conditions, not future expectations, were assumed for each system. This obvious fact may hardly seem worth mentioning, but it is an important point. For example, it might be contended that coal-fired plants of the future could produce less pollution than present ones, resulting in decreased health effects. Future steel mills might have a lower occupational risk than those which now exist. Future wind turbines might be more efficient than those which have been built to date. All of this might well be true, and all of it might not. We know the present only imperfectly (see below), and the future even less. As a result, it seems prudent to consider primarily today's energy systems with their associated risk, and re-calculate the values as new knowledge is generated.

This question is related to that of "differential risk", in which only the risk of building new facilities would be considered, without lumping the new in with the old. However, data on occupational or public risk of these hypothetical facilities is non-existant. Until it does become available, we must guard against comparing the future to the present – the future always wins – and retain a consistent methodology.

(g) A related point is the difference between actuarial and theoretical risk. Most risk calculation is based on historical or actuarial data. For example, occupational risk in the steel industry is based on what has happened in the past, not what might be achieved in the future. Occupational risk has declined slowly if at all, with the exception of coal mining[3].

In terms of catastrophic public risk, i.e., accidents which can harm more than a few people at a time, there exists, for all except one energy system, only historical data. For example, the risk of hydroelectric dam failure has not, as far as is known, been computed theoretically. As a result, studies[8,9] use the historical data for hydroelectricity, in which the total number of public deaths attributable to this source since 1890 is divided by the total hydroelectricity produced since that time.

The only system for which theoretical, as opposed to historical, calculations have been produced is nuclear power[12,13]. These studies have attempted to calculate the probabilities of a range of accidents, from negligible to severe.

The Rasmussen report[12] went on to estimate, by integration
over the probabilities, the average number of deaths to be expected
per reactor-year of operation. The recent German Risk Study[13] "more
or less confirms" the results of the U.S. study[12].

Any theoretical study of risk must eventually be compared to
the historical record if understanding is to improve. The U.S. and
German studies have proven conservative, i.e., not underestimating
risk in this respect. A brief calculation is in order. The U.S.
study estimated 0.025 deaths per reactor-year. Assuming a reactor
of 1000 MW capacity with a load factor, or ratio of actual to rated
output, of 0.7, this is $0.025/1000 \times 0.7 = 3.6 \times 10^{-5}$ deaths per
megawatt-year. The "central estimate" of the deaths that could be
caused by the accident at Three Mile Island (TMI) is 0.7[15]. The
total nuclear energy produced to the end of 1978 in reactors in the
Western World was about 170,000 megawatt-years[14]. If one assumes
that the TMI accident was the most significant to date in terms of
public risk, then the historical rate is $0.7/170,000 = 4.1 \times 10^{-6}$
deaths per megawatt-year, or $4.1 \times 100/36 = 11\%$ of the theoretical
rate. It could then be concluded that the theoretical rate does
not substantially underestimate public catastrophic risk.

(h)   The nuclear system considered is the light-water reactor
(LWR) presently used in the United States and other countries.
While the CANDU heavy-water reactor is used in Canada, there exists
comparatively little occupational or public risk data on this
reactor. As a result, the more heavily-studied LWR was used as a
model. Exactly how risk of the CANDU system will differ from that
of the LWR is not known at present. It seems likely, based on
simple physical reasoning, that it will not be overwhelmingly different.

(i)   Geographical aspects play an important part in many aspects
of risk, but have not been studied adequately up till now. For example, health effects from air pollutants from coal-fired plants will
depend strongly on whether the plant is in a heavily-populated area,
the direction of winds, etc. The question of geography has been most
extensively studied with respect to nuclear plants, but more work
needs to be done.

(j)   In order to avoid possible charges of pro-nuclear bias,
nuclear risks were handled differently from those of the rest of the
study. In general, they were "maximized", i.e., the highest values
were chosen from a variety of literature sources. This procedure
was not followed for other energy systems. For occupational risk,
this maximization did not affect the results strongly, since different estimates are fairly similar. However, there seems to be differences of opinion in terms of public risk, with a few estimates
being much higher than those commonly accepted. These former estimates can be termed "worst cases", and apparently have no experi-

mental or historical basis. The values of Comar and Sagan[6] were
used, as published in Annual Review of Energy. The maximum
values for public risk used by Comar and Sagan are much higher than
both the average value calculated by Rasmussen[12] or the historical
record (see above).

(k) Perhaps the most important caveat in this paper is that
much of the data dealing with risk is imprecise, to say the least.

Examples would fill pages, but a few must suffice: (a) the
energy collected per unit area in a solar collector is variable;
(b) the man-hours per unit energy output in uranium mines will depend strongly on the ore grade; (c) the lifetime of windmills is
still a matter of controversy.

As a result of these and many other uncertainties, the results
presented here can only be taken as approximations. While the absolute values of risk shown later in this paper are subject to change
as information is improved, the relative rankings have more validity.
They can be used as a general guide to orders of magnitude of risk.

CALCULATIONS OF RISK

How is total risk calculated? As can be deduced from Figure 1,
a variety of methods are employed. In terms of material acquisition,
labor statistics give the number of deaths, accidents and illnesses
per man-years worked. The number of man-hours required per operation is then multiplied by the deaths, accidents or disease per man-
hour, yielding the occupational risk. The calculations are shown
schematically in Figure 2.

As an example, suppose mining X tons of coal requires Y man-
days. If the number of man-hours lost per day of work is Z, then
the number of man-hours lost per ton of coal is YZ/X.

A similar analysis can be performed in terms of construction.
With knowledge of the trades - roofing, electrical work, plumbing
and so on - the man-hours of each required per unit energy output,
and the risk per man-hour, a calculation similar to that for material acquisition can be performed.

Transportation risk poses a different problem. In principle,
we should know the ways in which each material is transported -
rail, truck, air or barge - the distance it is moved, and the risk
per ton-mile for each of the transportation types. In practice,
this information is difficult to find, so approximations have to
be made.

Sand and other materials for making concrete are generally
moved short distances, so the risk attributable to their transport

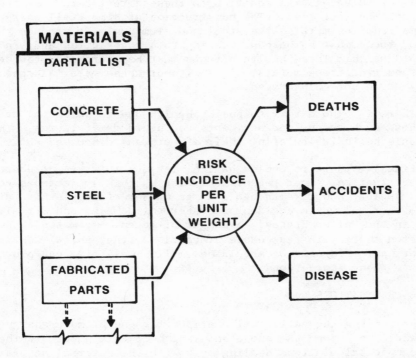

Fig. 2. Risk from material acquisition. Each of the raw materials
which go into an energy system has an associated risk, dependent on the accident, illness and death rate per unit
weight. Dashes indicate that other materials are used.

is probably small. As a crude approximation, it can be assumed that
non-sand materials are carried by train and are moved the same distance as coal. This assumption probably underestimates risk, as can
be deduced from Ramsay[16], since truck transport has a greater risk
per ton-mile than does rail.

Energy-related public health risk arises from a number of
sources. Transportation accidents occur not only occupationally,
but to members of the public as well. By far the largest effect on
the public is due to pollutants produced by burning coal and oil.
Values used here were originally generated by the U.S. National
Academy of Sciences. In addition to these direct emission effects,
there are indirect ones. The construction of almost all energy
systems requires metals like steel and aluminum. To produce these
metals, fuels must be burned, leading to air pollution and, in turn,
loss of health. These health effects must be attributed to the systems requiring these metals, since without these materials the
energy could not be produced.

There is also a risk to public health due to potential cata-
strophes such as nuclear accidents and hydro dam failures. The
rationale behind calculating their effects was discussed above.

Finally, there is public health risk due to waste disposition
and deactivation. Most recent publicity on this subject has concerned nuclear power, although a large number of people have died
due to the coal waste accidents at Aberfan in Wales and Buffalo
Creek in the United States. A number of recent estimates[17] have
suggested that, with reasonable precautions, the public risk from
nuclear waste disposition should be small. Only time can prove or
disprove these contentions.

SAMPLE CALCULATIONS

Presenting the entire calculations for one or more energy systems would be beyond the scope and length of this paper. Rather,
some sample calculations dealing only with the material acquisition
risk of solar space heating is shown in Table 1. Because there has
been some dispute about the values of Refs. 8 and 9, the calculations are taken from another source[16]. They tend to confirm some
general conclusions presented elsewhere[8,9], that the risk of solar
and other non-conventional energy systems can be substantial. All
the values in Table 1 are publicly available, so interested researchers can check these values for themselves.

A brief explanation of Table 1 is in order. The weight of the
solar panels per unit area is comparable to that of other estimates[19]. However, its energy output per unit area is substantially
higher than most other operating solar systems mentioned in a

Table 1. Do-it-yourself Risk Calculation for Material
Acquisition of Solar Panels[a]

	Aluminum	Steel	Glass
(1) Solar Panels (37 m^2, producing 1.27 kWyr/yr)	0.25 tonne	0.50 tonne	0.36 tonne
(2) Total U.S. Production	4.2×10^6 tonne	1×10^8 tonne	1.8×10^6 tonne
(3) Panels/Production (= (1)/(2))	$0.25/4.2 \times 10^6 = 6 \times 10^{-8}$	$0.5/1 \times 10^8 = 5 \times 10^{-9}$	$0.36/1.8 \times 10^6 = 2 \times 10^7$
		$5 \times 10^{-9} + 6 \times 10^{-8} = 6.5 \times 10^{-8}$	
(4) U.S. Deaths		235	70
(5) U.S. Accidents		1×10^5	5×10^3
(6) Solar Deaths/Panel (= (4) x (3))		$235 \times 6.5 \times 10^{-8} = 1.5 \times 10^{-5}$	$70 \times 2 \times 10^{-7} = 1.4 \times 10^{-5}$
(7) Solar Accidents/Panel (= (5) x (3))		$1 \times 10^5 \times 6.5 \times 10^{-8} = 6.5 \times 10^{-3}$	$5 \times 10^3 \times 2 \times 10^{-7} = 1 \times 10^{-3}$
(8) Solar Deaths/MWyr (= (6)/1.27 x 10^{-3} x 20, where 20 = lifetime in years)		$1.5 \times 10^{-5}/1.27 \times 10^{-3} \times 20 = 5.9 \times 10^{-4}$	$1.4 \times 10^{-5}/1.27 \times 10^{-3} \times 20 = 5.5 \times 10^{-4}$
(9) Solar Accidents/MWyr (= (7)/1.27 x 10^{-3} x 20, where 20 = lifetime in years)		$6.5 \times 10^{-3}/1.27 \times 10^{-3} \times 20 = 0.26$	$1 \times 10^{-3}/1.27 \times 10^{-3} \times 20 = 0.039$

Total Deaths/MWyr = $(5.9 + 5.5) \times 10^{-4} = 1.1 \times 10^{-3}$

Total Accidents/MWyr = $(0.26 + 0.039) = 0.30$

Total Man-days lost/MWyr = 6000 x deaths + 50 x accidents
= $6000 \times 1.1 \times 10^{-3} + 50 \times 0.30$
= 21

[a]Adapted from Ref. 16

recent survey[18]. The weight of tubing, heat exchangers and storage
are not included. The conditions outlined in the previous two sen-
tences produce a lower estimated risk for solar energy than is probably the case.

In lines 2 and 3 of Table 1, the proportion of U.S. production
of aluminum, steel and glass attributable to this solar collector
is shown. The proportions for aluminum and steel are combined because the occupational data are similarly combined.

Lines 4 and 5 show the number of deaths and accidents associated with the aluminum, steel and glass industries. Risk due to mining the raw materials required for their production (iron ore, coal, bauxite, sand, and so on) would be in addition to that shown.

Lines 6 and 7 indicate the number of deaths and accidents attributable to the materials in the panel considered. The calculated numbers of deaths and accidents are very small, because the energy output of the panel is so tiny. By way of comparison, a typical 1000 - megawatt coal-fired plant with a load factor of 0.7 produces 1000 x 0.7 x 1000/1.27 = 550,000 times the energy of this panel.

Lines 8 and 9 put the deaths and accidents on a unit energy basis. The total output of the collector over its lifetime is its annual output times 20.

The summarizing lines add the contributions of deaths and accidents from aluminum, steel and glass. The final entry attempts to find a "common unit" of man-days lost per megawatt-year, as noted above, by assigning each death 6000 and each injury 50 man-days lost. The total is about 21.

Ramsay[16] makes a rough estimation of transportation risk, assuming that aluminum, steel and glass are trucked average distances. It can be deduced that his calculations imply 19 man-days lost per megawatt-year, for a total of 40 man-days lost for these two sources of risk. Figure 1 notes that this is only part of the total risk.

The value of 40 man-days lost means little unless it is compared to quantities for other energy systems. This is done in the final section of this paper. Nonetheless, the data of Table 1 shows that a crude estimate of risk can be made using information that is readily accessible.

DISEASE/ACCIDENT RATIOS

Before presenting the final results of a comparison of eleven systems, it is of interest to discuss the ratio of disease risk to that of accidents. Deaths are included in each category. As mentioned previously, diseases are related in some way to the toxicity of substances in the energy systems.

Table 2 shows illness-caused deaths and diseases as a fraction of total risk, in terms of man-days lost, for the eleven energy systems considered. The first column shows that the proportions vary widely, from 0.01 to 0.99. In general, the low proportions are attached to those systems with a large amount of occupational risk in terms of accidents. The high proportions, such as those for coal and oil, are due to the public diseases from air pollution.

Table 2.   Proportion of Disease Related to
           Total Risk in Terms of Man-days Lost[a]

	Total Proportion	Proportion Excluding Air Pollutants
Coal	0.98	0.01 - 0.02
Oil	0.99	0
Natural Gas	0.08	0
Nuclear	0.34 - 0.52	0.27 - 0.45
Hydroelectricity	0.01	0
Wind	0.50 - 0.69	0
Methanol	0.07 - 0.29	0
Solar Space Heating	0.32 - 0.48	0.01
Solar Thermal Electric	0.50 - 0.71	0
Solar Photovoltaic	0.79 - 0.87	0
Ocean Thermal	0.18 - 0.32	0.01

[a]Includes both public and occupational risk.

The second column shows that almost all illness-caused deaths and
diseases are due to air pollution. Sulfur oxides were assumed to
be the prime source of health effects, due to lack of information
on the effect of other pollutants. Air pollution health loss is
direct in the case of coal and oil. For other systems, it is indirect. For example, solar thermal electric, solar photovoltaic and
wind are assumed to require back-up energy, made up of present-day
proportions of coal, oil, nuclear, hydro and natural gas-derived
electricity. Air pollution effects from this back-up are included
in the risk of the aforementioned three energy systems.

Another example of indirect air pollution health effects is the
production of materials, such as steel and aluminum, used in all
energy systems. Making these metals generates pollution, and this
is also included in risk calculations.

When these indirect and direct effects are eliminated, the proportion of illness-caused deaths and diseases is negligible for all
systems except nuclear. Nuclear power has a proportion of disease-
related risk, after air pollution effects are removed, of between
one-quarter and one-half. This is due to radiological disease in
uranium mining and from potential reactor accidents.

As noted at the beginning of this paper, the proportion of risk
due to toxicological (including radiological) effects seems to be
small. How much this would increase with further knowledge of toxicological effects is not known.

FINAL RESULTS

     Using the methodology sketched out above, occupational and pub-
lic risk can be calculated for a number of systems, both new and old.
Results are shown in Figures 3-5.

     Figure 3 shows that occupational risk is highest for methanol.
A considerable amount of logging is required for this system, and
logging is one of the riskiest occupations after mining.

     Lowest is natural gas, because comparatively little labour is
required in its production. Coal has a relatively high value, primarily because of the high danger of coal mining.

     The six new or non-conventional systems to the right of the
figures have relatively high values, ranging from 3-60 times that
of natural gas (in terms of maxima).   Depending in general on dilute
forms of energy like sun- and wind-power, these systems require large
collectors per unit energy output. In turn, building and operating
these collectors requires large amounts of labour, which tends to
produce substantial occupational risk. Each of these steps in the
reasoning has exceptions, but the overall deductions are generally
valid. Results are approximately similar to those of Hoy[20].

     Figure 4 shows the public risk, again using the same units.
For those systems assumed to require back-up, the risk is shown with
and without back-up.

     The highest values, by a substantial factor, are those of coal
and oil, primarily due to pollution effects. Lowest again is natural gas, followed by nuclear. In the case of the latter system, a
fairly pessimistic or high value was taken for the risk due to reactor accidents.

     The six non-conventional systems to the right have some public
risk, although much less than coal or oil. This is due to a number
of factors: (a) some systems require back-up, which produces public risk; (b) materials requirements produces air pollution; and
(c) transportation of materials produces public risk at railroad
crossings.

     Finally, Figure 5 shows the total risk, found by adding occu-
pational and public risk. This is a purely optional step, designed
to measure total effects on society. Others may wish to weight the
two components unequally, or avoid the addition entirely.

     As might be expected on the basis of Figures 3 and 4, natural
gas and nuclear have the lowest total risk, with coal and oil the
highest. In between are a "group of seven". There is not much
reason to discuss the ranking within this group, since there is

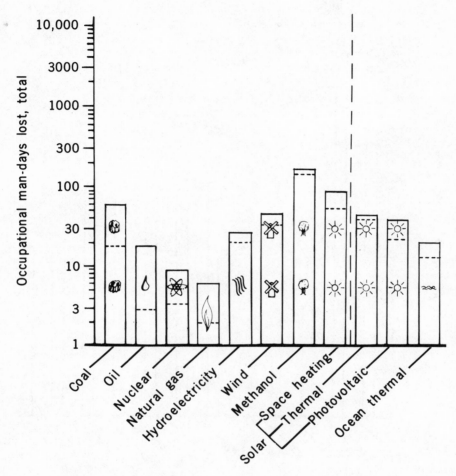

Fig. 3.   Occupational man-days lost per megawatt-year. The tops of
          the bars indicate the upper end of the range of values;
          the dotted lines within the bars, the lower. Those bars
          to the right of the vertical dotted lines indicate values
          for technologies less applicable to Canada. Solid and
          dashed jagged lines refer to the maximum and minimum values,
          respectively, if low-risk or no back-up is assumed. These
          jagged lines are not shown in this figure because occupa-
          tional risk changes little when no back-up is assumed; how-
          ever, they are shown in Figs. 4 and 5. Each death is
          counted as 6000 man-days lost. Note the logarithmic scale.

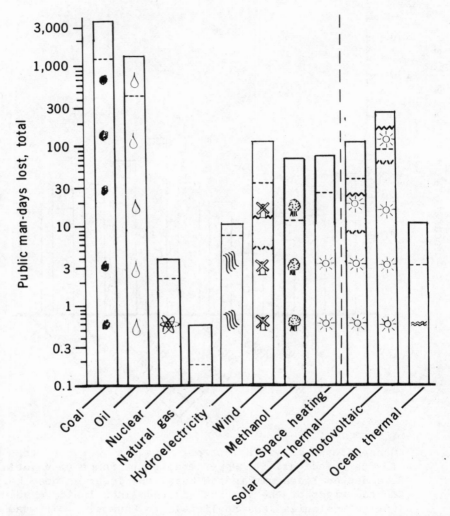

Fig. 4.   Public man-days lost per megawatt-year (see explanation in
           caption to Figure 3). Natural gas-fired electricity has
           the lowest value. Coal and oil have the highest values,
           due to air pollution effects.

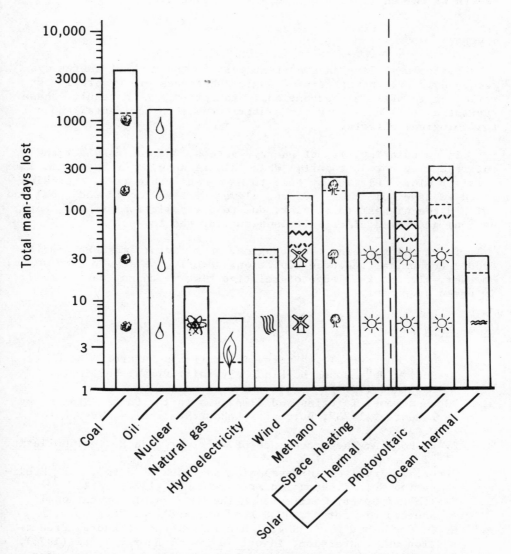

Fig. 5.   Total man-days lost per megawatt-year (see explanation in
          caption to Figure 3).   Quantities here are found by adding
          occupational and public risk.   Natural gas and nuclear
          have the lowest values.

some uncertainty in the values calculated. However, it is seen that the new or non-conventional systems can have substantial risk to health if the entire energy cycle is evaluated.

SUMMARY

Toxicology plays an important part in the risk of energy systems. However, the effects of toxic substances are generally not reflected in official occupational statistics. As a result, these statistics reflect energy risks attributable to accidental and not toxicological effects.

In calculating risk of energy systems, one can consider the entire cycle, not just part. When this is done, energy systems like solar or wind, believed by some to have negligible risk, are calculated to have some risk. Of the eleven systems considered, coal and oil had the highest total risk, due to air pollution effects, and natural gas-fired electricity and nuclear the lowest.

In choosing energy technologies, many factors must be considered: economics, resource depletion, security of supply, and so on. However, without knowledge of relative risk we cannot make a fully-informed judgement.

REFERENCES

1.   S. H. Schurr et al., "Energy in America's Future: The Choice Before Us", Johns Hopkins University Press, Baltimore, Maryland (1979).

2.   "Occupational Injuries and Illnesses in the United States, By Industry, 1973", Bureau of Labour Statistics, Washington, D.C., 1975.

3.   E. E. Pochin, The Acceptance of Risk, British Medical Bulletin, 31 (3) 184 (1975).

4.   "Problems involved in Developing an Index of Harm", ICRP Publication No. 27, Pergamon Press, London (1977), p.21.

5.   Health and Safety Commission, "The Hazards of Conventional Sources of Energy", HMSO London (1978), p. 28.

6.   C. L. Comar and L. A. Sagan, Health Effects of Energy Production and Conversion, Annual Review of Energy 1 581 (1976).

7.   S. C. Morris, K. M. Novak and L. D. Hamilton, "Databook for the Quantitation of Health Effects from Coal Energy Systems (Preliminary Draft)", Brookhaven National Laboratory, Upton, N.Y. (May 1979), p.20.

8.   H. Inhaber, Risk with Energy from Conventional and Non-Conventional Sources, Science, 203 718 (Feb. 23, 1979).

9. H. Inhaber, "Risk of Energy Production", Atomic Energy Control
    Board, Ottawa, Canada (March–Nov. 1978), Report AECB 1119,
    three editions.

10. Also found by T. Donakowski, Institute of Gas Technology,
    Chicago (private communication).

11. Ref.. 9, op.cit., Appendix L.

12. "Reactor Safety Study: An Assessment of Accident Risks in
    U.S. Commercial Nuclear Power Plants", Nuclear Regulatory
    Commission, Washington, D.C. (1975), Report WASH–1400.

13. Federal Minister of Research and Technology, "German Risk
    Study: Summary", Gesellschaft fur Reaktorsicherheit,
    Cologne, Federal Republic of Germany (August, 1979), p. 39.

14. Nucleonics Week, April 26, 1979, p. 17.

15. Ad Hoc Population Dose Assessment Group, "Population Dose and
    Health Impact of the Accident at the Three Mile Island
    Nuclear Station", Bureau of Radiological Health, U.S.
    Department of Health, Education and Welfare, Rockville,
    Maryland (May 10, 1979).

16. W. Ramsay, "Small–Scale Energy Technologies", draft prepared
    for National Energy Strategies Project, Resources for the
    Future, Washington, D.C. (June 1978), p. 18–93.

17. "High–Level Radioactive Waste Management Alternatives", U.S.
    Atomic Energy Commission, Washington, D.C., (1974),
    Report WASH–1297; R. C. Erdmann et al, "Status Report on
    the EPRI Fuel Cycle Accident Risk Assessment," Science
    Applications Inc., Palo Alto, Cal. (July 1979), Report
    NP–1128, p. 1–4.

18. S. V. Szokolay, "Solar Energy and Building", second edition,
    John Wiley, New York, (1977).

19. "Energy Requirements of a Solar Heating System", National
    Research Council, Ottawa (Feb. 1979), Report EPO–79–1.

20. As reported in Oak Ridge Review, 12 20 (1979).

DISCUSSION

COHEN: Consider occupational disease versus occupational accident
deaths. The occupational accident death rate in the United States
is something like 12,500 a year. The OSHA estimate of the number of
deaths per year from occupational disease is 100,000 per year. That
means that the occupational disease would be eight times the accident
fatality rate and you're saying it is a couple percent of the accident
fatality rate.

     The Bureau of Labor Statistics records occupational disease
deaths by a narrow definition. What they call occupational disease
is if a person working on the job gets some chemicals on his hands,
is burned, and dies from that. But there are many occupational diseases that are not so obvious, and they are not recorded.

INHABER: Well, of course, I am a Canadian and I hesitate to tell an
American agency how to get their act together, but I would say that
I have been basing these calculations on the Bureau of Labor Stat-
istics, and to a certain extent the National Safety Council.

COHEN: The National Safety Council record is just accidents. The
Bureau of Labor Statistics records only diseases which are obviously
and very closely related to occupations.

INHABER: I understand the problem and I am not exactly sure how I
can resolve it.

COHEN: OSHA gives the numbers.

INHABER: But 100,000 does seem rather high. There may be experts
on occupational health who want to comment on that.

COHEN: The total number of job-related accidental deaths last year
was 12,500.

INHABER: There seems to be a contradiction here which I cannot
resolve.

BERG: I wanted to make a technical distinction between the quantities
alluded to by the speaker and the commentator. Dr. Inhaber, in his
second statistic, was speaking of work days lost and not of deaths.
In considering occupation-related disease, Dr. Cohen spoke of deaths
but not work days lost. So you're not addressing the same statistic.
This is probably the reason for the discrepancy.

     Now, Dr. Inhaber converted the accident-related deaths into
work days lost by the 6,000 multiplier, and that's a big multiplier.
So perhaps your numbers are not that far apart. Is your point, then,

that he should compare deaths blamed on occupation to deaths on the job rather than work days lost?

COHEN: He's only blaming occupational disease deaths on diseases which are very obviously and closely related to occupational factors. And this in only the tip of the iceberg on occupational disease deaths.

BERG: He then used days lost on a job as another statistic.

KATES: You're both right, of course, but the morbidity figure on occupational disease is even more underestimated, it seems to me, because there is no regular reporting form. We only have national health surveys which give general population estimates. The international differences you cite can often be traced to the compensation system. When the compensation system is used for disease, the figures go up spectacularly, as opposed to where it is not in effect. Where compensation systems for accidents have been long in effect, the reporting systems for accidents are, I would think, much more accurate.

I'd like to comment on some of the caveats you mentioned. I basically welcome this kind of analysis, but I think it's very important to understand the caveats, as well as to understand how these analyses may be used in the media. You have probably seen some of the stuff in the papers. Maybe that, more than the content of the report, infuriated some people.

First of all, on your assumption of using the current state of the art, I, too, have been very worried about what I think is the misunderstanding among alternative energy proponents about the safety problem involved in alternative energy systems. I've been studying wood, for example. We have an epidemic of chain saw accidents in New England at the moment.

But my purpose is not to try to demonstrate the superiority of one system over another, but rather to consider all systems because it helps in hazard management. I think it is extraordinarily important to understand the amount of effort that's gone into reducing the risk of any technological system. In very few technological systems do you find the safety input occurring simultaneously with the technological development. In fact, nuclear power is probably the one in which you come closest to a prompt effort toward safety. Traditionally, there was an enormous time lag time in society between the introduction of a technology, or the revival and rediscovery of an old technology, and the catching up of safety efforts.

For example, consider the transition of a chain saw from a specialized instrument used by forestry workers to a tool used by

laymen. By the way, agriculture, forestry, and construction are the
classic industries where very little effort or investment in safety
has ever gone on. When the chain saw became a popular instrument,
an enormous epidemic of accidents occurred. But there will be changes
and the chain saw ten years from now will be a much safer chain saw
than the one used today.

So in that sense, because many of the so-called alternative
energy technologies are just becoming popular, the bias is that their
safety will lag considerably. It will especially lag if the proponents of that system do not appreciate the problems and don't invest time and money in solving those problems.

The second thing is, I was very much surprised when you described
the actuarial versus the theoretical projections. I find you don't
meet my objections to that. I agree that there's no way to avoid
putting actuarial and theoretical data together if we are going to
arrive at some judgements, but we have to do it very cautiously and
appreciate the many, many differentiations that exist between these
kinds of data.

There are at least three different kinds of theoretical data
that we should address, not just actuarial versus theoretical. We're
talking about simulated accident data, which are computer codes, or
calculations on backs of envelopes, or Rassmussen reports. We're
talking about dose-response curves, some weak, some strong, which
can be classed as correlative data. In the simulated data, we pre-
tend we understand the laws of physics that may go into the simulation, but we don't have any empirical results. In the correlations, we may not understand the laws of biology that linked our
cause with effect, but we have some empirical results. And both
types of data are theoretical.

The third kind of data is brought in by people who consider
"risk factors" as if they were theoretically related: for example,
the risk of being born a male in America, or any other of the hundreds of factors highly correlated with life expectancy, such as
socioeconomic class or education. The problem is that people begin
to take these seriously. For example, we have a rash of cases of
tetraethyl chloride being discovered in drinking water in New England.
The head of the environmental protection agency in Massachusetts says,
using, I guess, Richard Wilson's list, that the risk is equivalent
to visiting for two days in New York or smoking 1/4 of a cigarette,
and so on, mixing together actuarial and theoretical data without
any of the caveats that all of us in this room understand. It's as
if we have established a common currency of risk. We would make risk
into a common utility. And I would argue if we accept that, all of
the time we spent these last three days carefully arguing whether
we have enough evidence and so on, is water down the drain. We need

to make comparisons in order to make decisions, but first we must
get back to the original evidential basis of the projections. The
evidential basis may be weak.

And finally, my most important problem is the "with or without"
problem. In the absence of a technology, for example, in the absence
of solar panels, would we be still making that much copper sheeting,
or would that investment be going to something else?

That problem always worries me. If you think of the classical
cost-benefit analysis, it always has to include a "with or without"
analysis. If we did not put the copper into solar panels, one could
argue we would be putting it into something else and still have that
same base-level of risk. But of a different type. If the same trade-
off applied across the board, then there would be no problem. But
if certain technologies require unique production systems with distinctive quality mixes, we may be introducing a particular bias.

INHABER: In terms of the compensation system for disease, I believe
you are correct. In other words, when compensation was made for
black lung in the United States it was brought out that there were
far more cases than a lot of people were expecting. How many were
valid or invalid, I'm not in a position to say. But statistically,
a great many cases occurred once compensation was produced.

The second question you raised was how fast does the rate of
occupational accidents change? There is not too much evidence on
this, I must admit. I can quote a few figures from the National
Safety Council. Of course, one has problems with the reporting mandated by the various laws which have been passed in the last few
years. Some people have said this just encourages more reporting of
accidents rather than showing a greater rate of accidents. This is
a possibility. But I looked at 23 groups of industries between 1971
and 1976, and 18 of these showed an increase, which indicates that
most occupational accident rates are not dropping fast. In terms of
coal mining it has been dropping over the past half century, but in
most other occupations, that does not seem to be the case.

I don't have too much comment on your third point concerning
actuarial and theoretical projections because I thought the points
were well taken.

The fourth point about what I call incremental risk is a little
trickier and I have thought about it. In other words, would the
people have been killed if the solar panels had never been produced
in the first place? This is more of a philosophical point rather
than one which could be proved one way or the other. My philosophical inclination is to say that if you have a solar panel, or a turbine for a nuclear reactor, there are going to be so many people
killed or injured in producing the steel and coal or whatever, and

in being exposed to the waste products of the process. But these
people may have been killed or injured if the turbine had not been
produced or the collector had not been built. This is a theoretical
consideration that I have not put on paper.

CROW: If you're counting coal accident rates, is this per hour
worked or per ton of coal produced? I ask it partly because I read
somewhere that when measured the latter way, the accident rate went
down fairly rapidly for the past half century, but that it hasn't
for the past two years because of a recent drop in productivity.

INHABER: That's correct.

COHEN: There were 250 accidental fatalities a year before the 1969
Act and there are about 150 a year now, producing roughly the same
amount of coal -- actually 10% more coal. If you go back to early in
the century, there were as many as 1,400 per year producing roughly
the same amount of coal that is produced now, that is, 600 million
tons.

INHABER: The work force was much greater. I have read the deaths
per man hour have changed very slightly.

COHEN: I spoke of deaths per ton of coal.

WEINBERG: Would you take this opportunity first to state what you
consider to be the most telling or relevant of the criticisms that
the Berkeley group has offered on your study. And second, what your
response to that most telling or most violent criticism is.

INHABER: They made a considerable number of criticisms, some of
which were valid and some of which were invalid. I consider most of
them to be invalid or at best subject to great dispute, and in dispute long before I came on the scene.

The most telling criticism was that there was a fairly substantial error in the materials calculations for wind power, an error of
about a factor of 20. That error, however, was removed by the time
that the Science article was printed. The other error that I made
was that the construction risk for building the four conventional
systems that I considered -- that is, nuclear, coal, oil and natural
gas -- was not included due to an oversight on my part. The construction risk is not the risk due to obtaining the uranium or the coal
but actually building the reactor or the coal-fired plant. This was
left out by mistake.

Those were the criticisms. My answer to those criticisms is
that the values of those errors on a relative basis were very small.
For example, in terms of nuclear power, leaving out the construction

risk amounted to about 1.4 man days lost per megawatt year. Nuclear
power ranged between 4 and 10 man-days lost per megawatt year. So
it changed the value of the maximum, which is what most people concentrated on, for better or for worse, by about 20%. Obviously, the
minimum changed by about 50%.

In terms of wind power, again a comparable proportion of the
risk was due to construction. Again, the wind power risk did not
change substantially.

Therefore, I consider that there were errors in the absolute
values, which I have admitted, but the relative rankings remained
almost the same. I have the slide which shows the rankings from the
first edition compared to the fourth draft, which I have just shown.
The numerical risks clearly have changed somewhat, but the overall
order I would say is about the same. I ran statistical tests and I
find that the differences between power sources remained quite similar between the calculation of March, 1978, and the corrected calculations of June, 1980.

I might point to some work by Harry Hoy who went over some of
the occupational risks at the American Nuclear Society meeting in
Knoxville a month or two ago. His values are somewhat different from
mine but close enough. This was for the occupational rather than the
total risk.

HAVE THE NUCLEAR POWER RISK ASSESSORS FAILED?

Leonard A. Sagan

Electric Power Research Institute
3412 Hillview Avenue
Palo Alto, California   94303

Over the past several years, a number of investigators have
attempted estimates of the risks to health from the operation of
nuclear power plants[1].   Quite consistently these studies have
concluded that the generation of electricity from nuclear fuels is
no more hazardous, and may well be considerably less hazardous,
than generation of an equal quantity of electrical energy from
conventional sources, and in one study from solar generation[2].
Other studies demonstrate that nuclear generation is more economic
than generation from fossil fuels, and the growing worldwide
commitment to nuclear by private utilities suggests that their
experience is consistent with that conclusion.

If nuclear power generation poses a lesser threat to health
and costs less to produce than the alternatives, why is it that
the construction and operation of nuclear power plants has become
the object of widespread and growing public opposition, restrictive legislation and political debate both here and abroad?
Clearly, this intense opposition may spring from a number of
sources but among them there appears to be a scepticism of the
risk assessment.   That nuclear power poses a lesser threat than
the alternatives may be indisputable to the risk assessment community, but has failed to impress large segments of the public.
This divergence of perceptions by the risk assessment community
and by the public creates enormous conflicts and social costs
which deserve attention.   In this paper I will attempt to explore
and evaluate these differences in perception, often depending upon
personal observations and judgement in the absence of available
data.

I will conclude in the first part of this paper that many persons do not appear to accept all of the assumptions which underlie the risk model; for example, they may weight death from radiation exposure far more heavily than death from other causes whereas the model weights all causes of death equally. Others, while not differing with the assumptions, view the uncertainties in the data base as unacceptably large and will not tolerate that degree of uncertainty. Another large number of persons, perhaps the largest, are unable or unwilling to examine the model or data themselves but have made their personal "nuclear decision" on the basis of following opinion leaders whom they admire or trust, or, contrariwise, rejecting the opinions of experts or authorities whom they distrust.

In the second part of this paper, I will also conclude that the controversy over nuclear power cannot be solely understood in terms of risk to health, the issue most openly discussed. It will be suggested that the issue of nuclear power is largely symbolic and can only be fully understood in terms of often covert ideological and psychological conflicts. It is not my intention to demean or belittle the two parties to this conflict; rather, it is my belief that the basically political issues which divide them be better openly argued.

PART 1:   THE RISK ASSESSMENT MODEL.

A.   WHAT IS RISK ASSESSMENT?

Risk assessment is a relatively young discipline, made possible only in recent years by the availability of quantitative estimates of injury and illness under specified conditions and by access to computers. Fundamental to the construction of a technological risk assessment is the development of a "model", i.e., assumptions about which health impairments or "costs" will be included in the assessment and how these shall be weighted and aggregated. Shall all morbidity no matter how trivial be included? Shall psychological costs be included? Shall occupational as well as public health be evaluated? Shall effects in following generations (genetic effects) be estimated? Boundaries and arbitrary assumptions must be established by the risk assessor in creating his model. These assumptions will, implicitly or explicitly, be heavily value-laden and will reflect the priorities of the assessor. If his values are at variance with those of the constituency for whose consideration the assessment is constructed, the assessment will have failed and will be ignored. Have the values of the nuclear risk assessors been congruent with those of the public? If not, that would provide one explanation for the apparent rejection of nuclear power by a sector of the public. The relevant assumptions underlying nuclear assessments will be examined later in this paper.

A second possible explanation for the failure of risk assessment may arise from the judgment that the method of risk assessment implies that some risk is inevitable and unavoidable, therefore requiring evaluation against some set of standards whether they be economic or moral. Those who reject this notion of the inevitability of risk may well also reject risk assessment methodology since they will see such efforts as creating a basis for the acceptance of such risks which they may view as immoral. Much of our recent regulatory legislation was written with language which implies that zero risk is attainable and with the mandate that such levels be achieved. The Delaney amendment to the Food and Drug laws is the ultimate expression of this faith.

The more common view is that zero risk is not achievable and that some realistic compromise must be reached. The underlying credo is that health and safety can be considered as economic commodities (rather than as moral imperatives) that can be bought for a price. The ultimate questions then become "how much health and safety can we afford," or "are the risks associated with this technology as low as can reasonably be achieved?" To what extent this element accounts for the rejection of nuclear power is not known: it will not be further discussed.

Still a third reason that risk assessment appears to have had relatively little impact on the issue of nuclear power acceptability is that the question of health effects may not be seen as of over-riding importance to that issue. Health costs may be an important issue in technology acceptance: they are not the only issue. Questions of national interests, international balance of payments and other issues as tangential as "life style" and political preferences may be associated explicitly or implicitly with nuclear power. I will return to these questions in the discussion.

WHAT ARE THE ASSUMPTIONS UNDERLYING THE NUCLEAR POWER RISK ASSESSMENT MODEL?

We turn now to the model of nuclear power risks and examine how well the underlying assumptions regarding health, coincide with those of the public as a whole. Identical assumptions have often been made in evaluation of electricity generated by fossil fuels.

INCLUDE THE ENTIRE FUEL CYCLE

The assumption here is that assessment should include not only those risks associated with power generation but should logically begin at the "front end" of the fuel cycle, i.e., with the extraction, refining and transportation of fuel to the generating station. This logic gains weight from the knowledge that the extraction industries are often quite hazardous because of both the frequency of accidents and the dusty environment in which miners work. Not only are occupational personnel exposed to risk at mining sites, but both liquid and gaseous leachates from mining operations may affect public water and air supply. These health costs may be as great or greater than effects at the generating station.

The "back end" of the fuel cycle, which encompasses disposition of "ashes" whether nuclear or fossil also has potential health effects and again, logic requires that these be assessed.

What has been excluded from all nuclear risk assessments are the risks associated with transmission, distribution and end use of the electrical energy. Obviously there are risks here, the most conspicuous of which is electric shock, but these are common to all systems regardless of energy source. Since nuclear risk estimates are often constructed with the assumption of making comparison with other fuels, the end use effects have been ignored.

Since much public concern regarding nuclear power relates to the back end, i.e., waste disposal, there is little reason to speculate that this first assumption is at variance with the implicit public model.

INCLUDE OCCUPATIONAL RISKS, AND WEIGHT THEM EQUALLY WITH RISKS TO THE PUBLIC

This assumption may well be at variance with the implicit public model but data on this point are not available. This is an issue which deserves some study since there are relatively large differences in occupational risk among energy sources. If the public gives a lesser weight (value) to occupational risk than to risks imposed on the public, comparative risks among energy sources might well be shifted.

There are strong reasons to suspect that the occupational risks and public risks are not viewed with neutrality. The former have a large voluntary component; the latter are largely involuntary, a variable which Starr has shown to be important[3]. There is the opportunity for the employee to inform himself of the magnitude of his risk. Members of the public often are unaware of the risk of possible injury or ill health imposed by industrial activity.

INCLUDE ACCIDENTAL INJURIES AND WEIGHT THEM EQUALLY WITH CHRONIC DISEASE INDUCTION

This assumption springs from the logic that death or disability, whatever the cause, is to be given equal weight and merits the same avoidance effort. Since most of the accidental deaths occur among occupational personnel and most of the concern regarding chronic disease effects occurs among members of the public, the weakness of this assumption overlaps with that of the previous assumption just discussed, i.e., there is reason to believe that the public would not view deaths from trauma and deaths from all chronic diseases with neutrality (given that both occur at the same age).

For one thing, some chronic disease is associated with particular dread, e.g., cancer. A lingering painful death such as that from cancer would almost certainly be given much greater weight than the sudden death associated with, say, an airplane crash. It may well be that public concern is as much related to pain and suffering as to death itself.

There is still another element in the assumption regarding accidents that may be at variance with the public judgment, namely, that accidental injuries and deaths can be averaged over time. This would imply that the public is indifferent to one death per day for 100 days or 100 deaths occurring once each 100 days. The attention given to large scale accidents by the press compared to the apathy afforded over 50,000 deaths per year from auto accidents strongly suggests that this is not the case, i.e., that the more spectacular accident is viewed with greater alarm than the more frequent single accident.

This bears strongly on public attitudes toward nuclear power. Slovic[4] has shown that although public attitudes toward risks of normally operating nuclear power plants are not greatly different from those of experts, the public does have an exaggerated view of the probability and consequences of catastrophic accidents in general and of nuclear reactor accidents in particular. The sources of these fears are not well known, but visions of the devastated cities of Hiroshima and Nagasaki might erroneously contribute to public confusion between weapons and power plants.

THE DATA BASE

In addition to possible defects in the risk assessment model, there are weaknesses in the data base that make suspect conclusions drawn from operation of the model. Some of this scepticism is justified, some not.

While there appears to be considerable public uncertainty regarding knowledge of low level radiation effects, this portion of the data base is, as is frequently noted, probably better understood than is any other environmental agent. For example, the widespread consensus that the Three Mile Island accidental release of radioactivity could be confidently predicted to cause no more than one additional cancer death among the surrounding populations has not been seriously challenged.

Whereas that confidence grows out of the experience of observations among many tens of thousands of irradiated humans, predictions of serious nuclear accidents, which are thought to have extremely low probability are based on very limited experience. Although worldwide experience with normally operating nuclear reactors is now growing, the number of accidents is, fortunately, very limited. Estimates of reactor accidents must necessarily be based, then, upon theoretical constructs not susceptible to experiential test, i.e., the predictions must be considered to have wide margins of error.

Still another area of uncertainty relates to possible genetic effects of radiation exposure. A number of observations suggest that fear of genetic defects in coming generations underlies much of the fear among women.

Although estimates of the risk of genetic disease following radiation exposure have been developed by the United Nations[5], these estimates are based solely on observations in exposed animal populations. Absence of detectable genetic effects among exposed Japanese populations gives us assurance that mutation rates in humans are not greater than those in animals; still, it is not known with any degree of certainty how such induced genetic defects mights manifest themselves in humans.

Nevertheless, the magnitude of radiation exposures from nuclear power operation are small compared to other sources of exposure including natural sources. Furthermore, exposures from reactors are small even in comparison with natural geographic variations. Therefore, even though we should be seriously in error regarding genetic risk estimates, consequences of nuclear power operation would be small compared to those which occur due to natural causes.

Lastly, even in the unlikely event of a large accidental exposure to neighboring communities, the Japanese experience should reassure us that there would be no detectable effect following such an accident.

THE RISK AGGREGATION PROBLEM

In attempting to provide a summary or aggregate value of the health risks implicit in the nuclear fuel cycle, the assessment must find some means of providing a common dimension for such diverse effects as transient reversible disability and chronic disease producing suffering and death.

Some investigators and government agencies have attempted to apply some dollar value to these health costs, the dollar being our most usual currency for measuring the value of assets and liabilities. Clearly, courts and insurance companies constantly make such estimates of the dollar value of imposed health effects; there is extensive experience and precedent with the method. Yet, there seems to be reluctance on the part of the public to consider health (or its absence) in terms of dollars. American mythology places health above price, i.e., "health is priceless". Furthermore, even with some agreement on the use of a dollar value for various health defects, it is not clear against which standard this dollar value could be measured as acceptable.

An alternative and more widely used technique is to compare the estimates of health cost associated with the nuclear cycle with health costs similarly estimated for the fossil fuel cycle. This technique, too, has its limitations. Firstly, there are limitations similar to those noted above for the nuclear cycle: problem of arbitrary assumptions, data base and aggregation. If there exists controversy regarding the data base and interpretation of low level radiation effects, the controversy regarding possible public health effects of exposure to fossil fuel combustion products is even more intense and the uncertainty greater. Also, many of the anti-nuclear persuasion argue that this standard of comparison, i.e., with fossil fuel effects, does not represent an adequate standard of acceptable risk: both are considered unacceptable. There is some justice in this criticism and that brings us to the last problem area.

THE NOTION OF ACCEPTABLE RISK

There is some logic to the notion that technology must meet the test of acceptable safety, but there is no consensus nor has there been public discussion of what such a level should be. Starr has shown that risks to the public from industrial fatal

accidents fall within the range of risk posed by death from natural causes, suggesting an implicit standard[3]. Still, great
variations exist within those boundaries. Nuclear power risks,
which are small by that comparison, apparently fail to meet that
standard for a large section of the public. The frequency of
death and illness, a crude measure of risk, may have to be
weighted by many of the variables discussed above relating to the
special characteristics of the risk.

The preceding discussion was intended to provide some perspective on nuclear risk assessment and its weaknesses as an
introduction to the question, "do these weaknesses explain the
high level of concern and even hostility directed toward nuclear
power by certain anti-nuclear segments of the public?" In my
opinion the answer is in the negative. In the following paragraphs, I will discuss some hypotheses which I believe may provide
motives for the rejection of nuclear power. In each case, opposition grows from motives other than a concern for health. I wish
to emphasize, however, that I do not mean to dismiss all opposition to nuclear power as motivated by political or psychological
objectives. Clearly, as noted above, there are legitimate reasons
for concern. Nevertheless, other elements to be described below,
also appear to play a role, particularly among activists who are
part of the anti-nuclear "movement."

PART 2: THE ANTI-NUCLEAR MOVEMENT AS A "SEARCH FOR MEANING".

Throughout human history, mankind has had to cope with uncertainty in a very unpredictable world. Two sometimes related
defense mechanisms have been the use of religious dogma and/or
political ideology. Religion provides answers to the unanswera-
ble, e.g., where do we come from, where do we go, why does this
happen to me? (Ideology provides the goals and values toward which
meaningful and organized efforts can be directed.) When the faith
weakens or the level of anxiety grows, or both, cults, sects and
movements appear to capture the ideological needs of alienated
members of society. Affluence seems to generate both anxiety and
alienation.

Irving Kristol, in commenting on this phenomenon, observed,
"The better the system works, the more affluent and freer the
society, the more marked is the tendency to impose an ever greater
psychic burden upon the individual. He has to cope with his
'existential' human needs--with the life of the mind, the psyche,
and the spirit--on his own. At the same time, precisely because
the beurgeois-capitalist order is so 'boring' from this 'existential' point of view, what poet has ever sung its praises? What
novelist was ever truly inspired by the career of a businessman?
The psychic needs are more acute. A dangerous dialectic is

thereby created. Young people, no longer hard pressed to 'better
their condition' are all the more free to experience the limitations of their social world, to rebel against them, to participate
in what Lionel Trilling called 'The Adversary Culture'"[6].

But what evidence is there that the anti-nuclear movement is
a surrogate for such a "search for meaning" and why should nuclear
power be chosen to play that role? As noted earlier, such movements appear when the conventional faith fails as a remedy for
uncertainty and/or when the level of anxiety grows. I believe
that we are in such a period of uncertainty, a turning point in
our history where old values have failed and new ones are being
generated, a national identity crisis, if you will.

If one examines the constituency of the activist anti-nuclear
movement, its ranks are filled with those most critical and scep-
tical of existing political and social institutions and whose
needs for faith, a credo, are greatest: middle class youth and
older members of the liberal establishment. If there is doubt
that the word "movement" applies, watch an anti-nuclear demonstra-
tion--the preaching, the holding of hands, the singing, the right-
eousness and the instinct to martyrdom, going to jail, all reflect
the religious quality of a movement.

A sociological study of nuclear knowledge and nuclear attitudes concludes that those with pro-nuclear and those with anti-
nuclear views are about equally well informed on nuclear technology. The investigators speculate that underlying political and
social attitudes determine opinion of nuclear power acceptability. Their data suggests that information is selectively
perceived so as to support the pre-existing beliefs and that
individuals rarely permit contrary information to challenge their
beliefs[7].

Why Nuclear Power?

Why should nuclear power be chosen for such a role? "Why not
alligators?" someone asked me. Radiation, associated with war and
disease, invisible and deadly, is widely viewed with suspicion
and, I believe, with a good deal of misunderstanding. The assumption of a linear relationship between risk to a population and
radiation exposure is mistakenly taken to mean that low level
radiation produces some cumulative biological damage within each
exposed individual, rather than a stochastic risk to some individual. This notion represents a misunderstanding of radiation
risk which leaves unaffected all except the rare individual who
manifests a late effect.

The incongruence between the scientific understanding of the
magnitude and mechanisms of radiation damage and the perception of

these risks by the public reflects a serious defect in the ability
of the scientific community to communicate with the public. There
are a number of reasons for this, among which are the complexities
and jargon associated with science. An understanding of radiation
risk requires some minimal acquaintance with biological phenomena
including toxicology as well as with the tools of the trade such
as RADS, REMS and "dose-response relationships," fairly heady concepts. Secondly, many scientists, out of a sense of distrust of
the media, or an inability to simplify, or both, avoid media
contacts. Furthermore, there are no professional rewards for
successfully explaining science to the public. On the contrary,
scientists who make a serious effort at communicating with the
public (which foots the bill for their work) are viewed by their
colleagues as "popularizers". This leaves the media dependent
upon those few scientists who often have highly controversial
views which are at variance with those of the wider scientific
community and who turn to the media to obtain an airing for those
controversial views. The history of the nuclear power controversy
has been particularly blighted by such mavericks.

We come now to the most speculative, but perhaps most provocative observation regarding perception of risk. Professor Renee
Fox suggests that hazards that appear to threaten our biologic
heritage and therefore our ability to survive as a race are perceived as intolerable[9]. In his discussion of the intense controversy surrounding recombinant DNA research, he quotes
Thomas[10], "The recombinant line of research is . . . upsetting,
not because of the dangers now being argued about but because it
is disturbing in a fundamental way to face the fact that genetic
machinery in control of the planet's life can be fooled around
with so easily. We do not like the idea that anything so fixed
and stable as a species line can be changed. The notion that
genes can be taken out of one genome and inserted into another is
unnerving." There is much to suggest a parallel explanation
regarding the concern for nuclear power which may be viewed by
many as not only posing the possibility of creating a disaster,
but a threat to the human genetic machinery as well.

The second point that Fox makes is that the human source of
this potential hazard greatly enhances public apprehension. He
says, "This shuddering sense of metaphysical danger is premised
not only on the belief that human error is unnatural, ungovernable
and particularly difficult to rectify or reverse; but also on the
belief that it is made more lethal by the moral and spiritual
weaknesses of human beings and human societies--above all, by the
evils that result from their self-centeredness and their temptation to play God." Suffice it to say that this insight deserves a
good deal more evaluation.

Still another mechanism which may well be operating to generate fear of nuclear power is a conservative element in society which evokes concern with any new technology. Although there has been little scholarly study of this phenomenon, there has been some resistance to the introduction of all new technology particularly where public health and safety may be perceived as threatened. Examination of the contemporary literature associated with the development of smallpox vaccination, the pasteurization of milk, fluoridation of water or such technologies as electrification and automobile transportation will indicate widespread concern and resistance.

Populism.

In addition to the misconception regarding low level radiation effects, there are other characteristics of nuclear power which contribute to its becoming the object of a movement. Within American history there is a strong current of suspiciousness of authority and power, sometimes known as populism, which also includes the notion that these powerful institutions are both exploiting the masses and subverting the popular will. Beginning with King George III, many Americans react with concern to power as well as to symbols of power. Nuclear power may well be viewed as a proxy for many of the sources of economic and political power in America. Public utilities, giant vendors such as Westinghouse and General Electric, and federal agencies all have vested interests in nuclear power. Furthermore, the complexity of reactors and the intricacies of low level radiation may themselves create barriers to public understanding and acceptance. As a psychiatrist, Robert L. DuPont[8], has recently pointed out, those who are able to understand these issues will themselves be viewed with some suspicion as "one of them" rather than "one of us", and therefore suspect.

Not all members of the anti-nuclear movement are driven by the same motives. From my perspective, some of those in leadership roles are exploiting some genuine concerns for their own political motives. By "political motives" I mean that nuclear power is seen by some as a useful battleground on which to fight broader social and political conflicts. Many of the nuclear opponents make no secret of their interest in radical political change. One of them, Amory Lovins, has said that he would be opposed to nuclear power even if he were assured that it were absolutely safe and harmless[11]" i.e, his opposition is based on considerations other than health. The list could be easily expanded. The reader may search his own knowledge of the leading anti-nuclear spokespeople for evidence of political motives.

The Underlying Issues.

If indeed the nuclear debate has been politicized and if a
broad sector of the public in "search of meaning" have been
coopted for political purposes, just what are those political
purposes? Beginning in eighteenth century England there appeared
certain notions regarding the conduct of economic affairs, namely
that business operates most efficiently when left unfettered by
government, church or other institutional constraints. These
concepts developed in parallel with notions of political freedom
which have similar historical roots. In the subsequent two centuries, Western Europe and North America have witnessed an unprecedented explosion in productivity as well as in other indices
generally accepted as measures of the quality of life.

Yet, in the mid-ninteenth century, those liberal views which
generated both the economic and political benefits just noted,
came under attack particularly by certain German intellectuals
including Marx and Hegel. Their views included a centrally managed society and abandoned the Laissez-Faire doctrines of the
British economists. Although there are few who still believe that
what is now called "capitalism" will disintegrate through inherent
defects and internal inconsistencies, there are many who find
sufficient defects so that they prefer the Marxist or socialist
alternative. Those defects include distributional inequities,
recurrent business cycles and consequent unemployment as well as a
longer list which includes alienation of the individual, "corpor-
ate-exploitation", "imperialism", etc. In capsule form, this
polarization of views regarding political organization is the
central issue which I believe separates the stridently anti- from
the stridently pro-nuclear forces.

I hope not to be misunderstood: I see elements of the
nuclear establishment also engaged in a "search for meaning" in
terms of the political contest briefly described above. Staunch
defenders of the principles of free-enterprise and personal
liberty, they too have politicized the nuclear debate. Stereo-
typically, their faith lies with the benefits of technology and
capitalism. They are reluctant to recognize the defects of that
economic and political system which has produced modern western
society.

The Media.

The last issue on which I must comment, even if in brief
passing, is the media. Dr. Robert DuPont, who has taken a special
interest in media presentation of nuclear issues, finds that
television particularly dwells on the "what if's?"[8]. TV com-
mentators, says DuPont, seem to feel that only bad news is exciting and furthermore, their credibility depends upon warning of

worst possible consequences. If their predictions turn out to have exaggerated the risk, no harm done, but if the public had been reassured in the remote case of a serious accident, credibility would be lost, or so they seem to think.

The report of the President's Commission on the Accident at Three Mile Island[12] concluded that the errors and sensationalism reported by the news media merely reflected the confusion and ignorance of the facts by the official sources of information. It further concluded that the press did a creditable ("more reassuring than alarming") job of news coverage.

One of the commissioners, Mrs. Ann Trunk, a resident of Middletown, disagreed with this conclusion and observed. "In fact, these conclusions are not generally supported by the staff reports. There were reliable news sources available. Too much emphasis was placed on the "what if" rather than the "what is." As a result, the public was pulled into a state of terror, of psychological stress. More so than any other normal source of news, the evening national news reports by the major networks proved to be the most depressing, the most terrifying. Confusion cannot explain away the mismanagement of a news event of this magnitude."

Cui Bono?

Finally, in evaluating why a distorted view of the risks of nuclear power should not only persist but actually be thriving, it may be well to consider who it is that may benefit from this exaggerated public concern. Starr and Whipple have noted that, if risk assessments and public perceptions differ sufficiently, conflicts will arise and social costs will accrue[13]. When such costs are paid, some lose and some gain. In the case of nuclear power, there will be winners just as in all instances of exaggerated public fear. For example, William Clark[14], in examining the phenomenon of witch-hunting during the middle ages, observes that for young men, witch-hunting offered an excellent opportunity for exciting work, career development, advancement and training. When the provision for confiscating the property of the convicted witches was abolished, witch-hunting quickly disappeared.

Clark goes on to say: "Early preaching against witchcraft and its evils almost certainly put the idea of witches (read "radiation effects") into many a head that never would have imagined such things if left to its own devices. The harder the inquisition looked, the bigger its staff, the stronger its motivation, the more witches it discovered. A general question then arises concerning the causal relationship between assessment and risk: which is driving what? Since the resulting higher discov-

ery rate of witch risks obviously justifies more search effort,
the whole process becomes self-contained. Today, we ask, "Is this
a risk?" with no logical observation which could force an answer,
"No".

In the following paragraphs, we look at who benefits from the
anti-nuclear movement.

1) Clearly, radiation scientists benefit from public concern
with low level radiation. Federal research budgets are dictated
far more by public concern than by any objective measure of the
magnitude of a problem or the liklihood of a successful research
effort. Here I do not mean to discredit the motives or sincere
concerns of radiation scientists which intrigue them, but I would
suggest that scientists, like all the rest of us, require
resources to support their professional and economic activities.
Public concern about low level radiation will not go unnoticed nor
unmentioned in scientific testimony to legislators and administra-
tors.

2) Like scientists, regulators will benefit from great
public concern about nuclear safety and from demands for increasing regulatory control. Following the Three Mile Island accident,
the Nuclear Regulatory Commission staff increased, budget
increased and opportunities for promotion increased in spite of
the absense of any clear evidence that such changes will increase
public safety.

3) Lawyers always benefit from conflict and controversy
which it is their duty to resolve. Exaggerated concern for low
level radiation has created an avalanche of compensation and
liability suits alleging radiation produced health effects.

4) The electronic and printed media benefit from lurid
presentation of sensationalized fears. As one journalist has
pointed out, "No one will ever see a morning headline reading,
'World Trade Center Still Standing.'"

5) Public relations firms and lobbyists who attempt to
counter the anti-nuclear movement benefit from this public concern.

6) Lastly, as noted above, risk assessors clearly benefit
from the intense public inquiry into the true risks of nuclear
power.

To what extent the anti-nuclear movement is encouraged, if at
all, by these forces, is unknown, but, it is suggested here, the
issue deserves some attention if that movement is to be understood.

Finally, and in conclusion, I should like to answer the question posed by the title of this paper, "Have the risk assessors failed?" No. I do not believe that they have failed--they have been overtaken by powerful historical forces. If the risk assessors are to refine their trade, they must study and understand these forces and see them as an opportunity to improve the craft of risk assessment.

REFERENCES

(1)   Comar, C. and Sagan, L.: Health Effects of Energy Production and Conversion. Ann. Rev. of Energy, 1, 581-600, 1976.

(2)   Inhaber, H.: Risk with Energy from Conventional and Nonconventional Sources. Science, 203:718-23, 1979.

(3)   Starr, C.: Social benefit versus technological risk. Science, 165:1232-1238(1969)

(4)   Slovic, P.: Images of Disaster: Perception and acceptance of risks from nuclear power. In Perceptions of Risk, Proc. Fifteenth Annual Meeting of the National Council on Radiation Protection and Measurements. Washington, D.C., Mar. 14-15, 1979

(5)   United Nations Scientific Committee on the Effects of Atomic Radiation: Sources and effects of ionizing radiation. 1977 Report to the General Assembly, New York

(6)   Kristol, I.: Two Cheers for Capitalism. Basic Books, N.Y., pg. XI(1978)

(7)   Reed, J. and Wilkes, J.: Nuclear Knowledge and Nuclear Attitudes: An Examination of Informed Opinion. Unpublished Manuscript

(8)   DuPont, R.L.: Nuclear Phobia--Phobic Thinking About Nuclear Power. The Media Institute, Washington, D.C.(1980)

(9)   Fox, R.C.: The Evolution of Medical Uncertainty. Milbank Memorial Fund Quarterly 58 1-49, 1980

(10) Thomas, L.: The Medusa and the Snail. New York: Viking, 1979.

(11) Lovins, A.: Soft Energy Paths. Ballinger Publishing Co., Cambridge, Mass., p. 56(1977)

(12) Report of the President's Commission on the Accident at Three Mile Island. Washington, D.C., Oct. 30, 1979

(13) Starr, C. and Whipple, C.: Risks of Risk Decisions. Science, 208:1114-1119(1980)

(14) Clark W.: Witches, Floods, and Wonder Drugs. Proc. of Symposium on Societal Risk Assessment sponsored by General Motors Corp., Warren, Mich., Oct. 7-9, 1979 (in press, Plenum Press, 1980)

DISCUSSION

CRANMER: At the risk of sounding a little cynical, could you add another balloon to your figure and put in "Competing Industry"?

I heard an interesting discussion on television not too long ago where an individual representing the gas industry was quite anti-nuclear, voicing certain types of health concerns and why society had to turn to the expansion of his particular industry. He certainly had an axe to grind and something to gain from it.

SAGAN: Somebody from the gas industry, did you say?

CRANMER: The person was an executive for a gas and oil company, operating primarily in Canada, who argued that there were enough reserves if we expanded it and made it economical and that we should do things that way. It wasn't worth the risk, in his opinion, to go nuclear.

SAGAN: I've heard conspiratorial rumors about the antinuclear movement being funded by Middle Eastern oil interests. I've never seen evidence of that. Within the United States most of the nuclear industry is closely allied with the energy industry. Kerr McGee, for example, not only mines uranium, they mine oil and coal as well.

TOTTER: Leonard, you may have forgotten about the representatives from Pennsylvania. A few years ago they fought nuclear power tooth and toe nail - not because it was a competing energy thing, but because their state produced coal.

SAGAN: These days the demand for energy in this country is so enormous that I doubt that anybody really feels in a competitive bind with nuclear power or any other source.

COHEN: Are you telling us that if you came up to a person and said, would you rather I shot you dead now or let you live another twenty five years in good health and then die of cancer, they would say shoot me now? If you think so, take a poll here and see who would rather go right now and who would rather have the extra twenty five years.

SAGAN: I don't think that's a fair question. I think if I said to this roomful of people, which would you prefer, that I shoot one of you in this room now or that one of you must die of cancer, but I am not going to tell you which one for twenty five years -- I am not certain how that vote would come out.

COHEN: Take a poll.

ALBERT: I think you are missing a point about the discrepancy between the perception of risk by the risk assessors and the general
public. It might be related to some hard-headed thinking on the
part of the general public, namely that the perception or the assessment of risk is really a two pronged affair. It involves two
questions: one, how likely is the event to occur and second, if it
does occur, what are the consequences? I think it is this latter
part, namely, what are the consequences of risk if it does occur that
made the greatest impact. It is unfair of you to write this off as
a species of phobia when it is essentially a normal thought process,
namely, thinking out the consequences. To the public's perception,
and I think, to anybody's perception, there isn't any question but
what there is inherent in nuclear reactors a magnitude of danger
that far exceeds any other conventional device that we run into.
If all the isotopes were released from the Indian Point reactor in
Buchanan, New York, you would have to evacuate the entire metropolitan area.

    You can talk about the odds of this, but we are talking about
the consequences and the perception of consequences. There is, I
think, a realistic position that the public has taken, namely, that
they are faced with devices that are capable of causing incalculable
disaster; it is somewhat similar in a larger way to the perception
of airplane risks. Most people getting on an airplane are nervous.
The reason that they do board a plane is because they perceive that
the control of these risks has been dealt with very effectively.
There is a public image of the airplane industry in terms of its
servicing and maintenance of planes. There is a public image of
airplane pilots being a very stable, competent group. So, the thing
that counteracts this nervousness is an image that's been projected
by the industry.

    What is missing in the nuclear industry is something of this
sort, namely, that there is no perception by the public that these
very dangerous devices are in the hands of a very highly expert group
of people. There is a real perception in the public that the machinery, more often than not, is operated in a sloppy fashion. I
think the Three Mile Island incident is an example of that. Although
you are pessimistic about the future of nuclear energy, I would suggest that one of the areas that needs to be developed and, perhaps,
will counteract the nervousness which we are talking about in terms
of the public perception of nuclear risks is to develop an image of
an exceedingly competent group of technical people who are running
this industry so that this Pandora's box is very unlikely to open.

    I suggest that nothing really has been done in a very effective
way to develop this public perception and for the very good reason
that it simply doesn't exist. I don't think anybody in this room
really trusts people who run nuclear reactors.

<u>WEINBERG</u>: I don't run nuclear reactors, but I've been close to lots
of people who have run nuclear reactors and I think much of what
Professor Albert says is correct. I suppose what he is worried about
is epitomized by a conversation that I had ten years ago with the
Executive Vice President of a utility that was going nuclear. I said
to him, "Do you think there is any chance that you might have a meltdown and radioactivity will be distributed around the reactor?" He
said, "No, that's impossible." I said, "How do you know that it's impossible?" and he said, "My board of directors would not have gone
into nuclear energy if there were any possibility of this." So, in
a sense, you are right that the utility industry and the AEC had not
really fully recognized the degree of responsibility that's involved
in fifteen billion curies of radioactivity in a reactor that you
can't shut off when you shut down the reactor.

On the other hand, I think you err in two essential points.
First, in your assertion that nothing has been done. The fact is that
Three Mile Island has made believers out of the utilities and the
utilities have established the Nuclear Safety Analysis Center and the
Institute for Nuclear Power Operation. The utilities face the sanc-
tion of going out of business if this happens again and every president of a nuclear utility realizes that. That is marvelously powerful medicine for clearing the mind when you have to make a choice
between what is safe and what is cheap.

The other point I would argue with is that there is something
qualitatively, but not quantitatively, different between nuclear
energy and other energy sources. You asserted that the nuclear reactor has the capacity for causing damage of unprecedented proportion.
I remind you that the Folsom Dam on the American River has a probability of between one in one thousand and one in ten thousand of
failing. Should the Folsom Dam fail, 250,000 people would be wiped
out, and yet we appear prepared to live with situations like that.
Perhaps things will change -- in California, I understand, people are
getting dam-reservoir hypochondria. Why is it that people will accept the danger that is posed by the dam? As you pointed out, the
Vajont Dam in Italy killed 3,500 people -- boom -- just like that,
about fifteen years ago. What is different about the nuclear situation?

I think the thing that is different is an aspect of the nuclear
situation that you did not talk about. In case of the worst accident,
which has a low probability of ten to the minus eight or ten to the
minus seven per reactor per year, radioactivity is spread and land
is interdicted. It is not easy to see exactly how you recover that
land.

The question which ultimately is going to determine our attitude toward nuclear energy is: are we going to become sufficiently

understanding or sufficiently sophisticated about the character of
the low level radiation danger to accept with some equanimity the
possibility of living in areas where the background has been increased by a factor of two? That is the real issue. We have places
where 100 or 120 mR per year is the average background exposure.
When the worst thing that Professor Albert speaks about happens, most
of the casualties that are computed do not come from people who are
exposed to 200 rads but come from people who get an additional lifetime dose of 7 R over thirty years -- that is, about twice background.
In my view whether nuclear power in the long run is going to survive
depends on whether the public is willing to accept that possibility.
I don't know what the answer is.

I would hope that we can prove that the dose response is less
than linear for low LET radiation at very low levels and that, therefore, the hazard that one computes is very much lower than was used
in these estimates. Incidentally, in the original Raserman's report
the hazard was reduced by about a factor of five because the exposure
was protracted. The best thing that could happen as far as nuclear
energy is concerned is to be able to show that at levels of the order
of twice background the hazard is some ten or a hundred times lower
than people calculate by the linear hypothesis.

SAGAN: I didn't defend nuclear power today, but rather talked about
differences in perception. I am not insensitive to the fear of an
accident. On the contrary, I indicated that that was precisely most
people's concern. Remember, I talked about the image of a devastated
Hiroshima that is so vivid in many persons' minds.

I recognize, too, that there _is_ a catastrophic risk. Whether
that's an exaggerated risk or not, clearly, there is a risk. If you
could close down every nuclear power plant in the country tomorrow
you would eliminate that risk. We could achieve zero risk of a
meltdown, of devastation, but that, in turn, creates other risks.
Let me remind you that we live in a very risky world right now. We
live in a world where half of our oil supply comes from the Middle
East, a third of it comes through one tiny strait with shores held
by an unstable government and not far from large and potentially
hostile military forces.

I heard one economist say just the other day that should the
Saudis for some reason stop their production of oil that the price
of oil on the world market would go quickly to $200 a barrel. That
$200 a barrel of oil doesn't just mean that people don't drive to
the supermarket as often. It means a totally new civilization for
us. It means that your whole way of life, let alone your longevity,
would be drastically changed. The risk of that, in my view, is not
small. It's not one in ten to the minus eight. The risk of that
may be -- you name it -- one in twenty, one in ten. You have seen

the Saudi government, just a few weeks ago, come to the brink of that because of a movie they didn't like.

FROM THE FLOOR: You're exaggerating.

SAGAN: I'm exaggerating? They threatened to cut off British oil because of that movie.

CROW: I wonder whether you want to add one small balloon to the diagram, and that's the fact that the scientific and technical community have not exactly spoken with one voice on this question. I think that did not inspire public confidence.

SAGAN: I don't want to dismiss Dr. Albert's credibility problem. The question could have been assumed under my populism rubric but it deserves a rubric of its own. There is not widespread faith in the people who operate nuclear power plants, nor in the government nor in any large corporation. Is a part of this popular cynicism attributable to dissension among scientists? I think that's what you were suggesting. You know, when scientists talk in public they tend to bring up topics upon which they disagree. We would not call a meeting to talk about things about which we agree.

KATES: For a social scientist it is difficult to comment on these issues. Everybody so enjoys being his own social scientist. It was an intelligent discussion, but of the nine points you raised on the right hand side of the diagram social scientists have data on seven.

My group has just finished a study very similar to your speculations, trying to examine the value content in the nuclear controversy as opposed to the substantive content. One of the most puzzling things is the role of women. Sixty-five percent of nuclear opponents are women. It is one of the few issues in the United States in which there are fundamental differences between males and females.

We have not been able to find the trends that you suggest. We did a very simple frequency study of values. The values of both the pros and the antis were almost opposite. Maybe those PR people created it, but there is no basis to distinguish between the values on merit. There are good solid values that people have in both the pro and the anti sides, as you noted.

We went back through the Nuclear News, a pronuclear journal, and Critical Mass, an antinuclear publication, and argued that if values other than risk were important, we should find some articles dealing with populism or political conflict, articles of a general nature that were not just safety or hazard articles. The evidence

is that we could only find one article and that was in both journals
that seemed to be dealing with general issues rather than the substantive risks. While that doesn't prove anything, it raises a difficulty. We tend to conclude that probably nuclear hazard is still
the substance of the issue rather than being somehow profoundly manipulated as a surrogate for other values.

SAGAN: I don't accept that as a valid test.

BERG: Dr. Albert posed a great challenge to us, the challenge of
somehow reconciling the public with a useful technology. I know of
two communities where this has been done with some degree of success.
One is Oak Ridge, Tennessee. The other is right here in Rochester,
New York. They are two communities in which the environmental movement was not captured by the anti-nuclear group.

MORROW: Is another little balloon in your diagram called the mys-
tique of radiation?

SAGAN: There is no question about that.

SESSION V

GENETIC AND CANCER HAZARDS

CHAIRMAN:

SIR EDWARD E. POCHIN

INTRODUCTION TO SESSION V

Sir Edward E. Pochin
National Radiological Protection Board
Harwell Didcot
Oxfordshire OX11 ORQ, England

Both in cancer induction and in genetic effects we are dealing
with effects which are delayed for a long period. You have heard
discussion of the increased anxiety that this involves and the obviously increased difficulty in making assessments of the level of
risk accurately. Quite clearly, it is particularly important in both
of these fields to be able to give a definite estimate of the size
of the risk. Very often anxieties arise not so much because of what
people know of the size of the risk, but because they have no impression of the size of the risk. It has been very difficult to give a
proper perspective until recently when it has become clearer in the
somatic field what is the level of hazard, not only from the whole-
body exposure to radiation at moderate doses, but also, what is obviously important, from irradiation of single organs in which radio-
nuclides may be concentrated. There are reasonably valid estimates
for as many as twelve or fifteen body organs -- not precise estimates,
certainly, but I am not sure that any estimate of risk needs to be
made with great precision. One needs an order of magnitude, or a
factor of two or three, and not high precision to a few percent. I
think it was striking when Dr. Land put up the figure showing the
concordance between the estimates of risk of breast cancer from three
quite different kinds of exposure. Ten years ago it would have been
pretty startling to find any such precision of agreement, and now one
is worrying because estimates from one source differ by a factor of
two or three from estimates from another source.

In both genetic and somatic risks, the better one can estimate
and state objectively the size of the risk, the more, in the long run,
it will help in putting the perceived risk into perspective.

CYTOGENETIC BASES FOR RISK INFERENCE[*]

Michael A. Bender

Medical Department
Brookhaven National Laboratory
Upton, N.Y. 11973

INTRODUCTION

With the recent publicity given a cytogenetic study of residents of the Love Canal area, there seems little need to point out
that cytogenetics does indeed provide a basis for risk inference.
Just what may be inferred, however, and from just what sorts of
cytogenetic evidence, is not always so clear. If anything emerged
from the intense debate of recent weeks, it is that the observation
of chromosomal abnormalities in peripheral blood lymphocytes, as in
the first study of 36 Love Canal residents, does not in itself indicate any ill health; like many other clinical observations it is
simply a sign, not an illness. Though one can reasonably infer increased risk from such a sign, the inference is in the probability,
not in any way the certainty, of future ill health, any more than
riding a motorcycle, with its attendant increased risk of traumatic
injury, means that one must sooner or later suffer an accident.
It is furthermore important to recognize that there is no such
thing as zero risk; life guarantees death, and ultimately we must
all suffer ill health. Thus any increase in the risk of ill health
must be considered in relation to the natural risk in the absence of
whatever factor increased the risk.

The possible health effects of low level human exposure to
noxious environmental pollutants frequently of the greatest concern

* The submitted manuscript has been authored under Contract DE-
AC02-76CH00016 with the U.S. Department of Energy. Accordingly,
the U.S. Government retains a nonexclusive, royalty-free license
to publish or reproduce the published form of this contribution,
or allow others to do so, for U.S. Government purposes.

are cancers arising in those exposed, and genetic changes that
would appear among their descendants. There are a number of
reasons, but perhaps the most important is that in contrast to the
situation for most health effects, for which a threshold dose response is either demonstrated or deduced with some confidence, it
is generally held that the dose response for carcinogenesis and
mutagenesis are extremely unlikely to exhibit any threshold.
"Extremely unlikely" quite properly suggests both some uncertainty
about the basic mechanisms involved, especially in the case of carcinogenesis, and the lack of positive human data in the range of
exposure of concern that might settle the question. In estimating
hazard, then, we must assume that any exposure, however small, entails some finite risk, even though one of uncertain magnitude, and
even though we cannot hope to detect it against the spontaneous
incidences. Unfortunately, if large populations are exposed, the
absolute numbers of cases that might arise may be quite large even
though remaining statistically undetectable, and might thus constitute an unseen, but very large societal cost in terms of human suffering and medical care.

     Naturally, in order to infer risk, much less to estimate its
magnitude, one must have some indicator of exposure. In the case
of ionizing radiation physical dosimeters and dose measurement are
useful, but in the face of the multiplicity of possible chemical
carcinogens and mutagens to which people might be exposed, physical
dosimeters become virtually impossible. What is needed, obviously,
is some kind of universal dosimeter, and preferably one people must
"wear" all of the time. As a biological dosimeter, a person's
chromosomes seem almost ideally suited. Not only do they respond
to virtually all carcinogens and mutagens, but their aberrations
are in fact a class of mutation, even though usually seen in
somatic cells and thus not constituting a genetic effect in the
strict sense. Furthermore, the chromosomes contain virtually all
of a cell's DNA, and many, including myself, believe that chromosome aberrations are the result of alterations in the DNA, just as
are gene mutations and probably at least most cancers. Not only
does the close relationship inspire some confidence in chromosome
aberrations as a basis for risk inference, but the involvement of
DNA damage bolsters our confidence in the increasing use of another
cytogenetic endpoint, the sister chromatid exchange (SCE), as a
sensitive measure of exposure to many chemical carcinogens and
mutagens, because SCE seem to result from some form of repair of
damaged DNA.

CHROMOSOMAL ABERRATIONS

     Chromosomal aberrations are induced by so-called clastogenic
agents in several distinct patterns. These must be understood in

order to interpret the results of cytogenetic observations. Since the patterns involve not only temporal differences, but also differences in the types of aberrations seen, it is very important that studies involving aberrations as an endpoint carefully distinguish between aberration types. Naturally, confusion can be minimized if standard nomenclature is used in reports. Finally, some aberrations are lost as a function of cell division, while others may be converted to other types, so it is important to take into account the time factor in interpreting aberration data.

I.   The Ionizing Radiation Pattern

The classic pattern of aberration production as a function of stage in the cell cycle treated is the well known one characteristic of ionizing radiation (6). If cells are irradiated prior to the DNA synthetic (S) phase, in the G_1 or G_0 stages, the chromosome behaves as though composed of a single unit, and breaks and rearrangements involve both of the chromatids of a chromosome at the same point along their length when seen at the next metaphase. These are termed "chromosome type" aberrations. If cells are irradiated later in the cell cycle, during S or the G_2 phase, the chromosome behaves as though already split into two subunits, each of which can be broken and possibly rejoin independently of the other. Such aberrations are termed "chromatid type" aberrations. In addition, though perhaps of little interest in the present context, cells irradiated in the prophase display yet another class of aberration, called the half chromatid exchange. This pattern, though the classic one, is in fact not characteristic of most environmental clastogens; in addition to ionizing radiation, only a very few chemical agents, for example the anti-tumor drug bleomycin, produce it. The vast majority produce aberrations in a pattern sometimes referred to as "S-dependent" (10).

II.   The "Chemical" Pattern

Most chemical clastogens, and ultraviolet radiation as well, are characterized by a lack of any production of chromosome type aberrations at all (4, 7). Treatment of G_1 cells or S cells yields chromatid type aberrations exclusively, and treatment of G_2 cells (or prophase) yields few if any aberrations. It may be inferred that with respect to such agents the chromosome always behaves as though composed of two subunits. The important thing from the practical point of view, however, is the absence of chromosome type aberrations at the first post-treatment metaphase, because the induction of chromosome types in cells from a subject would be inconsistent with exposure of that subject to environmental chemicals, for example, and their presence would lead one to look for other causes, providing, however, one could be sure that one was in fact dealing with first post-exposure divisions.

III.   Fates of Aberrations

Aberrations are generally observed at metaphase, and include chromatid and chromosome breaks and recombinations between chromatid or chromosome broken ends constituting rearrangements. A broken chromatid or chromosome constitutes a deletion, because a portion of the genome is detached from the remainder of the chromosome or chromatid that bears the centromere and can thus be expected to segregate normally at anaphase. Such a deletion is usually detected by observing the so-called acentric fragment, which, lacking a centromere, is likely to be lost at anaphase. One or both restitution nuclei will then contain the deleted chromatid or chromosome, but not any fragment. The shortened chromosome will generally not be detected at the next metaphase in the absence of any acentric fragment (unless special procedures are used), so the apparent aberration frequency is reduced if one is not careful to score only first divisions. Similarly, some of the exchange type aberrations, the ones called "asymmetrical" by the cytogeneticist, also tend to be lost at anaphase. These include the chromatid type quadriradials and the rings and dicentric chromosomes. All involve acentric fragments, which are lost just as those generated as simple deletions. Furthermore, in the case of those that involve a dicentric chromatid or chromosome, the two centromeres can segregate to opposite poles of the anaphase spindle apparatus, creating a bridge that may either break, leaving two superficially normal monocentric chromosomes, or prevent completion of the division thus eliminating the cell bearing it from the population. Rings can similarly be lost through interlocking, creating a segregation problem at anaphase. Again, the effect of scoring metaphases later than the first following the induction of the aberration is usually to miss some of the aberrations originally present.

On the other hand, if a chromatid type aberration does segregate normally, and become a part of the genome of one of the two daughter cells following mitosis, the aberrant chromatid has in fact now become an aberrant G_1 chromosome. If, for example, the dicentric chromatid from a chromatid quadriradial survives anaphase, it is no different from the dicentric G_1 chromosome that might be generated by treating a G_1 cell with ionizing radiation, except that the companion acentric fragment will most likely be missing. During the subsequent S phase the dicentric will replicate, and appear at the next metaphase as a chromosome type dicentric.

Obviously, if one examines the chromosomes of cells from a subject exposed some time in the past to some clastogenic agent, long enough prior to sampling for some cell division to have occurred in vivo, one will see what appear to be chromosome type aberrations no matter whether the clastogen induced them as chromatid or as chromosome types. However these "old" aberrations are in general distinguishable from "new" ones by their lack of accompanying acentric fragments. The presence of induced chromatid aberrations must be taken to indicate either recent exposure to a clastogen or at least the persistence of DNA lesions up until the S phase prior to the metaphase examined. The presence of chromosome type aberrations with their acentric fragments, on the other hand, indicates that they were induced during the preceeding G_1 phase by some agent capable of generating this class of aberrations.

IV. Spontaneous Aberrations

An important point, and one often lost sight of in discussions of chromosomal aberrations and the risk that may be inferred from their observation, is that aberrations occur "naturally", in the absence of any known exposure to extraneous clastogens. This is naturally important in the simple statistical sense, for it is obvious that it is not just the presence of aberrations that needs to be demonstrated, but rather the presence of a significantly increased frequency of aberrations, before any increased risk can be inferred. Even more important, however, is the realization that all that clastogens do is to increase the frequency of something that occurs anyway; clastogens do not, so far as we know, create any novel aberration types, so whatever the inference one may draw from their presence in the cells of unexposed persons, the inferences from an increased frequency of them must be similar.

V. DNA Damage and Repair

The patterns of chromosomal aberration production discussed above are consistent with a rather simple molecular model ([3]). Though it cannot be said to be proven conclusively, most cytogeneticists would I think agree that it appears that the human chromosome is mononeme, containing but one DNA double helix at any given point along the length of a G_1 chromosome, or of a post-replication chromatid. It also appears that aberrations consist of breaks and recombinations between broken ends of DNA molecules, and that it is damage to the DNA polynucleotide strands themselves that gives rise, either directly or indirectly, to these DNA breaks. The production of chromosome type aberrations in G_1 by ionizing radiation (and the few truly radiomimetic chemicals) is understood in terms of direct production of DNA double strand breaks, as is the production of chromatid types in S and G_2 cells. The S-dependent pattern of aberration production is understood in terms of the production of lesions, not breaks, involving single polynucleotide chains; these lesions interfere with the template function of the chain during DNA synthesis, thus generating breaks, and since the lesion does involve only one of the two original polynucleotide chains, it follows that the aberrations would be of the chromatid, not the chromosome, type. Our understanding of the molecular mechanisms involved in the production of various kinds of aberrations

by various classes of DNA lesions is naturally a great deal more
involved and sophisticated than this, but the important point for
the present purpose is that aberration production may be equated
with damage to DNA.

As is well known, cells, including human ones, possess elaborate enzymatic mechanisms that can recognize and repair a number
of classes of DNA damage. Perhaps best known is the excision system that removes ultraviolet-light-induced pyrimidine cyclobutane
dimers, the system that is deficient in most people affected by
the autosomal recessive disease xeroderma pigmentosum. But others
are known that repair many other classes of DNA lesions, including
strand breaks, base damages and crosslinks. Since all of these
DNA lesions can under the right circumstances result in chromosomal
aberrations, since they can give rise to other classes of mutations,
and since it appears that many cancers result somehow from DNA
damage, it weems reasonable to believe that measures of DNA repair,
responding to DNA damage, may be a reasonable indicator of possible
genetic and carcinogenic hazard. The idea that gene mutations
arise from alterations in DNA is almost a truism, since mutations
are changes in DNA base sequences. The idea that cancers may arise
from DNA damage is admittedly less well founded. Nevertheless,
many DNA damaging agents are also carcinogens, and vice versa. In
addition, at least one particular DNA lesion, the pyrimidine cyclobutane dimer, is fairly rigorously implicated in the induction of
cancer (14). In addition, the fact that several human genetic
diseases, including ataxia telangiectasia and Fanconi's anemia, both
predispose to the development of cancer and involve specific DNA
repair deficiencies (1) seems strongly to support the idea that
unrepaired DNA lesions may somehow cause cancer. In consequence,
measures of DNA repair are often employed as indicators of DNA
damage and, by inference, of carcinogenic potential. One such
measure that is made on the cytogenetic level, the sister chromatid
exchange, has in fact become widely advocated as an especially sensitive indicator from which carcinogenic and mutagenic risk may be
inferred.

SISTER CHROMATID EXCHANGE

The phenomenon of sister chromatid exchange, or SCE, was discovered by Taylor, et al. (15), using the technique of allowing
chromosomes to incorporate tritium-labelled thymidine and then following the distribution of the radioactive DNA polynucleotide chains
to the daughter chromatids in subsequent metaphase by means of auto-
radiography. Though research using this rather tedious technique
had already implicated some form or forms of DNA repair as contributing to the production of these exchanges, it was not until easier
and quicker technical methods for the demonstration of SCE were discovered (8,11,16) that this cytogenetic endpoint became a practical
and widely used test system.

SCE are now usually demonstrated by allowing cells (in vitro or in vivo) to synthesize new DNA in two successive S phases in the presence of the analogue 5-bromodeoxyuridine, so that each G_2 chromosome consists of two DNA double helices in which only one of the four polynucleotide chains (the oldest one, of course) still contains only thymidine, without analogue substitution. The chromatid with this unsubstituted chain can be made to stain differently from the other chromatid of each chromosome by one of several techniques. SCE are then seen as points along the length of the metaphase chromatid at which this "label" switches from one chromatid to the other. Thus in a metaphase preparation of cells that have been so treated any exchanges that occurred in either of the two cell cycles involved are revealed.

It is clear that SCE induction is a very sensitive indicator of some, but not all, forms of DNA damage (12). Specifically, this indicator appears sensitive to DNA damage by those agents that induce chromosomal aberrations through the DNA-synthesis-dependent mechanism already discussed. SCE induction by ionizing radiation, and by implication also the very few known truly radiomimetic chemical agents, is on the other hand quite minimal. Like chromosomal aberrations, SCE also arise spontaneously, in the absence of any known exposure to carcinogens or mutagens. Thus it is an increase in frequency that must be measured. It appears that for those agents for which SCE induction is a sensitive endpoint, statistically significant increases can be detected at exposure levels about an order of magnitude lower than those that result in statistically significant increases in chromosomal aberration frequencies. In addition, the time and labor required for SCE scoring is substantially less than that involved in scoring a suitable sample for aberrations.

The same techniques that allow the demonstration of SCE also provide a rather nice solution to a practical problem that has long plagued chromosome aberration studies. By far the most widely employed system for measuring aberration frequencies in human subjects is the short-term culture of peripheral blood lymphocytes. Though other tissues, such as bone marrow, are useful if samples can be obtained, a simple venipuncture is usually the only sampling procedure to which well subjects will agree. Furthermore, the peripheral lymphocyte is a particularly suitable cell for cytogenetic purposes because these cells do not normally divide while in the blood, and are all in a G_1-like G_0 phase of the cell cycle when sampled. They are normally made to start new division cycles in short term culture by exposing them to a mitogen such as phytohemagglutinin. If sampled in their first in vitro mitosis, these cells then accurately reflect any aberration induction in vivo prior to the time the blood was drawn. Unfortunately, it is technically impossible to choose a fixation time for the cultures at which they will consistently have enough mitotic activity for scoring to be practical and still not contain any second or later in vitro mitoses. However, if 5-bromodeoxyuridine is added to the culture when it is made, it is possible to distinguish the first from the later mitoses on the basis of the same differential staining that is used to detect SCE. A fairly standard protocol for cytogenetic examination of samples from human subjects for evidence of possible exposure to environmental carcinogens and mutagens is to fix the lymphocyte cultures at some arbitrary time, such as 60 hours, to differentially stain the fixed preparations, and to score the first divisions for aberrations and the second divisions on the same slides for SCE.

RISK INFERENCE

Some of the bases for inferring the risk of future ill health from cytogenetic evidence has already been mentioned. These include, first, the fact that chromosomal aberrations are actually one class of mutational event. Even though they are usually screened for in somatic cells, most often in peripheral lymphocytes, their presence implies exposure to some agent that can also induce them in germ line cells as well, provided, of course, that these cells are also exposed. And though chromosomal aberrations are not believed to constitute the major class of mutations that can be expected to give rise to genetically related ill health in future generations, the induction of aberrations must surely also indicate a parallel induction of other classes of mutations.

Second is the remarkable degree to which agents capable of inducing aberrations are also carcinogens, and vice versa. From this we infer that DNA damage is a common denominator in both mutagenesis and carcinogenesis, and that the presence of an increased level of chromosomal aberrations in the somatic cells of an individual implies an increased risk of cancer.

A third point reinforces this inference. This is the existence of human genes that predispose the persons carrying them to cancer and also give rise to chromosomal aberrations. We have mentioned xeroderma pigmentosum, ataxia telangiectasia and Fanconi's anemia. All involve chromosomal sensitivity to one or another class of clastogenic and carcinogenic agent, apparently mediated in all three cases by a specific enzymatic DNA repair deficiency. In xeroderma pigmentosum it is clear that the individuals affected are at greater risk than normal individuals of cancer induction by an encironmental agent (ultraviolet light). Direct evidence of greater risk of induction of cancer in ataxia telangiectasia and Fanconi's anemia is lacking, but it is surely implied. Another inherited disease, Bloom's syndrome, provides evidence relating increased SCE frequency somehow to cancer risk. Patients with this disease are at increased cancer risk, and are characterized by extremely high "spontaneous" SCE frequencies (1). Just how the two are related remains to be elucidated, but it seems almost inconceivable that they are not related somehow.

In addition to these somewhat indirect bases, we also have at least some direct empirical human evidence relating at least cancer risk to cytogenetic endpoints. Most notable are the extensive studies of the survivors of the atomic bombings of Hiroshima and Nagasaki. This large population has been followed carefully for over 35 years since it was exposed to doses of ionizing radiation ranging up to hundreds of rads. Extensive genetic studies have thus far failed to demonstrate any effect on the health of the off-spring of these people (9). This result is, however, consistent with our expectations based upon induced and spontaneous mutation rates measured in the laboratory mouse. On the other hand, there is clear-cut evidence that the population's radiation exposures have resulted in significant increases in the incidence of cancer (2). Furthermore, even though cytogenetic studies were not under-taken until many years after the bombings (because the necessary techniques only became available in the late 1950's), the population has continued to display, as a group, a definitely elevated fre-quency of chromosomal aberrations in peripheral lymphocytes (13). Thus we have an example of a population exposed to a powerful car-cinogen and mutagen, displaying cytogenetic evidence of the ex-posure even many years later, and clearly at greater cancer risk than unexposed populations.

Although such studies are only beginning to be made, there is also at least some suggestive empirical evidence from human popula-tions that SCE levels may be significantly elevated among those at higher cancer risk, as a group, as well. For example, Carrano, et al. (5) have reported significantly elevated SCE frequency in a group of petroleum refinery workers as compared to a nonexposed control group. While clear-cut epidemiological evidence of in-creased cancer risk is lacking, there are certainly at least sug-gestions that it may be real.

The extensive evidence accumulated at Hiroshima and Nagasaki also demonstrates something the importance of which was unfortun-ately dramatically illustrated by the Love Canal cytogenetic study episode. This is simply that although cytogenetic measures of aberration frequency (and probably of SCE frequency as well) can provide an indication of exposure to carcinogens and mutagens, and although increased risk can be demonstrated in the population ex-posed, the cytogenetic evidence provides no real basis for conclud-ing that any particular person in the population will develop a cancer, or will have a genetically affected descendant. The cyto-genetic studies at Hiroshima and Nagasaki have already adequately demonstrated that the finding of residual aberrations in peripheral lymphocytes from a given subject is in no way a predictor of ill

health in that subject. Thus though as pointed out initially cytogenetic endpoints can provide a sort of biological dosimetry indicating human exposure to carcinogens and mutagens, and though
increased exposure is correlated with increased risk, these remain
correlations, and not predictions of ill health.

REFERENCES

1. Arlett, C.F. and Lehmann, A.R.: Human disorders showing in-
    creased sensitivity to the induction of genetic damage. Ann.
    Rev. Genetics, 12: 95 (1978)
2. Beebe, G.W., Kato, H. and Land, C.E.: Mortality Experience of
    Atomic Bomb Survivors 1950-74. RERF Technical Report RERF
    TR 1-77, Hiroshima (1977)
3. Bender, M.A, Griggs, H.G. and Bedford, J.S.: Mechanisms of
    chromosomal aberration production, III. Chemicals and ioniz-
    ing radiation. Mutation Res., 23: 197 (1974)
4. Bender, M.A, Griggs, H.G. and Walker, P.L.: Mechanisms of
    chromosomal aberration production, I. Aberration induction
    by ultraviolet light. Mutation Res., 20: 387 (1973)
5. Carrano, A.V., Harrison, L.B., Mayall, B.H., Minkler, J.L.
    and Cohen, F.: Sister chromatid exchange studies in petro-
    leum refinery workers. Proc. 11th Annual Meeting of the
    Environmental Mutagen Society, pg. 82 (1980)
6. Evans, H.J.: Chromosome aberrations induced by ionizing radia-
    tions. Int. Rev. Cytol., 13: 221 (1963)
7. Evans, H.J. and Scott, D.: Influence of DNA synthesis on the
    production of chromatid aberrations by x-rays and maleic
    hydrazide in Vicia faba. Genetics, 49: 17 (1964)
8. Kato, H.: Spontaneous sister chromatid exchanges detected by
    a BUdR-labelling method. Nature, 251: 70 (1974)
9. Kato, H.: Early genetic surveys and mortality study. J.
    Radiation Res., 16 (Suppl): 67 (1975)
10. Kihlman, B.: Caffeine and Chromosomes. Elsevier, Amsterdam
    (1977)
11. Latt, S.: Microfluorometric detection of deoxyribonucleic
    acid replication in human metaphase chromosomes. Proc. Natl.
    Acad. Sci., U.S.A., 70: 3395 (1973)
12. Perry, P. and Evans, H.J.: Cytological detection of mutagen-
    carcinogen exposure by sister chromatid exchange. Nature,
    258: 121 (1975)
13. Sasaki, M.S. and Miyata, H.: Biological dosimetry in atomic
    bomb survivors. Nature, 222: 1189 (1968)
14. Setlow, R.B.: Repair deficient human disorders and cancer.
    Nature, 271: 713 (1978)
15. Taylor, J.H., Woods, P.S. and Hughes, W.L.: The organization
    and duplication of chromosomes as revealed by autoradio-
    graphic studies using tritium-labeled thymidine. Proc. Natl.
    Acad. Sci. (U.S.), 43: 122 (1957)

16. Wolff, S. and Perry, P.: Differential Giemsa staining of
     sister chromatids and the study of sister chromatid ex-
     changes without autoradiography. Chromosoma, 48: 341
     (1974).

DISCUSSION

STEIN: Has it been shown either experimentally or in man that the
somatic chromosomal aberrations have any predictive effects in terms
of reproductive damage?

BENDER: We are virtually lacking any direct human evidence of genetic
mutation including chromosome aberration induction except in somatic
cells. As far as real genetic effects go, we just don't have any
information.

     However, it seems reasonable to infer that radiation exposure,
and probably exposures to chemicals that are known mutagens, will
produce these effects, always provided that the agent gets to the
germ line cells, even though we have no evidence in man.

     In animals and in plants, of course, we have loads of informa-
tion. It has been shown, for example, that you can induce aberrations in the mouse and that a few of these aberrations that are
induced in germ cells can, in fact, be transmitted genetically.
Generally, I think that chromosomal effects should be regarded as a
sort of dosimeter; a measure of exposure to potentially mutagenic and
carcinogenic agents, and predictive within limits and only in a statistical sense.

COHEN: Are there dose response data in humans for carcinogens other
than ionizing radiation?

BENDER: Very little. There is beginning to be a fair amount of --
I hesitate to call it anecdotal -- data on aberrations in peripheral
lymphocytes from small groups of exposed individuals, but dose is so
poorly known that you could not say we had a dose-response curve by
any means.

     The same is beginning to be true for SCE. There was an inter-
esting paper at the recent Environmental Mutagen Society meeting a
few weeks ago in which a group from Livermore, Tony Carrano in particular, detected statistically significant increases in SCE frequency
in peripheral lymphocytes of a group of 22 workers in a petroleum
refinery as opposed to non-exposed controls.

It is my understanding through personal communication, that he now has demonstrated a significant difference in a larger population, i.e., residents of the northern New Jersey area, as opposed to people who live in an area of Calfornia where exposure to carcinogens is believed to be much lower and where cancer incidence is lower.

TOTTER: You mentioned that bleomycin is producing chromosome breaks like radiation. I understand bleomycin enhances oxygen toxicity. Do you know whether there are any data on oxygen as to what kind of chromosome breaks it produced in animal cells?

BENDER: Yes. The data are not too clear, but it appears that the induction of aberrations is largely of the chromatid type by oxygen and oxidizing agents. One reason may be that oxygen need not attack DNA directly. It is possibly an activated intermediate of a reaction with oxygen -- something like malonaldehyde, for example -- that causes the damage.

WEINBERG: Does that mean that the oxygen effect in radiation enhances not the typical radiation type of aberration, but different kinds of aberrations?

BENDER: No, not at all. I think it enhances the production of or interferes with the repair of double-strand breaks, but it also interacts in other ways. There is evidence in the case of ataxia telangiectasia (AT), a human genetic disease which apparently involves a DNA repair deficiency. Affected people and their cells are abnormally sensitive to ionizing radiation, and the cells at least are relatively more sensitive when they are anoxic than when they are exposed to oxygen. This is what you might expect if oxygen interfered with the deficient repair process in the normal cells, but of course less in the deficient AT cells.

BOURDEAU: Do you consider that chromatid exchange is a good test to include in screening for mutagens or carcinogens?

BENDER: Yes. If I were going to survey a population, I would set up a standard protocol in which I sampled lymphocytes. The procedure would be to grow lymphocytes in the presence of bromodeoxyuridine and fix them at some appropriate time at which I would have some first and some second in vitro divisions. I would score the first divisions for aberrations and I would score the seconds for SCE.

BOURDEAU: I meant the other way around -- to test for hazardous substances.

BENDER: It is widely used for screening. I consider the evidence that it is a very good predictor quite compelling.

LAND: If you were to claim that the frequency of chromosome aberrations had a greater predictive value than knowing the dose, you would have to score a whole lot of people, wouldn't you?

BENDER: I wouldn't make that statement. If I had my "druthers", I would use a physical dosimeter. I would read the dose and I would infer risk from that and I'd save myself a lot of work. The chromosome measurements are bound to be less perfect because of all the complications I mentioned.

LAND: But if you were going to find out if that were true, you would have to score an awful lot of people, wouldn't you?

BENDER: It has been done in the case of ionizing radiation. If all you are after is the correlation with dose, it really has been demonstrated elegantly. There is a paper either out or about to come out in Radiation Research which pretty well wraps it up. It is by Mac Randolph and Grant Bruen down in Oak Ridge (or formerly of Oak Ridge). What they did was to look at all the Atomic Bomb Commission cytogenetic data, and making certain very reasonable assumptions about the average lifetime of various aberrations they showed a beautiful correlation frequency with dose. Of course, the correlation for cancer was strong there too.

At a lower dose range, the Harwell group looked at a great deal of data they have in the occupational exposure range. Again, making reasonable corrections for a loss of aberrations with time after exposure, they have a beautiful correlation with dose. Whether that is going to turn out to correlate with increased cancer risk in that dose range I can't say.

LAND: My point was that if you were going to use chromosomal changes as a measure of dose, you would have to score more people than is practicable. You need intermediate information about doses.

BENDER: Yes. It is very tedious business and if you really wanted to apply it on a wide scale, I think it would require automation, something that people have talked about for many years.

SCE are much easier to score, it is practical for bigger studies, and that's why people are beginning to do them.

BERG: You have what toxicologists call a subcritical effect. You called it the biological dosimeter effect. Such effects should show up in exposed individuals who suffered no damage.

Take Hiroshima and Nagasaki data. What are the numbers of people who score positive at a given dose level for this test as compared to the number of people who do come down with leukemia?

BENDER: It is far, far higher; perhaps several orders of magnitude.

LAND: In a study of chromosome aberrations we are not looking at anywhere near as many people as you would need in order to measure incidence.

BERG: I asked only for an estimate.   Can you tell us if the odds are something like a thousand to one for a chromosome aberration response as compared to a cancer response?

BENDER: I think it would be possible to draw some rather flexible conclusions of that kind.   The difficulty in thinking about the Hiroshima and Nagasaki data is that we like to think in terms of an acute dose and we were not, unfotunately, able to get aberration information for several decades because the techniques were not available.   So, it is by inference that we go back to the initial levels.

I think that anybody who had over ten rem would have turned out positive in the kind of test that was done in the early days of aberration scoring, if he had been sampled promptly.   Let's say everybody above ten.

What is the cumulative leukemia incidence at let's say ten rem and above?   That's a good statistic because the occurrence of radiation-induced leukemia is almost all at the higher doses.   It is a very small percentage, is it not?   The ratio is perhaps 100% divided by that small number.

PROBLEMS AND SOLUTIONS IN THE ESTIMATION OF GENETIC RISKS

FROM RADIATION AND CHEMICALS*

W. L. Russell

Biology Division
Oak Ridge National Laboratory
Oak Ridge, Tennessee 37830

ABSTRACT

Extensive investigations with mice on the effects of various
physical and biological factors, such as dose rate, sex and cell
stage, on radiation-induced mutation have provided an evaluation of
the genetics hazards of radiation in man. The mutational results
obtained in both sexes with progressive lowering of the radiation
dose rate have permitted estimation of the mutation frequency
expected under the low-level radiation conditions of most human
exposure. Supplementing the studies on mutation frequency are
investigations on the phenotypic effects of mutations in mice,
particularly anatomical disorders of the skeleton, which allow an
estimation of the degree of human handicap associated with the
occurrence of parallel defects in man. -- Estimation of the genetic
risk from chemical mutagens is much more difficult, and the research
is much less advanced. Results on transmitted mutations in mice
indicate a poor correlation with mutation induction in non-mammalian
organisms. On the one hand, mice show little or no mutagenic response to several compounds that are highly mutagenic in other systems. On the other hand, recent results with ethylnitrosourea show
that a single injection of 6 mg per mouse of this compound induces
a mutation rate 75,000 times greater than that considered as a
maximum permissible level of risk from a whole year of exposure to
radiation. Further investigation in mice is obviously needed, not

*Research sponsored by the Office of Health and Environmental
Research, U.S. Department of Energy under contract W-7405-eng-26
with the Union Carbide Corporation.

only on the screening for mutagenicity of other chemicals, but also
on the nature of the mutagenic action of ethylnitrosourea.

INTRODUCTION

The title of this conference, "Measurement of Risks," indicates
an emphasis, not on the end product of the measurement, the actual
risks, but on the measurement process itself. Accordingly, this
paper on genetic risks focuses on the methods of measuring, the
rationale for their choice, problems and solutions in interpreting
the results, gaps in our knowledge, and future possibilities for
better estimation of risks. Special attention is given to the suggestion, by the organizers of the conference, to "examine both the
logical soundness of the inferences of risk and the validity of the
experimental evidence of damage, with examples drawn from environmental hazards of toxic chemicals and ionizing radiation."

The experimental results discussed here come primarily from work
with mice, and, since these are so much more extensive for radiation
than for chemical exposures, the measurement of genetic risks from
radiation is treated first. Additional information is available in
excellent reviews by Searle (35) and Selby (38).

RADIATION

For two reasons, measurement of the risk from major chromosomal
aberrations is not discussed here. First, the presentation at this
conference by Bender covers part of this subject. Second, I agree
with the consensus of the current National Academy of Sciences Committee on the Biological Effects of Ionizing Radiation (45) that the
radiation hazard from this class of genetic effects is probably small
compared with that from gene mutations and small deficiencies. This,
of course, does not detract from the great importance of using
chromosomal aberrations in somatic cells of human beings to monitor
human exposure.

This paper is also limited to measurement of risks in the first-
generation offspring of irradiated parents. The paper by Crow at
this conference deals with estimates for later generations.

In spite of extensive studies, attempts to detect radiation-
induced transmitted genetic damage in humans have not, so far, been
conclusive, although there is a suggestion of some damage in the
children of irradiated fathers in the Hiroshima-Nagasaki surveys
(12). Estimates of genetic risk are consequently still based on
results from experimental organisms. Until 1950, measurements of
mutation rate used in the evaluation of human hazards came mainly
from Drosophila. Since then, the data accumulated on the mouse have

been the major basis for risk estimation. Radiation-induced mutation frequencies in the mouse were found to be much higher than those observed for Drosophila (17). Furthermore, several of what were thought to be basic principles of radiation genetics derived from the Drosophila work turned out not to apply to the mouse germ-cell stages of primary importance in risk estimation (23). However, although the mouse results presumably carry us much closer to a reliable prediction of mutagenic effects in man, extrapolation of these experimental findings to humans is still one of the problems in risk estimation. This is discussed later.

The questions that are important to answer by the measurement of radiation-induced genetic damage fall into two main groups: - (i) What are the factors affecting mutation rate and how do they affect it? (ii) What is the nature and extent of the phenotypic disorders caused by a given mutation rate? Much has been discovered in answer to the first question. The second question has proved more difficult, but two approaches to it have, in recent years, provided risk estimation committees with useful material.

Factors Affecting Mutation Rate

In order to investigate the effects that various physical and biological factors might have on mutation frequency, we developed the specific-locus method in the mouse (16). We started building the stocks of mice for it in 1947. If, at that time, anyone had predicted that 33 years later neither we nor anyone else would have devised a better method for its purpose, I would not have believed him. Yet we are still using it. It detects gene mutations and deficiencies. These are the two subgroups of radiation-induced mutational damage that comprise the major part of the genetic hazard from radiation. The phenotypic expression of the homozygotes of the mutations scored by the specific-locus method ranges all the way from lethality in early embryonic stage, through lethality at weaning age, to minor effects intermediate in expression between wild type and the viable alleles in the test stock used in the method.

Male

The rationale for the first use of the specific-locus method was not only to obtain, for the first time, a reliable estimate of radiation-induced gene mutation rate in the mouse, but also to have a rate that might be meaningfully compared with that in Drosophila. For a reason that will become apparent later, it was desirable to make this species comparison on mutations induced in the spermatogonial stage, and since there were no data on specific-locus mutations induced in this stage in Drosophila, we sponsored such a study

by Alexander (2) in our own laboratory. The mean mutation rate per
locus for 7 loci in the mouse came out about 15 times higher than
that for 8 loci in Drosophila (17), and this finding naturally had
an impact on the setting of standards for permissible levels of
radiation. If equal weight is given to a later, much smaller, study
of 5 additional loci in the mouse (8) the mouse to Drosophila ratio
is about 10.

     Another of the early studies with the specific-locus method in
the mouse was a comparison of mutation frequencies in spermatogonial
and postspermatogonial stages. For high-dose-rate irradiation, the
mutation rate from postspermatogonial stages was twice that from the
stem-cell spermatogonia (30). However, because human germ cells
spend only about 3 months of the average 30-year generation time (or
1/120) in postspermatogonial stages it was concluded that, from then
on, it would be most relevant for hazard estimation to focus on the
collection of data from irradiated spermatogonia. This conclusion
is still valid after a later finding that there is a dose-rate effect
in spermatogonia and none in postspermatogonial stages (33). This
result indicates that, under most conditions of human radiation
exposure, the mutation rate in spermatogonia may be only about 1/6
of that in postspermatogonial stages. Even with this much differential, however, the limited exposure time for the postspermatogonial
stages would result in a mutational damage in these stages that
would be only about 1/20 (i.e. 6 x 1/120) of that incurred in spermatogonia per human generation.

     In the early days of the mouse work it was discovered that the
mutation frequency in spermatogonia following high doses of acute
irradiation was not linearly related to dose, but actually showed a
marked decrease at 1000 R compared with 600 R (18, 34). This raised
many questions that were investigated by further experiments. It
immediately suggested differential response among the spermatogonia,
both to killing and mutation induction. Results from experiments
with fractionated doses supported this view (34). In terms of
hazards, it was important to find out at what lower dose levels the
humping of the dose-response curve might still exist. Data at 300 R
showed no significant departure from a linear fit with those at
600 R. However, the evidence of differential sensitivity among the
spermatogonia, along with the finding of extensive spermatogonial
killing at high doses (13), led directly to studies to find out what
might happen if the dose rate were lowered. Extensive Drosophila
results indicated that there would be no effect. A marked effect
was found in the mouse, however, in spermatogonia, but not in
spermatozoa (33). Because the Drosophila data had come from spermatozoa, it was widely believed that Drosophila spermatogonia might
show a dose-rate effect like that in the mouse. H. J. Muller
immediately started testing this possibility for sex-linked mutations in Drosophila. For various technical reasons, he chose
oogonia rather than spermatogonia. He ended this work very

disappointed that, despite intensive investigation, he was not able to show to his own satisfaction a clear-cut effect of dose rate, and he concluded that mice and flies are simply different. He generously congratulated us on finding a basic principle important for risk estimation that had been missed in Drosophila studies. Abrahamson and Meyer (1) have recently reanalysed Muller's data and have concluded that his treatment of them was "possibly in some ways wrong" and that there is a dose-rate effect. If their interpretation is correct, (and it would have been interesting to have had Muller's own evaluation of it), then, after 18 years, Drosophila results are finally brought in line with those in the mouse. However, any effect so far detected in Drosophila is small, and we still await a dose-rate study on specific-locus mutations in Drosophila.

The finding of a dose-rate effect, originally with results from 0.001 and 0.009 R/min compared with those from 90 R/min, led to investigations at other dose rates (20) and to the conclusion that below 0.8 R/min, even down to 0.0007 R/min in recent work (28), there is no further reduction in mutation frequency. Thus, there appears to be no threshold dose rate in the male. Accordingly, risk estimates for the offspring of irradiated males are based on a linear fit to the data obtained at dose rates of 0.8 R/min and below.

An obvious prediction based on the dose-rate effect was that small doses of high-dose-rate irradiation, or large doses delivered in small fractions, would give mutation frequencies per R approaching the lower response at low dose rates. This has proved to be the case (10). Therefore, under almost all conditions of human exposure, that is, low dose rates or small doses at high dose rates, the mutational risk is now estimated from the experimental data at low dose rates.

It was discovered that the distribution of mutations among the seven loci used in the specific-locus test was not significantly different at high and low dose rates. This indicates that there is no qualitative difference in the array of mutations obtained at the different dose rates. In other words, the reduction in mutation frequency at low dose rates is not the result of elimination of a particular class of mutational events, but simply a consequence of a lower probability of each event occurring (21). This conclusion is strengthened by the fact that distribution among the loci and other qualitative characteristics are capable of being changed. Thus, they are affected by factors such as radiation quality (neutron compared with X irradiation) and cell stage (spermatozoa and oocytes compared with spermatogonia).

Another factor that has been explored in the male is the possible effect of the interval between irradiation and fertilization. The rationale for this study was the possibility that the mutated stem-cell spermatogonia might be selectively reduced in number over the breeding period of approximately two years following exposure. No statistically significant effect has been found.

Age of the male at irradiation has also been studied for its possible effect on mutation frequency. No difference between the mutational sensitivity of young and old sexually mature males has been detected. Mutation frequencies of irradiated immature males of various ages and of males in fetal stages at the time of irradiation have also been studied (36, 37). In general, any departure from the mutation frequency observed following irradiation of adults is a decrease.

With regard to the extrapolation of the mouse results in spermatogonia to the risk in man, the germ-cell stages and the process of spermatogenesis appear to be so similar in the two species that the only obvious major question is whether their mutational sensitivity is similar. Probably the most satisfactory answer to this is that the finding of no clear-cut genetic effect in the offspring of exposed males in Hiroshima and Nagasaki, (merely the suggestion of an effect on the borderline of statistical significance), indicates that the human male cannot be much more mutagenically sensitive to radiation than the male mouse, and may be less so (12, 44).

Female

Use of the specific-locus method to measure the relative influence of the various factors affecting mutation rate has revealed sex and cell stage to be dramatically important variables. In fact, the largest difference in effect observed anywhere occurs between different phases within one prophase stage of one cell type, the primary oocyte. Before presenting this, it may be helpful to outline the general aspects of the problem of relating the experimental results in the female to risk estimation.

The female germ cells in both the mouse and human go through the early stages of prophase of the first meiotic division in the fetus. At about the time of birth in the mouse, and before birth in the human, the primary oocytes go into an arrested diplotene stage and remain in this state until they prepare to take part in one of the successive estrus or menstrual cycles by starting on the path of maturation toward ovulation. This process takes approximately two months in the mouse and possibly as long as a year in humans. Even if it takes as long as a year, it is clear that in the average 30-year generation most of the radiation exposure will be accumulated by the arrested oocytes, not by the maturing ones. The arrested oocyte stage in the mouse has accordingly been extensively investigated in our laboratory. The results were unexpected and remarkable. In more than a quarter

of a million offspring scored for specific-locus mutations following
X, γ, or neutron irradiation of arrested oocytes in their mothers
with a variety of doses and dose rates, only 3 mutations have been
observed (22). This is actually slightly, but not, of course,
significantly, below both of two estimates of the control, or
spontaneous, mutation rate (25).

These results on the arrested oocyte indicate the possibility
that the only genetic risk in the irradiation of women may reside
in the exposure of the maturing and mature oocytes, even though the
duration of these stages is short relative to the 30 years of a
generation. The mutational response of these stages is, therefore,
obviously worth considering. There was also another reason for
examining mutagenicity in these stages. The arrested oocyte in the
mouse is quite sensitive to killing by high-dose-rate irradiation,
while the human arrested oocyte appears to be much more resistant.
Furthermore, there are differences between the two species in the
cytological appearance of oocytes in this stage. Therefore, it was
desirable to look at the mutational response of other oocyte stages
in the mouse which might parallel the human more closely in one or
both of these two characteristics.

In extreme contrast to the mutational insensitivity of the
arrested oocytes, the mutation frequency at high doses and dose
rates in the maturing and mature oocytes of the mouse turns out to
be high, higher than that in spermatogonia. However, the dose-rate
effect is much greater than in spermatogonia and does not reach its
lower limit of effectiveness at 0.8 R/min. The mutation frequency
continues to drop as the dose rate is lowered to 0.009 R/min (25),
and at this dose rate, which is the lowest dose rate tested in
females, the mutation rate is not significantly above the control
spontaneous rate, except when compared with the lower of two estimates of the spontaneous rate, in which case a one-tailed statistical
test gave $0.05 > P > 0.01$. A similar low mutational response is
obtained when high-dose-rate irradiation is given in small fractions.
Lyon and Phillips (9) found only one specific-locus mutation in
35,875 offspring following exposure of maturing and mature oocytes
to an effective weighted mean dose of approximately 200 R of X rays
delivered in 20 fractions over either 5 days or 4 weeks. The number of spontaneous mutations expected in this many offspring is
0.5 or 1.4, depending on which estimate of the spontaneous rate
is used.

The cytological appearance of maturing and mature oocytes and
their sensitivity to killing by radiation appear to be similar in
mice and humans, as well as in other mammalian species studied.
If, on this basis, the mouse mutation results can be used for human
risk estimation, it is clear that low-level irradiation of maturing
and mature oocytes would, at most, present only a very small hazard
relative to that from irradiation of spermatogonia, because of the

low mutation frequency and the relatively short duration of these oocyte stages (25). The possibility of a threshold dose or dose rate is not excluded, even at the experimental levels used, which are much higher than most conditions of human exposure.

Because the maturing and mature oocytes of the mouse are much more resistant to killing than are the arrested oocytes, the possibility of using them as a model for the human arrested oocyte, which is also resistant to killing, has been considered. However, sensitivity to killing and to mutation induction show no consistent correlation, either negative or positive, among the various oocyte stages (25, 3). Therefore, to expect a similarity in mutational response solely on the basis of a similarity in sensitivity to cell killing does not seem to be well founded.

A possibly better model for estimating the mutational sensitivity of the human arrested oocyte is the mouse oocyte near the time of birth. This cell is quite resistant to killing, and its chromosomes are thought to bear a closer resemblance to those of the human arrested oocyte than do the chromosomes of the mouse arrested oocyte. In a recent investigation by Selby et al. (42), mice 18 1/2 days pregnant were given 300 R of 0.8 R/min gamma irradiation, and their daughters were mated in a specific-locus test. In the 37,218 offspring produced by those daughters, only one mutation was observed. In this size of sample, 0.5 or 1.5 spontaneous mutations would be expected depending on which estimate of the spontaneous rate is used.

In conclusion, although there are problems in trying to match oocyte stages in mice and humans, the low mutational sensitivity of all mouse oocyte stages to low-level irradiation provides reasonable confidence that radiation-induced mutation frequency in the human oocyte will be less than that in spermatogonia, probably much less, and possibly near zero.

Support for the view that this conclusion, based on the mouse results, does not underestimate the human risk comes from the Hiroshima and Nagasaki studies (12). The estimated doubling dose of low-level radiation for possible mutational damage resulting in death during the first 17 years after live birth of offspring of irradiated mothers is at least 1000 rem. Furthermore, while there is some evidence, on the borderline of statistical significance, for an effect in the children of irradiated fathers, there is no suggestion of any effect from maternal exposure.

Comparison with Measurement of Somatic Risks

A few words about the comparison between the measurement of genetic and somatic radiation risks seem in order. The two types of damage are often not separated in discussions of the effects of conditions such as very low levels of radiation. It is sometimes assumed that the violent controversy over the shapes of the dose response curves for cancers at low levels of radiation, and the pessimism about ever settling it, apply as well to genetic damage. I would argue that this is not the case. I believe we have fairly reliable answers for genetic effects of radiation in both sexes.

In the male, the marked effect of dose rate in spermatogonia over the range of 90 to 0.8 R/min, and the absence of any further reduction in mutation frequency as the dose rate is lowered to 0.0007 R/min (at which dose rate the effect is still highly significantly above the control) strongly suggest that the response will not change at even lower dose rates. In short, it would seem valid, and not an overestimation of genetic risk from irradiation of the male, to assume that there is no threshold dose rate, and that the response is linear with dose at all dose rates below the low ones for which we already have experimental data.

In the female, there is no evidence of mutation induction in arrested oocytes even with acute irradiation, and the sensitivity of other oocyte stages is so low at the lowest dose rates tested that the damage, at most, is small compared to that in the male. So, for mutation induction in both sexes, I think we have answers from experimental data as to what to expect at very low doses and dose rates, and there is nothing from the human data to contradict these estimates.

This view differs from that of Weinberg (46) who chose the estimation of the genetic effects of low-level radiation as a prime example of what he calls, "trans-science," that is, a problem "which cannot be answered by science." I agree, of course, with his statement that the number of mice that would have to be raised and examined to determine the mutation frequency induced by a yearly dose of 170 millirem is impossibly large. However, I think our indirect approach, by measuring the effect of successively lower dose rates, has brought the problem within the realm of science. The constancy of mutational response in spermatogonia over the more than 1000-fold drop in radiation dose rate from 0.8 R/min to 0.0007 R/min, coupled with the fact that, at 0.0007 R/min, the ionization tracks passing through the gene, with its limited target size, are presumably sparsely distributed in time, indicates that there is scientific validity in extrapolating these results to the lower dose rates involved in human hazards.

The problem of estimating the risk of cancer and other somatic effects from low-level radiation is much more difficult. From the kinetic and operational point of view, there are only two classes of genetic defect to measure: gene mutations and small deficiencies, on the one hand, and major chromosomal aberrations on the other.

Furthermore, we are concerned with only two organs, the testis and
ovary, and with only a limited number of cell types within each.
Contrast this with the myriad of somatic effects and the probably
large number of possible kinds of kinetic response and it is obvious
that the dose-response problem is much more complicated for somatic
than for genetic effects. It is possible, nevertheless, that the
approach of determining the effects of successively lower radiation
dose rates on some critically important cancers could make the
estimation of risk from them at human dose-rate levels reliable,
and thereby remove the estimation from the realm of trans-science.

When it comes to measuring the phenotypic expression of the
mutations, however, the variety of possible important medical
disorders from mutations is enormous. It must be much greater than
the number of important somatic effects. Here, geneticists still
have much to do, as is demonstrated in the next section of this
paper.

Nature and Frequency of Genetic Disorders

In addition to the information on mutation rate and how it is
affected by dose rate, cell stage, and all the factors discussed
earlier, we also need, for adequate risk estimation, some knowledge
of the nature and extent of the physiological detriment or anatomical
disorders caused by mutations.

Here I shall limit my discussion to direct measures of damage,
leaving a treatment of the doubling-dose method to Crow's presentation at this conference.

One approach has been to look for effects on such vital
statistics as early mortality, growth, and lifespan in the descendants of irradiated populations. This approach has not produced any
clear-cut positive evidence of genetic damage in the Hiroshima and
Nagasaki studies. Similar investigations in experimental mammals
have been generally inconclusive. A few have given apparently
positive effects, some of which were not, however, reproducible;
and most have yielded only equivocal results.

As an example, I published one report indicating a shortening
of life in the offspring of male mice exposed to neutron radiation
from an atomic bomb (19). Spalding (43) tried to confirm this with
a laboratory neutron source and found no effect. I could point out
that he irradiated a different strain of mice and a different germ-
cell stage, and that the mean lifetime in his controls was much
shorter than in mine, indicating a less viable strain or a less
favorable environment -- either of which might have accounted for
the greater variation than in my experiment, and consequently have
made it more difficult to detect an effect. But, without further

replications, one cannot feel convinced that my results were unequivocally positive. Even if they actually were, the fact that the
conditions of another experiment had obscured the effect would still
demonstrate the difficulty of using F_1 lifespan as an end point.

Long before the Spalding report appeared, I had decided on the
basis of my own experience that vital statistics, such as lifespan,
have so much natural variability and are so easily affected by
numerous factors, many of which are not under control, that a small
increment of damage due to mutation is not easily detectable.
Furthermore, even if a clear-cut positive effect on a vital statistic, such as longevity could be demonstrated in the mouse, how would
one translate this into human detriment? Therefore, I decided to
determine whether it would be possible to score radiation-induced
mutations affecting one of the major body systems in the mammal.
Both Dr. Liane Russell and I had had experience in observing skeletal
defects in mice, and in 1960 we collaborated with Dr. Ehling in
setting up an attempt to detect skeletal variants in the offspring
of male mice exposed to X irradiation.

Ehling's experiments were successful (4), and I urged the use
of his findings by committees involved in risk estimation. The
results were not generally accepted for this purpose, mainly because
the animals were killed for observation of their skeletons, and
there was, therefore, no unequivocal proof, by breeding tests, that
the defective animals were true mutants. I have discussed elsewhere (26) why I thought the evidence for mutational origin was
adequate. In any case, the point is now moot because the reluctance
to use skeletal results has been dispelled by the work of Selby and
Selby (39, 40, 41). They performed an extensive investigation
similar to that of Ehling, but they raised offspring from all animals that were to be killed for skeletal examination, thereby
permitting proof by further breeding tests that the skeletal defects
scored by them were true mutations.

The skeletal findings have now been used by risk estimation
committees such as the United Nations Scientific Committee on the
Effects of Atomic Radiation (44) and the U. S. Committee on the
Biological Effects of Ionizing Radiation (45). In order to convert
this information on one body system into an estimate of the total
damage in all systems, use was made of McKusick's (11) tabulation
of monogenic disorders in man. The proportion of clinically
important autosomal dominants that involve at least one part of the
skeleton has been used, with some modifications for relative ease
of detection of skeletal variants and for pleitropy, to derive a
factor by which the skeletal defects should be multiplied to estimate the number of disorers in all body systems. Some of the mouse
skeletal abnormalities are minor, and a consultation between Selby
and McKusick has provided an estimate of what proportion of the
mutational effects in the mouse would probably impose no real harm

if they occurred in humans. About half were in this category. The
parallelism between mouse and human skeletal mutations is often
striking, as, for example in the case of cleidocranial dysplasia,
a syndrome marked by absence of clavicles and by skull defects.

The validity of the method for extrapolating from one class of
defects to estimate disorders in all body systems has been strengthened by recent work of Kratochvilova and Ehling (7). They measured
the frequency of radiation-induced mutations that cause cataracts in
the lenses of mice. Even though this is a much more restricted
class of damage than that of the whole skeleton, application of the
results to estimate, by the use of McKusick's list, the total
disorders in all systems yielded an answer similar to that obtained
from the skeletal data.

Much more information is obviously needed on the nature and
frequency of genetic disorders that have their parallels in man,
but the skeletal and cataract studies have pioneered an extremely
important aspect of risk estimation. For important groups of
disorders, they provide estimates of the mutation rates, information
on the nature of the mutational events (gene or chromosomal), and
data on penetrance, expressivity, etc. Most important, they furnish
a detailed description of the phenotypic effects of the mutations
which can be examined by human geneticists for an estimation of the
degree of human handicap associated with the occurrence of parallel
defects in man.

CHEMICALS

Here again the discussion is limited to results obtained with
the specific-locus method, namely, presumed gene mutations and small
chromosomal deficiencies. The possibility should not be overlooked,
however, that some chemicals may turn out to have their major, or
even sole, genetic effect by inducing major chromosomal aberrations.
There is, in fact, already some evidence for this, but, so far, the
chromosomal damage measured has not resulted from exposure of
spermatogonia or arrested oocytes, the cell stages of primary importance in human genetic hazards.

In the specific-locus tests on the mouse completed so far, the
most striking feature is that most chemicals have either induced no
mutations in spermatogonia or have not increased the mutation frequency in this germ-cell stage significantly above the spontaneous
mutation rate (5, 15). Among the compounds showing no mutagenic
effect in mouse spermatogonia are several that are well-known potent
mutagens in other organisms. One example is ethyl methanesulfonate
(EMS) which is highly mutagenic in many organisms, including
Drosophila. In this case, and probably in several others, the lack
of mutagenic effect in mouse spermatogonia cannot be attributed to

failure of the chemical or its active metabolite to reach the testis. Thus, EMS does induce some mutations in postspermatogonial stages in the mouse.

Until recently, only three chemicals, out of more than 20 tested by the specific-locus method, have given a clear-cut positive mutagenic effect in mouse spermatogonia. These are triethylenemelamine, mitomycin C, and procarbazine (Natulan). At sublethal doses, the most mutagenic of these is procarbazine, but the most effective dose of this compound (6) produced only approximately one-third as many mutations as had been obtained with a sublethal, 600-R, dose of acute X-irradiation.

An impression was growing that perhaps no chemical could break through the mammalian body's defense barriers, or circumvent its genetic repair capabilities, to produce more than a moderate mutagenic effect in spermatogonia. Recent results with N-ethyl-N-nitrosourea (ENU) (32) refute this view. In comparison with other chemicals that have shown a positive mutagenic effect in the mouse, ENU may be classed as a supermutagen. Thus, the highest reported mutation frequency obtained from a single dose of any other chemical is 16 mutations in 45,413 offspring produced by an injected dose of 600 mg/kg of procarbazine (6). In our laboratory, the current mutation frequency from ENU at 250 mg/kg is 160 mutations in 29,577 offspring. This represents an induced mutation rate (experimental minus control) which is 18 times higher than that from procarbazine at 600 mg/kg, even though the ENU dose is slightly less than the molar equivalent of the procarbazine dose.

The supermutagenicity of ENU is also illustrated by the fact that the induced mutation frequency cited above is 6 times the mutation frequency induced by 600 R, the most effective single acute dose of X-irradiation; and 18 times as effective as 600 R of chronic γ irradiation. The results with ENU greatly increase our concern over the potential human genetic risk from chemicals, and it is appropriate at this point to review what general conclusions can be reached from the data presently available on all chemicals investigated in mice.

I have pointed out elsewhere (24, 26) that the problem of chemical mutagenesis in mammals is exceedingly complex and that there have been dangerous tendencies to oversimplify it. Perhaps the most important general conclusion is that results in other organisms are not reliably predictive of what to expect in mammals. This applies even to eukaryotes as high in the evolutionary development of their chromosome structure as Drosophila. For example, diethylnitrosamine, which is a potent mutagen in Drosophila, gives no elevation above the control mutation frequency in one of the most extensive specific-locus tests conducted in the mouse (29). Many examples could be cited of the failure of the Ames Salmonella

test to predict the mutagenic effect of a chemical in mice. The
most striking is procarbazine, which is negative in the Ames test,
but was, until the effect of ENU was discovered, the most powerful
mutagen known in mouse spermatogonia. ENU is mutagenic in many
organisms including Drosophila and Salmonella, but in Salmonella it
is a weak mutagen compared with extremely potent N-methyl-N'-nitro-
N-nitrosoguanidine (MNNG), whereas, in the mouse MNNG has given
zero mutations in 8302 offspring (5). The only short-term test
which has, so far, given good correlation with mutagenicity in mouse
spermatogonia is the in vivo somatic mutation method (spot test)
developed by L. B. Russell (14).

Even when mutagenicity of a particular chemical has been
demonstrated in the mouse, whether by the specific-locus or any
other method, a vast array of complexities must still be explored.
As with radiation, the effects of dose, dose fractionation, sex,
cell stage, etc. must be determined along with additional variables
encountered with chemicals, such as route of administration, and
factors affecting variation in pharmacodynamics. Furthermore, as
is already clear, the determination of the effects of the above
factors on mutagenesis for one chemical is not necessarily predictive of what will happen with another chemical that might have
given a similar response in the initial mouse test. Thus, procarbazine has a similar mutagenic effect in spermatogonial and postspermatogonial stages (6), but mitomycin C and ENU, both of which
are mutagenic in spermatogonia, have little or no effect on postspermatogonial stages (5, 31). Completing the contrast, EMS,
which is mutagenic in postspermatogonial stages has, so far, produced no mutations in spermatogonia (5).

It is clear, even from the limited number of examples of
complexities within the mouse cited above, that, although mutagenesis
studies on mammalian cells in culture are useful for investigating
basic mechanisms under the conditions of the tests, nevertheless
they are unlikely to be reliably predictive of the mutagenic events
that occur in the various germ-cell stages and which are transmitted to descendent generations. Even the in vivo somatic mutation (spot) test, which has already been cited as giving good
correlation with mutagenesis in spermatogonia, must be interpreted
with caution in risk estimation, because not all the mutational
events detected by it are necessarily of the kind that would
survive passage through gametogenesis and fertilization to final
expression in the offspring. It is, therefore, obvious that there
is a critical need for comprehensive studies on transmitted mutations in the mouse for an array of model compounds that show any
mutagenicity in this organism. By "comprehensive" is meant investigation into the effects of dose, dose fractionation, sex, cell
stage, and all the other factors known or expected to affect
mutation frequency.

Results along these lines have already been obtained by Ehling and coworkers on mitomycin C and procarbazine (5, 6), but progress is slow, compared to that possible with radiation studies·, owing to the lower mutagenicity of these compounds relative to that from X rays. In contrast, the high mutagenicity of ENU offers an excellent opportunity for an in-depth study of this compound. Such a study is being conducted in our laboratory and is making rapid progress. Reference has already been made to the report on preliminary results showing that ENU, like mitomycin C, is much less mutagenic in postspermatogonial stages than in spermatogonia (31). The same report also cites preliminary data indicating low mutagenicity in treated females, and, in contrast to the effect of radiation, this low response applies to mature and maturing oocytes as well as to arrested oocytes. Another recent finding (27) is that of a marked variation in response in replicate experiments using the same dose. The variation may be due to age of the males at the time of injection, a factor that has not been evaluated in other chemical mutagenesis studies. Data are also rapidly accumulating on the dose-response curve, on the distribution of mutations among the seven loci, on the viability of the mutations in homozygous condition, and on the proportion of mutations that are intermediate in expression between that of the test allele and wild type.

As with radiation, the second part of the information needed for estimation of genetic risk of a chemical is the nature and extent of the phenotypic disorders caused by the induced mutations. It is obvious that, here again, we need mammalian information, and virtually none is yet available. We do not know whether the disorders will be similar in expression and severity to those induced by radiation, or whether there will be marked differences in the effects of different chemicals. ENU again offers an opportunity, and Selby, in our laboratory, is now looking for skeletal disorders in the offspring of mice injected with ENU.

There are two unrelated arguments which the results on ENU have already settled, at least to my satisfaction. These were circulating among discussion groups, although they may not have appeared in formal publications. The first was the view that the series of negative results obtained with the mouse specific-locus method on compounds that were potent mutagens in other organisms raised the question of whether the method was failing to detect the kind of mutational events induced by chemicals. The incredibly high mutation frequency obtained with ENU vindicates the method, especially in view of our finding, to be reported elsewhere in detail, that a high proportion of the mutations detected are minor changes intermediate in expression between that of the test allele and wild type.

The second argument has to do with the approach I have used

for estimating an upper limit of risk on the basis of a negative
finding in the mouse. The most extreme example of this was based
on an observation of zero mutations in 314 offspring of male mice
exposed to large doses of 5-chlorouracil in their drinking water.
Taking the upper 95% confidence limit, namely 3.3, of the observed
zero number of mutations, it was calculated, on the basis of the
relative dose x exposure time for 5-chlorouracil in human drinking
water and in the mouse experiment, that the genetic risk in humans
would not, with 95% confidence, exceed 0.02% of the spontaneous
mutation rate (26). Some have objected to the conclusion on the
grounds that, with the specific-locus method, it was absurd to
expect anything other than zero mutations in the small sample of
314 offspring. This objection seemed irrelevant to me. If the
concentration of 5-chlorouracil in human drinking water had really
been potent enough to induce a mutation rate as high as, or higher
than, 0.02% of the spontaneous rate, then, accepting the assumptions involved, the much higher concentration in the mouse experiment would have induced some mutations in 314 offspring, provided
the mice could survive this concentration, which, in fact, they
did with no signs if ill health. In any case, the objection is no
longer valid. One of our experiments with ENU produced 78 mutations
in 12,054 offspring (27), a rate of slightly more than 2 per 314
offspring, thereby showing that this is not an absurd possibility
for the specific-locus method.

    It seems appropriate to end this paper by reemphasizing the
mutagenic potency of ENU. The mutation frequency cited in the
above paragraph, obtained from a single injection of 6 mg of ENU
per mouse, is 75,000 times greater than that considered as a maximum permissible level of risk from a whole year of exposure to
radiation. Fortunately, ENU is apparently not encountered outside
the controlled conditions of the laboratory, but its powerful
mutagenic effect in mice demonstrates that we can no longer regard
the mammalian body as resistant to all chemical mutagens. It is
sobering to reflect on the possibility that there may be other
chemicals with similar mutagenic potency to which man is exposed.
Further scientific investigation in mammals is obviously needed,
and this should involve not only the screening for mutagenicity
among other chemicals, but also continued studies on the various
important questions still to be answered with ENU.

REFERENCES

1. Abrahamson, S. and Meyer, H. U.: Quadratic analysis for induc-
        tion of recessive lethal mutations in Drosophila oogonia by
        X irradiation. In Biological and Environmental Effects of
        Low-Level Radiation. Vol. 1. International Atomic Energy
        Agency, Vienna, p. 9-18 (1976)

2. Alexander, M. L.: Mutation rates at specific loci in the mature and immature germ cells of Drosophila melanogaster. Genetics, 39:409-428 (1954)

3. Cox, B. D. and Lyon, M. F.: X-ray induced dominant lethal mutations in mature and immature oocytes of guinea pigs and golden hamsters. Mutat. Res., 28:421-436 (1975)

4. Ehling, U. H.: Dominant mutations affecting the skeleton in offspring of X-irradiated mice. Genetics, 54:1381-1389 (1966)

5. Ehling, U. H.: Specific-locus mutations in mice. Chapt. 10 in Chemical Mutagens, Vol. 5, Ed. by A. Hollaender and F. J. de Serres. Plenum Press, New York, p. 233-256 (1978)

6. Ehling, U. H. and Neuhäuser, A.: Procarbazine-induced specific-locus mutations in male mice. Mutat. Res., 59:245-256 (1979)

7. Kratochvilova, J. and Ehling, U. H.: Dominant cataract mutations induced by γ-irradiation of male mice. Mutat. Res., 63:221-223 (1979)

8. Lyon, M. F. and Morris, T.: Gene and chromosome mutation after large fractionated or unfractionated doses to mouse spermatogonia. Mutat. Res., 8:191-198 (1969)

9. Lyon, M. F. and Phillips, R. J. S.: Specific locus mutation rates after repeated small radiation doses to mouse oocytes. Mutat. Res., 30:373-382 (1975)

10. Lyon, M. F., Phillips, R. J. S. and Bailey, H. J.: Mutagenic effects of repeated small radiation doses to mouse spermatogonia. I. Specific-locus mutation rates. Mutat. Res., 15:185-190 (1972)

11. McKusick, V. A.: Mendelian Inheritance in Man: Catalogs of Autosomal Dominant, Autosomal Recessive and X-Linked Phenotypes. Fourth Edition. Johns Hopkins University Press, Baltimore (1975)

12. Neel, J. V., Kato, H. and Schull, W. J.: Mortality in the children of atomic bomb survivors and controls. Genetics, 76:311-326 (1974)

13. Oakberg, E. F.: Sensitivity and time of degeneration of spermatogenic cells irradiated in various stages of maturation in the mouse. Radiat. Res., 2:369-391 (1955)

14. Russell, Liane B.: In vivo somatic mutation systems in the mouse. Genetics, 92:s153-s163 (1979)

15. Russell, L. B., Selby, P. B., Von Halle, E., Sheridan, W. and Valcovic, L.: The mouse specific-locus test with agents other than radiations: interpretation of data and recommendations for future work. Mutat. Res., in press

16. Russell, W. L.: X-ray-induced mutations in mice. Cold Spring Harbor Symposia on Quant. Biol., 16:327-336 (1951)

17. Russell, W. L.: Comparison of X-ray-induced mutation rates in Drosophila and mice. Am. Naturalist, 90, Suppl.:69-80 (1956)

18. Russell, W. L.: Lack of linearity between mutation rate and dose for X-ray-induced mutations in mice. Genetics, 41:658-659 (1956)

19. Russell, W. L.: Shortening of life in the offspring of male mice exposed to neutron radiation from an atomic bomb. Proc. Nat. Acad. Sci. U.S., 43:324-329 (1957)

20. Russell, W. L.: The effect of radiation dose rate and fractionation on mutation in mice. In Repair from Genetic Radiation Damage, Ed. by F. Sobels. Pergamon Press (Oxford), pp. 205-217; 231-235 (1963)

21. Russell, W. L.: The nature of the dose-rate effect of radiation on mutation in mice. Suppl., Jap. J. Genet., 40:128-140 (1965)

22. Russell, W. L.: The genetic effects of radiation. (Fourth International Conference on the Peaceful Uses of Atomic Energy, Geneva, Sept. 6-16, 1971). In Peaceful Uses of Atomic Energy, Vol. 13. IAEA, Vienna, pp. 487-500 (1972)

23. Russell, W. L.: Mutagenesis in the mouse and its application to the estimation of the genetic hazards of radiation. In Advances in Radiation Research: Biology and Medicine, Vol. pp. 323-334. (J. F. Duplan and A. Chapiro, Eds.) Gordon & Breach, New York, London, Paris, (1973)

24. Russell, W. L.: The role of mammals in the future of chemical mutagenesis research. Arch. Toxicol. 38:141-147 (1977)

25. Russell, W. L.: Mutation frequencies in female mice and the estimation of genetic hazards of radiation in women. Proc. Nat. Acad. Sci., USA 74:3523-3527 (1977)

26. Russell, W. L.: Comments on mutagenesis risk estimation. Genetics 92:s187-s194 (1979)

27. Russell, W. L. and Hunsicker, P. R.: Possible effect of age at injection on mutation induction by ethylnitrosourea in the mouse. Genetics, in press (1980)

28. Russell, W. L. and Kelly, E. M.: Specific-locus mutation frequencies in mouse spermatogonia at very low radiation dose rates. Genetics, 83:s25 (1976)

29. Russell, W. L. and Kelly, E. M.: Ineffectiveness of diethyl-nitrosamine in the induction of specific-locus mutations in mice. Genetics, 91:s109-s110 (1979)

30. Russell, W. L., Bangham, J. W. and Gower, J. S.: Comparison between mutations induced in spermatogonial and post-spermatogonial stages in the mouse. Proc. Tenth Internatl. Congr. Genetics, 2:245-246 (1958)

31. Russell, W. L., Hunsicker, P. R. and Carpenter, D. A.: Additional results from specific-locus tests on the super-mutagenicity of ethylnitrosourea in the mouse. Environ-mental Mutagenesis, in press (1980)

32. Russell, W. L., Kelly, E. M., Hunsicker, P. R., Bangham, J. W., Maddux, S. C. and Phipps, E. L.: Specific-locus test shows ethylnitrosourea to be the most potent mutagen in the mouse. Proc. Natl. Acad. Sci. USA, 76:5818-5819 (1979)

33. Russell, W. L., Russell, Liane B., and Kelly, Elizabeth M.: Radiation dose rate and mutation frequency. Science, 128: 1546-1550 (1958)

34. Russell, W. L., Russell, Liane Brauch and Kelly, Elizabeth M.: Dependence of mutation rate on radiation intensity. (Symposium on "Immediate and Low Level Effects of Ionizing Radiation," Venice 1959) International J. Radiation Biol., Supplement:311-320 (1960)

35. Searle, A. G.: Mutation induction in mice. In Advances in Radiation Biology, Ed. by J. T. Lett, H. A. Adler and M. Zelle. Academic Press, New York, p. 131-207 (1974)

36. Selby, P. B.: X-ray-induced specific-locus mutation rate in newborn male mice. Mutat. Res., 18:63-75 (1973)

37. Selby, P. B.: X-ray-induced specific-locus mutation rates in young male mice. Mutat. Res., 18:77-88 (1973)

38. Selby, P. B.: Radiation genetics. In The Mouse in Biomedical Research, Ed. by H. L. Foster, J. D. Small and J. G. Fox. Academic Press, New York (in press)

39. Selby, P. B. and Selby, P. R.: Gamma-ray-induced dominant
    mutations that cause skeletal abnormalities in mice. I.
    Plan, summary of results and discussion. Mutat. Res., 43:
    357-375 (1977)

40. Selby, P. B. and Selby, P. R.: Gamma-ray-induced dominant
    mutations that cause skeletal abnormalities in mice. II.
    Description of proved mutations. Mutat. Res., 51:199-236
    (1978)

41. Selby, P. B. and Selby, P. R.: Gamma-ray-induced dominant
    mutations that cause skeletal abnormalities in mice. III.
    Description of presumed mutations. Mutat. Res., 50:341-
    351 (1978)

42. Selby, P. B., Lee, S. S. and Kelly, E. M.: Probable dose-
    rate effect for induction of specific-locus mutations in
    oocytes of mice irradiated shortly before birth. Genetics,
    in press (1980)

43. Spalding, J. F.: Longevity of first and second generation
    offspring from male mice exposed to fission neutrons and
    gamma rays. In Proc. Int. Symp. the Effects of Ionizing
    Radiations on the Reproductive System. Ed. by W. D.
    Carlson and F. X. Gassner. Pergamon Press, London (1964)

44. United Nations Scientific Committee on the Effects of Atomic
    Radiation: Sources and Effects of Ionizing Radiation.
    United Nations, New York (1977)

45. United States National Academy of Sciences Committee on the
    Biological Effects of Ionizing Radiations: Genetic effects.
    Chap. IV in The Effects on Populations of Exposure to Low
    Levels of Ionizing Radiation. National Academy of Sciences,
    Washington, D.C., p. 91-180 (1980)

46. Weinberg, A. M.: Science and trans-science. Minerva, 10:
    209-222 (1972)

DISCUSSION

FLOOR QUESTION: Please comment on the safety of handling mutagens.

W. RUSSELL: We handle only tiny amounts working with rubber gloves
and a hood, and take all the usual precautions for handling carcinogens. When our ENU results appeared in some newspapers and radio
programs last year, I got a call from a gentleman in Edmonton,
Alberta, who heard me on the radio. He wanted to tell me that as a
graduate student he was handling kilogram quantities of ethylnitrosourea, and taking no precautions.

    So some people have been exposed to this compound, but I think
it is a very limited number.

ABRAHAMSON: You briefly mentioned when you showed the dose response
with ENU that there were some clusters at the 250 milligram treatment. Were they large clusters?

W. RUSSELL: Yes, quite large clusters. At this dose there is a lot
of killing of spermatogonia.

    If I might digress for a moment, there is another aspect of
spermatogonial killing which I didn't have time to mention, but which
is apparently different for ENU and procarbazine. Ehling's results
with procarbazine show a lower mutation frequency at 800 than at 600
milligrams per kilogram. It happens that this corresponds with a
similar hump at 600 R in the dose-response curve with X-rays, and the
amount of spermatogonial killing is similar. The spermatogonia that
are resistant to killing also appear to be resistant to mutation
induction.

    At 250 mg/kg, ENU gives more spermatogonial killing than Ehling
gets with 800 mg/kg of procarbazine, but there is no evidence of a
humped dose-response curve. So, the type of killing in the spermatogonial stage with ENU is probably different from that with procarbazine.

ABRAHAMSON: You were describing the fact that EMS is different in
mouse versus Drosophila, but almost all of the Drosophila work is on
post-meiotic germ cells so that there may not be that much difference.
Rates drop off considerably when you get into gonia with both of
these.

    As to clusters, I know there are some clusters of specific locus
mutations induced by radiation, but I've never heard detailed reports
of them. Is there a major difference in the clusters between ENU
and X-rays?

W. RUSSELL: It's a little hard to compare. We are getting more

clusters in the ENU experiment, but largely because we raised many
more offspring for a given male than we did in the X-ray experiments.
We weren't expecting this fantastically high mutation rate with ENU.
When the first data showed it, we didn't want to have to inject
another batch of males and wait several months for fertility to return so the males whose fertility had already returned were mated
with four females per week. Consequently there was a tremendous
number of young for each male in this experiment. At 250 mg/kg, more
than half of the males have given at least one specific-locus mutation in their offspring. So we might have needed only two males to
find out that ENU was a mutagen.

BENDER: The possibility occurs to me that the strain of mouse you
are using may perhaps be deficient for genetic reasons in the ability
to repair some particular kind of DNA damage.

W. RUSSELL: We haven't tested this for specific-locus mutations yet.
We could do it with any strains that are wild-type for the seven loci.
We do have data on spermatogonial killing with ENU. I think four different strains have been tested for that, and there are some differences, but they are not large. Toxicity results on these strains are
also not markedly different.

BERG: It seems to me that fertilization by a sperm is the outcome
of the most sporting event known. There are several million competitors, only one winner, and the dead obviously don't compete. Is
the outcome a matter of pure chance? Or is it conceivable that the
chemical you have selected as an extremely potent mutagen is merely
much more selective; could it spare various loci that X-rays hit
where the mutated sperm is handicapped so that it becomes a slower
swimmer or sluggish or just a loser? Would a much higher specificity
to the loci that don't interfere with success in fertilization give
you a semblance of mutagenic potency?

W. RUSSELL: That is conceivable. Even with X-rays, however, the mutation rate based on seven loci is high enough to indicate that, when
we consider the whole genome, every spermatozoon probably has more
than one induced mutation. Perhaps there is no differential basis
for selection.

BERG: If with X-rays you were getting mutations just as frequently,
but spread over the hypothetical loci which interfere with fertilization, would you not get the same differential effect?

W. RUSSELL: That's possible, but I think it is very unlikely that
you are going to get selective effects in spermatozoa as a result of
mutations in spermatogonia.

BERG: Because they are all formed and the machinery is already there?

CROW: I think it is well established in Drosophila and reasonably
well in mice that the gene content of the sperm does not affect its
function. In Drosophila it has been shown unequivocally. In the
mouse the evidence is indirect, but the strongest evidence is that
no transcription or translation takes place post-meiotically.

You can also make a purely logical argument. If sperm did compete with each other, we would have a problem because genes selected
for their effect on sperm function might have harmful effects on
other body functions.

STEIN: I am puzzled that you showed us an effect of the age of the
male at treatment with ENU and did not show us any other age effects
for males and females. Was there any other work to relate the age
of the mouse to specific mutations?

The second question is, I wonder if in Hiroshima there were
enough babies conceived by women within a couple of months of being
exposed to the bomb. Maybe there really wasn't a genetic testing
situation at Hiroshima.

W. RUSSELL: The period of interest in Hiroshima would be closer to
conceptions occurring within a year after the bomb rather than two
months, if you are referring to effects on maturing oocytes. Were
there enough conceptions within, say, a year of the bomb?

ABRAHAMSON: The data looked at by Neel and Schull showed 35,000 conceptions overall in the period of some eighteen years after exposure
to radiation.

W. RUSSELL: Yes. I think the yield for the one-year period would not
be very big. It is a good point, however.

The other part of the question was on age. I don't know whether
Ehling has done anything with procarbazine, the only other chemical
mutagen for which there is likely to be data. The tendency has been
to standardize the age. Since ours was a preliminary experiment, we
happened to have different ages. When we saw the possible age effects, we explored them further.

The only other data we have are on radiation. In the male we
have not seen any effect of age at the time of exposure on mutation
frequency. We probably could detect only a factor of two difference,
and we've not seen anything of that size.

In the female we had a few experiments that suggested quite a
marked effect. I have mentioned the possibility that this might be
not so much an effect of age on mutation induction, but perhaps an
effect of maturation time.

Recently, this question came up in the BEIR committee, and I analyzed our data again much more thoroughly. With all of our data, the average effect for old versus young females is about a 15% increase. That is not statistically significant, and, if real, would be in the opposite direction from the effect with ENU.

BENDER: You had slides suggesting that there was an age effect, age at time of treatment, for spermatogonia. Was the interval between treatment and the average conception the same for those different ages?

W. RUSSELL: The length of the sterile period is remarkably variable from mouse to mouse. In any one of the age groups, there is a very wide spread in the time that individuals are temporarily sterile. There is some difference between group means, but that is not as clearly correlated with age as the mutation frequency is.

BENDER: The point I was getting at was that if the mutation induction was dependent on DNA synthesis, then if there was a longer interval between treatment and the average conception you might expect to get more rounds of DNA synthesis, because there was more sperm production.

EVALUATION OF GENETIC RISKS

James F. Crow and Carter Denniston

Department of Medical Genetics
University of Wisconsin
Madison, WI   53706

Measuring the impact of an increased mutation rate on future
human generations is a two-fold problem: First one must assess the
damage to the genetic material itself, and second, one must determine the likely effect of such damage on the welfare of future generations.

The assessment of damage to the genetic material can be divided
into two parts. The first part is the development of test systems to
detect environmental agents that can cause genetic damage. Some of
these systems, such as those utilizing bacteria, are exquisitely
sensitive. They provide a very efficient means for monitoring of
a large class of potential mutagens and carcinogens at a low cost.
A major difficulty, however, is the uncertainty as to how well these
tests predict potential human damage, and in particular, how well
they can provide quantitative predictions. So the second part of
the problem of assessing genetic damage arises out of the necessarily awkward extrapolation from the test system to human DNA. In
general, the closer the test system is to the human germ cell, the
more confidence we have in it. Finally, it is often the case that
the test is done at high doses, so there may be the additional
problem of extrapolating from high to low dose, the topic of tomorrow's session.

Dr. Bender has discussed the methods of detecting chromosome
aberrations in human or mammalian somatic cells. In this case the
observations are made on human cells, or cells of closely related
mammals, and the main extrapolation is from somatic to germinal
damage. There is still no direct evidence for environmentally-
induced germinal mutations in man, but Dr. Russell has described
relevant experiments with mice. Specific locus tests have been

especially useful for the study of radiation-induced mutations. In
particular these experiments have added important information about
the shape of the dose-response curve, the effects of dose rate and
dose fractionation, and the differential sensitivity of different
cell stages in the germ line of males and females. The detection
of dominant mutants that affect the skeleton, and which often have
effects on other body systems, provides a means of assessing a class
of genetic damage with a significant human counterpart. More recently these systems have been used for study of potentially mutagenic
chemicals.

These mouse tests are expensive and time consuming, so tests
that are cheaper, quicker, and more sensitive are needed for preliminary screening of putative mutagens. Among such test systems are
the Salmonella strains developed by Ames and his associates (1) which
are capable of detecting specific kinds of genetic changes and which
have been made extremely sensitive by incorporation of mutations
such as those that affect DNA repair systems and which increase the
permeability of the cell surface. Of less sensitivity and greater
expense are tests for mutations, chromosome aberrations, and sister
chromatid exchanges in mammalian cell lines. At the next level are
Drosophilia tests. Metabolic effects can be simulated by the addition of liver homogenates. Such test systems have often been reviewed recently. (e.g. 2,3,4,5)

The results do not always agree. Sometimes this is simply
because of differential sensitivity of the tests. At other times
it may be caused by qualitative differences; mutagens act in alternative ways to which the test systems are differentially responsive.
Sometimes the pattern of response permits an informed judgment about
the way the chemical acts and its probable effect in humans. Another
procedure is to use some sort of index based on combined results of
different systems. One such method (6) assigns, for each system,
weights to positive and negative results and to the minimal effective concentration of the chemical being tested. The substance is
then assigned to one of four classes according to its probable mutagenicity. A decision to act on this information or continue with
more expensive mammalian in vivo tests would depend on the number
of persons who would be exposed to the chemical, its benefits, and
other relevant considerations.

Such information is at present largely qualitative. Mutagens
can be quantified in test systems and can be ranked as probably,
strongly or weakly mutagenic in humans; but even qualitative extrapolation to human germinal damage is uncertain and quantitative
extrapolations are simply informed guesses. There are grounds for
optimism, however, for the rate of progress in developing tests that
are specific, sensitive, inexpensive, and more and more closely
related to human germ cells is rapid.

The determination of the effect of genetic damage on human welfare is a different sort of problem. Given knowledge of the damage to chromosomes or to the DNA, what can we say about the impact of this on the human population? The problem is complicated by our uncertainty about the range of effects produced by mutation and chromosome breakage, by uncertainty about the contribution of mutation to many kinds of diseases and disabilities, and by uncertainty as to the distribution of the effects in time. For risk/benefit assessments we should like to express the total damage in the same units as we use to measure benefits, but at the moment this doesn't seem feasible. Furthermore, there is the problem of inter-generation inequity; the people who receive the benefits and those who are at risk may be many generations apart.

In this discussion we consider only the second problem, the problem of assessing the impact of genetic damage on the welfare of future generations.

THE SPECTRUM OF MUTATION EFFECTS

At the chromosome level, mutations can be as small as the substitution of a single nucleotide, or its deletion, or a single addition. Or the change can involve several nucleotides within a gene, presumably in the inter-genic and untranslated regions. The change may involve a large enough chromosome region to be cytologically detectable, or it may involve the gain or loss of whole chromosomes, or sets of chromosomes. Although the spectrum is continuous, it is often convenient (as was done by the two previous speakers) to distinguish between those changes that are large enough to cause a detectable change in chromosome number or structure, and those that are small enough to behave as a Mendelian unit.

Since genes affect all aspects of human structure and function, the range of mutational effects extends over the same broad range. Mutations can affect all organs and tissues, structures, physiological processes, and behaviour. Although by no means all possible mutational consequences are known, the variety of known mutant effects is so broad as to include almost all systems.

The range of severity is similarly broad. There are mutations whose effects are trivial and barely detectable. Alternatively, there are mutants whose effects are so drastic as to cause death. Between these extremes is a continuous range of severity. On another level, some mutations produce effects that are curable, others have so far defied medical efforts. The fraction that can be cured or repaired increases steadily. Still others, such as severe physical and mental impairment or disease, may cause a lifetime of suffering and necessitate prolonged intensive care that is a burden on the individual, on the family, and on society.

One consequence of the diversity of effects and range of severity is that it is often difficult or impossible to distinguish mutational events from those that are environmentally induced. Almost
every mutant phenotype has an environmentally induced mimic (or pheno-
copy). With advances in physiological, cellular, and molecular understanding of disease it is possible in some cases to pin-point the
defect and blame it on a mutant gene. But, despite an enormous rate
of advance in this area, the great bulk of mutational effects cannot
be individually identified, and in most cases genetic and environmental effects cannot be distinguished. This is futher complicated
by the fact that, for complicated traits involving several genes, the
genetic and environmental effects may interact in complex ways that
cannot be disentangled.

With chromosome mutations, involving addition, subtraction, or
rearrangement of chromosomes or chromosome parts, the phenotypic
effects increase in severity roughly in proportion to the degree of
chromosomal imbalance. Cytological analysis is usually quite precise
and, to some extent, the phenotypic effects can be predicted from the
nature of the change. But, for the most part, detailed phenotypic
predictions cannot be made. Nor is it possible, except for a few
diseases, to tell from the external phenotype whether an effect is
chromosomal or has other causes. Since the chromosomes can be broken
at any point along their length, we would expect (and indeed find)
that there is a virtually continuous array of abnormalities.

Mutations that cause a change in a single gene often produce an
effect that can be easily detected and which is sufficiently well
characterized that a medical geneticist can recognize it, particularly if pedigree information is available. The latest compilation
of human Mendelian traits list nearly 3000 known defects (7) About
half are very well established; the rest are somewhat uncertain. Nobody knows what the total number of human genes is. It is almost
certainly 10,000 or more, so the great majority of mutant phenotypes
are yet to be recognized.

Mutant genes may be dominant, in which case a single mutant
gene is sufficient to produce the effect; or recessive, in which
case the effect is produce only in an individual with two homologous
mutant genes, one inherited from each parent (a homozygote). The
effect on the population of a new mutation is drastically different
for dominant and recessive mutants. The effect of a dominant mutation is manifest in the next generation following the occurrence
of the mutational event. The effect persists in ensuing generations until the gene is lost from the population by failure of
its bearers to survive or reproduce, or simply by chance in the
Mendelian lottery. On the other hand, a new recessive mutant may
not exert any effect for many generations. It can produce its
mischief in two ways: (a) when two individuals inherit the same

mutant gene and both transmit it to a child, and (b) when a child
who receives a new mutation from one parent inherits a preexisting
mutant gene of the same type from the other parent. The first will
occur only if there is a consanguineous mating. This means that
the effect will be delayed for at least 3 generations and the rate
of human consanguineous matings is so low that very few mutant
genes ever become homozygous this way. The second event is also
improbable because the frequency of pre-existing mutant genes is
very low. Therefore, there may be a delay of dozens and more
likely hundreds of generations before a recessive gene ever exerts
its effect. During this time the mutant gene may be lost from the
population by chance. The impact of the mutation is scattered over
hundreds of generations.

Actually, there is good evidence that most recessive genes are
not completly recessive, but have a slight effect in a single dose.
Such a slight effect will usually cause a small reduction in survival
and fertility. Therefore the recessive mutant gene is very likely
to be eliminated from the population by this means before it ever
has a chance to become homozygous.

There are two kinds of mutational effects that are often beyond
range of ordinary observation. One is a mutant whose effect
is so severe that it causes death in the very early embryonic period.
Ordinarily such a mutant would never be noticed; it is ironic that
that most drastic genetic effects produce no significant human burden.
At the other extreme are genes whose effects are too small to notice,
or whose effects are similar to many other genes doing much the same
thing. An example would be a gene that adds half an inch to the
height. Such an effect would never be noticed; there is too much
normal variability in height, partly gene-determined and partly
environmental. We know very little about mutations causing such
minor effects in any mammal.

In Drosophila the most frequent mutations by far are those
causing a slight decrease in survival and/or fertility. A typical
mutant of this kind reduces the probability of surviving from the
zygote stage to adulthood by 1-3 percent. Such an effect can be
detected only when it is possible to compare large numbers of otherwise identical organisms that differ in such a gene. No direct
demonstration of such genes is possible in man, but unless humans
are grossly different from Drosophila in this regard, the most
frequent kind of mutant is one causing small impairments of various
sorts. The average mutant of this type in Drosophila persists in
the population an average of some 50 generations (1500 years in
human terms), so the effects on viability and fertility are spread
out over a very long time with the effect decaying approximately
exponentially (8).

One might think that mutations that produce such minor effects are of no importance. But we can't dismiss them in such a cavalier way for the reason that mutants with very mild effects are only very slowly eliminated from the population by natural selection. Therefore they persist for many generations and the cumulative effect of such mutants can become very large. In Drosophila there is good reason to think that the major impact of mutation on the welfare of the population is through such individually minor but collectively important mutations.

If the same thing is true in the human this means that the impact of an increased mutation rate will be very hard to assess. But there is the mitigating factor that it would take many generations for such additional mutant genes to accumulate in numbers that would cause significant harm. In the meantime, we can hope for much better information.

THE MUTATION COMPONENT OF GENETIC DAMAGE

The phenotype of an individual is the result of the genotype inherited from his parents and the collective effect of all the environmental influences that have acted since the zygote formed. In specific instances it is often possible to assign the cause entirely to one or more defective genes or to specific environmental causes. Between these nature-nurture extremes lies the great bulk of human disease and disability; the causes are mixed and usually complex.

Traditionally, the unifying concept that quantifies the proportional contributions of genotype and environment is the idea of heritability. (Heritability is used in two senses; it is the broad sense that is meant here.) Heritability is the proportion of the population variance that is attributable to genetic differences among the individuals in the population. This concept is useful for some purposes, but for assessing the impact of mutation on the population it is unsatisfactory. A dominant trait causing severe impairment, so that the incidence of the trait is determined by the balance between new mutations and their elimination by sterility or premature death, has a high heritability -- 100 percent. If the mutation rate were suddenly to double, the incidence of the trait would also double after a few generations. An example is achondroplastic dwarfism. At the other extreme is a trait like sickle cell anemia. We designate the gene producing normal hemoglobin by A and abnormal by S. In the past the gene frequency was determined by a balance between selection against sickle cell anemia in the SS genotype and susceptibility to malignant malaria of the AA type. The genotype most favorable for survival had both genes, AS. For such a trait, if it is near equilibrium, the effect of a change in mutation rate is practically nil. (In the United States, where malaria is no longer a major cause of death, the gene is nowhere near equilibrium. The incidence of the sickle cell gene is presumably slowly

decreasing, and the effect of mutation is a slight slowing of the
rate of decrease.) So a dominant trait and one that depends on balance of opposing selective forces can both be largely, or completely,
determined by genes and therefore have a high heritability; yet the
effect of an increase in mutation rate is vastly different.

So, we need a different concept, and to fill this need we define the mutational component of a disease or disability. This
was first introduced in the 1972 BEIR Report (9), but we develop it
further here. The mutational component is that fraction of the
incidence (or more broadly, the fraction of the impact) that increases in proportion to the mutation rate, at least for small increments in the mutation rate. More explicitly, if the incidence
can be written in the form

$$I \;=\; a + bm \tag{1}$$

where m is the mutation rate and a and b are constants, the mutational component, M, is $bm/(a + bm)$. If the mutation rate
were increased by a fraction k, the incidence would eventually
increase by a fraction Mk.

We have used the letter I to stand for the incidence. We can
also let it stand for "Impact", where the impact is the incidence
weighted by some factor that measures the severity of the effect
or other attributes of the disease that are important for human
welfare.

A disease that is caused by recurrent mutations at a single
locus has a mutational component of one; its incidence at equilibrium is proportional to the mutation rate. If there are also cases
of the same phenotype caused by environmental influences, then this
contribution is measured by a. The constant, b, is twice the mean
number of individuals affected by the mutant gene before it disappears from the population. If the mutation rate were doubled, the
incidence after equilibrium is reestablished would become

$$I' \;=\; a + 2bm \tag{2}$$

If the mutant gene is dominant the new equilibrium will be attained
rather soon; the more severe the disease the sooner it is reached.
On the other hand, with a recessive mutant, the equilibrium may be
so far in the future as to make calculations meaningless, since conditions determining the equilibrium are likely to change much faster
than the rate of approach.

If the relation between incidence and mutation rate is linear
as in equation (1), then for an increment of mutation rate Δm, the
equilibrium increase in incidence or impact, ΔI, is given by

$$\frac{\Delta I}{I} = M \frac{\Delta m}{m} \tag{3}$$

This suggests that a more general definition of the mutational component applicable to cases where the mutational component is non-
linear is

$$M = \frac{m}{I} \frac{dI}{dm} = \frac{d \ln I}{d \ln m} \tag{4}$$

An economist would call M the elasticity.

The mutational component will be one for diseases that are
determined by genes that are recessive, dominant, or partially
dominant and that have no environmental influence. The more important the environment is in determining the incidence, the lower the
mutational component.

It is possible to have a low mutational component for a trait
that is strongly, or even completely, genetically determined. One
such situation occurs when the heterozygote is more viable or fertile
than either homozygote, as in the sickle cell anemia example mentioned above. Under this circumstance the frequency of the gene in
the population is determined by balanced selective forces, and a
change of mutation rate makes very little difference. The heritability is high, although all nonadditive, but the mutational component is virtually zero.

One of the great unanswered questions in human biology is
whether there is a significant fraction of disease and impairment
that is caused by genes that are involved in some sort of balancing
selection. If a large fraction of human misery is caused by such
genes then the impact of a change in mutation rate is correspondingly
reduced.

If there is an environmental component to the impact, measured
by a, this will reduce the heritability. The mutational component
is then not one, but the heritability, which in this case is
$bm/(a + bm)$. In general, if the trait is rare and the equilibrium
frequency is determined by the balance between recurrent mutation
and selection against the trait, the mutational component is approximately the heritability, regardless of the interactions of genes
responsible for the trait.

A particularly intriguing theoretical and practical question
has to do with polygenic traits, such as size, and presumably a
large number of physiological measures, where the optimum phenotype
is an intermediate value. It can be shown that if the fitness
decreases in proportion to the square of the deviation from the

optimum, the mutational component of the decreased fitness is about half the heritability for small increments in the mutation rate. This suggests that there may be an appreciable mutational component to ordinary variability and that a substantial part of the harmful impact of mutation may arise from increasing the variance for such traits. On the other hand if intermediate phenotypes are the result of selection for heterozygosity per se then the mutational component is close to zero. This is a question of some importance and, although it is very unlikely that direct human evidence will be forthcoming soon, there are possibilities for study in experimental systems.

Since so much of the human disease and disability burden is caused by diseases of complex origin -- cancer, degenerative diseases, congenital abnormalities, heart and kidney defects, mental defect and disease -- it is important to determine the mutational component of such conditions. At the moment we can only guess. We are reduced to estimates based on simple Mendelian and cytological defects, with the uneasy feeling that we are ignoring the submerged part of the mutational iceberg.

We need to introduce a word of caution here. The mutational component is one important item in assessing the total burden imposed by mutation or by a change in the mutation rate. But it is not the only relevant consideration. We also need to know something about the time distribution. If the effect of a pulse of mutations is spread over thousands of years the concern is quite different from what it would be if the effect were to be in the next two or three generations. Thus, dominant or partially dominant mutants with relatively mild effects have a high mutational component but the impact of this may be diluted by time (for example, by improved medical practice in the future). This is even more true for completely recessive mutants (if there are such), for the effect could be scattered over hundreds or thousands of generations. It is entirely reasonable, for risk assessment, to place the greatest emphasis on severe dominant conditions, and on cytogenetic effects which have similar kinetics.

THE OVERALL EFFECT OF A CHANGE IN MUTATION RATE

The impact of mutation on the population depends on (a) the severity of the effect and (b) the number of persons affected by the gene before it disappears from the population. We would expect these two quantities to be inversely related, because the more severe a disease is the greater the effect it will have on survival and reproduction and therefore the more quickly it will be eliminated from the population.

Of course, the relationship is not exactly inverse. Some diseases that cause great human misery cause very little reduction in
survival or fertility. Others, such as mutants causing embryonic
death, are quickly removed from the population, yet cause relatively
little human suffering. But, for purposes of discussion and to help
simplify complicated ideas, it is convenient to assume that the impact of the disease is measured by the reduction in "fitness" (i.e.
survival and fertility). H. J. Muller called this impact on fitness
the mutational load (10).

Haldane and Muller independently formulated the idea that the
reduction in fitness of the population is equal to twice the total
mutation rate. In Muller's formulation, each mutation leads to one
"genetic death," that is, an extinction of the gene through pre-
adult death or failure to reproduce. (This is in a population of
constant size; in a growing population the number of genetic deaths
increases in proportion).

This concept is appealing in its simplicity and was considered,
along with other methods and with some reservations, by the BEAR
Committee (11). However, in the ensuing years it has been largely
discarded. There are two principal reasons: (1) Gene interactions
upset the linearity on which the principle depends, and to an unknown extent. Some geneticists think that the load is considerably
less than the principle predicts. (2) Much more important is the
fact that the Haldane-Muller principle aggregates all gene extinc-
tions and implicitly counts them as equal. Nobody regards all
deaths as equal in their burden on the individual or society, and
many geneticists regard the composite as being so heterogeneous as
to lack meaning.

We then will not use this concept, which says that the effect on
fitness is eventually _equal_ to the mutation rate increase. Instead,
we make the weaker statement implicit in equation (3), that if the
mutation rate is increased by a small proportion the impact will
eventually rise in the same _proportion_, but multiplied by the mutational component.

We shall use the words "mutational impact" instead of "mutation
load" to emphasize the important distinction between equality and
proportionality.

More specifically, as explained earlier, if the mutation rate
were to change from m to $m(1 + k)$, where k is a small fraction and
environment remains constant, the mutational impact will rise
asymptotically from I to a new value $I(1 + Mk)$ where M is the mutational component. The time required to reach the new value depends
on how harmful the mutant is. If it is dominant and severely deleterious, the new equilibrium will be reached in a few generations.
For example, if the mutant causes a reduction of 25 percent in sur-

vival or fertility, the population will go half-way to the new equilibrium in about 3 generations. On the other hand if the impairment
is slight, and especially if the mutant is recessive, it may take
dozens or hundreds of generations for the population to go an appreciable way toward the new equilibrium, as emphasized earlier.

    We can ask the question in another way, perhaps more relevant
to what is likely to happen. Suppose there is a one-generation pulse
of mutations before the cause is discovered and corrected. There
will be an immediate rise in the mutational impact, followed by an
exponential decline back to the original value. In inquiring as to
how long a time the effect of the impact persists, we can utilize
the "half-damage" time. This is the time in which half the total
impact will have occurred. This is the same as the time for the
number of mutants to return half-way to their equilibrium value.
Thus a mutant that causes a 10 percent reduction in fitness will
exert 50 percent of its effect in about 7 generations. In simple
cases the total impact from the one-generation pulse of mutations
is equal to one generation of impact for an equal but permanent
increase in the mutation rate after the new equilibrium has been
reached.

    The new mutations are, of course, a heterogeneous group with
varying effects on survival and fertility. The return to equilibrium
after a pulse of mutants is a complex composite of the varying rates
of approach of the individual mutants. In the earlier generations
this is relatively rapid because of mutants having a large deleterious
effect, but later as these are eliminated and mutants with small
effects become relatively more important the approach is very slow.
For example, if 1/4 of the mutants cause a 4 percent reduction in
viability or fertility, 1/4 cause a 2 percent reduction and half
cause a one percent reduction, the average persistence is about 70
generations, but half the damage will have occurred in 40 generations.

EFFECT OF A CHANGE IN ENVIRONMENT

    A major difficulty with the foregoing theory comes from the fact
that in the human population many of the factors that determine an
equilibrium are changing faster than the equilibrium is approached.
The environmental improvements of the last few centuries have un-
doubtedly had a great effect (although in some cases, such as pharma-
cogenetic diseases, the effect is opposite) in decreasing the harm-
fulness of many mutants. A mutant that caused a high probability of
death a century ago may well have only a minor effect now.

    In so far as an improvement in environment ameliorates, rather
than completely obliterates, the harmful effect of a gene mutation
the total future damage will not be reduced in proportion to the
improvement. This is because the improvement is likely to cause an

increase in fertility so that some genes that would have been eliminated in a harsher environment will now persist longer. Although
there is a positive relationship between the effectiveness of the
improvement and the increased fertility, this is not likely to be
a simple proportion.

     The incidence of the trait will increase until it reaches a new
equilibrium determined by the mutation rate and the changed effect
of the mutants on fitness. If we simplify the situation and assume
that the increase in survival and fertility cause a strictly proportional reduction in the impact of the mutant genes on the population, then when the new equilibrium is reached the total impact will
be what it was before the environmental improvement. Of course, it
might be argued that it is better for a greater number to suffer less
than for a smaller number to suffer more; but this requires a
different set of arguments, along with value judgments.

     The present human population, especially in the technologically
more advanced countries, are considerably out of equilibrium in this
respect. The population is probably at a stage where current elimi-
nations are insufficient to balance the past and current mutation
rates. If the present environment can be maintained but is not further improved, the population will eventually return to a state
where the impact is equal to that in the past. Thus the current
generations are enjoying a respite. The harm is postponed rather
than prevented entirely, unless the environmental change is such
as to render a previous harmful gene completely innocuous. There
will be future improvements in the environment, probably much more
spectacular than those of the past. The continued postponement of
genetic deaths demands continuous new improvements of the environment, but whether such improvements can keep ahead for long times
in the future is a question about which one can only guess.

     As emphasized earlier, what we are primarily concerned about is
not reduction in fitness per se but the associated increase in human
misery. From the standpoint of long-time human welfare, the most
beneficial kind of environmental advance is one that reduces the
amount of suffering associated with a mutation by a greater fraction
than the fitness (mainly fertility) is increased. On the other hand,
if the fitness is greatly increased but the amount of suffering not
reduced correspondingly, the long-time total misery will increase.
It is ironic that treatment advances may ultimately produce more
human misery. This point is an embarrassing one to social progress
and should be of concern to social planners.

     The important question is this: Can we continue to improve the environment so that the mutational impact remains permanently reduced, or are we enjoying a tempory respite from the ravages of mutation by a one-time bonus of a happy coincidence of scientific and technological advance, industrial revolution, and exploitation of non-renewable resources?

SHOULD WE DISCOUNT GENETIC EFFECTS EXPRESSED IN THE DISTANT FUTURE?

The possibility of genetic damage that will be expressed many generations in the future raises a kind of issue that society does not usually consider. Ordinarily we don't look beyond the next few years, or decades at most.

There are many reasons for paying less attention to a disease or impairment a long time in the future. One reason is simply the uncertainty of our present predictions. More important, perhaps, is the belief that human knowledge will continue to increase and that our descendants will be better able to cope with genetic defects than we can now.

For these and similar reasons it is appropriate to apply some sort of discount to genetic (and somatic) impacts that are expected in the future. It is typical in economic calculations to discount future income or expenses in accordance with prevailing interest rates. The same kind of thinking could be applied to health risks. To many, this kind of calculation seems either crass, or unrealistic, or both. If we discount at prevailing commercial interest rates, we would give very little emphasis to diseases or defects more than twenty years in the future.

There is, however, another basis for discounting the importance of diseases and impairments in the future. This is to use the rate of progress in prevention, cure, and amelioration. If the amount of mortality or suffering of a genetic disease is being reduced at, say, one percent per year then it would be appropriate to apply a discount rate of one percent to future cases, on the grounds that this would equalize the suffering at the two times. It is hard to estimate what the proper discount value would be. It is certainly less than the discount rates of ordinary business economics, which are in the order of 10 percent. But a value of 1 percent or 1/2 percent per year might be reasonable.

The present value of a mutant gene expressed in the future at these two discount rates is as follows:

Time of expression	1% discount	.5% discount
Now	1.00	1.00
30 years hence (1 generation)	0.74	0.86
100 years hence	0.37	0.61
500 years hence	0.01	0.08

This suggests that we should concentrate our main attention on genetic risk assessment of conditions that are expressed in the next few generations. The impact of mutant effects caused by heterozygous effects of recessive mutants, minor deleterious mutants, and the occasional expression of a recessive condition are spread out over such a long time and the effect at any one time is thereby so diluted that the impact on a single generation is very slight. This argues that for the present this component not be specifically included in the risk assessment. The major impact is long delayed and we will surely know a great deal more about such genes in a few years, given the rapid growth of knowledge of genetics and cell biology.

The arguments above seem quite appropriate when, for example, assessing future somatic effects, such as carcinogenesis. The rate of improvement in cure and amelioration can be used as a rough discounting factor, and inter-generation equity is thereby preserved to a first approximation. Such discounting might be especially appropriate for somatic effects of slowly decaying radioactive compounds.

On the other hand, genetic damage has a complicating factor that does not appear in discussions of somatic damage. If the effect of a partial cure is to reduce sterilty then the overall impact of the cure is diminished correspondingly. As was emphasized before, environmental improvements are a two-edged sword. This makes us less certain about discounting genetic effects for the future than somatic effects.

On thing does seem clear, however. Our future health problems, insofar as they are caused by genetic disease, are likely to be far more influenced by high living standards and improved medical care than they are by induced mutation, unless the latter is comparable to the spontaneous rate.

One way to look at this is the following Gedanken experiment. Assume that the environment and medical care improve so that every individual has an equal chance of surviving to reproduce -- in other words, that natural selection is completely eliminated. In this case gene frequencies would not change except for chance processes,

which largely cancel each other. But mutation would go on, and each
generation would get a new supply of mutant genes. In this sense, a
complete relaxation of selection for one generation is equivalent
in its future effect to doubling the mutation rate (in a population
currently at equilibrium).

The contribution to this would be from spontaneous mutations,
plus whatever increment occurs from man-made sources. If environmental mutagens produce a small number of mutations relative to the
spontaneous rate, we can say that large improvements in environment
will have a larger effect on mutant frequency in the future than
environmental mutagens.

Whether the effect of environmental improvement on future generations is benign or traumatic depends on several factors. One is
whether the improvement is permanent. If the environment is good
for several generations and then returns to the prior condition, the
accumulated mutants would exert their former individual impacts, but
in increased numbers. So, an environmental improvement has to be
permanent. We would hope, of course, not simply to maintain the
present environment but to continue to improve things as we have in
recent centuries.

The second factor is the relationship between reduction of suffering, and increase of fertility. If environmental and medical
advances reduce suffering, but reduce sterility even more, then the
future will have more suffering than the present; and vice versa.
We see no way to make any confident predictions about the relationship between these two key factors, depending as it does on individual and social decisions about reproduction.

INTER-GENERATION EQUITY

If the costs of a chemical in terms of the risks that it causes
and the benefits of the chemical accrued to the same individual, the
problem would be (relatively) simple. The cost could be weighed
against the benefit, and the appropriate decision reached. Conceivably different persons would weight these differently, but a sufficiently flexible system would permit the resulting individual decisions to prevail. Under such circumstances, a cost-benefit calculation would appear to be superior to setting of arbitrary standards. The information may be inaccurate and insufficient. Yet, the
principle seems reasonable.

Genetic damage presents a new problem, however. The benefit
and risk do not affect the same people. The bulk of the risk is
not even to the immediate children of those who are exposed (and
who therefore may be presumed to share in the benefit) but to
more remote descendants. Therefore, there is very little impact

of the risk on the present person, except through his general concern for the future of mankind.   There is hardly any basis for
a rational risk-benefit decision.

Under these circumstances, setting some sort of upper limit on
the amount of genetic damage permitted would appear to be a more
rational approach to public policy.   The people of this generation
could agree not to pass on to future generations any more than a
certain number of new mutant genes, or a certain fraction of those
that occur spontaneously.

With such a policy, new chemicals could be permitted only if
their collective impact (along with radiation) is below a certain
fraction of the spontaneous mutation rate.   Of course, in granting
permits, a highly beneficial chemical is to be preferred to a less
beneficial one with the same mutagenic potential.

We shouldn't regard our contribution to future generations as
simply a parcel of harmful mutations.   Future generations will have
the benefit of long time capital improvements and, most important
of all, an improved technology.   There is every expectation that life
in the future for the average person will offer less pain, greater
life expectancy, higher living standard, more comforts, and more lux-
uries (that will by then be regarded as necessities).   If the genetic
damage to future generations could be measured quantitatively in the
same units as cultural, scientific, and technological benefits there
could perhaps be some reasonable cost-benefit calculation.   The
future benefits of a mutation-enhancing technology could be set
against the effect of the mutants.   At the present this seems too
uncertain to attempt.

WITH ALL THESE UNCERTAINTIES, WHAT CAN WE DO?

From the foregoing, the minimum requisites for extrapolating from
known mutation rates in the human genome to the impact of these mutations are:

   (1)   The mutational component of the human disease and disabil-
          ity burden.

   (2)   The time course of change until equilibrium, or at least
          for the next few generations.

   (3)   The change in environment to be expected over the period
          being considered.

Clearly these are not known and there is very little likelihood that
any existing research methodology can provide even approximate answers.   Must we then move entirely in the dark (as the 1956 BEAR
Committee asked)?

There are four things that can reasonably be said at this stage:

A.   Estimate only cytogenetic and dominant effects.   For some
classes of mutational damage we can attempt direct quantitative
assessments.   The class that seems best at present is cytogenetic
effects.   Techniques for detecting cytogenetic changes in human
somatic cells are now very well developed.   It should be possible
soon to correlate these with transmitted germ cell damage in organisms close to man, and to have a reasonable estimate of the phenotypic damage and its time distribution.

We can also use the mouse to give estimates of single locus
mutation rates, dominant and X-linked recessive, and rates for dominant mutants leading to certain classes of abnormalities, such as
skeletal defects.   This requires extrapolation from mouse to
man, but it is from germ cells in one species to those of another, which we could do with more confidence than from other test
systems.   A difficulty is that such studies require very large numbers of mice and this limits the number of chemicals that can be
tested.   This method has so far provided most of the quantitative
data for radiation risk assessment (9,12).

These two methods measure only part of the genetic impact, but
they measure the part that makes the largest impact on the first few
generations.   The other effects have such a large time lag that errors
made in this generation will be greatly diluted by time.   By the time
the effect becomes important, several generations hence, we can at
least hope that genetic knowledge will have advanced to the point
where quantitative assessments more closely approximating the total
risk can be made.   To improve these assessments we need not only
better data on induced mutations, but also more information on the
natural incidence of genetic disease and abnormalties.

B.   Comparison to the spontaneous rate.   The spontaneous mutation rate is something that the human species has lived with
throughout its history and despite this (and in a much more indirect way, because of it) has evolved both biologically and
culturally.   There is no reason at all to think that this rate
has been optimal, either from the standpoint of evolutionary
progress or from the standpoint of human welfare.   But, in any
case it has not been a catastrophe.

We know enough about chemical mutagens and chromosome breaking
agents to be quite sure that the kinds of changes produced will not
be qualitatively different from those that occur spontaneously.   So,
despite all sorts of quantitative uncertainties, we can state that:

As long as any addition to the mutation rate is a small
fraction of the spontaneous rate, we can be sure that

any impact of this will not differ in kind from and will
be a correspondingly small fraction of the damage caused
by spontaneous mutations.

This argues strongly for a system of mutation risk assessment that
uses the spontaneous rate as a standard of comparison. At the
present time we know little about either the spontaneous or induced
rate in man, but these are researchable subjects and we can with some
confidence expect useful answers (if not as accurate as we would
like) in the foreseeable future.

   C.   Use background radiation as a standard. For radiation
risk assessment we have the convenient standard of the natural background radiation throughout its history. There is good reason to
think that the contribution of background radiation to the human
mutation rate is small relative to other causes. We know, then,
that if we keep man-made radiation to amounts of the order of background radiation or less we will be adding to the genetic burden
only a fraction of what already exists.

   There is no such "natural" level for most mutagenic chemicals.
Many are new to the human experience. It might be possible to determine a basic level of natural mutagens in the body fluids and use
this as a beginning standard. Alternatively, since we already have
much better information about radiation risks than chemical risks, we
might compare chemical mutagenic potency with that of radiation (13).
This is fraught with a great many difficulties, as many have pointed
out. For one thing, there is usually not a simple relationship between a chemical and radiation -- one may be more effective in some
systems, while the other is in other systems. Nevertheless this might
serve as a rough guiding principle in determining acceptable risks.

   D.   Concentrate on somatic effects.. The kind of data from
mice that have been used for assessing early generation risks from
radiation require very large numbers and long times. Tests for carcinogenesis can be done more rapidly and with smaller numbers. When
the same chemical is tested for carcinogenesis and for mutagenesis in
highly sensitive systems the correlation is very high and is somewhat
quantitative -- the most potent mutagens tend to be the strongest
carcinogens. Therefore, a public policy of protection against chemical carcinogens will go a long way toward providing protection from
genetic damage to future generations. It may well be a useful stop-
gap measure while better genetic methods are being developed.

   This is paper number 2433 from the Laboratory of Genetics, University of Wisconsin.

REFERENCES

1. Ames, B. N., McCann, J., and Yamasaki, E.: Methods of detect-
    ing carcinogens and mutagens with the Salmonella-microsome
    mutagenicity test. Mutation Res., 31:347 (1975).

2. Scott, D., Bridges, B. A., and Sobels, F. H., Eds.: Progress
    in Genetic Toxicology. Elsevier/North Holland Biomedical Press,
    Amsterdam (1977).

3. Griffen, A. C., and Shaw, C. R., Eds.: Carcinogens: Identifi-
    cation and Mechanisms of Action. Raven Press, New York (1979).

4. Hiatt, H. H., Watson, J. D., and Winsten, J. A., Eds.: Origins
    of Human Cancer, Cold Spring Harbor Lab., New York (1977).

5. Hollaender, A., and deSerres, F. J., Eds: Chemical Mutagens
    Principles and Methods for their Detection. Plenum Press.
    New York (1978).

6. Brusick, D.: Unified scoring system and activity definitions
    for results from in vitro and submammalian mutagenesis test
    batteries. In Press.

7. McKusick, V: Mendelian Inheritance in Man, 5th ed. Johns Hop-
    kins Press. (1978).

8. Crow, J. F. : Minor viability mutants in Drosophila. Genetics
    92:s165 (1979).

9. BEIR: The Effects on Populations of Exposure to Low Levels of
    Ionizing Radiation. National Academy of Sciences, Washington
    (1972).

10. Muller, H. J: Our load of mutations. Amer. J. Human Genet.
    2:11 (1950).

11. BEAR: The Biological Effects of Atomic Radiation. National
    Academy of Sciences, Washington (1956).

12. UNSCEAR: Sources and Effects of Ionizing Radiation. United
    Nations, New York (1977).

13. Committee 17 of Environmental Mutagen Society : Environmental
    mutagenic hazards. Science 187:503 (1975).

DISCUSSION

WEINBERG: Does this mean you take a whole species of fruit flies all over the world and you suddenly find that they all, in unison, change their mutation rate?

CROW: Almost that. One has to make the matings the right way to bring this out. I exaggerated a bit. 100% have the capacity now to show a high mutation rate when crossed the right way. That particular right way to cross doesn't happen very often in nature, but I can imagine circumstances under which it would.

W. RUSSELL: I think Alvin is asking if it is simultaneous all over the world.

CROW: It is across the world. I don't know how long it took to spread.

BERG: You said right at the beginning that recombination is what really matters in human diversity. As I remember, Sewall Wright said that there is an optimum size of recombining subpopulations so that we maximize selection pressure and get the most good with the least bad out of mutation pressure. The optimum inbreeding units were small, the equivalent of a small primitive tribe. We seem to have gone a long way from this in the United States. How does our change of mating patterns influence fitness, as compared with increases in mutation rate?

CROW: Dr. Wright thinks about the optimum structure of a population from the standpoint of long range evolution, that is, for the creative development of novel adaptive types. A better type might evolve partly by chance in one subpopulation and spread through the rest of them. As an evolutionary strategy, that has a great appeal. As a strategy for the human population in the next thousand years, it has, to me, zero appeal.

I am not concerned with the evolution of wings as I said in the first part. I am really concerned with the preservation of these high standards of health, intelligence, all of the things that we think are good, without looking for ways of creating novel human types.

BERG: I thought that you also spoke to the frequency of deleterious recessive mutants. Would homozygotes not be formed and eliminated far less efficiently in our society?

CROW: What Wright didn't know when he was writing this is the heterozygous effect that I was describing. The ubiquity of heterozygous effects is such as to make population structure less important than

it would otherwise be from any standpoint except the evolution of
novelty, which I think is outside the field of consideration for the
human species.

UTIDJIAN: Why is it that mutations are more likely to be detrimental
than beneficial?

CROW: I think there is a fundamental reason. Besides, there are
good empirical data on this. It is simply an observed fact that
virtually every mutant that has an effect large enough to be detected
is deleterious. I would expect it to be true on purely evolutionary
grounds because you and I are the products of a small minority of
successful mutants in the past that happened to be well suited to
their niche. The whole existing human population is a group of
highly selected mutant genes of a beneficial sort. When you make a
random change in a highly selected group, it will be deleterious
much more often than beneficial.

L. RUSSELL: Do you think it is realistic to assume that the half a
percent per year improvement in life span will continue? We've entered a technological era in the last generation or so, but there
must be a biological limit to what the technological fix can accomplish.

CROW: We would soon have whole populations 150 years old at that
rate. I think it more probable that we will reach a limit at less
than that.

     I really think, Lee, that sooner or later the human population
is going to have to take its genetics into account -- our grandchildren or great grandchildren or great, great grandchildren. The
ideal we seem to be reaching for currently is for every zygote to
have an equal chance of growing up and for the population to reproduce at an average rate of 2.1 children per couple with a variance
of zero. That isn't possible. There will have to be some means for
eliminating deleterious mutations. I don't really expect that we
will be clever enough to provide custom-made environments for the
bearers of each defective gene.

W. RUSSELL: Jim, I realize you are simplifying things with the
mathematical treatment. Perhaps it is not always understood that
there might be an evolutionary advantage not in everybody reaching
optimum size, but having a variety of sizes -- tall people to build
roofs and short ones to dig tunnels. It is rather clear to me because I am very near-sighted. There may be a distinct advantage in
having some people far-sighted to do the hunting and other people
near-sighted, like me, to make the superior arrow heads. There is
an advantage in variety in a lot of situations.

CROW: I'd be the last to deny that variety is the spice of life, and that a diverse population is far preferable. But not all variants are desirable. Extreme deviants with respect to kidney function, say, might have a miserable life. Normal variability is good; I am concerned about abnormalities.

COHEN: You explained very well why bad mutations are bred out. You haven't explained why good mutations don't stay in and stabilize the genotype against further mutations.

CROW: I think they do, but at a very, very slow rate relative to the kind of things that we are concerned with in this discussion.

BENDER: Amniocentesis and in vitro genetic testing are beginning in a very, very small way to provide the kind of selective force that you are looking for in the future.

CROW: We are certainly chipping away at this problem. That's part of the reason for being so uncertain with answers to Lee's question whether technical advances can just keep finding, as we are doing now, new ways of coping with genetic disease to keep ahead of the currently increasing mutation rate.

BENDER: I wanted to make another point: one of my principal objections to the use of a radiation dose equivalent for chemical mutagens is that it implies that the spectrum of mutations, whatever that is, is the same. There is an awful lot of evidence to suggest it's not.

CROW: I wouldn't want the concept of dose to be that simplified.

STEIN: Several studies of inbreeding in humans have looked at consanguinity of parents for possible correlation with miscarriages. They have always come out negative; in fact, it is often a negative correlation. This suggests that uterine development is not a period of elimination of deleterious recessive genes. Natural selection doesn't seem to operate there.

CROW: Yes, I think the major way in which selection hasn't changed a great deal in the last hundred years is in prenatal death. I suspect that there are prenatal recessive lethals, but they are so lost in the large noise of chromosomal effects plus environmental effects and whatever the unexplained residual is that they are not measured. I am inclined to think that it is no accident that one doesn't find all of the possible trisomic aberrations nor all of the kinds of recessive lethals in abortions. Natural selection ought to operate so that if a developing foetus is going to die, a mother who has the capacity of having that embryo die in the preimplantation stage will have the next child sooner. Therefore, any combination of genes that would lead the mother to behave as if she knew how to make this determination would have selective value. It is no accident, I think, that the very worst kinds of genetic effects are never seen because they are the ones that are preimplantation losses or, at least, very early deaths.

ALBERT: Are humans genetically more diverse than other animals?

CROW: Not if you compare us with mammals that have had as wide a diversity of habitat as we have.

ALBERT: I refer to the choice of species for testing.

CROW: If your message is what I think it is, I want to agree with it -- that we know enough about human variability, whatever it is, to know that there are many kinds of unique genotypes and there are going to be special susceptibilities to mutagenic effects in individuals.

ALBERT: The question is whether or not humans are unique in that regard. Are we an extreme compared to pussycats?

CROW: I don't think we are unique, but uniquely interesting. Domestic dogs are pretty variable, but there's a special explanation for that. What I said a while ago is probably correct -- that the human species extends over the whole surface of the earth and very few other animal species do.

FROM THE FLOOR: What about porpoises?

CROW: I don't know much about porpoises. As soon as I spoke I realized that _Drosophila_ _melanogaster_ are all over the world and look very much alike. So, I guess I'd better change my mind and say that humans are more variable than some species.

SESSION VI

EXTRAPOLATION TO LOW DOSES

CHAIRMEN:

ALVIN M. WEINBERG

AND

JOHN R. TOTTER

INTRODUCTION TO SESSION VI

Alvin M. Weinberg

Institute for Energy Analysis
Oak Ridge Associated Universities
Oak Ridge, TN 37830

This morning we are talking about Extrapolation to Low Doses. I am not a biologist nor an expert on statistics. I have written a paper in which I raised the following question: how do you formulate public policy with respect to standards of exposure in those instances where science is not proficient, either as a matter of principle or because science hasn't progressed sufficiently far to determine the dose response relation? There are a large class of questions that outwardly look like scientific questions and yet, in principle, can not be answered by science. I called such questions trans-scientific. The two examples I gave were rare events, and questions that had indeterminate answers because the underlying mathematical structure was indeterminate. In the latter category were questions like "What is the climate going to be five years from now?" or "What is the GNP going to be three years from now?", the point being that in those cases although the mathematical equations that describe the phenomena (at least in the case of climate) are well known, they are highly non-linear and the solutions to the equations may be unstable with respect to small changes in the initial conditions. Tiny differences in the initial conditions magnify into very large changes in the final outcome, the result being that the system lacks predictability, and this is intrinsic. A system becomes, as the mathematicians nowadays say, chaotic.

The other class of questions were those that I describe as rare events. For example, you can ask what is the effect of a million milliroentgens on the health of John Totter. You can get a pretty good answer to that. Then, you can ask another question which has exactly the same structure, what will one milliroentgen do to John Totter and the answer is not that easy to give. Of course, the answer you give is that nothing will happen to John Totter as a result of one milliroentgen applied to him. Yet that's not quite the answer, at least not if you assume the linear hypothesis, because

then there is some probability that John Totter will contract cancer
some time in the future as a result of that one milliroentgen.

My argument was that questions dealing with rare events, and
cancer from low-level exposures has the character of being a rare
event, were fundamentally beyond the proficiency of science to answer.
Therefore, in order to deal with the matter from the point of view
of public policy one probably ought to recast the issue.

We've heard about cost-benefit analysis in the discussion.
Nuclear reactors are going to impose a certain cost in terms of
health and a certain benefit which is only indirectly related to
health. The advice that we get from the professional cost-benefit
analyst is that you must measure the cost and measure the benefit.
This was in the BEIR II report. Then you draw the line somewhere so
that you can decide if you are going to do it or not do it as a result of this weighing of cost and benefit. There is a great deal of
arbitrariness in this because the metric in which you measure the
cost and the benefit are not the same.

In situations like this it is arguable whether conclusive scientific data can ever be obtained. Should one not be more explicit
with respect to the arbitrariness and admit that the question of
where the line should be drawn is to some degree a matter of taste,
a matter of politics? Eventually, it is a matter of politics anyhow
when you have to draw the line between what's an acceptable cost and
what's an acceptable benefit.

Howard Adler and I have proposed that you go back to the original BEIR I report, which pointed out that there are two different
ways of arriving at standards for low-level radiation. One was to
start with the occupational doses and work downward, which is in
fact the way it has been done. The BEIR committee said that that
wasn't as logical as the other way, which was to relate the standard
to the ambient background.

Howard Adler has proposed setting the standard for public exposure at a level "small" compared to the natural background. The
argument hangs around the definition of "small". Adler did give an
explicit definition for "small". "Small" should be taken as one
standard deviation from the natural background. This turns out to
be about twenty milliroentgens per year, where the mean natural background is about a hundred milliroentgens. It is interesting that
this value is about what the EPA established for the allowable exposure to the public for the entire fuel cycle. I am told by people
within EPA that the resemblance is not purely coincidental.

I understand that NCRP and other people are beginning to take
seriously this idea of establishing the standards at a similar "de
minimis" level in places where it is arguable whether you will ever
have a definitive answer. In the Soviet Union the matter is appar-

ently handled more simply because an acceptable level of exposure is established and I am told that they do not record exposures below the acceptable level. Therefore, it is impossible to multiply the number of individuals by the number of millirems per year and establish a dose to the exposed population.

Public policy has been largely concerned with exposure levels far lower than the levels that will be talked about today. Bill Russell said last night that he protracted the dose and he got it down to seven ten thousandths of a rem per minute which seemed like an awfully low number. That, however, amounts to roughly 365 roentgens per year. This turns out to be about 3,000 times the natural background. By contrast, the casualties estimated in the famous Rasmussen study come from the very large numbers of people who receive a single exposure of the order of, maybe, one year's background.

EXTRAPOLATION FROM LONG TERM LOW DOSE ANIMAL STUDIES - I. REVIEW

M. F. Cranmer

Jefferson Professional Services
P.O. Box 3397
Little Rock, AR 72203

Undeniably chemical technology has in large measure contributed to the achievement of our present standard of living. It produced many of the tools and resources needed to reduce human suffering and modify selective pressures of our environment. Accompanying these benefits, however, is the possibility that toxic properties of certain chemicals have the potential to threaten our health. A rational policy of utilization of chemicals is to produce the highest standard of living consistent with a quantitatively acceptable hazard-to-benefit ratio.

Products containing chemicals should be approved for use if there is an acceptable margin of safety between the anticipated exposures and the levels estimated to be hazardous to humans or the environment (12).

The toxicologist is faced with the dilemma of estimating the hazard to an enormous and variable human population from studies conducted on small numbers of environmentally and genetically controlled experimental animals. There is a considerable potential for error in assessing the hazard side of the hazard/benefit ratio under the limitations of present experimental and theoretical technique (11, 39).

The limitations of toxicological evaluations should be stated clearly. It was not, is not and will not be possible to guarantee absolute safety (11). Small populations of experimental subjects, either animal or man, may provide an imprecise estimate of hazard for comparison to a large human population of variable genetic/ disease states, cultural backgrounds and ages (18). Ways of

overcoming these limitations are becoming recognized. Techniques
for extrapolation must make maximum use of available data (13).
Social value judgements should be applied after the hazard analysis
has been completed and not injected surreptitiously under the guise
of science (16).

Advanced technologies offer an opportunity to improve our
standard of living and our health while reducing environmental
risks (15). For humans, just as for inbred mice kept under SPF
conditions, this will increase populational risks due to environmental pressures. If released to a natural environment, our inbred
animals would be fated to vanish as population in a few
generations. A retreat from technology is similarly not an option
for civilized mankind. The task of not fouling mankind's lair
remains.

PITFALLS IN THE PURSUIT OF ABSOLUTE SAFETY

The Delaney Clause of the Food, Drug and Cosmetic Act is an
example of an all-or-none approach to safety in the case of inten-
tional additives to commercially formulated foods. The Clause contains two segments, one for human and one for animal foods. The
segment addressing animal food additives states that in evaluating
the safety of such compounds used in feed, consideration must be
given to possible residues in the products of those animals which
are a source of food for man. No compound may be administered to
animals which are raised for food production if such a compound has
been shown to induce cancer when ingested by man or animal, unless
such compound will not adversely affect the animal and no residues,
as determined by methods of analysis prescribed or approved by the
Secretary (DHEW), are found in the edible products of such animals
under conditions of use specified in labeling and reasonably
certain to be followed in practice.

Let us consider the ways by which one might attain the
complete absence of a residue. The first would be to never permit
exposure, and the second would be to rely on the "complete" removal
by dilution or transformation after an appropriate waiting period.
The first approach eliminates the use of a chemical additive in
feeds. The second approach depends on the selection of analytical
methodologies which would be acceptable for determining "complete
removal". Any practical method will be open to challenge, because
it will fall short of analytical sensitivity to one molecule.

There are beneficial uses of biologically active chemicals and
there is the concomitant need to insure that the population is not
exposed to hazardous residue levels (12, 15). Some of the uses are
essential, in so far as no substitute process can be considered
less hazardous. For such chemicals, a compatible approach would be

to permit that use for which the absence of hazardous quantities of
a residue can be assured. The major requirements of this strategy
are to define the hazard, then determine the amount of exposure
which is expected to be hazardous, and finally to determine the
sensitivity of a method required for analysis to assure the absence
of potentially hazardous residue levels. Rephrased, the requirement for methodology and limitation of use would be defined toxico-
logically rather than as a function of the state of the art of
analytical chemistry.

A general application of zero-residue rules as found in the
Delaney Clause is likely to be inadequate in several respects (17).
It provides a false sense of security by ignoring the problem of
"false negatives" which may result from chance or inadequate testing; encourages poor experimentation since the less we do and the
less precise we are the less chance we have of determining anything
at a statistically significant level; and ignores uses with
benefits which might be documented to outweigh a worst case calculation of a carcinogenic hazard.

VALUE JUDGEMENT AND BIAS

Ambiguities in the process of anticipating an acceptable
safety policy will arise if the proposed criteria incorporate the
unobtainable goal of attempting to prove scientifically that no
deleterious effect will take place, i.e., to prove a nonoccurrence
in some future time. Examples were described by Dr. Alvin Weinberg
as "Transscience". Such a policy postulates society's need to
ensure an absence of positive findings beyond the range of our
methods for data collection. The toxicologists' tools, however,
are experiments employing the scientific method. They are usually
designed to establish that phenomena resulting from repeated experimental manipulations are real, are not artifacts and have not
occurred simply by chance.

We are all aware that positive findings may be artifacts and
therefore in most scientific disciplines there is a positive reward
for investing in adequate techniques and replication of experiments. Insistence on any desired degree of assurance against
making a wrong conclusion is standard operating procedure. The
quality of safety evaluations suffers as a result of an ingrained
attitude of some regulators that once they find a positive carcinogenic effect, no number of negative studies will provide an
adequate counter balance. No more telling example exists than the
unsuccessful attempt of ex-FDA Commissioner Kennedy to ban
saccharin (14). This attitude inappropriately ignores false positives, and discourages rigorous and repeated experimentation by
even the most responsible sponsor. In addition this bias places
the sponsor and the conscientious regulator alike in the position

of being bludgeoned with experiments carried out by third parties under conditions often not appropriate for safety evaluation or for which the results have not been validated. The sorry story of the attempted ban of nitrates by FDA is a case in point (31).

TRADITIONAL MODELS

When direct measurements are impossible, assumptions must be made if we are to extrapolate cancer hazard from animal studies at relatively high dose rates to human population hazards at intermittent and variable low dose rates. One set of assumptions concerns the description of the function relating real hazard as measured at high dose rates to theoretically estimated animal risk at low dose rates. The magnitude of low dose risk is extremely dependent upon the assumed shape of this dose-response function (21). Unfortunately this shape at low dose rates is much more sensitive to manipulating the extrapolation procedure than to the experimental data. This has led to the discouraging observation that extensive experimentation and quality assurance means less than arbitrary mathematical manipulation.

The extreme differences between models for extrapolating to low risks have been reviewed in detail elsewhere (11, 12, 13) and a summary is presented in Table 1. The probit, logistic, and one-hit curves all equally predict a 50% tumor response at a unit dose and 16% tumor response at ¼ that unit dose. The families of curves generated by these models are indistinguishable in the 8% to 92% tumor response range. Several thousand animals would be required to distinguish between the probit and logistic curves in the 2% to 4% response range with no absolute guarantee that either model would be applicable at lower levels. Extreme differences between models in estimated doses are noted when extrapolating to a 1 in a million risk.

TABLE 1
Doses Required to Give Upper Limits to Estimated Risks

Estimated Risk	Probit	Logistic	One-Hit
10^{-3}	1/67	1/323	1/714
10^{-6}	1/714	$1/9.8 \times 10^5$	$1/7.14 \times 10^5$
10^{-8}	1/2440	$1/6.3 \times 10^6$	$1/7.14 \times 10^7$

The "extreme value" curve, another possible model, would generally lie between the probit and logistic, depending on the slopes selected (7). The choice of an extrapolation model is critical, but the parameters adjusted in the use of the model, particularly the slope and upper confidence intervals, are even more critical.

Purists reject the logit analysis because the logit
function as originally proposed by Reed and Berkson in 1929 is an
empirical form of a series of at least six equations obtained by
data fitting and not from any formal derivation. In addition the
forms of the logit are uncertain since different investigators use
different equations, and different slopes and intercepts thus
obtained are without physical meaning even in well-defined chemical
or biochemical systems. However, a logit function derived from
the mass-action law is used in the Hill equation. Another
application of this function by Chou is discussed below in the
context of time-to-tumor models.

Even given a particular model, e.g., the probit, the slope
selected for extrapolation produces widely different results (Table
2).

TABLE 2
Fraction of Experimental Dose Using Probit Extrapolation with
Different Slopes for an Estimated Risk not to Exceed
1 in 100 Million

Observed Tumors	Slope = 1	Slope = 1.5	Slope = 2.0
0/50	1/18,000	1/690	1/135
0/100	1/8,300	1/410	1/91
0/500	1/1,800	1/150	1/42
0/1000	1/1,000	1/100	1/32

For comparative purposes, dose reduction factors for a risk of
1 in a million are given in Table 3 using a probit of slope of 1.

TABLE 3
Fraction of Experimental Dose Using Probit Extrapolation
with a Slope of One for an Estimated Upper Limit Risk of
One in a Million

Observed Tumors	Fraction of Experimental Dosage
0/50	1/2,500
0/100	1/1,140
0/500	1/250
0/1,000	1/140

There is no mathematical reason to set cancer aside as different from many other toxicological effects. A no-effect dose for any effect in the absence of a threshold, not just cancer, is sample size dependent.

THRESHOLDS

A few comments on "threshold" and value judgements are an appropriate prelude to a discussion of several newer methods available for mathematical extrapolation. The concept of a threshold dose is based on the premise that some smaller dose under similar conditions will not produce the measured effect. If the conditions change likely there will be a change in the threshold. This does not mean thresholds don't exist! This does not mean that thresholds can't be estimated! It does not mean that bounds cannot be established! It means only that thresholds are not absolute.

It is obvious that more refined methods of observation or changing diagnostic criteria may lower the observed threshold. For example if we consider hyperplasia as an obligate precursor to neoplasia we shift the threshold. Repeating the bioassay, as in the ED_{01} study (19), will demonstrate variability even among genetically equivalent individuals. Phenotypic heterogeneity of any population and microenvironments will be expressed and will influence the responses observed. Almost all toxicologists believe that for any compound for given conditions a "biologically insignificant dose" exists. There is little doubt that this is true; however no acceptable approach has emerged for risk assessment since we possess no consensus of the definition of insignificant.

LOW DOSE MODELS

Investigators have and will continue to utilize mathematical models of carcinogenesis to gain insight into whether or not a linear, nonthreshold relationship prevails between dose and excess response at low constant dose rates of a test agent. Crump et al. (21) and Guess et al. (29) and Peto (34) have invoked certain hypotheses of carcinogenesis, to argue that there exists the possibility of linear responses at low doses. For example Crump et al. (21) and Guess et al. (29) offer the proposition that the probability P(d) of response at dose rate is given by

$$P(d) = 1-\exp[-(a_0 + a_1 d + a_2 d^2 + ...)], \quad a_i \geqq 0. \quad \text{When}$$

P(d) is small, the excess risk P(d)-P(0) is approximately

$$P(d)-P(0) = a_1 d + a_2 d^2 + ..., \quad \text{and the question}$$

of nonthreshold low-dose linearity is determined by whether or not the coefficient a_1 is zero. There are plausible assumptions, such as detoxification mechanisms, DNA repair, or the necessity for multiple molecular interactions, that lead to $a_1 = 0$. There are also plausible assumptions for some agents that can lead to positive values for a_1. We will almost never have the knowledge to completely discriminate between these alternatives. The only acceptable approach is to use extrapolation procedures that make efficient use of what we have or can get, the experimental data. Injection of value judgements such as the value of various upper confidence limits in place of central expected values for the coefficients a_1 will incorporate a bias value judgement into the extrapolation procedures that almost always outweighs the information inherent in the data. When one applies upper confidence limits rather than central expected value for a_1 it is equivalent to accepting that a_1 is positive. At low dose rates this value judgement (an arbitrary upper confidence limit) dominates the remaining terms. The requirement of the use of upper confidence limits rather than central expected value guarantees that models will yield nonthreshold linearity at low dose rates. Why are masquerades necessary? If a user has a bias for nonthreshold linear models, let him state so clearly and forthrightly.

The lack of logic supporting this type of value judgements becomes apparent when they are applied to the procedures of Crump et al. and Guess et al. since the techniques become so insensitive to response at experimental dosages that they fail to distinguish between low levels of potent carcinogens and noncarcinogenic substances. Guess et al. (29) have documented this by using the procedure on two dose response data sets for a noncarcinogenic agent. One simulation involved 150 responses at each of ten dose rates. The second involved 300 responses at each of 5 dose rates. In both cases the 90% upper confidence limit on a_1 was positive, so that the two upper confidence curves relating extra response to dose rate were virtually linear at low dose rates. Such false positive risk estimates support the contention that the value judgement inherent in the use of upper confidence limits is not appropriate and should be separated from the quantitative use of mathematical models.

Another example is provided by Gaylor and Kodell (28) in their study of 14 sets of toxicological dose response data previously described by the Scientific Committee of the Food Safety Council (27). The behavior of a gamma multihit model was compared to the Armitage-Doll multistage model for low dose extrapolation using the technique given by Crump et al. (20). The Gaylor and Kodell Armitage-Doll multi-stage model results do not exactly agree with the Scientific Committee of the Food Safety Council (27) because the limits calculated by Gaylor and Kodel, did not assume a maximum degree of dose in the exponential term, whereas the limits calculated

by the Food Safety Council took the degree of dose as fixed. Gaylor
and Kodell (28) concluded "Conceptually linear extrapolation would
(should)* be more conservative, but this is not the case in actuality
apparently because more stringent mathematical assumptions and conditions are required" (by the gamma one-hit model)*. Selected examples
are given in Table 4.

These examples reinforce the recommendation, made by the
Scientific Committee of the Food Safety Council (40), calling for
reason when mathematical games impact on real life decisions.
"Although the value judgement involved in the use of conservative
risk assessments may seem appropriate in the light of the many
scientific unknowns involved, once formalized as a specific
mathematical procedure it escapes the control of the decision-maker
and can lead to undesirable and unsound results by distorting the
balance between risk and benefit. We therefore recommend the separation of the mathematical and societal aspects of the problems,
with the extrapolation procedure chosen to provide 'best estimates'
of risk as well as their upper or lower limits".

Toxicological and mathematical uncertainties associated with
extrapolating risks from relatively high experimental dosages in
animals to low human exposure levels are often the principal
rationale of those who call for complete prohibition when a chemical
has been "demonstrated" to be a carcinogen. A slight modification
of this idea, which seems recently to be more acceptable to some
regulators, is to use a series of conservative assumptions for
data presentation followed by linear extrapolation from upper
confidence limits of the experimental results to a zero response
at zero dosage. Since rodents, the principal bioassay species,
have substantial rates of neoplastic disease at many sites this
offers the regulator the discretionary option to declare almost
any thoroughly studied compound a carcinogen (see Table 14).

FDA EXTRAPOLATION

FDA policy was stated by Cairns: "Explanation of the dose-
response relationship at low doses is fundamental to the regulatory
agencies' posture that there is not a threshold level below which a
carcinogen cannot exert its carcinogenic effect. Concurrent with
this philosophy, linear extrapolation is also a non-threshold method"
Cairns interpreted the ED_{01} study as follows: "The evidence from the
ED_{01} study, although never intended to directly answer or validate
these views, has provided a massive and overwhelming experimental
profile and data base which lends support to regulatory policies"
(6). The ED_{01} was a dose response study on 24,000 mice fed the
carcinogen $2-AAF$. Its results are interpreted quite differently
in Part II of this report (19).

---

*Comments in parentheses added for clarity.
**Scientific Committee of the Food Safety Council (40).

TABLE 4
Lower 97.5% Confidence Limit for Dosages Predicted
to Have a Risk of Less Than One Million in Rodent Populations

Substance	Dose Unit	Sci. Com. FSC 1978**	Linear	Armitage-Doll
Aflatoxin B_1	ppb	3.4×10^{-5}	7.9×10^{-6}	5.9×10^{-6}
Vinyl Chloride	ppm	1.6×10^{-3}	7.1×10^{-4}	5.2×10^{-4}
Ethylenethiourea	ppm	4.4×10^{-4}	1.0×10^{-4}	3.2×10^{-4}
Dieldrin	ppm	9.4×10^{-6}	5.7×10^{-6}	2.9×10^{-6}
DDT	ppm	2.0×10^{-2}	3.4×10^{-5}	2.6×10^{-5}

EPA EXTRAPOLATION

An example of such a divergent procedure is one that EPA has used in estimating risks of NTA (24). Two separate stages were included by EPA in deriving quantitative estimates of carcinogenic risk to humans. The first stage involved the extrapolation of a dose response curve over a region of extremely low dietary concentrations, far below the concentrations used in actual bioassays.

For the first stage, two separate low-dose extrapolation procedures were used to derive a dose-response curve. These extrapolations were performed separately with incidence data for males, females, tumors of all types and selected system tumors alone. One extrapolation procedure used was the "one-hit" dose-response model proposed by the EPA Carcinogen Assessment Group (CAG) (3).

Following is a brief discussion of the theory, as explained by EPA, underlying the one-hit model. In this discussion "tumor incidence" is synonomous with "risk" and "dietary concentration" is synonomous with "dosage". If one assumes that some risk of cancer results from even a slight exposure to a carcinogen, the exponential probability law;

$$P_{(d)} = 1 - e^{(-\lambda d)}$$

gives the probability, P, that a carcinogen at a dosage, d, will induce a tumor in these animals. It will often be the case that some of the tumors in the treatment group were not induced by the carcinogen, but had developed spontaneously. Where P_c is the probability that a tumor develops spontaneously in a control group and P_t is the probability that a tumor develops in the treament group, the probability that a tumor does not develop in the treatment group was shown by Abbott (1) to be

$$(1 - P_t) = (1 - P_c)(1 - P)$$

Solving,

$$P = \frac{P_t - P_c}{1 - P_c}$$

Substituting gives the probability of observing a tumor in the treatment group,

$$P_t = 1 - (1 - P_c)e^{(-\lambda d)}$$

Solving,

$$\lambda = \frac{1}{d} \ln (1 - Pt)/(1 - Pc).$$

At very low dosages, P is almost directly proportional to the dosage d and λ will be the slope of the dose-response curve obtained when P is plotted against values of d close to zero. Because this form of the one-hit model approximates a straight line through the origin at very low dosages, it is often referred to as the linear non-threshold dose-response model. EPA interprets this to state that any exposure to a carcinogenic substance will result in some risk of tumor incidence, and the risk of probability of cancer induction at low dosages increases almost linearly with increasing dose.

Use of the EPA CAG one-hit model with data from bioassays requires that the treatment group be defined as the group at the lowest dietary concentration whose tumor incidence had been shown to be a statistically significant increase over the spontaneous tumor incidence in the control group. Separate extrapolations are also performed with the CAG one-hit model using the incidence for all tumor types in males and females.

The second extrapolation procedure used by EPA to derive a dose-response curve is a computer based one-hit model developed by Dr. Charles Brown of the Biometry Branch, Division of Cancer Cause and Prevention, National Cancer Institute. The mathematics of the Brown one-hit model differ from the CAG one-hit model in that Brown's model takes into account the tumor incidences at all dietary concentrations simultaneously without regard to the statistical significance of any. It is considered by EPA to be especially useful as it does not demand an answer to the question of types exposed at a given dietary concentration. The computer program for the Brown one-hit model also allows derivation of values of λ derived by the CAG one-hit model. Therefore, 95% and 99% upper cofidence limits are placed on all derived values of λ regardless of the form of the one-hit model used.

The larger the value of λ, the steeper the dose-response curve at low-dosages. By either the CAG one-hit model or the Brown one-hit model, the values of λ will be consistently less for one sex than the values similarly derived using data from the other sex. Therefore, EPA has elected to incorporate an additional measure of "conservatism", by utilizing the most senstive data for all calculations involved in the derivation of final estimates of carcinogenic risk to humans associated with potential exposures.

The second stage in an EPA derivation of estimates of carcinogenic risks associated with potential human exposure involves the transformations of each experimental animal derived value of λ to a λ for humans. This transformation is accomplished by the application of a species conversion factor. This species conversion factor is based upon the EPA stated knowledge that the specific dose in mg/kg/day of a direct acting agent required to produce an effect in

humans is smaller than the specific dose of that agent that would
be required to produce a similar effect in a given animal species.
According to EPA if dietary concentrations or exposure levels are
expressed in mg/kg/day, then the potency of a chemical or direct-
acting drug in humans is higher than in animal by the ratio:

$$[(Average\ human\ weight)/(Average\ animal\ weight)]^{1/3}$$

If the average human weight is assumed to 70kg (70,000g) and the
average weight of a rat is assumed to be 350g, then the conversion
factor is $(70,000g/350g)^{1/3} = (200)^{1/3} = 5.85$ (3).

Each point estimate of the value λ from the data, along with
associated 95% and 99% upper confidence limits on λ is multiplied
by the species conversion factor to yield a point estimate of the
value of λ for humans along with associated 95% and 99% upper confidence limits. To arrive at final quantitative estimates of carcinogenic risk from potential human exposures, each point estimate
of λ and associated upper 95% confidence limits is combined with
the range of exposure estimates, d, and applied to

$$P_{(d)} = 1-e^{-\lambda d}$$

the exponential probability law. After performing these calculations EPA states "The respective resultant values of P are the
point estimates and upper 95% and 99% confidence limits of risk or
probability that a lifetime of human exposure at dosage level, d,
would induce a tumor in a human so exposed."

The EPA approach selects two worst case models, the worst case
data points, the worst case tumor yields, the most senstive species,
most sensitive sex, upper confidence limits, relates all data to a
direct acting drug hypothesis and applies species conversion factors.
After all of this we are not being cynical when we state that the
actual data really make very little difference.

The sensitivity of a model to data is of great importance
in estimating risk by extrapolation. Treatment of data on dieldrin
and DDT(i) provided provocative examples of small modifications that
altered the risk estimates. The technique utilized in Tables 5 and
6 to demonstrate sensitivity is to add or substract one tumor from
a data set and analyze by the one hit model and compare the changes
to that of the multi-hit model. It is clear that the one hit model
is relatively insensitive to data.

TABLE 5

Estimated Virtually Safe Dose at Different Allowable Levels of Risk
% change from estimates from original data in parentheses
(Van Ryzin's Data Set #13)

Data Set	Model	Added Risk Over Background		
		10^{-4}	10^{-6}	10^{-8}
Original	One-hit	2.76×10^{-2}	2.76×10^{-4}	2.76×10^{-6}
	Multi-hit	7.39×10^{-1}	4.79×10^{-2}	3.10×10^{-3}
One fewer tumor, control group	One-hit	2.71×10^{-2} (-2%)	2.71×10^{-4} (-2%)	2.71×10^{-6} (-2%)
	Multi-hit	4.88×10^{-1} (-34%)	2.50×10^{-2} (-48%)	1.29×10^{-3} (-58%)
One more tumor, control group	One-hit	2.80×10^{-2} (1%)	2.80×10^{-4} (1%)	2.80×10^{-6} (1%)
	Multi-hit	9.92×10^{-1} (34%)	7.54×10^{-2} (36%)	5.75×10^{-3} (85%)
One fewer tumor, 50 ppm	One-hit	2.80×10^{-2} (1%)	2.80×10^{-4} (1%)	2.80×10^{-6} (1%)
	Multi-hit	1.29 (75%)	1.14×10^{-1} (133%)	1.00×10^{-2} (223%)
One more tumor, 50 ppm	One-hit	2.72×10^{-2} (-1%)	2.72×10^{-4} (-1%)	2.72×10^{-6} (-1%)
	Multi-hit	4.14×10^{-1} (-44%)	1.95×10^{-2} (-59%)	9.18×10^{-4} (-70%)

TABLE 6

Estimated Virtually Safe Dose at Different Levels of Risk
% change from estimates from original data in parentheses
(Van Ryzin's Data Set #12)

Data Set	Model	Added Risk Over Background		
		10^{-4}	10^{-6}	10^{-8}
Original	One-hit	5.67×10^{-4}	5.67×10^{-6}	5.67×10^{-8}
	Multi-hit	4.81×10^{-2}	6.34×10^{-3}	8.44×10^{-4}
One fewer tumor, control group	One-hit	5.58×10^{-4} (-2%)	5.58×10^{-6} (-2%)	5.58×10^{-8} (-2%)
	Multi-hit	4.37×10^{-2} (-9%)	5.49×10^{-3} (-13%)	6.95×10^{-4} (-18%)
One more tumor, control group	One-hit	5.77×10^{-4} (2%)	5.77×10^{-6} (2%)	5.77×10^{-8} (2%)
	Multi-hit	5.27×10^{-2} (10%)	7.31×10^{-3} (15%)	1.02×10^{-3} (19%)
One fewer tumor, 1.25 ppm	One-hit	5.74×10^{-4} (1%)	5.74×10^{-6} (1%)	5.74×10^{-8} (1%)
	Multi-hit	6.10×10^{-2} (27%)	9.20×10^{-3} (45%)	1.40×10^{-3} (66%)
One more tumor, 1.25 ppm	One-hit	5.60×10^{-4} (-1%)	5.60×10^{-6} (-1%)	5.60×10^{-8} (-1%)
	Multi-hit	3.69×10^{-2} (-23%)	4.21×10^{-3} (-34%)	4.83×10^{-4} (-43%)

NCTR EXTRAPOLATION

When referring to the problem of model choice and referencing the ED_{01} Cairns (6) stated "Most of the objections to cancer risk assessment reflect a reluctance to accept extrapolation from high to low doses. The four most widely employed models in descending order of conservatism are the linear, multi-stage, Mantel-Bryan and Cornfield models. It is true that risk estimates using these four models vary dramatically. The debate centers on the fact that inadequate experimental evidence was available to determine which model most accurately delineated the dose-response relationship at extremely low exposure levels. The availability of the ED_{01} data base should help resolve this controversy in favor of the conservative linear model."

NCTR's Gaylor and Kodel (28) in defending linear extrapolation (interpolation) and relying on ED_{01} for support state "The development of more sophisticated mathematical models to extrapolate to low doses with quantal bioassay data does not appear to be justified". This is a curious attitude considering the mission of NCTR was to provide just such capabilities.

Gaylor and Kodell have suggested a linear interpolation technique which is described mathematically over the low unobservable dose range by

$$P = \frac{UCL}{d_e} x \ d$$

where P is the upper bound on the potential proportion of animals with excess tumors caused by the administration of a dosage, d, of a chemical and UCL is the upper confidence limit at a dosage, d_e, in the experimental dose range. Linear interpolation is suggested for use between zero and the upper confidence limit of the excess tumor rate estimated for the lowest experimental dosage. In most cases interpolation proceeds from that point on the upper confidence limits in the experimental dose range which has the smallest slope (UCL : d_e), i.e., which gives the lowest risk. Any mathematical model can be used which adequately fits the data in the experimental dose range since it makes relatively little difference on the resultant value. The only purpose of this model is to obtain an upper confidence line for the experimental region. The fitted line from the selected model is not extended below the experimental region.

CONCLUSIONS ABOUT LINEAR EXTRAPOLATION

Statements of NCTR, EPA and FDA notwithstanding, a rational assessment of cancer risk associated with environmental exposures necessarily entails the use of best estimates instead of worst case mathematical models. Linear extrapolation or interpolation is an intellectual capitulation and should not always, if ever, be the model of choice. Any mathematical model, or for that matter quantitative hypothesis of carcinogenesis thought applicable should be rationalized on the basis of an explicit set of assumptions which consider the mechanisms by which cancer is induced. In addition such procedures should estimate the consequences of these assumptions at predicted levels and durations of exposure and permit the calculation of predicted cancer hazard for specific groups and general populations. While we are only too aware of our limited understanding of the processes by which cancers occur and that most of the assumptions necessary in model utilization themselves have not yet been directly verified, we must not ignore our expanding knowledge. The limits and values assigned to these assumptions are critical in influencing predictions of hazard. This impact is ignored when a model is selected or abandoned for the sake of producing a desired prediction.

TIME TO TUMOR MODELS

Additional hazard from cancer accrues to those additional people who might eventually contract cancer. Cancers, created by low doses of carcinogens in experimental animals generally occur late in life and are not lethal. The impact of these cancers is most appropriately measured as a reduction of quality of remaining life. Murray and Axtell (33) were among the first to investigate this question. Time to tumor development becomes the critical component for consideration.

Extrapolating to low dosages from a classical fixed time dose-response curves (linear, logistic, probit, one hit) does not adequately consider that period of a lifetime during which the tumors exist with the potential to impair the quality of life. Experimental animal or human responses are most often evaluated by comparing gross percentage of tumors occurring over the lifetime or at the termination date of an experiment or some combination of both. One must immediately recognize difficulties with gross rates. For example animals or humans at the highest doses are more likely to have shorter life spans due to toxicity of the chemical or agent and therefore have less opportunity to express slowly developing tumors. Therefore, the highest exposure rate may at the time of death exhibit a lower incidence of tumors. Should more weight be given to the earlier tumors since they influence quality of life for a longer time or should more weight be given to late developing but lethal tumors? If more weight should be given to either lethal or early tumors, how much? Also, tumors occurring at lower doses not only tend to be less life threatening but occur later. Low dose groups may not develop lethal tumors and may in fact, due to competing risks, even live longer than controls as in the ED_{01} study. How does one evaluate an increase in nonlethal tumors accompanied by increased lifespan? Certainly linear extrapolation from upper confidence limits does not provide much help in resolving these questions.

The simplest carcinogensis bioassay protocol which can be employed to access the dynamics of tumor development measures tumors in animals sacrificed at fixed points in time and observes the percentages of those animals possessing particular tumors. This sampling technique yields estimates of the proportion with tumors at given times which can then be plotted against dose. The ED_{01} is an example of an experiment combining lifespan and serial sacrifice techniques (Table 7). A disadvantage of such experiments is that they usually require large numbers of animals.

The literature containing several examples of time to tumor experiments. Blum, in his 1959 (4) work on "Carcinogenesis by Ultraviolet Light", demonstrated a log normal distribution of severity of exposure and time of cancer development. It was Druckrey however who dramatized the relationships of time, dose, and dose rate for chemicals in a 1967 (25) monograph representing 25 years work and 10,000 experimental animals.

Druckrey accomplished the first of two critical conceptual steps when he demonstrated with 4-dimethylaminobenzene the dependency of time and dose. According to the relationship developed, the product of daily dosage and induction time is a constant $(k = dt)$. He reported the second step with his description that increased carcinogenic response could be obtained for smaller dose rates and total doses if time of observation was extended $(k = dt^n)$.

Druckrey extended his observations with 4-dimethylamino-stilbene (DAST). 4-dimethylaminostilbene (26) produces a parallel and linear relationship between probits of ear duct and mammary carcinoma and log total dose. Druckrey clearly demonstrated at least for 4-DAST and the dose rates used that the total dose required to produce a given incidence is clearly smaller at smaller dose rates if one waits long enough. A replotting of log total dose, and median induction time vs. log dose rate demonstrate a direct relationship between the log median induction time and log dose rate.

The power law describes this condition as follows, $(f_a = bd^k)$ and predicts that a plot of log (f_a) vs log (D) will give a straight line with a slope k and y-intercept at log b. However, the theoretical data generated by the mass-action law, when plotted by application of the power law yield curves instead of straight lines. The slopes of curves by Chou (9) decrease as the dose increases (or as the f_a value increases). The maximal slope occurs at an extremely low f_a value at which the k values approach the m

TABLE 7

Extrapolation Methods Discussed in
Text or Utilized in Analyzing ED_{01} Data

Probit Function (point exposure)	$f_a = 1 - \exp[-QD]$
Log-Probit Model	$P_{(d)} = \phi(\alpha + \beta \log_{10} d)$
Power Law	$f_a = bD^k$
Doll	$I_t = b(t-v-w)^k$
Doll-Weibull	$I = bd^m (t-w)^k$
One Hit Linear	$P_{(d)} = 1 - e^{(-\lambda d)}$
Extreme Value	$P_{(d)} = 1 - \exp[-\exp(a + \beta \log d)]$
Linear Interpolation	$P_{de} = UCL \times d$
Multi Stage	$P_{(d)} = 1 - \exp[-(a + B_1 d) \ldots (\lambda_k + \beta_k d)]$
Multi-hit (k-hit) Model	$P_{(d)} = 1 - \Sigma^{k-1}(\lambda d)^i e^{-\lambda d}/i$
Median Effect Principle of the Mass-action Law	$f_a/(1-f_a) = (D/D_m)^m$
Chou Equation	$fa = [1 + (D_m/D)^m]^{-1}$

values. From Chou's work (8, 9) and application of the power law it can be shown, that the ratio k/m of the slopes of the power law plot and the median-effect plot for the same set of data is:

$$k/m = \frac{d \log (f_a)/d \log D}{d \log [(f_a)^{-1}-1)]^{-1}/d\log D} = 1-f_a = f_u$$

where f_u is the fraction that is unaffected by the dose.

If a system follows the mass-action law and if f_a values are high, then k/m>>1 and the k value will be grossly underestimated by a plot of log (f_a) vs log (D). Low-dose risk assessment of a carcinogen obtained by application of the power law will result in underestimation. The k values will approximate the m values only when the f_a value is very low.

The power law, $(f_a = bD^k)$, takes into account those affected (i.e., f_a) but not those unaffected (i.e., $1-f_a$) when the dose is varied. By contrast, the median-effect equation takes into account both f_a and $1-f_a$ simultaneously.

In the critical relationships identified by Druckrey, independent of model correctness and even for clearly dosage-dependent rates, the limiting component is obviously lifespan. Time is the limiting and most relevant experimental variable, a fact that toxicologists and statisticians and regulators should work together to exploit while formulating policy.

Comparative data also exist for man. Doll explored the concepts relating time and dose in his 1970 paper read before the Royal Statistical Society (23), where he proposed that $I_t = b (t-v-w)^k$ where v is time of beginning exposure, and w is the minimum time for clinical recognition for a tumor in humans. Doll first applied this concept to data on the incidence of bronchial carcinoma in cigarette smokers. Doll also developed k's for data reported by Day in 1967 on tumors from tar painted on the skin of mice. The k obtained for cigarette smoking in man and skin tumors in mice were considered similar and this was especially encouraging to those who were active in efforts to describe mathematical similarities in cancer responses. Doll stressed however that much of the data available fit a wide range of pairs of values for k and w in the formula $I_t = b (t-v-w)^k$ and suggested that a desirable experimental approach would be to design protocols to estimate the values independently (10).

Research in statistical techniques to analyze time to tumor data continues. One useful measure of the impact of carcinogenesis

on a population is age-specific incidence rates of the amount of
life shortening due to a tumor. Time-to-tumor studies do not, as
often suggested, require life time data to estimate a relationship
between tumor rates, time and dosage. Indeed extrapolations to low
dosages often project values for median time to tumor beyond the
normal lifespan of an animal. Time-to-tumor distributions must
however estimate the proportion of animals expected to develop
tumors within their lifespan before dying of other causes.
Approaches tend to be complicated and, just as all models do,
depend on mathematical factors subject to bias. These factors can
often be established experimentally, and need not automatically be
relegated to value judgements. Relevant experiments simply require
survival and tumor data at several dosages. It is important to
observe the effects of dosage rate on the time pattern of response,
especially incidence and severity and time to tumors at all incidence levels.

     There was a resurgence of interest in time to tumor when
Albert and Altshuler (2) developed a mathematical model for predicting tumor incidence and life shortening. This work was based
on the reports of Blum (4) on skin tumor response with chronic
ultraviolet irradiation in mice and Druckrey (25) on a variety of
chemical carcinogens in rodents. Albert and Altshuler investigated
cancer in mice exposed to radium and also in cigarette smokers. In
review, the basic relationship used was Druckrey's $dt^n = k$. The
purpose in this case was to determine the time it takes for a small
proportion of the population to develop tumors. As the dosage is
increased, the time to tumor occurrence may be expected to be
shortened. In their 1973 paper Albert and Altshuler used the
log-normal distribution to represent time to tumor occurrence
assuming the standard deviation to be independent of dosage. A log
normal distribution of tumor times corresponds to the probit transformation so employed in the Mantel-Bryan procedure. A Weibull
distribution for time to tumors has been suggested by those
studying human cancers (10, 32) where I is the incidence rate of
tumors at time t, b is a constant depending on experimental conditions, d is dosage, w is the minimum time to the occurrence of an
observable tumor, m and k are parameters to be estimated. Day
(22), Peto, Lee and Paige (36) and Peto and Lee (35) are among
those to have considered the Weibull distribution for time to tumor
occurrence. Theoretical models of carcinogenesis have been interpreted to predict Weibull distributions (38). Theoretical arguments and some experimental data suggest the Weibull distribution
where tumor incidence is a polynomial in dose times a function of
age. Weibull distributions for time to tumor can lead under some
conditions to an extreme value distribution relating tumor response
to dosage (7). Hoel (30), among others has provided techniques to
be apllied when adjustments must be made for competing causes of
death. Albert and Altshuler (2) also discussed other distributions
of time to tumor.

$$I = bd^m (t-w)^k.$$

Chou (9) reported an interesting model to evaluate experimental dose-effect relationships of carcinogens following either acute (single dose) or chronic (time-to-tumor) exposure. Results appear to conform with the median-effect principle (8) of the mass-action law:

$$f_a / (1-f_a) = (D/D_m)^m,$$

where D is dose or cumulative dose, D_m is the D for the median effect, m is a Hill-type coefficient, and f_a is the fraction that responded to D. The parameters m and D_m are the basic characteristics for each carcinogen at specified experimental conditions.

A plot of $y = \log [(f_a)^{-1}-1]^{-1}$ vs. $x = \log (D)$ gives the slope m,

and the intercept $\log D_m$, at y=0. The Chou proposal is based on the fact that the dose-effect relationship described by the median-effect equation is consistent with well defined biological systems. The median-effect equation has been shown earlier to be a generalized form of the biochemical enzyme kinetic equations of Michaelis-Menten and Hill, the physical absorption equation of Langmuir, the chemical pH-ionization equation of Henderson-Hasselbalch, the equilibrium-ligand binding equation of Scatchard and the pharmacological drug-receptor interaction.

A plot of $\log [(f_a)^{-1}-1]^{-1}$ vs $\log (D)$, has been shown to be a general and simple method for determining pharmacological median doses for lethality (LD_{50}), toxicity (TD_{50}), effect of agonist drugs (ED_{50}) and effect of antagonists (ID_{50}). Thus, the median-effect principle of the mass-action law encompasses a vast range of applications. This rationale has led to the hypothesis by Chou that the action of chemical carcinogens, like other chemicals, follows the mass-action law.

Using previously reported data of Bryan and Shimkin (5) and Peto et al. (37), Chou has shown that dose-effect relationships of carcinogens obtained from various experimental designs (e.g., mode of exposure, route of administration, age of beginning of exposure to carcinogen, type of tumor produced, and strain and sex of animal used) can be normalized and compared directly and their consistency with the mass-law principle clearly demonstrated. Chemical carcinogens, then like non-carcinogenic chemicals can exert their effects according to the principle of the mass-action law. If true this suggests that the interaction of the ultimate carcinogens and the critical molecules is either a multi-event or a slow-transition process (i.e., m>1). Mathematically then

$$f_a = [(1 +(D_m/D)^m]^{-1}$$

provides a simplified general method for assessment of low-dose
risk of carcinogens.

Chou's efforts may be of great value in welding theory and
practical observable reality. When a chemical carcinogen follows
the mass-action law, it is reasonable to expect, if molecules are
active electrophiles, that the molecules are capable of attaching
the critical molecular site at any level. Thus, if (even for an
electrophilic carcinogen) an experimental system exhibits a dose
threshold phenomenon, it does not need to be due to the carcinogenic mechanism per se but could be due to insufficient hits at a
redundant site or post-carcinogenic events such as reversion,
repair and immunologic effects, etc.

Chou (9) proposes that low-dose risks at a given dose of a
carcinogen can be estimated from experimental dose ranges by using
the median-effect equation and m and D_m values by:

$$f_a = [1 + (D_m/D)^m]^{-1}$$

The theoretical analysis offered by Chou indicates that the
difference between the mass-action law and the power law increases
greatly with dose. Recognition of this fact is again of particular
significance since estimates of carcinogenic effect at very low
doses (such as with environmental carcinogens) can only be obtained
by extrapolating from experiments using much higher doses.

In demonstrating this point Chou (9) calculated that acute
administration of benzpyrene in a single dose by injection gave a
D_m = 98.9 µg and m = 1.39 ± 0.05. If a safety limit (D) is set for
0.001 D_m (i.e., 0.0989 µg), then the expected f_a value (the
resulting fraction of the population that incurs cancer) is 6.76 x
10^{-5}. However, when a low dose of benzpyrene was repeatedly
applied to animals over a period of D_m = 41.18 weeks (or a cumulative median-effect dose of 1640 µg), an m of 4.859 + 0.158 was
obtained. If a safety limit (D) is set for 0.01 D_m ($\bar{i}$.e., 16.4

µg), then the expected f_a value will be 1.91 x 10^{-10} which is quite

low. It has again demonstrated the variability derived from
different modeling conditions utilized in assessing low-dose
risk or in setting safety limits for carcinogens by extrapolation.

It might be easier to explain to scientist and public alike
that a safe dose is defined on the basis that one must live to some
multiple of a normal lifespan to have a remote chance of developing
a tumor just before death occurred by another cause. Not only is
it easier to explain, it is more consistent with the facts.

Most procedures provide estimates of the average risk and do not consider segments of the population which may be at high risk. Real risks simply are not often, if ever, linear or proportionally distributed. Mathematically, the proper approach in calculating the risk for the total population is to calculate the risk for a continuum of dosages and then to multiply that risk by the proportion of the time that dosage occurs followed by integration over the distribution of dosages. Unfortunately the distribution of dosages for an environmental chemical in a human population is often unknown. Introducing variation in exposure adds another critical dimension to an already complicated problem.

Quantitative determination of acceptable exposure levels to carcinogens is of particular importance to those involved in meeting our extensive chemical needs and should be basic to the policy of regulatory agencies. As justified in the introduction, many uses of chemical products (drugs, pesticides, food additives) have become a necessity and, consequently, the use of techniques that yield objectively best estimates of associated hazards should be recognized as obligatory.

REFERENCES

1. Abbott, (1925): A method of computing the effectiveness of
       an insecticide. J. of Economic Entomology, 18:265-267.

2. Albert, R.E. and Altshuler, B., (1973): Considerations
       relating to the formulation of limits for unavoidable
       population exposures to environmental carcinogens. In
       Rationale of Carcinogenesis, Ballou, J.E. et. al eds.,
       AEC Symposium Series, CONF-72050, NTIS, Springfield, Va.,
       pp. 223-253.

3. Anderson, (1979): Discontinuities in dose response curves
       from toxicological tests. Paper presented at the Soap
       and Detergents Manufacturers Association (Boca Raton,
       Florida). January 27, 1979.

4. Blum, H.F., (1959): Carcinogenesis by ultraviolet light.
       Princeton University Press, Princeton, New Jersey.

5. Bryan, W.R. and Skimkin, M.B., (1943): Quantitative analysis
       of dose-response data obtained with three carcinogenic
       hydrocarbons in strain C3H male mice. J. Natl. Cancer
       Inst., $\underline{3}$:503-531.

6. Cairns, (1979): The ED_{01} Study: Introduction, objectives,
       and experimental design. In Innovations in Cancer Risk
       Assessment (ED_{01} Study), (J. Staffa and M. Mehlman, eds.),
       pp. 1-7, Pathotox Publishers, Inc., Park Forest South,
       Illinois.

7. Chand, N. and Hoel, D.G., (1973): A comparison of models for
       determining safe levels of environmental agents. Con-
       ference on Reliability and Biometry, Florida State
       University, Tallahassee.

8. Chou, T.-C., (1976): Derivation and properties of Michaelis-
       Menten type and Hill type equations for reference
       ligands, J. Theoret. Biol., $\underline{59}$:253-276.

9. Chou, T.-C., (1980): Comparison of dose-effect relation-
       ships of carcinogens following low-dose chronic exposure
       and high-dose single injection: an analysis by the
       median-effect principle. Carcinogenesis, $\underline{1}$:203-213.

10. Cook, P.J., Doll, R., and Fellingham, S.A., (1969): A
     mathematical model for the age distribution of cancer
     in man. Int. J. Cancer, $\underline{4}$:93-112.

11. Cranmer, M.F., (1974): Reflections in Toxicology. Journal
     of Washington Academy of Sciences $\underline{64}$(2):158-179.

12. Cranmer, M.F., (1977): Hazards of Pesticide Development and
     Mammalian Toxicity: Carcinogenicity, Teratogenicity, and
     Mutagenicity. Proceedings of XV International Congress of
     Entomology, 719-736.

13. Cranmer, M.F., (1977): Estimation of risks due to environ-
     mental carcinogensis. Medical and Pediatric Oncology,
     $\underline{3}$(2):169-198.

14. Cranmer, M.F., (1978): Report to the Commissioner, Food and
     Drug Administration on the Hazards and Risks of Saccharin,
     800 Pages. FDA Publication.

15. Cranmer, M.F., (1978): Toxicology of families of chemials
     used as herbicides in forestry. Proceedings USDA/EPA
     Symposium, the Use of Herbicides in Forestry. USDA
     Publication.

16. Cranmer, M.F., (1979): Scientific basis for regulatory
     decisions on saccharin. Health and Sugar Substitutes.
     S. Karger, 281-287.

17. Cranmer, M.F., (1979): The design criteria and application
     of dose response relatioships to interpretation of
     carcinogenesis bioassay. Regulatory Aspects of Carcino-
     genesis and Food Additives: The Delaney Clause.
     Academic Press, 147-172.

18. Cranmer, M.F.: Use of animal and laboratory tests to screen
     for toxic effects. Proceedings of the Third Joint
     US-USSR Symposium on Comprehensive Analysis of the
     Environment, Tashkent, Russia. EPA Publication.

19. Cranmer, M.F., (1981): Extrapolation from long term low
     dose animal studies. II. The ED_{01} study. In:
     Measurement of risks, G.G. Berg, et al., eds., Plenum
     Press, New York.

20. Crump, K.S., Guess, H.A., and Deal, K.L., (1977): Confidence
     intervals and test of hypotheses concerning dose response
     relations inferred from animal carcinogenicity data.
     Biometrics $\underline{33}$:437-451.

21. Crump, K.S., Hoel, D.G., Langley, C.H., and Peto, R., (1976): Fundamental carcinogenic processes and their implications for low dose risk assessment. Cancer Res. 36:2973-2979.

22. Day, T.D., (1967): Carcinogenic actions of cigarette smoke condensate on mouse skin. Br. J. Cancer, 21:56-81.

23. Doll, R., (1971): The Age Distribution of Cancer: Implications for Models of Carcinogensis. J. Royal Stat. Soc. 134:136-166.

24. Draft Final Report: NTA. April 22, 1980.

25. Druckrey, H., (1967): Quantitative aspects in chemical carcinogenesis. Potential hazards from drugs, in U.I.C.C. Monograph Ser. 7:60-78.

26. Druckrey, H., Schmahl, D. and Discher, W., (1963): Dose action relation of the cancer production by 4-dimethyl-aminostibene in rats. Z. Krebsforsch, 65:272.

27. Food Safety Council: Report of the Scientific Committee (1978). Food Cosmet. Toxicol. 16:Supplement 2, 1-136.

28. Gaylor, D.W. and Kodell, R.L., (1980): Linear interpolation algorithm for low dose risk assessment of toxic substances.

29. Guess, H.A., Crump, K.S., and Peto, R., (1977): Uncertainty estimates for low-dose-rate extrapolations of animal carcinogenicity data. Cancer Res. 37:3475-3483.

30. Hoel, D.G., (1972): A representation of mortality data by competing risks. Biometrics, 28:475-488.

31. Kennedy, Donald (1980): Nitrites: FDA beats a surprising retreat. Science, 209, No. 4461:1100-1101, September 5.

32. Lee, P.N. and O'Neill, J.A., (1971): The effect both of time and dose applied on tumor incidence rate in benzopyrene skin painting experiments. Br. J. Cancer 25:759-770.

33. Murray, J.L. and Axtell, L.M., (1974): Impact of cancer: years of life lost due to cancer mortality. J. Natl. Cancer Inst. 52:3-7.

34. Peto, R., (1978): Carcinogenesis effects of chronic exposure to very low levels of toxic substances. Environ. Health Perspectives, 22:155-159.

35. Peto, R. and Lee, P.N., (1973): Weibull distributions for continuous carcinogenesis experiments. Biometrics, 29:457-470.

36. Peto, R., Lee, P.N. and Paige, W.S., (1972): Statistical analysis of the bioassay of continuous carcinogens. Br. J. Cancer, 26:258-261.

37. Peto, R., Roe, F.J.C., Lee, P.N., Levy, L., and Clack, J., (1975): Cancer and aging in mice and men, Br. J. Cancer, 32:411-426.

38. Pike, M.C., (1966): A method of analysis of a certain class of experiments in carcinogenesis, Biometrics, 22:142-161.

39. Sontag, J.M., Cranmer, M.F., Page, N.P., and Cueto, C., (1976): Experimental design and toxicology. In: Report of the temporary committee for the review of data on carcinogenicity of cyclamate, DHEW Publication No. (NIH)-77-1437.

40. Wodicka, V.O., Goldberg, L., and Carr, C.J., (1978): Proposed system for food safety assessment. Food Cosmet. Toxicol. 16(Suppl. 2):1-136.

EXTRAPOLATION FROM LONG TERM LOW DOSE ANIMAL STUDIES –

II. THE ED_{01} STUDY

M.F. Cranmer

Jefferson Professional Services
P.O. Box 3397
Little Rock, AR   72203

BACKGROUND

A Pilot Study in which 2AAF was administered in the feed of male and female C57/B6 and BALB/c mice for eighteen months established the suitability of the strain and sex and provided for prediction of the dosage-time range used in the ED_{01} Study. The results of the pilot study have been published elsewhere (8). Based on the Pilot Study results, the main objective, that is the validation of a chemical carcinogen dose-response curve to permit extrapolation from high to low levels of response, was determined to be achievable.

Seven dosages expressed as ppm of 2-AAF in the feed were selected to yield target tumor prevalences of 64% through 1% (1). The dose-response relationship expressed was based on the 18-month pilot study in which the animals used were not SPF-DF animals maintained under barrier conditions. Although the pilot study mice were BALB/c females, they were from a commercial source and were not derived from the NCTR mice breeding colony. The predicted dose response relationship was considered the best approximation which could be made when all the available data were considered. The accuracy of this approximation was validated by the ED_{01} - 2-AAF Chronic Study (5).

The original experimental design was to be replicated six times. That is, equal segments of the experiment were to be conducted in six barrier rooms. This should have provided adequate numbers of animals to estimate dose-response slopes within +50% and to estimate the ED_{01} levels within a factor of two which was important since mathematical models that differ by a factor of three at the ED_{01} levels can be discriminated. A computer data management system provided the ability to exercise rigorous control (3, 4).

Table 1 presents the number of different dose groups and the number of different experimental components originally planned in each of the six rooms (1).

Unfortunately the FDA decided to modify the experimental design after three rooms had completed the 18 month sacrifice. This decision reduced the number of comparable animals by 50%, weakened the model testing aspects of the experiment and introduced a strong potential for room effect. This decision was prompted after Hoel, Gaylor, Kirschstein, Saffiotti, and Schneiderman published a report (7) suggesting linear extrapolation as the method of choice and great criticism was placed on FDA for using Mantel-Bryan in the proposed Sensitivity of the Method Regulation. The NCTR reported to FDA Commissioner that at 18 months the ED_{01} was more consistent with a threshold model than any other, that a time to tumor relationship existed at the top doses for bladder lesions regressed at lower doses. The decision to alter the experiment to attempt to find responses at lower doses was made, after FDA decided that the advantages of desired positive results were worth the risk that many of the original goals of the ED_{01} would be invalidated or compromised. The primary interest shifted from a low background tumor (bladder) and model testing, to a high background tumor (liver) and an attempt to justify a linear extrapolation model.

MATERIALS AND METHODS

Experimental Design. - The design contained two basic types of experiments: survival (lifespan) and serial sacrifice. The serial sacrifice portion was subdivided into continuous and discontinuous feeding (1).

Animals. - Mice were selected for this study because of the need for large numbers of animals required for the statistical validity of dose-response studies at low levels of exposure. The BALB/c strain was selected because of the lack of spontaneous bladder tumors in contrast to its high susceptibility to 2-AAF induction of these tumors. The dosage range studied in the pilot experiment gave better data distributions for the female than for the male BALB/c mice, therefore females were selected for the ED_{01} Study.

All animals allocated to the experiment were weanlings, three to four weeks of age. All were specific pathogen free defined flora" animals derived in the breeding colony of NCTR from a Charles River substrain of BALB/c mice (BALB/cStCrlfC3H/Nctr).

TABLE 1
(CAGES/ROOM)

TREATMENT	SURVIVAL		SERIAL SACRIFICE							SERIAL TREATMENT			DIAGNOSTIC	TOTAL
WKS. OF SACRIFICE	NONE	LIFE	78	74	70	65	60	52	39	78	78	78	DO IS AT GI NC	T O T A L
WKS. ON 2-AAF			78	74	70	65	60	52	39	78	52	39		
2-AAF in Feed, PPM														
150		6	12	6	6	6	6	6	6	6	6	6	6	78
100		6	12	6	6	6	6	6	6	6	6	6		72
75		12	24	12	12	6	6	6	6	12	12	12		120
60		12	24	18	18	12	12	12	12	18	18	18		174
45		18	36	24	18									96
35		36	72	36										144
30		72	144											216
0		18	36	12	12	6	6	6	6				6	108
TOTAL	180		360	114	72	36	36	36	36	42	42	42	12	1008

Time denoted as weeks on a particular treatment from the beginning of the experiment.
Dosages based on expected percent of bladder tumors at 18 months.
Four mice per cage; 72 cages per rack; 14 racks per room.
Repeat experiment in 6 rooms for a total of 24,192 animals.
For diagnostic purposes, use two mice every two weeks during first 39 weeks; then share available sacrificed mice with Pathology.
Use BALB/c female weanling mice.

Type and Duration of Treatments. - The survival phase of the study involved a lifespan exposure to 2-AAF in the feed. The animals in this phase of the study were removed from the experiment as they become moribund. The serial sacrifice phase involved treatment for and sacrifice at 6, 7, 8, 9, 12, 15, 18, 24, and 33 months. The serial treatment or recovery study involved treatment for 6, 9, and 12 months followed by recovery and sacrifice at the eighteenth month of entering the experiment (Table 1).

Statistics.

1. Grouping and Randomization of Animals. - As animals were received from Animal Husbandry Division, they were randomly allocated to the various experimental groups. This was hoped to minimize any differences in animals, feed, laboratory conditions, or handling. For ease of operation, treatments were grouped in tiers of six cages on a rack. This tended to average out floor-to-ceiling differences in temperature, light, and humidity (2).

2. Sequential Entry. - The animals were placed on experiment, a room at a time. Each barrier room pertinent to the study was loaded at the rate of two racks per week, requiring seven weeks to load a room. The randomization of animals to treatments was expected to mediate most changes that occur with time within a room and had the protocol not been modified would have allowed for substantial comparison between rooms.

3. Replication. - The original protocol is shown in Table 1. The altered final protocols for the six barrier rooms are shown in Tables 2-7.

                              RESULTS

General. The record of response of the entire population is summarized in Tables 8-12. Table 11 provides the Kaplan-Meier Median Survival Time for 0, 30, 34, 45 and 60 ppm. There is a slight increase in survivability of treated over controls. This phenomenon appears to be due to a protective effect against reticulum cell sarcomas due to 2-AAF treatment. Table 12 documents that there was more variability between replicates that between doses.

Table 8 lists the major spontaneous neoplasms occurring in female BALB/c mice. Table 9 documents that of those animals with an opportunity to die: 90% died of neoplastic disease. There are no differences in deaths due to neoplasia among the dose groups. Table 10 provides the incidence of cancers of various types at the time of death by all causes. With the exception of bladder cancer, there is no difference in total cancer rates.

TABLE 2
Room 141
No. Bladders Examined - Sacrificed Animals Only
Time (mo.)

Dose Level	9	12	14	15	16	17	18	24	Life
150 ppm	24	24		47				47	
100 ppm	24	24						72	
75 ppm	23	23						121	
60 ppm	47	48						16	2
45 ppm								150	3
35 ppm								20	2
30 ppm								29	8
0 ppm	24	23						14	2
TOTAL	142	142		47				120	17

TABLE 3
Room 142
No. Bladders Examined - Sacrificed Animals Only
Time (mo.)

Dose Level	9	12	14	15	16	17	18	24	Life
150 ppm	24	24	23					51	
100 ppm	23	23	24					56	
75 ppm	24	23	22					116	1
60 ppm	48	46	38					161	
45 ppm								156	1
35 ppm								202	5
30 ppm								281	11
0 ppm	24	24	23					137	3
TOTAL	143	140	130					1160	21

TABLE 4
Room 143
No. Bladders Examined - Sacrificed Animals Only

Time (mo.)

Dose Level	9	12	14	15	16	17	18	24	Life
150 ppm	23	23	24	22	22			32	
100 ppm	24	22	24	28	23			32	1
75 ppm	23	24	22	24	44			74	1
60 ppm	47	48	47	46	65			91	
45 ppm					67			139	2
35 ppm								230	8
30 ppm								321	6
0 ppm	23	23	21	24	44			104	5
TOTAL	140	140	138	144	165			1023	23

TABLE 5
Room 144
No. Bladders Examined - Sacrificed Animals Only

Time (mo.)

Dose Level	9	12	14	15	16	17	18	24	Life
150 ppm	23	23	24	23	20	21	45		
100 ppm	24	23	24	23	24	24	43		
75 ppm	24	23	22	24	43	47	86		2
60 ppm	47	43	45	43	65	70	87		1
45 ppm					69	8	118		
35 ppm						127	264		7
30 ppm							529		18
0 ppm	23	22	23	23	46	43	129		-2
TOTAL	141	134	138	136	267	421	1301		31

TABLE 6
Room 145
No. Bladders Examined - Sacrificed Animals Only
Time (mo.)

Dose Level	9	12	14	15	16	17	18	24	Life
150 ppm	24	24	20	24	22	24	38		
100 ppm	23	23	23	22	22	20	45		4
75 ppm	23	22	20	24	42	44	90		3
60 ppm	46	48	45	46	69	70	91		5
45 ppm					66	90	133		5
35 ppm						134	264		14
30 ppm							525		26
0 ppm	24	24	23	21	46	42	137		8
TOTAL	140	141	131	137	167	426	1323		65

TABLE 7
Room 146
No. Bladders Examined - Sacrificed Animals Only
Time (mo.)

Dose Level	9	12	14	15	16	17	18	24	Life
150 ppm	22	23	23	21	21	20	39		
100 ppm	24	23	22	24	21	23	43		3
75 ppm	22	22	24	22	46	43	91		6
60 ppm	47	35	46	46	66	66	91		3
45 ppm					69	85	132		1
35 ppm						128	268		9
30 ppm				23			496		23
0 ppm	23	24	23	20	47	42	134		4
TOTAL	138	127	138	156	207	407	1294		49

TABLE 8

Incidence[1] of Major Spontaneous Neoplasms in Sacrificed and Dead and Moribund Female BALB/c Mice

TUMOR TYPE	MONTHS										TOTAL
	1-11	12-13	14-15	16	17	18	19-21	22-29	30-34	1-34	No.
Reticulum Cell Sarcoma			2.3	6.1	5.3	7.8	17.0	58.0	70.5	26.9	641
Alveolar Cell Neoplasm	3.6	5.6	12.0	8.9	8.8	16.3	20.3	36.6	52.4	22.3	527
Adrenocortical Adenoma							1.5	12.9	33.3	5.8	121
Uterine Stromal Polyp	7.5	16.6	18.0	23.4	29.0	23.5	21.6	30.1	31.6	24.0	561
Harderian Gland Neoplasm	2.1	3.2	5.3	8.0	10.0	9.3	7.9	16.5	24.0	10.7	250
Hepatocellular Neoplasm							1.0	2.6	16.8	1.9	45
Mammary Adeno-Carcinoma				1.8			.56	5.0	12.2	2.3	53
Intestinal Polyp							1.29	3.6	9.0	1.9	45
Adrenal Carcinoma								1.6	6.0	.8	16
Lymphoma	11.7	3.8	3.0	3.5	4.9	5.9	6.3	8.3	5.9	6.7	160
Hemangio-sarcoma							2.5	4.3	5.8	2.3	55
Ovarian Neoplasms							.8	2.8	5.3	1.4	31
ANIMALS AT RISK	195	159	133	113	205	153	554	762	102		2376

[1] The % incidence for animals at risk in each time group is shown to one decimal place. Whole numbers show the total counts of animals.

TABLE 9
Frequency Distribution of Cause of Death (%)

Dose (ppm)	Unknown	Inflammation	Neoplasm	Inflammation + Neoplasm
0	8	2	89	0
30	8	2	89	1
35	7	3	89	1
45	5	4	91	0
60	7	3	89	1
75	5	2	92	1
100	3	1	95	1
150	1	4	92	2

TABLE 10
Cancer Incidence at Time of Death by All Causes (%)

Dose (ppm)	Other	Lymphoma	Lung	Mammary	Hepato-Cellular	RCS	TOTAL	Bladder Ca.
0	6	16	10	2	2	52	88	1
30	7	14	8	2	6	52	89	1
35	4	15	10	3	6	50	88	1
45	8	16	7	4	5	51	91	1
60	5	14	9	5	9	51	93	1
75	9	15	7	3	8	52	94	2
100	9	16	13	2	13	43	96	6
150	7	15	6	4	10	42	84	21

TABLE 11
Kaplan-Meier Median Survival Times (Average Days)

Concentration (ppm)	146	145	144	Room 146-4	143	142	141	143-1
0	764	832	746	780	726	742	710	726
30	801	801	796	799	748	761	728	746
35	778	791	773	781	745	742	695	727
45	737	809	769	772	744	774	734	751
60	794	790	776	787	749	708	750	736

TABLE 12
Frequency Distributions of Neoplastic Causes
of Death for Each Replicate(%)

Room	Bladder Carcinoma	Hepato-cellular Carcinoma	Mammary Adeno-carcinoma	Alveolar Cell Tumor	Lymphoma	Reticulum Cell Sarcoma	Other
146	2	6	3	9	17	43	7
145	2	6	3	9	14	47	8
144	1	7	3	10	15	50	6
143	2	8	3	10	15	52	6
142	1	5	3	7	14	56	6
141	1	6	2	8	14	56	5

Analysis of Bladder Tumor by Individual Room

Room 146

In Room 146, 6 of the animals that were removed prior to 19 months of age had bladder tumors.

(150 ppm, 4, Grade 0; 100 ppm, 1, Grade 1; 45 ppm, 1, Grade 0)

Conclusion: Only at 150 ppm were there excess bladder tumors in dead and moribund (D&M) animals prior to 9 months. There were no life threatening tumors prior to 9 months.

During the entire experiment, 42 of the animals that were removed as D&M had bladder tumors.

(150 - 23/43; 100 - 10/56; 75 - 0/52; 60 - 1/54; 45 - 2/91; 35 - 0/147; 30 - 6/270; 0 - 0/72)

Conclusion: There was an increase in tumor incidence associated with dead and moribund animals receiving doses below 100 ppm.

Of all animals dead and moribund and sacrificed through 19 months, 74 had tumors.

(150 - 41 grade 0, 23 grade 1, 1 grade 3; 100 - 2 grade 0, 2 grade 1, 1 grade 4; 75 - 1 grade 0; 60 - 0; 45 - 2 grade 0; 35 - 0; 30 - 1 grade 1; 0 - 0)

Conclusion: There was no increase in tumor incidence associated with any groups receiving doses below 100 ppm.

From 19 months sacrifice there were 40 additional tumor bearing animals removed.

(150 - 3 grade 0, 9 grade 1, 1 grade 2, 2 grade 3, 4 grade 4; 100 - 7 grade 0, 5 grade 1; 75 - 1 grade 0; 60 - 1 grade 0; 45 - 1 grade 4; 35 - 0; 30 - 5 grade 0, 1 grade 1; 0 - 0)

Conclusion: There was no increase of tumor incidence associated with all groups receiving doses below 100 ppm.

Room 145

Six animals were removed as dead and moribund through 19 months which had bladder tumors.

(150 - 2 grade 3, 1 grade 4; 100 ppm - 1 grade 1, 1 grade 2, 75 - 1 grade 0)

Conclusion: There was a positive effect in dead and moribund animals at 150 ppm.

Seventy-nine animals were removed through 19 months for all reasons including dead and moribund.

(150 - 34 grade 0, 25 grade 1, 1 grade 2, 3 grade 3, 3 grade 4;
100 - 5 grade 0, 2 grade 1, 1 grade 2; 75 - 1 grade 0;
 60 - 1 grade 0; 45 - 1 grade 0; 35 - 0; 30 - 1 grade 0,
1 grade 1; 0 - 0)

Conclusion: There was no increase in tumor incidence in any group receiving less than below 100 ppm.

Thirty-five animals were removed after the 19 month sacrifice.

(150 - 4 grade 0, 10 grade 1, 1 grade 1; 100 - 4 grade 0,
3 grade 1, 0 grade 2, 2 grade 3, 1 grade 1; 75 - 4 grade 0,
2 grade 1, 0 grade 2, 1 grade 3; 60 - 1 grade 1; 35 - 1 grade 1;
 30 - 1 grade 1, 1 grade 4)

Conclusion: 75, 100, 150 ppm were effect doses in animals in the sacrificed at 19 months of age.

Room 144

Eight animals were removed as dead and moribund with bladder tumors through 19 months of age.

(150 - 1 grade 0, 2 grade 1, 1 grade 3; 45 - 1 grade 0,
1 grade 1; 30 - 1 grade 0; 0 - 1 grade 1)

Conclusion: There was a positive effect observed at 150 ppm in dead and moribund animals at 19 months of age.

Sixty animals removed for all reasons through 19 months had bladder tumors.

(150 - 25 grade 0, 22 grade 1, 1 grade 2, 2 grade 3; 100 - 0;
 75 - 0; 60 - 2 grade 0; 45 - 2 grade 0, 1 grade 1;
 35 - 1 grade 0, 1 grade 1; 30 - 1 grade 0; 0 - 2 grade 0)

Conclusion: There was a positive effect observed at 150 ppm in animals sacrificed at 19 months of age.

Twenty-five animals were removed with bladder cancer after the 19 month sacrifice.

(150 - 4 grade 0, 3 grade 1, 6 grade 3; 100 - 5 grade 0, 1 grade 1; 75 - 1 grade 0; 60 - 2 grade 0; 45 - 0; 35 - 1 grade 0; 30 - 1 grade 1; 0 - 1 grade 0)

Conclusion: There was a positive effect observed at 150 and 100 ppm in animals removed after the 19 month sacrifice.

There were no bladder tumors present significantly contributing to death except at 150 ppm.

Analysis of Combined Bladder Tumors (Tables 13-17)

Rooms 144, 145, and 146 can be considered identical for the purpose of analysis. When 144-6 are combined the following conclusions are reasonable.

1. 2-AAF produces effects on bladder tumors at 75, 100 and 150 ppm.

2. There is no tumor related life shortening at any dose except 150 ppm. (Four bladder tumors metastasized during the entire study).

3. There is a dose related reduction in the minimum time necessary for the appearance of bladder tumors.

4. The dose-response relationship for bladder tumors is not linear for incidence or time and an apparent total absence of demonstratable effect occurs at 60 ppm and below at all time periods.

5. It was possible to experimentally demonstrate an ED$_{01}$ for bladder tumors because of the steepness of the dose response curve and the apparent absence of effect beginning at about 60 ppm but below 75 ppm.

TABLE 13
% Sacrificed Animals with Bladder Cancer at 0, 30, 35, 45, 60 ppm

	Dose	19 Mo. Sac.*	25 Mo. Sac.**	34 Mo. Sac.+	Median Survival
Room 141-3	0		.3	0	726
	30		1.1	1.1	746
	35		.3	0	727
	45		.2	0	751
	60		.7	0	736
Room 144-6	0	.3		0	781
	30	.3		0	799
	35	.1		0	781
	45	.3		0	772
	60	1.1		12.5(1/8)	787

+ 2/184 tumors is within the expected 34 month spontaneous rate of approximately 1%.

**No significant difference or trend.
*No significant difference or trend.

TABLE 14

% of Animals with Bladder Cancer

Dose	Rms. 144-6 Prior to 19 Mo. D&M	Rms. 144-6 19 Mo. S	Rms. 141-3 25 Mo. S	Rms. 144-6 19-34 D&M&S	All Rooms 34 Mo. S
150	1.7	51	77	65	–
100	-*	3.8	16	39	80
75	-*	-*	-*	6.3	33
60	-*	1.1	-*	2.8++	9.1**(1/11)
45	-*	-*	-*	-*	-*
35	-*	-*	-*	-*	-*
30	-*	-*	-*	-*	1.1**(1/92)
0	-*	-*	-*	-*	-*

*less than 1%.
**two grade zero tumors in 184 animals at terminal sacrifice was not different than the 1% spontaneous rate occurring in animals past 29½ months of age.
++all three grade zero tumors were later reclassified as hyperplasia with lymphoreticular disease present.
D - dead; M - moribund; S - sacrificed on schedule.

TABLE 15
Weibull Distribution of Calculated Time to
Appearance and Time to Death Following Tumor Appearance

	Concentration (ppm)	Months to Tumor Appearance	Time to Death After Tumor Appearance
Bladder	30	*	7
Carcinoma	35	*	7
	45	*	7
	60	*	6
	75	*	7
	100	31	9
	150	21	7

Calculated Median Times to Appearance of Bladder
Neoplasms and Times to Death Following Appearance

	Concentration (ppm)	Months to Tumor Appearance	Time to Death After Tumor Appearance
Bladder	30	*	7
Carcinoma	35	*	7
	45	*	7
	60	*	6
	75	*	7
	100	30	8
	150	20	7

*Exceeded Lifespan of the Experimental Animal

TABLE 16

Bladder Cancers - Linear Regressions

Room & Months on Treatment	Slope	Dose Y Intercept	Signi-ficance	Age Slope	Dose Y Intercept	Room Probability Significance	R	R Age	R Room	R Dose
Room 141-143										
SAC 9-17	.09	-.02	.04	.17	-.24	.03	.42	.28	.13	.30
SAC 18-33	.42	-.12	0.	.50	-8.3	0.	.71	.03	.21	.65
ALL SAC	.14	-.03	.0003	.28	-4.8	0.	.53	.23	.12	
Room 144-146										
SAC 9-17	.33	-.06	0.	.40	-.009	0.	.63	.23	-.01	.57
SAC 18-33	.24	-.03	.0007	.40	-.02	.001	.63	.31	.0057	.49
ALL SAC	.15	-.03	0.	.38	-.05	0.	.62	.46	.0016	.38
ALL BLADDER	.14	-.03	0.	.32	-1.6	0.	.57	.32	.05	.38

TABLE 17
Incidence of Bladder Tumors
in Age Sensitivity and Regression
Progression Study

I II	0	60	75	100	150
			Dose		
9- 9	.7	--	--	--	.7
12-12	--	--	--	--	6.4
15-15	--	--	1.1	1.1	31.1
18-18	.3	1.1	.4	3.8	51.2
24-24	.3	.7	1.0	15.6	76.9
9-18	.3	--	1.6	1.6	6.3
12-18	.3	--	--	1.5	22.2
15-18	.3	--	--	--	33.8
18-18	.3	1.1	.4	3.8	51.2
9-24	.3	.9	--	--	18.2
12-24	.3	--	--	3.0	24.1
15-24	.3	--	--	2.9	39.3
24-24	.3	.7	1.0	15.6	76.9

I = Months of Continuous Exposure

II = Months of Sacrifice

Analysis of Liver Tumors (Tables 18-23)

If 2-AAF treatment produced a liver tumor related life shortening effect on female BALB/C mice, one would expect the survival of
the treated to be reduced compared to the controls and a dose
response relationship should exist. It has been demonstrated instead
that the average lifespan of the 30, 35, 45, 60 ppm groups equalled
or exceeded the controls.

Examination of liver tumor rates in dead and moribund animals
in rooms 141-143 supports the conclusion that there is no statistically significant increase in liver tumors at dose rates of 0,
30, 35, 45, and 60 ppm during the later stages of life.

There was a dose related increase in the number of tumor
bearing animals between 19 and 29½ months. The animals bearing
liver tumors did not die sooner than non tumor bearing animals at
any dose.

Two outlying readings were noted:

(1) In rooms 141-3 there was a significantly lower incidence of
liver tumors in control animals living to 29-½ months when compared
to

a.   control animals in rooms 144-6.
b.   control animals in rooms 141-3 from 24-29½ months.
c.   control animals in rooms 141-3 at the 33 month sacrifice.

There is no apparent explanation for this observation.

(2) In rooms 141-3 there was no difference in liver tumors
between the 30-60 ppm treated animals at 29-½ months.

The following conclusions are derived from the analysis of data
shown in Tables 18-23.

1.   The liver tumor bearing animals live as long as the non-
      tumor bearing animals.
2.   Treated animals live as long or longer than controls.
3.   90% of the liver tumors appeared after 80% of the animals
      had died by other causes. The majority of animals bearing
      liver tumors died of RCS.
4.   2-AAF at all doses studied increased the incidence and
      rate of appearance of nonlethal liver tumors in a dose
      related manner between 18-29½ months.
5.   No increase in incidence occurs at 0, 30, 35, 45, 60 ppm
      after 29½ months of age.

TABLE 18
Incidence of Liver Tumors

% Incidence at 19 Month Sacrifice

DOSE	Room 145	Room 145	Room 144	Total
0	.75	0	0	.25
30	1.0	1.3	1.1	1.2
35	.37	1.1	1.1	.88
45	1.5	3.0	4.2	2.9
60	0	6.6	3.4	2.6
75	1.1	6.6	0	2.6
100	7.0	0	6.9	4.6
150	0	2.6	15.5	6.6

% Incidence at 25 Month Sacrifice

DOSE	Room 143	Room 142	Room 141	Total
0	1.9	.73	4.9	2.6
30	5.3	.82	6.4	6.6
35	8.7	.69	8.7	8.1
45	13	10	12	12
60	15	19	18	17
75	20	22	17	20
100	31	29	31	30
150	·53	44	32	44

% Incidence at 34 Month Sacrifice

Dose	Rms. 141-3	Rms. 144-6
0	30	36
30	56	40
35	33	30
45	50	33

Only 33 animals remained in six rooms for the highest four dose
levels.

TABLE 19
Summary of Liver Tumors

Dose	19 Mo. Sac.	17-25 Mo. D&M	25 Mo. Sac.	24-29-1/2 Mo. D&M	34 Mo. Sac.	Mean Surv.
			Rooms 141-3			
-	-	1.7	2.6+	0$^{\pm}$	30	725
30	-	2.8	6.6+	30	56	746
35	-	2.9	8.1+	38	33	727
45	-	2.9	12+	38	50	751
60	-	2.8	17+	41	±±	736
			Rooms 144-6			
0	-*		-	20	36	781
30	1.2+		-	23	40	799
35	-*		-	30	30	781
45	2.9		-	43	33	772
60	2.6+		-	31	±±	787

* less than 1%.
+ no significant dose response.
± significantly different than all other groups in all rooms at
  times equal to or greater than 25 months.
±± too few animals to evaluate.

TABLE 20
Incidence of Liver Tumors
in Age Sensitivity and Regression/
Progression Study

I	II	0	60	75	100	150
				Dose		
9- 9		--	--	--	.7	--
12-12		--	.7	--	2.2	.7
15-15		.5	.5	1.1	4.4	1.1
18-18		.2	2.6	2.2	4.6	5.8
9-18		.2	.5	2.3	1.6	6.3
12-18		.2	.5	4.5	--	3.2
15-18		.2	2.0	3.8	1.6	6.2
18-18		.2	2.6	2.2	4.6	5.8
9-24		2.3	12.0	15.2	14.3	27.3
12-24		2.3	9.3	18.9	15.2	31.0
15-24		2.3	13.2	16.3	17.2	21.4

I = Months of Continuous Feeding

II = Months of Sacrifice

TABLE 21
Weibull Distribution of Calcuated Time to
Appearance and Time to Death Following Tumor Appearance

	Concentration (ppm)	Months to Tumor Appearance	Time to Death After Tumor Appearance
Hepato-cellular Neoplasm	30	35	6
	35	34	6
	45	33	5
	60	33	7
	75	32	8
	100	30	7
	150	27	6

Calculated Median Times to Appearance of Liver
Neoplasms and Times to Death Following Appearance

	Concentration (ppm)	Months to Tumor Appearance	Time to Death After Tumor Appearance
Hepat-cellular Neoplasm	30	34	5
	35	33	5
	45	31	5
	60	31	6
	75	30	7
	100	28	7
	150	25	5

TABLE 22
Incidence of Malignant Metastasing Liver Tumors

Dose	Months	% Malignant Tumors	% Metastatic Tumors	Ratio of Metastatic to Malignant
0	18	.5	0	
	24	2.2	0	= 0
	33	11.9	0	
30	18	1.2	.099	$\frac{1.63}{30.4} = 0.54$
	24	5.2	.43	
	33	24.1	1.1	
35	18	1.4	.091	$\frac{1.3}{38.3} = 0.34$
	24	6.1	.22	
	33	30.8	1.0	
45	18	1.8	.18	$\frac{1.6}{35.9} = 0.45$
	24	7.9	.45	
	33	26.2	.97	
60	18	2.4	.49	$\frac{5.15}{54.4} = 0.95$
	24	10.8	.26	
	33	41.2	4.4	
75	18	3.4	.26	$\frac{1.73}{60} = .029$
	24	15.3	.17	
	33	41.3	1.3	
100	18	8.0	2.3	$\frac{12}{93.9} = .128$
	24	18.2	0	
	33	67.7	9.7	
150	18	8.1	.47	$\frac{1.43}{111.7} = .013$
	24	30.9	.96	
	33	72.7	---	

TABLE 23

Liver Tumors - Linear Regressions

Room & Months on Treatment	Dose			Age		Room Probability	R	R Age	R Room	R Dose
	Slope	Intercept	Significance	Slope	Y Intercept	Significance				
Room 141-143										
SAC 9-18	.00009	.017	.95	.15	.87	.06	.39	.38	.18	.01
SAC 24-33	.09	.18	.06	.48	-5.11	0.	.69	.53	.12	.31
All SAC	.0001	.15	.92	.51	-0.5	0.	.72	.67	.0001	.012
Room 144-146										
SAC 9-17	.008	.005	.41	.05	2.7	.23	.22	.14	-.15	.09
SAC 18-33	.00006	.28	.96	.66	2.0	0.	.81	.79	-.02	.01
ALL SAC	.003	.13	.55	.63	2.2	0.	.79	.79	-.05	-.05
All Liver	.001	.14	.49	.58	.50	0.	.76	.75	-.08	-.04

RESULTS

Cancer Incidence.

The linear interpolation technique of Gaylor and Kodell was applied to the data published by Littlefield, et al., (9) to estimate the dosage of 2-AAF producing a lifetime tumor risks of less than one in a million at 97.5% confidence. The estimated dosages were 11 ppb for bladder carcinoma and 0.25 ppb for hepato-cellular tumors. Applying the multi-stage model of Crump et al. (6) to the same data yielded estimates of 0.08 ppb for bladder carcinoma and 0.003 ppb for hepatocellular tumors.

Linear extrapolation using the 97.5% confidence limits on the same data yielded less than a 1 in 1,000,000 lifetime risks for 10 ppb for bladder cancer and .4 ppb for liver cancer.

Analysis of the data in this report suggests a highly signi-ficant absence of effect at 60 ppm and below for a lifetime cancer incidence.

TABLE 23

1/1,000,000 Risk

	Linear Extra-polation	Linear Inter-polation	Crump et al.	Best Est.
Bladder	10 ppb	2.7 ppb	.08 ppb	>30 ppm
Liver	.4 ppb	.28 ppb	.003 ppb	>30 ppm

Control animals from 24 months on have a 200% chance of having some type of spontaneous neoplasm. Therefore an increased risk is not an increased risk of having a neoplasm but the risk of having multiple neoplasms. A 1/1,000,000 risk means that we are 97.5% sure that in a million treated mice we will not have more than 2,000,001 vs. 2,000,000 cancers.

<u>Dose Response</u>. - Bladder and liver tumor prevalence in terms of response to dose rate and total dose are very different and neither is linear. Neither bladder or liver tumors are produced in excess during the last four months of life at the four lowest doses. The ED_{01} data remain to be completely evaluated to determine the best mathematical model(s) for the extrapolation from dose-tumor-time data from high to lower exposure levels and durations. Eventually models to conditionally approximate a "socially acceptable risk" need to be fitted to the data. Care should be taken in analyzing ED_{01} data reported in a publication edited by Staffa and Mehlman (10). Errors in (10) are responsible for several departures from the data reported here.

<u>Time to Tumor</u>. - Increased utilization of time to tumor dose-response relationship in chronic studies is justified. Early tumors have much more impact on quality and quantity of life than do late tumors, lethal tumors more than nonlethal tumors. Furthermore, for 2-AAF liver tumors at low levels of exposure, the lifetime liver tumor prevalence is not different at the four doses. The prevalence of bladder or liver tumors as a function of age (time to tumor) provides a better description of the tumorigenic process than prevalence at a single point in time or the total prevalence of tumors over the lifespan. Two problems remain to be resolved. First, the relationship between dosage and median time to tumor must be established. Secondly, given a dosage, the distribution of times to tumors must be established to estimate the prevalence of tumors. The survival group (lifespan group) in the ED_{01} experimental design provides data for such analyses. This problem is especially perplexing when treatment results not only in an increased incidence of treatment related tumors but also in a reduction in spontaneous lethal tumors and a resultant net increase in lifespan.

<u>Life Shortening</u>. - The lifespan portion of the ED_{01} experimental design provided data for the evaluation of life shortening as an endpoint sensitive to dose. The information gathered on time to tumor development demonstrated life shortening for spontaneous lethal tumors but not for nonlethal, treatment-related tumors except perhaps at the highest dose. Except for 150 ppm the treated groups lived at least as long as untreated groups. 2-AAF at the four lower doses appeared to have extended lifespan. There is some suggestion 2-AAF protects against reticulum cell sarcomas.

<u>Age Sensitivity</u>. - Hazards involved in exposure to a chemical carcinogen depend not only on the nature of the chemical itself, the route of exposure, and the extent of exposure in terms of amount and time, but also on the susceptibility of the animals at the time of exposure. Age sensitivity studies conducted as in a separate component of the ED_{01} experiment permitted evaluation of possible age sensitivity to 2-AAF in relation to specific periods

of treatment. Serial sacrifices and serial treatment phases of the
ED_{01} - 2-AAF study demonstrated no age sensitivity.

Regression or Progression of Effects. - The experimental design
permitted groups fed 2-AAF for 9, 12, and 15 months and sacrificed
to be compared with groups fed the same length of time but sacrificed at 18 and 24 months. Possible regression or progression of
pretumorous lesions such as hyperplasia in relation to dosage and
time have been compared and while all lesions regress to some
extent bladder lesions regress to a greater extent than liver
tumors. Discontinued treatment not surprisingly results in a
lesser incidence.

Tumor Growth Rate. - The experimental design permits an approach to
the question of the possible dependence of tumor growth rate on
dosage and treatment. The serial sacrifice and serial treatment
phases of the study revealed that growth rates of bladder and liver
tumors were not related to dose rate except possibly at the highest
dose.

Relative Malignancy. - There was an increase for liver tumors at
the highest dose in the number of increasingly malignant lesions.
The ratio of metastases to malignant tumors decreased at higher
doses not because the absolute number of metastases decreased but
due to the much larger number of tumors of different grades of
malignancy.

This pioneering study, designed initially to seek a crucial
test between two ways of modeling dose-response relationships in
carcinogenesis, yielded results which are consistent with threshold
models. It provided no support to linear no-threshold extrapolations
in the low range of doses of a potent carcinogen.

REFERENCES

1. Cranmer, M.F., (1974): Reflections in Toxicology. Journal
    of Washington Academy of Sciences 64(2):158-179.

2. Cranmer, M.F., (1976): Advances in animal care techniques
    at NCTR. Laboratory Animal Science, 26(2)(II):355-373.

3. Cranmer, M.F., Herrick, S.S., Lawrence, L.R., Konvicka, A.J.
    and Taylor, D.W., (1976): Research data integrity: A
    result of an integrated information system. Journal
    of Toxicology and Environmental Health, 2:285-299.

4. Cranmer, M.F., Lawrence, L.R., Konvicka, A.J., and Herrick,
    S.S., (1978): NCTR computer systems designed for toxico-
    logic experimentation, I. Overview. Journal of Environ-
    mental Pathology and Toxicology, 1:543-549.

5. Cranmer, M.F., (1979): The design criteria and application
    of dose response relationships to interpretation of
    carcinogenesis bioassay. Regulatory Aspects of Carcino-
    genesis and Food Additives: The Delaney Clause.
    Academic Press, 147-172.

6. Crump, K.S., Guess, H.A., and Deal, K.L., (1977): Confidence
    intervals and test of hypotheses concerning dose response
    relations inferred from animal carcinogenicity data.
    Biometrics 33:437-451.

7. Hoel, D.G., Gaylor, D.W., Kirschstein, R.L., Saffiotti, U.
    and Schneiderman, M.A., (1975): Estimation of risks
    irreversible, delayed toxicity. J. Toxicol. Environ.
    Hlth., 1:133-151.

8. Littlefield, N.A., Cueto, C., Jr., Davis, A.K. and Medlock, K.,
    (1975): Chronic dose-response studies in mice fed
    2-AAF. J. Tox. & Environ. Hlth., 1:25-37.

9. Littlefield, N.A., Greenman, D.L., and Farmer, J.H., (1979):
    Effects of continuous and discontinued exposure to
    2-AAF on urinary bladder hyperplasia and neoplasia.
    J. Environ. Path. & Tox. 3:35-54.

10. Staffa, J.E. and Mehlman, M.A., eds., (1980): Innovations
    in cancer risk assessment (ED$_{01}$ study). J. Environ.
    Path. Toxicol. 3 No. 3.

DISCUSSION

CROW: Is the fact that cancers concentrate in the bladder and liver a property of the strain or a property of the chemical that is being tested?

CRANMER: It is a property of the species and strain. These compounds primarily produced bladder tumors in mice or at least they produce them in a more detectable way than other types of tumors, so we were worried about bladder tumors for humans. In fact, this compound does not produce any tumors at all in the guinea pig where it is not n-hydroxylated. In the rat the tumors are primarily in the male and they are liver tumors. Females have benign nodules, but these do not progress as fast. The female rat fed male hormones gets tumors the same way as the male. Even among similar species, the cotton rat is very, very resistant to the compound and various rat strains are quite sensitive. You can produce ear duct tumors, mammary gland tumors, bladder cancer, etc., but in setting up this experiment we found only reports indicating very poor ability to produce bladder cancer with the compound.

However, we were able to demonstrate bladder hyperplasia in several strains of animals and play little games which suggested that we would get bladder cancer. After we tested both sexes of the C57 Black and BALB/c mice we determined that either sex of either strain would produce relatively the same types of responses. We chose the BALB/C strain because it had a lower background incidence of both hepatocellular carcinoma and bladder cancer.

FORBES: What variability do you get if you replicate the same dose as opposed to different doses? You mention, in your abstract, inter- and intra-laboratory variability. Do you have any data on that?

CRANMER: On the variability of cancer tumors, yes. Six strains can be compared to one another. We did everything to keep conditions constant and what we found was dramatic differences between the strains for liver carcinogenesis (or promotion or whatever mechanism we want to postulate) for the same doses.

With respect to bladder cancer, the effects were much more uniform.

BERG: You haven't mentioned the word "threshold", but since you do know quite a bit about the mechanism of action of this compound, is there any biochemical rationale why it would have a threshold for malignancy?

CRANMER: Well, there is significant literature that the lesion that is caused by 2-(acetylamino)fluorene can be repaired. The experimental evidence is that if you treat animals with effective doses

of the compound and you remove the compound, the observable pathological lesion regresses. It also goes away at lower doses.

So you may have produced an effect for which there wasn't a
threshold, but removing the insult allows the animal to create a
threshold, if you will, because it is able to repair.

BERG: Are you saying that there is, at least in principle, a level
of exposure that the repair mechanism can keep up with?

CRANMER: I think this experiment has clearly demonstrated that with
respect to bladder cancer and 2-(acetylamino)fluorene in BALB/C mice
that is absolutely so.

The experiment was designed to show whether the linear model
would be confirmed or not. It was not. The results excluded it.

BERG: This is a carcinogen. Therefore, it is not a stochastic carcinogen in the sense of the model -- not a pure chance single hit
mechanism.

CRANMER: Let's look at what's happening, if we can. We give this
compound, 2-(acetylamino)fluorene. It goes in the animal and it's
absorbed. Let's assume that the absorption characteristics are the
same in high and low doses and that everything gets in that went in
there.

Now the metabolism of the compound is not the same at high and
low doses. You have an intoxication pathway by n-hydroxylation, and
a detoxication pathway by ring hydroxylation. The ring hydroxylation
pathway is more efficient than the n-hydroxylation pathway. However,
if you keep adding substrate you will get more and more of the n-
hydroxylation pathway. Additionally, the unchanged substrate, the
parent compound, is also being ring hydroxylated and the ability of
the n-hydroxylated compound to be ring hydroxylated and detoxified
decreases with dose. So, the ability of a toxic molecule to escape
metabolic removal becomes higher.

Additionally, if you assume that there is DNA repair of the
lesion once it is created, it is reasonable to assume that you can
saturate some of these, or escape repair, if that is the word you
want to use. Carcinogenic activity should be a dynamic process,
dependent on the ability to produce a critical number of lesions.

BERG: So, if there is a stochastic mutation event, it takes place
after several intervening steps which can be saturated.

CRANMER: That's correct.

SPIELMAN: Did you explicitly try to fit your data to any of the

models in the literature which take account of the repair mechanism
like Kornfield's recently proposed model?

CRANMER: I haven't done it. Whether individuals at the National
Center of Toxicological Research have done that or not, I don't know.
It might be difficult to do because the slope of the dose-response
curve was precipitous for bladder tumors and compound for liver
tumors. One can ask, though, are the results consistent with this
model given these parameters? You might start excluding certain
models in that way.

WEINBERG: If I understand your results, the mean survival of treated
mice was about the same as for controls, or longer. Nevertheless, you
did find some extra cancers of the sort that you were looking for.
That means, I suppose, since you showed at the beginning that 89%
of your controls die of cancer, that cancers of the type induced,
presumably, by this agent appeared in place of some other cancers.

CRANMER: That's correct.

WEINBERG: Do you have a picture of what was the spectrum of the
cancers that didn't appear?

CRANMER: Yes, there appears to be a treatment-related effect -- a
depression of reticulum cell sarcoma, the most vicious neoplasm in
this particular strain of mice.

WEINBERG: Does EPA, or do any of the regulatory agencies, recognize
this possibility that some agents can inhibit certain cancers?

CRANMER: I welcome this as an issue which I believe to be true. At
certain doses the compound allowed the animal to live longer because
there was a lower incidence of reticulum cell sarcoma. Since the
incidence of liver cancer increases dramatically and spontaneously
with older age, if you allow the animal to live longer he is going
to get it. If you adjust the effect of reticulum cell sarcoma on
age, the increase of hepaticellular carcinoma can be controlled for.
In other words, the carcinogenic effect of 2-AAF goes away. It is
just as if those animals died young of heart attacks. They would not
have lived to get liver cancer unless treated, then a cure of heart
disease could be called a carcinogenic treatment.

WEINBERG: This possibility is certainly not in the Delaney amendment.

BERG: The Delaney amendment is unfortunately misunderstood and since
this is the second time it has been brought up, perhaps a correction
is in order.

It is not true that the Delaney clause speaks to any zero threshold or to any non-permissible levels of carcinogens in food. It has nothing to do with levels of exposures. It is a model law as far as I am concerned because it simply exludes from commercial use a risk which is not warranted -- not because it is above zero, but because it is not warranted.

What it says is that if you mass-produce a food and deliberately add a known carcinogen or something that even could be a carcinogen, where you don't really know the threshold, you are taking an unnecessary chance. It is unnecessary because there is always an alternative way to prepare food. This is why DDT may not be used as a food additive in any amount, while the clause does not stop the FDA from setting a tolerance level for DDT in accidentally contaminated cheese, and it certainly does not interfere with licensing a DDT lotion for sale as a delousing cosmetic.

WEINBERG: But George, the evidence here seems to be that if you would add a little 2-AAF to the food, then you will live a little bit longer. Isn't that what the evidence shows?

BERG: What the evidence shows is that if you dispense AAF as a drug under the care of a qualified physician you might get some beneficial effects with proper management. If you sell it over the counter as an additive in food, any number of people will eat the wrong amount at the wrong time and get hurt.

WEINBERG: Fair enough.

ALBERT: This suggestion of beneficial effects at very low doses has come up again and again in terms of consideration of carcinogens for regulatory acttion. As a matter of fact, it has come up with ionizing radiation too, but it has never come up in a way that is sufficiently persuasive to make any impact.

THE SHAPES OF THE RADIATION DOSE-MUTATION RESPONSE CURVES IN DROSOPHILA: MECHANISMS AND IMPLICATIONS

S. Abrahamson, H. U. Meyer, C. DeJongh

Department of Zoology, University of Wisconsin, Madison, WI

The major thesis we wish to make in this presentation is that radiation induced mutations, namely sex-linked recessive lethals in Drosophila and forward mutations at specific loci in Drosophila, mammals and lower eucaryotes, are the result of two sub-lesions or hits, induced by either single ionization tracks or by the inter-action of two independent tracks for low LET radiations, when the dose is delivered in an acute fashion. This statement formally reduces to the well recognized linear quadratic expression: $Y = C + \alpha D + \beta D^2$ where C is the spontaneous frequency of events scored and α and β represent the coefficients of the dose. In practice, the curve is more complex because saturation occurs at high doses. This linear-quadratic relationship is most often applied to the yield of gross chromosome aberrations in plant and animal systems and was first demonstrated by Sax (1940). Lea (1955) and subsequently Neary (1965) and Kellerer and Rossi (1972) have developed the biophysical and microdosimetric framework for the empirically derived dose-response relationship.

For high LET radiations, a single densely clustered track is capable of producing all the necessary hits in the target structure, throughout the dose-range usually investigated, so that the above equation reduces to a simple linear expression, $Y = C + \alpha D$. Neary (1963) first pointed out that the best description of RBE would be the ratio of the high LET slope to the low LET slope, i.e. $\alpha N/\alpha$ X-ray.

For low LET radiations the consequences of the linear qua-dratic model of mutation and chromosome aberration induction are the following: (1) The yield of events in the dose-response curve within the α slope region, will be dose dependent but dose-rate independent (assuming that the biological targets are not disturbed by such factors as cell division and chromosome condensations). Thus the yield will be additive.

(2) In metabolically active cell systems the region of the dose response curve that is predominantly the result of the inter-action of two or more independent ionization tracks should be modi-fiable by the manner in which the dose is delivered. As the dose rate is lowered the β term diminishes, becoming zero when no interactions between independent tracks occur. Lea (1955) has developed equations which permit estimates of the influence of different dose rates on β.

(3) The value α/β, the dose where one or two ionization tracks are equally likely to traverse the target, denotes the region below which predominantly linear dose-response kinetics will be observed and above which predominantly dose-squared kinetics will obtain.

(4) When the intervals between them are sufficiently long, fractionated acute doses will produce a yield of events that is the sum of their individual doses (i.e. of each linear-quadratic com-ponent) and their frequency will be lower than that from a single acute dose, in the dose-squared region of the curve. The smaller the dose per fraction, the lower the composite yield.

In table 1 we present our X-ray data on sex-linked recessive lethals induced in oogonia of Drosophila. These experiments have been carried out so that only a single daughter derived from each P_1 female parent, treated or control, was bred to determine whether she contained a recessive lethal mutation. Though considerably more arduous, this procedure, nevertheless, eliminates the problem of recovering identical clusters of either spontaneous or induced gonial mutation origin. Clusters inflate the variance of the mutation frequencies and could obscure important relationships particularly at low doses.

Eleven doses, were studied with exposures ranging from 20R to 9000R. The dose rate was 80R/minute for doses up to 1500R and from 280/480R/minute for the higher doses. Because the mutation fre-quency appears to have plateaued at or above 6000R, we have excluded the 7500R and 9000R frequencies from subsequent analysis.

Over the dose-range of zero to 6000R the mutation response curve was significantly different from linearity. The curve was fitted by weighted regression analysis to the linear-quadratic relationship: $Y = 1.29 \times 10^{-3} + 2.81 \times 10^{-6}D + 6.28 \times 10^{-10}D^2$. Other mathematical expressions may of course be fitted to the data, but we believe that the linear-quadratic expression is the most relevant because it is predictive and provides a consistent and

Table 1. Sex-linked Lethal Frequencies in Oogonia
(1) Acute X-ray Doses

Dose (R)	No. Replicate Experiments	No. Leth./Tot. Tests	Lethal Frequencies, %	
			Observed ± S.E.	Computed*
0**	442	268/190,610	.141 ± .009	.129
20	147	102,67,553	.151 ± .015	.134
100	224	141/102,491	.138 ± .012	.158
200	164	165/92,685	.178 ± .014	.188
500	318	320/118,549	.270 ± .015	.285
1,500	77	282/36,967	.763 ± .045	.692
3,000	61	485/31,478	1.541 ± .069	1.537
4,500	41	598/21,006	2.847 ± .115	2.665
6,000	31	627/21,006	3.859 ± .151	4.076
7,500	5	84/2,062	4.074 ± .435	5.769
9,000	7	49/1,082	4.529 ± .632	7.744

*Model: $Y = 1.2894 \times 10^{-3} + 2.8116 \times 10^{-6}D + 6.2774 \times 10^{-10}D^2$, based on data for doses 0 to 6000R only.

**Entire data pooled.

unifying radiobiological interpretation to both induced mutation
and cytogenetic events.

We originally undertook our studies to determine if Oftedal's
experiments (1964a,b) which suggested the existence of a population
of highly sensitive cells recovered only at low doses could be
confirmed. Our studies on the dose-response curve in oogonia are
however in sharp contrast to his spermatogonial studies. In
Oftedal's studies, for acute delivery, the dose response curve at
56, 109 and 163R was quite flat but above control and dropped to
the control value at 307R. He suggested that the results were due
to differential killing and cell heterogeneity. In a further series
of chronic exposures protracted over 8 hours employing 5 doses
ranging from 144 to 542R, the curve reached a peak at about 300R
and fell to the control frequency at 400 and 542R. Our considerably
larger scale studies fail to demonstrate any humped shape curve
over the 20-500R dose range, nor do they show any unique sensitivities at the 20 or 100R doses with respect to the control and
therefore, do not provide support for the Oftedal model.

While it is possible that methodological differences between
the experiments account for the lack of agreement, for example he
irradiated young male larvae, we treated adult females; we believe
the more likely explanation is that his smaller scale experiments
suffer from large statistical uncertainties at these very low
doses.

From the data presented in Table 1 it would appear that below
a dose of approximately 4000R (the α/β dose) the single track 2
break (or hit) events appear to dominate, whereas the 2 track
events become increasingly important at higher doses.

This should mean that dose rate and dose fractionation
regimens should have only minimal influence on the yield in the
linear region of the curve. The dose-rate experiments that have
bearing on this statement were actually completed nearly a decade
before our experiments were undertaken. The studies of Purdom
and colleagues (1963) on Drosophila spermatogonia were unable to
demonstrate consistent reductions in mutation frequency by reducing
dose-rate by a factor of 200,000 when the doses studied were in
the 200-750R range. On the other hand, a significant reduction in
mutation yield at 4000R was obtained by Muller et al. (1963) by
varying the dose-rate. In a subsequent analysis of the Muller
data (Abrahamson, 1976) it was shown that the observed yields for
both the chronic and acute exposures were in good agreement with
our predictions.

Thus to summarize the dose-rate studies, no dose-rate influence on mutation induction was found when the doses were in the
linear portion of the curve and a significant lowering of mutation

yield was observed by reducing the dose-rate of a 4000R exposure.
Our recent dose-fractionation studies (Meyer and Abrahamson, 1980)
provide further support. In Table 2 a significant reduction in the
mutation yield is observed below the unfractionated 6000R frequency
when the dose is given either in 3 or 4 equal fractions. Two equal
fractions while lower were not significantly so. However a
dose of 4500R, delivered in multiply fractionated doses, significantly
reduced the yield below the single acute dose. Finally at 1500R,
fractionation was ineffective (3 doses of 500R) with respect to
the single acute dose. Thus there appears to be reasonably good
consistency with the expectation that in the region of the dose
response curve that is dominated by dose squared kinetics, dose
fractionation will reduce the yield; while in the linear region no
appreciable influence of dose-fractionation is observed.

Drosophila is the organism frequently cited for demonstrating
the linearity concept. All of the very early work was carried out
on Drosophila mixed samples of spermatozoa and spermatid stages
which have different mutation sensitivities (e.g. Spencer and
Stern, 1948). As effort was made to study homogeneous samples of
sperm it was demonstrated (Traut, 1963) that a quadratic contribution became evident in the range of 3500R or above. The experiments
of Gonzales (1972) over a dose range of 500-2500 not surprisingly
were consistent with a linear fit. These experiments permit an
estimate of the linear slope around $2-4 \times 10^{-5}$, which is about ten
times larger than the gonia values. We interpret this to mean
that the more highly condensed chromosomes of sperm and spermatids
allow a larger target to be deleted per unit dose. Cytological
observations support this view. Finally it is not surprising that
dose-rate and dose fractionation studies are ineffective on these
germ cell stages since sperm and maturing spermatids are incapable
of metabolic repair of chromosome damage. The repair systems of
the oocyte are required to join breaks induced in these male germ
cell stages.

For Drosophila oocytes Parker (1963) reported that "the
increase in frequency of recessive lethals in stage 7 and stage 14
oocytes seems primarily dependent on the increased frequency of
two-hit events, hence may be due to an increased production of
chromosomal aberrations, perhaps small deficiencies." E. H.
Markowitz (1970) using stage 7 oocytes was unable to confirm the
results of Herskowitz and Abrahamson (1955) of a dose-rate effect
on sex-linked recessive lethals in oocytes. However the experiments were probably performed on too small a scale in the dose
range of interest to provide the needed discrimination.

To summarize for all Drosophila germ cell stages tested, the
X-ray dose-response curves become significantly different from
linearity at high doses. The curves can all be fitted by the
linear quadratic equation. Appropriate dose rate and dose frac-

Table 2. Sex-Linked Lethal Frequencies in Oogonia
(2) Effect of Dose Fractionation

X-ray Treatment	No. Replicate Exp.	No. Leth./Tot. Tests	% Lethals ± S.E.	P-Value Acute vs. Fract. [**]
0R[*]	442	268/190,610	.141 ± .009	--
1 x 6000R (Acute)	31	627/16,249	3.859 ± .151	--
2 x 3000R	53	935/26,519	3.526 ± .113	.75
3 x 2000R	10	209/7,387	2.829 ± .193	<<.0001
4 x 1500R	21	328/9,991	3.283 ± .178	.016
1 x 4500R (Acute)	41	598/21,006	2.847 ± .115	--
3 x 1500R	21	317/13,317	2.380 ± .132	.009
9 x 500R	20	214/11,560	1.851 ± .113	<<.0001
1 x 1500R (Acute)	77	282/36,967	.763 ± .045	--
3 x 500R	20	59/8,567	.689 ± .089	.473

[*] Entire data pooled.

[**] Based on chi-square test

tionation regimens in metabolically active cells reduce the yield
of mutations below the single acute doses in the primarily quadratic
region of the curve (see Figure 1).

It has long been known that high LET radiations cause predominantly linear dose response curves when either chromosome rearrangements or mutations are the end points in either germ cells or
somatic cell studies.

Employing the germ cell stage and mating scheme as used in
the X-ray experiments we initiated a series of neutron experiments
on the RARAF accelerator carried out at Brookhaven National
Laboratory in collaboration with Mr. Steve Marino. We did not
however restrict the experiment to one F_1 daughter for each P_1
female exposed because this would have seriously curtailed the
size of the experiment. Our purpose was to determine the dose-
response curve for a variety of specific monoenergetic neutron
energies and thus the RBE of each energy. A minimum of 4 doses
were employed, the highest dose was usually limited by the time
required to achieve the dose. The data for each neutron energy
are presented in Table 3. Both linear and linear-quadratic
regression analyses were used to evaluate the data. While there
may be evidence of a quadratic component in the neutron curves, it
does not appear to be of major significance and we have therefore
used the slopes derived from the linear regression analysis to
compute the RBE's for the respective neutron energies of .43 MeV,
.68 MeV, 2 MeV, 6 MeV and 15 MeV radiations; the corresponding
RBE's are 4.8, 4.0, 3.2, 2.9 and 2.0 relative to the X-ray slope.
The relationship of RBE to specific neutron energies parallels
that observed by plant geneticists (see ICRP #18, Table 5). The
LET (keV/μm) is greatest for .43 MeV neutrons and decreases with
increasing neutron energy (see Figure 1).

These comparative studies lend additional support to the
notion that radiation induced mutations require two hits to
accomplish the mutational event since the more densely clustered
neutron tracks are more efficient than sparsely ionizing X-rays
in supplying the submicroscopic hits. Put another way, if only a
single ionization in the target were required to produce a
mutation one would expect the neutron irradiations to be more
wasteful and thus lead to RBE's consistently lower than one.

Based on similar analyses to those already presented,
Abrahamson and Wolff (1976) stated that the similar kinetics
observed for mutation induction and gross chromosome aberrations
"is not fortuitous, but a reflection of both their common mode of
origin and their subsequent common response to modifying physiological factors." In that paper the authors fitted both the mouse

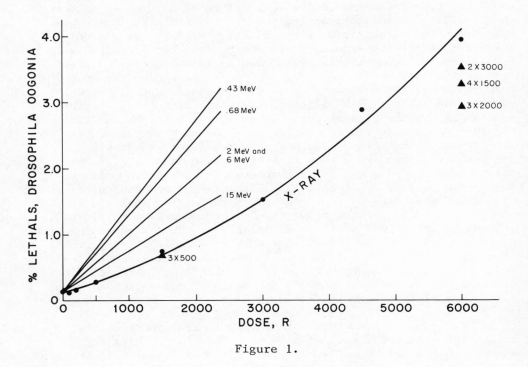

Figure 1.

oocyte and spermatogonial data to linear-quadratic equations in
an attempt to demonstrate that specific locus mutations were primarily deletions resulting from a mixture of one and two track
events.

TABLE 3. Neutron-Induced X-Linked Recessive Lethal Mutations In Oogonia

Dose	.43 MeV		.66 MeV		2 MeV		6 MeV		15 MeV	
	M/N	Obs. % Lethals ± 95% C.L.	M/N	Obs. % Lethals ± 95% C.L.	M/N	Obs. % Lethals ± 95% C.L.	M/N	Obs. % Lethals ± 95% C.L.	M/N	Obs. % Lethals ± 95% C.L.
0R	106/60,491 (13-2, 3-3)	.18 ± .04								
250R			14/3,437	.41 ± .21	11/5,066 (3)	.22 ± .16	38/7,062 (4-2,3,4,7)	.54 ± .27	7/5,117 (2)	.14 ± .12
500R	49/7,315	.67 ± .19	60/9,147 (3-2,4)	.66 ± .19	23/5,693 (2-3)	.40 ± .20	17/5,472 (3)	.31 ± .18	41/10,105 (3-2)	.40 ± .14
1000R	90/6,473 (3-2)	1.39 ± .29	109/8,721 (3-2)	1.25 ± .24	138/13,544 (4-2,3)	1.02 ± .18			89/9,576 (11-2,4)	.93 ± .24
1500R	216/9,168 (25-2,3)	2.36 ± .35	151/7,405 (10-2)	2.04 ± .34	83/4,959 (2-2)	1.67 ± .36	64/4,371	1.46 ± .36	130/13,466 (2)	.96 ± .16
1675R					165,8995 (7-2,2-3)	1.83 ± .30				
1900R	130/4,412 (16-2)	2.95 ± .53								
2000R					97/4,455 (6-2)	2.18 ± .45				
2500R					201/7,975 (14-2)	2.52 ± .37				
3000R							95/2,982 (8-2,3)	3.18 ± .70	63/3,053 (4-2,3)	2.06 ± .56
$\frac{\alpha N/\alpha X}{RBE}$	$\frac{1.35 \times 10^{-5}}{2.81 \times 10^{-6}} \alpha X$ 4.8		$\frac{1.11 \times 10^{-5}}{\alpha X}$ 4.0		$\frac{9.11 \times 10^{-6}}{\alpha X}$ 3.2		$\frac{8.10 \times 10^{-6}}{\alpha X}$ 2.9		$\frac{5.67 \times 10^{-6}}{\alpha X}$ 2.0	

NOTE in these experiments more than one F1 daughter per female was used and some clusters of identical mutations were obtained.

Brewen and his collaborators (Brewen et al., 1976, 1977; Brewen, 1977; Brewen and Payne, 1979) have demonstrated that the yield of chromosome aberrations in maturing mouse oocytes increases in curvilinear fashion (fitted with either linear-quadratic or dose^2 relationships) with increasing acute X-ray doses, while a linear response was obtained with chronic irradiation. Moreover, reduced yields were obtained when a 400R dose was fractionated into two equal doses separated by 180 minute intervals, but no reduction was observed when the interval was 90 minutes. In addition identical results were obtained with 100 + 300R and 300 + 100R fractions over varying intervals. This would not be expected if the repair process were dose-dependent (see below). Finally the α/β values for induced rearrangements in mouse oocytes are in the range of 16-44R.

For specific locus mutations in maturing mouse oocytes recovered within one week after irradiation, Lyon et al. (1979) have extended the acute dose response curve up to 600 rad X-ray and found that the data for 200, 400 and 600 rad was best fitted by either linear-quadratic or dose squared relationships. Linear regression analysis provided the poorest fit (P .05-.06) to these data. Previous studies by Russell (1972) over the 50-400R range also could not be fitted by a linear relationship. The linear-quadratic relationship derived by Lyon et al. was $Y = 2.1 \times 10^{-6} + 6.0 \times 10^{-8}D + 9.0 \times 10^{-10}D^2$ for a per locus mutation rate. These workers state, "Thus, the data are consistent with the view that a single quadratic curve can be obtained which fits all data from mature or nearly mature oocytes at high or low doses or dose rates." Abrahamson (in NCRP64, 1980) had independently derived a similar equation over the 50-400R dose response for oocytes of essentially the same developmental stage as used by Lyon et al. The α value was 2.8×10^{-8} for that fit. Thus the α/β values range from about 25-70R for oocyte specific locus mutations, which is in agreement with the values cited earlier for oocyte rearrangements.

Abrahamson and Wolff (1976) and Brewen (1977,1978) have endorsed the view that the mouse specific locus mutation data are explicable in terms of 2 break events. Russell (1977) and Lyon et al. (1979) suggest as an alternative view that the variety of effects noted can be explained by invoking dose and dose-rate dependent repair mechanisms. Such hypotheses at present appear to lack the capability of predicting quantitatively the outcomes for modified radiation regimes.

For mouse spermatogonia studies we again note that the cytogenetic studies provide a useful backdrop with which to view the specific locus mutation studies. Preston and Brewen (1973,1976) demonstrated that the induced translocation frequency over a 10

fold dose range (50-500R) was best fitted by the linear-quadratic
relationship. The α/β values for different studies are in the
range of 100-200R. Saturation of yield (19%) occurred in the
500-600R region and the frequency plummeted for the higher 1000R
dose. Since seven 400R fractions separated by long intervals
produced an 81% translocation frequency, the data indicate that
selective elimination of cells containing broken chromosomes was
responsible for the saturation by the lower single acute doses.
Pomerantzeva et al. (1972) and Brewen et al. (1979) demonstrated
that after chronic exposures, the curve assumed a linear slope
predicted by the α coefficient. Small fractionated doses of 300R
all significantly reduces the yield below the single acute dose
value (Lyon et al., 1970). The expected frequencies predicted by
the model were in agreement with those observed (Abrahamson in
NCRP64, 1980).

Information on the shape of the acute dose response curve
for specific locus mutations is equivocal. Three doses have been
examined. The curve rises between 300 and 600R and at 1000R falls
back to the value observed at 300R. Chronic exposures ranging
from 37.5 to 861R produce a linear response that remains significantly below the 300 and 600R acute points (see extensive reviews
in NCRP64 and Searle, 1974). If it is assumed (Abrahamson and
Wolff, 1976) that the acute dose response for specific locus
mutations parallels that of chromosome rearrangements it is possible
to derive the β coefficient from the 300R acute dose point, the
dose least likely to be influenced by saturation conditions. This
procedure produced a per locus estimate of β equal to 6.6×10^{-10},
after a 6.8×10^{-8} value for α was estimated directly from the
chronic exposure data by linear regression analysis. Thus the α/β
value of 100 for specific locus mutations, agrees with that obtained
from gross chromosome rearrangements. This equation too provides
a reasonable fit for all of the data obtained from fractionated
exposures in the 600R and 1000R studies. In the absence of this
model a variety of ad hoc hypotheses are required to explain why
some of the observed mutation values for fractionated 600R doses
are significantly above whilst others are significantly below the
single dose value.

Fast fission neutron studies in mouse spermatogonial cells
suggest that the RBE based on a comparison with chronic γ radiation
is in the range of 20 (ICRP #18, 1972). For oocytes, as discussed
earlier, the α coefficient for X-rays are based on a limited stage
(Lyon et al., 1979), the published neutron data for different
doses (Russell, 1965; Russell, 1972) extend over a wider range of
stages including more sensitive ones. In addition Russell (1965)
notes that there is some uncertainty in the actual dose received
by the caged mice, who tend to huddle and thus shield each other.
A linear regression analysis performed on three acute neutron
doses, crudely corrected for stage sensitivity suggests that the

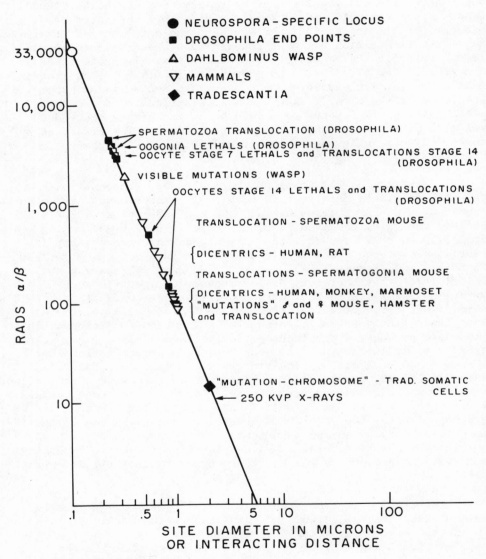

GRAPH OF KELLER & ROSSI (1972)
α/β - COMPUTED BY ABRAHAMSON

Figure 2.

RBE for oocytes is likely to be in the range of 15-20 but we cannot exclude a maximum of 34.

We have previously noted (Abrahamson, 1976, see figure 2) that the α/β values appear to be related to a nuclear target size For example the α/β value for Tradescantia is 16, for a variety of mammalian systems the values cluster around 100 for Drosophila around 4000 and for neurospora around 30,000. The RBE's for comparable neutron energies are 50, 20 and 2-5 for Tradescantia, mouse and Drosophila. From prokaryotes to plants both the DNA content and the induced gene mutation rate per rad vary by four orders of magnitude (Abrahamson et al., 1973, opposing interpretations have been expressed by Schalet and Sankaranarayanan, 1976). We interpret this to mean that for a larger target cross sectional area (more DNA per locus) there will be a smaller α/β value and higher RBE (for high LET radiations) relative to organisms with smaller DNA contents per target (per locus).

In summary we conclude that in the interest of scientific parsimony that for low LET radiations, X or gamma rays, the linear-quadratic model can be used to predict the genetic response of germ cells and somatic cells to a variety of radiation regimes. The point of inflection in the curve, α/β value, will be determined specifically by target dimensions which vary with respect to DNA content. High LET radiations (densely ionizing) induce genetic damage in a linear fashion because the two or more breaks required are produced more efficiently by a single track. The difference in RBE values observed for different species is considered to be a reflection of their different target sizes.

ACKNOWLEDGMENT

The preparation of this publication was stimulated by discussions within the Drosophila workshop for the GENETOX program conducted by the Environmental Protection Agency (EPA). Original research from the University of Wisconsin, Madison, reported herein was supported by succession by the U.S. Atomic Energy Commission, the U.S. Energy Research and Development Administration, and the Department of Energy under contracts No. 1748 and No. 2001. Additional support came from the National Institutes of Health (Project Program GM 15288) and the Graduate School of the University of Wisconsin.

REFERENCES

Abrahamson, S., 1976, Mutation process at low or high radiation
    doses, in: "Biological and Environmental Effects of Low-
    Level Radiation, Vol. I, IAEA/STI/PUB/409 (International
    Atomic Energy Agency, Vienna).
Abrahamson, S., Bender, M.A., Conger, A.D., and Wolff, S., 1973,
    Uniformity of radiation-induced mutation rates among different
    species, Nature, 245: 460.
Abrahamson, S., and Meyer, H.U., 1976, Quadratic analysis for the
    induction of recessive lethal mutations in Drosophila
    oogonia by X-irradiation, Vol. I, IAEA/STI/PUB/409 (Inter-
    national Atomic Energy Agency, Vienna).
Abrahamson, S., and Wolff, S., 1976, Reanalysis of radiation
    induced specific locus mutations in the mouse, Nature, 264:
    715.
Brewen, J.G., 1977, The application of mammalian cytogenetics to
    mutagenicity studies, in: "Proc. II Int. Conf. on Environ.
    Mutagens, Progress in Genetic Toxicology", D. Scott,
    B.A. Bridges, F.H. Sobels, eds., Elsevier, North Holland.
Brewen, J.G., and Payne, H.S., 1979, X-ray stage sensitivity of
    mouse oocytes and its bearing on dose-response curves,
    Genetics, 91: 149.
Brewen, J.G., Preston, R.J., and Littlefield, L.G., 1972,
    Radiation-induced human chromosome aberration yields fol-
    lowing an accidental whole-body exposure to ^{60}Co γ rays,
    Radiat. Res., 49: 647.
Brewen, J.G., Payne, H.S., and Preston, R.J., 1976, X-ray induced
    chromosome aberrations in mouse dictyate oocytes. I. Time
    and dose relationship, Mutat. Res., 35: 111.
Brewen, J.G., Payne, H.S., and Adler, J.D., 1977, X-ray induced
    chromosome aberrations in mouse dictyate oocytes. II.
    Fractionation and dose rate effects, Genetics, 87: 699.
Gonzalez, F.W., 1972, Dose response kinetics of genetic effects
    induced by 250 kVp x rays and 0.68 MeV neutrons in mature
    sperm of Drosophila melanogaster, Mutat. Res., 15: 303.
Herskowitz, I.H., and Abrahamson, S., 1955, The effect of X-ray
    intensity on the rate of sex-linked recessive lethal
    mutations induced by treatment of Drosophila oocytes,
    Drosophila Information Serv., 29: 125.
ICRP, 1972, International Commission on Radiological Protection,
    The RBE of high-LET radiations with respect to mutagenesis,
    ICRP Publication 18, Pergamon Press, New York.
Kellerer, A.M., and Rossi, H.H., 1972, The theory of dual
    radiation action, Curr. Topics Radiat. Res. Quart., 8: 85.
Lea, D.E., 1955, "Actions of Radiations on Living Cells", The
    University Press, Cambridge.
Lyon, M.F., Morris, J., Glenister, P., and O'Grady, S.E., 1970,
    Induction of translocations in mouse spermatogonia by X-ray
    doses divided into many small fractions, Mutat. Res., 9: 219.

Lyon, M.F., Phillips, R.J.S., and Fisher, G., 1979, Dose-response
    curves for radiation-induced mutations in mouse oocytes and
    their interpretation, Mutat. Res., 63: 161.
Markowitz, E.H., 1970, Gamma ray-induced mutations in Drosophila
    melanogaster oocytes: The phenomenon of dose rate, Genetics,
    64: 313.
Meyer, H.U., and Abrahamson, S., 1978, Linear-quadratic dose
    kinetics for X-ray induced recessive mutations in Drosophila
    oogonia, Mutat. Res. 53: 229.
Muller, H.J., Oster, I.I., and Zimmering, S., 1963, Are chronic
    and acute gamma irradiation equally mutagenic in Drosophila?,
    in: "Repair from Genetic Radiation Damage", F.H. Sobels, ed.,
    Pergamon Press, Oxford.
NCRP, 1980, National Council on Radiation Protection and Measure-
    ments, Influence of dose and its distribution in time on
    dose-response relationships for low-LET radiations, NCRP
    Report No. 64, Washington, D.C.
Neary, G.H., 1965, Chromosome aberrations and the theory of RBE.
    I. General Considerations, Int. J. Rad. Biol. 9: 477.
Oftedal, P., 1964a, Radiosensitivity of Drosophila spermatogonia.
    I. Acute doses, Genetics 49: 181.
Oftedal, P., 1964b, Radiosensitivity of Drosophila spermatogonia.
    II. Protracted doses, Hereditas, 51: 13.
Parker, D.R., 1963, On the nature of sensitivity changes in oocytes
    of Drosophila melanogaster, in: Repair from Genetic Radiation
    Damage, F.H. Sobels, ed., Pergamon Press, Oxford.
Pomerantzeva, M.D., Ramaiya, L.K., and Ivanov, V.N., 1972, The
    mutagenic effect of different types of irradiation on the
    germ cells of male mice. VII. The effect of dose-rate on
    gamma-irradiation on the induction of reciprocal transloca-
    tions in spermatogonia, Genetika, 8: 128.
Preston, R.J., and Brewen, J.G., 1973, X-ray induced translocation
    in spermatogonia. I. Dose and fractionation responses in
    mice, Mutat. Res. 19: 215.
Preston, R.J. and Brewen, J.G., 1976, X-ray induced translocations
    in spermatogonia. II. Fractionation responses in mice,
    Mutat. Res., 36: 333.
Purdom, C.E., 1963, the effect of intensity and fractionation on
    radiation-induced mutation in Drosophila, in: "Repair from
    Genetic Radiation Damage", F.H. Sobels, ed., MacMillan
    Press, New York.
Russell, W.L., 1962, An augmenting effect of dose-fractionation
    on radiation-induced mutations in mice, Proc. Natl. Acad.
    Sci., 48: 1724.
Russell, W.L., 1963, The effect of radiation dose rate and
    fractionation on mutation rate in mice, in: Repair from
    Genetic Radiation Damage, F.J. Sobels, ed., Pergamon Press,
    Oxford.

Russell, W.L., 1965c, Effect of the interval between irradiation
    and conception on mutation frequency in female mice, Proc.
    Natl. Acad. Sci., 54: 1552.
Russell, W.L., 1972, The genetic effects of radiation, in:
    "Peaceful Uses of Atomic Energy", United Nations, New York.
Russell, W.L., 1977, Mutation frequencies in mouse oocytes and the
    estimation of genetic hazards of radiation in women, Proc.
    Natl. Acad. Sci., 74: 135.
Russell, W.L., 1977, Mutation frequencies in mouse oocytes and
    the estimation of genetic hazards of radiation in women,
    Proc. Natl. Acad. Sci., 74: 3523.
Sax, K., 1940, An analysis of X-ray induced chromosomal aberrations
    in Tradescantia, Genetics, 25: 41.
Schalet, A.P., and Sankararanarayanan, K., 1976, Evaluation
    and re-evaluation of genetic radiation hazards in man. I.
    Interspecific comparison of estimates of mutation rates.
    Mutat. Res., 35: 341.
Searle, A.G., 1974, Mutation induction in mice, Adv. in Radiat.
    Biol., 4: 151.
Spencer, W.P., and Stern, C., 1948, Experiments to test the
    validity of the linear gamma dose-mutation frequency relation
    in Drosophila at low dosage, Genetics, 33: 43.
Traut, H., 1963, Dose dependence of the frequency of radiation-
    induced recessive sex-linked lethals in Drosophila
    melanogaster with special consideration of the stage sensi-
    tivity of the irradiated germ cells, in: "Repair from Genetic
    Radiation Damage", F.H. Sobels, ed., Pergamon Press, Oxford.

DISCUSSION

W. RUSSELL: There are other models which Seymour didn't discuss, such as a dose rate dependent repair system, which I proposed many years ago because we thought the lesions themselves were probably not two track events.   I based that, at the time, primarily on Drosophila results, but now there is other evidence for this.

Both his and our hypotheses are still tenable.   In our argument we rejected his model because of the nature of the mutational events which I can't go into in detail here -- one reason I gave yesterday was that the qualitative nature of the mutational events does not change with the dose rate.   If the acute response was primarily from two track events and the chronic result from one track events, I would expect some change in distribution of mutations among our seven loci, and there is none.

ABRAHAMSON: No more than I would expect translocation qualities to change whether it is a one track event or a two track event.   The densely ionizing part of one x-ray track can produce those breaks leading to the deficiency equally as well as would two tracks and I see no reason why there should be a qualitative difference between the two.

W. RUSSELL: The point is that we see qualitative differences when we go to neutrons, or when we compare spermatozoa with spermatogonia or oocytes with spermatogonia, so the spectrum does change.

ABRAHAMSON: Bigger deletions?

W. RUSSELL: More deletions, and the distribution among the loci changes markedly.

The other point that I think is more important to this conference is the impact of your hypothesis on risk estimation.   We both agree, at the present time, that the response is linear for low doses and low dose rates in spermatogonia.   The linear portions of our hypotheses agree.   Your alpha is derived essentially from responses at low doses and low dose rates.   There is no effect of that hypothesis on risk estimation in the male.

However, I point out that other hypotheses such as the simple quadratic relationship also fit the data, although under that hypothesis there would be essentially no effect at low dose rates and low doses.

ABRAHAMSON: The oocyte data can be fitted to a quadratic model.   I don't think you could fit the spermatogonia data quadratically.   I haven't tried that.

W. RUSSELL: Yes, you can -- rather well.

Turning to another question, Seymour has at times fitted the
acute data to a linear quadratic plot, derived the alpha term from
this and assumed that this would be the risk. Now the alpha that
you derive from this fit has extremely wide confidence limits. It
is a very reliable estimate of what happens at low doses and dose
rates. I would ask whether you still think that this is a feasible
way to use the data?

ABRAHAMSON: You and I are going to have a lot of controversy over
oocytes for a long time. Mary Lyon just did it in her 1979 paper in
which she fitted by linear quadratic regression the acute dose response and then predicted all the results of your low dose rate exposure. I've done the same sort of thing. However, she doesn't
believe in linear quadratic models. She believes in dose rate dependent repair, but this mechanism has no predictability that I can see.
You can't predict from it what a fractionated exposure is going to
do or what a particular range of chronic exposures will do.

W. RUSSELL: Yes, you can make predictions.

ABRAHAMSON: Well, nobody has done it yet with respect to your model.
Nobody has predicted on that basis. That's why you and I disagree on
models. We do agree that in the low dose range of the curve we are
going to extrapolate linearly. That's the point that you are primarily interested in.

KATES: In the context of the challenge of our chairman, given that
you agree on effects in the lower range of exposures, but you profoundly disagree on the resolution of this controversy, would you
consider this a trans-scientific controversy?

ABRAHAMSON: I would not, even though we can't experiment by pushing
the doses any lower down for our test system. We have no scientific
reason to predict that there is going to be a fundamental change in
radiobiology when we get to single events produced by one ionization
track traversing the cell and not having another traversal through
it for another six weeks. As long as the event that we are describing is a change in DNA structure produced by a single track through
that cell, I see no difference whether you put ten tracks through
ten different cells or all ten through one. The dose-response relation whould still be linear.

BENDER: There is an evident increase in gene size (or target size
if you put it that way) for mutation with ionizing radiation as you
increase the DNA content per genome. I find it profoundly interesting. I think it has some predictive value from the point of view
of risk estimation. The thing that makes it really interesting is
that the size of the structural genes specifying the proteins in

higher organisms doesn't seem to be appreciably larger than that
for lower organisms. What it means, very likely, is that a lot of
DNA in higher organisms is doing something else which is important
to the function of a gene, but is not specifying the amino acid sequence of a protein.

With the advent of molecular biological techniques we are beginning to learn something about this extra DNA. For example, it turns
out that those mammalian genes that have been studied are much
longer in DNA sequences than they need to be to specify the protein.
They have long intervening sequences of bases whose function we don't
yet know. Indeed it does appear that the gene is getting bigger as
the complexity of an organism increases.

Another point has to do with drawing an analogy between two-
break chromosome aberrations and other classes of mutational events.
One way of thinking about the linear quadratic kinetics, if that
happens to be your preference in curve fitting, is that you must
break a chromosome twice, for example, and therefore produce a deletion. This isn't the only way that it can happen and it's not the
only mechanism by which you can generate what would appear to be a
deletion. For example, just as an exercise in speculation, let us
suppose that the x-ray treatment produces both double- and single-
strand DNA breaks, and let us suppose that with large acute doses
some of the single-strand breaks are close enough in complementary
strands so they effectively constitute a double-strand break. Let
us further suppose that in the repair of a double-strand break the
ends are trimmed so as to leave sticky ends, and that sufficient com-
plementarity is thus revealed to get the ends together and then polymerization, ligation and repair. That mechanism was proposed first
for chromosome aberration generation by Herbert Taylor about 18 years
ago and was scoffed at at that time by cytogeneticists, I'm afraid.
In fact, it is used commonly now as a technique in molecular biology
for splicing genes in the test tube.

Provided that was the only way double-strand breaks could be
repaired, that would mean that every repaired double-strand break
would in fact be a deletion of a substantial number of bases. I
think that such a mechanism is consistent with linear quadratic
kinetics.

CROW: This is an attempt to answer Dr. Kates.

This is a trans-scientific question in the sense that I or anyone else in this room could postulate a different dose rate-dependent
repair model that would fit these data and you could also postulate
appropriate coefficients of alpha and beta that will fit the data.
But it is far from trans-scientific if you bring other kinds of
evidence in.

If Bill can find reverse mutations of his mutants, that proves his point. If we could sequence DNA as easily as will someday be true, and see whether these mutations are single base changes or whether they are losses of small segments, we could attribute the true dose-response kinetics to a demonstrated mechanism. So the question is trans-scientific only in the sense that looking for more dose-response data won't answer it. There are many other approaches that surely can and eventually will.

THE CANCER RISK FROM LOW LEVEL RADIATION

Bernard L. Cohen

Department of Physics and Astronomy
University of Pittsburgh
Pittsburgh, PA 15260

EFFECTS AT HIGH LEVELS AND THE LINEARITY HYPOTHESIS

There have been many situations in which large numbers of people have been exposed to high levels of radiation, and through studies of them[1,2] the health effects of high level radiation are rather well known. Among the survivors of the atomic bomb attacks on Japan, there were 24,000 people who received an average exposure of 130 rem, and about 120 extra cancers developed among them up to 1972. There were 15,000 British patients treated with X-rays for ankylosing spondylitis (arthritis of the spine) with doses averaging 370 rem, and they had about 115 extra cancers. Over 900 Germans were treated for that same disease with injections of radium-224 giving an average dose to the bone of 4400 rem*, and 45 of them got bone cancer (vs 0.1 expected). About 1700 U.S. women employed during the 1920s in painting radium on clock and watch dial numerals to make them self-luminous used their tongues to put a fine tip on the brush, getting radium into their bodies; their average bone dose was 17,000 rem and 48 of them died of bone cancer (vs 0.4 expected). Among 4100 U.S. uranium miners exposed to excess levels of radon gas due to poor mine ventilation, the average exposure to bronchial surfaces was 4700 rem and up to 1972 there were 135 lung cancer deaths among them vs 16 expected. There have been several other miner groups which have experienced excess lung cancers, like a group of 800 Canadian fluorspar miners whose average bronchial exposure was 2800 rem, resulting in 51 lung cancer

---

*For loose discussion as in this Section, we use 1 rad = 10 rem (IC-59) for alpha particle radiation of the lung and bone (with radium).

deaths vs 2.8 expected. There have been a number of situations in
which there have been high exposures resulting in something like 10
extra cancers, such as women in a Nova Scotia tuberculosis sanitorium
exposed to excessive X-rays in the course of fluoroscopic examinations, U.S. women treated with X-rays for inflammation of the breasts
following childbirth, women treated with X-rays for gynecological
maladies, various types of pelvic X-ray treatments, children treated
with X-rays for enlargement of the thymus gland, infants radiated
with X-rays for ringworm of the scalp, patients in several countries
fed a thorium compound to aid in X-ray contrast studies, and Marshall
Island natives exposed to fallout from a nuclear bomb test. As a
result of numerous studies of these groups, there is a great deal of
information available on induction of cancer by high levels of radiation. This is periodically reviewed and updated by prestigious
study-evaluation groups.[1,2]

If one seeks to find similar information on low level radiation,
one is immediately confronted with statistical limitations. For
example, suppose one found a group of 10,000 white males who had
received an extra 10 rem of whole body radiation. The easiest evidence to find would be excess leukemias because that disease develops earliest and is among the most sensitive to radiation. As a
first approximation we might use the results of high level radiation
studies that leukemias are induced at a rate of about 1.0×10^{-6}/
year per rem of exposure. We would then expect $10,000 \times 10 \times 10^{-6}$
= 0.1 extra leukemias per year among this group. In the absence of
radiation, one would expect 0.88 leukemias if we take statistics
for the entire U.S. In the 25 years over which radiation is effective in causing leukemias, we then expect 22 ± 4.7 cases from
natural causes vs 2.5 from the 10 rem radiation exposures. Clearly,
the statistics here are marginal at best. But the problem goes
much deeper — the total U.S. population is hardly a suitable control group. Cancer is largely caused by environmental factors and
hence is subject to wide variations in incidence rates. Even for
entire states, the 0.88 cases given above as the expectation varies
from 1.0 (MN, DC) to 0.77 (ME, NM). In our above examples, this
could vary the number of expected cases from 19 to 25, making it
still more difficult to ascertain that there are 2 or 3 extra.
Moreover, a group of people with 10 rem of extra radiation would
typically have more environmental factors in common than merely
living in the same state.

Any experimental study of effects of low level radiation would
therefore need large populations, like millions of subjects, and
there would still be considerable difficulty in selecting a control
group. One way to achieve large numbers of subjects would be to use
variations in natural radiation; for example citizens of Colorado,
Wyoming, and New Mexico are exposed to about 5 rem more than the

U.S. average over their lifetimes. However, the leukemia rates in
those states are considerably <u>below</u> the U.S. average, 8.11 vs
8.81 x 10^{-5}/year for white males and 5.13 vs 5.74 for white females.
The same is true for all cancers; the high natural radiation states
have annual rates of 140 x 10^{-5} for white males and 114 x 10^{-5} for
white females, while the U.S. average is 174 and 130 respectively.
The fact that states with high natural radiation have considerably
<u>lower</u> cancer rates than average is generally dismissed as indicating
only that radiation is very far from being the principal cause of
cancer, and this point is logically correct. However, it is doubt-
ful whether that attitude would be accepted if states with high
natural radiation happened to have somewhat <u>higher</u> than average
cancer rates.

Since there is little direct evidence on effects of low-level
radiation, the simplest option is to use our abundant data on
effects of high level radiation to derive estimates of effects of
low levels by assuming a linear dose-effect relationship; i.e. if
some high level dose D causes a cancer risk R, we assume that a
dose 0.1D will cause a risk 0.1R, that a dose 0.01D will cause a
risk 0.01R, etc down to extremely low doses.

This "linearity hypothesis" was recommended by the National
Academy of Sciences Committee on Biological Effects of Ionizing
Radiation (BEIR) in 1972 with a statement that it is a "conservative" approach, more likely to over-estimate than to under-estimate
the effects of low levels.[1] This statement seems to represent the
general thinking in the involved scientific community, although
there is considerable variation in opinions of <u>how</u> <u>much</u> more likely
the over-estimate is. There is a considerable body of opinion that
the over-estimate is gross, say by a factor of 2-10, or even infinity, while there is also an important body of opinion that
linearity does not give an over-estimate. Let us review the evidence behind these positions.

EVIDENCE THAT LINEARITY IS CONSERVATIVE

Let me now review the principal evidence bearing on whether
the linearity assumption is conservative as a means of estimating
effects of low level radiation. This evidence comes from various
sources, each of which is discussed in a separate sub-section.

Repair Processes

There is a great deal of evidence that nature provides mechanisms for repair of radiation damage to biological molecules.

There have been many experiments in which it was shown that single doses in the 1000 rem range cause fatal radiation sickness in mice and other animals whereas fractionating these doses over several days or more does not.[3] Perhaps the best demonstration of repair mechanisms with regard to cancer is the dose rate effect; a given dose of radiation is generally much less carcinogenic when spread out in time than when given rapidly which implies that damage from earlier doses was repaired before the later doses were administered. The dose rate effect is well established in many animal studies with X-rays and gamma rays[4-7] although there is some contrary evidence with alpha particle radiation which will be explained later. It has been pointed out[9] that effects from the high dose rates received by the Japanese A-bomb survivors were no larger than from low dose rate medical exposures, but this could have other explanations. Increased effects of high dose rates are well established in studies of genetic effects, a mutagenic process somewhat linked to cancer induction.[10]

In addition to this indirect evidence from dose rate effects, there is direct evidence for repair processes in that broken chromosomes have been observed to re-unite into a single strand.[11,12] There is also a vast amount of evidence for DNA repair in bacteria.[13-17]

In view of the well established existence of repair mechanisms, there is a general feeling that effects of low doses should be largely repaired, whereas repair of the much more extensive damage from high doses would be far less complete. This implies that the linearity hypothesis over-estimates effects of low level radiation. On the other hand, it is argued that large doses may kill cells, which prevents them from becoming cancerous; this could cause linearity to under-estimate effects of small doses. However, there is good evidence that cell killing is not an important effect below about 100 rem,[18,19] so if data in the 100 rem range is utilized, it would be difficult to use cell killing as a reason for linearity under-estimating effects of low level radiation.

Mechanism for Radiation Induction of Cancer

One of the strongest reasons for believing that the linear hypothesis is conservative derives from our understanding of the processes by which radiation induces cancer.[20] Radiation affects matter largely by knocking electrons out of molecules and thereby disturbing molecular structure. In the process, the radiation gives up energy, transferring it to the material. The number of electrons knocked out of position is proportional to this energy deposited, and the latter is the basis for defining radiation dose. If the biological effects of radiation were simply due to single electrons being knocked out of position — this is called a "single hit" process — the cancer risk would be proportional to the total number of single hits, which is proportional to the energy deposited, regardless of the type of radiation. However, this is well known not to be the case;[21] for a given energy deposited, alpha particles and neutrons (known as high LET — linear energy transfer — radiation) are an order of magnitude more effective in doing biological damage than gamma rays or electrons (low LET). This is strong evidence that biological effects of radiation are not caused by single hits, but rather by multiple hits.

The basic difference between high and low LET radiation is that the former concentrates its damage within a much smaller volume of tissue. Since high LET is more effective, we may presume that effects are caused by multiple hits very close together, within some small sensitive volume.

Confirmatory evidence for a multi-hit process derives from the dose rate dependence discussed above. If cancer induction were a single hit process, it could not matter whether these hits were close together or far apart in time; each hit would have a certain probability of resulting in a cancer. However, as noted previously effects are much larger at high dose rate. With a multi-hit model, this is readily explainable by repair processes. If the two hits are well separated in time, damage from the first may be repaired before the second hit occurs.

Granted that radiation induced cancer is a multi-hit process (we assume a two-hit process), the multiple hits may be by the same particle of radiation or by separate particles. If they are by the same particle, effects are linearly proportional to dose, with the proportionality constant much larger for high LET than for low LET radiation because the former has a much better chance of making two hits close together.

On the other hand, if the two hits are by separate particles of radiation, effects are proportional to the square of the number of single hits and therefore proportional to the square of the dose, regardless of whether the radiation is high LET or low LET. These considerations lead to dose-effect curves with the following characteristics: At very low doses the linear term must be predominant, and at very high doses the term proportional to dose-squared (quadratic terms) must predominate. The transition between the two should occur at a dose where it is not unreasonable to expect two hits by separate particles of radiation within the sensitive volume. This would occur somewhere near the dose where there is an average of one hit per sensitive volume. The latter dose, of course, depends on the sensitive volume: for example, if it is 1 micron in diameter as suggested by some experiments,[20,22,23]

the dose for an average of one hit within it is 8 rad for a 1 MeV
gamma ray and 300 rad for a 5 MeV neutron whereas if the sensitive
volume is 5 microns in diameter, the size of an entire cell nucleus,
the required dose is 0.3 rad for a 1 MeV gamma ray and 12 rad for
a 5 MeV neutron. We don't really know what the sensitive volume
is, but these examples give the general impression that the transition from a linear to a quadratic dependence occurs at relatively
low levels for betas and gammas, and at relatively high levels
for alphas and neutrons. This means that over the range of principal interest, the dose-effect curves should be linear for the latter
and concave upward (quadratic) for the former, which leads to the
conclusion that application of the linear hypothesis based on data
at high doses will over-estimate effects of low doses for beta and
gamma ray exposure.

It may be noted that the above-outlined discussion assigns
most alpha particle radiation effects as due to multiple hits by
the same alpha particle at the same time. This implies that there
would be no dose-rate effect for alpha particles, in agreement with
experimental evidence.[8]

Data on Cancer Induction by Radiation

One basis for judging the validity of the linearity hypothesis
is to observe how well it behaves in explaining data down to the
lowest doses at which effects are statistically meaningful. There
is a rather large body of animal data extending down to the 10 rem
region with reasonable statistical significance. These data for
X-rays, gamma rays, and beta rays preponderantly indicate that
linearity over-estimates effects at low levels;[24-29] the dose-effect
curves are concave upward. In some cases results are close to
linear,[30] and there is one well known situation in which the observed dose-effect curve is concave downward.[31] The latter case
involves mammary cancers in Sprague-Dawley rats, a special breed
in which all females are virtually certain to die of that disease
even in the absence of radiation exposure; it is widely recognized
that this is an exceptional situation in many ways.[20]

The animal data for alpha particle radiation usually show
something close to a linear dependence.[32,33] It should be noted
that here, as in all other cases, there are no significant data
below about 100 rem (~10 rad for alphas).

Probably the best human data is that for leukemia among the
Japanese A-bomb survivors.[34] Unfortunately this has a controversial
aspect; the mortality data for subjects in the group chosen for
careful follow-up — the so-called "extended life-span study" —

indicate that linearity grossly over-estimates effects at low
doses. However, there are leukemia registries in both Hiroshima
and Nagasaki which keep track of the number of cases of leukemia
among people living at various distances from the bomb explosion
and compare them with the total population living at these distances (in 1950) and these data indicate no clear deviation from
linear dependence. In compiling these data, there is no consideration of age distribution, number of people who left the city,
etc, but it is presumed that these factors do not vary systematically with dose.

In the data on bone cancer among the radium dial painters,[35]
the data points for low doses lie consistently below the prediction of the linearity hypothesis. While the statistical significance of this conclusion is not very great, there is reasonably
good evidence that the linearity hypothesis is, if anything, conservative. Note that these data are for alpha particle exposure.

Information from Natural Environmental Exposure

The clearest evidence that linearity over-estimates effects
of low doses, if the basic assumptions of the study are accepted,
comes from a comparison of radon-induced lung cancer between
miners exposed to high doses and the non-cigarette smoking members
of the general public exposed to natural radon in the environment
at low doses.[36] It has been found[37] that 70% of the excess cancers
among the miners were of one particular histological type, small
cell-undifferentiated (SCU), and if linearity is applied to this
disease based on the miner data, the number of SCU lung cancers
due to normal environmental radon exposure among non-smokers is
over-predicted by a factor of 10.

The significance of this conclusion depends on some basic
assumptions that require justification. The most important
assumption is that radon induced lung cancer has the same risk
factor for smokers and non-smokers; that is, that there is no
synergism between smoking and radon exposure. Actually, there
were indications in the early U.S. miner data that smoking accent-
uated the effects of radon, but the most recent data do not seem
to support that viewpoint. One strong evidence against a
smoking-radon synergism is that lung cancer incidence vs radon
exposure is very similar between modern U.S. miners and a group
of 19th century miners in the Erz mountains of Central Europe
who suffered their fate before cigarette smoking began (in the
early 20th century). There is independent evidence against a
smoking-radon synergism from the studies of the Japanese A-bomb
survivors: the difference in lung cancer rates between those

with very low and very high exposure is the same for
non-smokers, although the percentage increase is only 40% for
smokers vs 200% for non-smokers. If there were a synergism, the
percentage increase should be similar for the two groups. It
may also be noted that the male/female ratio of excess lung cancer
from radiation was about unity, whereas that ratio in the general
population was about 3, due to heavier smoking by males. If
there were a strong synergism, these ratios should be the same.

Another basic assumption in the high level vs low level radon
comparison was that the percentage of lung cancers that are SCU
cell type does not decrease with decreasing dose. The evidence
for this is that among the uranium miner victims, the fraction of
the excess lung cancers that were SCU was 77% for the lowest dose
group, 68% for the intermediate dose group, and 68% for the highest
dose group.[37]

The above outlined evidence would seem to justify the conclusion that a linear dose-effect relationship normalized to the high
dose data on miners over-estimates the effects of environmental
radon exposure by a factor of 10.

The reason why this test is so sensitive is that average environmental radon exposures are quite high, well over 1 rem/year
to the bronchial epithelium. The lowest dose range for which there
is significant evidence on the linearity hypothesis is leukemia
caused by natural background gamma rays, levels of about
0.1 rem/year. Radiation induced leukemia is much better understood
than other types of radiocarcinogenesis because it develops much
sooner after exposure; thus we know the age dependence rather
well. It has been rather easily diagnosed since the 1890s, which
allows us to go back in time to the early years of this century
when it was a much rarer disease than it is now. It is therefore
possible to establish that a linear dose-effect relationship
normalized to the high dose data on Japanese A-bomb survivors and
radiation therapy patients requires that essentially all of the
leukemia observed among 20-35 year old British females in the
1911-20 time period was due to natural environmental gamma ray
exposure.[36] This is evidence that the linear hypothesis does not
under-estimate effects of radiation levels in the 2-3 rem range.

Latent Period Increases with Decreasing Dose

An entirely separate reason for believing that the linear
hypothesis is conservative derives from evidence that the latent
period for radiocarcinogenesis, the delay between radiation exposure and development of cancer symptoms, increases as radiation

dose decreases. There is evidence for this from many animal experiments.[26,31,38-42] For example, dogs injected with ^{239}Pu,
^{228}Th, and ^{226}Ra such that their total dose to the bone was not
more than 5000 rem did not develop bone cancer until they reached
an age when they would normally die of other causes.[40]

There is evidence on this effect from human data for the group
of German ankylosing spondylitis patients injected with ^{224}Ra,[43]
for skin cancer in Japanese radiological workers,[44] and for the
U.S. radium dial painters.[45]

If the latent period increases with decreasing dose at the
rate indicated by these data, at low doses this latent period will
far exceed the normal life span so there will be no cancers caused
by low level radiation.

"NEW EVIDENCE" INDICATING LINEAR HYPOTHESIS UNDER-ESTIMATES EFFECTS

The news media have recently given heavy publicity to several
reports from different sources purporting to indicate that the
linear hypothesis grossly under-estimates health effects of low
level radiation. Let us consider these reports, treating each
in a separate section.

Mancuso-Stewart-Kneale (MSK) Studies of Hanford Workers

Probably the best known report of the type under discussion
is a study of the effects of occupational radiation exposure to
workers at the Hanford Laboratory (near Richland, WA) by Mancuso,
Stewart, and Kneale,[46,47] which we refer to hereafter as MSK. It
is based essentially on the 3500 male deaths from the work force
of 25,000, searching for correlations between causes of death
as obtained from death certificates and radiation exposures as
recorded by film badges. MSK found that those who died of cancer
had slightly higher radiation doses than those who died of other
causes — 2.1 rad vs 1.6 rad, and that those who received more
radiation more frequently had cancer as their cause of death.
Note that these statements do not necessarily imply that those who
received more radiation had a larger probability of dying of
cancer. In fact that is not the case, at least within the statistical accuracy of the available data[48]: the age-adjusted cancer
mortality rates per year per thousand white males aged 25-70 were
1.7±0.4 for 0-2 rem exposure, 2.1±0.8 for 2-5 rem, and 1.4±0.6
for >5 rem, as compared to 2.1 for the total U.S. population
(± denotes 95% confidence limits). There are some tricky aspects
in considering only those who have died in that no consideration

is given to the great majority of those exposed since they are still
alive. Moreover, a higher proportion dying of cancer can mean
either a higher probability of cancer death or a lower probability
of dying from other causes.

MSK break their data down in various ways, and when this is
done they obviously find some ages, some employment periods, some
time interval between exposure and death, etc., which give larger
results than average. This especially applies to types of cancer;
for example, they find large excesses for cancer of the bone
marrow (22 observed vs 13.4 expected), pancreas (49 obs. vs
37.3 exp.), and lung (192 obs. vs 144 exp.); they give no further
consideration to types where results are in the opposite direction,
as for lymphatic leukemia (3 obs. vs 9.4 exp.), other RES neoplasms (5 obs. vs 20.3 exp.), and genito-urinary cancers
(15 obs. vs 30.9 exp.).

Since the difference in radiation dose between cancer and
non-cancer deaths is so small and they explain the entire effect
by these small differences, they naturally find very small "doubling doses". Some of these are listed in the following Table,[49]
in which we include also the results of their later revision

Cancer type	Number of Cases		Doubling Dose (rad)	
	total	due to rad.	Ref.46	Ref.47
Bone marrow	14	9.7	0.8	3.6
Pancreas	31	6.0	7.4	15.6
Lung	130	12.6	6.1	13.7
All RES	47	11.1	2.5	-
All cancer	442	25.8	12.2	33.7

The MSK work has drawn criticism from a wide variety of
sources.[49-66] We attempt here to summarize it only briefly.
There has been widespread criticism of the statistical methodology and handling of data; to cite one example, for multiple
myeloma there were 8 cases among men with <1 rem exposure and
3 cases with about 30 rem, and this was treated, using averaging,
as equivalent to 11 cases with 8 rem each. This procedure, plus
some non-standard disease grouping — "bone marrow" cancer is
not a standard classification — led to the estimate in our

Table of 9.7 radiation induced deaths due to bone marrow cancer whereas the 3 myeloma victims were the only ones with appreciable exposure.[57]

There was no consideration given to the "healthy worker" effect[48] — the fact that the Hanford workers had steady jobs means that they had less chronic disease than average which would result in their dying less frequently from some other causes and hence relatively more frequently from cancer. MSK used 1960 national statistics for comparisons, although most of the worker deaths occurred closer to 1970; since lung cancer was increasing rapidly over that period, this error alone explains their entire lung cancer effect.[61]

MSK paid no attention to the fact that dose correlates with many other factors such as years of service, job type, and socio-economic class, and these in turn correlate with exposures to other carcinogens and to general mortality from cancer; for example, technicians were exposed to much more radiation than office workers, and they were also exposed to far more chemical carcinogens. Several critics pointed to lack of increased leukemia incidence as a strong point against the validity of the study. It was never made very clear what MSK meant by "doubling dose" as regards the role of natural background radiation, and in fact the derivation of doubling doses below total background exposure has a ring of unreality.

At least two independent analyses were made of the Hanford worker data used by MSK,[48,61] and they each concluded that the only results worthy of consideration were those for cancer of the pancreas and multiple myeloma. For the former there were 5 cases with exposures above 10 rad vs 1.4 expected, and for the latter there were 3 cases vs 0.4 expected;[61] for exposures above 15 rem there were 3 cases vs 1.0 expected for the former and 2 cases vs 0.4 expected for the latter.[48] These results are clearly not explainable as statistical fluctuations, although they could easily be due to a factor which correlates with radiation dose such as exposure to chemical carcinogens.

One way of deciding whether radiation is the causative agent is to check for evidence of these diseases among other groups exposed to radiation. Data on cancer of the pancreas among Japanese A-bomb survivors give a doubling dose well over 1000 rad.[66]

Data on multiple myeloma[67] are much more sparse — 4 cases vs 1.9 expected up to 1965 — but the doubling dose is of the order of 100 rad which is 30 times the MSK doubling dose for bone marrow cancers. The rate derived for the A-bomb survivors was 3×10^{-6} cases/man-rem. In studies of patients exposed in thorotrast treatments, the rate was only 0.25×10^{-6} cases/man-rem, and among the German patients treated for ankylosing spondylitis with ^{224}Ra, there were 54 bone cancers but no cases of multiple myeloma which corresponds to less than 0.04×10^{-6} cases/man-rem.[68] Castleman searched the X-ray exposure history of multiple myeloma patients, and found no correlations.[69]

By very complicated and questionable procedures, MSK derived a doubling dose for all cancers as 12.2 rad,[46] later revised to 33.7 rad.[47] The data from the Japanese A-bomb survivors for all cancers except leukemia[34] indicate a doubling dose of about 800 rad.[66] It should be noted that MSK make no effort to compare their results with those for the Japanese A-bomb survivors or with any of the other groups with high radiation exposure.

The reaction to MSK of the prestigious national and international groups charged with evaluating health effects of radiation has been cool. The minutes of the Stockholm meeting of ICRP states "the Commission has concluded that the information available up to May 1978 does not call for changes in the risk factor given in ICRP Publication 26". The latter was published in Jan. 1977 and MSK was published in Nov. 1977. They made no mention of MSK.

The United Kingdom National Radiological Protection Board[49] report on MSK concludes "Despite the claims of the authors, a wide body of experts agree that there is no evidence in the Hanford data to support the suggestion that ICRP [26] values do seriously underestimate the risk."

The National Academy of Sciences BEIR Committee 1979 report has not yet appeared, but in a press conference it was stated that it found "no substance" in the MSK work.

Rotblat Comments on A-bomb Survivor Data

Rotblat has pointed out[70] that the survivors of the A-bomb attacks on Japan are a select group in that they survived the injuries and trauma of the attack. He points out that for some types of cancer, evidence from medical patients treated with radiation indicates higher risks, and explains the difference as due to the fact that the A-bomb survivors are such a select group. He does not seem to consider the fact that the medical patients are also a select group in that they are already suffering from another serious disease. He concludes that if there had been no early deaths from injuries and trauma in the original bombing episodes, the cancer deaths from radiation would have been five times higher.

It is interesting to point out that the Rotblat effect should
be very much larger for the high dose cases than for the low dose
cases, since the former were close to ground zero while the latter
were far away and thus much less likely to be directly injured by
the blast, heat, and other effects of the bomb.[71] Thus, if Rotblat
is correct, the high dose data would be moved up by an order of
magnitude while the low dose data would be little affected. This
would give a curve very much concave upward. In any case, the
effects of low doses would not be much changed.

The Rotblat thesis has not been accepted by the prestigious
evaluation groups, and there has been little indication of significant acceptance by the Scientific Community.

Najarian Studies of Workers at Portsmouth Navy Yard

Thomas Najarian, a physician practicing in Boston, got the
impression from discussions with patients, that there might be an
excess of leukemia among workers at the Portsmouth (NH) Naval
shipyard where nuclear ships are serviced, and suspected that it
might be due to their occupational radiation exposure. With the
help of a team of reporters from the Boston Globe, he searched
through 90,000 death certificates and found 1700 former Portsmouth
workers. Of these, 22 died of leukemia as compared with only 5
expected, according to the Feb. 1978 story in the Boston Globe;
according to a more scientific account published in Lancet,[72]
there were 1450 workers identified, and among these there were 20
leukemias vs 10.8 expected. The latter number is subject to considerable variation for specific groups: for Rhode Island males,
the leukemia rate is 23% above the U.S. average. Age distribution
is also a sensitive parameter,[73] as the leukemia rate increases
rapidly with increasing age — the average age of Portsmouth
workers is clearly above the average age of all males which
includes children, and it was not explained how the "expected"
number was derived. It is also well known that rates for various
cancer types show strong occupational correlations; in a study
in Washington State,[74] poultrymen were found to have over double
the average leukemia rate, and such diverse groups as dairymen,
bankers, and bus drivers also seemed to suffer far above average
leukemia rates.

Najarian attempted to separate out radiation workers by
asking their close relatives whether they remembered them wearing
film badges, a somewhat marginal methodology. He thereby identified 146 radiation worker deaths among which there were 6 leukemias vs 1.1 expected.

At this stage, data finally became available on doses measured
with film badges, and it turned out that only 3 of the 6 radiation
worker leukemia victims had any radiation exposure, and the average
exposure for the group was 1.3 rem. This raises the question of
the role of natural and X-ray radiation, which exposed the average
worker to about 10 rem by the time of his death. How is it possible
that 10 rem causes at most 1.1 leukemias, whereas an extra 1.3 rem
to make the total 11.3 rem causes 6 leukemias? No imaginable
dose-effect relationship could explain such a situation, especially
in view of the variability of natural radiation with geography
which is not correlated with leukemia rates.

It may be noted that there are many chemical carcinogens in
a shipyard environment, including benzene and other organic sol-
vents, welding debris, and asbestos.

On June 19, 1979, Najarian, appearing before Sen. Edward
Kennedy's subcommittee, withdrew most of his claims, and those
not withdrawn were heavily criticized in other testimony. As
reported in the Boston Globe which first promoted Najarian's work,
a highly agitated Sen. Kennedy chided Najarian with "I don't think
we ought to be alarming families unduly...we have seen you repudiate
two areas of your study, and the National Cancer Institute has re-
pudiated the third".[75]

Bross-Re-analysis of Tri-State Study

Bross and collaborators[76] reported a re-analysis of the well
known "Tri-State Study" carried out in NY, MD, and MN in 1959-62.
They emphasize that different people respond to radiation in
different ways, and attempt to take this into account by considering 5 different categories of people — this multiplies the number
of parameters available for adjustment by 5. They then consider
the triple correlation between number of X-rays received, cancer,
and heart disease. They treat the problem with what they call a
new statistical methodology, which they explain only cursorily.
They finally conclude that the linear hypothesis under-estimates
the effects of low level radiation by an order of magnitude.

Immediately following the Bross article in American Journal
of Public Health, there was a scathing critique of it by Boice and
Land[77] of National Cancer Institute. It is ironic that the New
York Times published a long article on the Bross paper,[78] but
made no mention whatsoever of the Boice-Land critique. If there
is a question of relative credibility, it should be pointed out
that Bross has a long record of anti-nuclear political activism,
whereas their critics have not participated politically in the
nuclear debate.

Boice and Land questioned the Bross statistical methodology and method of choosing parameters (the latter seems to be highly arbitrary). They note that there are clearly too many parameters for the individual values of each to have statistical significance. They point out that there is a great deal of independent evidence that radiation does <u>not</u> cause heart disease; for example, among the Japanese A-bomb survivors, there is no more heart disease among those exposed to >200 rad than among those with less than 1 rad exposure.

They point out many problems in the data collection process: X-rays may have been given for a pre-leukemic disease — half of all X-rays were made within the five years previous to development of leukemia; most information was obtained from interviews with relatives, a generally unreliable source, with a strong tendency to look for causes; there may well have been a tendency for interviewers to probe harder for radiation information on those whom they knew to be leukemia victims than on controls; and the dosimetry was very crude. They also point out that the Bross analysis considers only 206 of the 399 cases in the Tri-State study, and gives no explanation for not considering the others.

The National Academy of Sciences BEIR Committee Report considered the Bross paper and reported in a press conference that it found "no substance" in the work.

The 1979 paper by Bross and collaborators is the culmination of a series of previous papers re-analyzing the Tri-State Study.[78,79,80] Details of the Bross 1972 paper were critiqued by MacMahon[81] and by Mole.[82]

REFERENCES

1. NAS (National Academy of Sciences) "The Effects on Populations of Exposure to Low Levels of Ionizing Radiation", Washington, DC, (1972).
2. UNSCEAR (United Nations Scientific Com. on Effects of Atomic Radiation), "Sources and Effects of Ionizing Radiation", United Nations, New York, (1977).
3. J.F. Fowler and J. Denekamp, Chapter 5, p.139, <u>in</u>: "Cancer", S.S. Becker, ed., Plenum Publishing Co., New York (1977).
4. D. Grahn, R.J.M. Fry, and R.A. Lea, Volume X, <u>in</u>: "Life Sciences and Space Research," A.C. Strickland, ed., Akademie-Verlag, Berlin (1972).
5. C.J. Shellabarger, V.P. Bond, G.E. Aponte, and E.P. Cronkite, Cancer Res. 26:509 (1966).
6. A.C.Upton, et al., Rad. Res. 41, 467 (1970).

7. R. H. Mole, Brit. Jour. of Radiology, 32:497 (1959).
8. H. Speiss and C.W. Mays, in "Radionuclide Carcinogenesis,"
    C.L. Sanders et al, ed., USAEC Report CONF-720505, p.437
    (1973).
9. J.M. Brown, Health Phys. 31:231 (1976).
10. W.L. Russell, Peaceful Uses of Atomic Energy, IAEA Publ.
    ST1/PUB 1300, Vol. 13, p. 487, Vienna (1972).
11. D.E. Lea, "Actions of Radiation on Living Cells," Cambridge
    Univ. Press, London (1955).
12. S. Wolff, p. 157, in: "Radiation Protection and Recovery,"
    A. Hollaender, ed., Macmillan, New York (1961).
13. B.W. Fox and L.G. Lajtha, Brit. Med. Bul. 29:16 (1973).
14. M.M. Elkind and J.L. Redpath, Chapter 3, p. 51, in: "Cancer,"
    S.S. Bicker, ed., Plenum Publishing Co., New York (1977).
15. United Nations Scientific Com. on Effects of Atomic Rad.,
    "Ionizing Radiation: Levels and Effects," United Nations,
    New York (1972).
16. R.A. McGrath and R.W. Williams, Nature 212:534 (1966).
17. C.D. Town, K.C. Smith, and H.S. Kaplan, Radiation Res. 52:99
    (1973).
18. John Marshall (Argonne National Lab), private communication
    (1978).
19. M.M. Elkind, G.F. Whitmore, "The Radiobiology of Cultured
    Mammalian Cells," Gordon and Breach, New York (1967).
20. A.M. Kellerer & H.H. Rossi, Current Topics in Radiation Re-
    search, 8:85 (1972).
21. ICRP (International Commission on Radiological Protection),
    Report of Committee II on Permissible Dose for Internal
    Radiation, ICRP Publication 2, Pergamon Press, NY (1959).
22. E. Schmid, G. Rimpe, and M. Bauchinger, Rad. Res. 57:228
    (1973).
23. A.M. Kellerer and H.H. Rossi, Vol. 1, p. 405, in: "Cancer,"
    F.F. Becker, ed., Plenum Publ. Co., NY (1975).
24. A.C. Upton, Cancer Res. 21:717 (1961).
25. M.P. Finkel and B.O. Biskis, Prog. Exp. Tumor Res. 10:72
    (1968).
26. F.J. Burns, R.E. Albert, R.D. Heimbach, Rad. Res. 36:225
    (1968).
27. P. Maldague, in:"Radiation Induced Cancer," IAEA, Vienna,
    (1969).
28. C.W. Mays, T.F. Dougherty, G.N. Taylor, B.J. Stover, W.S.S.
    Jee, W.R. Christensen, J.H. Dougherty, W.Stephens, and
    C. Nabors, Hearings on Env. Effects of Producing Electric
    Power, Joint Com. on Atom. En., U.S. Congress, Vol. II,
    Part 2, p. 2192 (1970).
29. C.W. Mays and R.D. Lloyd, in "Biochemical Implications of
    Radiostrontium Exposure," M. Goldman and L.K. Bustad, eds.,
    USAEC Report CONF-710201 (1972).

30. J.B.Storer in "Cancer," F.F. Becker, ed., Plenum Publ. Co.,
     New York, 453 (1975).

31. C.J. Shellabarger, V.P. Bond, E.P. Cronkite, and G.E. Aponte,
     in: "Radiation Induced Cancer," IAEA, Vienna, p.61 (1969).

32. C.W. Mays, Argonne National Lab Symposium on "National Energy
     Issues - Plutonium as a Test Case," R.G. Sachs, ed., Sept.
     (1978).

33. M.P. Finkel, B.O. Biskis, and P.B. Jenkins, in "Radiation In-
     duced Cancer," A. Ericson, ed., Int. At. En. Ag., Vienna,
     p. 369 (1969).

34. G.W. Beebe, H.Kato, and C.E. Land, Radiation Effects Research
     Found. Report RERF TR1-77 (1977).

35. R.E. Rowland, A.F. Stehney, and H.F. Lucas, Rad. Res. 76:368
     (1978).

36. A.F. Cohen and B.L. Cohen, Tests of the Linearity Assumption
     in the Dose-Effect Relationship for Radiation-Induced
     Cancer, Health Physics 38:53-69 (1980).

37. V.E. Archer, G.Saccomanno, and J.H. Jones, Cancer 34:2056
     (1974).

38. A.C. Upton, Nat'l. Cancer Inst. Monog. 14:221 (1964).

39. E.V. Hulse, Brit. Jour. Cancer 21:531 (1967).

40. T.F. Dougherty and C.W. Mays, in "Radiation Induced Cancer,"
     Int. At. En. Agency (1969). Paper IAEA-SM-118/3, p.361.

41. O.Hug, W.Gossner, W.A. Muller, A.Luz, and B.Hindringer, in
     "Radiation Induced Cancer," IAEA, Vienna, p.393 (1969).

42. A.Nilsson, Acta Radiol. Ther. Phys. Biol. 9:155 (1970).

43. C.W. Mays, H.Speiss, and A.Gerspach, Health Physics 35:83
     (1978).

44. T.Kitabatake, T.Watanabe, and S.Koga, Strahlentherapie
     146:599 (1973).

45. R.D. Evans, Health Phys. 27:497 (1974).

46. T.F. Mancuso, A.Stewart, and G.Kneale, Health Phys. 33:369
     (1977). Referred to as MSK.

47. G.Kneale, A.Stewart, and T.F. Mancuso, IAEA Symposium on the
     Late Biological Effects of Ionizing Radiation, Vienna,
     March (1978).

48. E.S. Gilbert, Testimony for U.S. House of Representatives
     Subcommittee on Health and the Environment; also available
     as document PNL-SA-6341 Rev. (1978).

49. E.S. Gilbert, "Methods of Analyzing Mortality of Workers Ex-
     posed to Low-levels of Ionizing Radiation," Battelle
     Pacific Northwest Lab Report BNW1-SA-634, May (1977).

50. S.Marks, E.S.Gilbert, and B.D.Breitenstein, "Cancer Mortality
     in Hanford Workers," Int. Atomic En. Agency Document
     IAEA-SM-224. (1978).

51. A.Brodsky, Testimony for U.S. House of Representatives Sub-
     committee on Health and the Environment, Feb. 8 (1978).

52. L.A. Sagan, "Low Level Radiation Effects: The Mancuso Study,"
       Electric Power Research Institute Report (1978); Atom,
       No. 262, August (1978).
53. B.S. Sanders, Health Phys. 34:521 (1978).
54. D.J. Kleitman, "Critique of Mancuso-Stewart-Kneal Report,"
       Submission to U.S. Nuc. Reg. Com., March 2 (1978).
55. J.A. Reissland and G.W. Dolphin, Radiation Protection
       Bulletin No. 23, U.K.Natl. Rad. Prot. Bd., Harwell (1978).
56. Hon. Mr. Justice Parker, "The Windscale Inquiry," Her
       Majesty's Stationery Office, London, Jan. 26 (1978).
57. T.W. Anderson, Health Phys. (in print).
58. NRC (U.S. Nuc. Reg. Com.), Staff Committee Report of Nov.,
       (1976).
59. NRC (U.S. Nuc. Reg. Com.), Staff Committee Report of May,
       (1978).
60. D.Rubenstein, Report to U.S. Nuclear Regulatory Commission
       (1978).
61. G.B. Hutchinson, B.MacMahon, S.Jablon, and C.E. Land,
       Health Physics 37:207 (1979).
62. G.W.C. Tait, Health Phys. 37:251 (1979).
63. B.L. Cohen, Health Phys. 35:582 (1978).
64. R. Mole, Lancet 1978-I, p. 582 (1978).
65. S.M. Gertz, Health Phys. 35:723 (1978).
66. B.L. Cohen, "The Low-level Radiation Link to Cancer of the
       Pancreas," Health Phys. (in print).
67. H. Nishiyama, et al, Cancer 32: 1301 (1973).
68. C.W. Mays, private communication.
69. B.Castleman, private communication.
70. J.Rotblat, Bul. Atomic Scientists,September (1978).
71. B.L.Cohen, Bul. Atomic Scientists, February, p. 53 (1979).
72. T.Najarian and T.Colton, Lancet 1978-I, p.1018, (1978).
73. R.E. Lapp, "The Radiation Controversy," Reddy Communications,
       Greenwich, Connecticut (1979).
74. S.Milham, "Occupational Mortality in Washington State
       1950-71," Report to Dept. HEW-NIOSH, Cincinnati, April
       (1976).
75. S.Wermiel, "Doctors Shift on Shipyard: Kennedy Chides
       Portsmouth Researcher,"Boston Globe,June 20 (1979).
76. I.D.J.Bross, M.Ball, and S.Falen, Am. Jour. Pub. Health
       69:130 (1979).
77. J.D.Boice, and C.E.Land, Am. Jour. Pub. Health 69:137 (1979).
78. R.Gibson, I.D.J.Bross, et al, New Eng. J. Med. 279:906 (1968).
79. I.D.J.Bross and N.Natarajan, New Eng. J. Med., 287:107 (1972).
80. I.D.J.Bross and N.Natarajan, Jour. Am. Med. Assn. 237:2399
       (1977).
81. B.MacMahon, New Eng. Jour. Med. 287:144 (1972).
82. R.H.Mole, Brit. J. Cancer 30:199 (1974).

DISCUSSION

BENDER: I was puzzled in the original analysis of the Mancuso-
Stewart-Kneale report by the fact that not only did they calculate
doubling doses like three rem for particular cancers, but they also
calculated negative doubling doses for those cancers which were less
dose related. Obviously if you look at a group of cancers and just
subdivide them by class, sooner or later you are bound to find some
that statistically, for sampling reasons, are less frequent and some
that are more frequent. It seems a mistake to talk about multiple
myelomas, for example, as showing a significant increase in incidence.

COHEN: Of course, you can calculate the probability that the increase
was due to chance and in the case of multiple myelomas and cancer of
the pancreas the authors claimed that the probability it was due to
chance was very low -- something like one percent. With the same
statistical treatment, it did not appear anything quite that improbable among the ones where there was a deficiency. I think they
could have paid more attention to the deficiencies. This calls for
critical examination by a statistician.

SAGAN: I am addressing this comment particularly to people here in
this room who don't follow the radiation controversy carefully. This
last presentation suggests that there is a great deal of controversy
about low dose effects -- that we don't really understand what the
shape of the dose-response curve is at low doses. What is obscured
to the uninitiated is the fact that the effects are so low at those
doses that there are no detectable effects; the differences between
concave upward and concave downward models are extremely small.

     To take a realistic example, the predicted effect of the radi-
ation exposure resulting from the accident at Three Mile Island was
0.7 cases. Even taking the extreme models that Dr. Cohen just
presented that could rise to perhaps one case.

COHEN: No, much more. If you use the Mancuso-Stewart-Kneale doubling time, it would be over ten cases.

SAGAN: All right, but the point is that's a very small number.

BERG: Ten cases in sixty years.

SAGAN: Ten cases throughout the remaining lives of the people living
within fifty miles. That's 2.3 million people among which there are
expected some 300,000 cancers from spontaneous causes.

     So, even the extreme views of the data would suggest a range of
somewhere between zero and ten cases. That point tends to get lost.
People listening to a presentation of this kind might come away with

the notion that we really don't know anything about low level radiation. The point is that we know a great deal about radiation effects and that fact often tends to become obscured.

COHEN: I hoped I was giving the impression we do know a lot about it.

KATES: I am respectful of the thought that you put into this presentation, but it occurred to me that an outsider would have found
considerable discrepancy in the presentation of the two sides of the
controversy. For example, I think in the Mays data you say there
were seven studies that did this and three studies that did this and
one study that did this. You didn't pull them apart, but with the
Mancuso study you had this elaborate analysis.

     So the question I have is this: what do you think would be the
nature of an epidemiological study that would be supportive for the
majority hypothesis in which you would just respond by saying we will
have to suspend judgement and just wait until we get more studies?

COHEN: Mays reported on carefully designed animal studies.

KATES: I appreciate that, but describe to me what you would see as
the ideal kind of epidemiological study where you would just set it
aside and suspend judgement until we had considerably more studies.

COHEN: I don't think you should have one study and say that tells
us everything. I think you should look at the weight of evidence.

KATES: I am saying, with what study would you suspend judgement?

     I am not saying that you would conclude that it was so and throw
out the weight of evidence, but just set it aside and say I accept
that as a challenge study, but we need to do more; there will be more
information forthcoming in the future.

COHEN: In the Mancuso study, the conclusions did not stand up to
criticism. If they had, I would say that that would be a very important result, extremely important.

BERG: May I also speak to Dr. Sagan's point? I think that what he
said scientists are doing badly was exemplified in Dr. Cohen's
presentation. It's a temptation, when you grade essay exams and a
student hands you a confused answer, to spend a lot of extra time
grading it. We know it is not worth it, but we do it, and this is
what we have done here. We have discussed at great length a paper
which is so flawed that I use it in a graduate course as an example
of how not to edit a journal. Aside from problems with data, there
was no excuse for publishing oddball, novel statistics until the
manuscript was expanded to include an analysis of the same data with

conventional statistics. In the case of the MSK report, the missing
comparison was eventually published in the same journal by John
Gofman, and the doubling doses calculated by Stewart and Kneale's
method turned out to have no statistical significance. The confidence limits for estimates based on Mancuso's data included a range
from zero risk, through currently standard estimates, to the high
risks projected by MSK (J. W. Gofman, Health Physics 37:617, 1979;
see also Health Physics articles by B. S. Saunders, T. W. Anderson,
G. B. Hutchison et al., and G. W. Kneale, et al.).

Now, when a group of scientists such as ourselves pays all that
attention to numerology unsupported by independent data, that is not
trans-science. It is bad housekeeping.

COHEN: The New York Times Information Bank is computer-accessible.
I looked up Mancuso in it. There were eleven entries on Mancuso.
I looked up all the critiques. There was one entry. So, the picture
seen by the news media is very different.

INHABER: I wanted to pursue the point about the Colorado data. As
you probably know, Frigerio from Argonne some years back considered
the radiation levels in all American states and relative cancers,
subdividing it and so on. You are probably familiar with his graph.

COHEN: I have a graph of my own in my paper also. What it really
indicates is that the mountain states have lower cancer rates than
the rest of the country, but we don't have a suitable control group.
Almost everybody would say that's what it means. However, I used
to wonder what if it had come out the other way. What if cancer rates
in Colorado had been higher than the U.S. average? Now you don't
need to wonder any more, because it turns out there is a study in
Sweden which shows in the counties of Sweden there is a slight correlation between higher natural radiation and higher cancer rates
and the authors are saying this shows that low radiation causes
cancer. To them I say, how about the U.S. data? They offer no
rational answer.

ABRAHAMSON: Chuck Mays, of the University of Utah would always say
if you want to have less cancer, become a Mormon and live out in
Colorado or Utah because you live better and you have better medical
care. There are a lot of Mormons in Colorado, too.

BERG: Did you say that medical care prevents cancer?

ABRAHAMSON: You have a different lifestyle if you are a Mormon.

When you extrapolated expected lung cancers among uranium miners
and said "my number is less than I expected", did you already build
in an RBE value because the uranium miners were getting alpha radiation?

COHEN: All of them are exposures to radon. In fact, it is all done in working level months (WLM). You don't even have to convert from working level months to rem.

ALBERT: A technical point about that comparison of predicted and observed occurrence of small cell lung cancer. When you pointed out that there probably isn't that much of an effect of cigarette smoking, you used the Joachimsthal Schneeberg data as an example of very high yields of lung cancer in a population that was exposed to radon, but didn't smoke. I think it is worth pointing out that those mines had a lot of arsenic in them. As a matter of fact, for many years it was thought that the disease was due to arsenic and there is very convincing epidemiologic evidence to the effect that arsenic produces lung cancer.

So I wouldn't use that set of old data to argue about the lack of effect of cigarette smoking.

COHEN: Tell that to a BEIR III committee. There are all sorts of causes for cancer in mines. In my paper I have a list of about twenty things in mines that could cause lung cancer. The powers that be seem to have decreed that it was due to the radon.

CROW: I missed some point about this. How much is known about the miners themselves as to which ones smoked and which ones didn't?

COHEN: It is known. The earlier data seemed to show a very strong synergism between smoking and lung cancer.

Now the problem is that the later data have not been published. I don't have any direct access to them, but I've been told that that situation has turned around and the BEIR III report which is based mainly on new data gives only a 30% difference between smokers and non-smokers. Those are the numbers Edward Radford gave me, at least. Is that right Dr. Land?

LAND: As I recall, there aren't all that many uranium miners who don't smoke and that's the problem. These statistics do bounce around an awful lot. Every time you look at them they change.

COHEN: There are also data on other populations of miners, Swedish or British. At least Radford concluded that smoking was not very important.

BERG: What would happen to your projections if the high dose to the uranium miners was about double what it is estimated to be, and what would happen to your projections if the high dose to people who had myeloma was tripled or quadrupled? Let's take just those two outlying points and see what would happen if the high doses were shifted way up.

COHEN: In the case of lung cancers of miners, if the dose to these miners was doubled, that would mean that the discrepancy would be cut in half. Instead of the discrepancy being a factor of eight, it would be a factor of four or if you take that 30% difference for smoking, it would be a factor of three.

BERG: Now, in the case of myeloma?

COHEN: If the dose was twice as much?

BERG: It may be four times as much. It would begin to bring them in the range where you would, perhaps, expect some myelomas.

COHEN: Yes.

BERG: I do not think that the dosimetry was good in either case.

In the case of uranium miners, the lore out there is that the guys with the high doses, the old hands, had bootleg pits from which they took uranium ore and sold it on the side. They got whopping doses because they used crawl pits, but these doses were off the record. Also, if you look at the way the doses were recorded in the mine, those were not dosimeter readings, but estimates based on work station.

The experimental evidence is that when Dr. Donald Morken tried to give rats lung cancer with clean radon gas, he couldn't. You will probably find some uranium dust exposure in all experiments where radon exposures produced cancer in animals. On all these counts, the official estimates of the hazard of radon may be unduly inflated.

As to the doses associated with myeloma, I remember from the old days in Brookhaven that fellows on the spent fuel handling crew did not like to lose working time and made sure that their badges did not get exposed. Again, this was the case with the old hands who accumulated high doses. I remember when a friend from the crew walked into the radioiodine counting laboratory and the counters went off scale.

Perhaps you give too much credit to the official estimates of doses. Especially where the recorded doses are high, a check of the actual conditions of exposure will often show that the real doses were several times higher. Outlying data are just bad data unless double checked.

A SIMPLE THRESHOLD MODEL FOR THE CLASSICAL BIOASSAY PROBLEM

W. A. Thompson, Jr. and R. E. Funderlic

University of Missouri-Columbia and Union Carbide
Corporation-Oak Ridge

Statistics Department, University of Missouri, Columbia,
Missouri 65211 and Union Carbide Corporation, Nuclear
Research Department, Oak Ridge, Tennessee 37830

SUMMARY

A biologically motivated dose response model is proposed for
rough work where it is too difficult to take account of other
relevant factors such as timing of exposure and delay of response.
This model leads in a logical way to a Weibull dose response curve
with parameters which can be naturally interpreted in terms of
threshold and order of contact (for example linearity) in the low
dose range. The traditional logit and probit models do not allow
explicit study of these important issues. The several simple
alternative models are compared by fitting them to sets of data.
The Weibull does as well as but no better than the probit and logit
but these three are superior to the other alternatives considered.

INTRODUCTION

Consider that organisms are exposed to "doses" alleged to have
detrimental effect; the doses may, for example, be of radiation or
a chemical substance. The organism may or may not "respond," for
example, by developing a cancer. (Illustrations appear in Tables
1-6).

Determination of the true relation between response and dose
is an important but difficult task. It is important because it is
a basic issue in assessing the risk of an activity for safety or
health, and therefore it is of fundamental concern for the government regulation of industrial activity, nuclear generators for
instance.

It is difficult because it is interdisciplinary, bordering on biology, medicine, genetics, physics, and chemistry; it has a strong statistical component. Data is hard to obtain and frequently it is only indirectly to the point.

For cancer studies, what is needed is the effect on large human populations of normal doses of an alleged cancer causer. But we cannot perform experiments on humans and at normal doses cancers are events of low probability. Thus, at normal doses, a huge number of expensive test animals would have to be exposed to get any response at all. Further, if no response is observed in the experiment, we cannot infer that the dose is then safe for the human population; aside from the animal to man extrapolation, the human population will be much larger. A small increase in the probability of response could go unnoticed in the experiment and yet cause thousands of cancers in a population of perhaps two hundred million. So, test animals are subjected to mammoth doses, and it is inferred that substances which cause cancers in small numbers of animals at high doses will constitute a risk for large human populations at low doses. As we have seen in the saccharin study, the extent to which this risk extrapolation can be made is controversial. Success of such an extrapolation must depend on a knowledge of the structure of the dose-response relation.

Realistic determination of the dose-response relation is further complicated by the varied natures of dose and of response. The dose may be administered at roughly an instant, continuously over a long period of time, or at intervals. The response can occur immediately or it can consist of a general increase in the force of mortality subsequent to exposure. Whittemore and Keller (1978) present models which attempt to explain these more complex biological relationships and this is a worthwhile thing to do. But for some purposes simpler, more approximate models are needed. For example to determine the safety of fission reactors see Lewis (1980), a linearity hypothesis is used. This analysis adds exposures "linearly, independent of the number of people exposed, the length of the exposure, the dosage, or any other factor." This paper takes a similar view but considers dose and allows responses which are other than linear in the low dose range.

Here, we consider that organisms exposed to doses may or may not "respond" as in Tables 1-6. Let $\rho(x)$ be the true but unknown probability of response to dose x; $\rho(\cdot)$ is the true dose-response curve. Provisionally assume that $\rho(\cdot)$ is a specified function $p(\cdot)$. We sometimes find it convenient to express the model in terms of $q(x) = 1 - p(x)$.

For example, consider that n people are exposed to a total of E man-rems and that s latent fatal cancers result. If $p(x) = kx$ (for small x) then $s/n \simeq p(x) = kx = kE/n$ and $s \simeq kE$, the linearity hypothesis. But if $p(x) = kx^2$, say, then $s/n \simeq k(E/n)^2$ and $s = KE^2/n$, a slightly more complicated expression.

2. CHOICE OF FITTED DOSE-RESPONSE CURVE

Before introducing our threshold model we briefly review some of the simple competitors. For a general discussion of hit theory model building in the dose-response context see Turner (1975). Concerning hit theory, Rupert and Harm (1966) say: "Far from the passive targets pictured in the early days of radiation biology, cells must be viewed as actively meeting the challenge of radiation damage." An additional criticism is that one can demonstrate from hit-theory that thresholds do not exist; there is no positive dose level at which the probability of response is zero. Thus, either thresholds do not exist or hit-theory is an inadequate model, depending on your basic premise. One of the simpler classes of models to come from hit theory is the gamma with α a positive integer:

$$q(x) = \int_{x}^{\infty} \rho^{\alpha} z^{\alpha-1} \exp(-\rho z)/\Gamma(\alpha) \, dz,$$

$\rho > 0$, $x \geq 0$. The one hit model is the case $\alpha = 1$.

The traditional choice is the normal, see Finney (1964).

$$q(x) = 1 - \Phi[(x - \mu)/\sigma], \quad \sigma > 0$$

where

$$\Phi(x) = (2\pi)^{-\frac{1}{2}} \int_{-\infty}^{x} \exp(-t^2/2) \, dt.$$

The choice with the nice statistical properties, Cox (1970), is the logistic

$$q(x) = [1 + \exp(ax + b)]^{-1}, \quad a > 0. \tag{3}$$

We now wish to consider the following threshold model:

i)   an organism has a large number of critical targets,

ii) each target has a dose threshold (if threshold is exceeded, response occurs in that target),

iii)   a single target response results in organism response,

iv)   thresholds of targets are randomly chosen from some unknown initial distribution.

The critical targets might (or might not) be associated with cells or molecules. One explanation of ii) could be that the elimination or repair capacity of the target is overwhelmed. Assumption iii) would be the case, for example, if response were infectuous so that a single target response spreads through the organism. Thus, $q(x)$ is the probability that the minimum target threshold exceeds the dose. Since the number of targets is large, the probability of response should be well approximated by a minimum extreme value distribution, see Thompson (1969). There are three limiting minimum extreme value distributions: the exponential, Cauchy, and Weibull. Which of these limiting distributions would apply depends on the unknown initial distribution.

The Cauchy is an entirely unsatisfactory solution for this practical problem since it concentrates all probabilities on the negative axis but dose is a positive quantity. The double exponential

$$q(x) = \exp[-\exp(\frac{x - \xi}{\eta})], \eta > 0 \tag{4}$$

is a possibility since, although it does place some probability on the negative axis, that probability can be made small by choosing ξ large relative to η.

The best extreme value solution from a theoretical viewpoint is the Weibull

$$q(x) = \begin{cases} \exp[-(\frac{x - \beta}{\alpha})^{\gamma}], & x > \beta \\ 1 & , x \leq \beta \end{cases} \tag{5}$$

where $\alpha, \gamma > 0$ and $\beta \geq 0$. The parameters have the following interpretations: α is a scale parameter, β is an organism threshold since if dose is less than β then response has probability 0, γ is the "order of contact" of $p(x)$ at $x = \beta$ since

$$\lim_{x \to \beta+} p(x)/(\frac{x - \beta}{\alpha})^{\gamma} = 1.$$

This is the only part of our paper which is specific to low dose. In the neighborhood of threshold, probability of response is linear if $\gamma = 1$ or quadratic if $\gamma = 2$, but in contrast with hit theory, noninteger values of γ also make sense.

The Weibull is a frequently suggested model for continuous data, Peto et al. (1974), where one observes the time or dose at which response or failure occurs. But note that the data here is different: at a given dose we observe whether response occurs. The Weibull has previously been suggested by Chand and Hoel (1974) as a possible dose-response curve. Their derivation is an indirect argument involving the distribution time to cancer. Nor does our model seem to be equivalent to the familiar tolerancing model, Cox (1970), where individuals have dose tolerances below which they do not respond; the tolerences over individuals being distributed as, say, the Weibull distribution.

The models (2) and (3) assign positive probabilities of response to negative doses, an unpleasant feature. Probably for this reason the usual custom is to work with log-dose as independent variable. Thus (2) becomes the log-model ordinarily used in probit analysis

$$q(x) = 1 - \Phi[(\log x - \mu)/\sigma], \ \sigma > 0. \tag{6}$$

Similarly, the logit analysis model is

$$q(x) = [1 + \exp(a \log x + b)]^{-1}, \ a > 0. \tag{7}$$

Note that fitting a double exponential distribution to log-dose is equivalent to fitting a Weibull to dose.

The probit and logit analysis models (6) and (7) prejudge the question of whether a positive organism threshold might exist; for example, the only solution of $\Phi[\log x - \mu)/\sigma] = 0$ is $x = 0$. Of the curves discussed so far, the Weibull (5) is the only one which allows explicit study of the important and open issues of organism threshold and linearity in the low dose range and these arise in a natural way. A current regulatory view that thresholds do not exist, Maugh (1978), corresponds to taking $\beta = 0$ so that we have a two parameter Weibull distribution. We can, of course, introduce a threshold parameter into models (6) and (7). For example, the three parameter probit would be

$$q(x) = \begin{cases} 1 - \Phi\{[\log(x - \beta) - \mu]/\sigma\}, & x > \beta \\ 1 & , \ x \le \beta \end{cases} \tag{8}$$

3.   FITTING DOSE-RESPONSE CURVES

The experimental setup is that n_j organisms are exposed to dose x_j and R_j responses are observed ($j = 1,\ldots,g$); responses at different doses are independent and binomially distributed. Let $p(x_j) = p_j$. Having observed r_j responses and $f_j = n_j - r_j$ non-responses at dose x_j, then the log likelihood is, apart from a constant,

$$\ell = \sum_{\{j:r_j > 0\}} r_j \log \rho_j + \sum_{\{j:f_j > 0\}} f_j \log(1 - \rho_j).$$

Maximum likelihood estimates will be obtained by maximizing ℓ.

The unconstrained parameter space is $\Omega = \{(\rho_1, \ldots, \rho_g\}$ and the unconstrained maximum is

$$\max_{\Omega} \ell = \sum_{\{j:r_j > 0\}} r_j \log(r_j/n_j) + \sum_{\{j:f_j > 0\}} f_j \log(f_j/n_j). \quad (9)$$

This is the best that we can do; no fitted curve can yield a value of ℓ which is larger than this. The best that we can do, fitting a monotone nondecreasing function, $p(x)$, is obtained by maximizing ℓ subject to this constraint. This last can be accomplished by pooling methods explained in Barlow et al. (1972).

The best fitting dose-response curve of the specified form $p(\cdot)$ will be obtained by maximizing ℓ over the subset $\omega = \{(p(x), \ldots, p(x_g)\}$. The likelihood ratio statistic for testing goodness of fit is

$$\log \lambda = \max_{\omega} \ell - \max_{\Omega} \ell$$

and $-2 \log \lambda$ approaches a χ^2 statistic as all n's approach infinity. The degrees of freedom equals g minus the number of fitted parameters.

A similar test of whether the Weibull threshold parameter is positive would be based on the increase of log likelihood in going from three to two parameters. The test statistic would have a single degree of freedom.

4.   THE DATA SETS AND THEIR ANALYSES

From Totter and Finamore (1978) we have found eight sets of data which are sufficiently complete and of the desired form; these data sets appear in Tables 1-6. The optimum likelihoods appear in Tables 7 and 8. To save on minus signs these tables contain the negative of the log of the maximum likelihood so that the smaller tabled values indicate the better fits. The column labeled "Monotone" indicates the best that we can hope for. Examination of Tables 7 and 8 shows that the Weibull (5), probit (6, 8), and logit (7) can be made to fit each set of data about equally well but uniformly better than the other alternatives examined. It appears not to make any difference which of these three models we attempt to fit to data of this kind. The goodness of fit and threshold tests

Table 1.   Data Set 1.

Number of sperms with chromosomal aberrations.[a]

Dosage (1000 r)	Number of breaks	Normal sperm	Total
1	12	319	331
2	24	253	277
3	193	532	725
4	64	151	215
5	87	130	217

[a]Taken from Baur and Kaufmann (1938).

Table 2.   Data set 2.

Summarized results on tumor incidence of mice injected with methylcholanthrene[a].

Dose (mg.)	Mice injected	Mice with tumors
.00024	79	0
.00098	41	0
.00195	19	0
.0039	19	0
.0078	17	3
.0156	18	6
.031	20	13
.062	21	17
.125	21	21
.25	21	21
.5	21	21
1.0	20	20

[a]Taken from Bryan and Shimkin (1943).

Table 3. Summarized results obtained on tumor incidence of
mice injected with dibenzathracene and benzpyrene[a]

| | Data set 3. | | Data set 4. | |
| | dibenzanthracene | | benzpyrene | |
Dose (mg.)	Mice injected	Mice with tumors	Mice injected	Mice with tumors
.00195	79	2	81	2
.0078	40	6	40	0
.0156	19	6	19	0
.031	21	16	16	0
.062	20	20	20	4
.125	23	21	19	15
.25	21	19	21	14
.5	21	20	19	19
1.0	22	22	20	18
2.0	19	19	19	19
4.0	20	17	19	16
8.0	21	16	21	20

[a]Taken from Bryan and Shimkin (1943).

Table 4. Data Set 5.

Lymphoid tumor incidence[a].

Dose (roentgens)	Number of mice	Number of lymphomas
283	24	3
336	26	4
400	35	8
475	29	12
566	10	4

[a]Taken from Kaplan and Brown (1952).

Table 5.   Data Set 6.

Neoplasms induced by single application of
benzo[a]pyrene on mice[a]

Benzo[a]pyrene applied (mg.)	Number of mice treated	Number of mice responding
0	7	0
94	14	1
188	14	1
376	13	2
752	13	3
3008	11	5

[a]Taken from Poel (1959).

Table 6.   Occurrence of mammary carcinoma in mice fed varying
concentrations of diethylstilbestrol (DES) in the diet[a]

	Data Set 7.		Data Set 8.	
	C_3H males		Strain A castrate males	
DES (ppb)[b]	Number of mice	Number with tumors	Number of mice	Number with tumors
0	115	0	136	0
6.25	59	0	78	0
12.5	58	1	78	1
25	62	0	70	2
50	62	3	77	3
100	60	3	74	6
500	60	23	52	7
1000	71	30	76	15

[a]Taken from Gass, Coats, and Graham (1964).

Table 7.   Minus log maximum likelihood.

Data Set	g	Unconstrained (9)	Monotone	Normal (2)	Logistic (3)	exponential (4)	gamma (1)
			MODEL				
1	5	830.4	830.4	843.3	845.8	848.1	836.6
2	12	42.6	42.6	54.7	55.9	61.0	45.0
3	10[b]	67.0	68.6	116.2	110.2	128.3	85.2
4	10[b]	49.0	52.1	90.2	82.6	102.0	64.8
5	5	65.4	65.4	65.9	a	66.0	65.9
6	6	27.4	27.4	28.5	a	28.7	
7	8	117.3	118.0	132.9	a	137.3	
8	8	106.2	106.2	114.8	a	115.4	

[a]Preliminary plot shows poor fit.

[b]Omitting the last two points.

of the previous section are outlined in Table 8. Small observed significance level indicates lack of fit. Excellent fits are obtained for data sets 2, 6, and 8. But we have not been able to fit all data sets. In fact, for data sets 3 and 4, response is not increasing with dose and this effect is sufficiently pronounced that we judge it is not due to chance. For this reason we omit the last two data points in our analysis of sets 3 and 4. Essentially we think that data sets 3 and 4 represent a different kind of easily explained biological phenomena which goes beyond our story but we retain them for completeness.

The maxima for the various distributions and data sets in Tables 7 and 8 were obtained by use of Brent's (1973) optimization routine PRAXIS. The calculations were carried out in Fortran on a Digital Equipment PDP-10 using a Stanford University version of PRAXIS.

For the Weibull distribution threshold test, small observed significance level indicates positive threshold. Data set 2 appears to have a positive threshold.

The estimated Weibull parameters appear in Table 9. Note that estimated threshold is generally small. Probability of response near threshold is close to linear except perhaps for data set 5. Values of γ occur on both sides of 1.

Table 8. Minus log maximum likelihood and observed significance level

MODEL

Data Set	g	Unconstrained (9)	Monotone	2 parameter			3 parameter		2 vs. 3 parameter Weibull
				probit (6)	logit (7)	Weibull (5)	probit (8)	Weibull (5)	
1	5	830.4	830.4	835.5 .017	836.1 .010	837.2 .004	835.5 .006	835.9 .004	.107
2	12	42.6	42.6	44.3 .996	45.1 .891	45.5 .832	44.2 .956	43.3 .998	.036
3	10[a]	67.0	68.6	75.7 .026	74.2 .072	83.0 .000	75.5 .017	78.7 .001	.003
4	10[a]	49.0	52.1	65.2 .000	62.4 .001	64.7 .000	65.2 .000	64.7 .000	1.0
5	5	65.4	65.4	65.9 .801	65.8 .849	65.9 .801	65.9 .607	65.9 .607	1.0
6	6	27.4	27.4	27.5 .995	27.5 .995	27.5 .995	27.5 .978	27.5 .978	1.0
7	8	117.3	118.0	120.2 .446	120.6 .359	121.0 .285	120.2 .326	120.9 .206	.729
8	8	106.2	106.2	107.2 .920	107.5 .857	107.5 .857	106.4 .995	106.7 .963	.201

[a]Omitting the last two points.

Table 9.   Estimated parameters of fitted Weibull
            dose-response curves

Data Set	3 parameter			2 parameter	
	α	β	γ	α	γ
1	7.52	.607	1.15	7.11	1.58
2	.028	.004	.937	.036	1.37
3[a]	.036	.002	.615	.048	.772
4[a]	.218	.000	.946	.218	.945
5	589	109	1.75	672	2.4
6	6592	.002	.645	6307	.656
8	1436	6.25	.938	1573	.952
9	10894	6.25	.579	10986	.607

[a]Omitting the last two points.

We wish to thank D. G. Gosslee, V. R. R. Uppuluri, and J. R. Totter for introducing us to the problem and its literature.

REFERENCES

Barlow, R. E., Bartholomew, D. J., Bremner, J. M., and Brunk, H. D., 1972, "Statistical Inference Under Order Restrictions," Wiley, New York.

Bauer, H. and Kaufmann, B. P., 1938, X-ray induced chromosomal alterations in drosophila melanogaster, Genetics, 23:610-30.

Brent, R. P., 1973, "Algorithms for Minimization without Derivatives," Prentice Hall, New Jersey.

Bryan, W. R. and Shimkin, M. B., 1943, Quantitative analysis of dose-response data obtained with three carcinogenic hydorcarbons in strain C3# male mice, J. of the Nat. Cancer Inst., 3:503-31.

Chand, N. and Hoel, D. G., 1974, A comparison of models for determining safe levels of environmental agents, Reliability and Biometry, F. Proschan and R. J. Serfling, eds., 681-700. SIAM.

Cox, D. R., 1970, "The Analysis of Binary Data," Methuen, London.

Finney, D. J., 1964, "Probit Analysis," Cambridge, New York.

Gass, G. H., Coats, D., and Graham, N., 1964, Carcinogenic dose-response curve to oral diethylstilbesterol, J. of the Nat. Cancer Inst., 33:971-77.

Kaplan, H. S. and Brown, M. B., 1952, A quantitative dose-response study of lymphoid-tumor development in irradiated C57 black mice, J. of the Nat. Cancer Inst., 13:185-208.

Lewis, H. W., 1980, The safety of fission reactors, Sci. Amer., 242: 53-65.

Mann, N. R., Schafer, R. E., and Singpurwall, N. D., 1974, "Methods for Statistical Reliability and Life Data," Wiley, New York.

Maugh, T. H., 1978, Chemical carcinogens: How dangerous are low doses?, Science, 202:37-41.

Peto, R., Lee, P. N., and Paige, W. S., 1972, Statistical analysis of the bioassay of continuous carcinogens, Br. J. of Cancer, 26:258-61.

Poel, W. G., 1959, Effect of carcinogenic dosage and duration of exposure on skin-tumor induction in mice, J. of the Nat. Cancer Inst., 22:19-43.

Rupert, C. S. and Harm, W., 1966, Reactivation after photobiological damage, Advances in Radiation Biology, 2:2-75.

Thompson, W. A., Jr., 1969, "Applied Probability," Holt, Rinehart and Winston, New York.

Totter, J. R. and Finamore, F. J., 1978, "Dose Responses to Cancerogenic and Mutagenic Treatments," Oak Ridge Associated Universities, Oak Ridge.

Turner, M. E., Jr., 1975, Some classes of hit-theory models, Math. Biosciences, 23, 219-35.

Whittemore, A. and Keller, J.B., 1978, Quantitative theories of carcinogenesis, SIAM Review, 20:1-30.

A BIOLOGICAL BASIS FOR THE LINEAR NON-THRESHOLD DOSE-RESPONSE RELATIONSHIP FOR LOW-LEVEL CARCINOGEN EXPOSURE

Roy E. Albert, M.D.

Institute of Environmental Medicine
New York University Medical Center
New York, N.Y. 10016

There is no escaping the need to quantitatively assess the risks from low-level carcinogen exposure in order to judge how much regulatory effort is appropriate to reduce cancer hazards to acceptable levels. However, it is clearly recognized that the levels of exposure and the associated cancer risks from contamination of the environment by carcinogens are almost invariably far below the level which are directly measurable either by animal experiments or epidemiological studies in exposed human populations. We are therefore forced to use mathematical extrapolation models to define the relationship between dose and effect at levels which can never be ascertained directly. There are a number of mathematical extrapolation models which fit dose-response data for tumor induction and yet which predict risks differing by order of magnitude at very low levels of exposure.[1] None of these models has a sound basis in biological fact since we do not understand the pathogenesis of neoplasia at the cellular level. Perhaps the most plausible is the linear non-threshold dose-response model which was first adopted for use in the assessment of cancer risks from ionizing radiation[2] and then more recently from chemical carcinogens.[3] Its plausibility rests largely on the association between tumorigenicity and mutagenicity as common manifestations of genotoxicity and the linearity at low dose levels of the dose-response relationships for mutagenicity by ionizing radiation[4] and chemicals.[5] There are a few epidemiological studies, particularly in the radiation field, which show a consistency with a linear dose-response relationship at low doses such as those involving breast cancer[6] and leukemia.[7] Few animal tumorigenesis studies have been done on a sufficiently large scale to adequately define the shape of the dose-response relationships at relatively

535

low levels of exposure. The very large ED_{01} study with 2-acetyl-
aminofluorene did, however, show linearity in the dose-response
pattern for liver tumors in the mouse, but a response which was
sharply curvilinear upward for tumors of the bladder in the same
strain.[8]

In our laboratory we have examined low-level dose-response
relationships in terms of the two-stage mouse tumorigenesis model.
This represents an attempt to dissect the tumorigenic process into
its component parts and to characterize the quantitative aspects
of the dose-response relationships for each of the separate components and thus hopefully to obtain the basis for characterizing
responses at levels below those which can be observed directly.
The mouse skin is a model which readily lends itself to the
approach of dissecting the tumorigenic process using a polycyclic
aromatic carcinogen and the promoting agent phorbol myristate
acetate (PMA). The general properties of the initiation-promotion
model in mouse skin have been thoroughly described.[9] The
characteristics of the model are the following: mouse skin can be
initiated by a single carcinogen exposure at dose levels which are
virtually non-tumorigenic. The presence of initiated foci can be
displayed as papillomas by the repeated application of a promoting
agent such as PMA which in itself is virtually non-tumorigenic,
but when applied after (not before) the initiator, will produce a
relatively large yield of tumors in a relatively brief period.
The process of initiation has been likened to the induction of
somatic mutations: initiation occurs promptly and is irreversible,
remaining unchanged without further treatment for as long as a
year. Initiation is nonprogressive and, therefore, latent unless
promoted.

In our studies, both the interaction of B(a)P with epidermal
DNA of the mouse skin and the dose-response relationship for the
initiation stage of mouse skin tumorigenesis showed a linear non-
threshold dose-response relationship (Figs. 1 and 2). By contrast,
the dose-response relationship for skin tumorigenesis in the mouse
with chronic application of B(a)P at graded dose levels is sharply
convex upward unless there is concomitant exposure to a promoting
agent which converts the response to a linear form (Fig. 3). The
dose-response for DNA interaction in the rat liver with dimethyl-
nitrosamine is linear,[10] as is the relation between the induction
of enzyme deficient islands and the dose of diethylnitrosamine.[11]
The dose-response for diethylnitrosamine-induced rat liver cancers
also has a sharp upward curvature with the incidence being a
squared or cubed power of dose.[12] The liver also shows initiation-
promotion characteristics.[13] Hence, we have two very dissimilar
organs which behave in accordance with the two-stage initiation-
promotion tumorigenesis model where both have a linear non-
threshold initiation stage and a sharply upward curvilinear

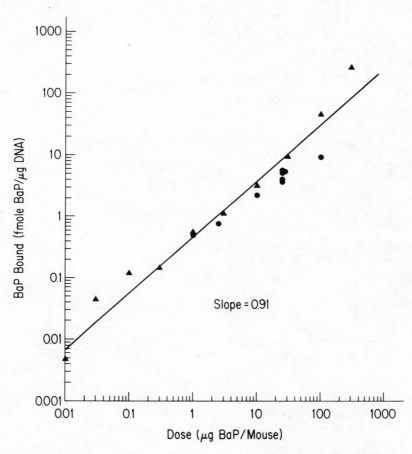

Fig. 1 Dose dependency of B(a)P guanine adducts formation in epidermal DNA. Groups of mice, 15 to 20 each, were treated topically with 1, 2, 5, 10, 25 and 100 µg ^{3}H-B(a)P (50 to 100 µCi) and sacrificed 24 hr. later. Enzymatically digested epidermal DNA was chromatographed on a Sephadex LH-20 or a Waters C_{18}-µBondapak column.[16]

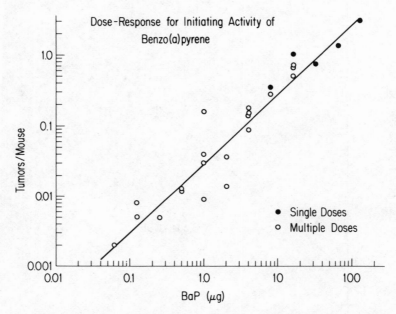

Fig. 2 The yield of skin papillomas per mouse per unit dose
        applied versus dose per fraction illustrating
        differences between single versus multiple fractionated
        doses of B(a)P. Following B(a)P treatment, 5 μg
        TPA was topically applied three times per week.

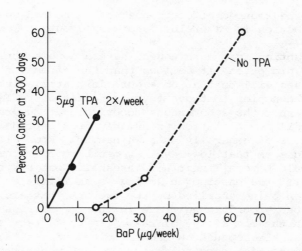

Fig. 3. The dose-effect data at 350 d for carcinoma induction in
mouse skin exposed to a weekly dose of B(a)P on Monday
with or without 5.0 µg TPA on Wednesday and Friday. Doses
refer to the amount of B(a)P given per week. The treatments were started at 56 d of age.

dose-response for tumors produced by chronic carcinogen exposure.
The dose-response characteristics for promoting agents have not
been extensively studied but the one for PMA in the mouse skin
shows a sharp upward curvature with increasing dose.[14]

It would follow from the two-stage initiation-promotion
schema that the response to carcinogen exposure consists of a
linear initiation component and an upwardly curvilinear promotion
component. The initiation components are cryptic whereas the
overt appearance of tumors can be construed to reflect the
promoting action of the carcinogen on the initiated cells. There
is evidence from the shape of the dose-response relationships for

promoters and the reduced effectiveness of increased spacing of doses that promotion is reversible and washes out at low doses.[15]

From the notion that carcinogens have a double action of initiation and promotion, it follows that the effect of a carcinogen at very low doses will be that of a pure initiator. It also follows from the notion that overt tumor formation reflects promoting action, that the spontaneous occurrence of tumors reflects promotion as well as initiation presumably from intrinsic and/or extrinsic factors of generally unknown nature. From all of the above, it would seem that low level exposure to environmental carcinogens would have a linear non-threshold dose-response relationship with the carcinogen acting as an initiator and the promoting action being supplied by the factors that are responsible for the background cancer rate in the target tissue. The extent to which the above line of reasoning is correct and generally applicable depends on the validity and generality of the two-stage model for carcinogen action, and whether background tumor occurrence does reflect the action of promoting factors which can operate on a broad spectrum of initiators.

REFERENCES

1. Panel on Carcinogenesis, Report on Cancer Testing in the Safety Evaluation of Food Additives and Pesticides, Toxicol. Appl. Pharmacol. 20:419-438 (1971).

2. National Research Council, Advisory Committee on the Biological Effects of Ionizing Radiations, "The Effects on Populations of Exposure to Low Levels of Ionizing Radiation," National Academy of Sciences, Washington, D.C. (1972).

3. R. E. Albert, R. E. Train, and E. Anderson, Rationale Developed by the Environmental Protection Agency for the Assessment of Carcinogenic Risks, J. Natl. Cancer Inst. 58(5):1537-1541 (1977).

4. National Research Council, Advisory Committee on the Biological Effects of Ionizing Radiations, "The Effects on Populations of Exposure to Low Levels of Ionizing Radiation," National Academy of Sciences, Washington, D.C. (1980).

5. J. McCann and B. N. Ames. A Simple Method for Detecting Environmental Carcinogens as Mutagens, Ann. N. Y. Acad. Sci. 271:5-13 (1976).

6. C. E. Land, J. D. Boice, Jr., R. E. Shore, J. E. Norman, and
    M. Tokunaga, Breast Cancer Risk from Low-dose Exposure to
    Ionizing Radiation: Results of Parallel Analysis of Three
    Exposed Populations of Women, J. Natl. Cancer Inst. 65:353-
    376 (1980).

7. G. W. Beebe, H. Kato, and C. E. Land, Studies of the Mortality
    of A-bomb Survivors. 6. Mortality and Radiation Dose,
    1950-1974, Radiat. Res. 75:138-201 (1978).

8. J. A. Staffa and M. A. Mehlman, eds., "Innovations in Cancer
    Risk Assessment (ED$_{01}$ Study)," J. Environ. Pathol.
    Toxicol. 3(3):1-250 (1980).

9. B. L. Van Duuren, Tumor Promoting Agents in Two-Stage
    Carcinogenesis, Prog. Exp. Tumor Res. 11:31-68 (1967).

10. M. I. Diaz Gomez, P. F. Swann, and P. N. Magee, The Absorption
    and Metabolism in Rats of Small Oral Doses of Dimethyl-
    nitrosamine, Biochem. J. 164:497-500 (1977).

11. E. Scherer and P. Emmelot, Kinetics of Induction and Growth
    of Enzyme-deficient Islands Involved in Hepatocarcino-
    genesis, Cancer Res. 36:2544-2554 (1976).

12. H. Druckrey, Quantitative Aspects of Chemical Carcinogenesis,
    in: "Potential Carcinogenic Hazards from Drugs, Evaluation
    of Risks," (VICC Monograph Series, Vol. 7) R. Truhart, ed.,
    Springer-Verlag, New York (1967).

13. H. C. Pitot and A. E. Sirica, The Stages of Initiation and
    Promotion in Hepatocarcinogenesis, Biochim. Biophys. Acta
    605:191-215 (1980).

14. T. J. Slaga, S. M. Fischer, L. Triplett, and S. Nesnow,
    Comparison of Complete Carcinogenesis and Tumor Initiation
    Promotion, a Reliable Short Term Assay, J. Environ. Pathol.
    Toxicol., in press.

15. R. K. Boutwell, Some Biological Aspects of Skin Carcinogenesis,
    Prog. Exp. Tumor Res. 4:207-250 (1964).

16. M. A. Pereira, F. J. Burns, and R. E. Albert, Dose Response
    for Benzo(a)pyrene Adducts in Mouse Epidermal DNA, Cancer
    Res. 39:2556-2559 (1979).

DISCUSSION

CROW: What does TPA stand for?

ALBERT: It is one of the phorbol esters.

CROW: I suppose the fact that even in the absence of TPA you still
get an eventual tumor just means that there are other natural promoters around?

ALBERT: There may be a source of confusion here because one can give
the carcinogen at a dose low enough not to produce any detectable
yield of tumors. If one really follows these animals carefully,
there is a low background frequency of spontaneous tumors. It would
increase, but not by very much when one administers the phorbol ester.
When one follows the low dose of the carcinogen with the phorbol
ester, one gets a big increase in tumors.

CROW: I thought that you treated both of them with BaP, but followed
with TPA in one case and not in the other.

ALBERT: On a later slide I showed there was concurrent exposure to
both the promoter and the carcinogen. The carcinogen was capable of
inducing tumors, but the response was linear with a power of the dose.
If you apply the promoter with it, of course, you get a shift to
tumors occurring at smaller doses of carcinogen, and the response
becomes linear with dose.

FORBES: In terms of mathematical models, if you have a log plot
with a slope of 9 or higher, that argues strongly against the multi-
stage theory of cancer because that would mean ten or so independent
rate determining stages which is biologically improbable.

ALBERT: Yes, the alternative is that it has to do with the degree
of homogeneity in the population. If all the animals are behaving
similarly, one would get a very steep time pattern because they are
almost all alike and they are all responding almost simultaneously.

    I agree that I find it difficult to reconcile those steep time
curves with so many different stages.

BOURDEAU: You have shown that once the agent gets to the target, the
linear non-threshold model seems to be the logical conclusion.

ALBERT: For the first stage in the process.

BOURDEAU: Right, but in practical terms, couldn't you accept the
idea of the threshold for specific agents because of detoxification
methods that are functional for them?

ALBERT: Not really. The difficulty with what you are saying is
that there are simply effects that modify the dose or the effect of
dose, namely, if an agent has to be activated in order to be an effective carcinogen, the extent of activation may drop off as the
dose goes down and that simply modifies the effective dose.

Sure, it may change the overall shape of the dose response to
the tested compound, but it doesn't necessarily change the inherent
linearity of the dose response to the activated compound.

From a practical standpoint such information would be highly
valuable in terms of doing risk assessments, but in fact it is
virtually never available.

I think emphasis is being placed more and more on trying to get
such data, but we really haven't seen it, as I mentioned, in the
assessment of over a hundred suspected carcinogens at the EPA.

SAGAN: Roy, you interpret your data as demonstrating linearity, but
I thought I saw evidence for a threshold; that is to say, there is
an inverse relationship between the dose and the time of appearance
of the first tumor so that there is clearly a dose that would provide tumors at a time beyond the life span of the animal, a biological
threshold if you like.

ALBERT: When you are dealing with high levels of exposure there is
a systematic relationship between the time of occurrence and the dose
rate.

This was observed first by Bloom with UV-induced skin tumors.
Then, Druckrey did it for a whole series of carcinogens with the liver,
but this is all high dose stuff and the question is, what happens
when you get really down low in the dose and you are beginning to
merge in with the spontaneous occurrence of tumors?

That rigamarole that I presented at the end would suggest that
when you are dealing with really low levels of carcinogen all you
would be doing would be interacting with the other things that cause
neoplastic conversions at about the time these cells pop off anyhow
in the process of senescence so that you really wouldn't be looking
at any acceleration in time. It would simply be just an increased
probability at about the same time you'd be getting tumors anyhow.
For example, Peto has made the point that there really isn't any
individual life shortening in lung cancer victims who smoke cigarettes compared to those who do not smoke. In other words, the average age of onset of cancer seems to stay the same, although the number of cases goes up.

THOMPSON: When you say linear, you mean linear when plotted on the log-log paper or do you mean linear when plotted on semi-log paper?

ALBERT: I mean linearly linear, that is, cumulative incidence
plotted against the dose. If such data are suitably normalized, a
log-log plot ought to have a slope of one.

ABRAHAMSON: Roy, when you showed this latency period being shortened
is that because with higher doses you are killing off more stem cells
and there is a stimulus for repopulation, so that you are moving more
cells toward their point of dividing and popping off in one direction
or the other?

ALBERT: I would think so. One could speculate that the effect of
radiation is to cause proliferative death of cells and at the higher
doses proliferative death occurs after fewer divisions. I don't know
that there are extensive data, but with lower doses you seem to get
more replications before death.

ABRAHAMSON: Do your promoters act in cell culture to change mutation
rates or change slopes in any way? Have they been used concurrently?
I recall experiments that used what they now call co-mutagens, but
I just don't remember the data.

ALBERT: Well, they certainly promote for neoplastic transformation
in vitro. I don't know whether something like phorbol esters actually increases the yield of mutations. I don't think it does.

CRANMER: If you take Ames' system, it does not. If you add phorbol
esters to nitrosamines or AEF or other types of carcinogens, you
don't increase mutagenic capacity.

Front Row: Abrahamson; Bourdeau; Sagan; Stein; Pochin; Hackney; Inhaber; Weinberg
Second Row: —————; Forbes; Clarkson; Totter; Albert; Bender; Spielman; Broman; Berg
Third Row: Pott; Crow; L. Russell; W. Russell; Utidjian; Seidenfeld; Land; Ferris; Thompson
Back Row: Maillie; Morrow; Cohen; Nash; Marsden; Cranmer; Oberdoerster

INDEX